Little Lulu ®

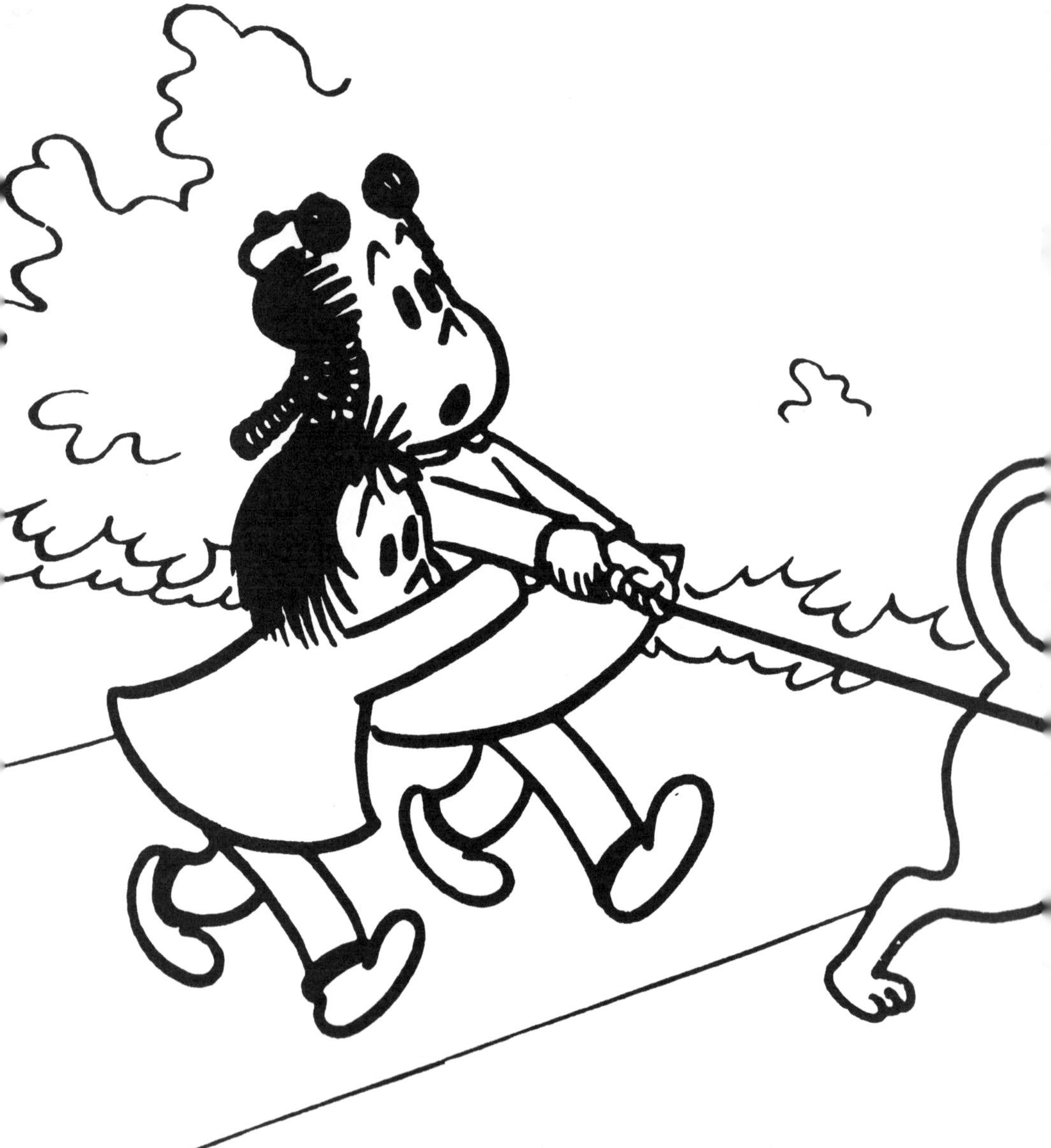

Little Lulu®

Leave It to Lulu

Story and Art
John Stanley
and
Irving Tripp

Based on the character
created by
Marge Buell

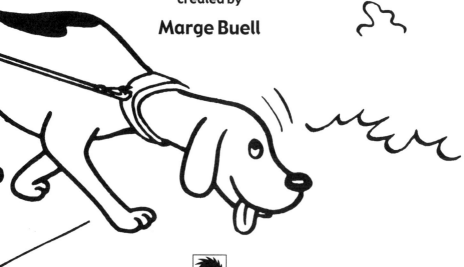

Publisher
Mike Richardson

Editor
Dave Marshall

Collection Designer
Krystal Hennes

Art Director
Lia Ribacchi

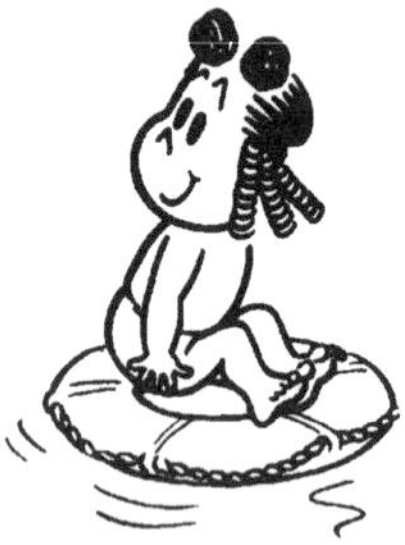

Published by
Dark Horse Books
A division of Dark Horse Comics, Inc.
10956 SE Main Street
Milwaukie, OR 97222

darkhorse.com

Little Lulu ® Vol. 12: Leave It to Lulu

The one-page comics on pages 209 to 215
originally appeared in *Dell Comics* issues 146, 158, 165,
and *Marge's Little Lulu* issue 1.

First edition: October 2006
ISBN-10: 1-59307-620-7
ISBN-13: 978-1-59307-620-7

1 3 5 7 9 10 8 6 4 2
Printed in U.S.A.

A note about Lulu

Little Lulu came into the world through the pen of cartoonist Marjorie "Marge" Henderson Buell in 1935. Originally commissioned as a series of single-panel cartoons by *The Saturday Evening Post*, Lulu took the world by storm with her charm, smarts, and sass. Within ten years, she not only was the star of her own cartoon series, but a celebrity spokesgirl for a variety of high-profile commercial products.

Little Lulu truly hit her stride as America's sweetheart in the comic books published by Dell Comics starting in 1945. While Buell was solely responsible for Lulu's original single-panel shenanigans, the comic-book stories were put into the able hands of comics legend John Stanley. Stanley wrote and laid out the comics while artist Irving Tripp provided the finished drawings. After a number of trial appearances in Dell Comics, Lulu's appeal was undeniable, and she was granted her very own comic-book series, called *Marge's Little Lulu*, which was published regularly through 1984.

This volume contains every comic from issues forty-nine through fifty-three of *Marge's Little Lulu*.

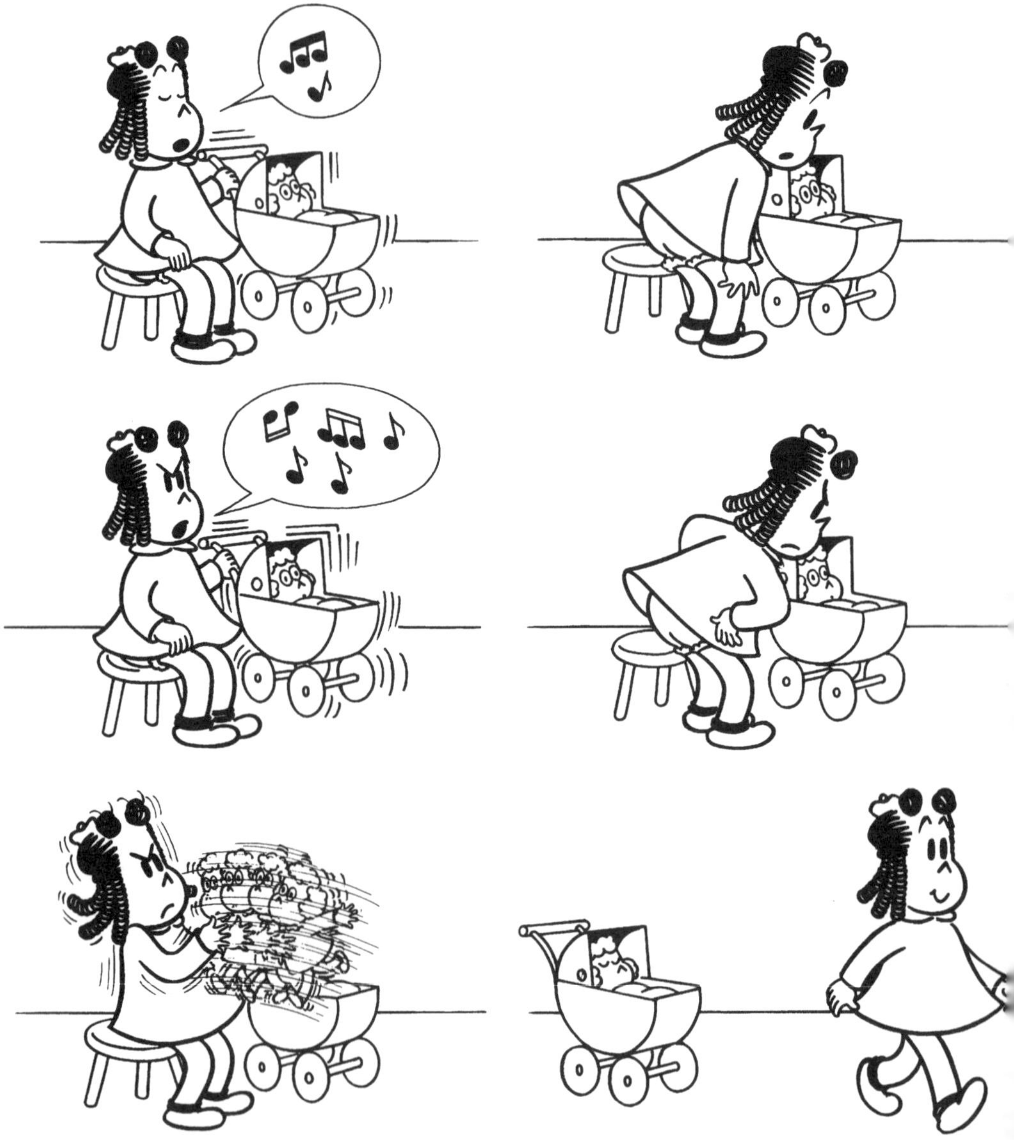

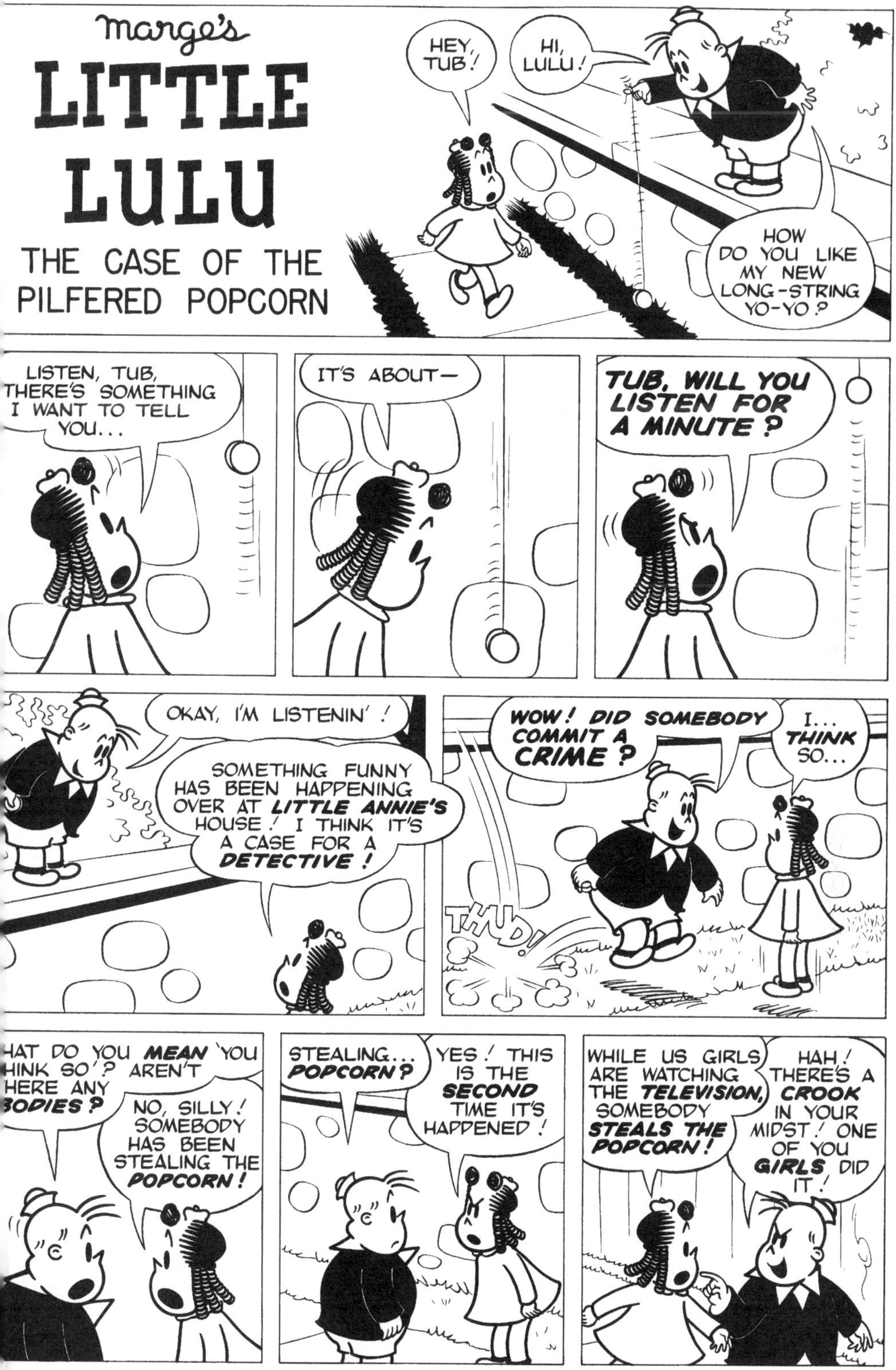
marge's
LITTLE LULU
THE CASE OF THE PILFERED POPCORN
HEY, TUB!
HI, LULU!
HOW DO YOU LIKE MY NEW LONG-STRING YO-YO?
LISTEN, TUB, THERE'S SOMETHING I WANT TO TELL YOU...
IT'S ABOUT—
TUB, WILL YOU LISTEN FOR A MINUTE?
OKAY, I'M LISTENIN'!
SOMETHING FUNNY HAS BEEN HAPPENING OVER AT LITTLE ANNIE'S HOUSE! I THINK IT'S A CASE FOR A DETECTIVE!
WOW! DID SOMEBODY COMMIT A CRIME?
I... THINK SO...
THUD!
HAT DO YOU MEAN 'YOU HINK SO'? AREN'T HERE ANY BODIES?
NO, SILLY! SOMEBODY HAS BEEN STEALING THE POPCORN!
STEALING... POPCORN?
YES! THIS IS THE SECOND TIME IT'S HAPPENED!
WHILE US GIRLS ARE WATCHING THE TELEVISION, SOMEBODY STEALS THE POPCORN!
HAH! THERE'S A CROOK IN YOUR MIDST! ONE OF YOU GIRLS DID IT!

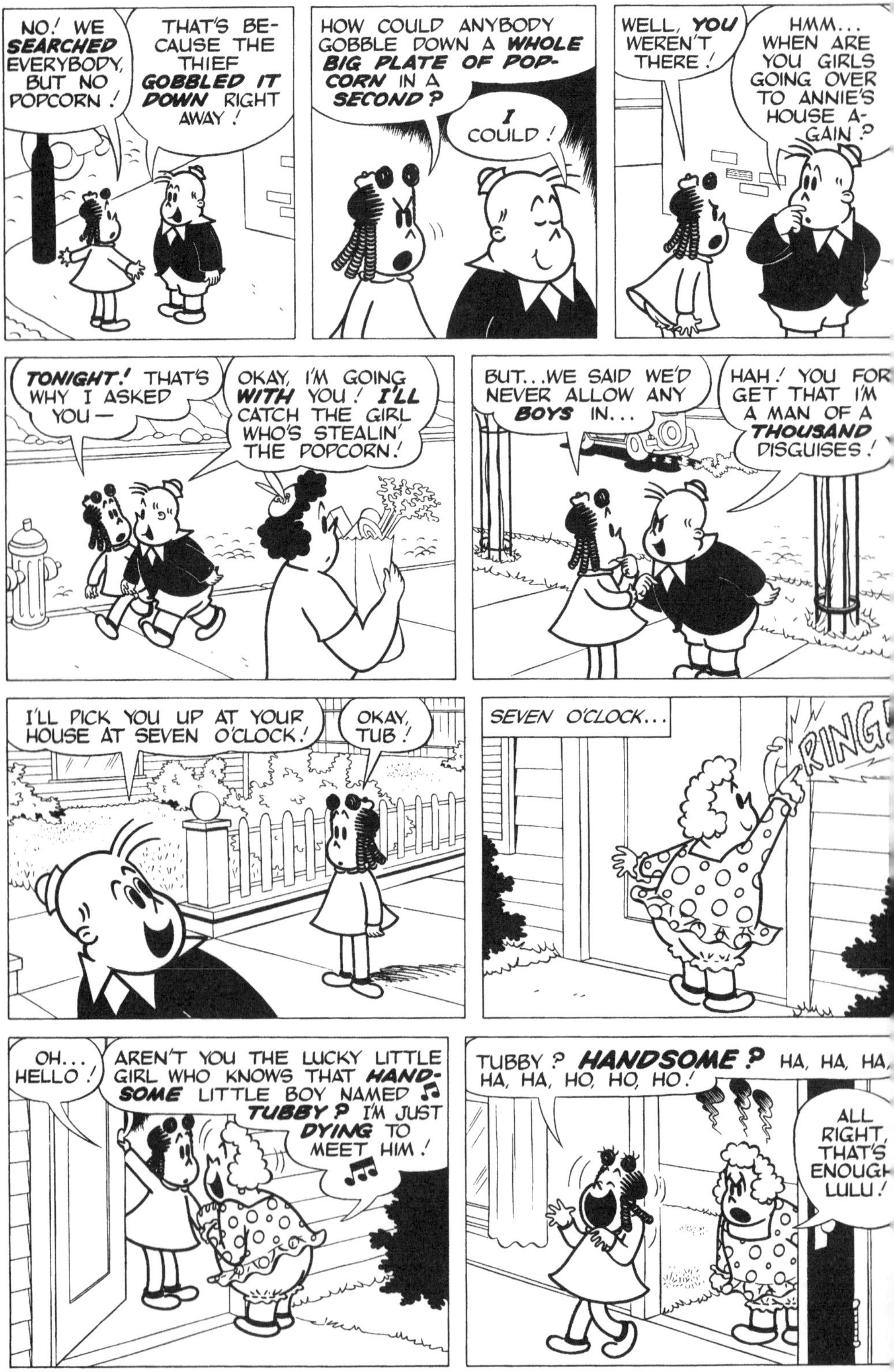
NO! WE SEARCHED EVERYBODY, BUT NO POPCORN!
THAT'S BECAUSE THE THIEF GOBBLED IT DOWN RIGHT AWAY!
HOW COULD ANYBODY GOBBLE DOWN A WHOLE BIG PLATE OF POPCORN IN A SECOND?
I COULD!
WELL, YOU WEREN'T THERE!
HMM... WHEN ARE YOU GIRLS GOING OVER TO ANNIE'S HOUSE AGAIN?
TONIGHT! THAT'S WHY I ASKED YOU—
OKAY, I'M GOING WITH YOU! I'LL CATCH THE GIRL WHO'S STEALIN' THE POPCORN!
BUT...WE SAID WE'D NEVER ALLOW ANY BOYS IN...
HAH! YOU FOR GET THAT I'M A MAN OF A THOUSAND DISGUISES!
I'LL PICK YOU UP AT YOUR HOUSE AT SEVEN O'CLOCK!
OKAY, TUB!
SEVEN O'CLOCK...
RING
OH... HELLO!
AREN'T YOU THE LUCKY LITTLE GIRL WHO KNOWS THAT HANDSOME LITTLE BOY NAMED TUBBY? I'M JUST DYING TO MEET HIM!
TUBBY? HANDSOME? HA, HA, HA, HA, HA, HO, HO, HO!
ALL RIGHT, THAT'S ENOUGH LULU!

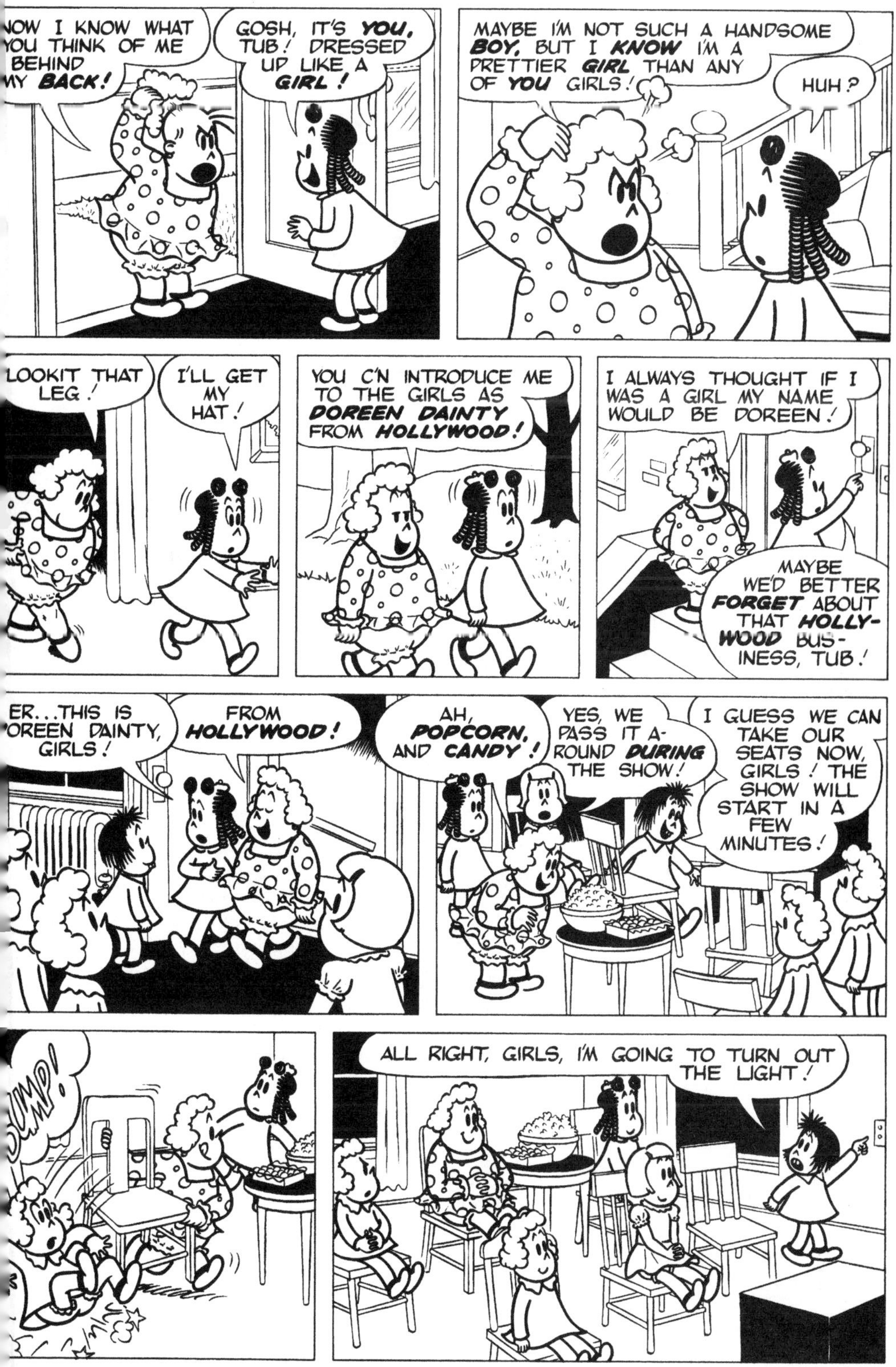

NOW I KNOW WHAT YOU THINK OF ME BEHIND MY **BACK!**
GOSH, IT'S **YOU,** TUB! DRESSED UP LIKE A **GIRL!**
MAYBE I'M NOT SUCH A HANDSOME **BOY,** BUT I **KNOW** I'M A PRETTIER **GIRL** THAN ANY OF **YOU** GIRLS!
HUH?
LOOKIT THAT LEG!
I'LL GET MY HAT!
YOU C'N INTRODUCE ME TO THE GIRLS AS **DOREEN DAINTY** FROM **HOLLYWOOD!**
I ALWAYS THOUGHT IF I WAS A GIRL MY NAME WOULD BE DOREEN!
MAYBE WE'D BETTER **FORGET** ABOUT THAT **HOLLY-WOOD** BUS-INESS, TUB!
ER...THIS IS DOREEN DAINTY, GIRLS!
FROM **HOLLYWOOD!**
AH, **POPCORN,** AND **CANDY!**
YES, WE PASS IT A-ROUND **DURING** THE SHOW!
I GUESS WE CAN TAKE OUR SEATS NOW, GIRLS! THE SHOW WILL START IN A FEW MINUTES!
ALL RIGHT, GIRLS, I'M GOING TO TURN OUT THE LIGHT!

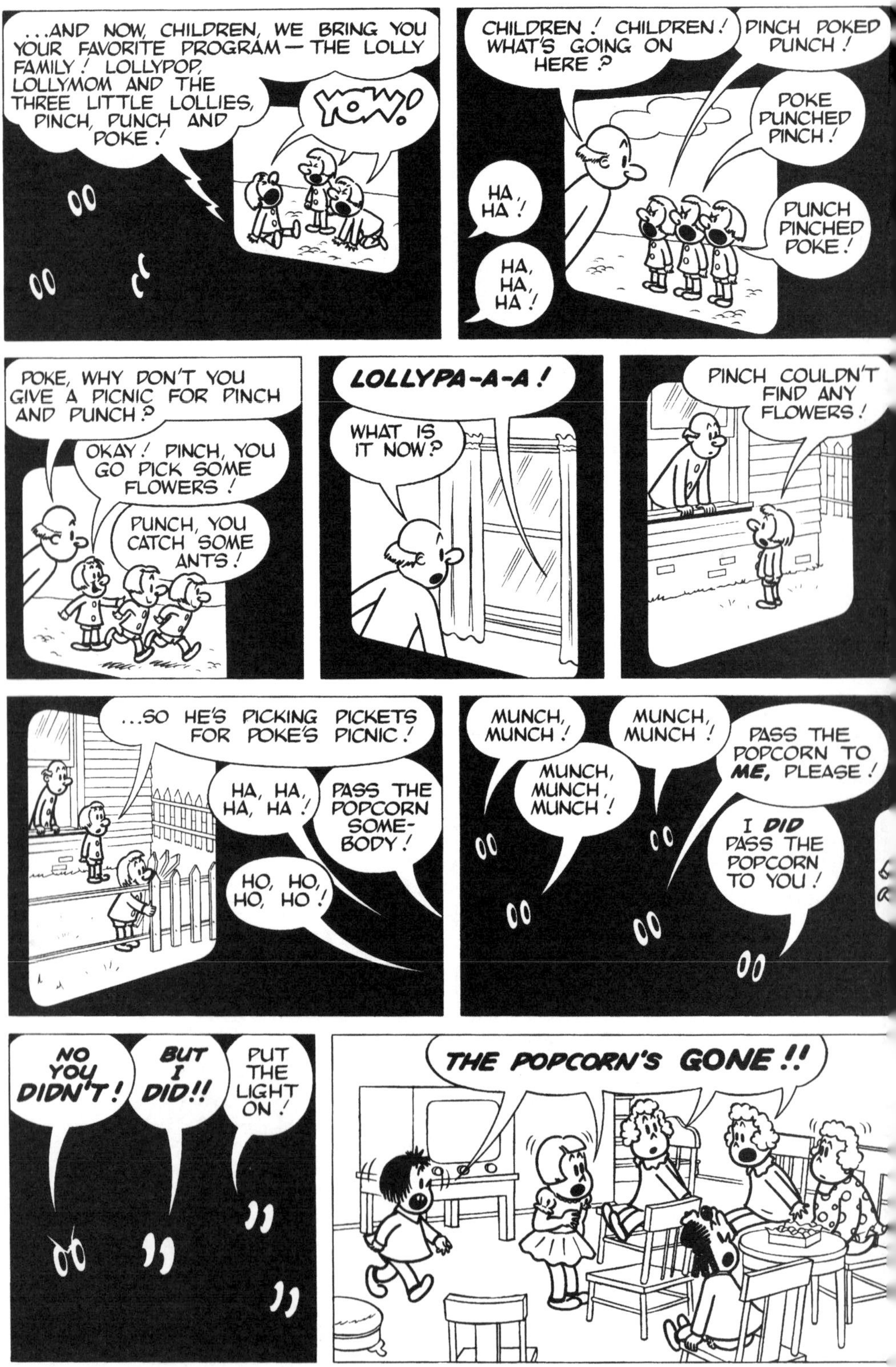
...AND NOW, CHILDREN, WE BRING YOU YOUR FAVORITE PROGRAM — THE LOLLY FAMILY! LOLLYPOP, LOLLYMOM AND THE THREE LITTLE LOLLIES, PINCH, PUNCH AND POKE!
YOW!
CHILDREN! CHILDREN! WHAT'S GOING ON HERE?
PINCH POKED PUNCH!
POKE PUNCHED PINCH!
HA, HA!
PUNCH PINCHED POKE!
HA, HA, HA!
POKE, WHY DON'T YOU GIVE A PICNIC FOR PINCH AND PUNCH?
OKAY! PINCH, YOU GO PICK SOME FLOWERS!
PUNCH, YOU CATCH SOME ANTS!
LOLLYPA-A-A!
WHAT IS IT NOW?
PINCH COULDN'T FIND ANY FLOWERS!
...SO HE'S PICKING PICKETS FOR POKE'S PICNIC!
HA, HA, HA, HA!
PASS THE POPCORN SOME-BODY!
HO, HO, HO, HO!
MUNCH, MUNCH!
MUNCH, MUNCH, MUNCH!
MUNCH, MUNCH!
PASS THE POPCORN TO ME, PLEASE!
I DID PASS THE POPCORN TO YOU!
NO YOU DIDN'T!
BUT I DID!!
PUT THE LIGHT ON!
THE POPCORN'S GONE!!

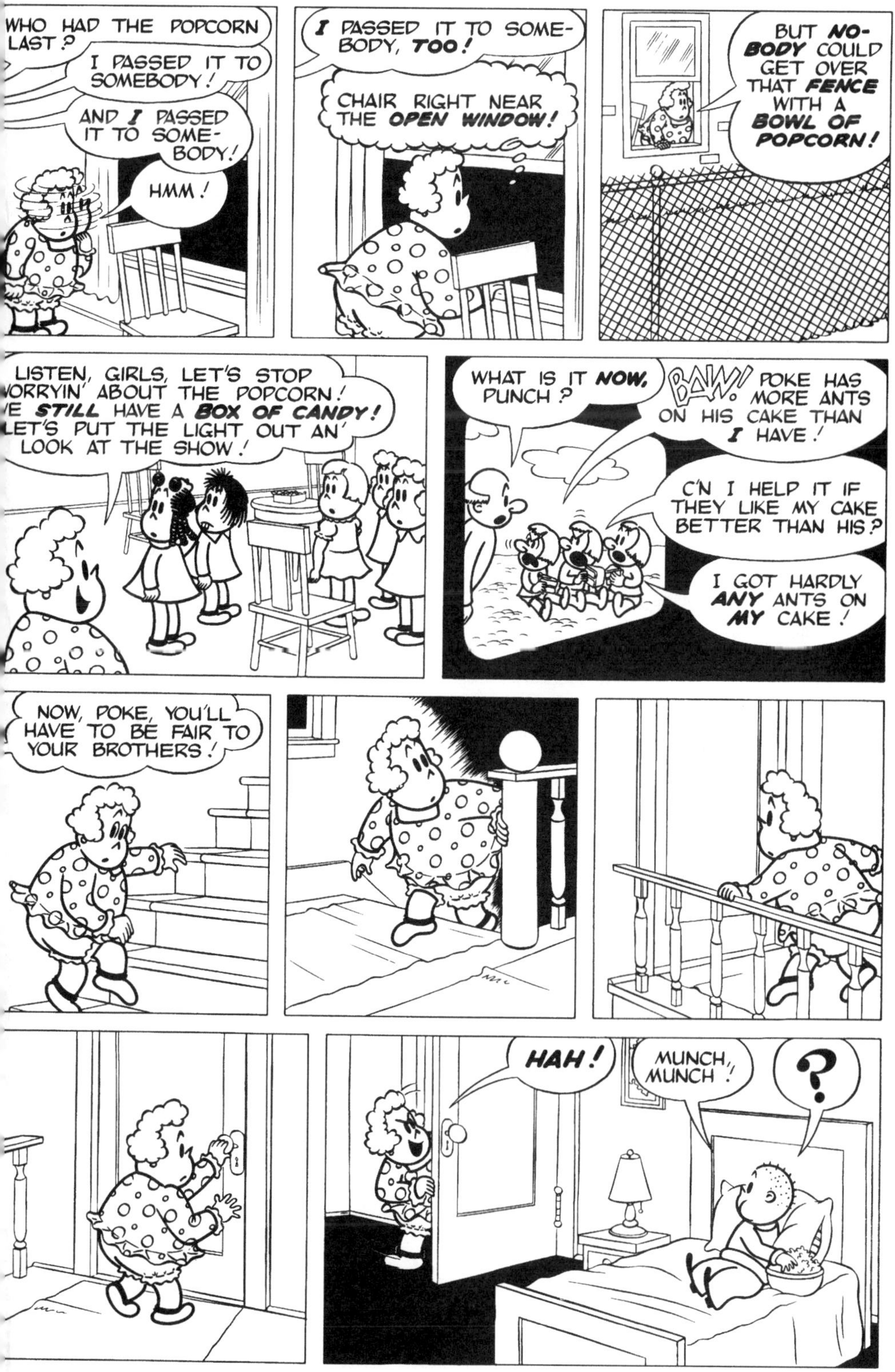
WHO HAD THE POPCORN LAST?
I PASSED IT TO SOMEBODY!
AND I PASSED IT TO SOMEBODY!
HMM!
I PASSED IT TO SOMEBODY, TOO!
CHAIR RIGHT NEAR THE OPEN WINDOW!
BUT NOBODY COULD GET OVER THAT FENCE WITH A BOWL OF POPCORN!
LISTEN, GIRLS, LET'S STOP WORRYIN' ABOUT THE POPCORN! WE STILL HAVE A BOX OF CANDY! LET'S PUT THE LIGHT OUT AN' LOOK AT THE SHOW!
WHAT IS IT NOW, PUNCH?
BAW! POKE HAS MORE ANTS ON HIS CAKE THAN I HAVE!
C'N I HELP IT IF THEY LIKE MY CAKE BETTER THAN HIS?
I GOT HARDLY ANY ANTS ON MY CAKE!
NOW, POKE, YOU'LL HAVE TO BE FAIR TO YOUR BROTHERS!
HAH!
MUNCH, MUNCH!
?

IGGY! SO **YOU** STOLE THE POPCORN!

WH–WHO ARE YOU?

PRIVATE DETECTIVE TUBBY!

TUBBY? GOSH, WHAT'S THE IDEA, TUB?

I WAS BROUGHT IN TO CATCH THE CROOK WHO WAS STEALIN' THE POPCORN!

YOU'RE NOT GONNA TURN ME IN, ARE YOU, TUB?

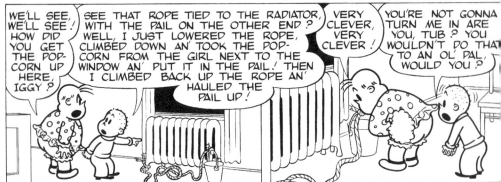

WE'LL SEE, WE'LL SEE! HOW DID YOU GET THE POPCORN UP HERE, IGGY?

SEE THAT ROPE TIED TO THE RADIATOR, WITH THE PAIL ON THE OTHER END? WELL, I JUST LOWERED THE ROPE, CLIMBED DOWN AN' TOOK THE POPCORN FROM THE GIRL NEXT TO THE WINDOW AN' PUT IT IN THE PAIL! THEN I CLIMBED BACK UP THE ROPE AN' HAULED THE PAIL UP!

VERY CLEVER, VERY CLEVER!

YOU'RE NOT GONNA TURN ME IN ARE YOU, TUB? YOU WOULDN'T DO THAT TO AN OL' PAL, WOULD YOU?

THERE'S ONLY **ONE** WAY YOU C'N **SQUARE** YOURSELF, IGGY!

WHAT'S THAT, TUB?

THEY GOT A BOX OF **CANDY** DOWN THERE!

YOU MEAN—

LET IT DOWN EASY! DON'T MAKE ANY NOISE!

DON'T WORRY, I'VE DONE THIS BEFORE!

CAREFUL NOW, IGGY!

CAREFUL!

I'M NEXT!

WAP!

OW! OW! OW!

the End

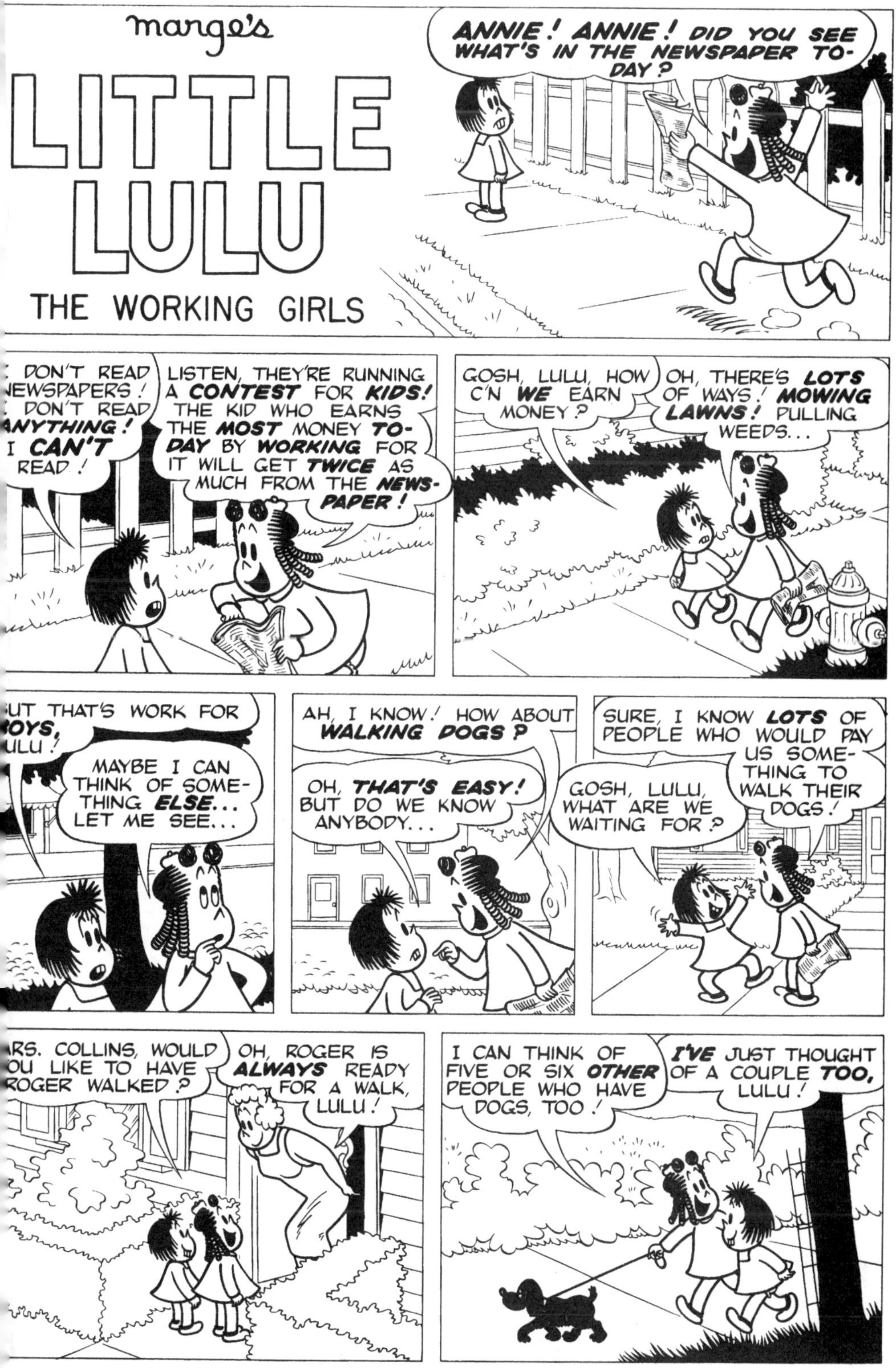
marge's
LITTLE LULU
THE WORKING GIRLS
ANNIE! ANNIE! DID YOU SEE WHAT'S IN THE NEWSPAPER TO-DAY?
DON'T READ NEWSPAPERS! DON'T READ ANYTHING! I CAN'T READ!
LISTEN, THEY'RE RUNNING A CONTEST FOR KIDS! THE KID WHO EARNS THE MOST MONEY TO-DAY BY WORKING FOR IT WILL GET TWICE AS MUCH FROM THE NEWS-PAPER!
GOSH, LULU, HOW C'N WE EARN MONEY?
OH, THERE'S LOTS OF WAYS! MOWING LAWNS! PULLING WEEDS...
UT THAT'S WORK FOR OYS, ULU!
MAYBE I CAN THINK OF SOME-THING ELSE... LET ME SEE...
AH, I KNOW! HOW ABOUT WALKING DOGS?
OH, THAT'S EASY! BUT DO WE KNOW ANYBODY...
SURE, I KNOW LOTS OF PEOPLE WHO WOULD PAY US SOME-THING TO WALK THEIR DOGS!
GOSH, LULU, WHAT ARE WE WAITING FOR?
RS. COLLINS, WOULD OU LIKE TO HAVE ROGER WALKED?
OH, ROGER IS ALWAYS READY FOR A WALK, LULU!
I CAN THINK OF FIVE OR SIX OTHER PEOPLE WHO HAVE DOGS, TOO!
I'VE JUST THOUGHT OF A COUPLE TOO, LULU!

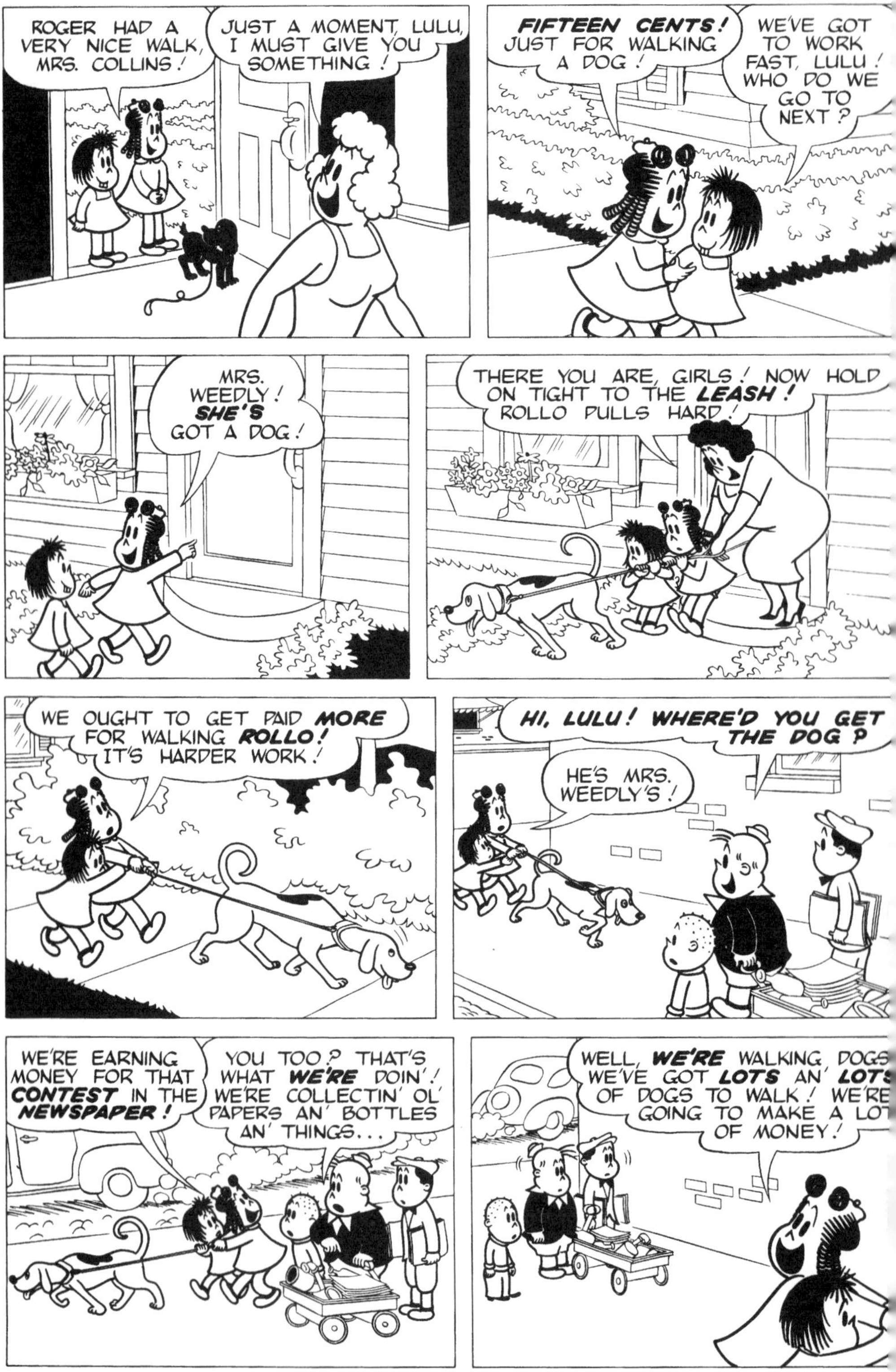
ROGER HAD A VERY NICE WALK, MRS. COLLINS!
JUST A MOMENT, LULU, I MUST GIVE YOU SOMETHING!
FIFTEEN CENTS! JUST FOR WALKING A DOG!
WE'VE GOT TO WORK FAST, LULU! WHO DO WE GO TO NEXT?
MRS. WEEDLY! SHE'S GOT A DOG!
THERE YOU ARE, GIRLS! NOW HOLD ON TIGHT TO THE LEASH! ROLLO PULLS HARD!
WE OUGHT TO GET PAID MORE FOR WALKING ROLLO! IT'S HARDER WORK!
HI, LULU! WHERE'D YOU GET THE DOG?
HE'S MRS. WEEDLY'S!
WE'RE EARNING MONEY FOR THAT CONTEST IN THE NEWSPAPER!
YOU TOO? THAT'S WHAT WE'RE DOIN'! WE'RE COLLECTIN' OL' PAPERS AN' BOTTLES AN' THINGS...
WELL, WE'RE WALKING DOGS! WE'VE GOT LOTS AN' LOTS OF DOGS TO WALK! WE'RE GOING TO MAKE A LOT OF MONEY!

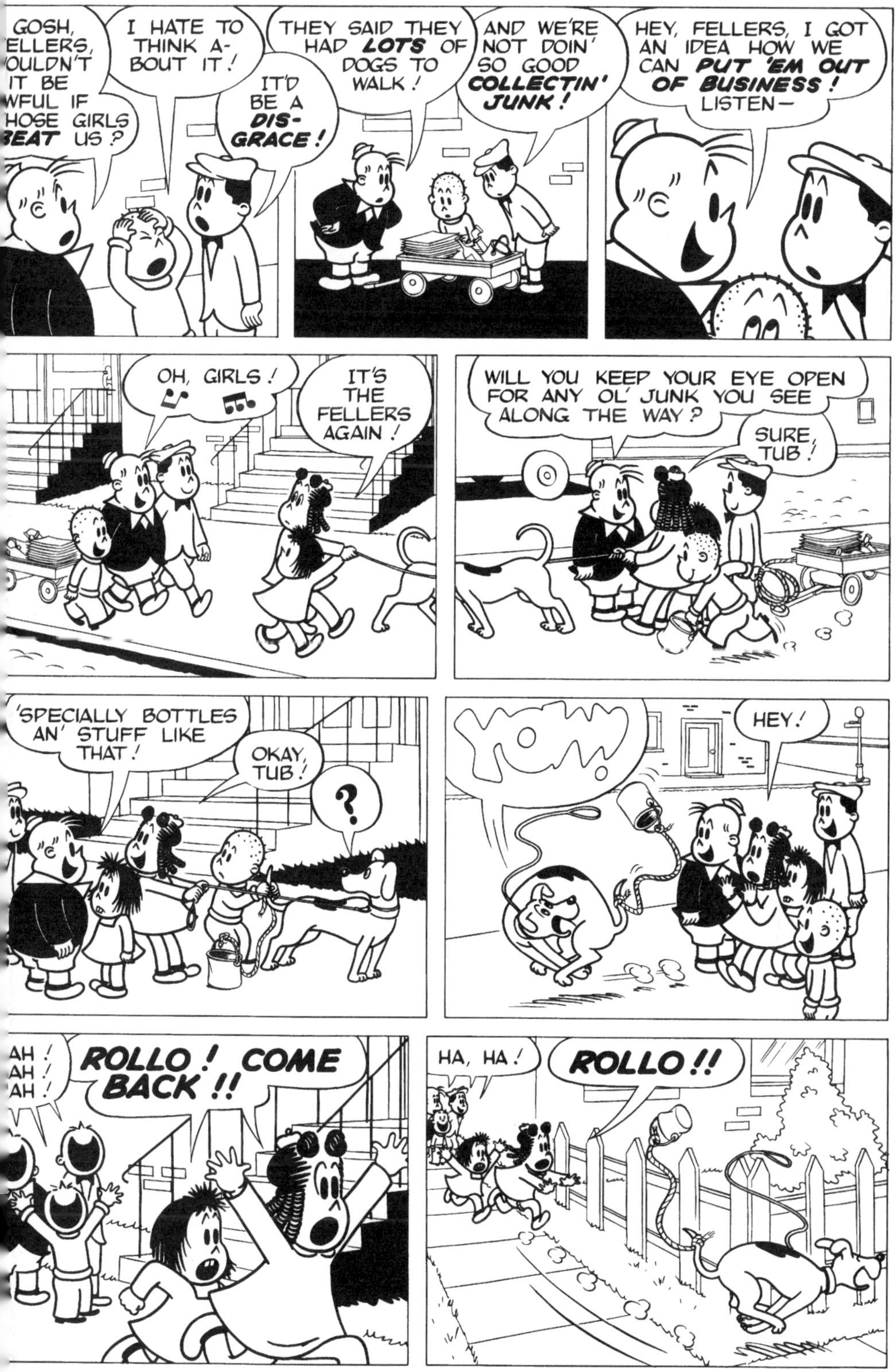
GOSH, FELLERS, WOULDN'T IT BE AWFUL IF THOSE GIRLS BEAT US?
I HATE TO THINK ABOUT IT!
IT'D BE A DIS-GRACE!
THEY SAID THEY HAD LOTS OF DOGS TO WALK!
AND WE'RE NOT DOIN' SO GOOD COLLECTIN' JUNK!
HEY, FELLERS, I GOT AN IDEA HOW WE CAN PUT 'EM OUT OF BUSINESS! LISTEN—
OH, GIRLS!
IT'S THE FELLERS AGAIN!
WILL YOU KEEP YOUR EYE OPEN FOR ANY OL' JUNK YOU SEE ALONG THE WAY?
SURE, TUB!
'SPECIALLY BOTTLES AN' STUFF LIKE THAT!
OKAY, TUB!
?
YOW!
HEY!
HAH! HAH! HAH!
ROLLO! COME BACK!!
HA, HA!
ROLLO!!

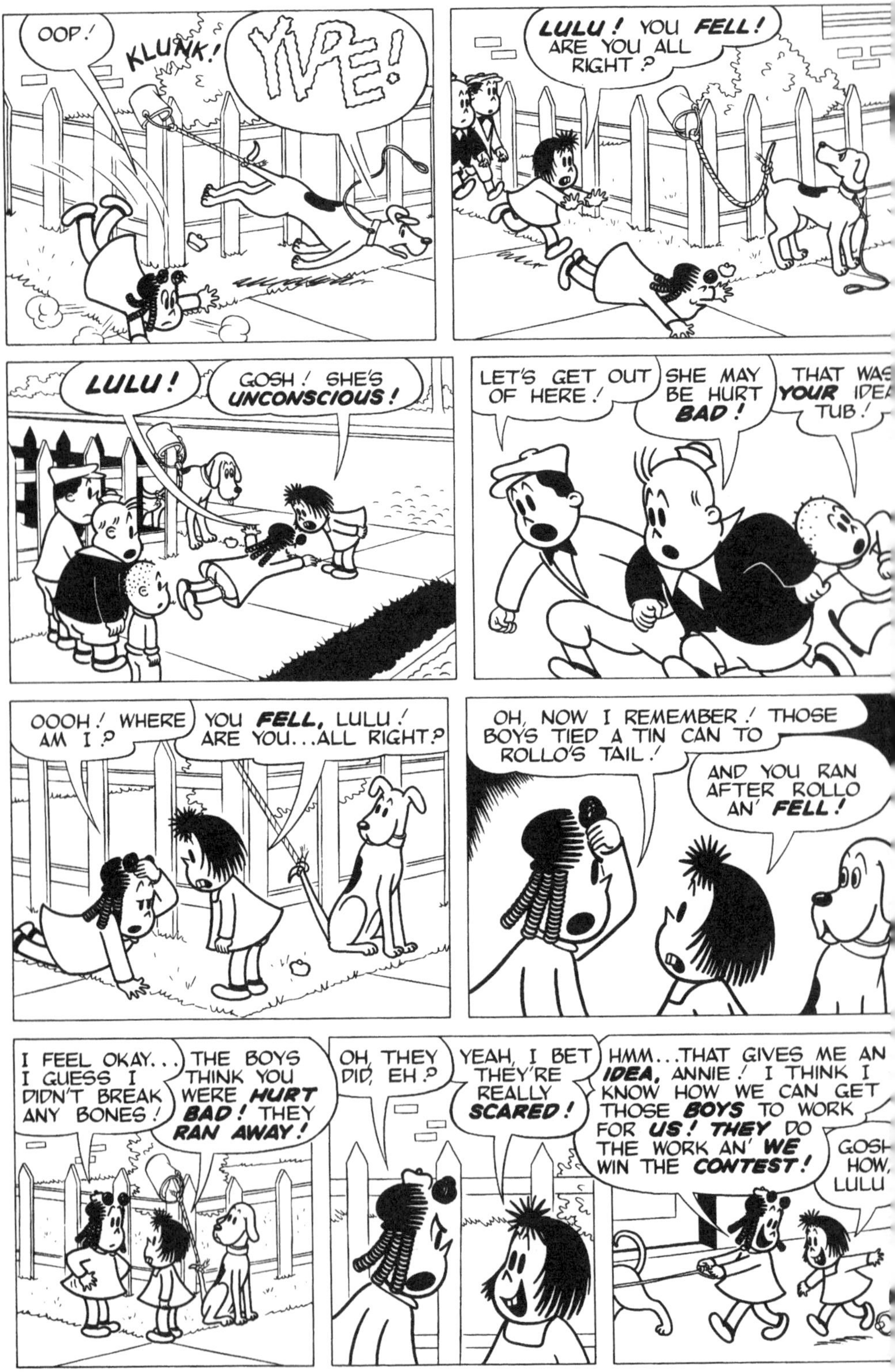
OOP!
KLUNK!
YIPE!
LULU! YOU FELL! ARE YOU ALL RIGHT?
LULU!
GOSH! SHE'S UNCONSCIOUS!
LET'S GET OUT OF HERE!
SHE MAY BE HURT BAD!
THAT WAS YOUR IDEA TUB!
OOOH! WHERE AM I?
YOU FELL, LULU! ARE YOU...ALL RIGHT?
OH, NOW I REMEMBER! THOSE BOYS TIED A TIN CAN TO ROLLO'S TAIL!
AND YOU RAN AFTER ROLLO AN' FELL!
I FEEL OKAY... I GUESS I DIDN'T BREAK ANY BONES!
THE BOYS THINK YOU WERE HURT BAD! THEY RAN AWAY!
OH, THEY DID, EH?
YEAH, I BET THEY'RE REALLY SCARED!
HMM...THAT GIVES ME AN IDEA, ANNIE! I THINK I KNOW HOW WE CAN GET THOSE BOYS TO WORK FOR US! THEY DO THE WORK AN' WE WIN THE CONTEST!
GOSH HOW, LULU

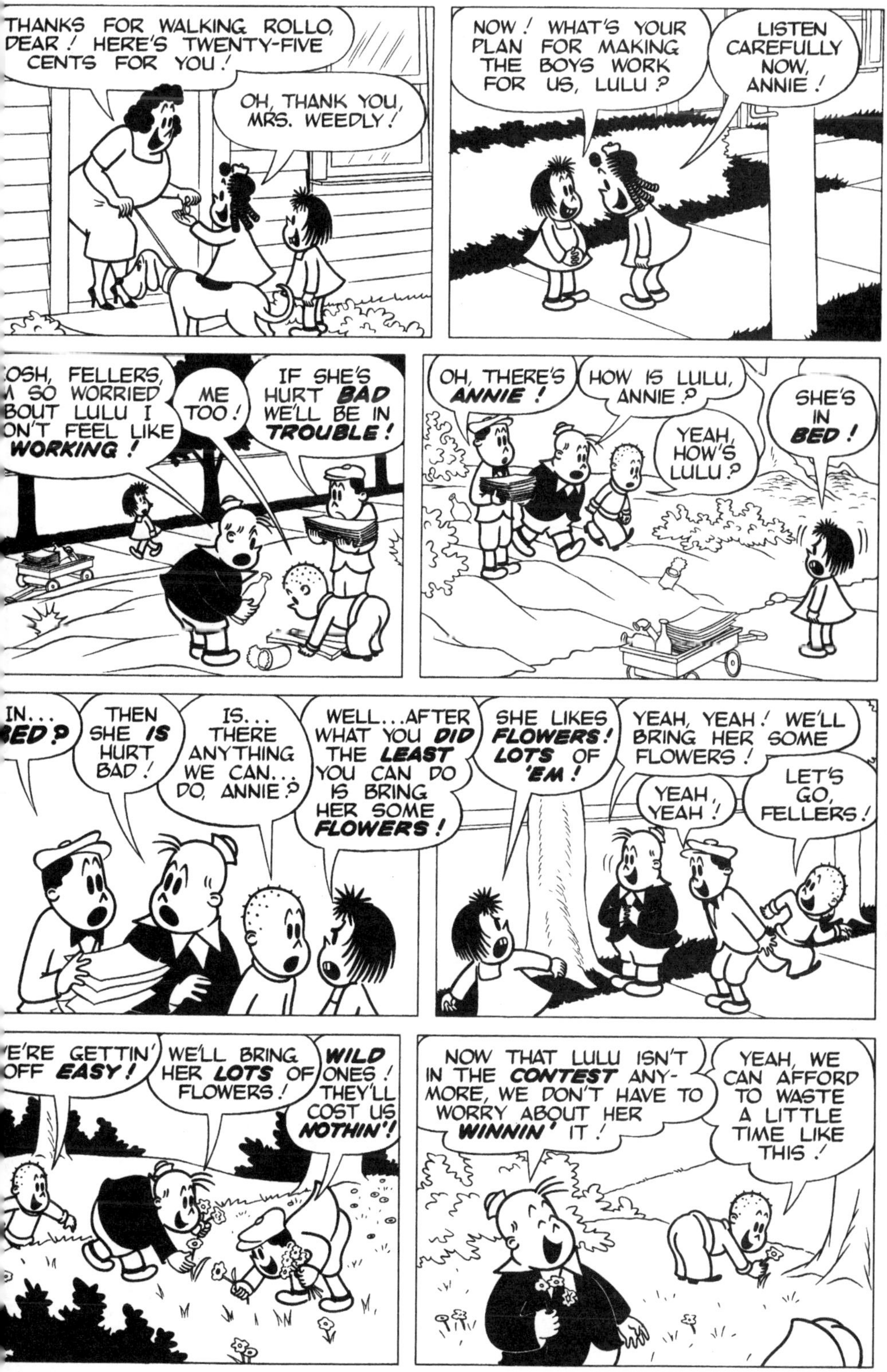
THANKS FOR WALKING ROLLO, DEAR! HERE'S TWENTY-FIVE CENTS FOR YOU!
OH, THANK YOU, MRS. WEEDLY!
NOW! WHAT'S YOUR PLAN FOR MAKING THE BOYS WORK FOR US, LULU?
LISTEN CAREFULLY NOW, ANNIE!
OSH, FELLERS, M SO WORRIED BOUT LULU I ON'T FEEL LIKE WORKING!
ME TOO!
IF SHE'S HURT BAD WE'LL BE IN TROUBLE!
OH, THERE'S ANNIE!
HOW IS LULU, ANNIE?
YEAH, HOW'S LULU?
SHE'S IN BED!
IN... BED?
THEN SHE IS HURT BAD!
IS... THERE ANYTHING WE CAN... DO, ANNIE?
WELL... AFTER WHAT YOU DID THE LEAST YOU CAN DO IS BRING HER SOME FLOWERS!
SHE LIKES FLOWERS! LOTS OF 'EM!
YEAH, YEAH! WE'LL BRING HER SOME FLOWERS!
YEAH, YEAH!
LET'S GO, FELLERS!
E'RE GETTIN' OFF EASY!
WE'LL BRING HER LOTS OF FLOWERS!
WILD ONES! THEY'LL COST US NOTHIN'!
NOW THAT LULU ISN'T IN THE CONTEST ANY-MORE, WE DON'T HAVE TO WORRY ABOUT HER WINNIN' IT!
YEAH, WE CAN AFFORD TO WASTE A LITTLE TIME LIKE THIS!

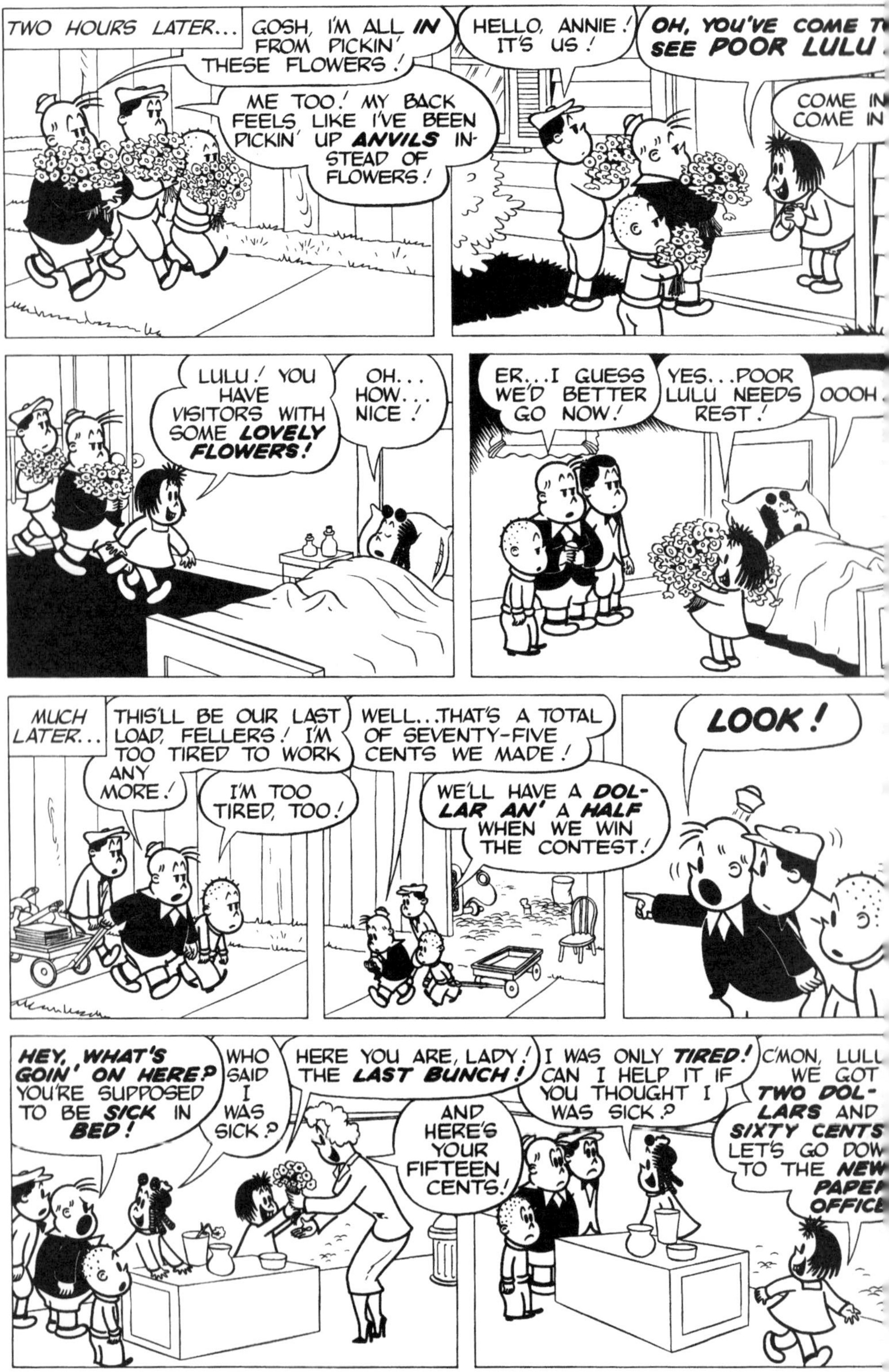
TWO HOURS LATER...
GOSH, I'M ALL **IN** FROM PICKIN' THESE FLOWERS!
ME TOO! MY BACK FEELS LIKE I'VE BEEN PICKIN' UP **ANVILS** INSTEAD OF FLOWERS!
HELLO, ANNIE! IT'S US!
OH, YOU'VE COME T
SEE POOR LULU
COME IN
COME IN
LULU! YOU HAVE VISITORS WITH SOME **LOVELY FLOWERS!**
OH... HOW... NICE!
ER...I GUESS WE'D BETTER GO NOW!
YES...POOR LULU NEEDS REST!
OOOH
MUCH LATER...
THIS'LL BE OUR LAST LOAD, FELLERS! I'M TOO TIRED TO WORK ANY MORE!
I'M TOO TIRED, TOO!
WELL...THAT'S A TOTAL OF SEVENTY-FIVE CENTS WE MADE!
WE'LL HAVE A **DOLLAR AN'** A **HALF** WHEN WE WIN THE CONTEST!
LOOK!
HEY, WHAT'S GOIN' ON HERE? YOU'RE SUPPOSED TO BE **SICK** IN **BED!**
WHO SAID I WAS SICK?
HERE YOU ARE, LADY! THE **LAST BUNCH!**
AND HERE'S YOUR FIFTEEN CENTS!
I WAS ONLY **TIRED!** CAN I HELP IT IF YOU THOUGHT I WAS SICK?
C'MON, LULU
WE GOT
TWO DOL-
LARS AND
SIXTY CENTS
LET'S GO DOW
TO THE **NEW**
PAPE
OFFIC

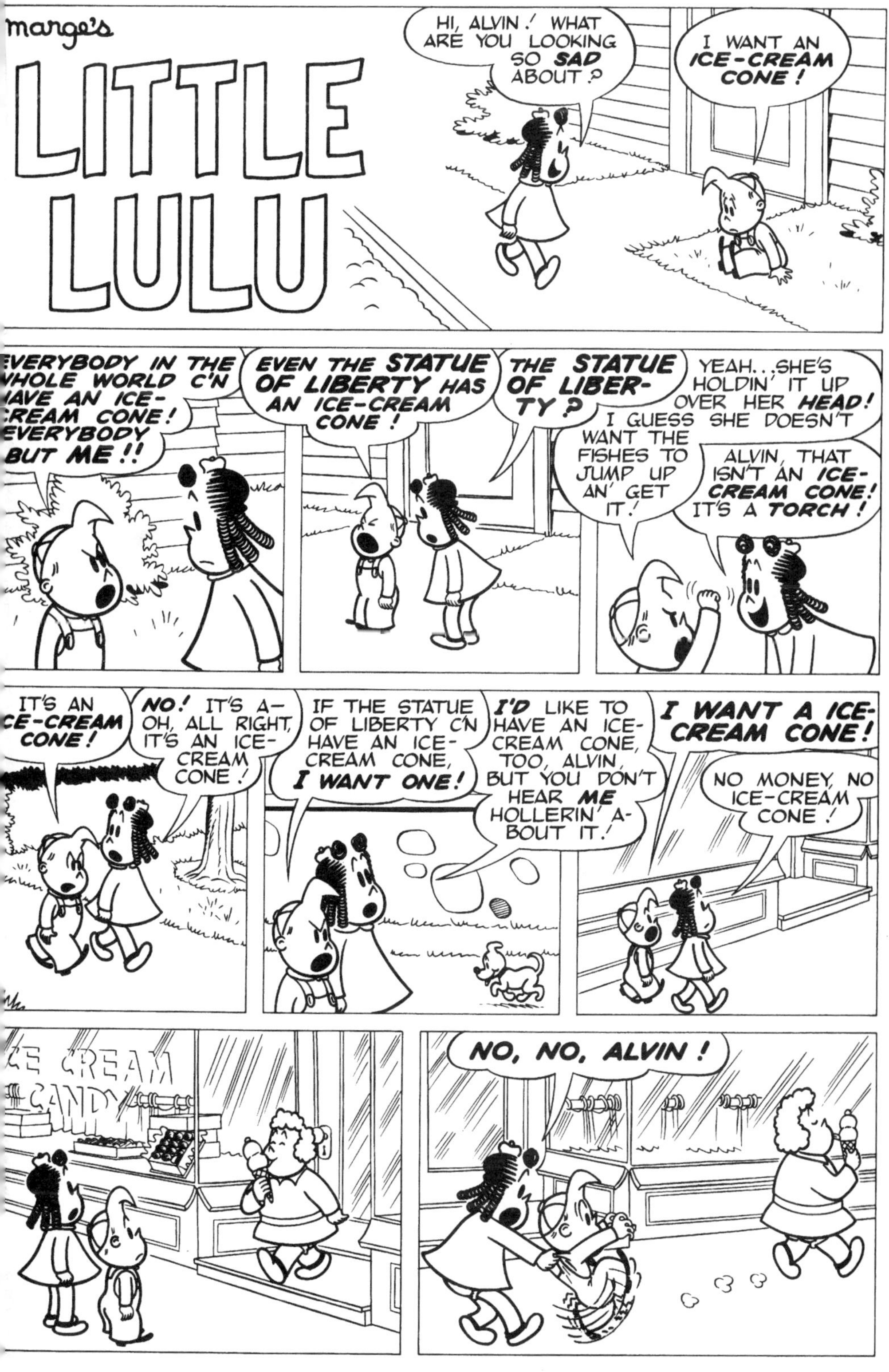
marge's
LITTLE LULU
HI, ALVIN! WHAT ARE YOU LOOKING SO SAD ABOUT?
I WANT AN ICE-CREAM CONE!
EVERYBODY IN THE WHOLE WORLD C'N HAVE AN ICE-CREAM CONE! EVERYBODY BUT ME!!
EVEN THE STATUE OF LIBERTY HAS AN ICE-CREAM CONE!
THE STATUE OF LIBER-TY?
YEAH...SHE'S HOLDIN' IT UP OVER HER HEAD! I GUESS SHE DOESN'T WANT THE FISHES TO JUMP UP AN' GET IT!
ALVIN, THAT ISN'T AN ICE-CREAM CONE! IT'S A TORCH!
IT'S AN ICE-CREAM CONE!
NO! IT'S A— OH, ALL RIGHT, IT'S AN ICE-CREAM CONE!
IF THE STATUE OF LIBERTY C'N HAVE AN ICE-CREAM CONE, I WANT ONE!
I'D LIKE TO HAVE AN ICE-CREAM CONE, TOO, ALVIN, BUT YOU DON'T HEAR ME HOLLERIN' A-BOUT IT!
I WANT A ICE-CREAM CONE!
NO MONEY, NO ICE-CREAM CONE!
CE CREAM
CANDY
NO, NO, ALVIN!

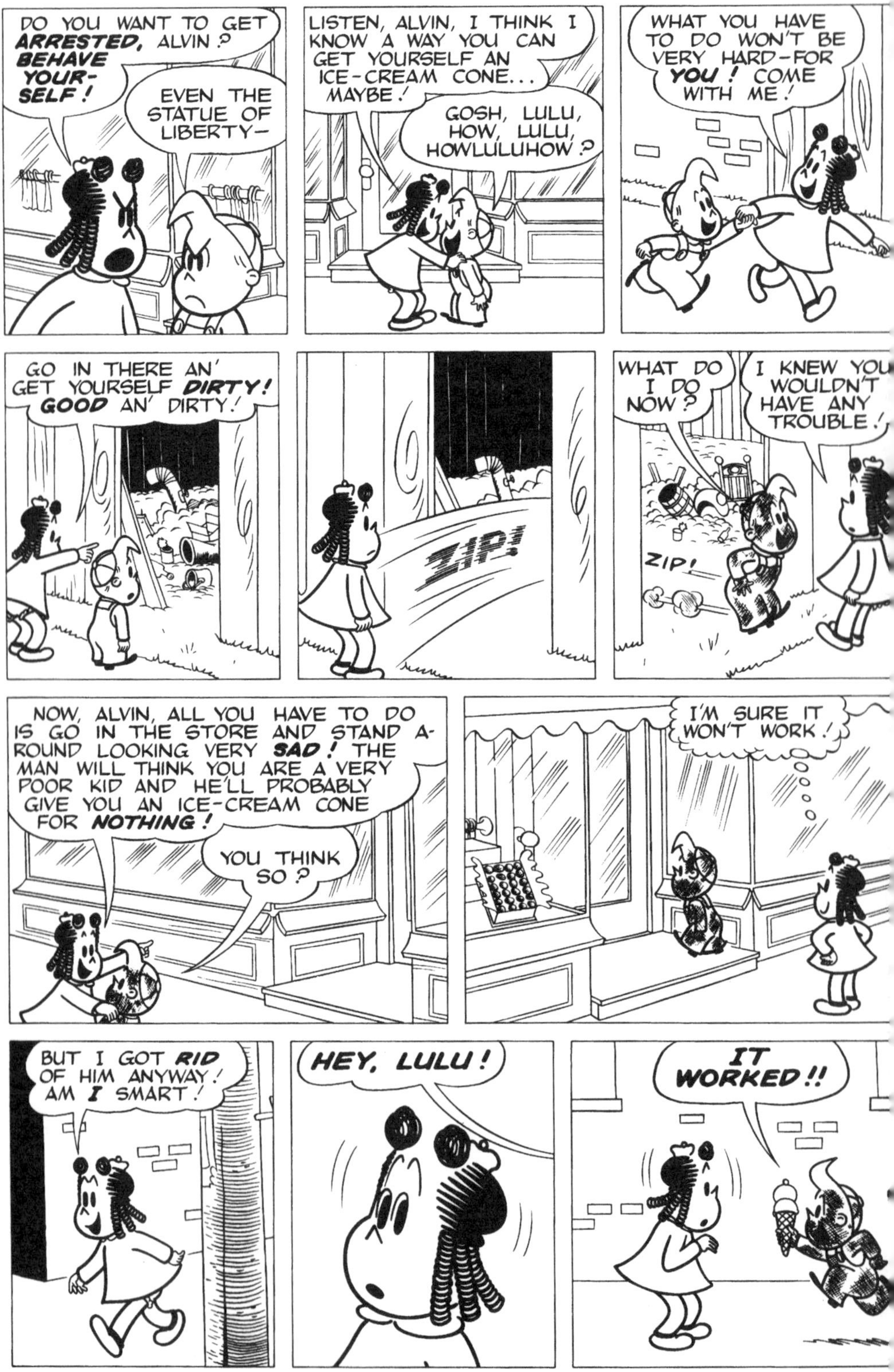
DO YOU WANT TO GET ARRESTED, ALVIN? BEHAVE YOURSELF!
EVEN THE STATUE OF LIBERTY—
LISTEN, ALVIN, I THINK I KNOW A WAY YOU CAN GET YOURSELF AN ICE-CREAM CONE... MAYBE!
GOSH, LULU, HOW, LULU, HOWLULUHOW?
WHAT YOU HAVE TO DO WON'T BE VERY HARD—FOR YOU! COME WITH ME!
GO IN THERE AN' GET YOURSELF DIRTY! GOOD AN' DIRTY!
ZIP!
WHAT DO I DO NOW?
I KNEW YOU WOULDN'T HAVE ANY TROUBLE!
ZIP!
NOW, ALVIN, ALL YOU HAVE TO DO IS GO IN THE STORE AND STAND AROUND LOOKING VERY SAD! THE MAN WILL THINK YOU ARE A VERY POOR KID AND HE'LL PROBABLY GIVE YOU AN ICE-CREAM CONE FOR NOTHING!
YOU THINK SO?
I'M SURE IT WON'T WORK!
BUT I GOT RID OF HIM ANYWAY! AM I SMART!
HEY, LULU!
IT WORKED!!

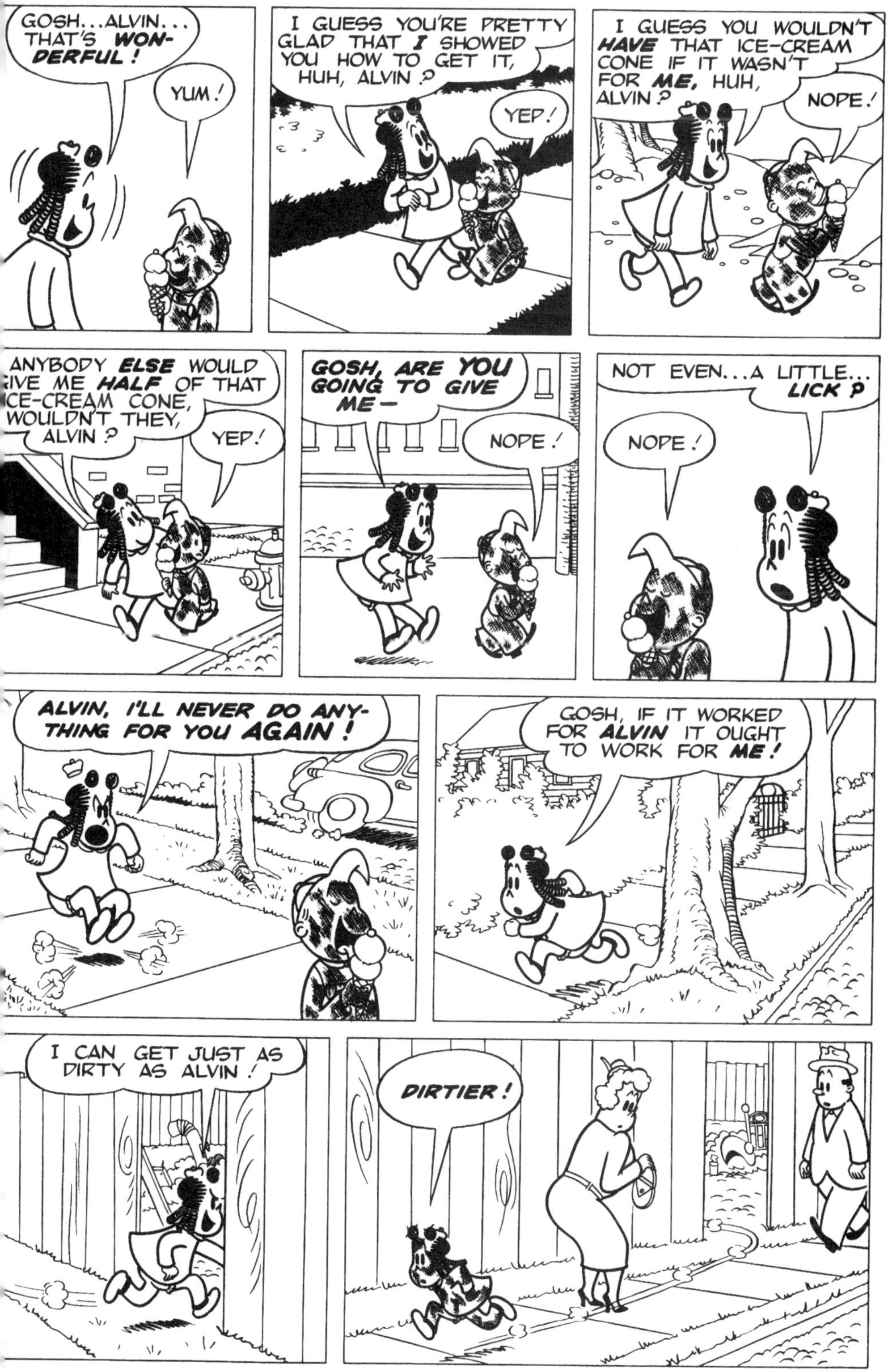

GOSH...ALVIN... THAT'S **WONDERFUL!**
YUM!
I GUESS YOU'RE PRETTY GLAD THAT ***I*** SHOWED YOU HOW TO GET IT, HUH, ALVIN?
YEP!
I GUESS YOU WOULDN'T ***HAVE*** THAT ICE-CREAM CONE IF IT WASN'T FOR ***ME,*** HUH, ALVIN?
NOPE!
ANYBODY ***ELSE*** WOULD GIVE ME ***HALF*** OF THAT ICE-CREAM CONE, WOULDN'T THEY, ALVIN?
YEP!
GOSH, ARE YOU GOING TO GIVE ME—
NOPE!
NOT EVEN...A LITTLE... ***LICK?***
NOPE!
ALVIN, I'LL NEVER DO ANYTHING FOR YOU AGAIN!
GOSH, IF IT WORKED FOR ***ALVIN*** IT OUGHT TO WORK FOR ***ME!***
I CAN GET JUST AS DIRTY AS ALVIN!
DIRTIER!

YUM, YUM!

WALNUT SUNDAE 25¢

LULU!!

M-MOTHER!

WHAT IN THE WORLD HAPPENED TO YOU? HOW DID YOU GET SO *DIRTY*?

MOTHER, I— I—

WHAT WERE YOU DOING IN THAT STORE, LOOKING JUST LIKE *ALVIN*?

MOTHER, ALVIN WANTED AN ICE-CREAM CONE VERY BAD, AND I THOUGHT OF A PLAN—

I THOUGHT IF ALVIN LOOKED LIKE A *POOR HOMELESS LITTLE CHILD* THE MAN WOULD GIVE HIM AN ICE-CREAM CONE FOR *NOTHING*!

WELL, THE M— *DIDN'T* GIV HIM AN ICE-CREAM CONE FOR NOTHIN

A *BATH!* RIGHT SMACK IN THE *MIDDLE OF THE DAY!*

LATER...

WHY DIDN'T YOU TELL N THAT IT WAS *MY MOTHE* WHO BOUGHT YOU THAT ICE-CREAM CONE?

YOU DIDN' ASK ME!

the End

22

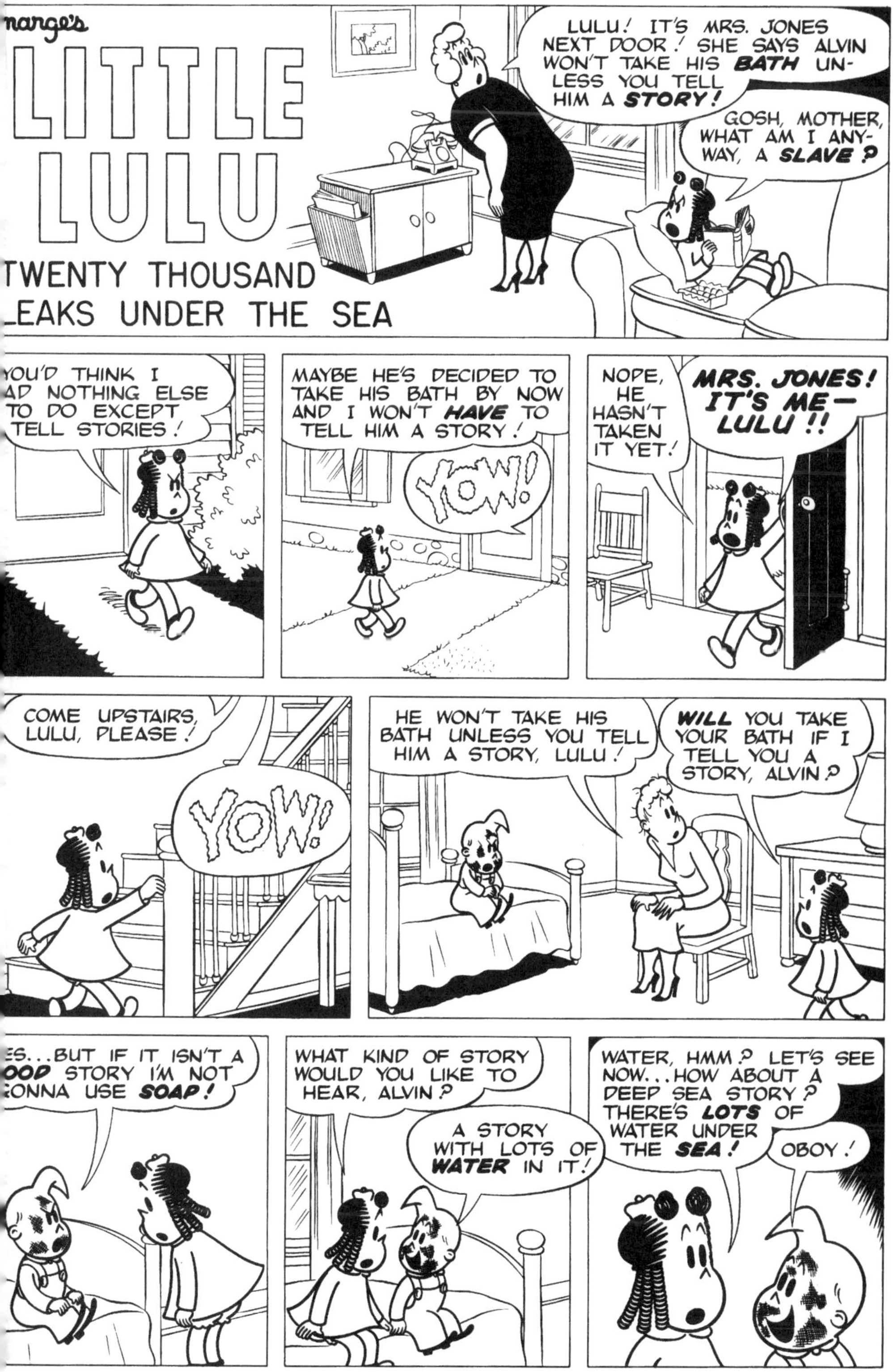
marge's
LITTLE LULU
TWENTY THOUSAND
LEAKS UNDER THE SEA
LULU! IT'S MRS. JONES NEXT DOOR! SHE SAYS ALVIN WON'T TAKE HIS BATH UNLESS YOU TELL HIM A STORY!
GOSH, MOTHER, WHAT AM I ANYWAY, A SLAVE?
YOU'D THINK I AD NOTHING ELSE TO DO EXCEPT TELL STORIES!
MAYBE HE'S DECIDED TO TAKE HIS BATH BY NOW AND I WON'T HAVE TO TELL HIM A STORY!
YOW!
NOPE, HE HASN'T TAKEN IT YET!
MRS. JONES! IT'S ME— LULU!!
COME UPSTAIRS, LULU, PLEASE!
YOW!
HE WON'T TAKE HIS BATH UNLESS YOU TELL HIM A STORY, LULU!
WILL YOU TAKE YOUR BATH IF I TELL YOU A STORY, ALVIN?
ES...BUT IF IT ISN'T A OOD STORY I'M NOT ONNA USE SOAP!
WHAT KIND OF STORY WOULD YOU LIKE TO HEAR, ALVIN?
A STORY WITH LOTS OF WATER IN IT!
WATER, HMM? LET'S SEE NOW...HOW ABOUT A DEEP SEA STORY? THERE'S LOTS OF WATER UNDER THE SEA!
OBOY!

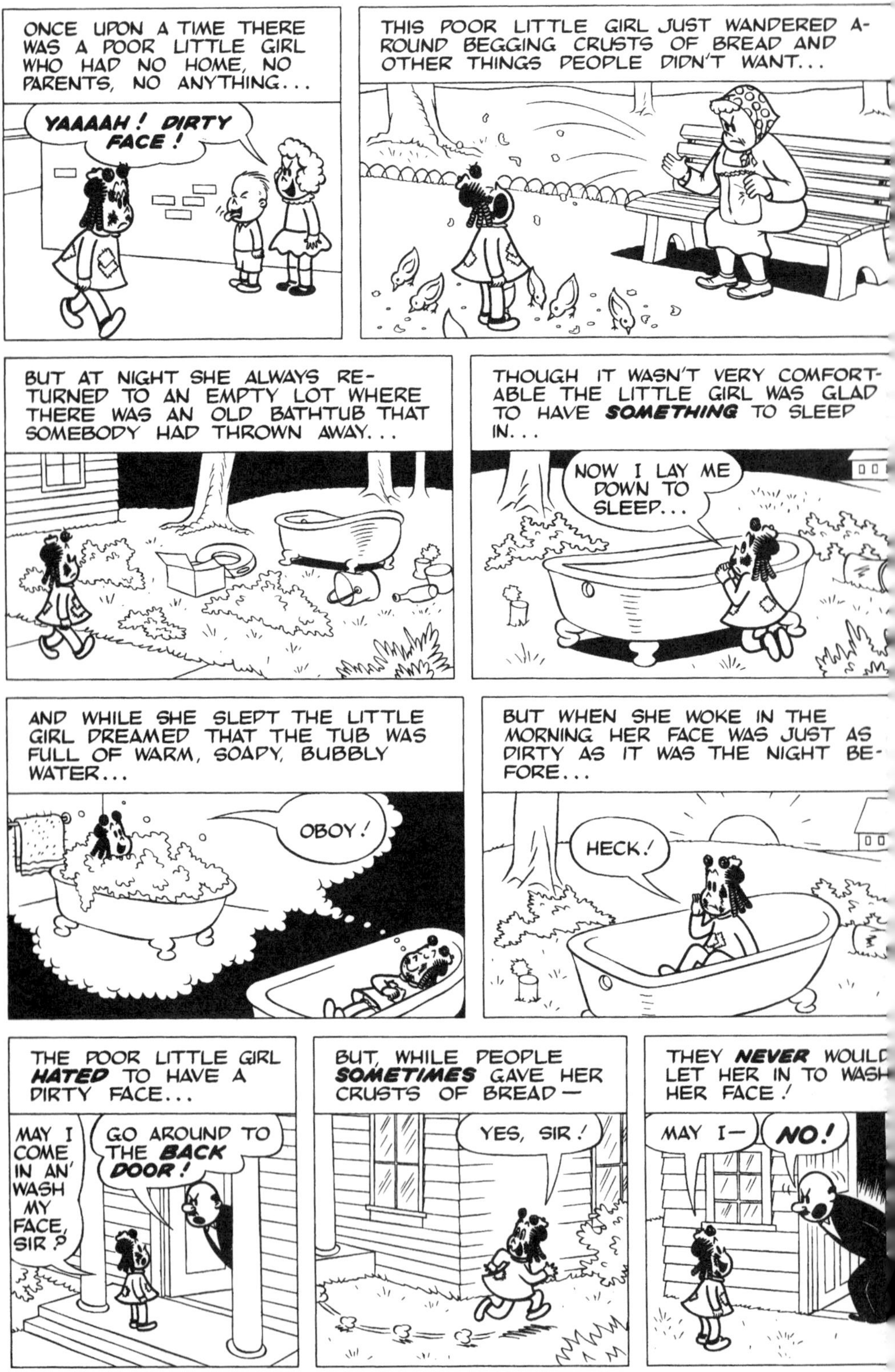
ONCE UPON A TIME THERE WAS A POOR LITTLE GIRL WHO HAD NO HOME, NO PARENTS, NO ANYTHING...
YAAAAH! DIRTY FACE!
THIS POOR LITTLE GIRL JUST WANDERED AROUND BEGGING CRUSTS OF BREAD AND OTHER THINGS PEOPLE DIDN'T WANT...
BUT AT NIGHT SHE ALWAYS RETURNED TO AN EMPTY LOT WHERE THERE WAS AN OLD BATHTUB THAT SOMEBODY HAD THROWN AWAY...
THOUGH IT WASN'T VERY COMFORTABLE THE LITTLE GIRL WAS GLAD TO HAVE SOMETHING TO SLEEP IN...
NOW I LAY ME DOWN TO SLEEP...
AND WHILE SHE SLEPT THE LITTLE GIRL DREAMED THAT THE TUB WAS FULL OF WARM, SOAPY, BUBBLY WATER...
OBOY!
BUT WHEN SHE WOKE IN THE MORNING HER FACE WAS JUST AS DIRTY AS IT WAS THE NIGHT BEFORE...
HECK!
THE POOR LITTLE GIRL HATED TO HAVE A DIRTY FACE...
MAY I COME IN AN' WASH MY FACE, SIR?
GO AROUND TO THE BACK DOOR!
BUT, WHILE PEOPLE SOMETIMES GAVE HER CRUSTS OF BREAD—
YES, SIR!
THEY NEVER WOULD LET HER IN TO WASH HER FACE!
MAY I—
NO!

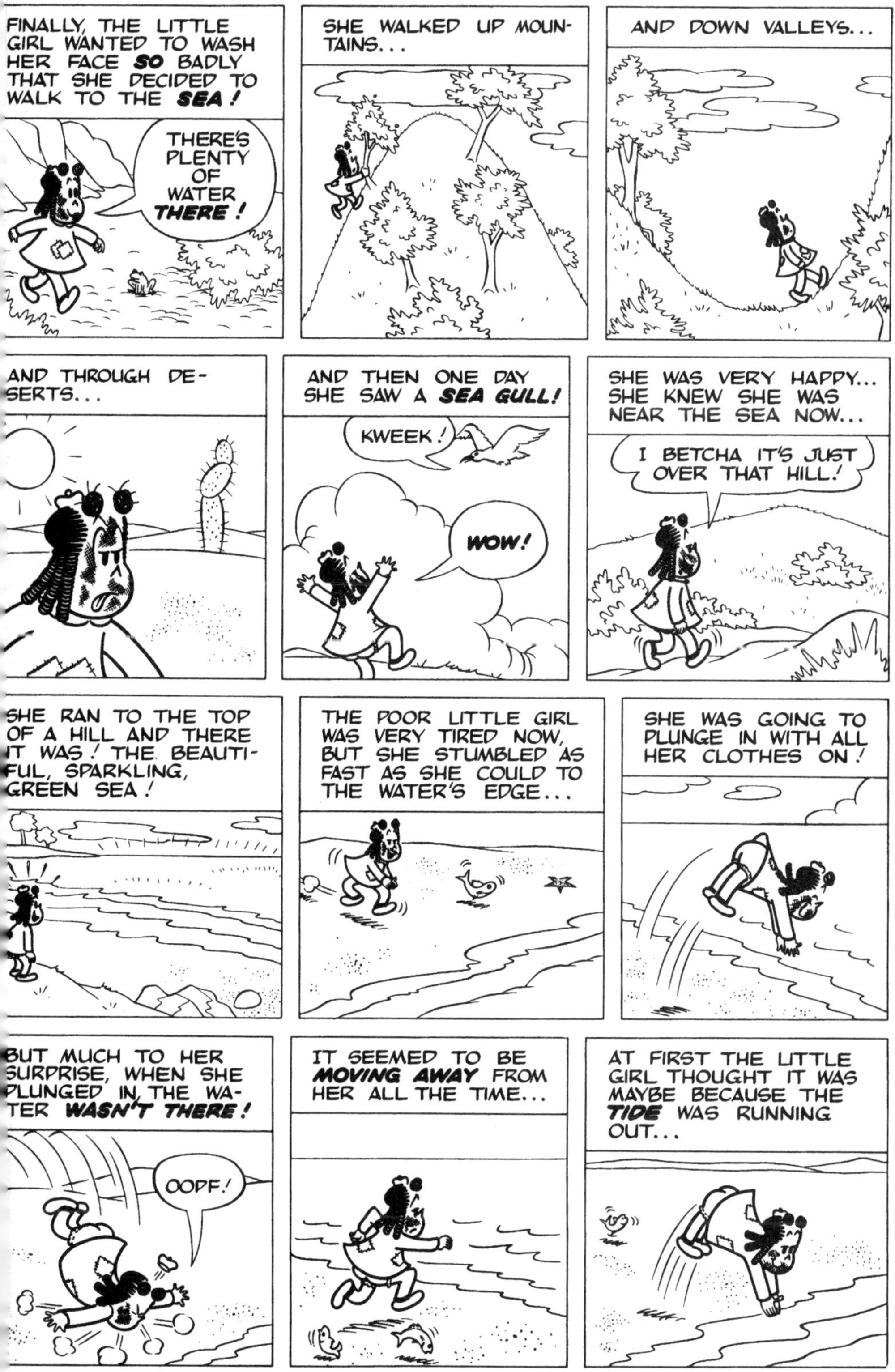
FINALLY, THE LITTLE GIRL WANTED TO WASH HER FACE SO BADLY THAT SHE DECIDED TO WALK TO THE SEA!
THERE'S PLENTY OF WATER THERE!
SHE WALKED UP MOUNTAINS...
AND DOWN VALLEYS...
AND THROUGH DESERTS...
AND THEN ONE DAY SHE SAW A SEA GULL!
KWEEK!
WOW!
SHE WAS VERY HAPPY... SHE KNEW SHE WAS NEAR THE SEA NOW...
I BETCHA IT'S JUST OVER THAT HILL!
SHE RAN TO THE TOP OF A HILL AND THERE IT WAS! THE BEAUTIFUL, SPARKLING, GREEN SEA!
THE POOR LITTLE GIRL WAS VERY TIRED NOW, BUT SHE STUMBLED AS FAST AS SHE COULD TO THE WATER'S EDGE...
SHE WAS GOING TO PLUNGE IN WITH ALL HER CLOTHES ON!
BUT MUCH TO HER SURPRISE, WHEN SHE PLUNGED IN THE WATER WASN'T THERE!
OOPF!
IT SEEMED TO BE MOVING AWAY FROM HER ALL THE TIME...
AT FIRST THE LITTLE GIRL THOUGHT IT WAS MAYBE BECAUSE THE TIDE WAS RUNNING OUT...

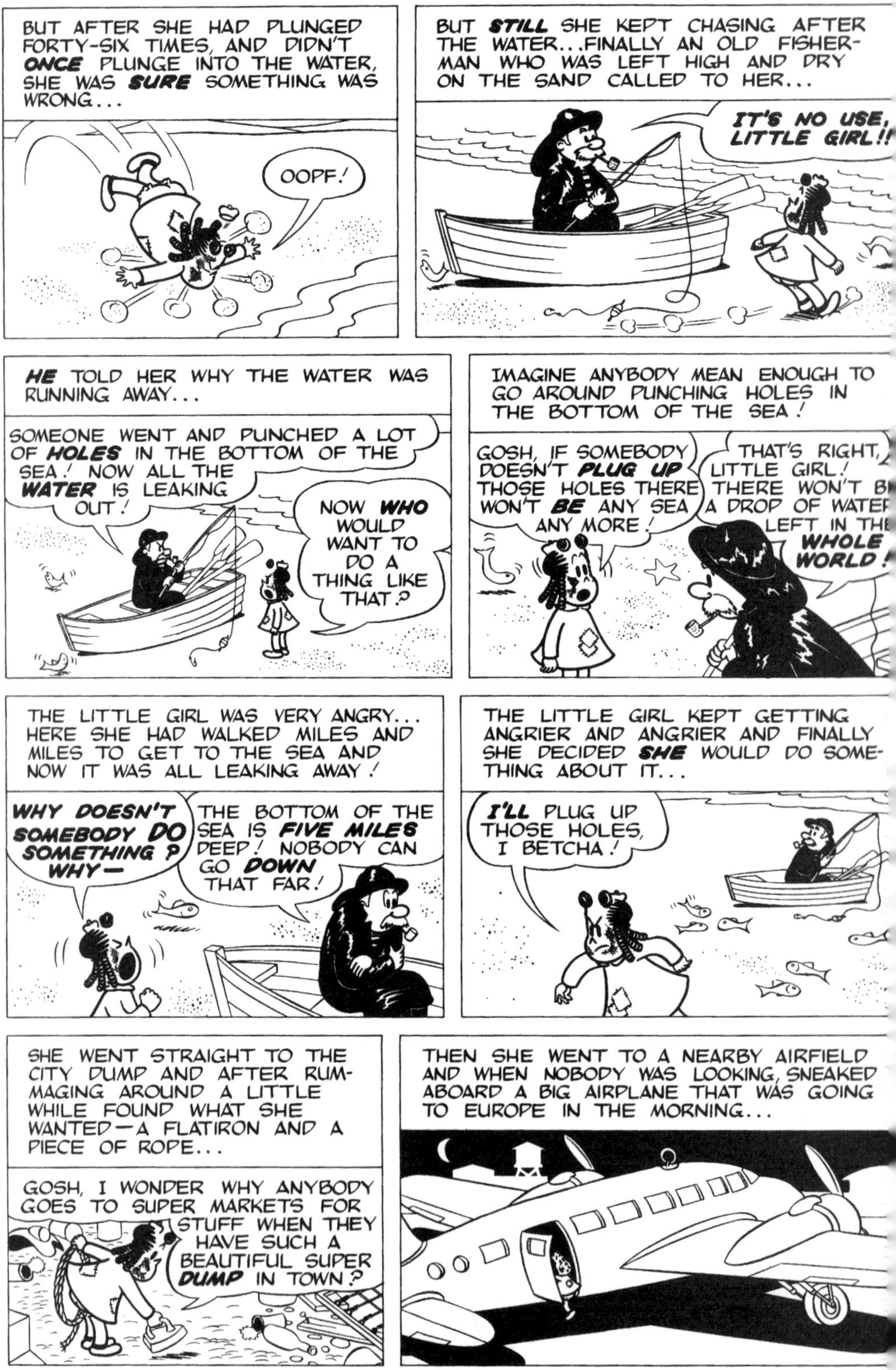
BUT AFTER SHE HAD PLUNGED FORTY-SIX TIMES, AND DIDN'T ONCE PLUNGE INTO THE WATER, SHE WAS SURE SOMETHING WAS WRONG...
OOPF!
BUT STILL SHE KEPT CHASING AFTER THE WATER...FINALLY AN OLD FISHERMAN WHO WAS LEFT HIGH AND DRY ON THE SAND CALLED TO HER...
IT'S NO USE, LITTLE GIRL!!
HE TOLD HER WHY THE WATER WAS RUNNING AWAY...
SOMEONE WENT AND PUNCHED A LOT OF HOLES IN THE BOTTOM OF THE SEA! NOW ALL THE WATER IS LEAKING OUT!
NOW WHO WOULD WANT TO DO A THING LIKE THAT?
IMAGINE ANYBODY MEAN ENOUGH TO GO AROUND PUNCHING HOLES IN THE BOTTOM OF THE SEA!
GOSH, IF SOMEBODY DOESN'T PLUG UP THOSE HOLES THERE WON'T BE ANY SEA ANY MORE!
THAT'S RIGHT, LITTLE GIRL! THERE WON'T BE A DROP OF WATER LEFT IN THE WHOLE WORLD!
THE LITTLE GIRL WAS VERY ANGRY... HERE SHE HAD WALKED MILES AND MILES TO GET TO THE SEA AND NOW IT WAS ALL LEAKING AWAY!
WHY DOESN'T SOMEBODY DO SOMETHING? WHY—
THE BOTTOM OF THE SEA IS FIVE MILES DEEP! NOBODY CAN GO DOWN THAT FAR!
THE LITTLE GIRL KEPT GETTING ANGRIER AND ANGRIER AND FINALLY SHE DECIDED SHE WOULD DO SOMETHING ABOUT IT...
I'LL PLUG UP THOSE HOLES, I BETCHA!
SHE WENT STRAIGHT TO THE CITY DUMP AND AFTER RUMMAGING AROUND A LITTLE WHILE FOUND WHAT SHE WANTED—A FLATIRON AND A PIECE OF ROPE...
GOSH, I WONDER WHY ANYBODY GOES TO SUPER MARKETS FOR STUFF WHEN THEY HAVE SUCH A BEAUTIFUL SUPER DUMP IN TOWN?
THEN SHE WENT TO A NEARBY AIRFIELD AND WHEN NOBODY WAS LOOKING, SNEAKED ABOARD A BIG AIRPLANE THAT WAS GOING TO EUROPE IN THE MORNING...

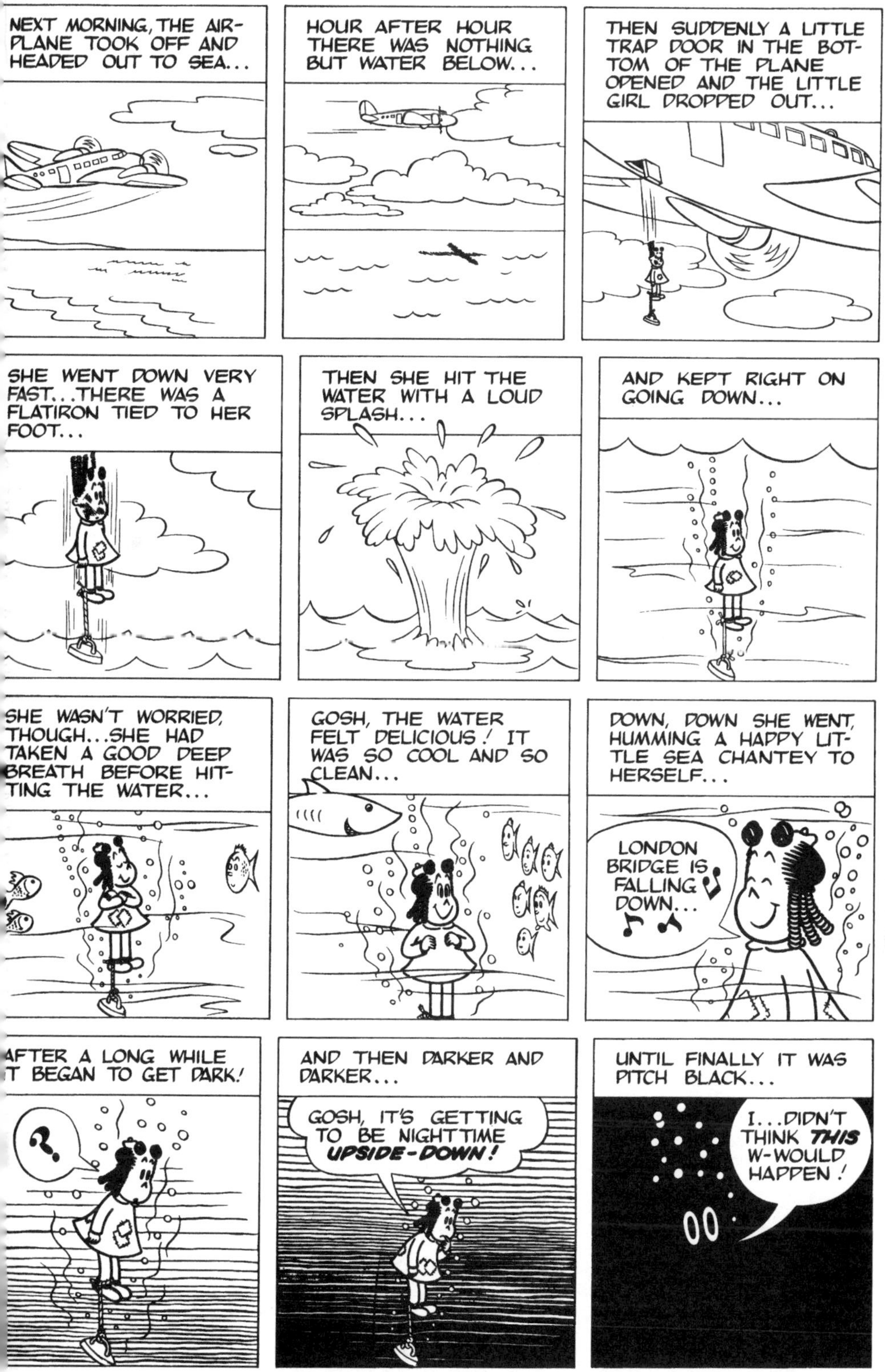
NEXT MORNING, THE AIRPLANE TOOK OFF AND HEADED OUT TO SEA...
HOUR AFTER HOUR THERE WAS NOTHING BUT WATER BELOW...
THEN SUDDENLY A LITTLE TRAP DOOR IN THE BOTTOM OF THE PLANE OPENED AND THE LITTLE GIRL DROPPED OUT...
SHE WENT DOWN VERY FAST...THERE WAS A FLATIRON TIED TO HER FOOT...
THEN SHE HIT THE WATER WITH A LOUD SPLASH...
AND KEPT RIGHT ON GOING DOWN...
SHE WASN'T WORRIED, THOUGH...SHE HAD TAKEN A GOOD DEEP BREATH BEFORE HITTING THE WATER...
GOSH, THE WATER FELT DELICIOUS! IT WAS SO COOL AND SO CLEAN...
DOWN, DOWN SHE WENT, HUMMING A HAPPY LITTLE SEA CHANTEY TO HERSELF...
LONDON BRIDGE IS FALLING DOWN...
AFTER A LONG WHILE IT BEGAN TO GET DARK!
?
AND THEN DARKER AND DARKER...
GOSH, IT'S GETTING TO BE NIGHTTIME *UPSIDE-DOWN!*
UNTIL FINALLY IT WAS PITCH BLACK...
I...DIDN'T THINK *THIS* W-WOULD HAPPEN!

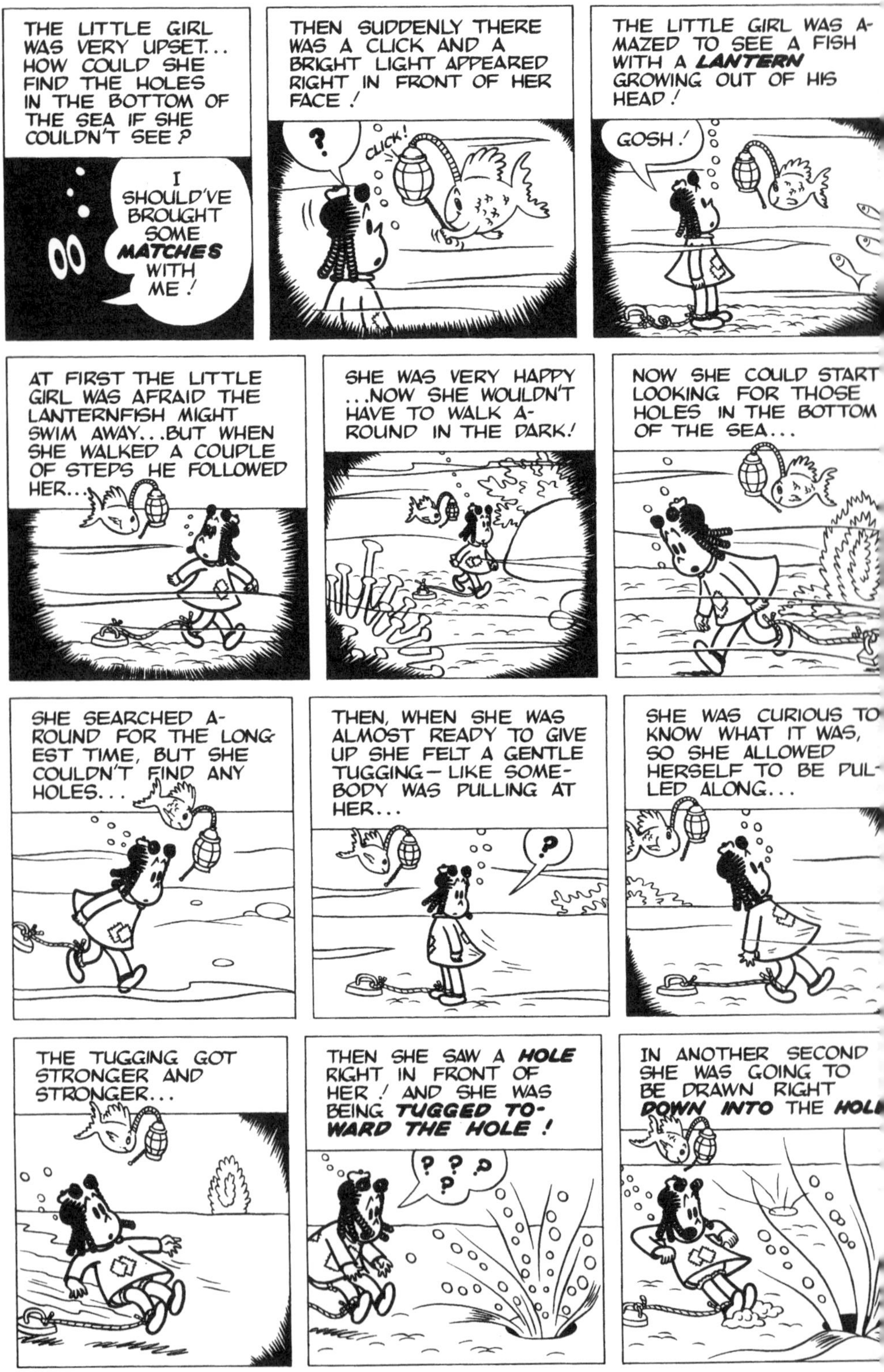
THE LITTLE GIRL WAS VERY UPSET... HOW COULD SHE FIND THE HOLES IN THE BOTTOM OF THE SEA IF SHE COULDN'T SEE?
I SHOULD'VE BROUGHT SOME MATCHES WITH ME!
THEN SUDDENLY THERE WAS A CLICK AND A BRIGHT LIGHT APPEARED RIGHT IN FRONT OF HER FACE!
?
CLICK!
THE LITTLE GIRL WAS A-MAZED TO SEE A FISH WITH A LANTERN GROWING OUT OF HIS HEAD!
GOSH!
AT FIRST THE LITTLE GIRL WAS AFRAID THE LANTERNFISH MIGHT SWIM AWAY...BUT WHEN SHE WALKED A COUPLE OF STEPS HE FOLLOWED HER...
SHE WAS VERY HAPPY ...NOW SHE WOULDN'T HAVE TO WALK A-ROUND IN THE DARK!
NOW SHE COULD START LOOKING FOR THOSE HOLES IN THE BOTTOM OF THE SEA...
SHE SEARCHED A-ROUND FOR THE LONG EST TIME, BUT SHE COULDN'T FIND ANY HOLES...
THEN, WHEN SHE WAS ALMOST READY TO GIVE UP SHE FELT A GENTLE TUGGING—LIKE SOME-BODY WAS PULLING AT HER...
?
SHE WAS CURIOUS TO KNOW WHAT IT WAS, SO SHE ALLOWED HERSELF TO BE PUL-LED ALONG...
THE TUGGING GOT STRONGER AND STRONGER...
THEN SHE SAW A HOLE RIGHT IN FRONT OF HER! AND SHE WAS BEING TUGGED TO-WARD THE HOLE!
? ? ? ?
IN ANOTHER SECOND SHE WAS GOING TO BE DRAWN RIGHT DOWN INTO THE HOL

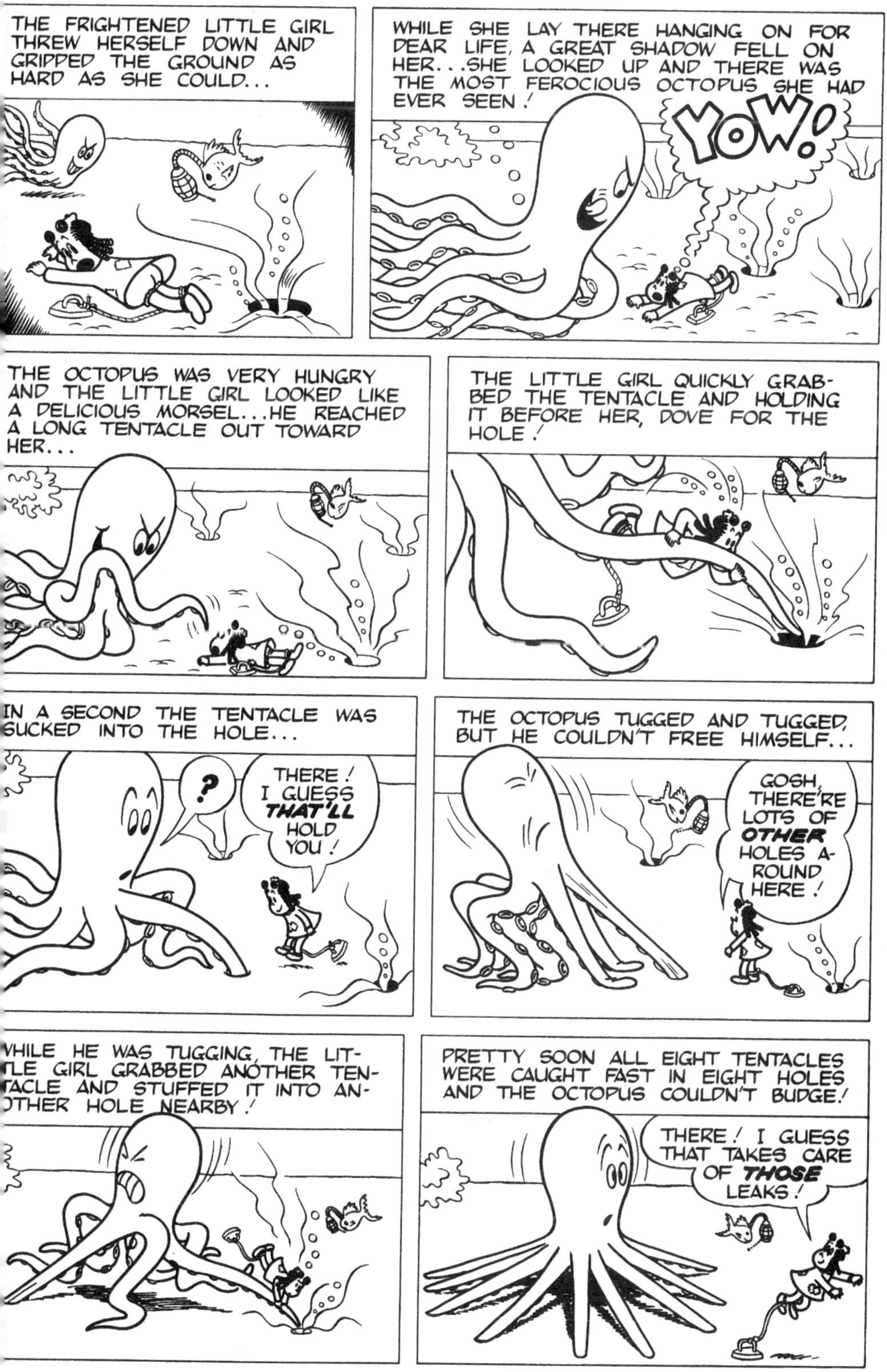
THE FRIGHTENED LITTLE GIRL THREW HERSELF DOWN AND GRIPPED THE GROUND AS HARD AS SHE COULD...
WHILE SHE LAY THERE HANGING ON FOR DEAR LIFE, A GREAT SHADOW FELL ON HER...SHE LOOKED UP AND THERE WAS THE MOST FEROCIOUS OCTOPUS SHE HAD EVER SEEN!
YOW!
THE OCTOPUS WAS VERY HUNGRY AND THE LITTLE GIRL LOOKED LIKE A DELICIOUS MORSEL...HE REACHED A LONG TENTACLE OUT TOWARD HER...
THE LITTLE GIRL QUICKLY GRAB-BED THE TENTACLE AND HOLDING IT BEFORE HER, DOVE FOR THE HOLE!
IN A SECOND THE TENTACLE WAS SUCKED INTO THE HOLE...
?
THERE! I GUESS THAT'LL HOLD YOU!
THE OCTOPUS TUGGED AND TUGGED, BUT HE COULDN'T FREE HIMSELF...
GOSH, THERE'RE LOTS OF OTHER HOLES A-ROUND HERE!
WHILE HE WAS TUGGING, THE LIT-TLE GIRL GRABBED ANOTHER TEN-TACLE AND STUFFED IT INTO AN-OTHER HOLE NEARBY!
PRETTY SOON ALL EIGHT TENTACLES WERE CAUGHT FAST IN EIGHT HOLES AND THE OCTOPUS COULDN'T BUDGE!
THERE! I GUESS THAT TAKES CARE OF THOSE LEAKS!

THE LITTLE GIRL HUNTED AROUND AND FOUND OTHER LEAKS, AND THEN SHE PLAYED THE SAME TRICK ON OTHER OCTOPUSES...

FINALLY, AFTER PLUGGING UP TWENTY THOUSAND LEAKS WITH TWENTY-FIVE THOUSAND OCTOPUSES SHE FOUND OUT WHAT WAS **CAUSING** THE LEAKS!

SO *THAT'S* WHAT'S BEEN GOING ON!

UGH.

IT WAS A **NEARSIGHTED SWORDFISH**! HE WANTED TO GO **UP**, BUT INSTEAD, HE WAS GOING DOWN, AND POKING HOLES IN THE BOTTOM!

LOOK, YOU'RE GOING THE WRONG WAY! LET ME—

THE LITTLE GIRL GENTLY TURNED HIM AROUND AND HE SWAM UP TO THE TOP WITH THE LITTLE GIRL CLINGING TO HIS TAIL...

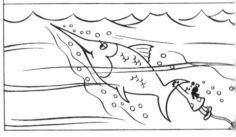

AFTER FLOATING AROUND FOR SIXTEEN DAYS, THE LITTLE GIRL WAS PICKED UP BY A BIG OCEAN LINER!

HEY! HERE I AM!

...AND WHEN SHE TOLD EVERYBODY HOW SHE HAD PLUGGED UP ALL THE LEAKS IN THE BOTTOM OF THE SEA SHE WAS GIVEN A BIG REWARD AND LIVED HAPPILY EVER AFTER!

ER...ARE YOU GOING TO TAKE YOUR BATH, ALVIN?

YEAH!

...BUT *NO* SOAP!

the End

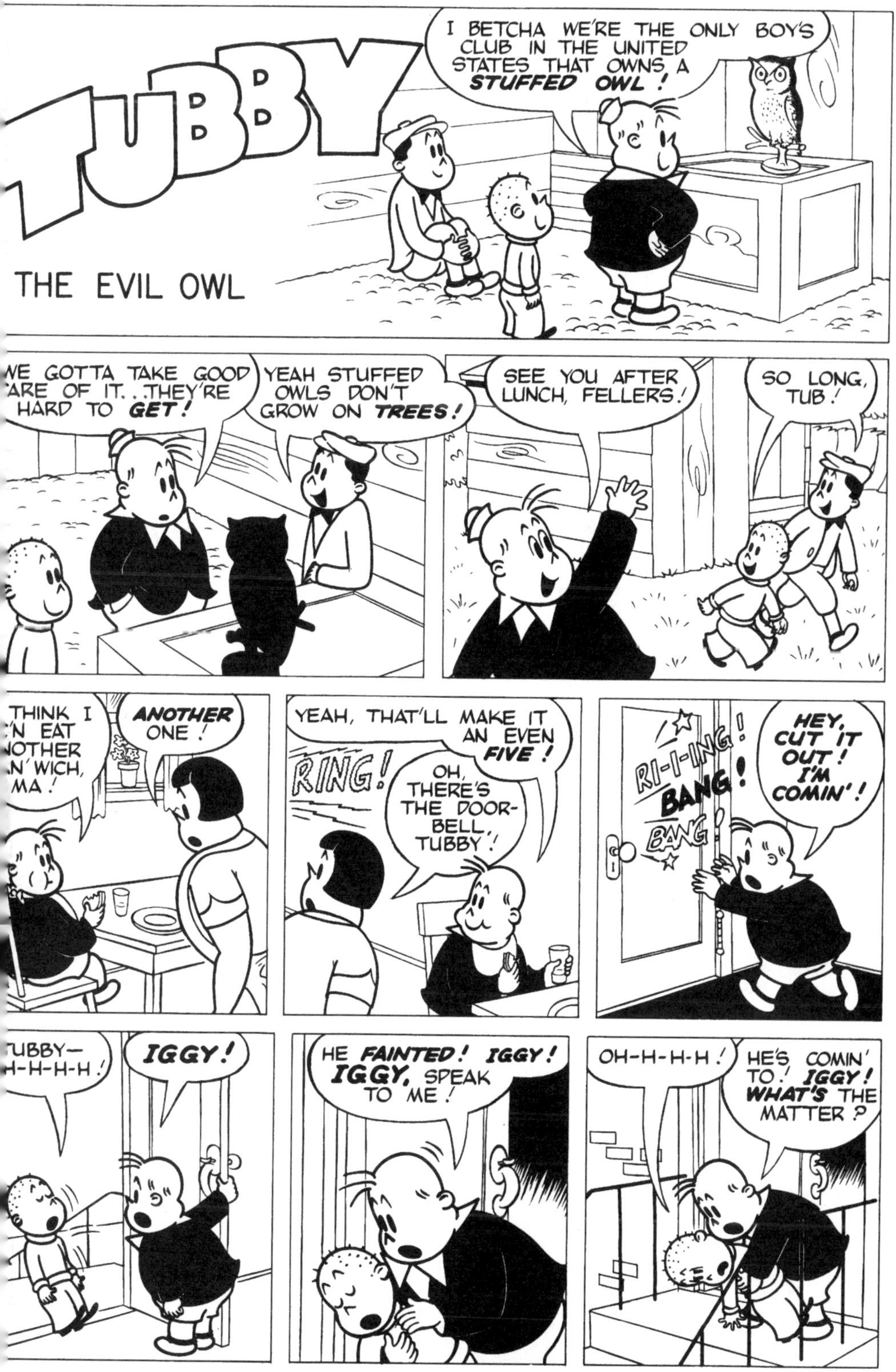
TUBBY
THE EVIL OWL
I BETCHA WE'RE THE ONLY BOY'S CLUB IN THE UNITED STATES THAT OWNS A STUFFED OWL!
WE GOTTA TAKE GOOD CARE OF IT...THEY'RE HARD TO GET!
YEAH STUFFED OWLS DON'T GROW ON TREES!
SEE YOU AFTER LUNCH, FELLERS!
SO LONG, TUB!
THINK I 'N EAT NOTHER N' WICH, MA!
ANOTHER ONE!
YEAH, THAT'LL MAKE IT AN EVEN FIVE!
RING!
OH, THERE'S THE DOOR-BELL, TUBBY!
RI-I-ING!
BANG!
BANG!
HEY, CUT IT OUT! I'M COMIN'!
TUBBY—H-H-H-H!
IGGY!
HE FAINTED! IGGY! IGGY, SPEAK TO ME!
OH-H-H-H!
HE'S COMIN' TO! IGGY! WHAT'S THE MATTER?

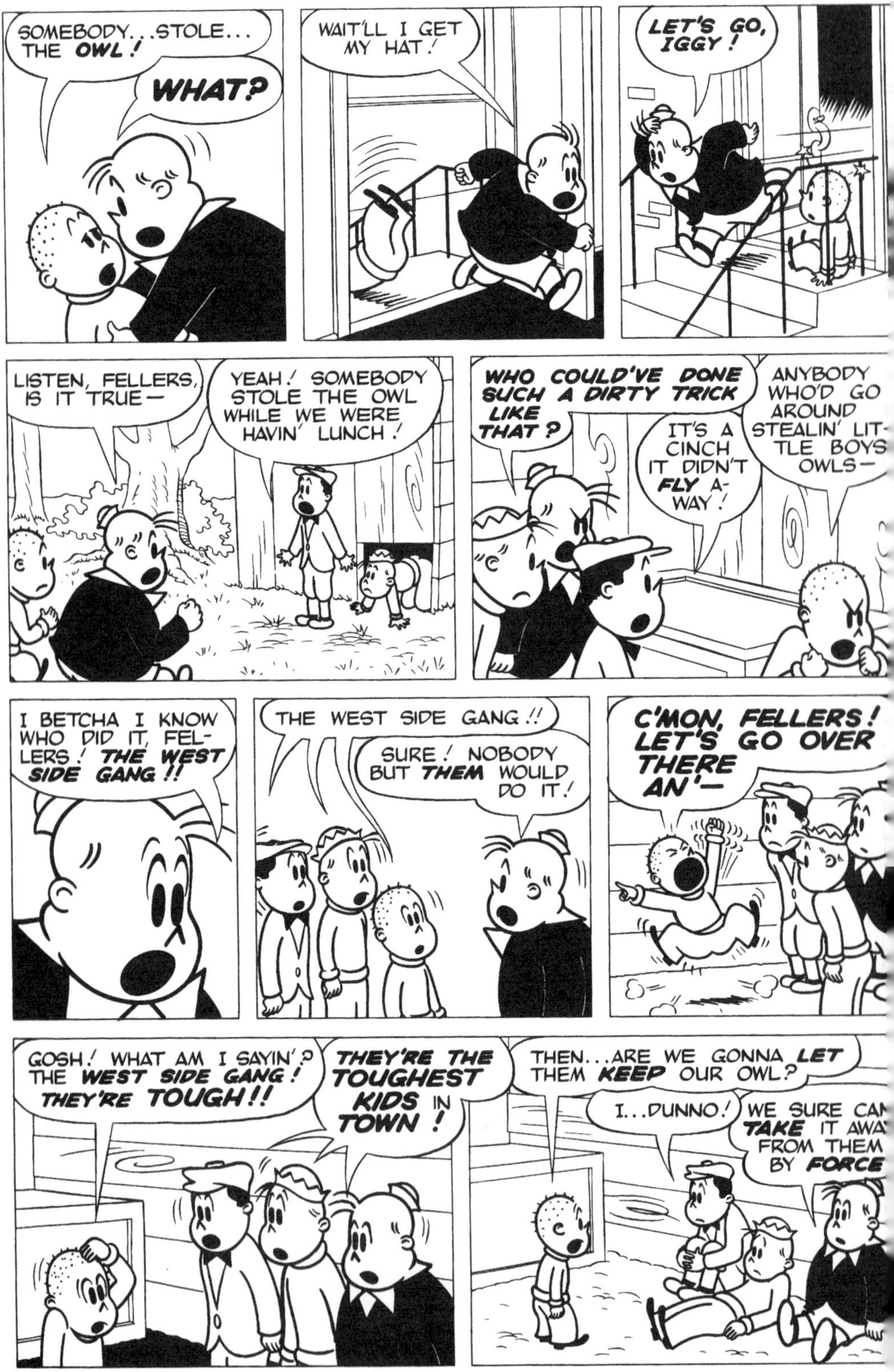
SOMEBODY...STOLE... THE OWL!
WHAT?
WAIT'LL I GET MY HAT!
LET'S GO, IGGY!
LISTEN, FELLERS, IS IT TRUE—
YEAH! SOMEBODY STOLE THE OWL WHILE WE WERE HAVIN' LUNCH!
WHO COULD'VE DONE SUCH A DIRTY TRICK LIKE THAT?
IT'S A CINCH IT DIDN'T FLY A-WAY!
ANYBODY WHO'D GO AROUND STEALIN' LIT-TLE BOYS OWLS—
I BETCHA I KNOW WHO DID IT, FEL-LERS! THE WEST SIDE GANG!!
THE WEST SIDE GANG!!
SURE! NOBODY BUT THEM WOULD DO IT!
C'MON, FELLERS! LET'S GO OVER THERE AN'—
GOSH! WHAT AM I SAYIN'? THE WEST SIDE GANG! THEY'RE TOUGH!!
THEY'RE THE TOUGHEST KIDS IN TOWN!
THEN...ARE WE GONNA LET THEM KEEP OUR OWL?
I...DUNNO!
WE SURE CAN TAKE IT AWAY FROM THEM BY FORCE

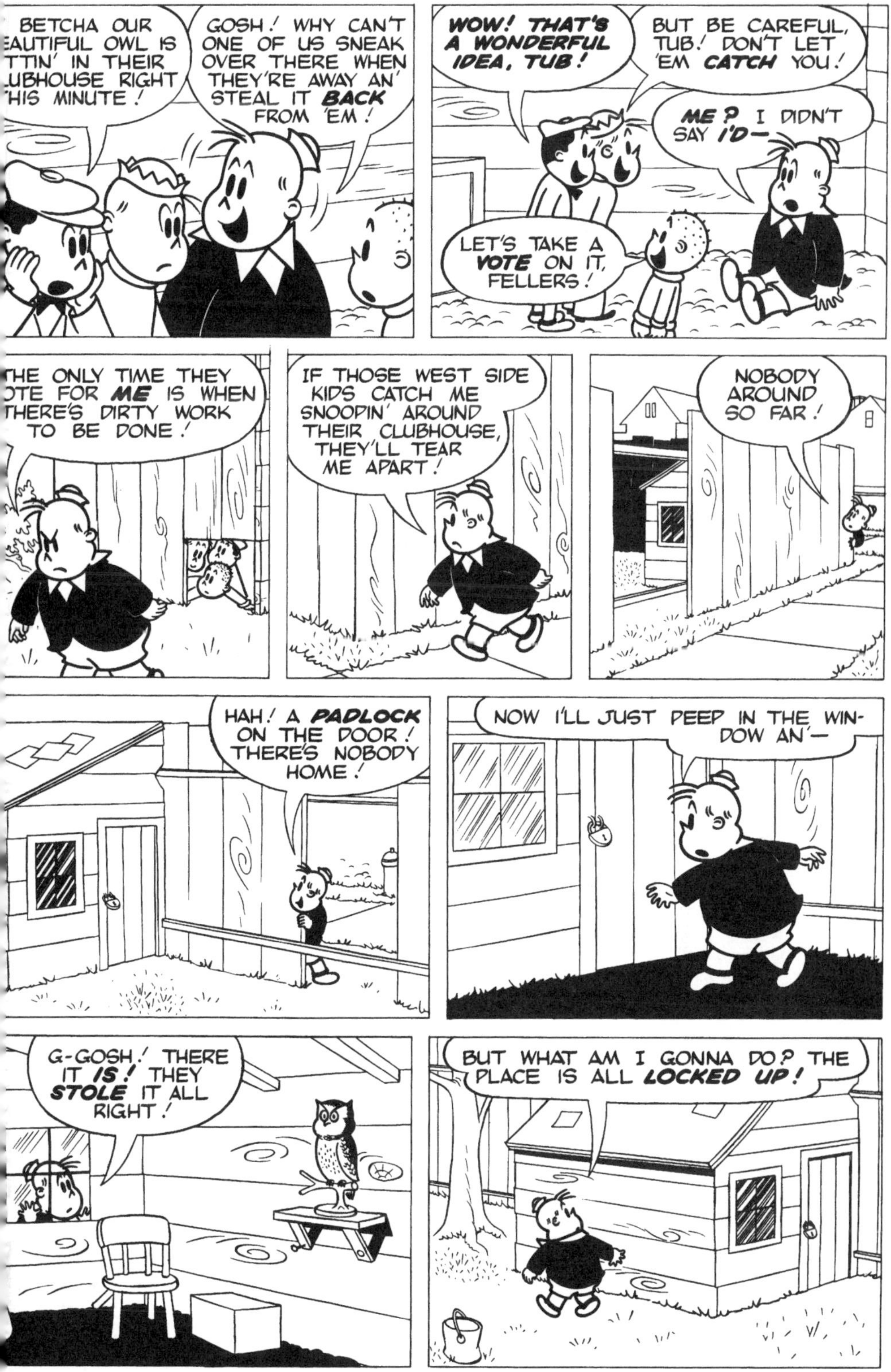
BETCHA OUR EAUTIFUL OWL IS TTIN' IN THEIR LUBHOUSE RIGHT HIS MINUTE!
GOSH! WHY CAN'T ONE OF US SNEAK OVER THERE WHEN THEY'RE AWAY AN' STEAL IT BACK FROM 'EM!
WOW! THAT'S A WONDERFUL IDEA, TUB!
BUT BE CAREFUL, TUB! DON'T LET 'EM CATCH YOU!
ME? I DIDN'T SAY I'D—
LET'S TAKE A VOTE ON IT, FELLERS!
THE ONLY TIME THEY OTE FOR ME IS WHEN THERE'S DIRTY WORK TO BE DONE!
IF THOSE WEST SIDE KIDS CATCH ME SNOOPIN' AROUND THEIR CLUBHOUSE, THEY'LL TEAR ME APART!
NOBODY AROUND SO FAR!
HAH! A PADLOCK ON THE DOOR! THERE'S NOBODY HOME!
NOW I'LL JUST PEEP IN THE WIN- DOW AN'—
G-GOSH! THERE IT IS! THEY STOLE IT ALL RIGHT!
BUT WHAT AM I GONNA DO? THE PLACE IS ALL LOCKED UP!

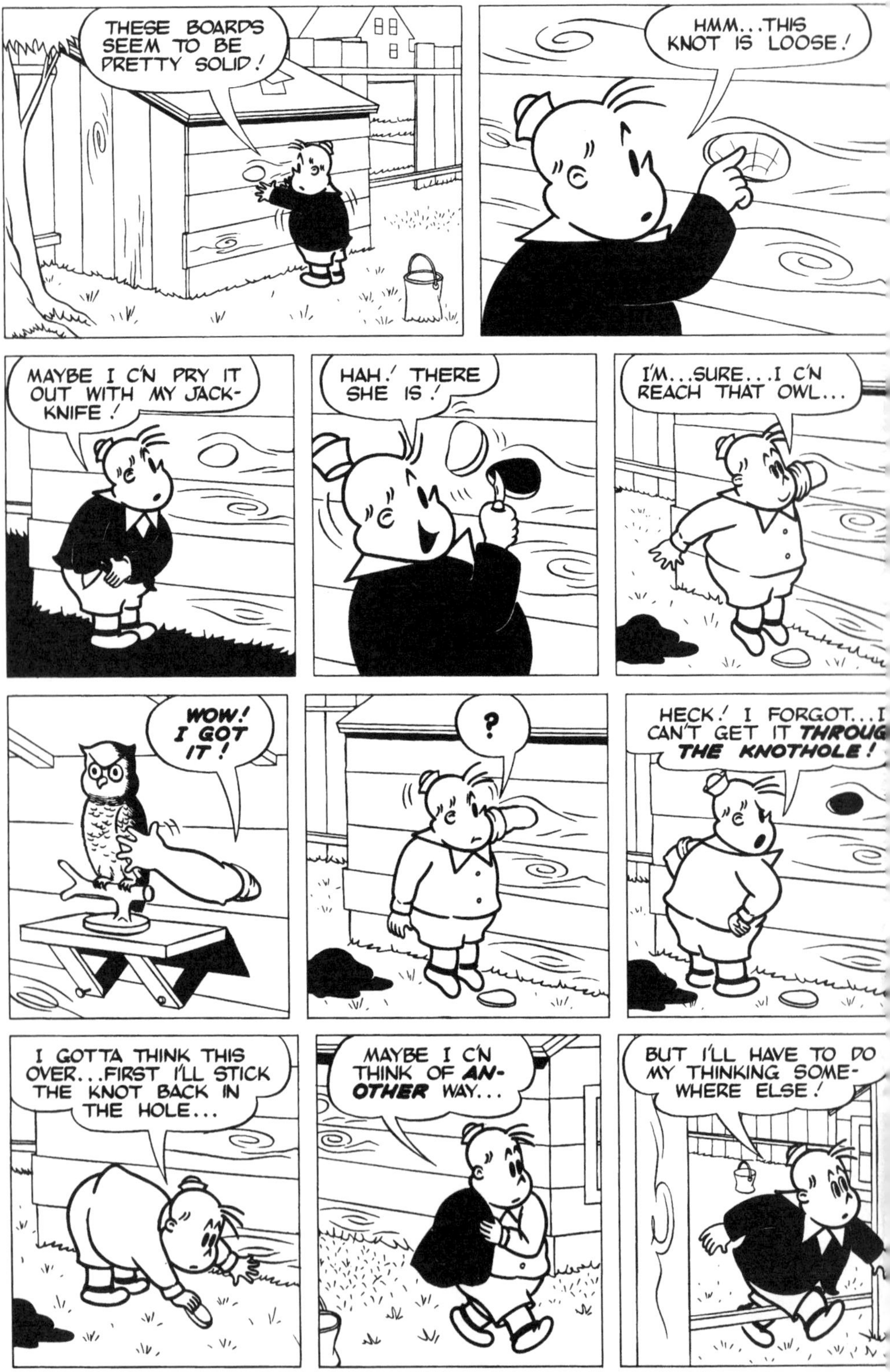
THESE BOARDS SEEM TO BE PRETTY SOLID!
HMM...THIS KNOT IS LOOSE!
MAYBE I C'N PRY IT OUT WITH MY JACK-KNIFE!
HAH! THERE SHE IS!
I'M...SURE...I C'N REACH THAT OWL...
WOW! I GOT IT!
?
HECK! I FORGOT...I CAN'T GET IT THROUG THE KNOTHOLE!
I GOTTA THINK THIS OVER...FIRST I'LL STICK THE KNOT BACK IN THE HOLE...
MAYBE I C'N THINK OF AN-OTHER WAY...
BUT I'LL HAVE TO DO MY THINKING SOME-WHERE ELSE!

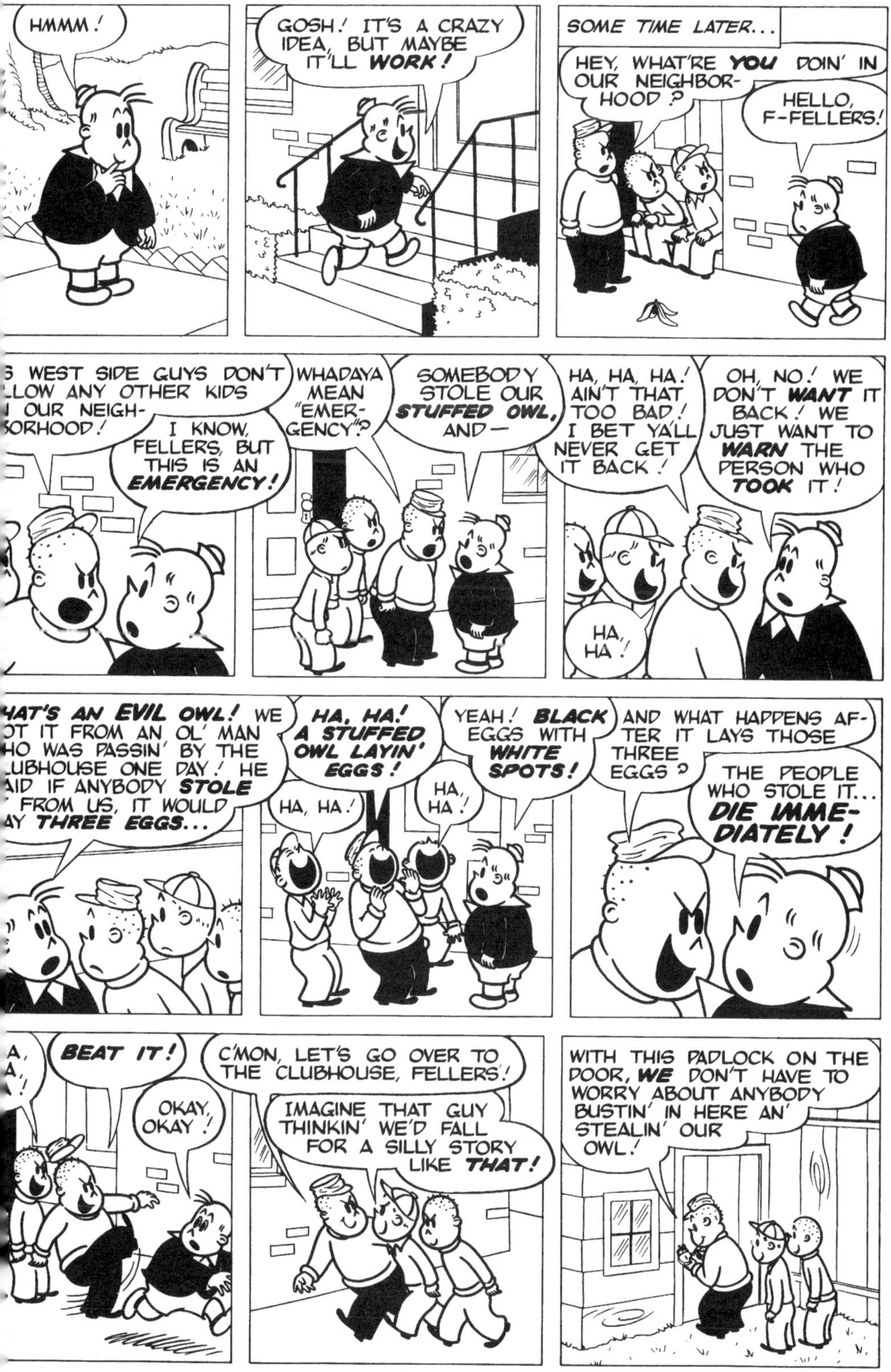
HMMM!
GOSH! IT'S A CRAZY IDEA, BUT MAYBE IT'LL WORK!
SOME TIME LATER...
HEY, WHAT'RE YOU DOIN' IN OUR NEIGHBOR-HOOD?
HELLO, F-FELLERS!
S WEST SIDE GUYS DON'T LLOW ANY OTHER KIDS OUR NEIGH-ORHOOD!
I KNOW, FELLERS, BUT THIS IS AN EMERGENCY!
WHADAYA MEAN "EMER-GENCY"?
SOMEBODY STOLE OUR STUFFED OWL, AND—
HA, HA, HA! AIN'T THAT TOO BAD! I BET YA'LL NEVER GET IT BACK!
HA, HA!
OH, NO! WE DON'T WANT IT BACK! WE JUST WANT TO WARN THE PERSON WHO TOOK IT!
HAT'S AN EVIL OWL! WE OT IT FROM AN OL' MAN HO WAS PASSIN' BY THE LUBHOUSE ONE DAY! HE AID IF ANYBODY STOLE FROM US, IT WOULD AY THREE EGGS...
HA, HA! A STUFFED OWL LAYIN' EGGS!
HA, HA!
HA, HA!
YEAH! BLACK EGGS WITH WHITE SPOTS!
AND WHAT HAPPENS AF-TER IT LAYS THOSE THREE EGGS?
THE PEOPLE WHO STOLE IT... DIE IMME-DIATELY!
A, A!
BEAT IT!
OKAY, OKAY!
C'MON, LET'S GO OVER TO THE CLUBHOUSE, FELLERS!
IMAGINE THAT GUY THINKIN' WE'D FALL FOR A SILLY STORY LIKE THAT!
WITH THIS PADLOCK ON THE DOOR, WE DON'T HAVE TO WORRY ABOUT ANYBODY BUSTIN' IN HERE AN' STEALIN' OUR OWL!

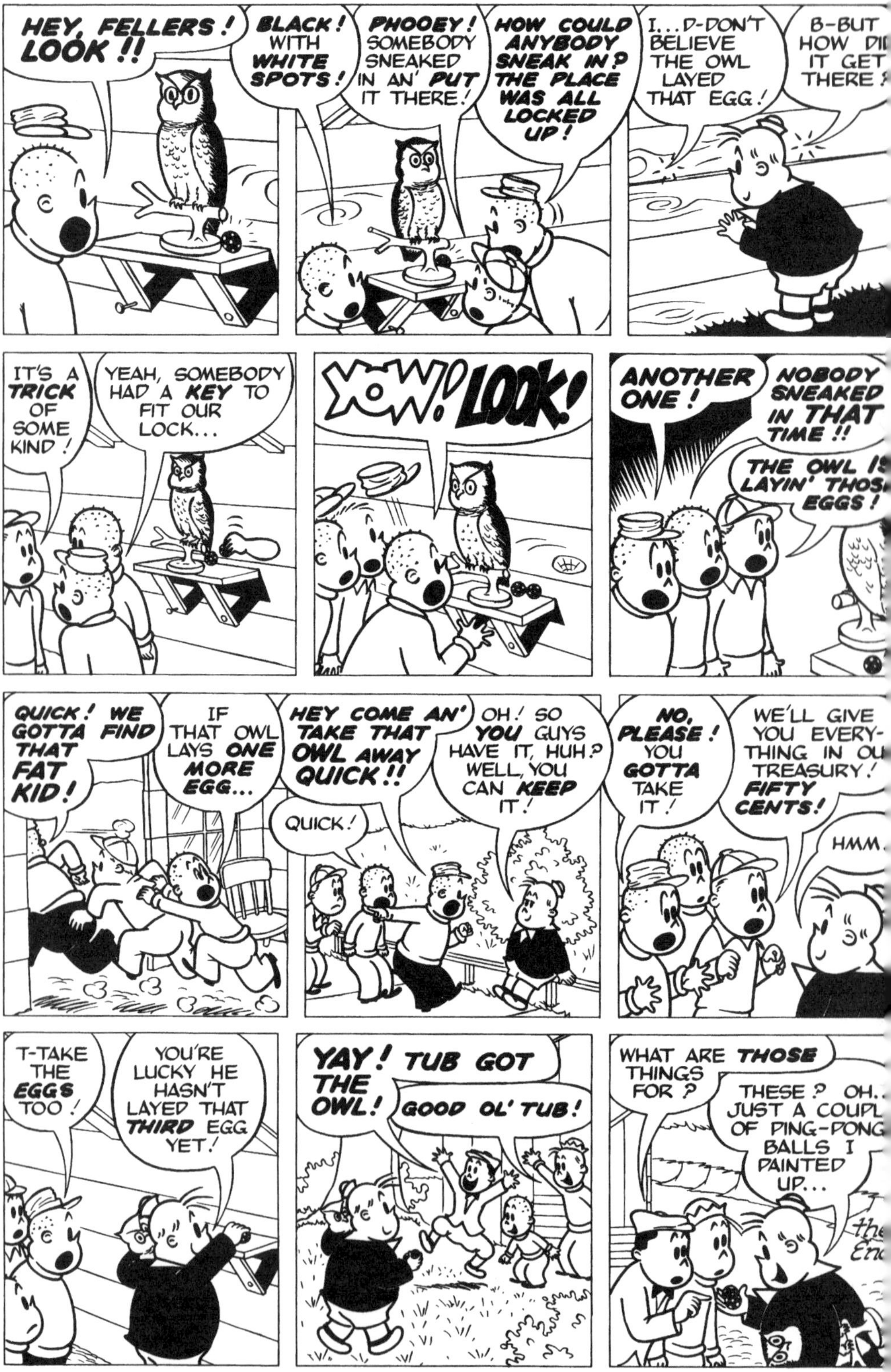
HEY, FELLERS! LOOK!!
BLACK! WITH WHITE SPOTS!
PHOOEY! SOMEBODY SNEAKED IN AN' PUT IT THERE!
HOW COULD ANYBODY SNEAK IN? THE PLACE WAS ALL LOCKED UP!
I... D-DON'T BELIEVE THE OWL LAYED THAT EGG!
B-BUT HOW DI IT GET THERE?
IT'S A TRICK OF SOME KIND!
YEAH, SOMEBODY HAD A KEY TO FIT OUR LOCK...
YOW! LOOK!
ANOTHER ONE!
NOBODY SNEAKED IN THAT TIME!!
THE OWL IS LAYIN' THOS EGGS!
QUICK! WE GOTTA FIND THAT FAT KID!
IF THAT OWL LAYS ONE MORE EGG...
HEY COME AN' TAKE THAT OWL AWAY QUICK!!
QUICK!
OH! SO YOU GUYS HAVE IT, HUH? WELL, YOU CAN KEEP IT!
NO, PLEASE! YOU GOTTA TAKE IT!
WE'LL GIVE YOU EVERY-THING IN OU TREASURY! FIFTY CENTS!
HMM.
T-TAKE THE EGGS TOO!
YOU'RE LUCKY HE HASN'T LAYED THAT THIRD EGG YET!
YAY! TUB GOT THE OWL!
GOOD OL' TUB!
WHAT ARE THOSE THINGS FOR?
THESE? OH.. JUST A COUPL OF PING-PONG BALLS I PAINTED UP...
The End

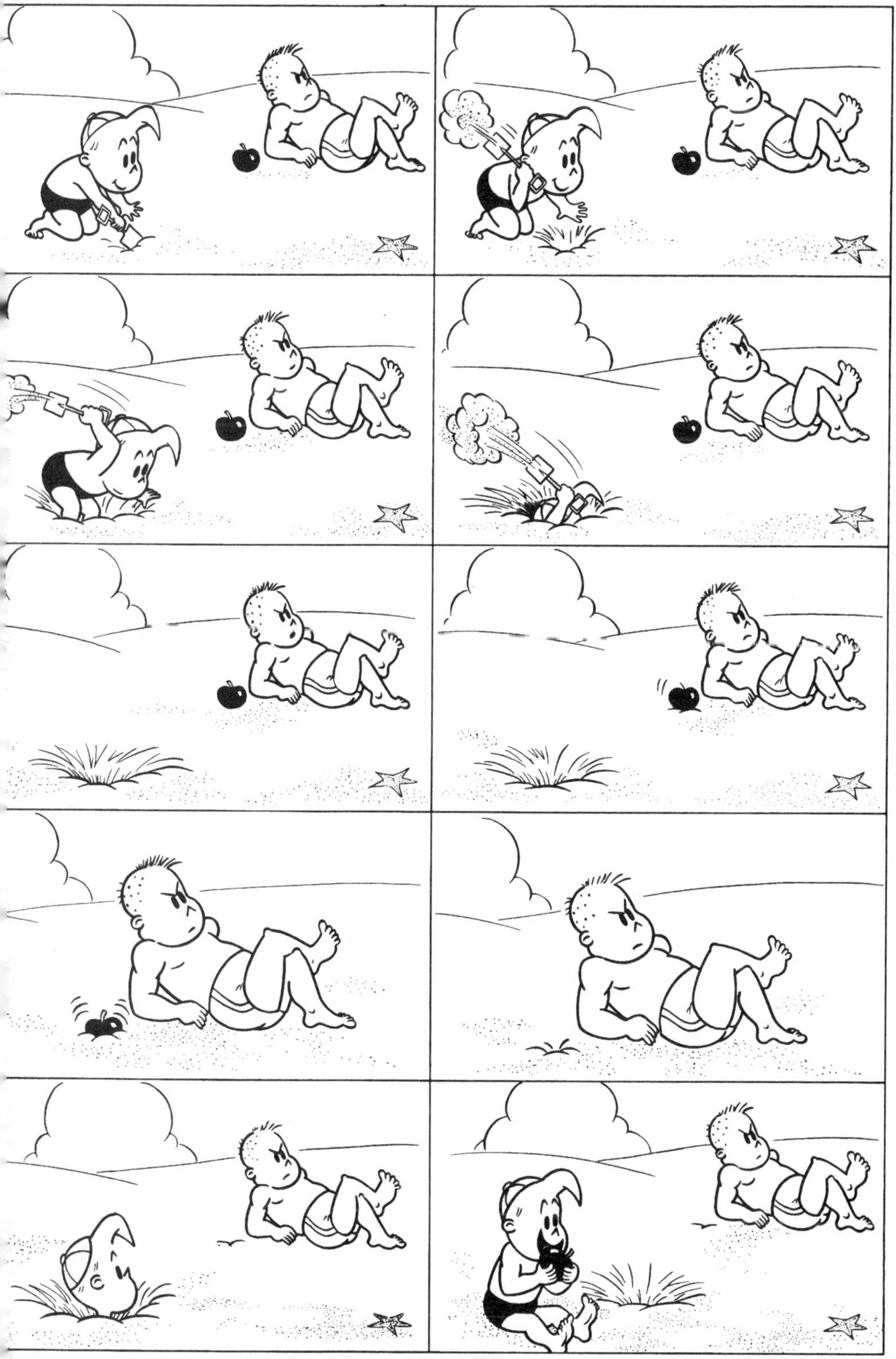

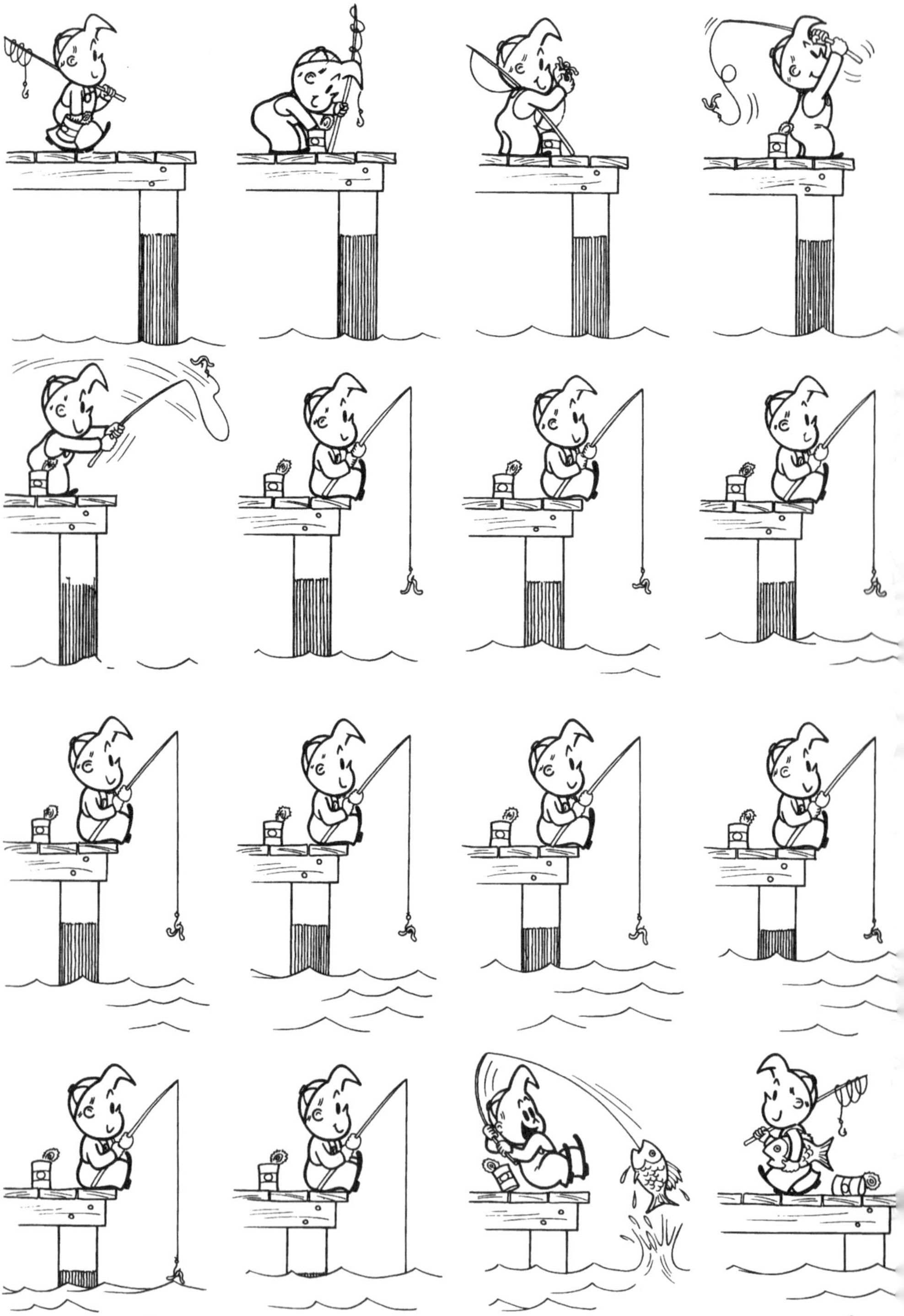

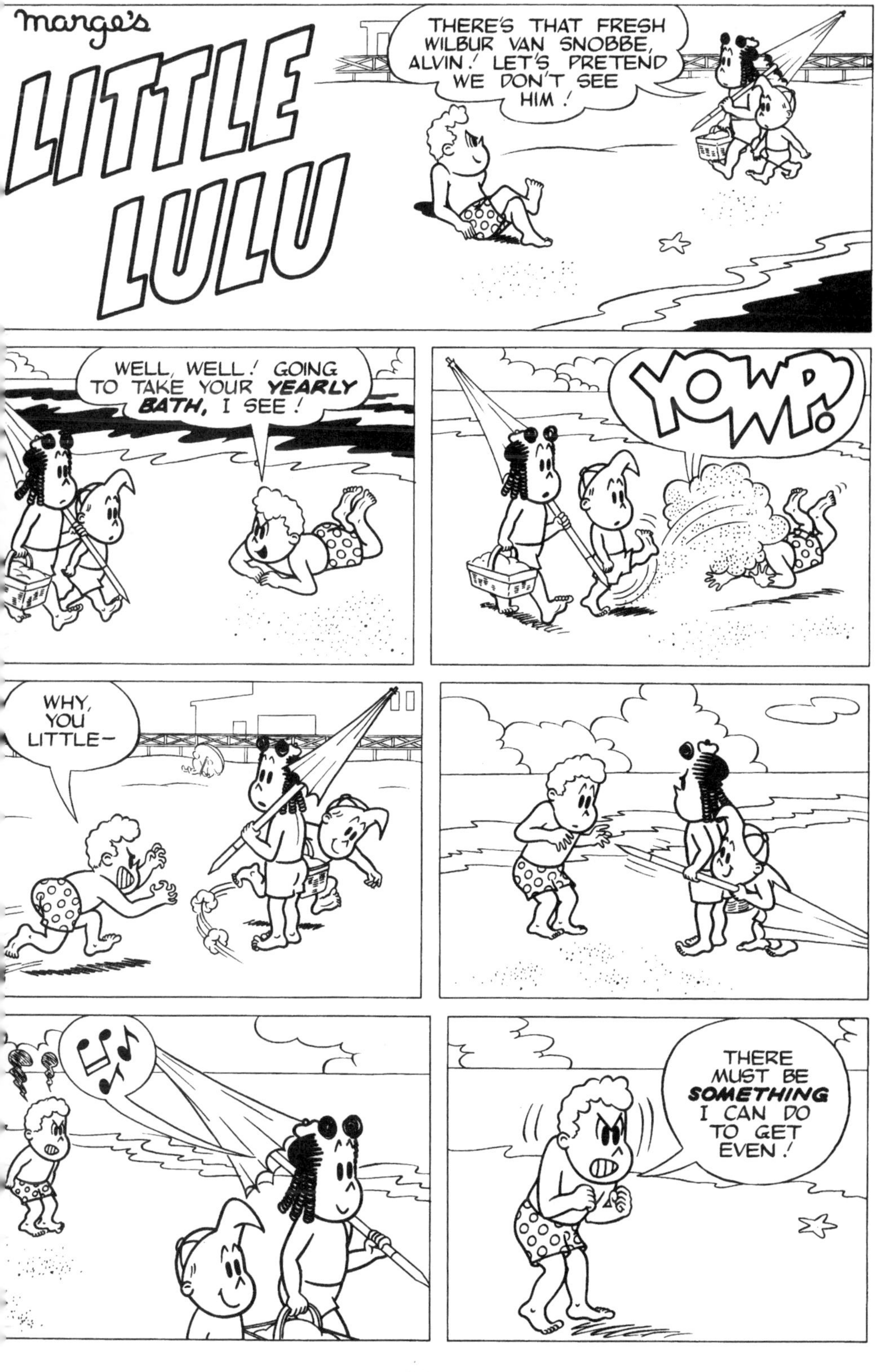
marge's
LITTLE LULU
THERE'S THAT FRESH WILBUR VAN SNOBBE, ALVIN! LET'S PRETEND WE DON'T SEE HIM!
WELL, WELL! GOING TO TAKE YOUR YEARLY BATH, I SEE!
YOWP!
WHY, YOU LITTLE—
THERE MUST BE SOMETHING I CAN DO TO GET EVEN!

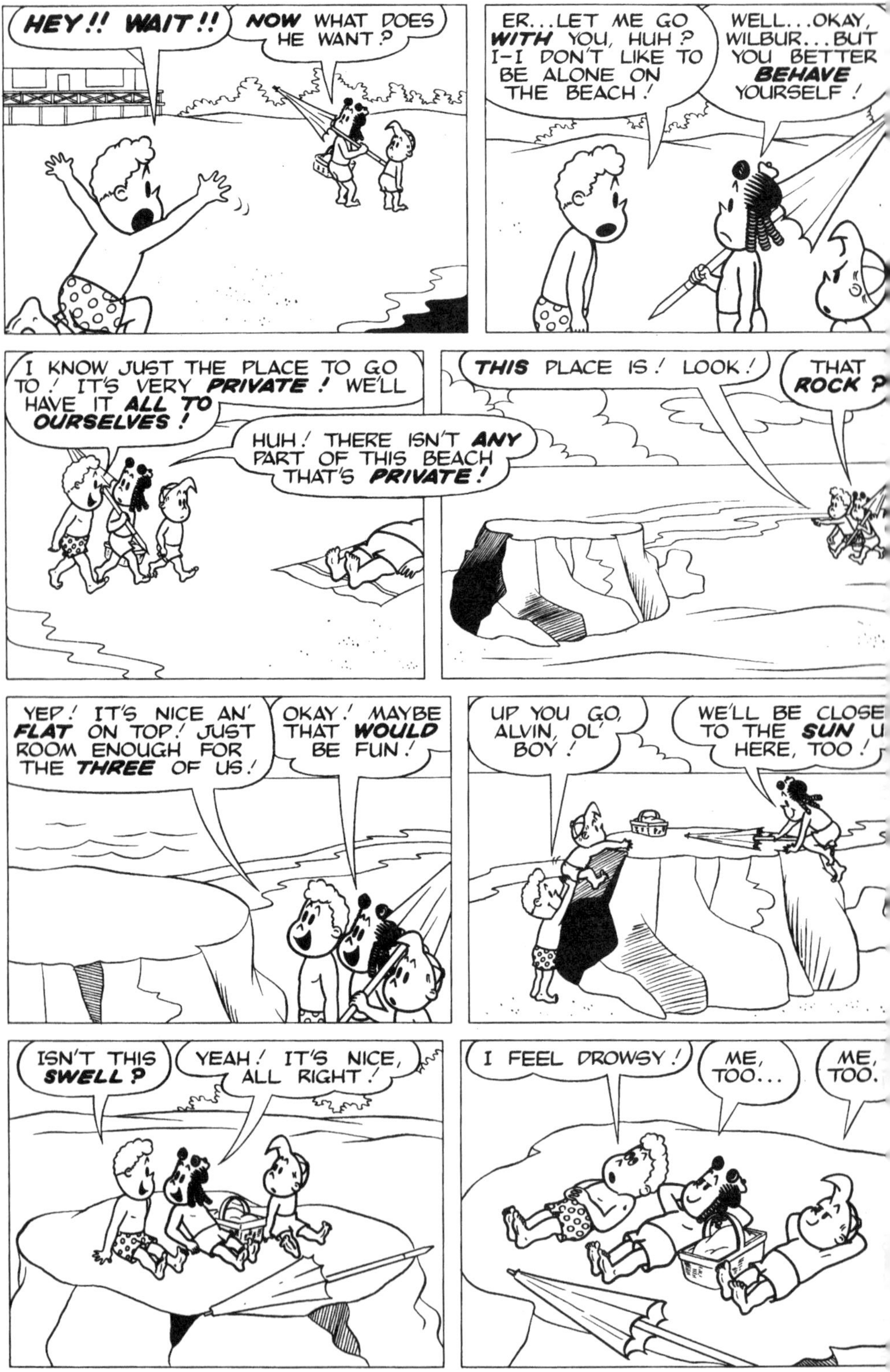
HEY!! WAIT!!
NOW WHAT DOES HE WANT?
ER...LET ME GO WITH YOU, HUH? I-I DON'T LIKE TO BE ALONE ON THE BEACH!
WELL...OKAY, WILBUR...BUT YOU BETTER BEHAVE YOURSELF!
I KNOW JUST THE PLACE TO GO TO! IT'S VERY PRIVATE! WE'LL HAVE IT ALL TO OURSELVES!
HUH! THERE ISN'T ANY PART OF THIS BEACH THAT'S PRIVATE!
THIS PLACE IS! LOOK!
THAT ROCK?
YEP! IT'S NICE AN' FLAT ON TOP! JUST ROOM ENOUGH FOR THE THREE OF US!
OKAY! MAYBE THAT WOULD BE FUN!
UP YOU GO, ALVIN, OL' BOY!
WE'LL BE CLOSE TO THE SUN U HERE, TOO!
ISN'T THIS SWELL?
YEAH! IT'S NICE, ALL RIGHT!
I FEEL DROWSY!
ME, TOO...
ME, TOO.

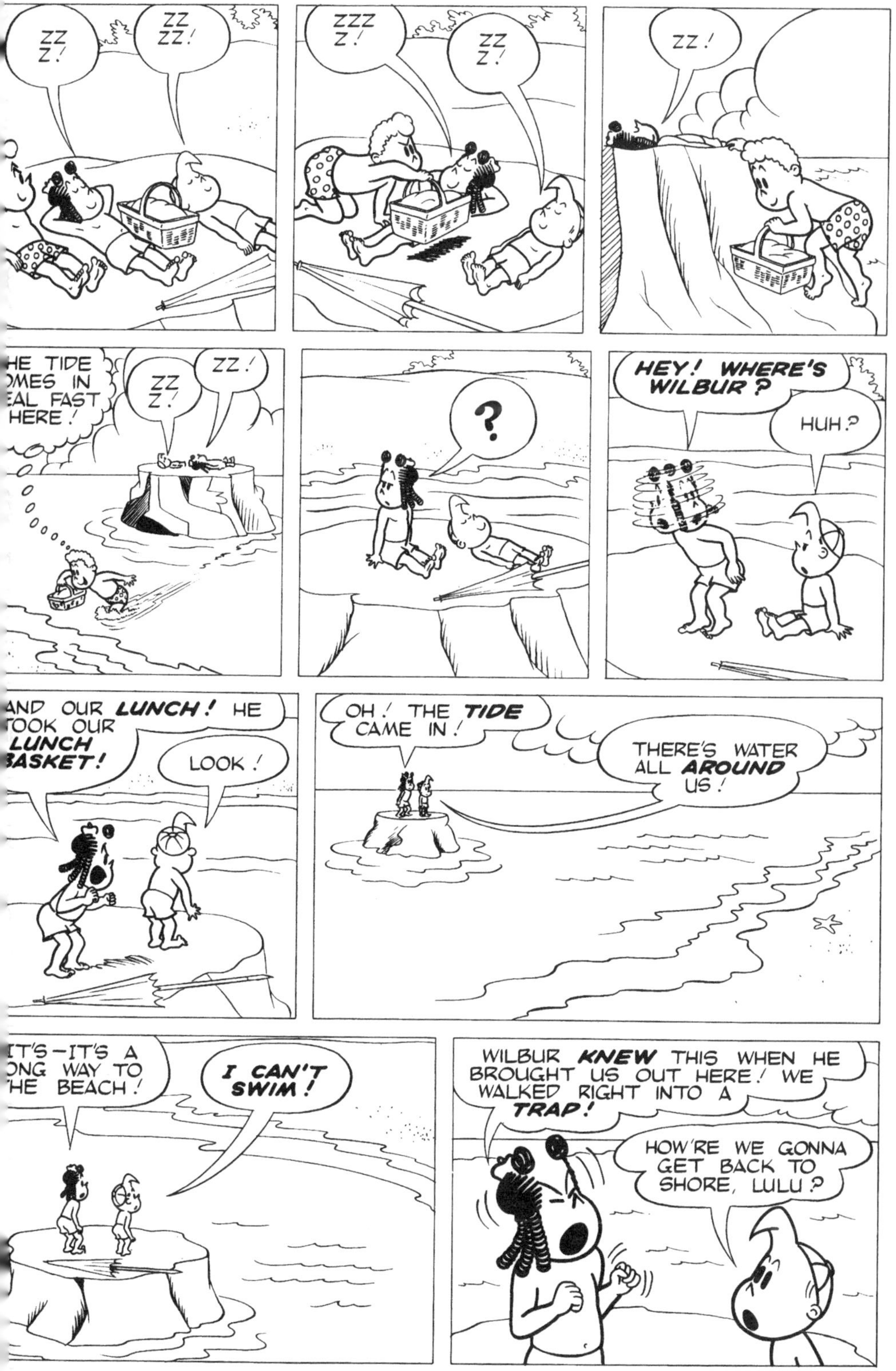
ZZ
Z!
ZZ
ZZ!
ZZZ
Z!
ZZ
Z!
ZZ!
HE TIDE
OMES IN
EAL FAST
HERE!
ZZ
Z!
ZZ!
?
HEY! WHERE'S WILBUR?
HUH?
AND OUR LUNCH! HE
TOOK OUR
LUNCH
BASKET!
LOOK!
OH! THE TIDE CAME IN!
THERE'S WATER ALL AROUND US!
IT'S—IT'S A
ONG WAY TO
HE BEACH!
I CAN'T SWIM!
WILBUR KNEW THIS WHEN HE BROUGHT US OUT HERE! WE WALKED RIGHT INTO A TRAP!
HOW'RE WE GONNA GET BACK TO SHORE, LULU?

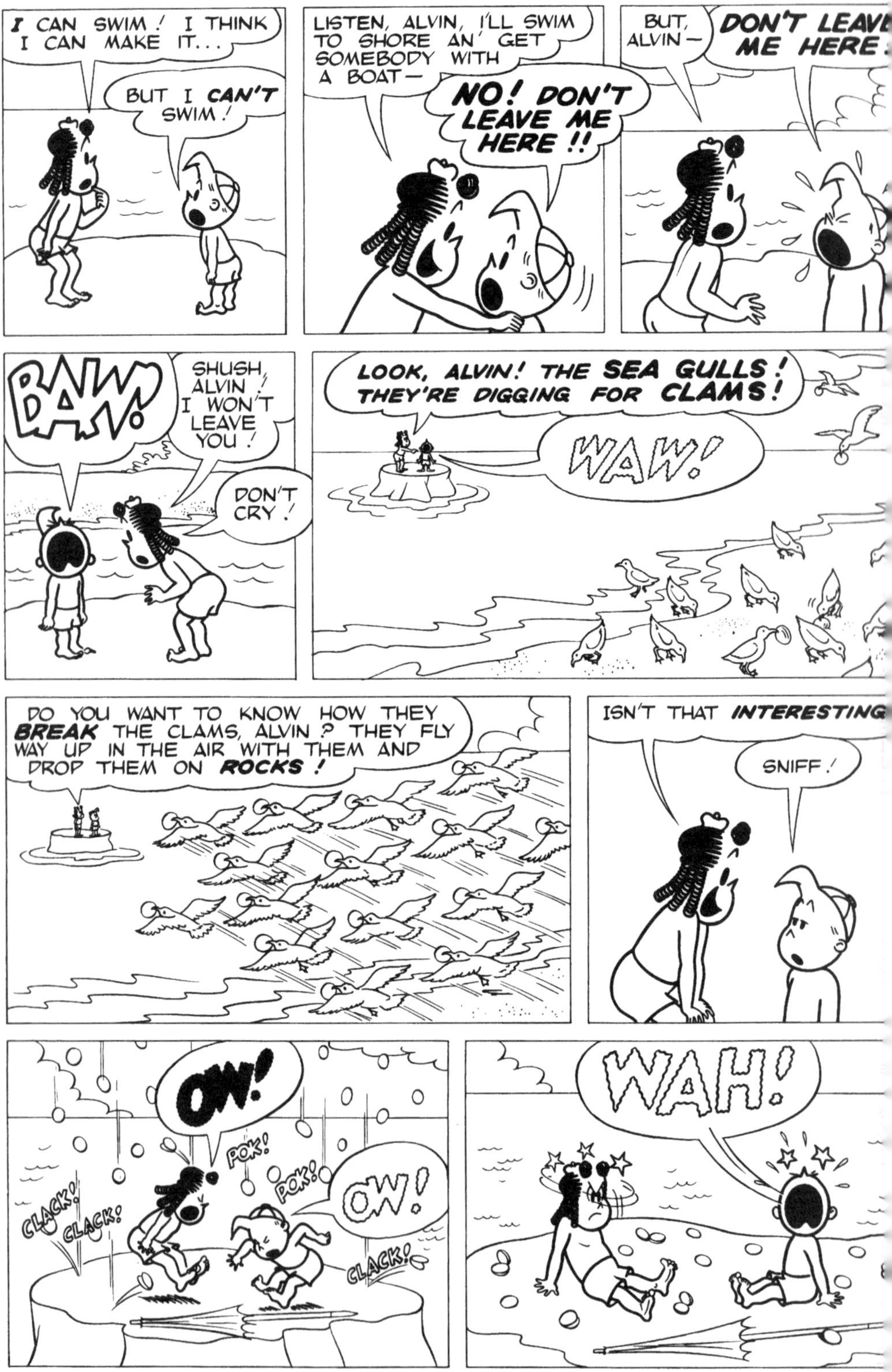
I CAN SWIM! I THINK I CAN MAKE IT...
BUT I CAN'T SWIM!
LISTEN, ALVIN, I'LL SWIM TO SHORE AN' GET SOMEBODY WITH A BOAT—
NO! DON'T LEAVE ME HERE!!
BUT, ALVIN—
DON'T LEAVE ME HERE!
BAW!
SHUSH, ALVIN! I WON'T LEAVE YOU!
DON'T CRY!
LOOK, ALVIN! THE SEA GULLS! THEY'RE DIGGING FOR CLAMS!
WAW!
DO YOU WANT TO KNOW HOW THEY BREAK THE CLAMS, ALVIN? THEY FLY WAY UP IN THE AIR WITH THEM AND DROP THEM ON ROCKS!
ISN'T THAT INTERESTING
SNIFF!
OW!
POK!
POK!
CLACK!
CLACK!
OW!
CLACK!
WAH!

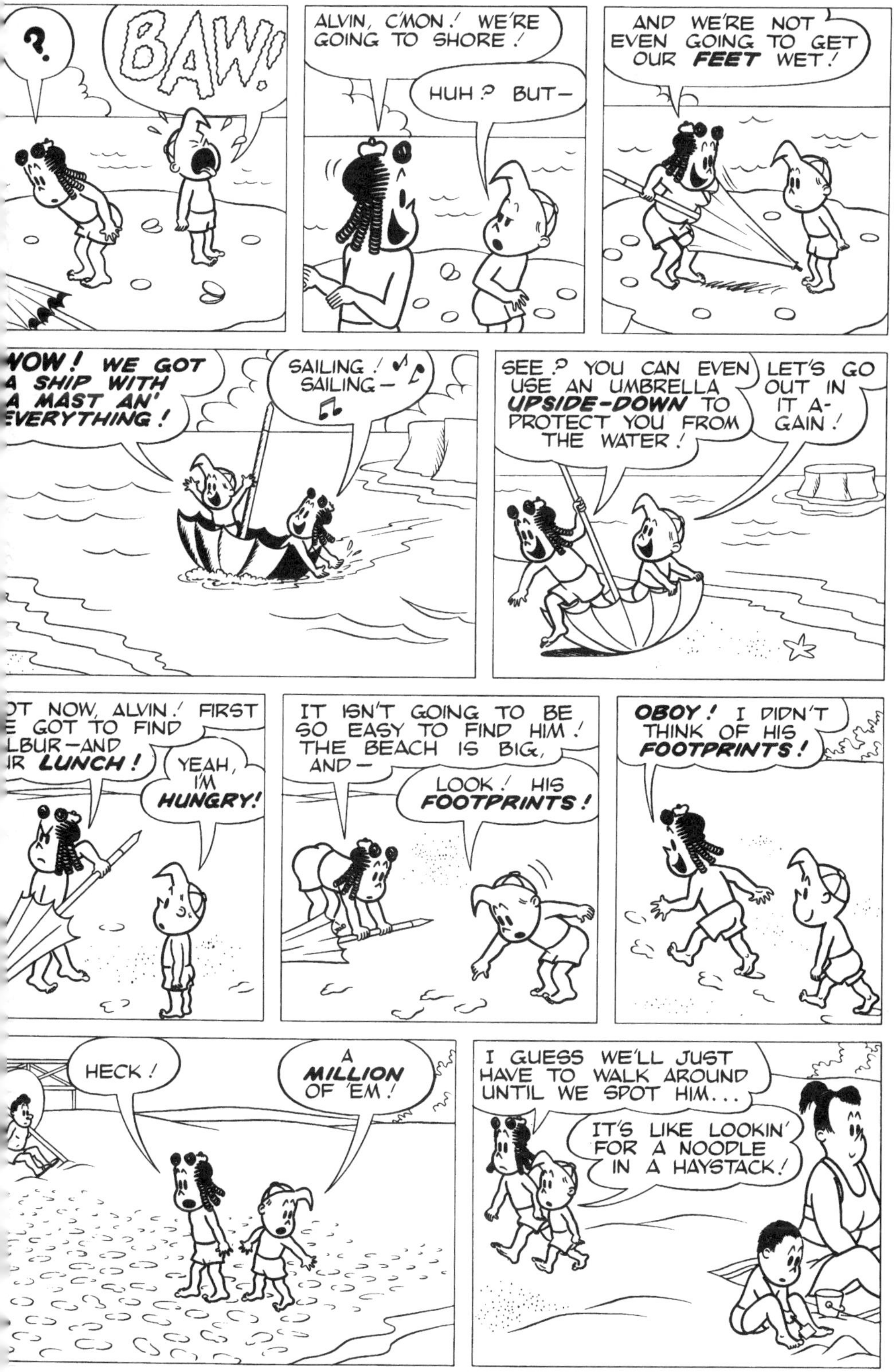
?
BAW!
ALVIN, C'MON! WE'RE GOING TO SHORE!
HUH? BUT—
AND WE'RE NOT EVEN GOING TO GET OUR **FEET** WET!
WOW! WE GOT A SHIP WITH A MAST AN' EVERYTHING!
SAILING! SAILING—
SEE? YOU CAN EVEN USE AN UMBRELLA **UPSIDE-DOWN** TO PROTECT YOU FROM THE WATER!
LET'S GO OUT IN IT A-GAIN!
OT NOW, ALVIN! FIRST E GOT TO FIND LBUR—AND IR **LUNCH!**
YEAH, I'M **HUNGRY!**
IT ISN'T GOING TO BE SO EASY TO FIND HIM! THE BEACH IS BIG, AND—
LOOK! HIS **FOOTPRINTS!**
OBOY! I DIDN'T THINK OF HIS **FOOTPRINTS!**
HECK!
A **MILLION** OF 'EM!
I GUESS WE'LL JUST HAVE TO WALK AROUND UNTIL WE SPOT HIM...
IT'S LIKE LOOKIN' FOR A NOODLE IN A HAYSTACK!

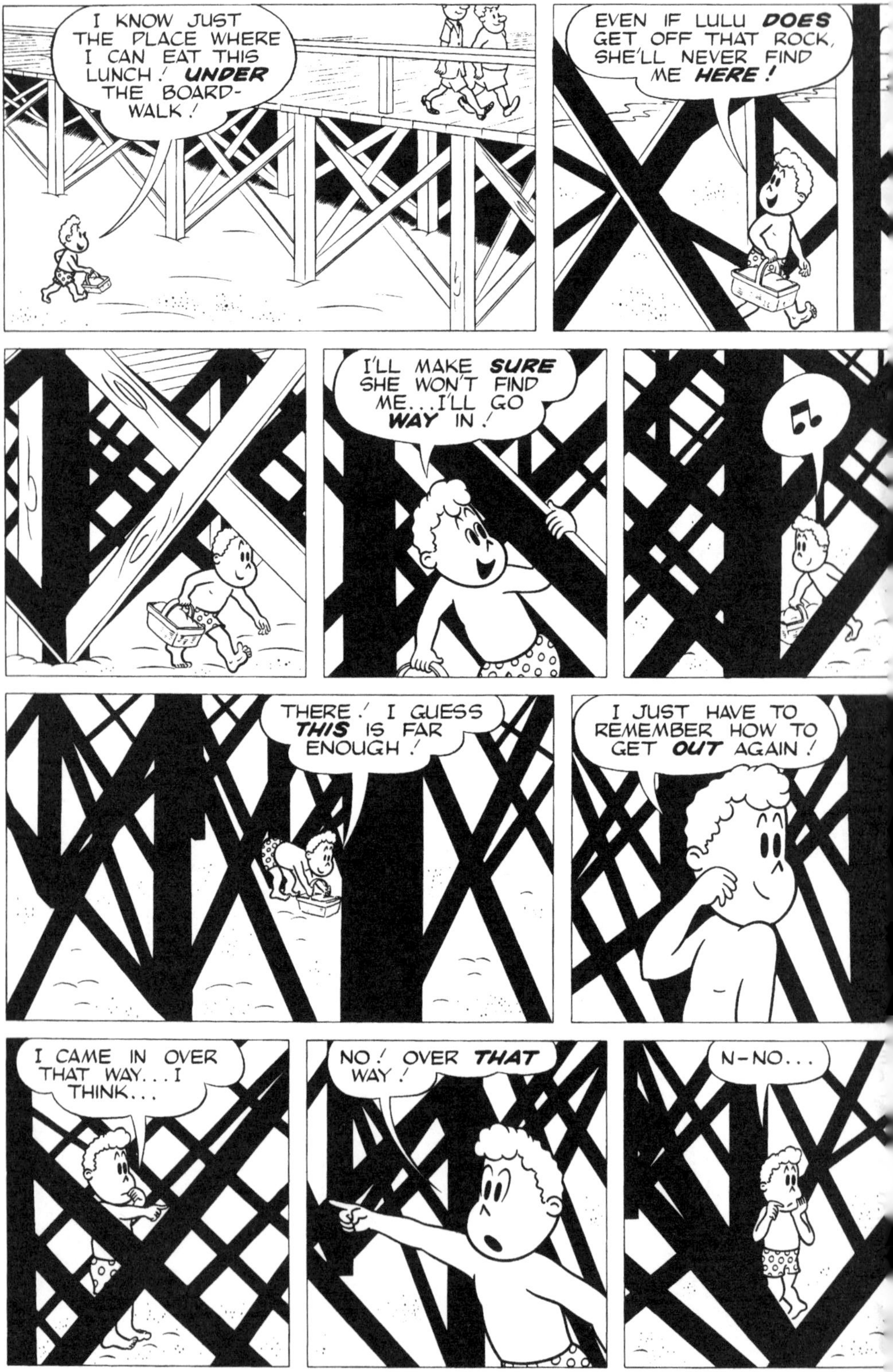
I KNOW JUST THE PLACE WHERE I CAN EAT THIS LUNCH! **UNDER** THE BOARD-WALK!
EVEN IF LULU **DOES** GET OFF THAT ROCK, SHE'LL NEVER FIND ME **HERE**!
I'LL MAKE **SURE** SHE WON'T FIND ME...I'LL GO **WAY** IN!
THERE! I GUESS **THIS** IS FAR ENOUGH!
I JUST HAVE TO REMEMBER HOW TO GET **OUT** AGAIN!
I CAME IN OVER THAT WAY...I THINK...
NO! OVER **THAT** WAY!
N-NO...

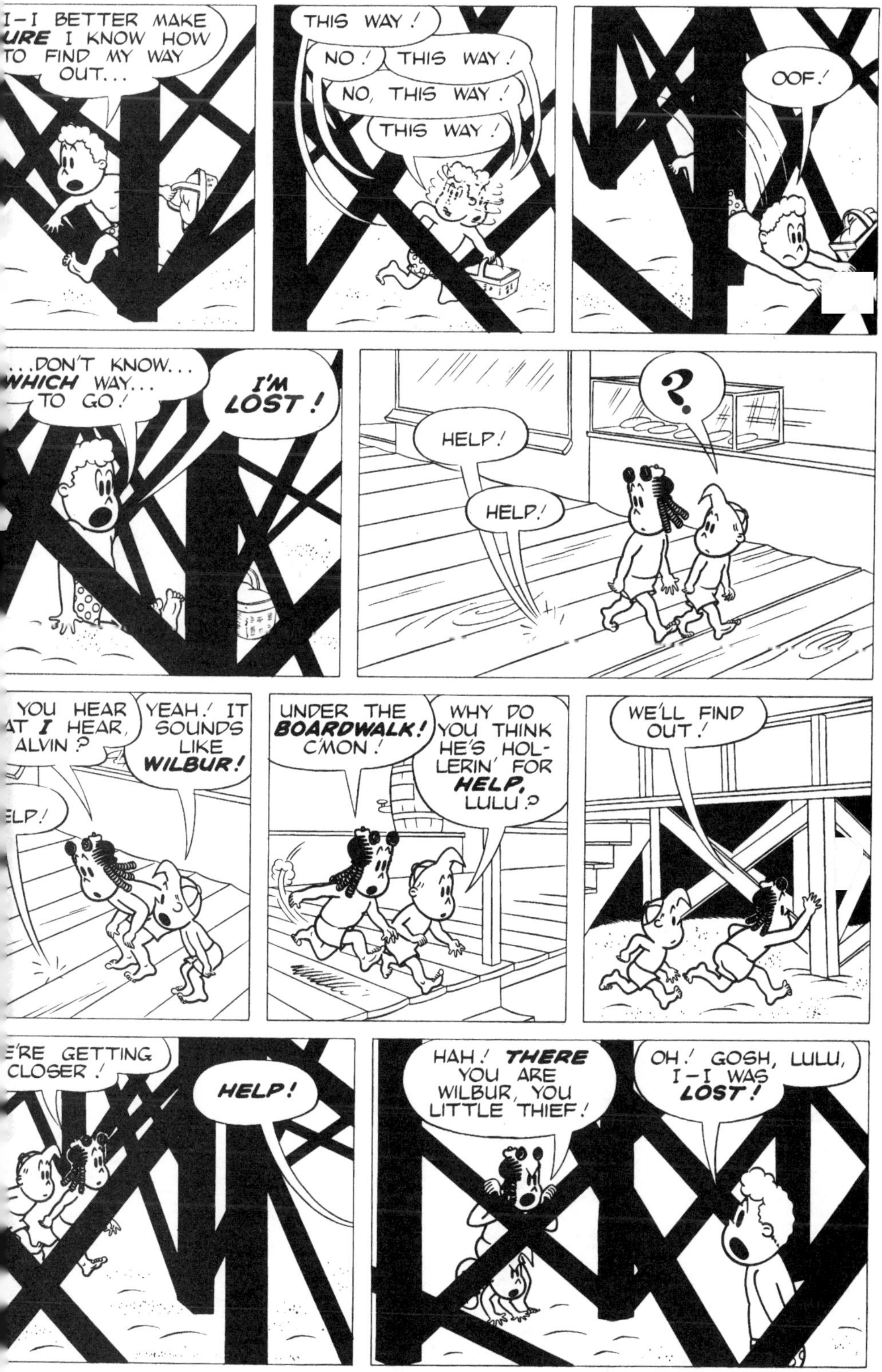
I–I BETTER MAKE URE I KNOW HOW TO FIND MY WAY OUT...
THIS WAY!
NO!
THIS WAY!
NO, THIS WAY!
THIS WAY!
OOF!
...DON'T KNOW... WHICH WAY... TO GO!
I'M LOST!
HELP!
HELP!
?
YOU HEAR AT I HEAR, ALVIN?
YEAH! IT SOUNDS LIKE WILBUR!
ELP!
UNDER THE BOARDWALK! C'MON!
WHY DO YOU THINK HE'S HOL-LERIN' FOR HELP, LULU?
WE'LL FIND OUT!
E'RE GETTING CLOSER!
HELP!
HAH! THERE YOU ARE WILBUR, YOU LITTLE THIEF!
OH! GOSH, LULU, I–I WAS LOST!

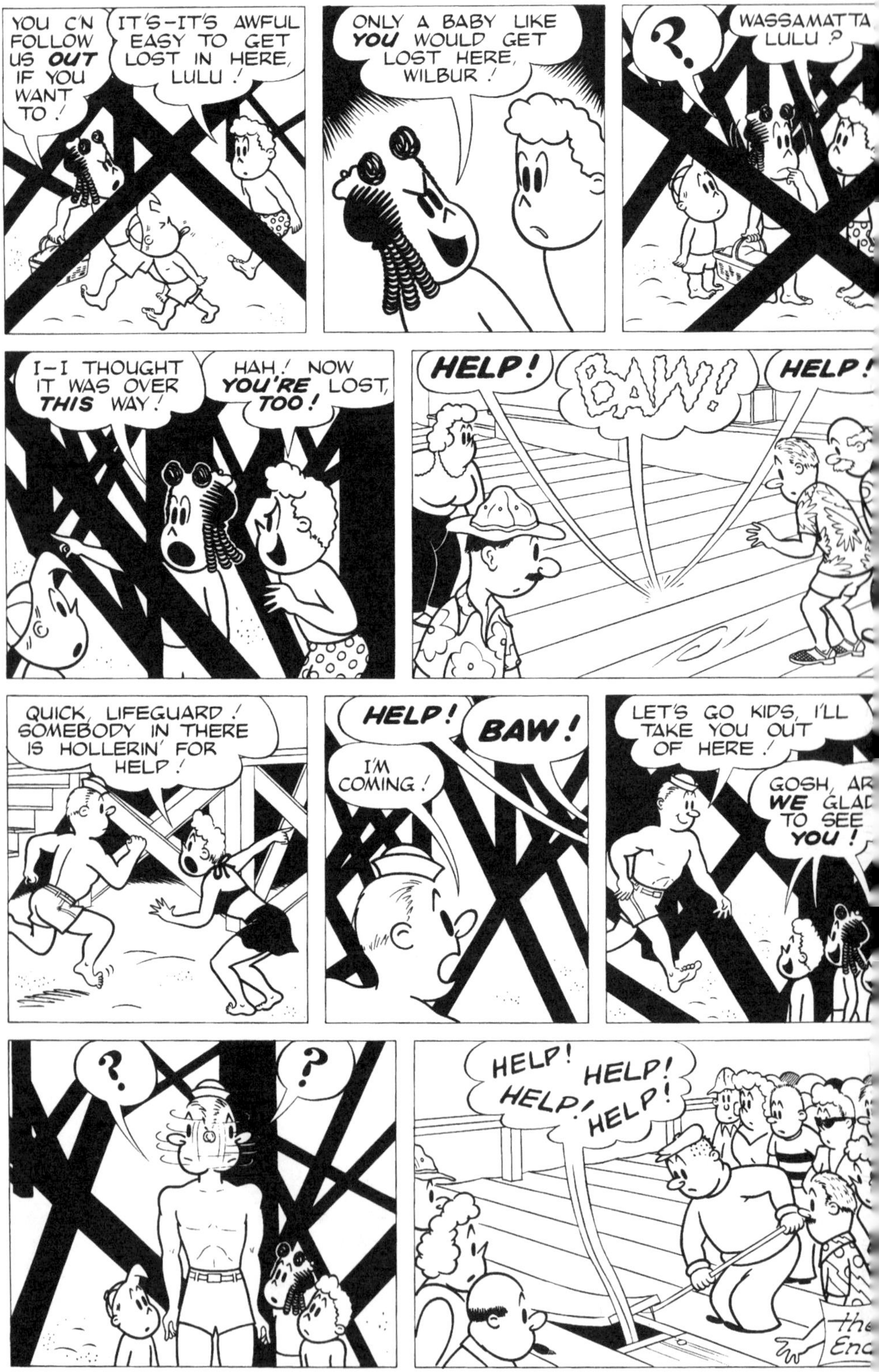
YOU C'N FOLLOW US OUT IF YOU WANT TO!
IT'S-IT'S AWFUL EASY TO GET LOST IN HERE, LULU!
ONLY A BABY LIKE YOU WOULD GET LOST HERE, WILBUR!
?
WASSAMATTA LULU?
I-I THOUGHT IT WAS OVER THIS WAY!
HAH! NOW YOU'RE LOST, TOO!
HELP!
BAW!
HELP!
QUICK, LIFEGUARD! SOMEBODY IN THERE IS HOLLERIN' FOR HELP!
HELP!
BAW!
I'M COMING!
LET'S GO KIDS, I'LL TAKE YOU OUT OF HERE!
GOSH, AR WE GLAD TO SEE YOU!
?
?
HELP! HELP! HELP! HELP!
the End

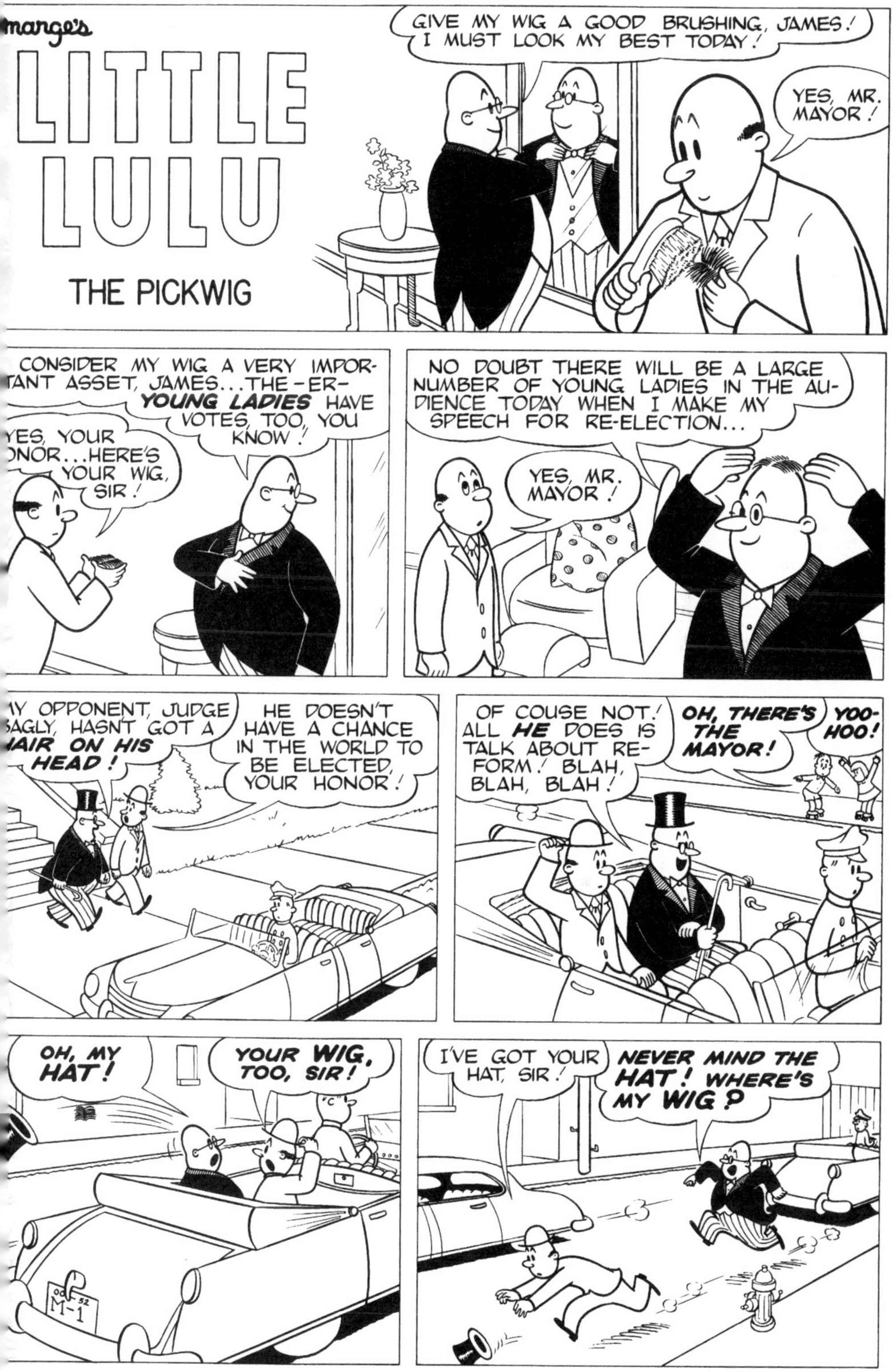
marge's
LITTLE LULU
THE PICKWIG
GIVE MY WIG A GOOD BRUSHING, JAMES! I MUST LOOK MY BEST TODAY!
YES, MR. MAYOR!
CONSIDER MY WIG A VERY IMPOR-TANT ASSET, JAMES...THE-ER- **YOUNG LADIES** HAVE VOTES, TOO, YOU KNOW!
YES, YOUR ONOR...HERE'S YOUR WIG, SIR!
NO DOUBT THERE WILL BE A LARGE NUMBER OF YOUNG LADIES IN THE AUDIENCE TODAY WHEN I MAKE MY SPEECH FOR RE-ELECTION...
YES, MR. MAYOR!
Y OPPONENT, JUDGE AGLY, HASN'T GOT A **AIR ON HIS HEAD!**
HE DOESN'T HAVE A CHANCE IN THE WORLD TO BE ELECTED, YOUR HONOR!
OF COUSE NOT! ALL **HE** DOES IS TALK ABOUT RE-FORM! BLAH, BLAH, BLAH!
OH, THERE'S THE MAYOR!
YOO-HOO!
OH, MY HAT!
YOUR WIG, TOO, SIR!
M-1
I'VE GOT YOUR HAT, SIR!
NEVER MIND THE HAT! WHERE'S MY WIG?

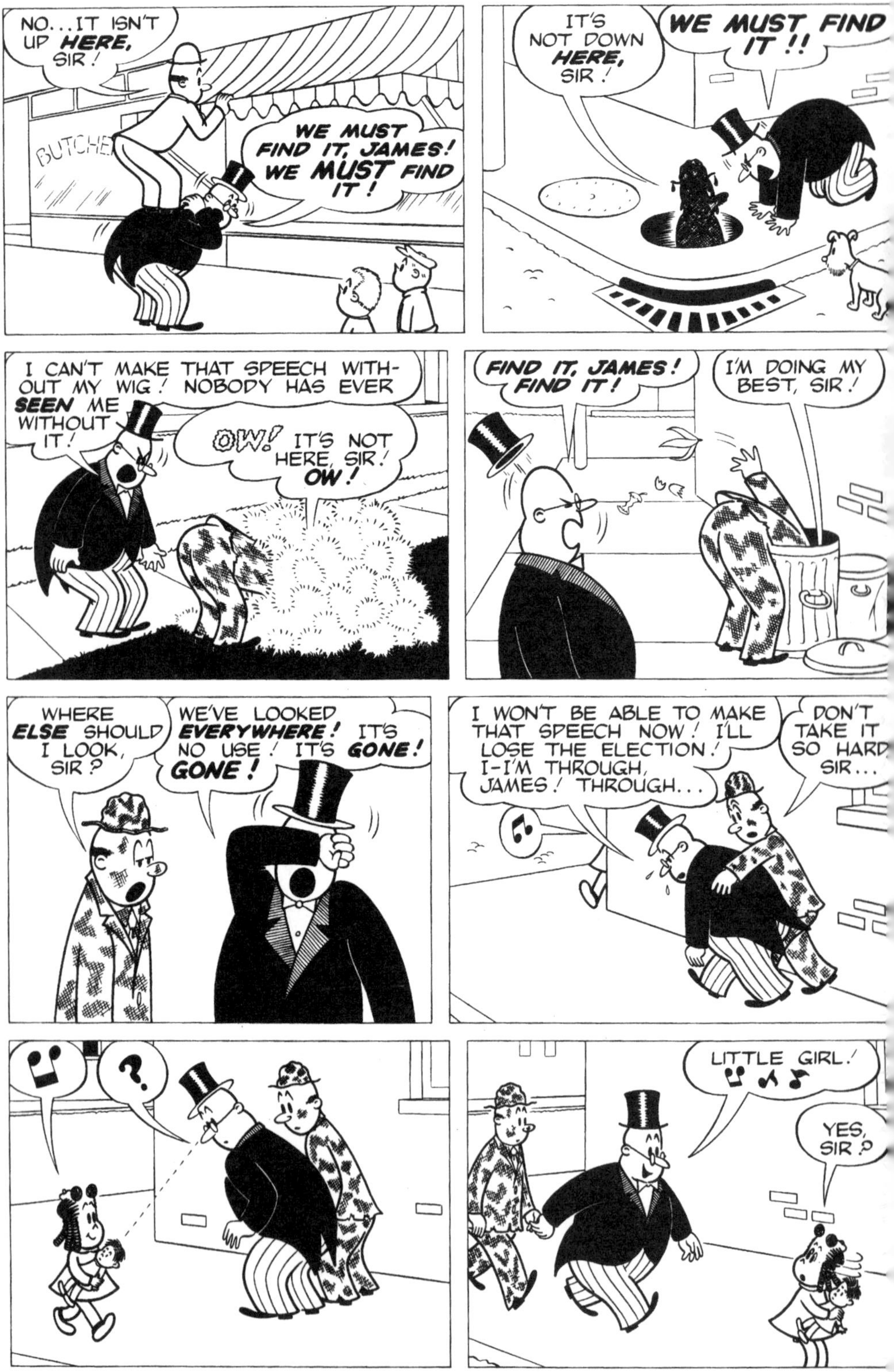
NO...IT ISN'T UP **HERE,** SIR!
BUTCHE
WE MUST FIND IT, JAMES! WE MUST FIND IT!
IT'S NOT DOWN **HERE,** SIR!
WE MUST FIND IT !!
I CAN'T MAKE THAT SPEECH WITHOUT MY WIG! NOBODY HAS EVER **SEEN** ME WITHOUT IT!
OW! IT'S NOT HERE, SIR! **OW!**
FIND IT, JAMES! FIND IT!
I'M DOING MY BEST, SIR!
WHERE **ELSE** SHOULD I LOOK, SIR?
WE'VE LOOKED **EVERYWHERE!** IT'S NO USE! IT'S **GONE! GONE!**
I WON'T BE ABLE TO MAKE THAT SPEECH NOW! I'LL LOSE THE ELECTION! I-I'M THROUGH, JAMES! THROUGH...
DON'T TAKE IT SO HARD, SIR...
?
LITTLE GIRL!
YES, SIR?

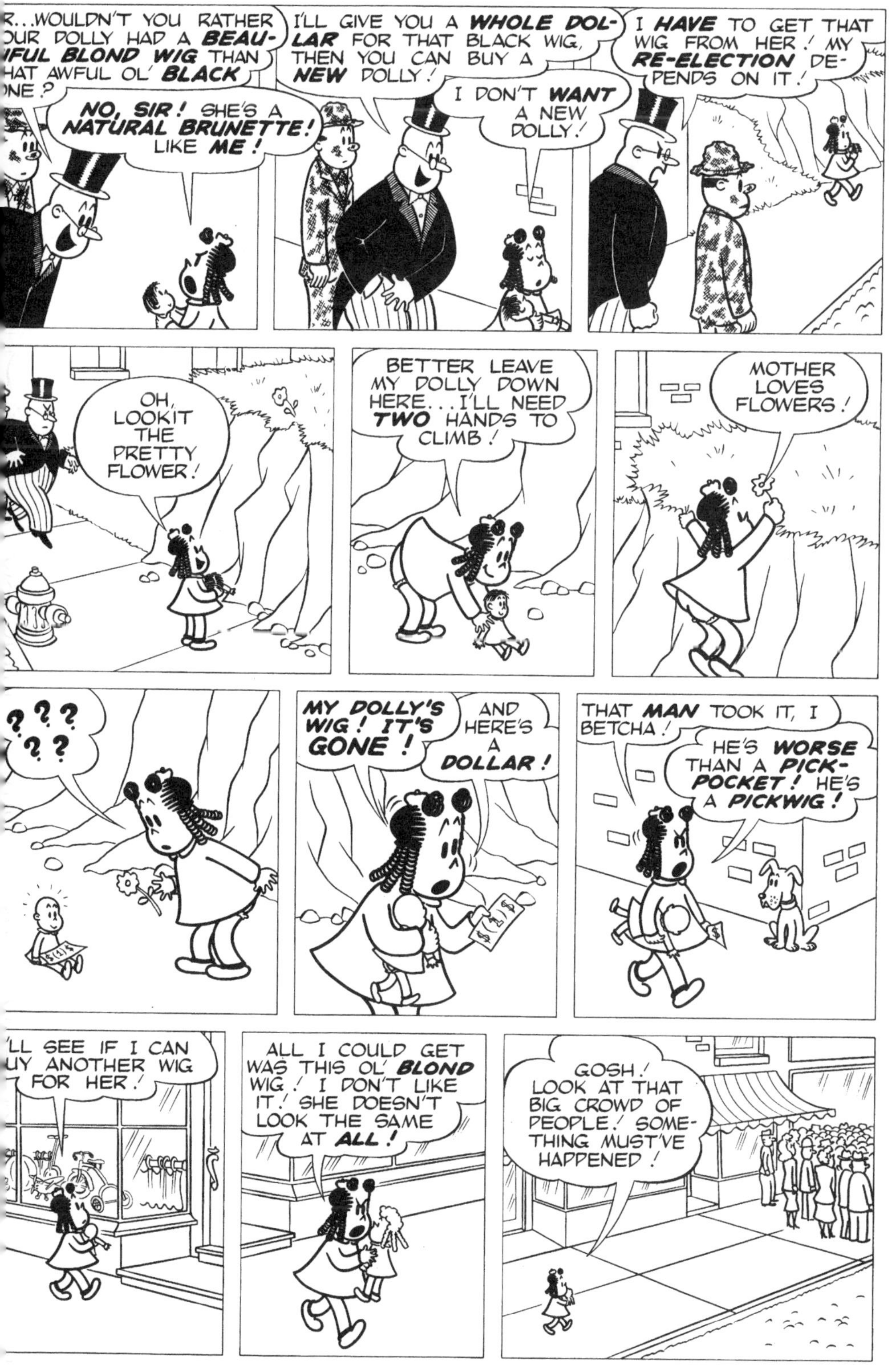
R...WOULDN'T YOU RATHER OUR DOLLY HAD A BEAU-IFUL BLOND WIG THAN HAT AWFUL OL' BLACK ONE?
NO, SIR! SHE'S A NATURAL BRUNETTE! LIKE ME!
I'LL GIVE YOU A WHOLE DOL-LAR FOR THAT BLACK WIG, THEN YOU CAN BUY A NEW DOLLY!
I DON'T WANT A NEW DOLLY!
I HAVE TO GET THAT WIG FROM HER! MY RE-ELECTION DE-PENDS ON IT!
OH, LOOKIT THE PRETTY FLOWER!
BETTER LEAVE MY DOLLY DOWN HERE...I'LL NEED TWO HANDS TO CLIMB!
MOTHER LOVES FLOWERS!
???
??
MY DOLLY'S WIG! IT'S GONE!
AND HERE'S A DOLLAR!
THAT MAN TOOK IT, I BETCHA!
HE'S WORSE THAN A PICK-POCKET! HE'S A PICKWIG!
'LL SEE IF I CAN UY ANOTHER WIG FOR HER!
ALL I COULD GET WAS THIS OL' BLOND WIG! I DON'T LIKE IT! SHE DOESN'T LOOK THE SAME AT ALL!
GOSH! LOOK AT THAT BIG CROWD OF PEOPLE! SOME-THING MUST'VE HAPPENED!

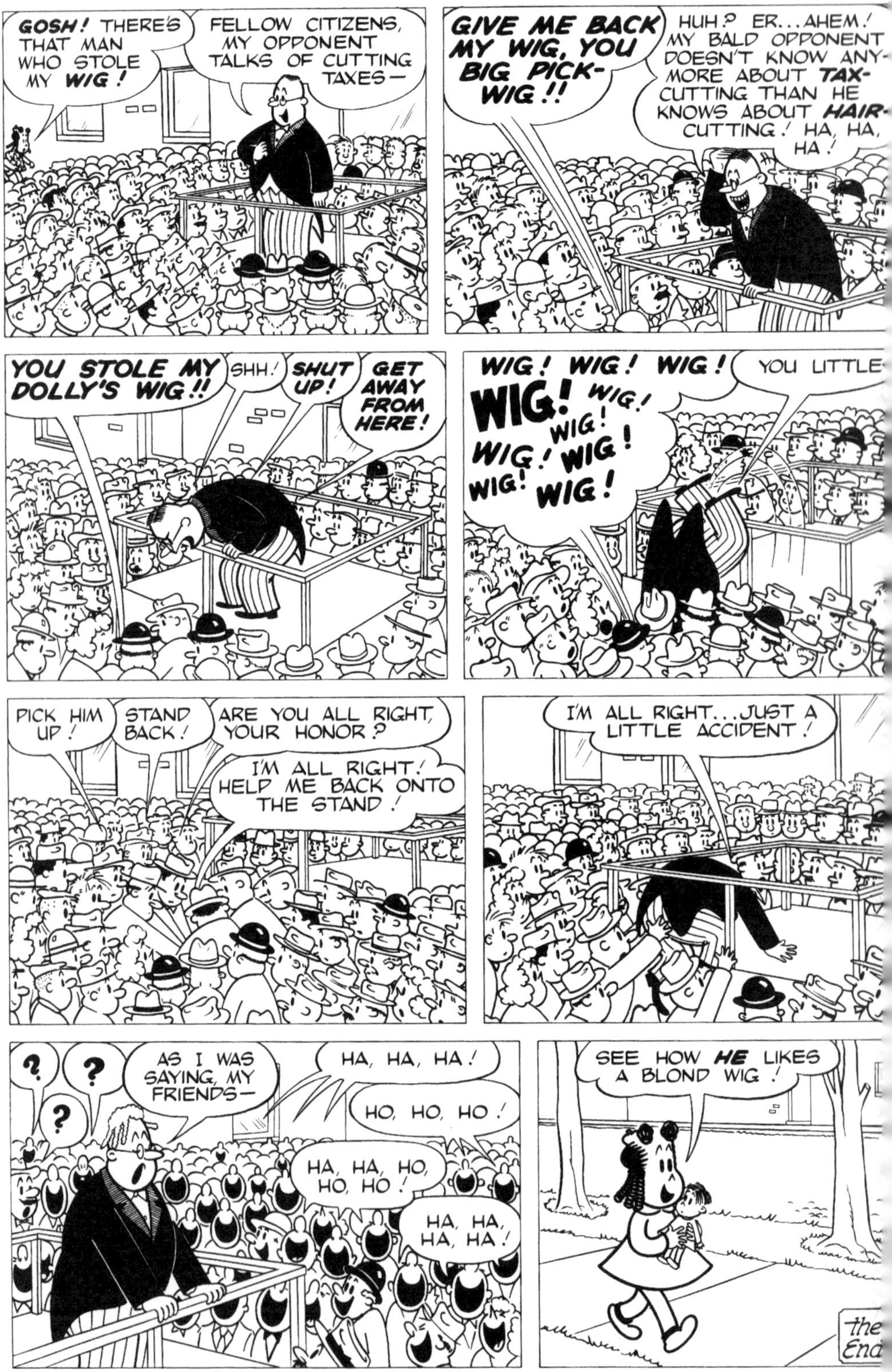
GOSH! THERE'S THAT MAN WHO STOLE MY WIG!
FELLOW CITIZENS, MY OPPONENT TALKS OF CUTTING TAXES—
GIVE ME BACK MY WIG, YOU BIG PICK-WIG!!
HUH? ER...AHEM! MY BALD OPPONENT DOESN'T KNOW ANY-MORE ABOUT TAX-CUTTING THAN HE KNOWS ABOUT HAIR-CUTTING! HA, HA, HA!
YOU STOLE MY DOLLY'S WIG!!
SHH!
SHUT UP!
GET AWAY FROM HERE!
WIG! WIG! WIG!
WIG! WIG! WIG! WIG! WIG! WIG! WIG!
YOU LITTLE-
PICK HIM UP!
STAND BACK!
ARE YOU ALL RIGHT, YOUR HONOR?
I'M ALL RIGHT! HELP ME BACK ONTO THE STAND!
I'M ALL RIGHT...JUST A LITTLE ACCIDENT!
?
?
?
AS I WAS SAYING, MY FRIENDS—
HA, HA, HA!
HO, HO, HO!
HA, HA, HO, HO, HO!
HA, HA, HA, HA!
SEE HOW HE LIKES A BLOND WIG!
the End

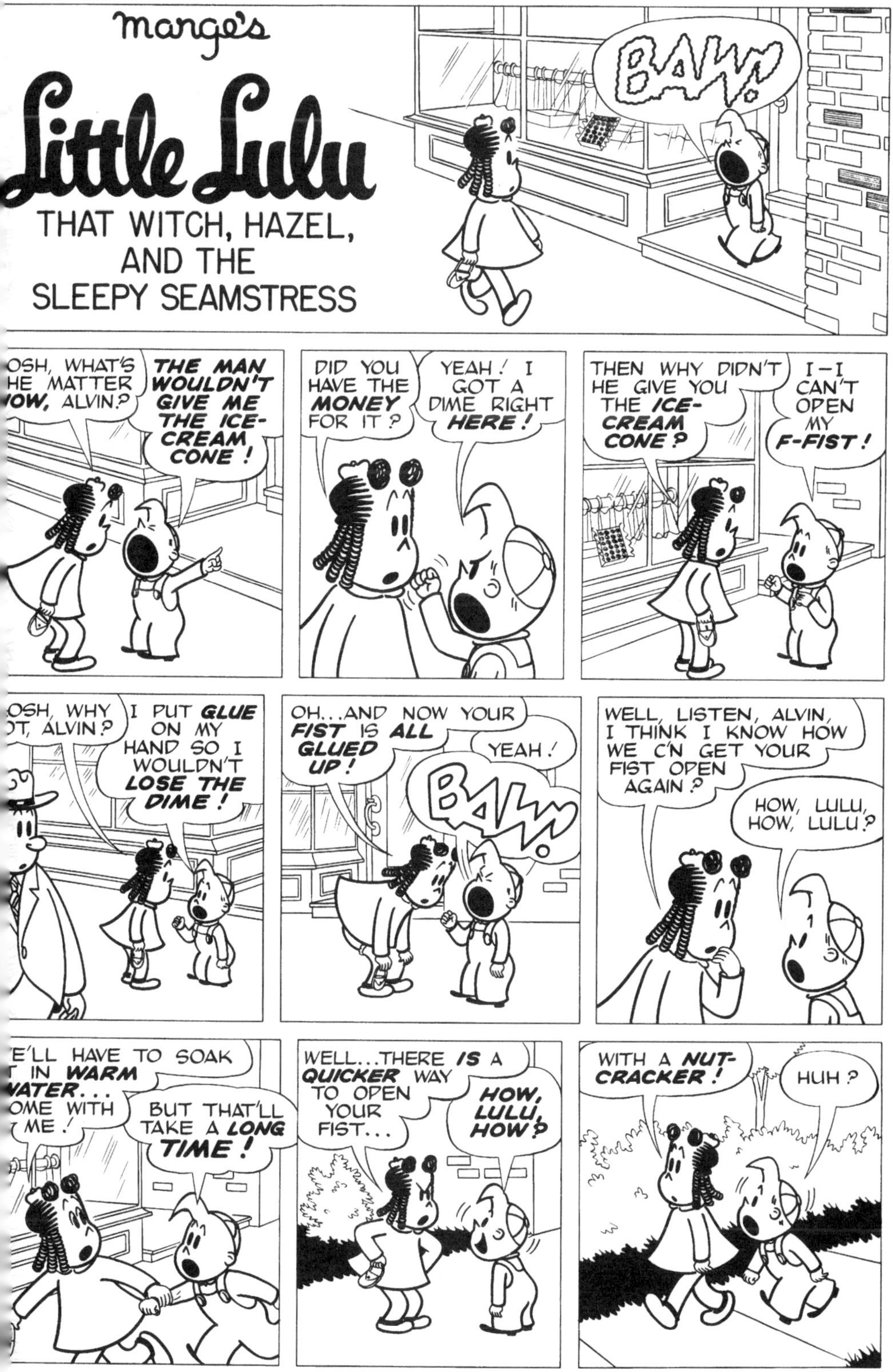
marge's
Little Lulu
THAT WITCH, HAZEL, AND THE SLEEPY SEAMSTRESS
BAW!
OSH, WHAT'S HE MATTER OW, ALVIN?
THE MAN WOULDN'T GIVE ME THE ICE-CREAM CONE!
DID YOU HAVE THE MONEY FOR IT?
YEAH! I GOT A DIME RIGHT HERE!
THEN WHY DIDN'T HE GIVE YOU THE ICE-CREAM CONE?
I—I CAN'T OPEN MY F-FIST!
OSH, WHY OT, ALVIN?
I PUT GLUE ON MY HAND SO I WOULDN'T LOSE THE DIME!
OH...AND NOW YOUR FIST IS ALL GLUED UP!
YEAH!
BAW!
WELL, LISTEN, ALVIN, I THINK I KNOW HOW WE C'N GET YOUR FIST OPEN AGAIN!
HOW, LULU, HOW, LULU?
E'LL HAVE TO SOAK T IN WARM VATER... OME WITH ME!
BUT THAT'LL TAKE A LONG TIME!
WELL...THERE IS A QUICKER WAY TO OPEN YOUR FIST...
HOW, LULU, HOW?
WITH A NUT-CRACKER!
HUH?

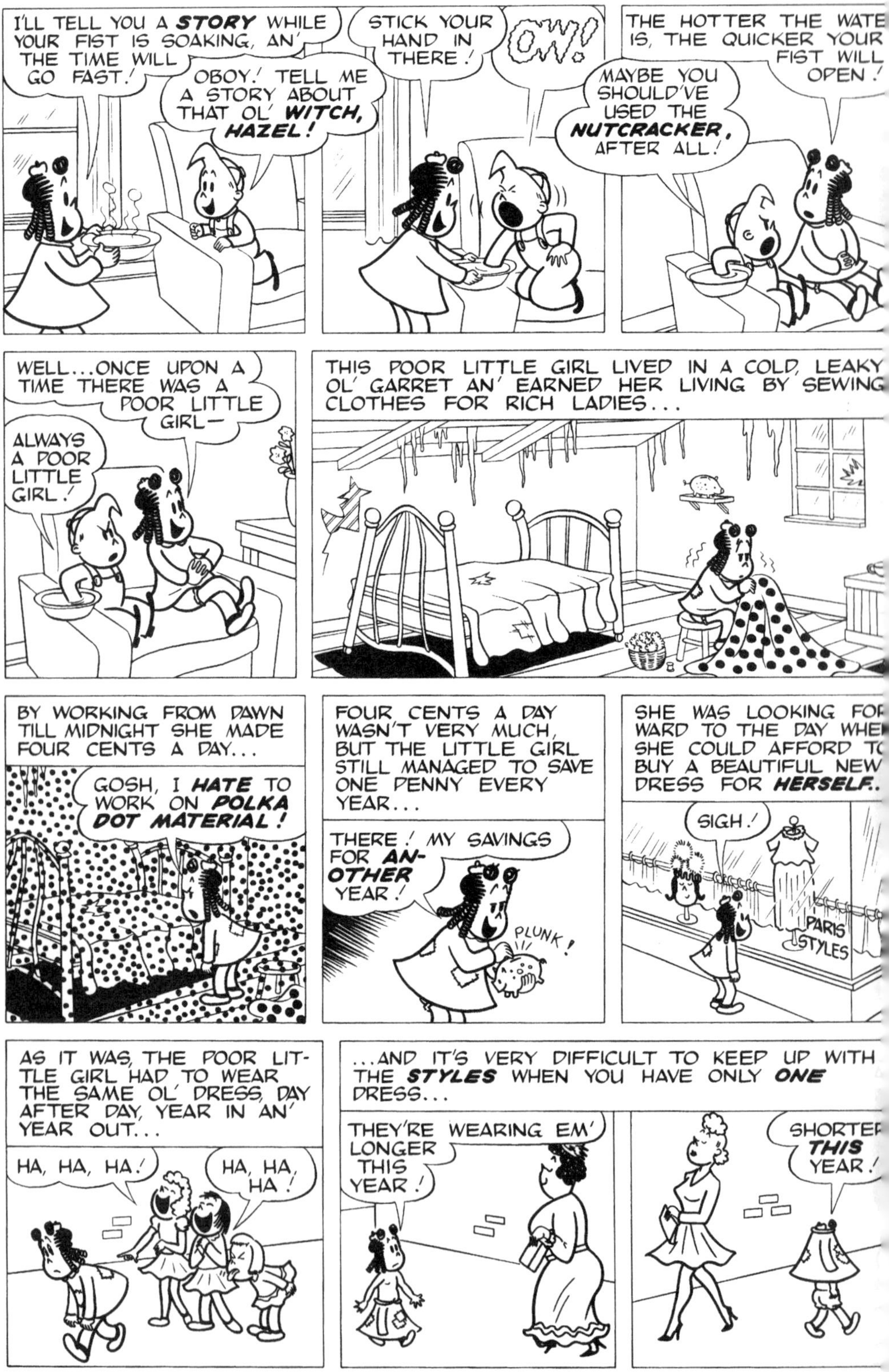

I'LL TELL YOU A **STORY** WHILE YOUR FIST IS SOAKING, AN' THE TIME WILL GO FAST!
OBOY! TELL ME A STORY ABOUT THAT OL' **WITCH, HAZEL!**
STICK YOUR HAND IN THERE!
OW!
THE HOTTER THE WATE
IS, THE QUICKER YOUR FIST WILL OPEN!
MAYBE YOU SHOULD'VE USED THE **NUTCRACKER,** AFTER ALL!
WELL... ONCE UPON A TIME THERE WAS A POOR LITTLE GIRL—
ALWAYS A POOR LITTLE GIRL!
THIS POOR LITTLE GIRL LIVED IN A COLD, LEAKY OL' GARRET AN' EARNED HER LIVING BY SEWING CLOTHES FOR RICH LADIES...
BY WORKING FROM DAWN TILL MIDNIGHT SHE MADE FOUR CENTS A DAY...
GOSH, I **HATE** TO WORK ON **POLKA DOT MATERIAL!**
FOUR CENTS A DAY WASN'T VERY MUCH, BUT THE LITTLE GIRL STILL MANAGED TO SAVE ONE PENNY EVERY YEAR...
THERE! MY SAVINGS FOR **ANOTHER** YEAR!
PLUNK!
SHE WAS LOOKING FOR
WARD TO THE DAY WHE
SHE COULD AFFORD TO
BUY A BEAUTIFUL NEW DRESS FOR **HERSELF**...
SIGH!
PARIS STYLES
AS IT WAS, THE POOR LITTLE GIRL HAD TO WEAR THE SAME OL' DRESS, DAY AFTER DAY, YEAR IN AN' YEAR OUT...
HA, HA, HA!
HA, HA, HA!
...AND IT'S VERY DIFFICULT TO KEEP UP WITH THE **STYLES** WHEN YOU HAVE ONLY **ONE** DRESS...
THEY'RE WEARING EM' LONGER THIS YEAR!
SHORTER **THIS** YEAR!

THE POOR LITTLE GIRL'S
LIFE WAS VERY MISERABLE!
IT WAS SO COLD IN THE
GARRET AT NIGHT THAT SHE
HAD TO WEAR HER *THIMBLE*
TO BED...

AT LEAST THE TIP
OF MY *FINGER*
IS WARM!

...AND SOMETIMES AN ICICLE WOULD BREAK OFF
THE CEILING AND FALL ON HER, AND SHE WOULD
HAVE TO WORK *STANDING UP* ALL THE NEXT DAY!

OW!

SNIFF!

.AND SOMETIMES THE MICE WHO LIVED IN THE GARRET WOULD STEAL HER ROLL
AND SHE WOULDN'T HAVE ANYTHING TO EAT THE WHOLE DAY...

HEY!

MY
ROLL!

SNIFF!

MUNCH,
MUNCH,
CRUNCH!

AND IT WAS *ALWAYS* VERY HARD TO
PLEASE THE RICH LADIES SHE WORKED
FOR...

IS THE DRESS FINISHED
I ASKED YOU TO MAKE
FOR ME YESTERDAY?

YES'M!
HERE
IT
IS!

THEY WERE *ALWAYS* FINDING SOME-
THING WRONG WITH HER WORK...

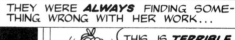

THIS IS *TERRIBLE*!
IT MAKES ME
LOOK LIKE A
CIRCUS TENT!
YOU'LL HAVE
TO MAKE IT
OVER!

YES'M!

BUT THE POOR LITTLE GIRL WAS AL-
WAYS VERY PATIENT...

DID YOU MAKE THAT
DRESS OVER
FOR ME?

YES'M!
HERE
IT IS!

SHE ALWAYS DID HER BEST TO PLEASE
THE RICH LADIES...

THAT'S BETTER! I'M
SURE I DON'T LOOK
LIKE A CIRCUS
TENT *NOW*!

NO'M!

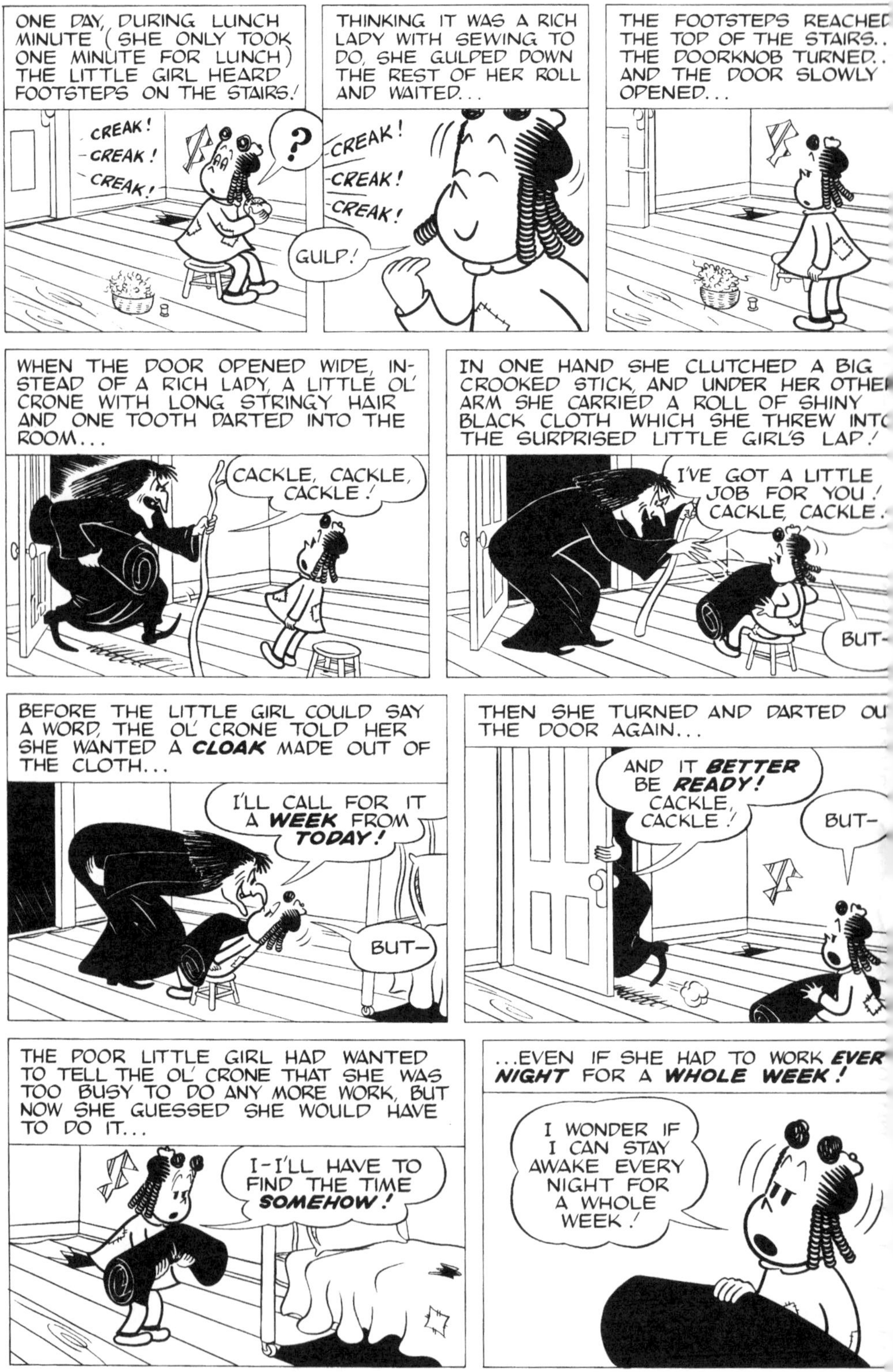
ONE DAY, DURING LUNCH MINUTE (SHE ONLY TOOK ONE MINUTE FOR LUNCH) THE LITTLE GIRL HEARD FOOTSTEPS ON THE STAIRS!
CREAK! CREAK! CREAK!
?
THINKING IT WAS A RICH LADY WITH SEWING TO DO, SHE GULPED DOWN THE REST OF HER ROLL AND WAITED...
CREAK! CREAK! CREAK!
GULP!
THE FOOTSTEPS REACHED THE TOP OF THE STAIRS... THE DOORKNOB TURNED... AND THE DOOR SLOWLY OPENED...
WHEN THE DOOR OPENED WIDE, INSTEAD OF A RICH LADY, A LITTLE OL' CRONE WITH LONG STRINGY HAIR AND ONE TOOTH DARTED INTO THE ROOM...
CACKLE, CACKLE, CACKLE!
IN ONE HAND SHE CLUTCHED A BIG CROOKED STICK, AND UNDER HER OTHER ARM SHE CARRIED A ROLL OF SHINY BLACK CLOTH WHICH SHE THREW INTO THE SURPRISED LITTLE GIRL'S LAP!
I'VE GOT A LITTLE JOB FOR YOU! CACKLE, CACKLE!
BUT-
BEFORE THE LITTLE GIRL COULD SAY A WORD, THE OL' CRONE TOLD HER SHE WANTED A **CLOAK** MADE OUT OF THE CLOTH...
I'LL CALL FOR IT A **WEEK** FROM **TODAY!**
BUT-
THEN SHE TURNED AND DARTED OUT THE DOOR AGAIN...
AND IT **BETTER** BE **READY!** CACKLE, CACKLE!
BUT-
THE POOR LITTLE GIRL HAD WANTED TO TELL THE OL' CRONE THAT SHE WAS TOO BUSY TO DO ANY MORE WORK, BUT NOW SHE GUESSED SHE WOULD HAVE TO DO IT...
I-I'LL HAVE TO FIND THE TIME **SOMEHOW!**
...EVEN IF SHE HAD TO WORK **EVERY NIGHT** FOR A **WHOLE WEEK!**
I WONDER IF I CAN STAY AWAKE EVERY NIGHT FOR A WHOLE WEEK!

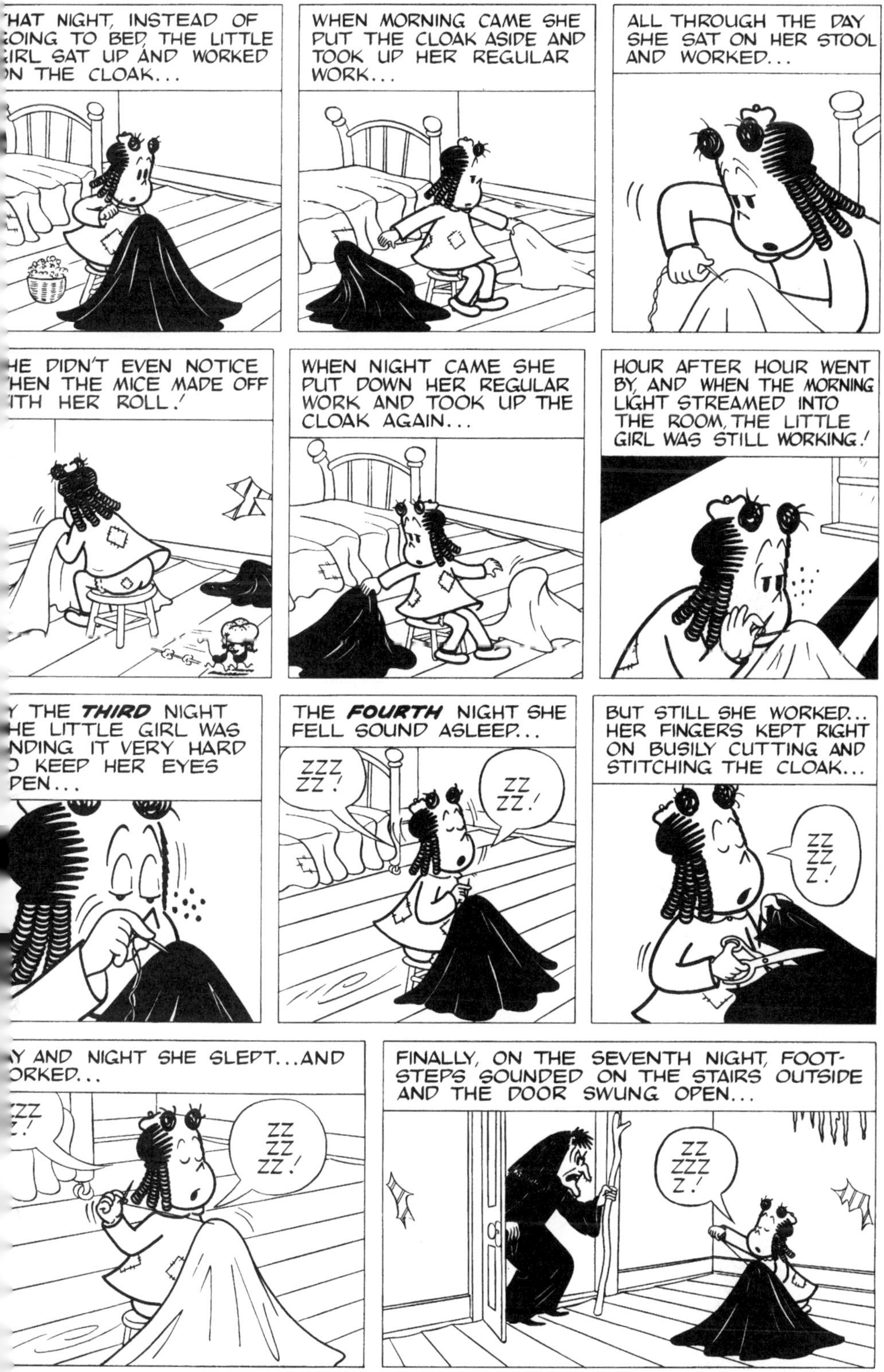

HAT NIGHT, INSTEAD OF OING TO BED, THE LITTLE IRL SAT UP AND WORKED N THE CLOAK...
WHEN MORNING CAME SHE PUT THE CLOAK ASIDE AND TOOK UP HER REGULAR WORK...
ALL THROUGH THE DAY SHE SAT ON HER STOOL AND WORKED...
HE DIDN'T EVEN NOTICE HEN THE MICE MADE OFF ITH HER ROLL!
WHEN NIGHT CAME SHE PUT DOWN HER REGULAR WORK AND TOOK UP THE CLOAK AGAIN...
HOUR AFTER HOUR WENT BY, AND WHEN THE MORNING LIGHT STREAMED INTO THE ROOM, THE LITTLE GIRL WAS STILL WORKING!
Y THE ***THIRD*** NIGHT HE LITTLE GIRL WAS NDING IT VERY HARD O KEEP HER EYES PEN...
THE ***FOURTH*** NIGHT SHE FELL SOUND ASLEEP...
ZZZ ZZ!
ZZ ZZ!
BUT STILL SHE WORKED... HER FINGERS KEPT RIGHT ON BUSILY CUTTING AND STITCHING THE CLOAK...
ZZ ZZ Z!
Y AND NIGHT SHE SLEPT...AND ORKED...
ZZ ZZ ZZ!
FINALLY, ON THE SEVENTH NIGHT, FOOT-STEPS SOUNDED ON THE STAIRS OUTSIDE AND THE DOOR SWUNG OPEN...
ZZ ZZZ Z!

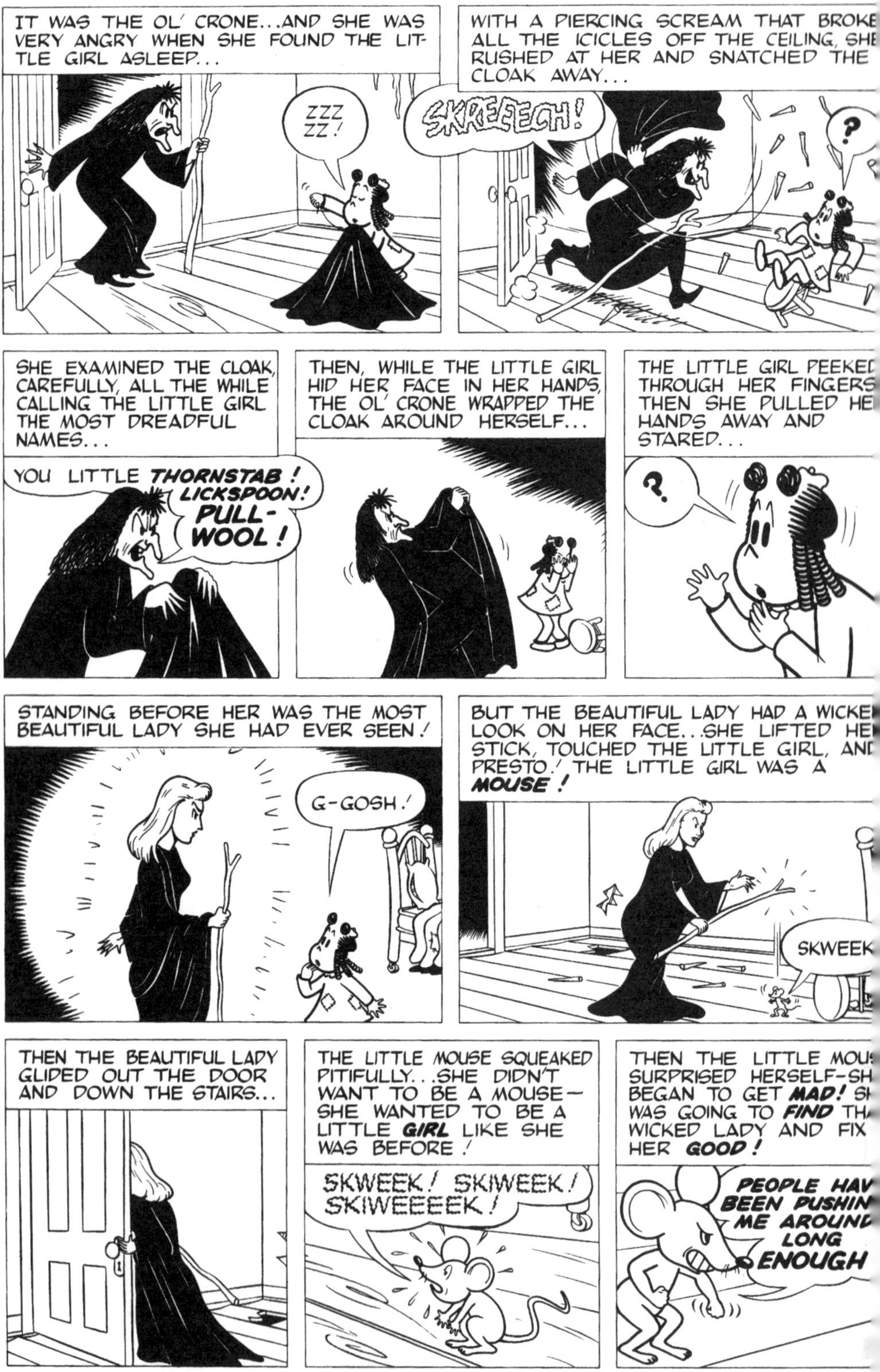
IT WAS THE OL' CRONE...AND SHE WAS VERY ANGRY WHEN SHE FOUND THE LITTLE GIRL ASLEEP...
ZZZ ZZ!
WITH A PIERCING SCREAM THAT BROKE ALL THE ICICLES OFF THE CEILING, SHE RUSHED AT HER AND SNATCHED THE CLOAK AWAY...
SKREEEECH!
?
SHE EXAMINED THE CLOAK, CAREFULLY, ALL THE WHILE CALLING THE LITTLE GIRL THE MOST DREADFUL NAMES...
YOU LITTLE THORNSTAB! LICKSPOON! PULL-WOOL!
THEN, WHILE THE LITTLE GIRL HID HER FACE IN HER HANDS, THE OL' CRONE WRAPPED THE CLOAK AROUND HERSELF...
THE LITTLE GIRL PEEKED THROUGH HER FINGERS THEN SHE PULLED HE HANDS AWAY AND STARED...
?
STANDING BEFORE HER WAS THE MOST BEAUTIFUL LADY SHE HAD EVER SEEN!
G-GOSH!
BUT THE BEAUTIFUL LADY HAD A WICKE LOOK ON HER FACE...SHE LIFTED HE STICK, TOUCHED THE LITTLE GIRL, AND PRESTO! THE LITTLE GIRL WAS A MOUSE!
SKWEEK
THEN THE BEAUTIFUL LADY GLIDED OUT THE DOOR AND DOWN THE STAIRS...
THE LITTLE MOUSE SQUEAKED PITIFULLY...SHE DIDN'T WANT TO BE A MOUSE—SHE WANTED TO BE A LITTLE GIRL LIKE SHE WAS BEFORE!
SKWEEK! SKIWEEK! SKIWEEEEK!
THEN THE LITTLE MOUS SURPRISED HERSELF—SH BEGAN TO GET MAD! SH WAS GOING TO FIND TH WICKED LADY AND FIX HER GOOD!
PEOPLE HAV BEEN PUSHIN ME AROUND LONG ENOUGH

BUT FIRST THERE WAS SOMETHING **ELSE** SHE MUST DO BEFORE SHE WENT LOOKING FOR THE LADY...

THE MICE WHO HAD BEEN STEALING HER ROLLS SURE WERE SURPRISED WHEN A STRANGE MOUSE WALKED IN AND PUNCHED THEM IN THE EYE!

SKWEEK?

SKWEEK?

THE LITTLE GIRL-MOUSE FELT BETTER AFTER THAT...SHE THREW OUT HER CHEST AND WALKED OUT THE DOOR...

...AND FELL DOWN SIX FLIGHTS OF STAIRS...

OW!

OH!

OW!

SHE HAD FORGOTTEN THAT SHE WAS TOO SMALL TO WALK DOWN-STAIRS A STEP AT A TIME LIKE A LITTLE **GIRL** COULD...

OOOOH!

THE LITTLE MOUSE REACHED THE SIDEWALK JUST IN TIME TO CATCH A PASSING TROLLEY CAR...

SHE WASN'T SURE IF THE TROLLEY WAS GOING IN THE RIGHT DIRECTION...

BUT IF IT **WASN'T** THE RIGHT DIRECTION, SHE COULD ALWAYS GET OFF AND TAKE A TROLLEY GOING THE OTHER WAY...

THE POOR LITTLE MOUSE REACHED THE END OF THE LINE SOONER THAN SHE THOUGHT...

?

BEFORE SHE KNEW IT SHE WAS OUT ON THE SIDEWALK AGAIN!

AND THE TROLLEY MOTORMAN SEEMED TO BE MAD AT HER... PROBABLY BECAUSE SHE HADN'T PAID ANY FARE...

HE KEPT THROWING HIS TROLLEY AT HER, BUT SHE DODGED INTO A CROWD OF PEOPLE AND SOON WAS SAFE...

IT WAS A VERY BIG CROWD...THE LITTLE MOUSE WONDERED WHY THERE WERE SO MANY PEOPLE STANDING AROUND...

THEN SHE DECIDED TO CLIMB UP ON SOMEBODY AND SEE WHAT SHE COULD SEE...

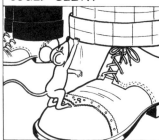

SHE PICKED OUT A MAN WITH A VERY BIG PAIR OF SHOES AND STARTED TO CLIMB...

SHE THOUGHT THAT A MAN WITH VERY BIG SHOES WOULD BE VER *TALL*...

BUT ALAS, *THIS* ONE WASN'T...

BUT SHE FOUND SHE COULD JUMP FROM HIS HAT ONTO A HAT A LITTLE HIGHER UP...

AND SO ON...

PRETTY SOON THE LITTLE MOUSE WAS SITTING ON THE HIGHEST HAT...AND SHE COULD SEE EVERYTHING...

SHE WAS *AMAZED* AT WHAT SHE SAW!

THERE WAS THE **KING** STANDING ON THE PALACE BALCONY, AND RIGHT **NEXT** TO HIM WAS THE BEAUTIFUL, WICKED LADY WHO HAD CHANGED THE LITTLE GIRL INTO A MOUSE!

GOSH! WH-WHAT IS SHE DOING UP **THERE**?

THE LITTLE MOUSE LISTENED TO WHAT THE PEOPLE AROUND HER WERE SAYING...

SHE WILL MAKE A **BEAUTIFUL QUEEN**!

I'M GLAD THE KING IS MARRYING HER!

I HOPE THEY LIVE HAPPILY **EVER AFTER**!

THE KING WAS GOING TO MARRY THAT WICKED LADY!!

NO, NO!

HE **CAN'T**!

THE LITTLE MOUSE QUICKLY SLID DOWN OFF THE TALL MAN...

I'VE GOT TO **STOP** IT!

THEN SHE TRIED TO MAKE HER WAY TOWARD THE BALCONY...

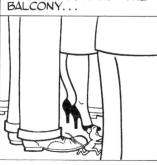

BUT SHE JUST COULDN'T MAKE ANY HEADWAY THROUGH THE FOREST OF LEGS AND FEET...

GOSH, I'LL **NEVER** MAKE IT!

THEN SHE LOOKED UP AND SAW AN OL' LADY WITH A BIG BUNCH OF BALLOONS!

HAH!

QUICK AS A MOUSE, SHE RAN UP TO THE FOLDS OF THE OL' LADY'S DRESS...

THEN ACROSS THE OL' LADY'S SHOULDER, DOWN HER ARM AND UP TO HER HAND...

THE OL' LADY DIDN'T EVEN NOTICE WHEN THE MOUSE TUGGED ONE OF THE STRINGS OUT OF HER HAND...

UP, UP THE BALLOON SHOT, WITH THE MOUSE DANGLING ON THE END OF THE STRING!

IN NO TIME AT ALL, THE BALLOON HAD RISEN HIGH UP ABOVE THE PALACE...

TAKING CAREFUL AIM, THE MOUSE LET GO OF THE STRING...

DOWN, DOWN SHE FELL.

AND PLUNKED RIGHT DOWN THE COLLAR OF THE ROYAL MINISTER WHO WAS ABOUT TO PERFORM THE WEDDING CEREMONY...

BUT THE ROYAL MINISTER DIDN'T *DARE* CRY OUT... HE JUST STOOD THERE WHILE THE MOUSE WRIGGLED DOWN HIS BACK AND DOWN HIS PANTS LEG...

THE LITTLE MOUSE JUMPED OUT ON THE FLOOR AND RAN AROUND BEHIND THE BEAUTIFUL LADY...

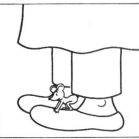

THEN VERY QUICKLY THE MOUSE CHEWED APART ONE OF THE STITCHES IN THE BEAUTIFUL LADY'S CLOAK...

CHOFF! CHOFF!

THEN SHE TUGGED AT THE LOOSE THREAD AND ONE BY ONE THE STITCHES UNRAVELLED...

THE ROYAL MINISTER WAS JUST ABOUT TO SAY "DO YOU TAKE THIS BEAUTIFUL LADY TO BE YOUR LAWFUL WEDDED QUEEN?" WHEN THE BLACK CLOAK FELL APART AND SLIPPED TO THE GROUND...

INSTEAD OF THE BEAUTIFUL LADY, THE KING WAS AMAZED TO SEE HIS OLD ENEMY, THAT WITCH, HAZEL, STANDING THERE!

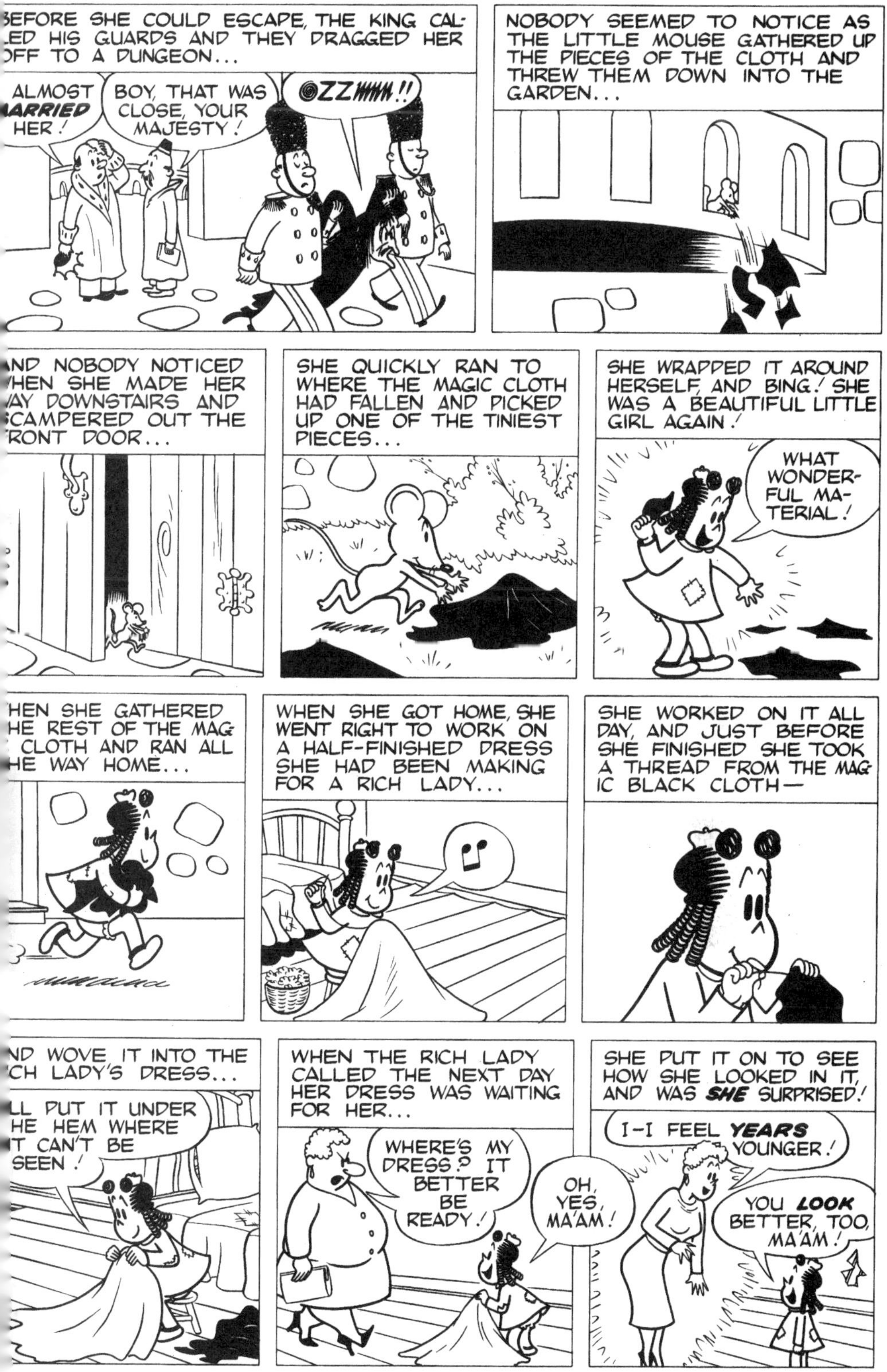
BEFORE SHE COULD ESCAPE, THE KING CALLED HIS GUARDS AND THEY DRAGGED HER OFF TO A DUNGEON...
ALMOST MARRIED HER!
BOY, THAT WAS CLOSE, YOUR MAJESTY!
ØZZWWW!!
NOBODY SEEMED TO NOTICE AS THE LITTLE MOUSE GATHERED UP THE PIECES OF THE CLOTH AND THREW THEM DOWN INTO THE GARDEN...
AND NOBODY NOTICED WHEN SHE MADE HER WAY DOWNSTAIRS AND SCAMPERED OUT THE FRONT DOOR...
SHE QUICKLY RAN TO WHERE THE MAGIC CLOTH HAD FALLEN AND PICKED UP ONE OF THE TINIEST PIECES...
SHE WRAPPED IT AROUND HERSELF, AND BING! SHE WAS A BEAUTIFUL LITTLE GIRL AGAIN!
WHAT WONDERFUL MATERIAL!
THEN SHE GATHERED THE REST OF THE MAGIC CLOTH AND RAN ALL THE WAY HOME...
WHEN SHE GOT HOME, SHE WENT RIGHT TO WORK ON A HALF-FINISHED DRESS SHE HAD BEEN MAKING FOR A RICH LADY...
SHE WORKED ON IT ALL DAY, AND JUST BEFORE SHE FINISHED SHE TOOK A THREAD FROM THE MAGIC BLACK CLOTH—
AND WOVE IT INTO THE RICH LADY'S DRESS...
I'LL PUT IT UNDER THE HEM WHERE IT CAN'T BE SEEN!
WHEN THE RICH LADY CALLED THE NEXT DAY HER DRESS WAS WAITING FOR HER...
WHERE'S MY DRESS? IT BETTER BE READY!
OH, YES, MA'AM!
SHE PUT IT ON TO SEE HOW SHE LOOKED IN IT, AND WAS SHE SURPRISED!
I-I FEEL YEARS YOUNGER!
YOU LOOK BETTER, TOO, MA'AM!

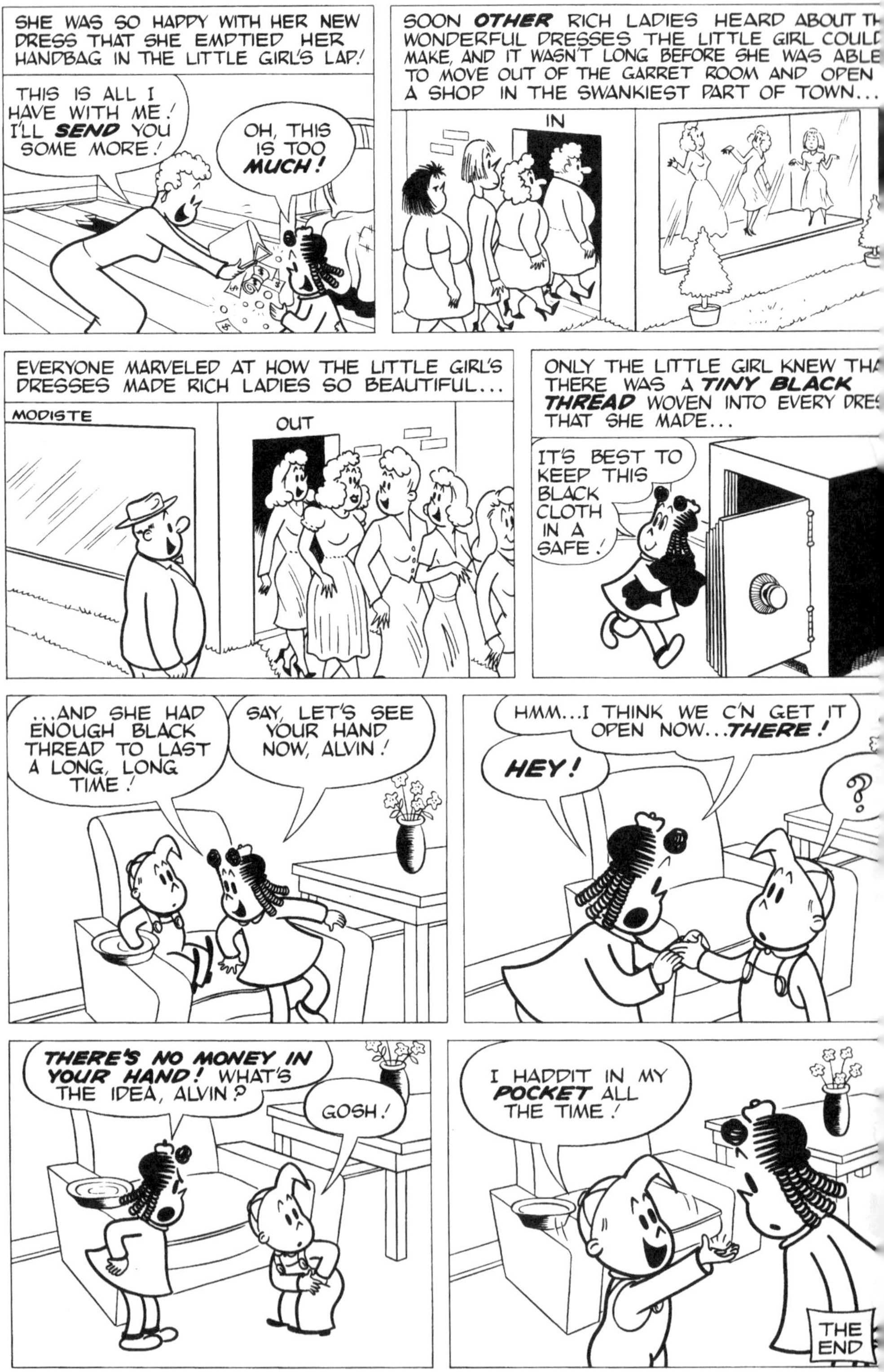
SHE WAS SO HAPPY WITH HER NEW DRESS THAT SHE EMPTIED HER HANDBAG IN THE LITTLE GIRL'S LAP!
THIS IS ALL I HAVE WITH ME! I'LL **SEND** YOU SOME MORE!
OH, THIS IS TOO **MUCH!**
SOON **OTHER** RICH LADIES HEARD ABOUT TH WONDERFUL DRESSES THE LITTLE GIRL COUL MAKE, AND IT WASN'T LONG BEFORE SHE WAS ABLE TO MOVE OUT OF THE GARRET ROOM AND OPEN A SHOP IN THE SWANKIEST PART OF TOWN...
IN
EVERYONE MARVELED AT HOW THE LITTLE GIRL'S DRESSES MADE RICH LADIES SO BEAUTIFUL...
MODISTE
OUT
ONLY THE LITTLE GIRL KNEW THA THERE WAS A ***TINY BLACK THREAD*** WOVEN INTO EVERY DRES THAT SHE MADE...
IT'S BEST TO KEEP THIS BLACK CLOTH IN A SAFE!
...AND SHE HAD ENOUGH BLACK THREAD TO LAST A LONG, LONG TIME!
SAY, LET'S SEE YOUR HAND NOW, ALVIN!
HMM...I THINK WE C'N GET IT OPEN NOW...***THERE!***
HEY!
?
THERE'S NO MONEY IN YOUR HAND! WHAT'S THE IDEA, ALVIN?
GOSH!
I HADDIT IN MY ***POCKET*** ALL THE TIME!
THE END

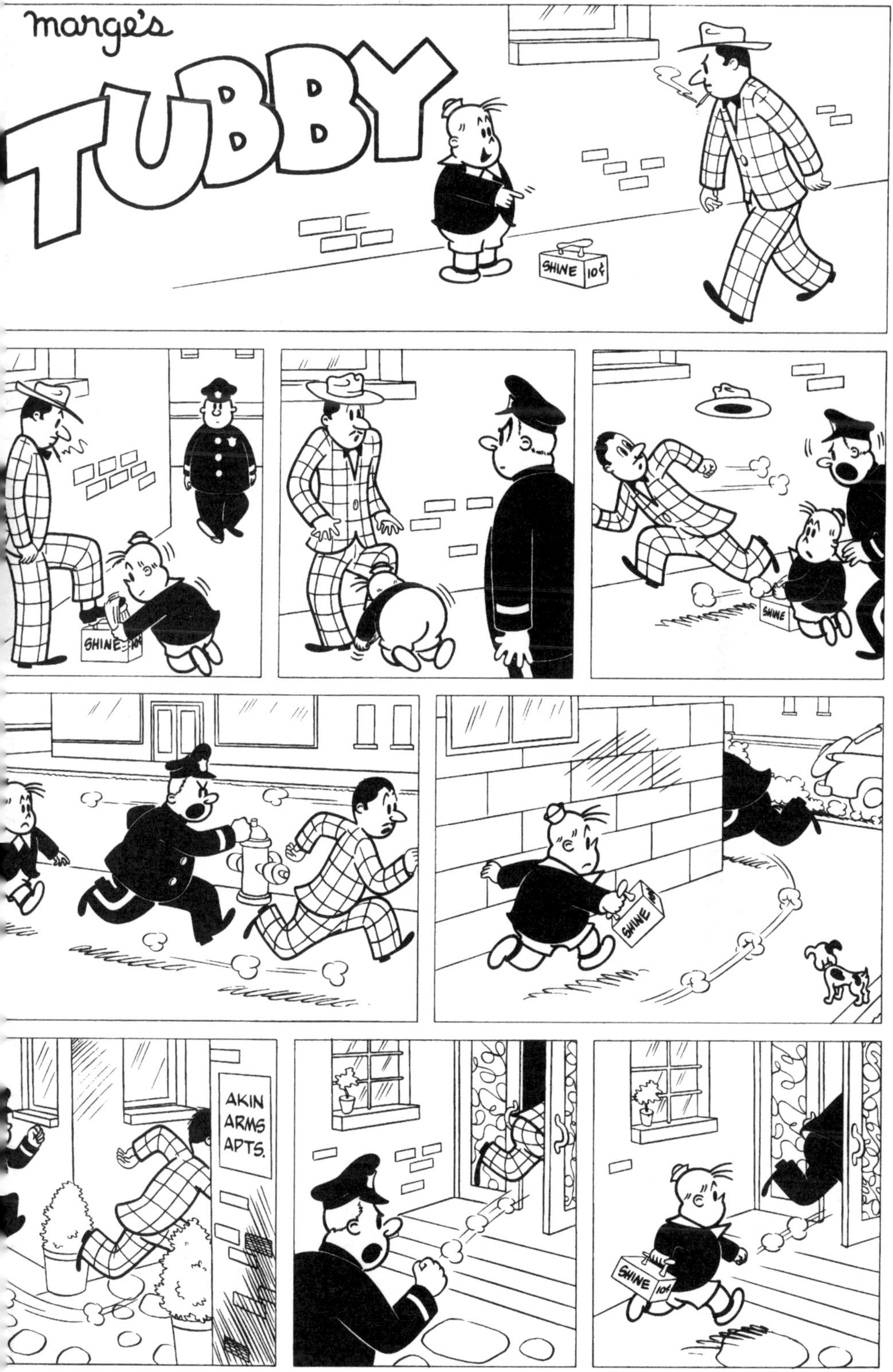
marge's
TUBBY
SHINE 10¢
SHINE 10¢
SHINE
SHINE
AKIN ARMS APTS.
SHINE 10¢

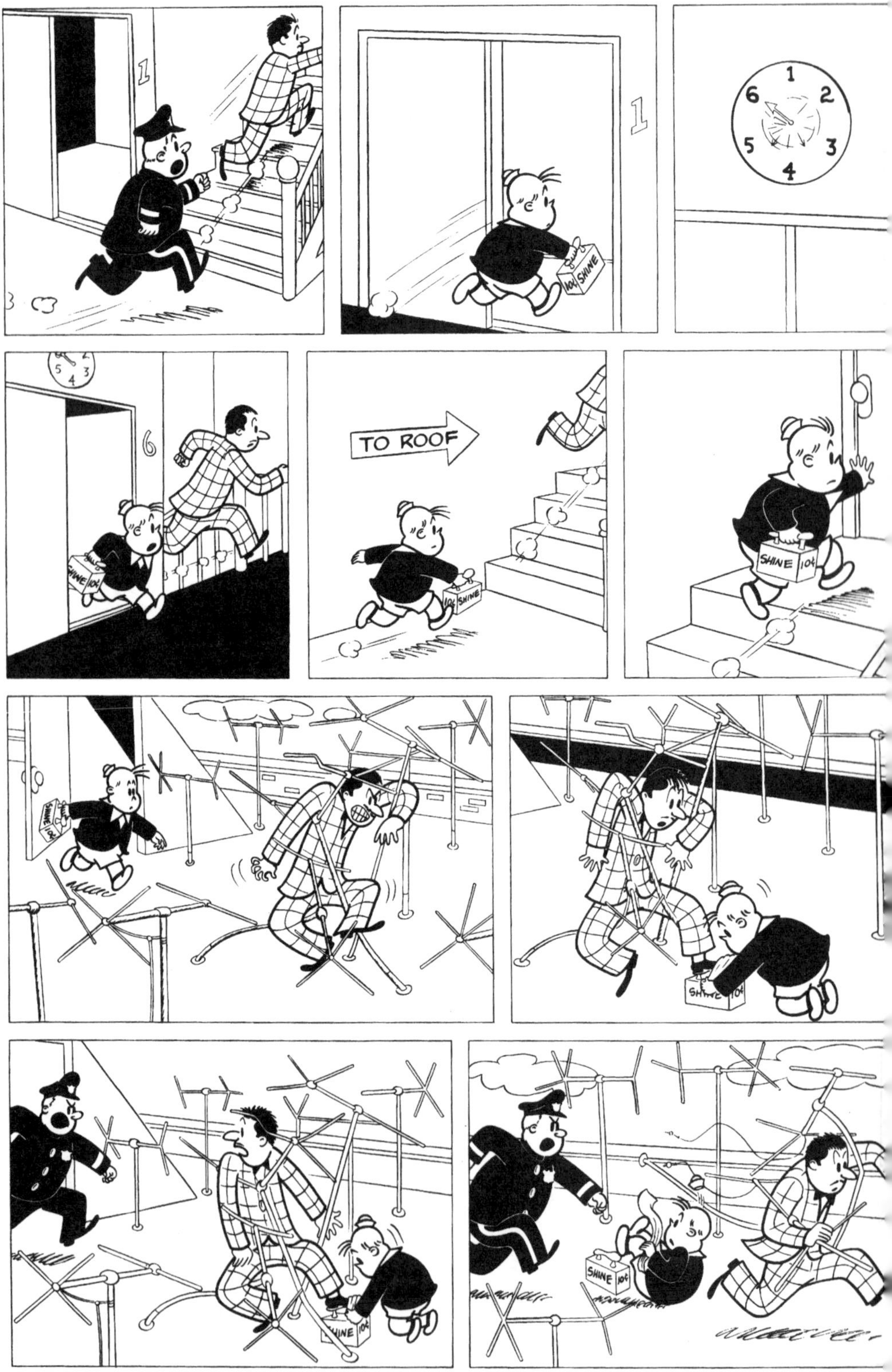
1
10¢ SHINE
TO ROOF
6
SHINE 10¢

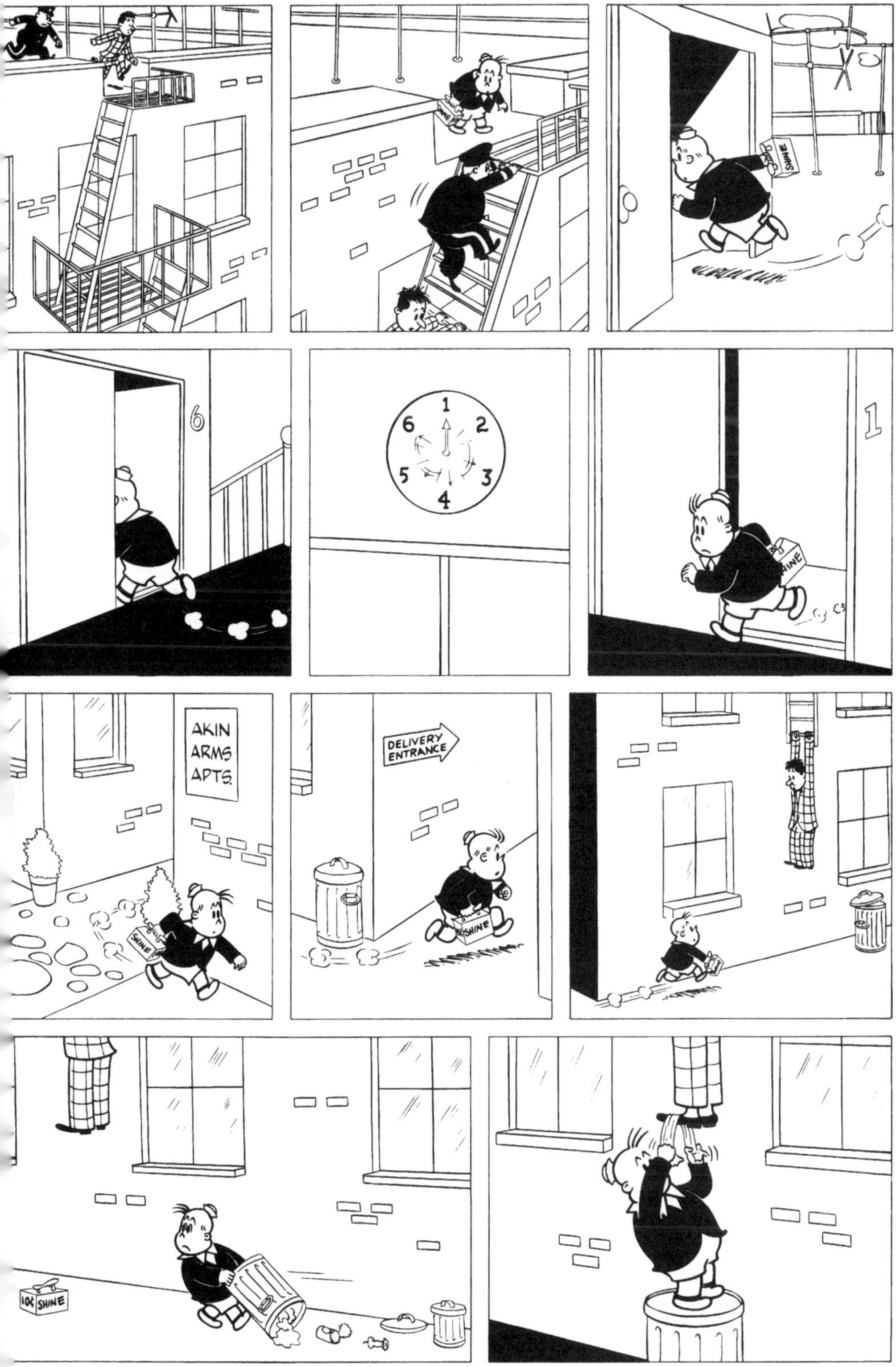
SHINE
SHINE
6
1
2
3
4
5
6
1
SHINE
AKIN
ARMS
APTS.
SHINE
DELIVERY
ENTRANCE
SHINE
10¢ SHINE

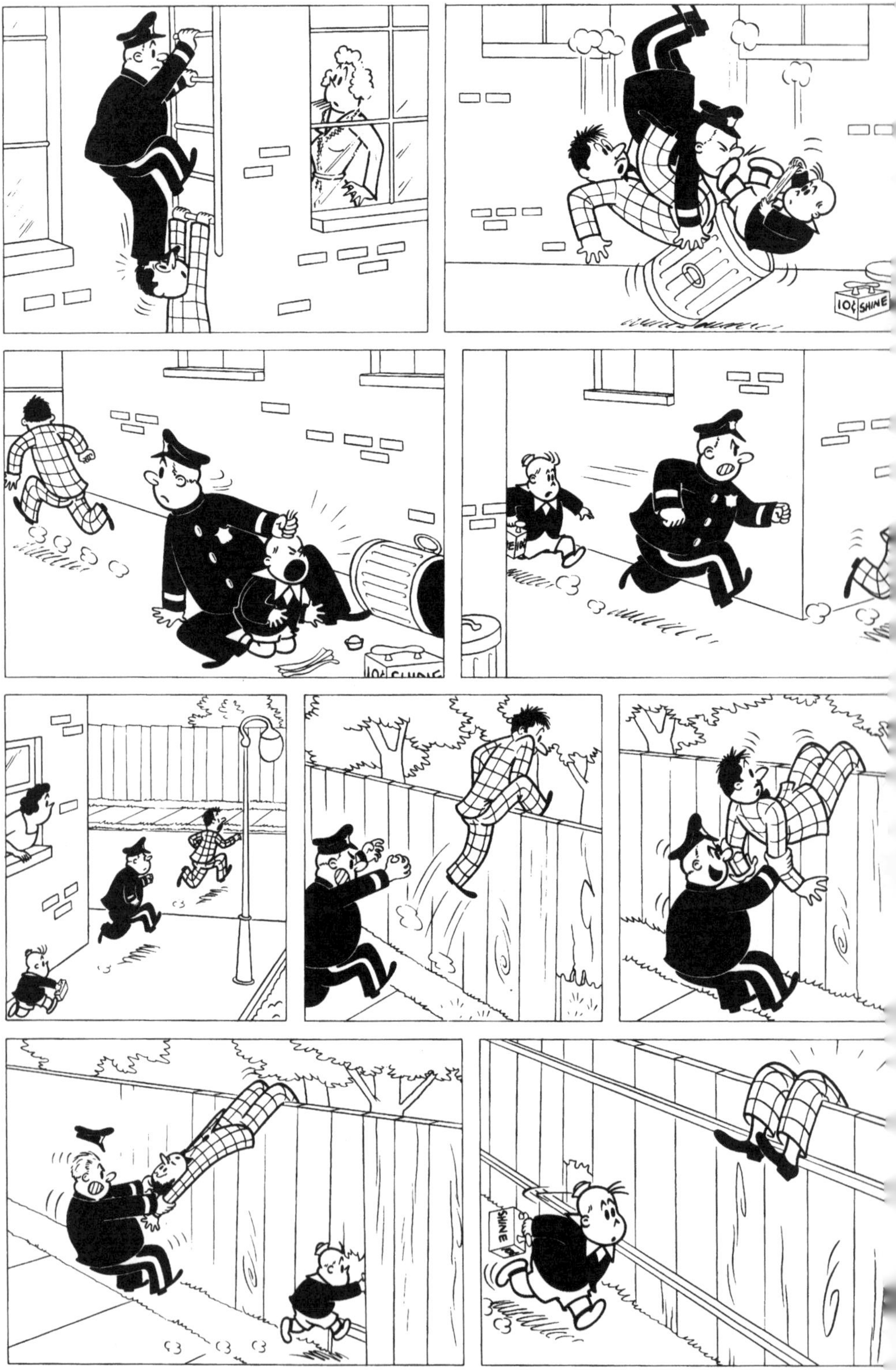
10¢ SHINE

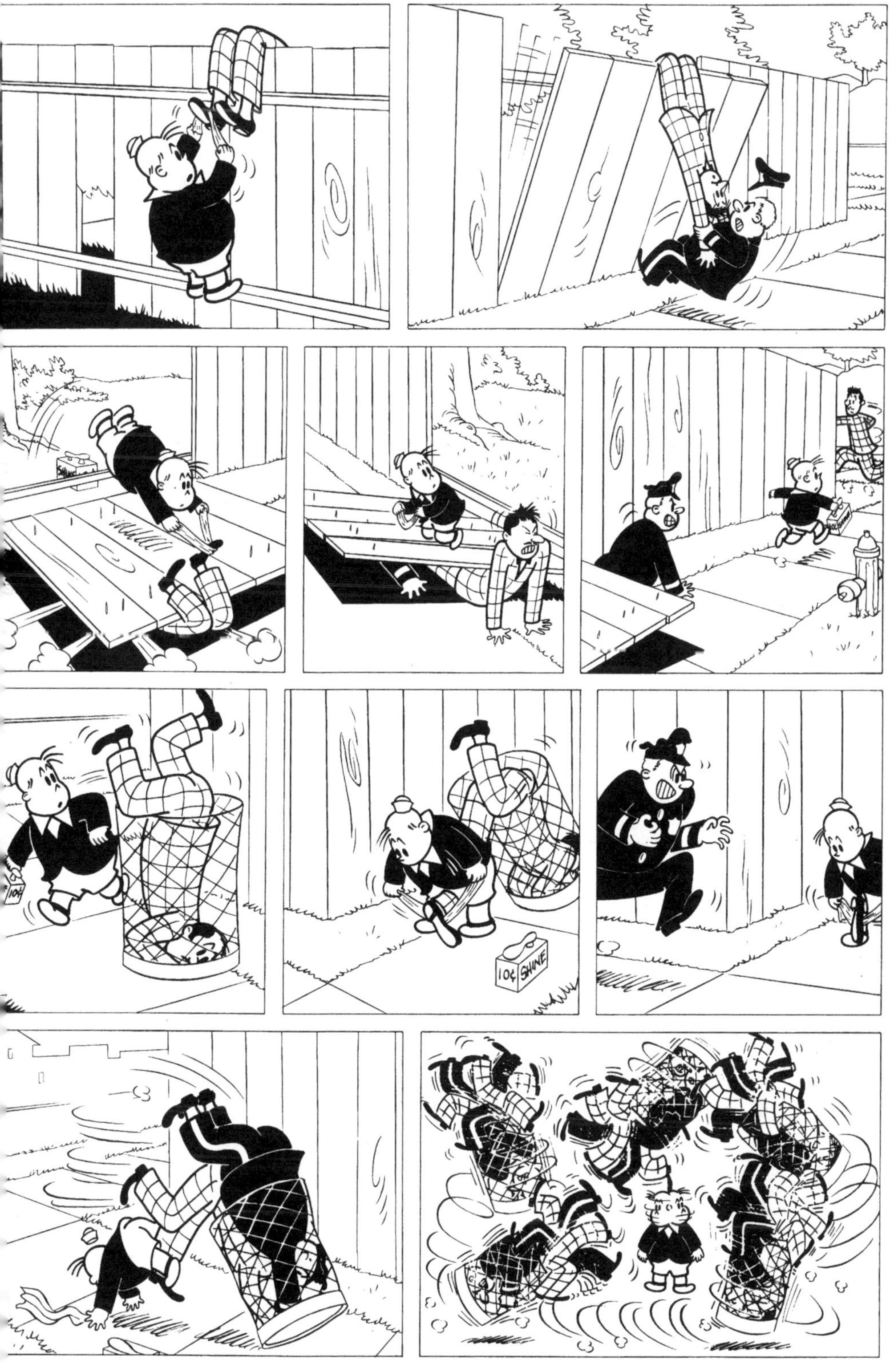
10¢ SHINE

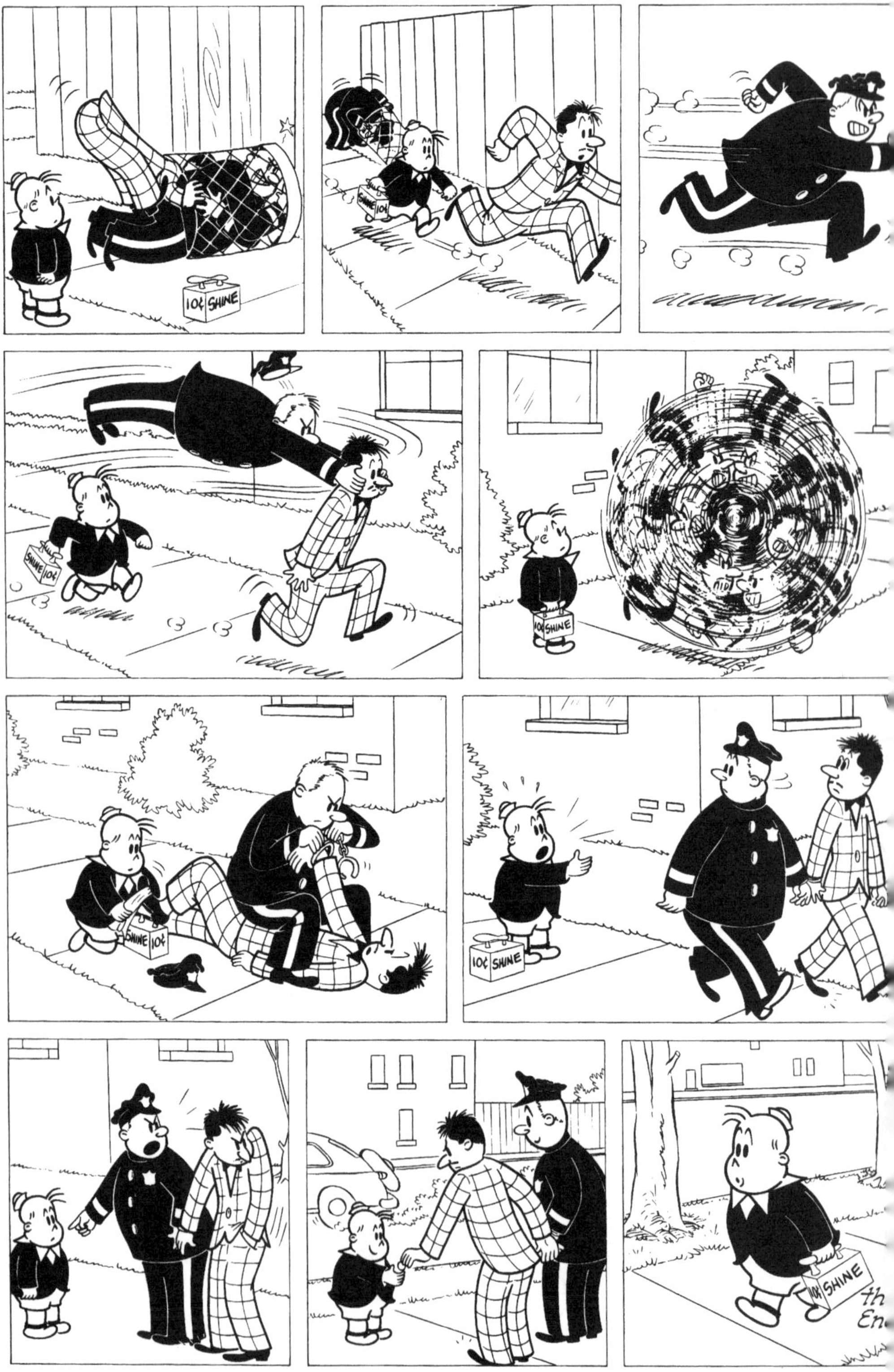
10¢ SHINE
SHINE 10¢
SHINE 10¢
10¢ SHINE
SHINE 10¢
10¢ SHINE
10¢ SHINE
th
En

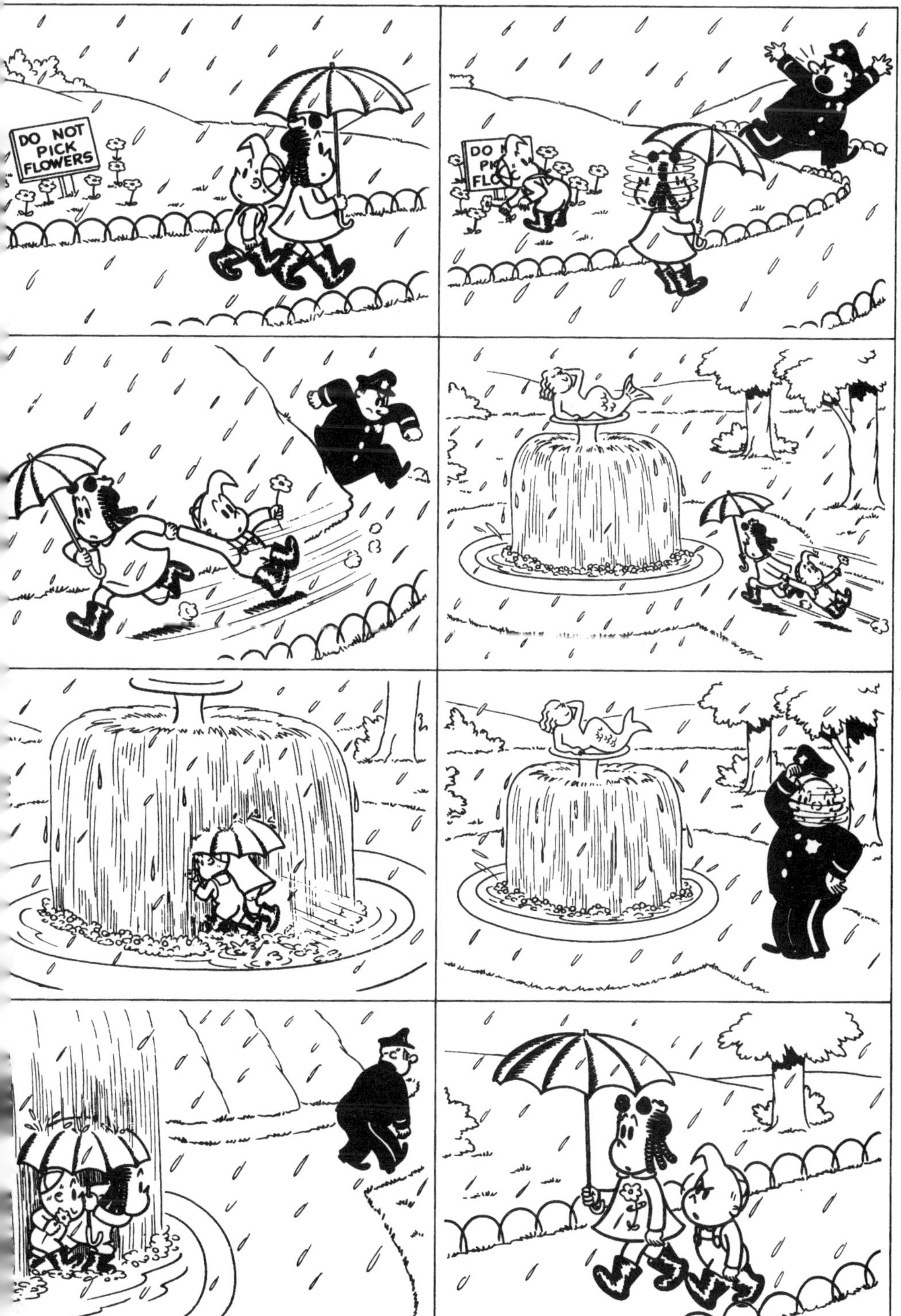
DO NOT PICK FLOWERS

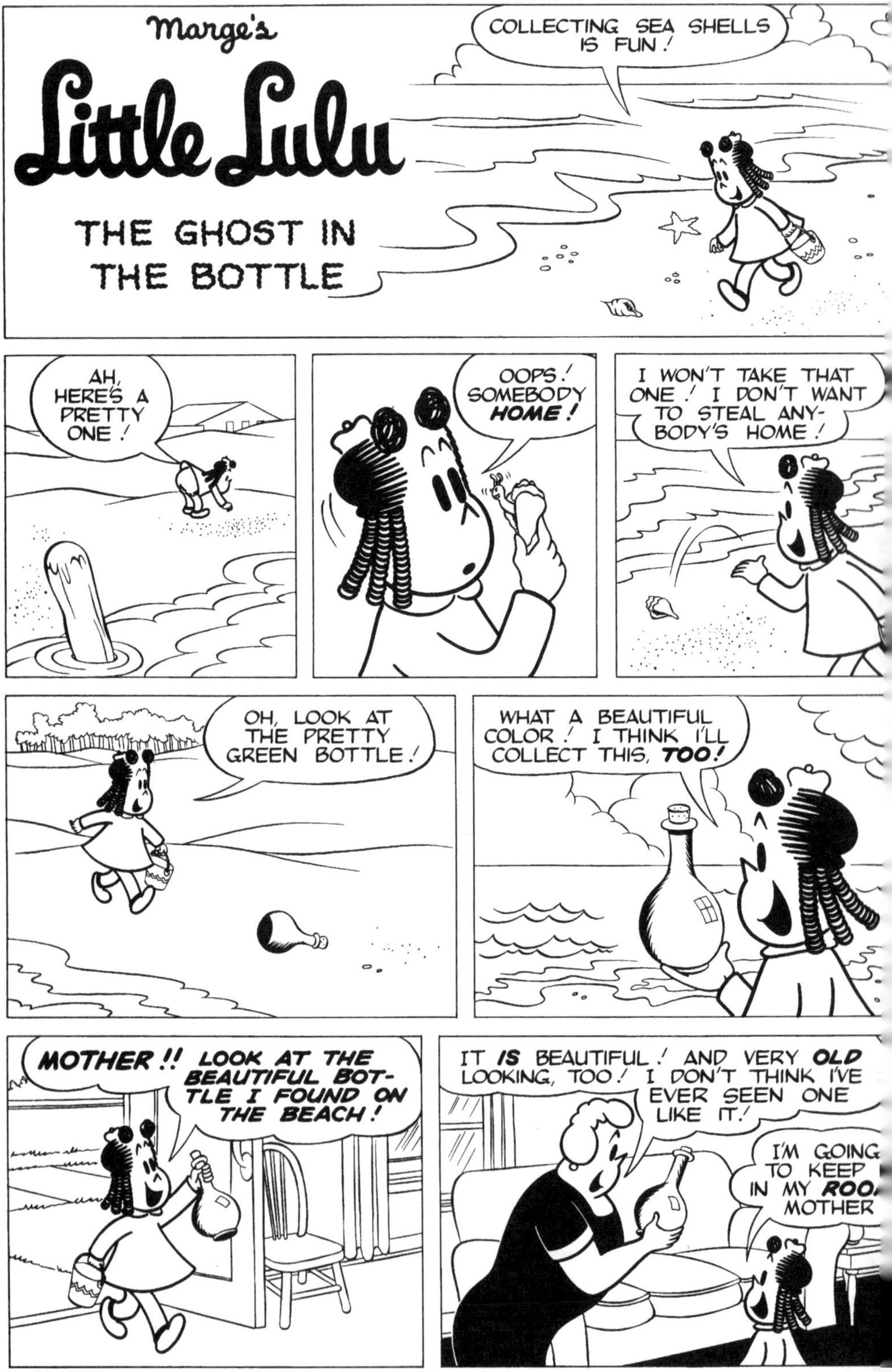

Marge's
Little Lulu
THE GHOST IN THE BOTTLE
COLLECTING SEA SHELLS IS FUN!
AH, HERE'S A PRETTY ONE!
OOPS! SOMEBODY **HOME!**
I WON'T TAKE THAT ONE! I DON'T WANT TO STEAL ANY-BODY'S HOME!
OH, LOOK AT THE PRETTY GREEN BOTTLE!
WHAT A BEAUTIFUL COLOR! I THINK I'LL COLLECT THIS, **TOO!**
MOTHER!! LOOK AT THE BEAUTIFUL BOT-TLE I FOUND ON THE BEACH!
IT **IS** BEAUTIFUL! AND VERY **OLD** LOOKING, TOO! I DON'T THINK I'VE EVER SEEN ONE LIKE IT!
I'M GOING TO KEEP IN MY **ROO** MOTHER

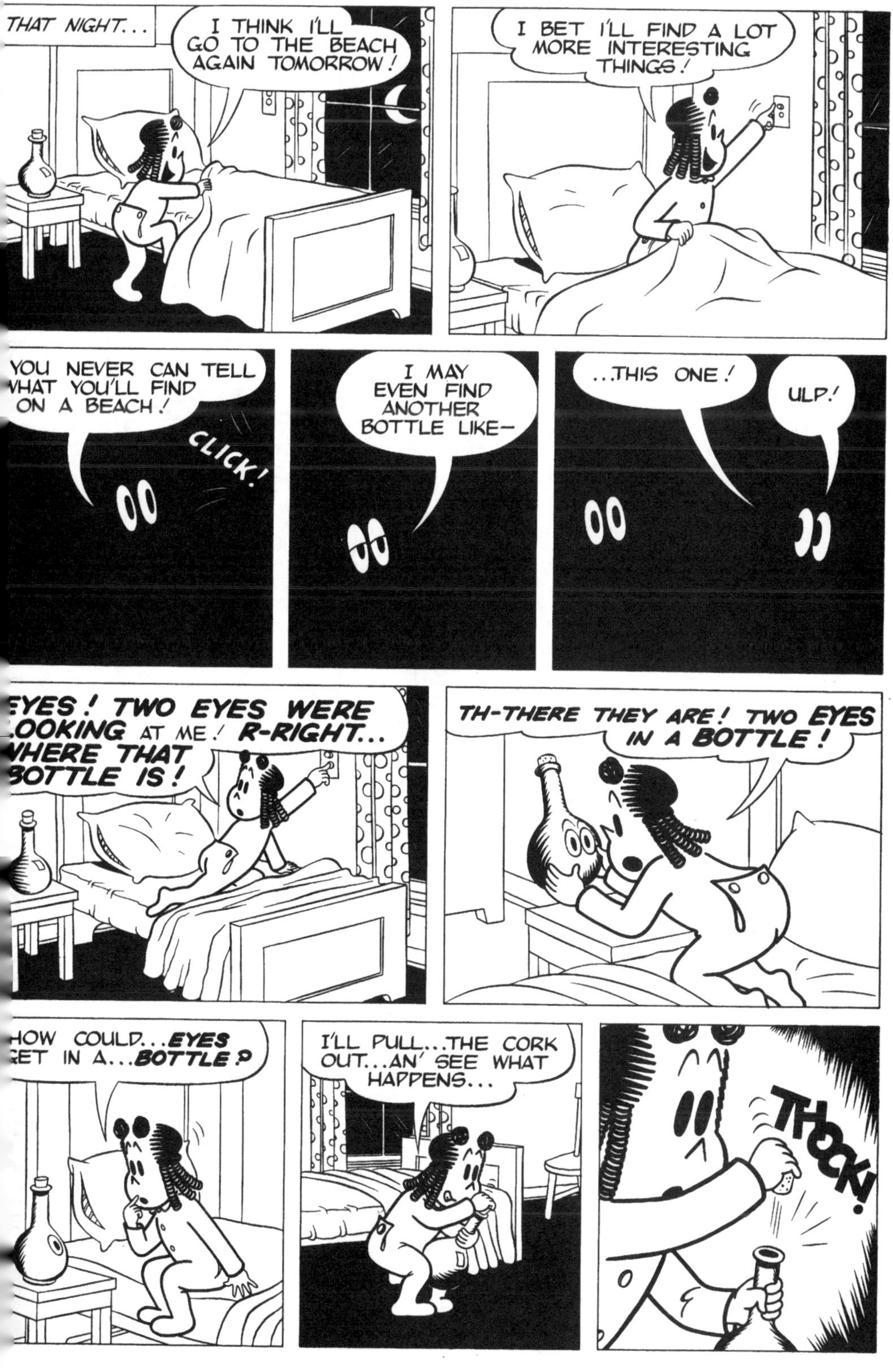
THAT NIGHT...
I THINK I'LL GO TO THE BEACH AGAIN TOMORROW!
I BET I'LL FIND A LOT MORE INTERESTING THINGS!
YOU NEVER CAN TELL WHAT YOU'LL FIND ON A BEACH!
CLICK!
I MAY EVEN FIND ANOTHER BOTTLE LIKE—
...THIS ONE!
ULP!
EYES! TWO EYES WERE LOOKING AT ME! R-RIGHT... WHERE THAT BOTTLE IS!
TH-THERE THEY ARE! TWO EYES IN A BOTTLE!
HOW COULD...EYES GET IN A...BOTTLE?
I'LL PULL...THE CORK OUT...AN' SEE WHAT HAPPENS...
THOCK!

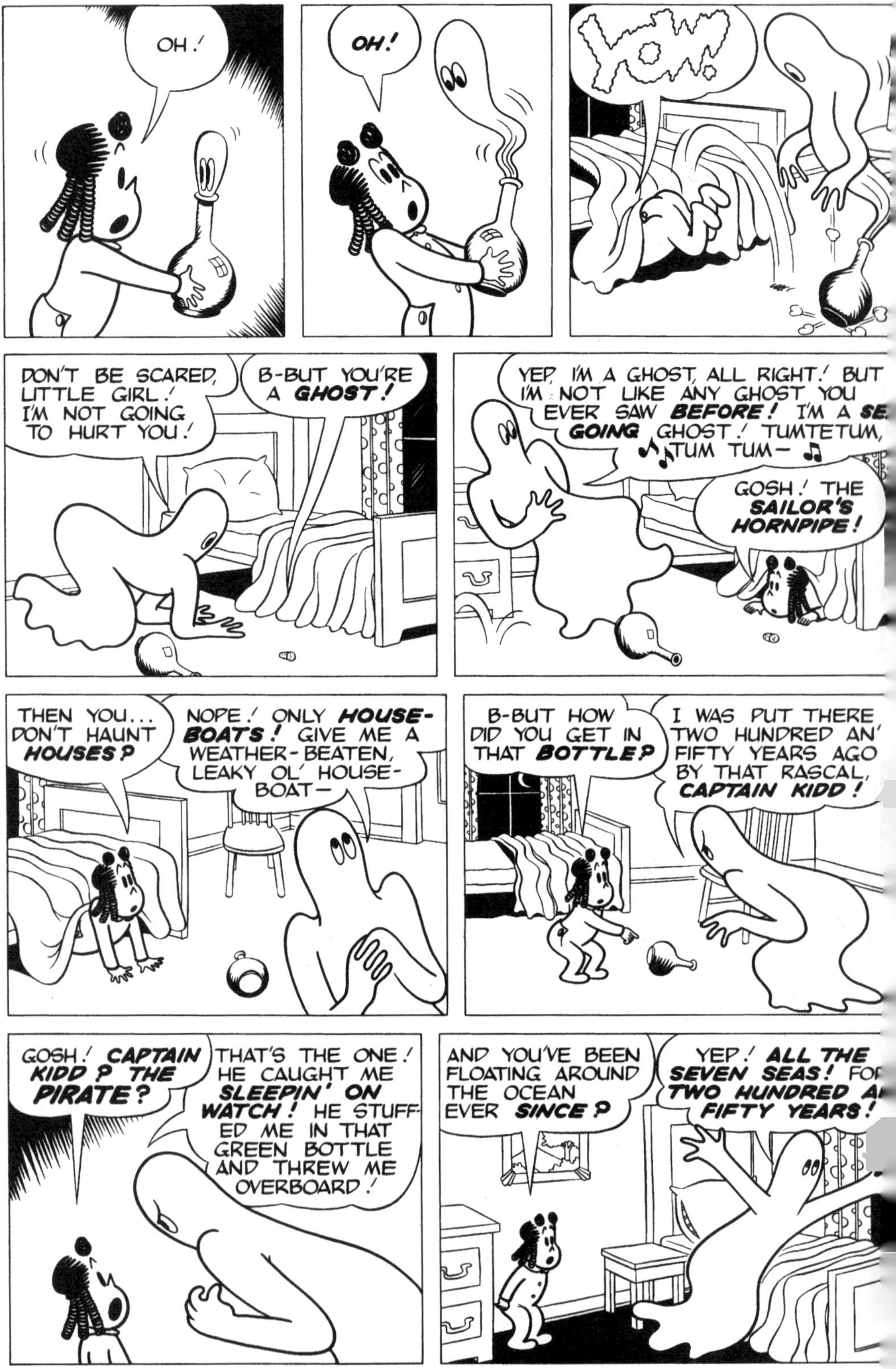
OH!
OH!
YOW!
DON'T BE SCARED, LITTLE GIRL! I'M NOT GOING TO HURT YOU!
B-BUT YOU'RE A GHOST!
YEP, I'M A GHOST, ALL RIGHT! BUT I'M NOT LIKE ANY GHOST YOU EVER SAW BEFORE! I'M A SEA GOING GHOST! TUMTETUM, TUM TUM—
GOSH! THE SAILOR'S HORNPIPE!
THEN YOU... DON'T HAUNT HOUSES?
NOPE! ONLY HOUSE-BOATS! GIVE ME A WEATHER-BEATEN, LEAKY OL' HOUSE-BOAT—
B-BUT HOW DID YOU GET IN THAT BOTTLE?
I WAS PUT THERE TWO HUNDRED AN' FIFTY YEARS AGO BY THAT RASCAL, CAPTAIN KIDD!
GOSH! CAPTAIN KIDD? THE PIRATE?
THAT'S THE ONE! HE CAUGHT ME SLEEPIN' ON WATCH! HE STUFF-ED ME IN THAT GREEN BOTTLE AND THREW ME OVERBOARD!
AND YOU'VE BEEN FLOATING AROUND THE OCEAN EVER SINCE?
YEP! ALL THE SEVEN SEAS! FOR TWO HUNDRED AN FIFTY YEARS!

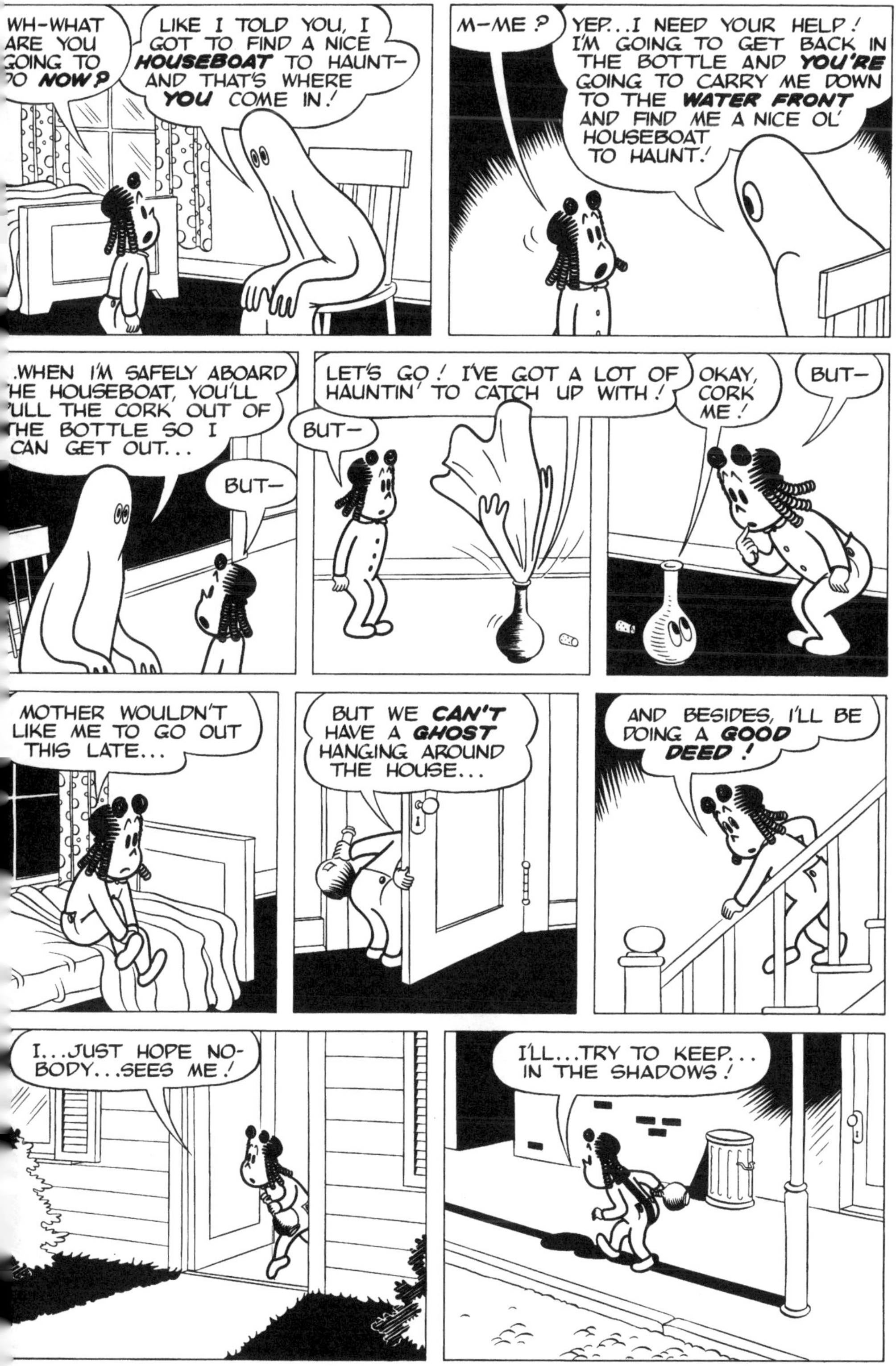
WH-WHAT ARE YOU GOING TO DO NOW?
LIKE I TOLD YOU, I GOT TO FIND A NICE HOUSEBOAT TO HAUNT– AND THAT'S WHERE YOU COME IN!
M-ME?
YEP... I NEED YOUR HELP! I'M GOING TO GET BACK IN THE BOTTLE AND YOU'RE GOING TO CARRY ME DOWN TO THE WATER FRONT AND FIND ME A NICE OL' HOUSEBOAT TO HAUNT!
...WHEN I'M SAFELY ABOARD THE HOUSEBOAT, YOU'LL PULL THE CORK OUT OF THE BOTTLE SO I CAN GET OUT...
BUT–
LET'S GO! I'VE GOT A LOT OF HAUNTIN' TO CATCH UP WITH!
BUT–
OKAY, CORK ME!
BUT–
MOTHER WOULDN'T LIKE ME TO GO OUT THIS LATE...
BUT WE CAN'T HAVE A GHOST HANGING AROUND THE HOUSE...
AND BESIDES, I'LL BE DOING A GOOD DEED!
I... JUST HOPE NOBODY... SEES ME!
I'LL... TRY TO KEEP... IN THE SHADOWS!

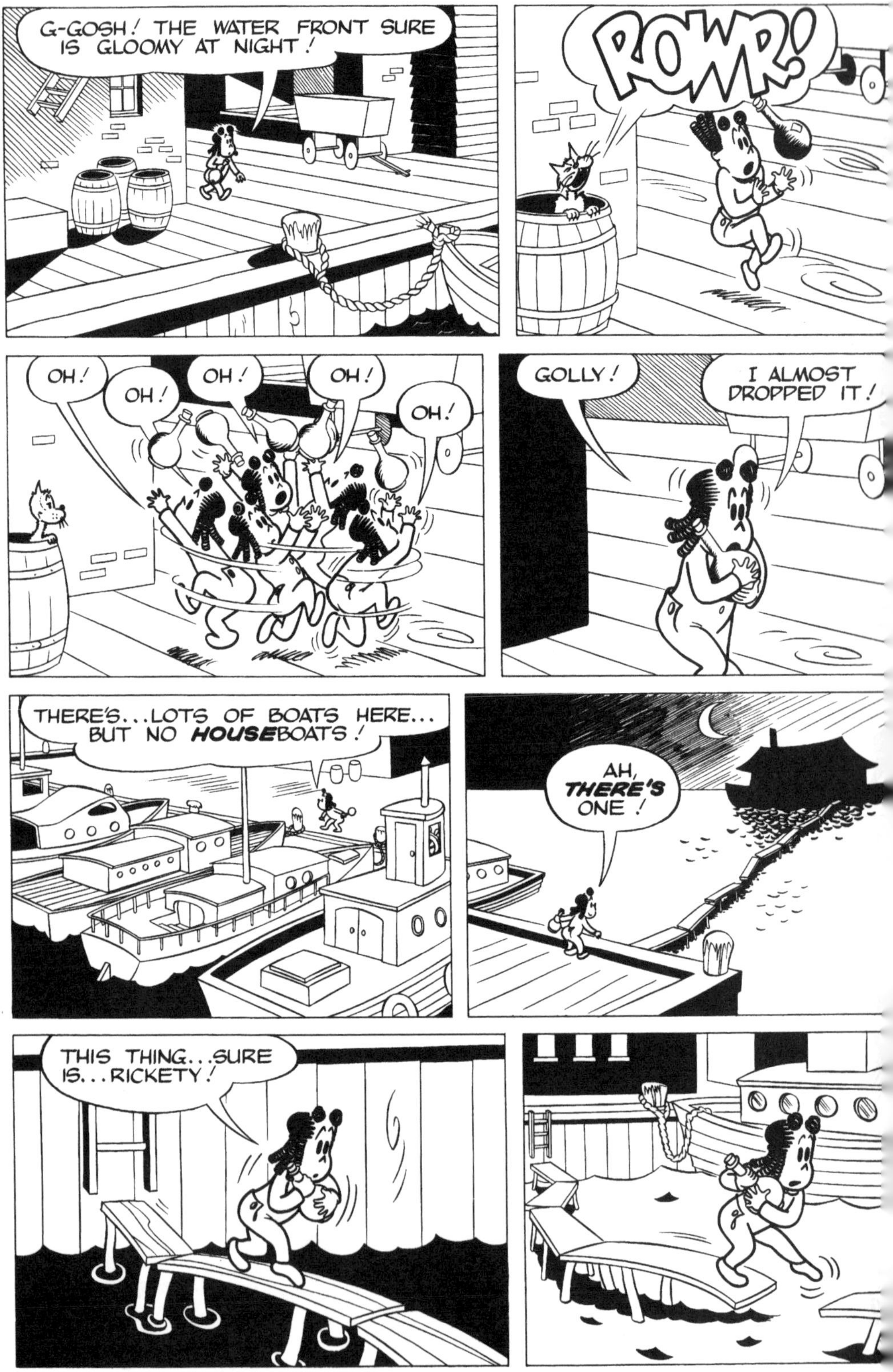
G-GOSH! THE WATER FRONT SURE IS GLOOMY AT NIGHT!
ROWR!
OH!
OH!
OH!
OH!
OH!
GOLLY!
I ALMOST DROPPED IT!
THERE'S...LOTS OF BOATS HERE... BUT NO **HOUSE**BOATS!
AH, ***THERE'S*** ONE!
THIS THING...SURE IS...RICKETY!

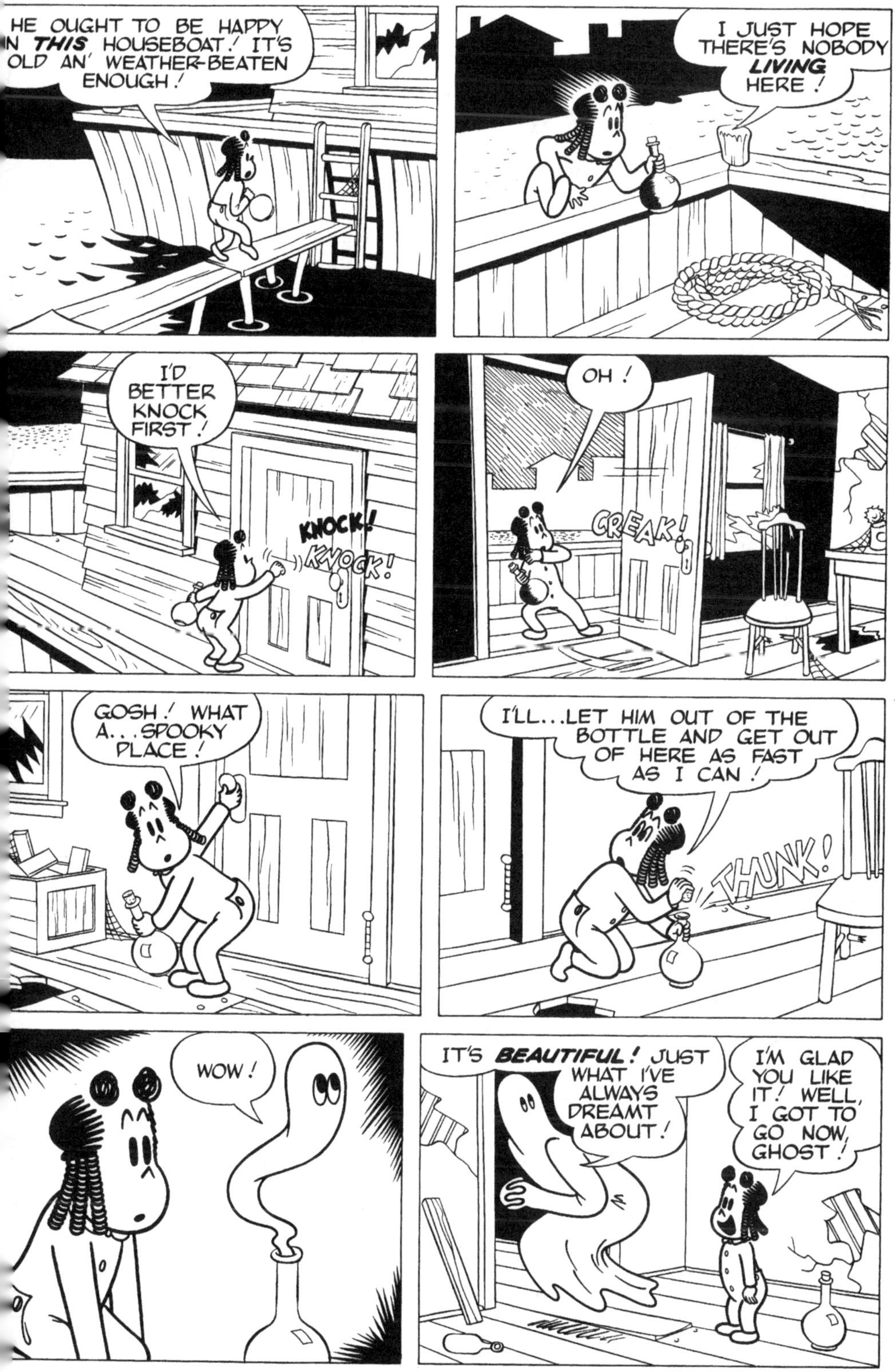
HE OUGHT TO BE HAPPY IN THIS HOUSEBOAT! IT'S OLD AN' WEATHER-BEATEN ENOUGH!
I JUST HOPE THERE'S NOBODY LIVING HERE!
I'D BETTER KNOCK FIRST!
KNOCK! KNOCK!
OH!
CREAK!
GOSH! WHAT A...SPOOKY PLACE!
I'LL...LET HIM OUT OF THE BOTTLE AND GET OUT OF HERE AS FAST AS I CAN!
THUNK!
WOW!
IT'S BEAUTIFUL! JUST WHAT I'VE ALWAYS DREAMT ABOUT!
I'M GLAD YOU LIKE IT! WELL, I GOT TO GO NOW, GHOST!

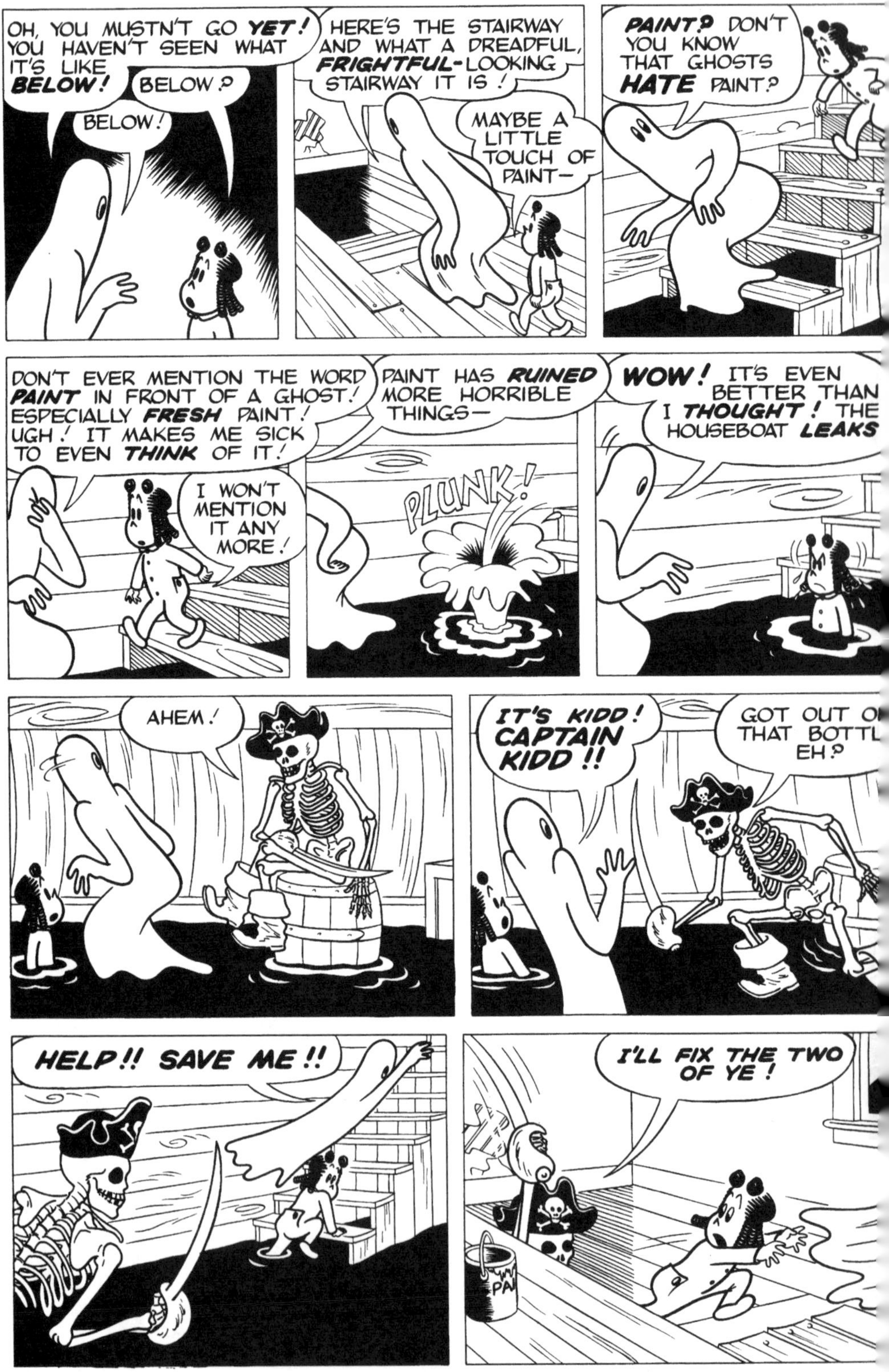
OH, YOU MUSTN'T GO YET! YOU HAVEN'T SEEN WHAT IT'S LIKE BELOW!
BELOW?
BELOW!
HERE'S THE STAIRWAY AND WHAT A DREADFUL, FRIGHTFUL-LOOKING STAIRWAY IT IS!
MAYBE A LITTLE TOUCH OF PAINT—
PAINT? DON'T YOU KNOW THAT GHOSTS HATE PAINT?
DON'T EVER MENTION THE WORD PAINT IN FRONT OF A GHOST! ESPECIALLY FRESH PAINT! UGH! IT MAKES ME SICK TO EVEN THINK OF IT!
I WON'T MENTION IT ANY MORE!
PAINT HAS RUINED MORE HORRIBLE THINGS—
PLUNK!
WOW! IT'S EVEN BETTER THAN I THOUGHT! THE HOUSEBOAT LEAKS
AHEM!
IT'S KIDD! CAPTAIN KIDD!!
GOT OUT OF THAT BOTTL EH?
HELP!! SAVE ME!!
I'LL FIX THE TWO OF YE!

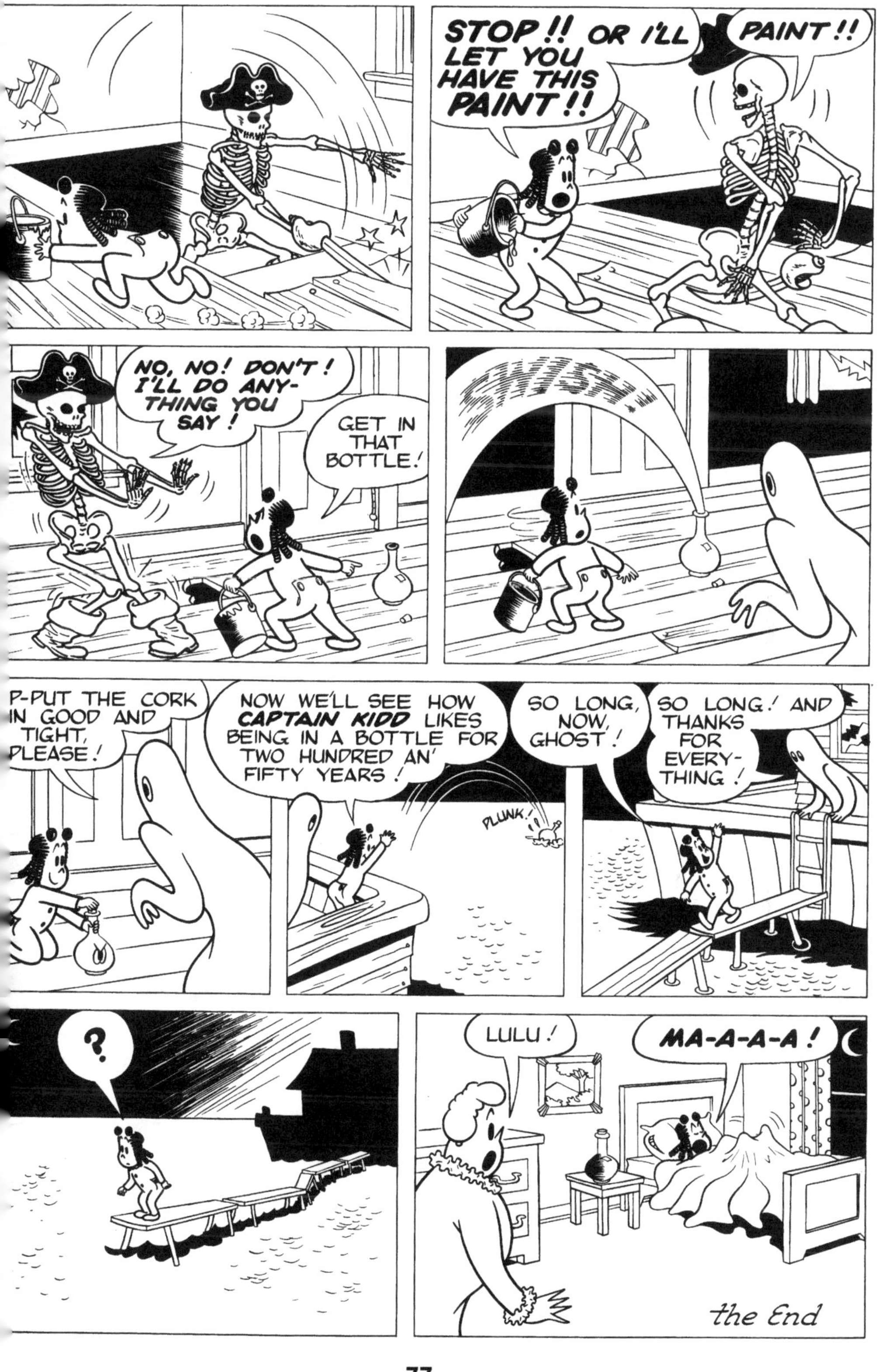
STOP!! OR I'LL LET YOU HAVE THIS PAINT!!
PAINT!!
NO, NO! DON'T! I'LL DO ANY-THING YOU SAY!
GET IN THAT BOTTLE!
SHISH
P-PUT THE CORK IN GOOD AND TIGHT, PLEASE!
NOW WE'LL SEE HOW CAPTAIN KIDD LIKES BEING IN A BOTTLE FOR TWO HUNDRED AN' FIFTY YEARS!
PLUNK!
SO LONG, NOW, GHOST!
SO LONG! AND THANKS FOR EVERY-THING!
?
LULU!
MA-A-A-A!
the End

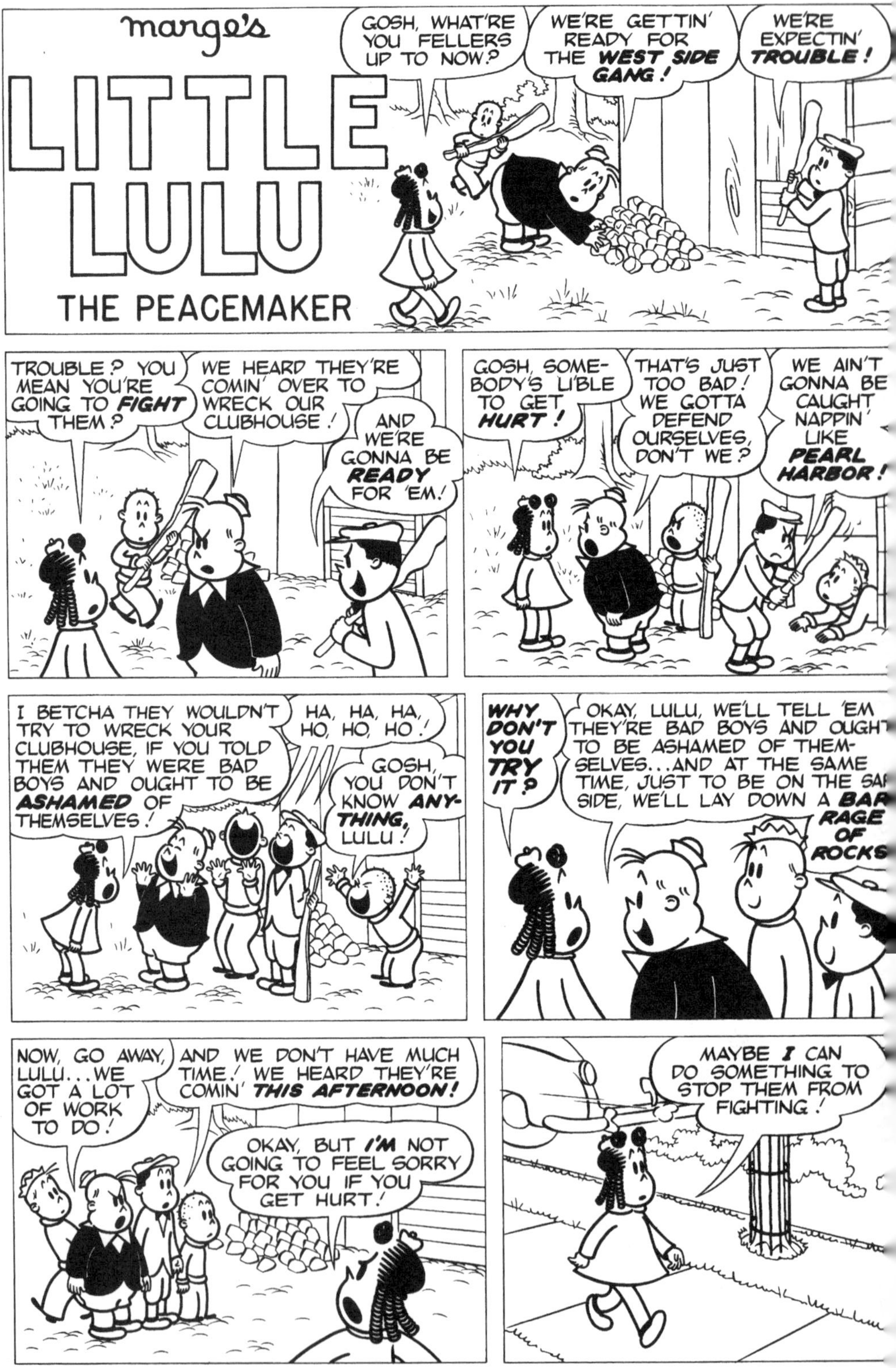
marge's
LITTLE LULU
THE PEACEMAKER
GOSH, WHAT'RE YOU FELLERS UP TO NOW?
WE'RE GETTIN' READY FOR THE WEST SIDE GANG!
WE'RE EXPECTIN' TROUBLE!
TROUBLE? YOU MEAN YOU'RE GOING TO FIGHT THEM?
WE HEARD THEY'RE COMIN' OVER TO WRECK OUR CLUBHOUSE!
AND WE'RE GONNA BE READY FOR 'EM!
GOSH, SOME-BODY'S LI'BLE TO GET HURT!
THAT'S JUST TOO BAD! WE GOTTA DEFEND OURSELVES, DON'T WE?
WE AIN'T GONNA BE CAUGHT NAPPIN' LIKE PEARL HARBOR!
I BETCHA THEY WOULDN'T TRY TO WRECK YOUR CLUBHOUSE, IF YOU TOLD THEM THEY WERE BAD BOYS AND OUGHT TO BE ASHAMED OF THEMSELVES!
HA, HA, HA, HO, HO, HO!
GOSH, YOU DON'T KNOW ANY-THING, LULU!
WHY DON'T YOU TRY IT?
OKAY, LULU, WE'LL TELL 'EM THEY'RE BAD BOYS AND OUGHT TO BE ASHAMED OF THEM-SELVES...AND AT THE SAME TIME, JUST TO BE ON THE SA SIDE, WE'LL LAY DOWN A BAR RAGE OF ROCKS
NOW, GO AWAY, LULU...WE GOT A LOT OF WORK TO DO!
AND WE DON'T HAVE MUCH TIME! WE HEARD THEY'RE COMIN' THIS AFTERNOON!
OKAY, BUT I'M NOT GOING TO FEEL SORRY FOR YOU IF YOU GET HURT!
MAYBE I CAN DO SOMETHING TO STOP THEM FROM FIGHTING!

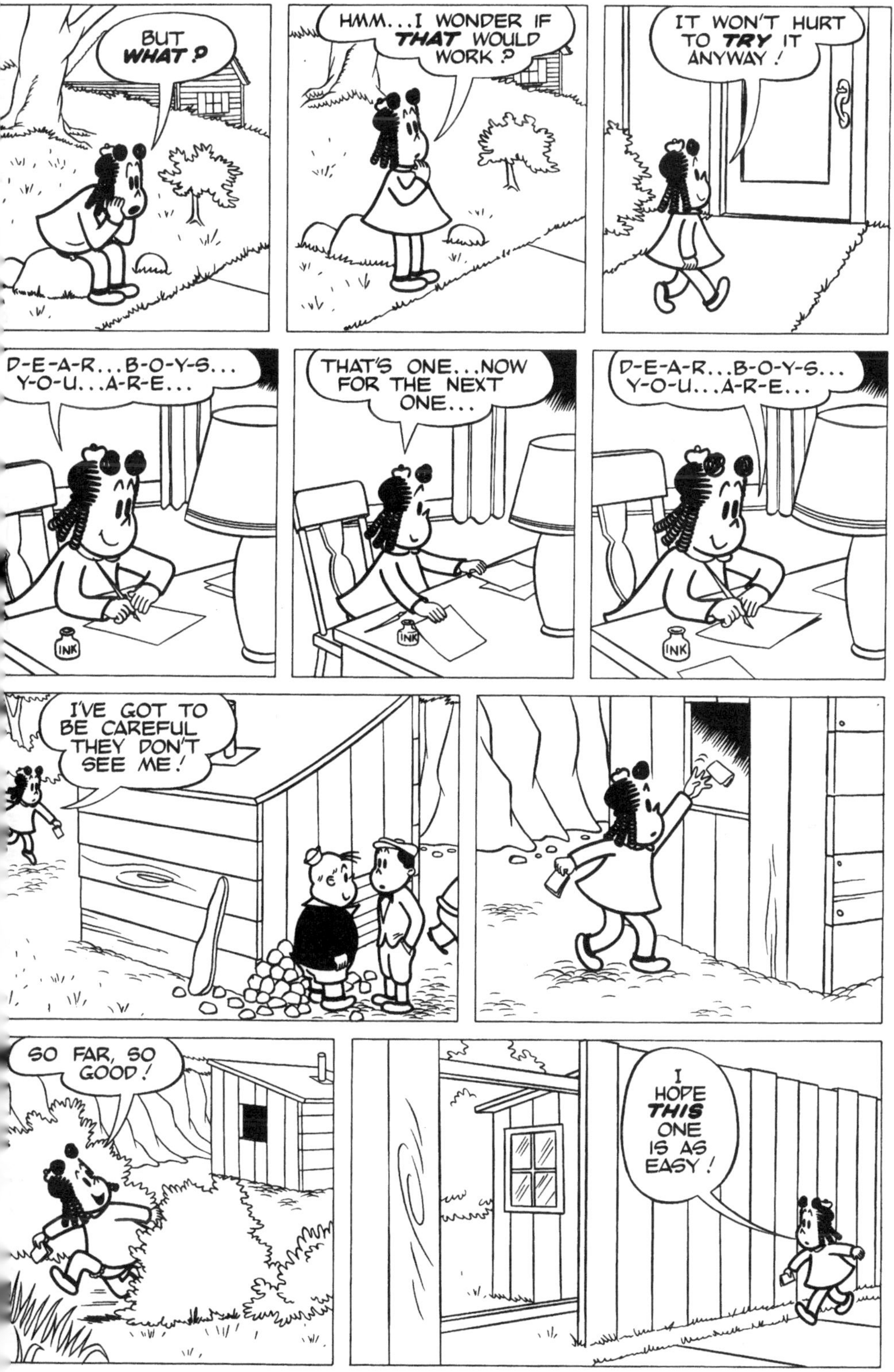
BUT *WHAT?*
HMM...I WONDER IF *THAT* WOULD WORK?
IT WON'T HURT TO *TRY* IT ANYWAY!
D-E-A-R...B-O-Y-S... Y-O-U...A-R-E...
INK
THAT'S ONE...NOW FOR THE NEXT ONE...
D-E-A-R...B-O-Y-S... Y-O-U...A-R-E...
INK
I'VE GOT TO BE CAREFUL THEY DON'T SEE ME!
SO FAR, SO GOOD!
I HOPE *THIS* ONE IS AS EASY!

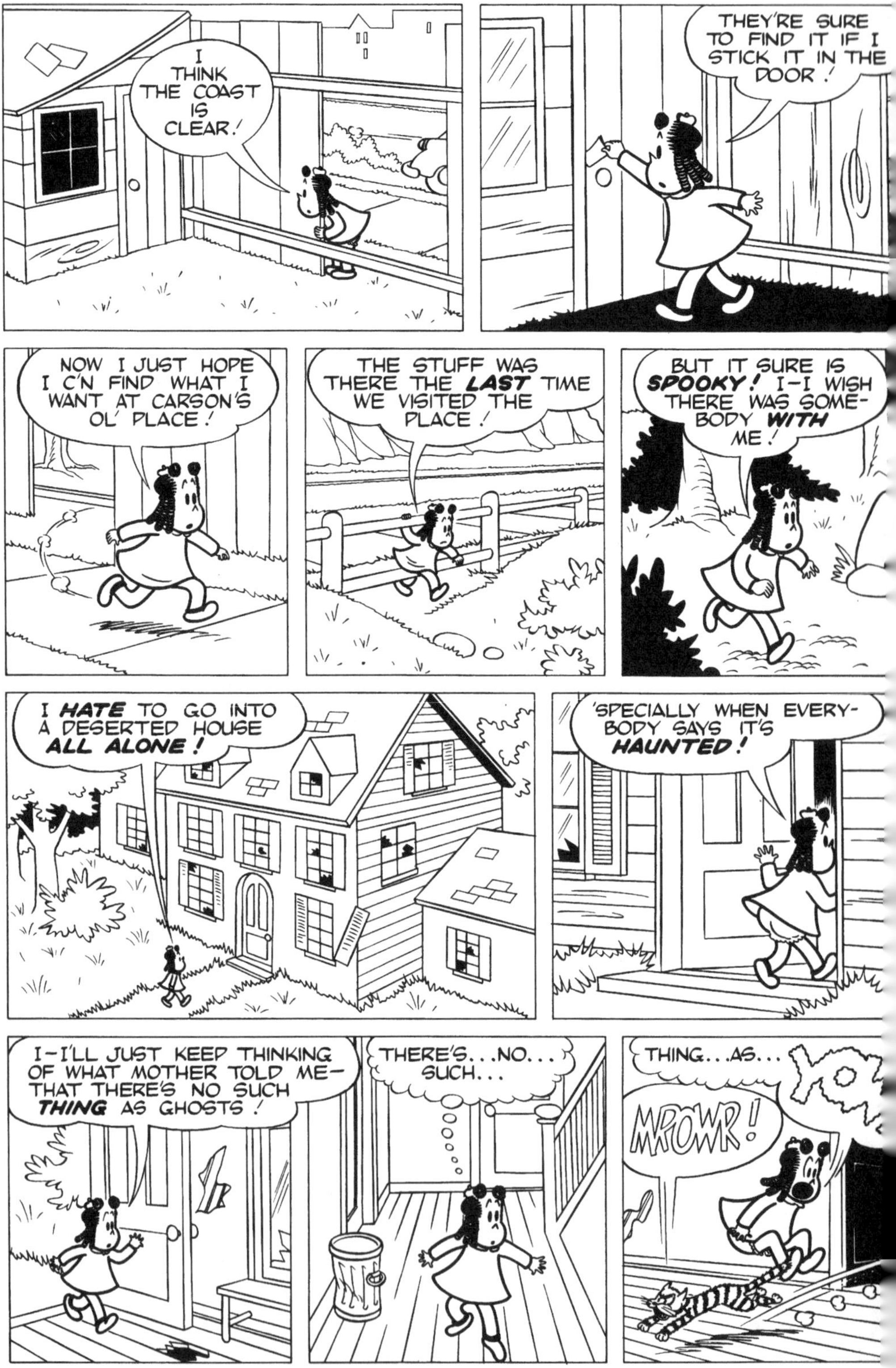

I THINK THE COAST IS CLEAR!
THEY'RE SURE TO FIND IT IF I STICK IT IN THE DOOR!
NOW I JUST HOPE I C'N FIND WHAT I WANT AT CARSON'S OL' PLACE!
THE STUFF WAS THERE THE LAST TIME WE VISITED THE PLACE!
BUT IT SURE IS SPOOKY! I-I WISH THERE WAS SOMEBODY WITH ME!
I HATE TO GO INTO A DESERTED HOUSE ALL ALONE!
'SPECIALLY WHEN EVERYBODY SAYS IT'S HAUNTED!
I-I'LL JUST KEEP THINKING OF WHAT MOTHER TOLD ME— THAT THERE'S NO SUCH THING AS GHOSTS!
THERE'S...NO... SUCH...
THING...AS...
YOW
MROWR!

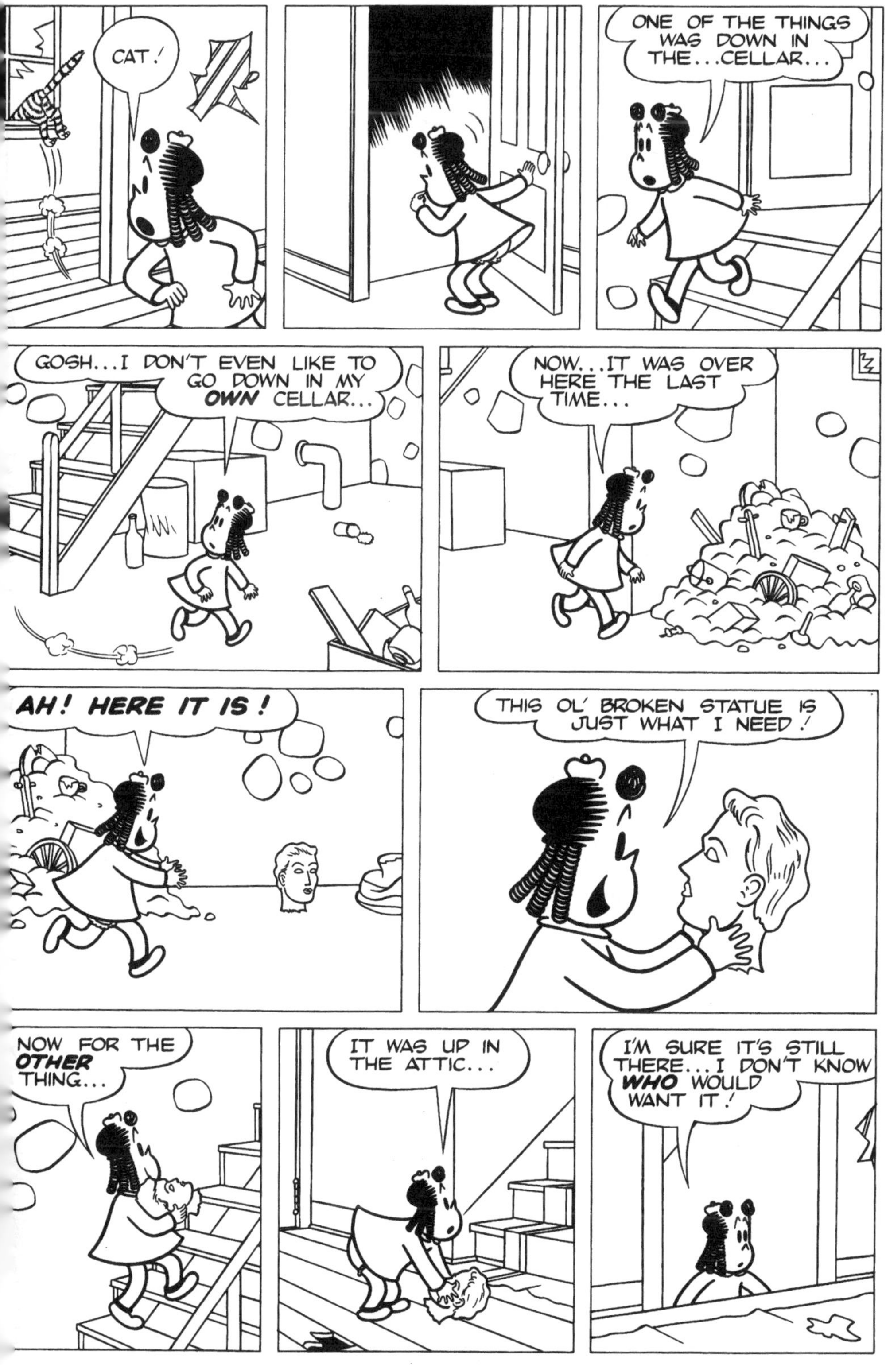

CAT!
ONE OF THE THINGS WAS DOWN IN THE...CELLAR...
GOSH...I DON'T EVEN LIKE TO GO DOWN IN MY **OWN** CELLAR...
NOW...IT WAS OVER HERE THE LAST TIME...
AH! HERE IT IS!
THIS OL' BROKEN STATUE IS JUST WHAT I NEED!
NOW FOR THE **OTHER** THING...
IT WAS UP IN THE ATTIC...
I'M SURE IT'S STILL THERE...I DON'T KNOW **WHO** WOULD WANT IT!

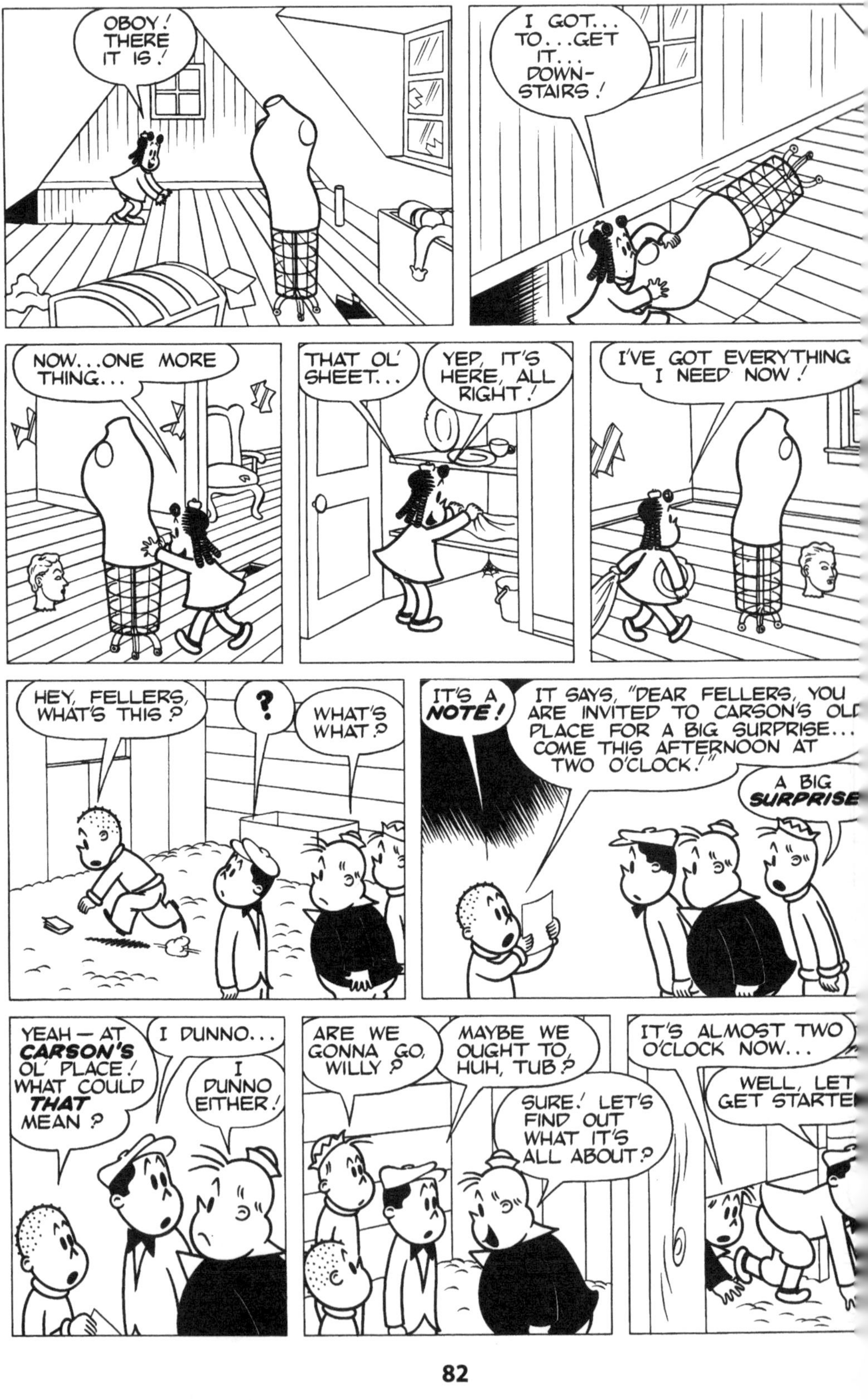
OBOY! THERE IT IS!
I GOT... TO...GET IT... DOWN-STAIRS!
NOW...ONE MORE THING...
THAT OL' SHEET...
YEP, IT'S HERE, ALL RIGHT!
I'VE GOT EVERYTHING I NEED NOW!
HEY, FELLERS, WHAT'S THIS?
?
WHAT'S WHAT?
IT'S A NOTE!
IT SAYS, "DEAR FELLERS, YOU ARE INVITED TO CARSON'S OL PLACE FOR A BIG SURPRISE... COME THIS AFTERNOON AT TWO O'CLOCK!"
A BIG SURPRISE
YEAH—AT CARSON'S OL' PLACE! WHAT COULD THAT MEAN?
I DUNNO...
I DUNNO EITHER!
ARE WE GONNA GO, WILLY?
MAYBE WE OUGHT TO, HUH, TUB?
SURE! LET'S FIND OUT WHAT IT'S ALL ABOUT!
IT'S ALMOST TWO O'CLOCK NOW...
WELL, LET GET STARTE

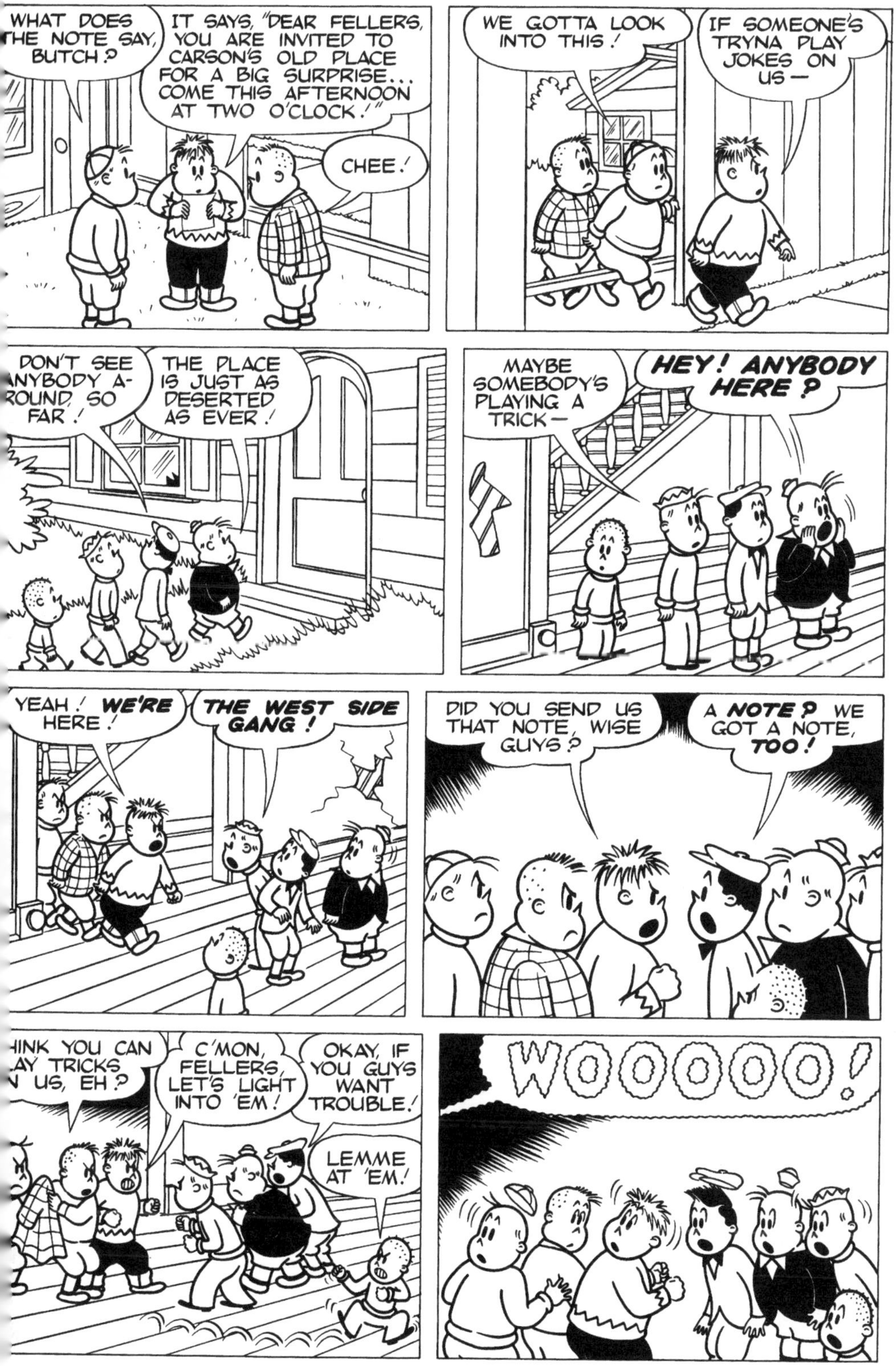
WHAT DOES THE NOTE SAY, BUTCH?
IT SAYS, "DEAR FELLERS, YOU ARE INVITED TO CARSON'S OLD PLACE FOR A BIG SURPRISE... COME THIS AFTERNOON AT TWO O'CLOCK!"
CHEE!
WE GOTTA LOOK INTO THIS!
IF SOMEONE'S TRYNA PLAY JOKES ON US—
DON'T SEE ANYBODY A-ROUND SO FAR!
THE PLACE IS JUST AS DESERTED AS EVER!
MAYBE SOMEBODY'S PLAYING A TRICK—
HEY! ANYBODY HERE?
YEAH! WE'RE HERE!
THE WEST SIDE GANG!
DID YOU SEND US THAT NOTE, WISE GUYS?
A NOTE? WE GOT A NOTE, TOO!
HINK YOU CAN LAY TRICKS N US, EH?
C'MON, FELLERS, LET'S LIGHT INTO 'EM!
OKAY, IF YOU GUYS WANT TROUBLE!
LEMME AT 'EM!
WOOOOOO!

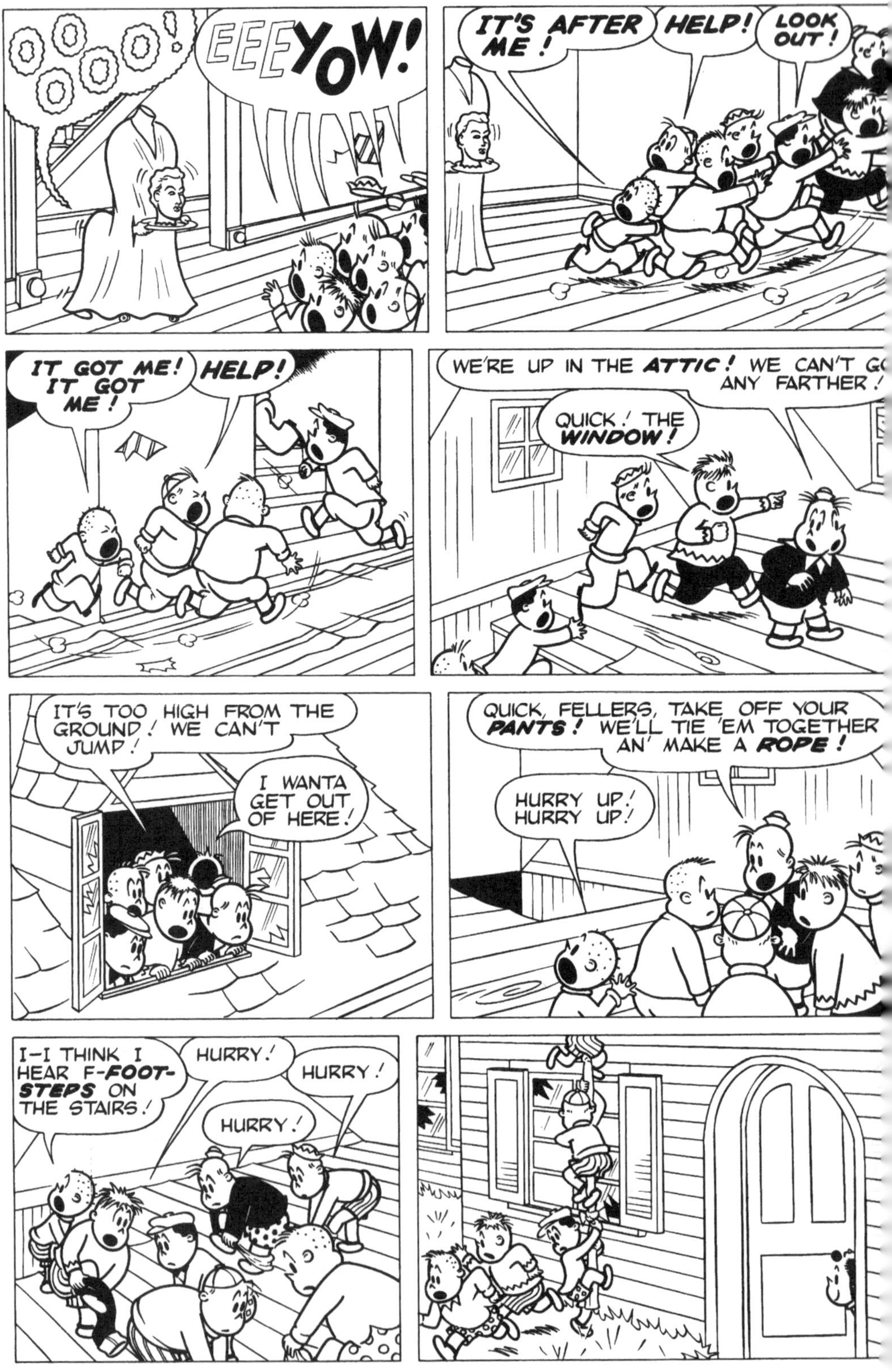
EEEYOW!
IT'S AFTER ME!
HELP!
LOOK OUT!
IT GOT ME! IT GOT ME!
HELP!
WE'RE UP IN THE ATTIC! WE CAN'T GO ANY FARTHER!
QUICK! THE WINDOW!
IT'S TOO HIGH FROM THE GROUND! WE CAN'T JUMP!
I WANTA GET OUT OF HERE!
QUICK, FELLERS, TAKE OFF YOUR PANTS! WE'LL TIE 'EM TOGETHER AN' MAKE A ROPE!
HURRY UP! HURRY UP!
I-I THINK I HEAR F-FOOTSTEPS ON THE STAIRS!
HURRY!
HURRY!
HURRY!

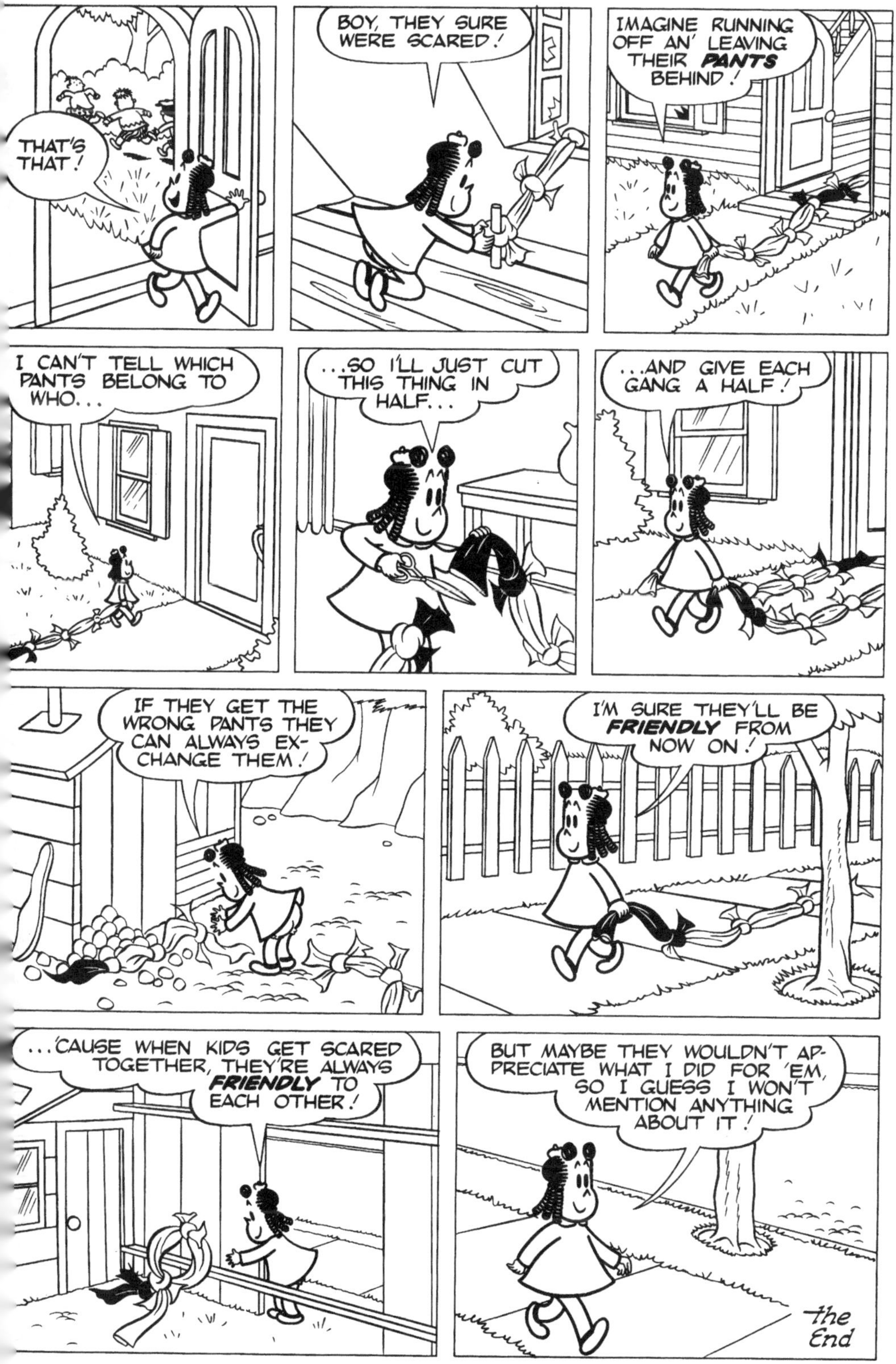
THAT'S THAT!
BOY, THEY SURE WERE SCARED!
IMAGINE RUNNING OFF AN' LEAVING THEIR **PANTS** BEHIND!
I CAN'T TELL WHICH PANTS BELONG TO WHO...
...SO I'LL JUST CUT THIS THING IN HALF...
...AND GIVE EACH GANG A HALF!
IF THEY GET THE WRONG PANTS THEY CAN ALWAYS EX-CHANGE THEM!
I'M SURE THEY'LL BE **FRIENDLY** FROM NOW ON!
...'CAUSE WHEN KIDS GET SCARED TOGETHER, THEY'RE ALWAYS **FRIENDLY** TO EACH OTHER!
BUT MAYBE THEY WOULDN'T AP-PRECIATE WHAT I DID FOR 'EM, SO I GUESS I WON'T MENTION ANYTHING ABOUT IT!
The End

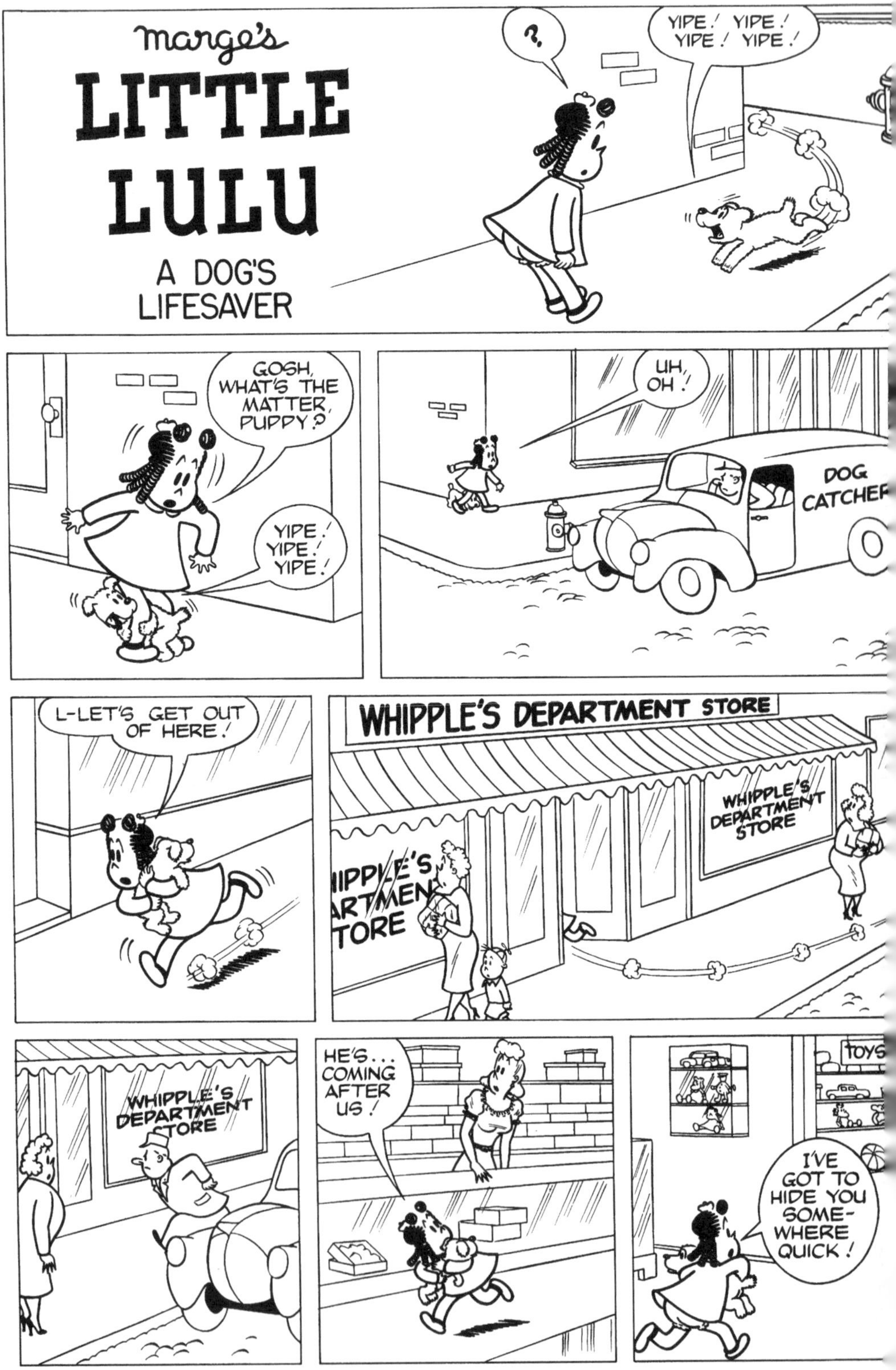
marge's
LITTLE LULU
A DOG'S LIFESAVER
?
YIPE! YIPE! YIPE! YIPE!
GOSH, WHAT'S THE MATTER, PUPPY?
YIPE! YIPE! YIPE!
UH, OH!
DOG CATCHER
L-LET'S GET OUT OF HERE!
WHIPPLE'S DEPARTMENT STORE
WHIPPLE'S DEPARTMENT STORE
WHIPPLE'S DEPARTMENT STORE
HE'S... COMING AFTER US!
TOYS
I'VE GOT TO HIDE YOU SOMEWHERE QUICK!

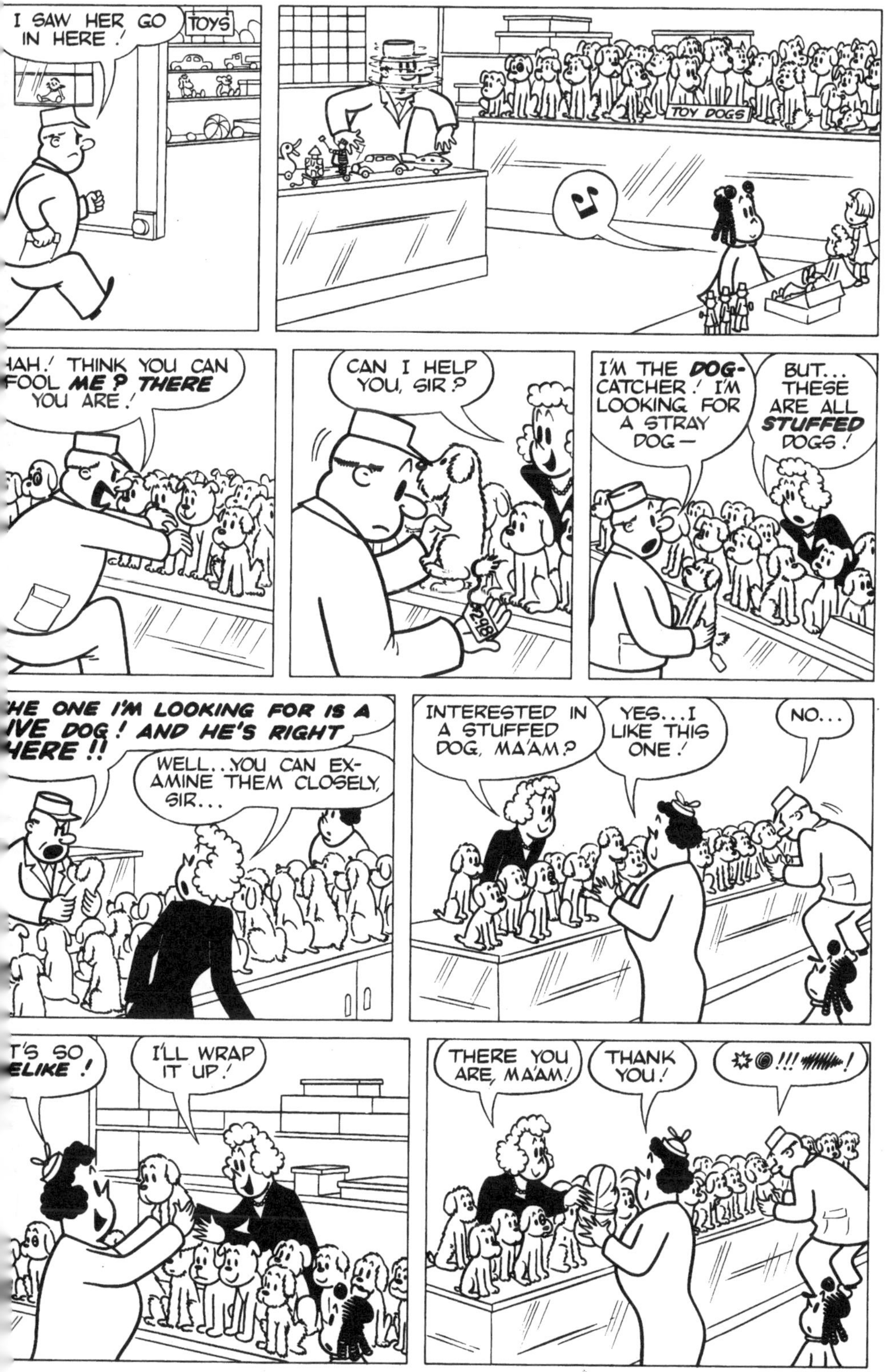
I SAW HER GO IN HERE!
TOYS
TOY DOGS
HAH! THINK YOU CAN FOOL ME? THERE YOU ARE!
CAN I HELP YOU, SIR?
I'M THE DOG-CATCHER! I'M LOOKING FOR A STRAY DOG—
BUT... THESE ARE ALL STUFFED DOGS!
HE ONE I'M LOOKING FOR IS A IVE DOG! AND HE'S RIGHT HERE!!
WELL...YOU CAN EX-AMINE THEM CLOSELY, SIR...
INTERESTED IN A STUFFED DOG, MA'AM?
YES...I LIKE THIS ONE!
NO...
T'S SO ELIKE!
I'LL WRAP IT UP!
THERE YOU ARE, MA'AM!
THANK YOU!

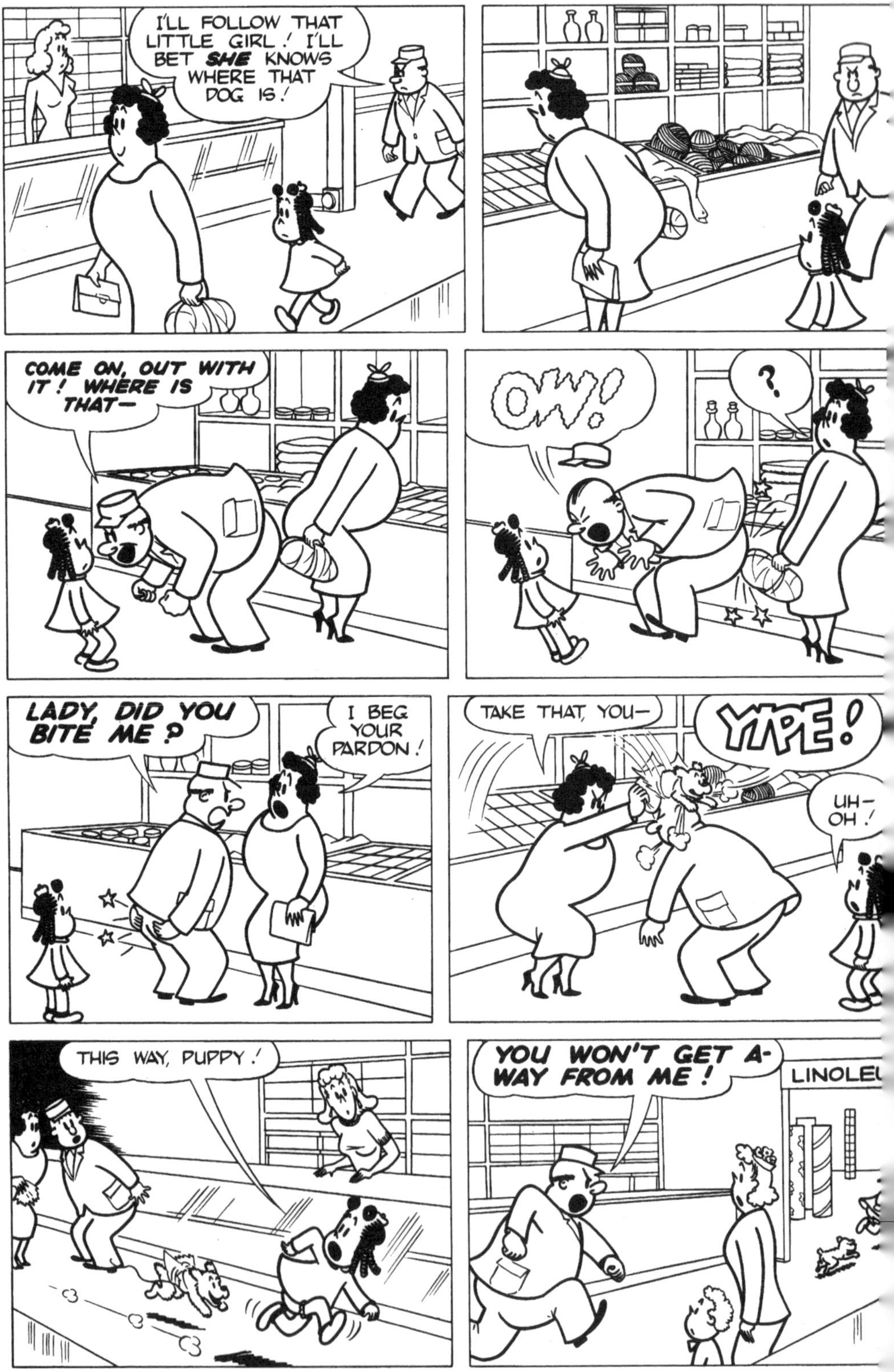
I'LL FOLLOW THAT LITTLE GIRL! I'LL BET SHE KNOWS WHERE THAT DOG IS!
COME ON, OUT WITH IT! WHERE IS THAT—
OW!
?
LADY, DID YOU BITE ME?
I BEG YOUR PARDON!
TAKE THAT, YOU—
YIPE!
UH-OH!
THIS WAY, PUPPY!
YOU WON'T GET A-WAY FROM ME!
LINOLEU

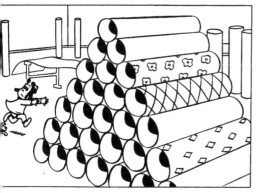

I'M THE DOG-CATCHER!

LOOK OUT!

NOW LOOK WHAT YOU'VE DONE!

THEY'RE HIDING IN ONE OF THESE ROLLS!

LL FIND 'EM N' SHAKE EM OUT!

HAH!

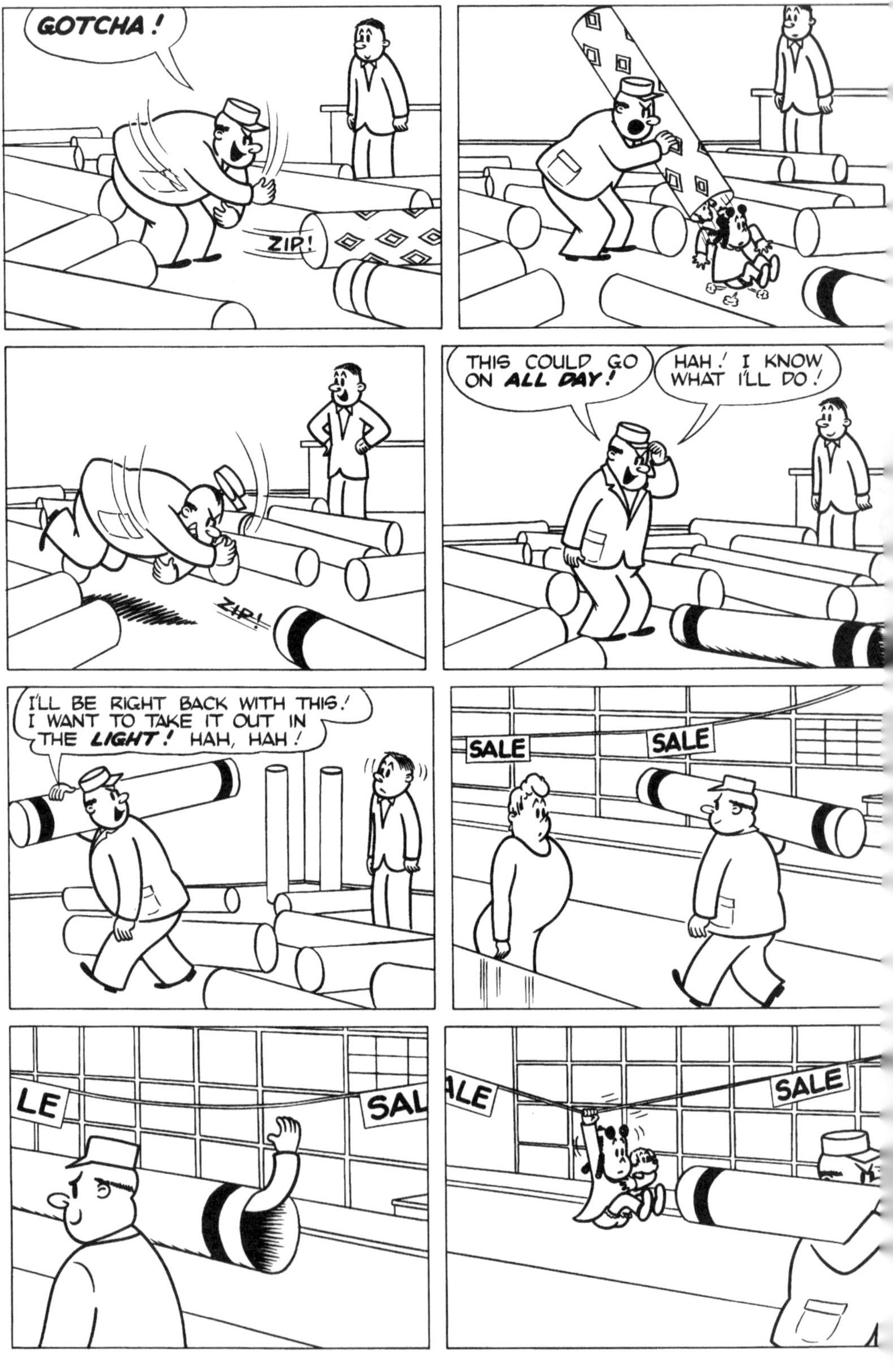
GOTCHA!
ZIP!
ZIP!
THIS COULD GO ON ALL DAY!
HAH! I KNOW WHAT I'LL DO!
I'LL BE RIGHT BACK WITH THIS! I WANT TO TAKE IT OUT IN THE LIGHT! HAH, HAH!
SALE
SALE
LE
SAL
ALE
SALE

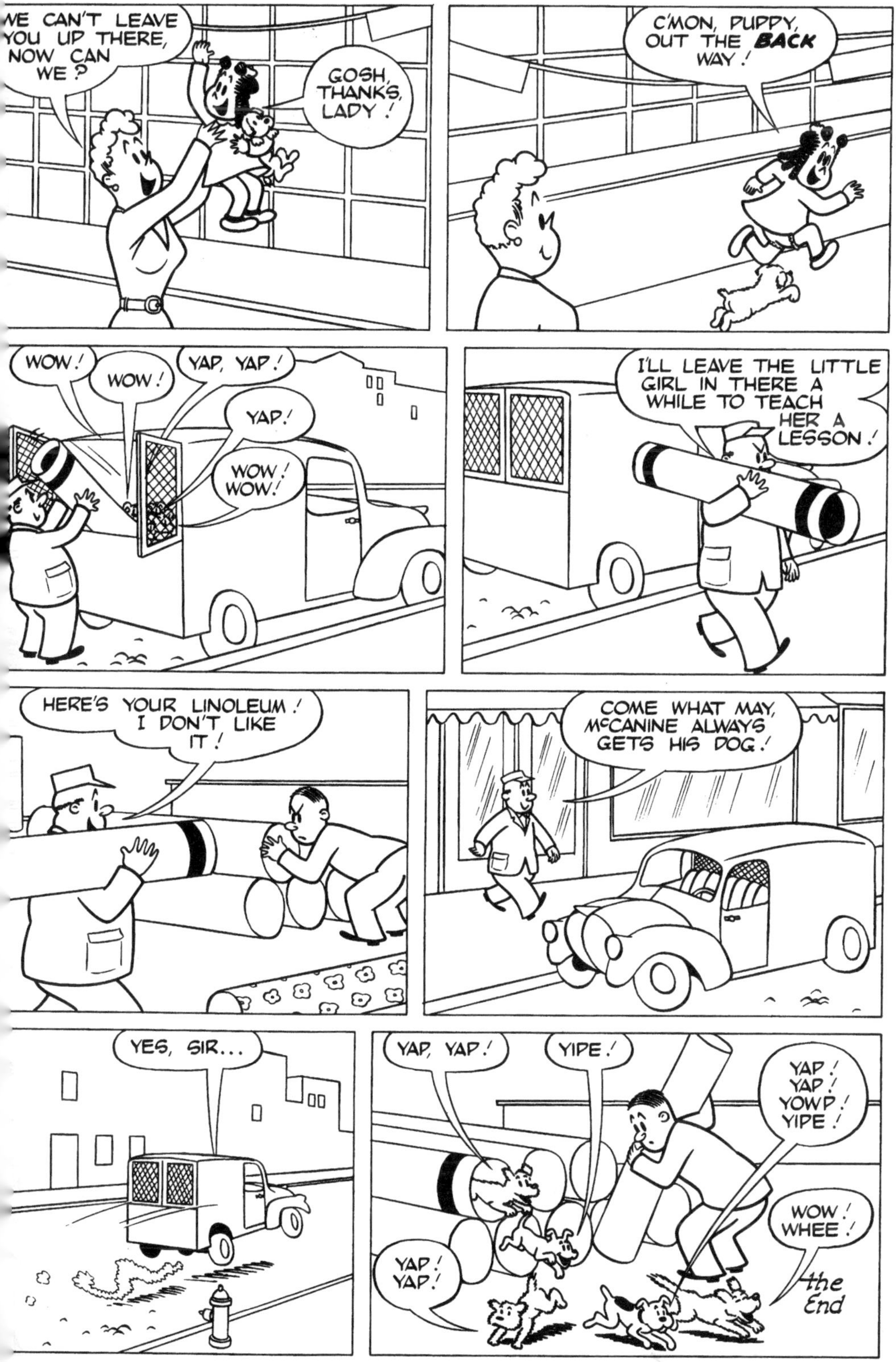
WE CAN'T LEAVE YOU UP THERE, NOW CAN WE?
GOSH, THANKS, LADY!
C'MON, PUPPY, OUT THE **BACK** WAY!
WOW!
WOW!
YAP, YAP!
YAP!
WOW! WOW!
I'LL LEAVE THE LITTLE GIRL IN THERE A WHILE TO TEACH HER A LESSON!
HERE'S YOUR LINOLEUM! I DON'T LIKE IT!
COME WHAT MAY, McCANINE ALWAYS GETS HIS DOG!
YES, SIR...
YAP, YAP!
YIPE!
YAP! YAP! YOWP! YIPE!
WOW! WHEE!
YAP! YAP!
the End

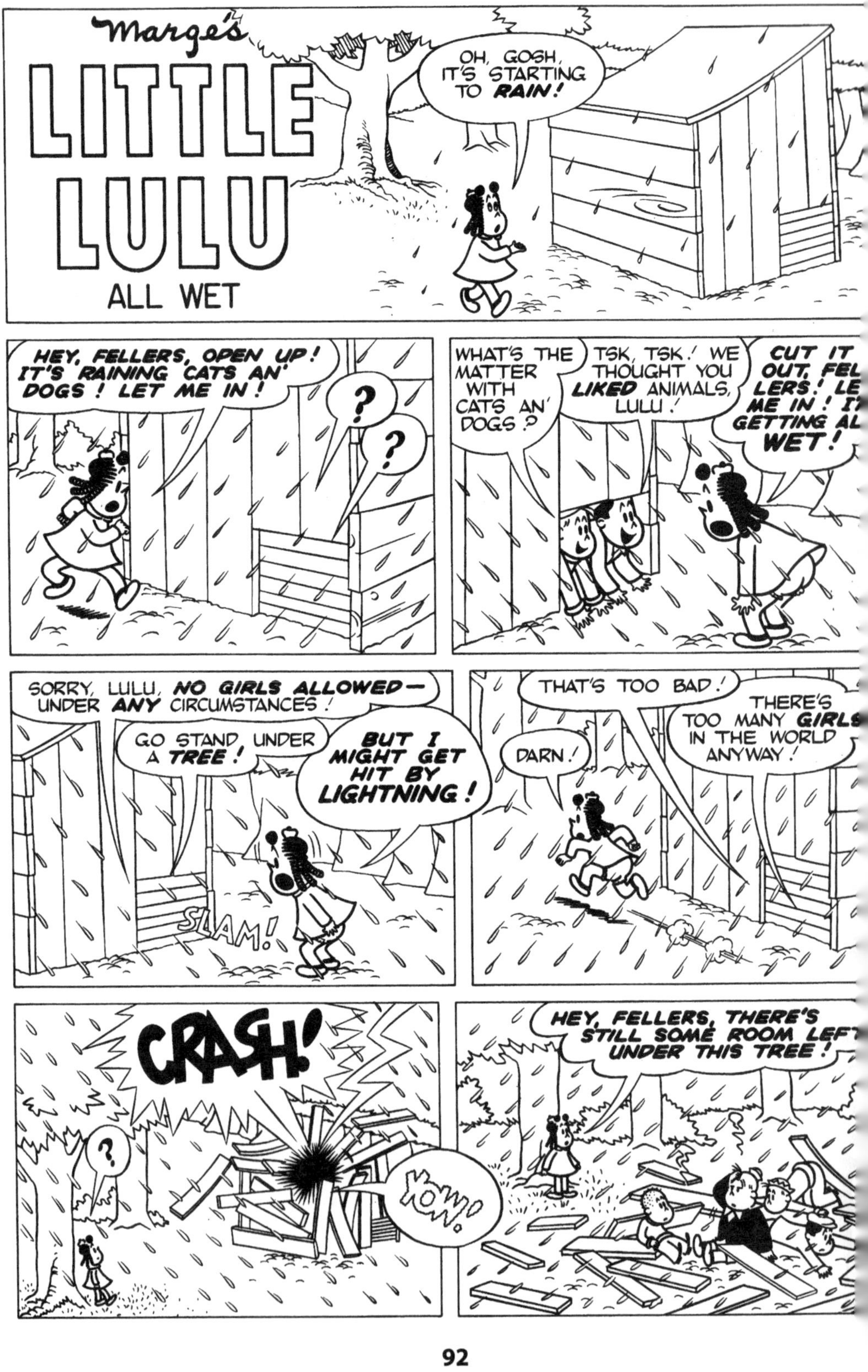
Marge's
LITTLE LULU
ALL WET
OH, GOSH, IT'S STARTING TO RAIN!
HEY, FELLERS, OPEN UP! IT'S RAINING CATS AN' DOGS! LET ME IN!
?
?
WHAT'S THE MATTER WITH CATS AN' DOGS?
TSK, TSK! WE THOUGHT YOU LIKED ANIMALS, LULU!
CUT IT OUT, FEL LERS! LE ME IN! I GETTING AL WET!
SORRY, LULU, NO GIRLS ALLOWED— UNDER ANY CIRCUMSTANCES!
GO STAND UNDER A TREE!
BUT I MIGHT GET HIT BY LIGHTNING!
SLAM!
THAT'S TOO BAD!
THERE'S TOO MANY GIRLS IN THE WORLD ANYWAY!
DARN!
CRASH!
?
YOW!
HEY, FELLERS, THERE'S STILL SOME ROOM LEF UNDER THIS TREE!

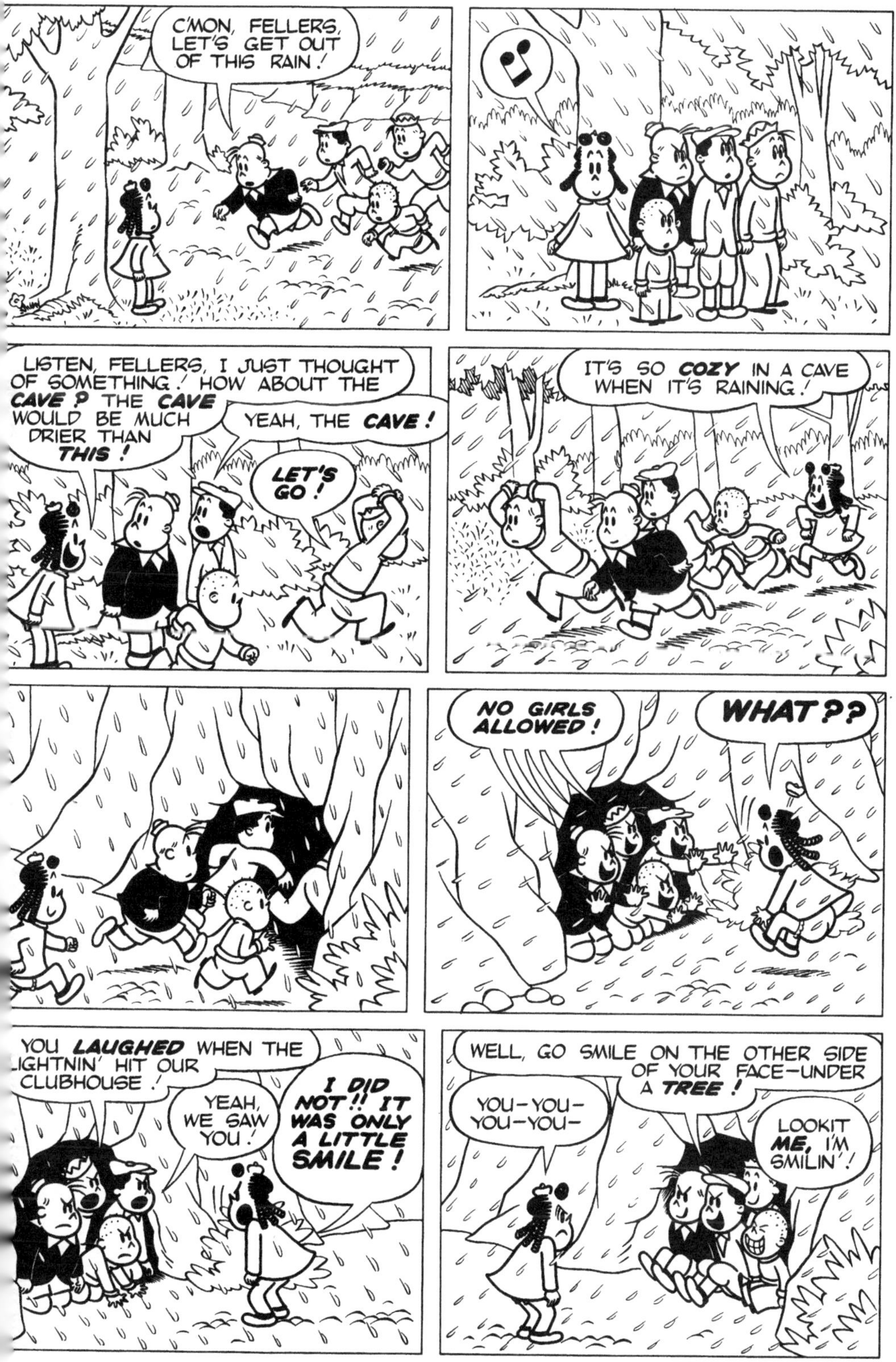
C'MON, FELLERS, LET'S GET OUT OF THIS RAIN!
LISTEN, FELLERS, I JUST THOUGHT OF SOMETHING! HOW ABOUT THE CAVE? THE CAVE WOULD BE MUCH DRIER THAN THIS!
YEAH, THE CAVE!
LET'S GO!
IT'S SO COZY IN A CAVE WHEN IT'S RAINING!
NO GIRLS ALLOWED!
WHAT??
YOU LAUGHED WHEN THE LIGHTNIN' HIT OUR CLUBHOUSE!
YEAH, WE SAW YOU!
I DID NOT!! IT WAS ONLY A LITTLE SMILE!
WELL, GO SMILE ON THE OTHER SIDE OF YOUR FACE—UNDER A TREE!
YOU-YOU-YOU-YOU-
LOOKIT ME, I'M SMILIN'!

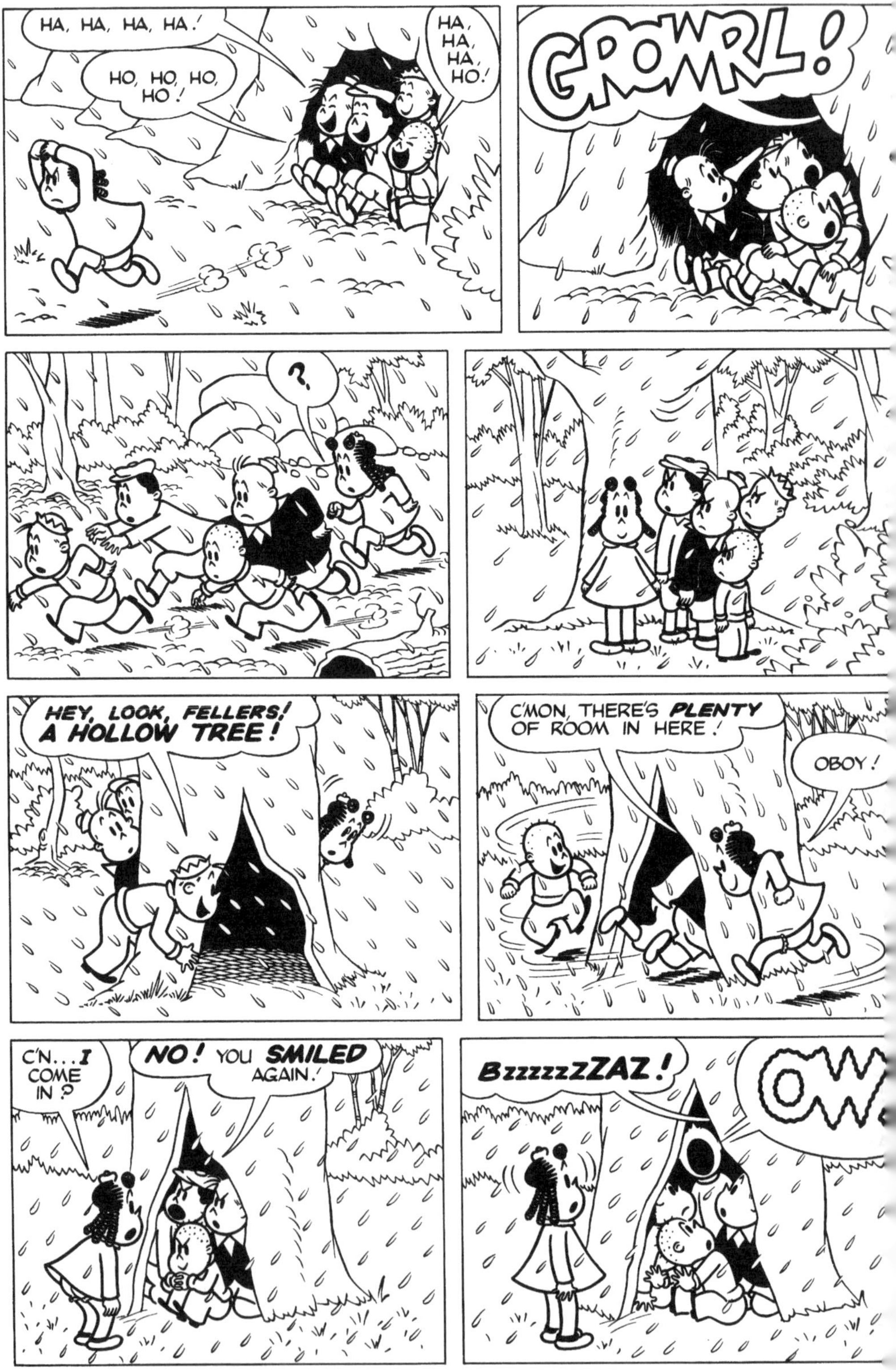
HA, HA, HA, HA!
HO, HO, HO, HO!
HA, HA, HA, HO!
GROWRL!
?
HEY, LOOK, FELLERS! A HOLLOW TREE!
C'MON, THERE'S PLENTY OF ROOM IN HERE!
OBOY!
C'N... I COME IN?
NO! YOU SMILED AGAIN!
BzzzzzZZAZ!
OW

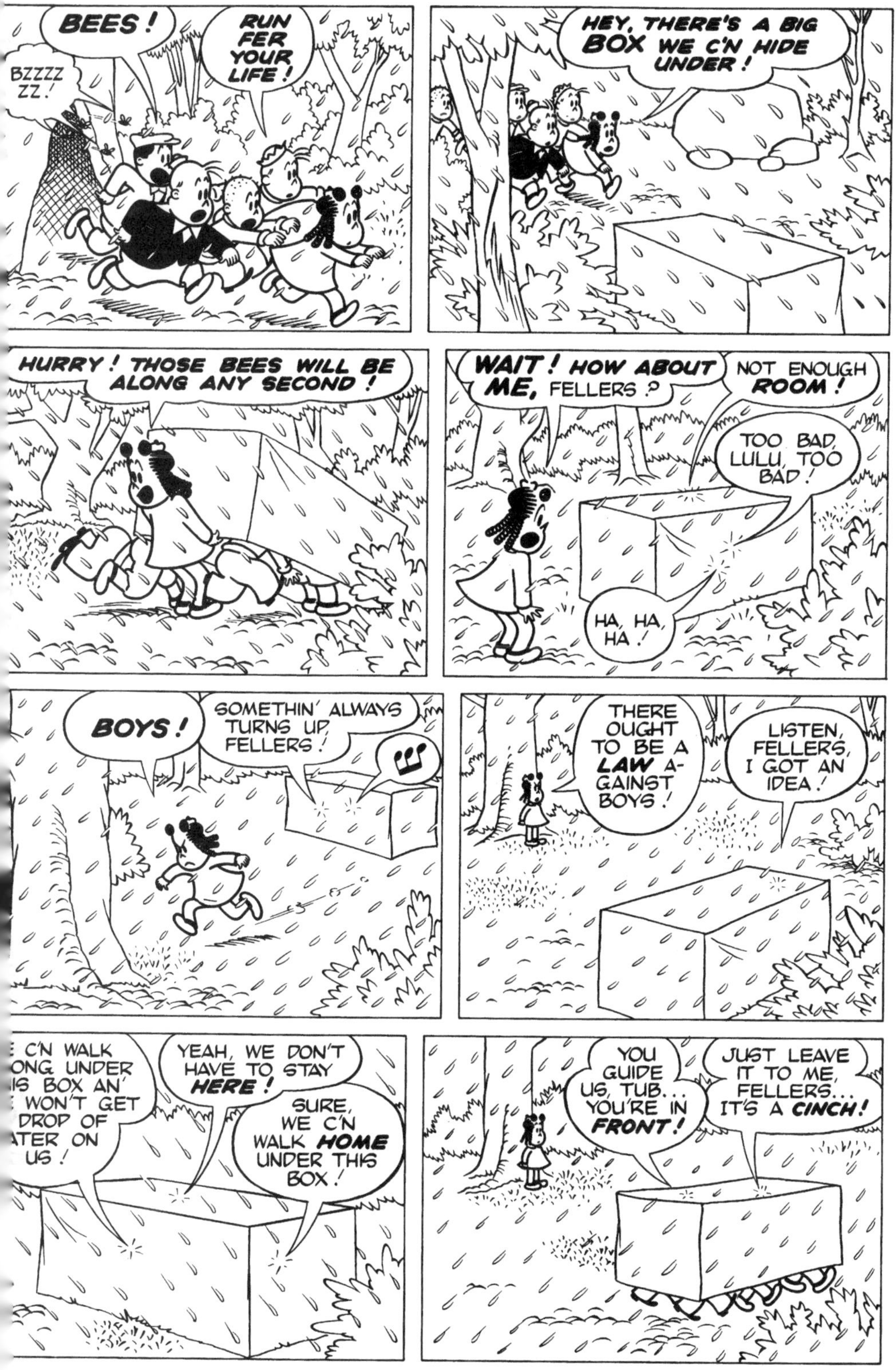

BZZZZ ZZ!
BEES!
RUN FER YOUR LIFE!
HEY, THERE'S A BIG BOX WE C'N HIDE UNDER!
HURRY! THOSE BEES WILL BE ALONG ANY SECOND!
WAIT! HOW ABOUT ME, FELLERS?
NOT ENOUGH ROOM!
TOO BAD, LULU, TOO BAD!
HA, HA, HA!
BOYS!
SOMETHIN' ALWAYS TURNS UP, FELLERS!
THERE OUGHT TO BE A LAW AGAINST BOYS!
LISTEN, FELLERS, I GOT AN IDEA!
C'N WALK ONG UNDER IS BOX AN' WON'T GET DROP OF ATER ON US!
YEAH, WE DON'T HAVE TO STAY HERE!
SURE, WE C'N WALK HOME UNDER THIS BOX!
YOU GUIDE US, TUB... YOU'RE IN FRONT!
JUST LEAVE IT TO ME, FELLERS... IT'S A CINCH!

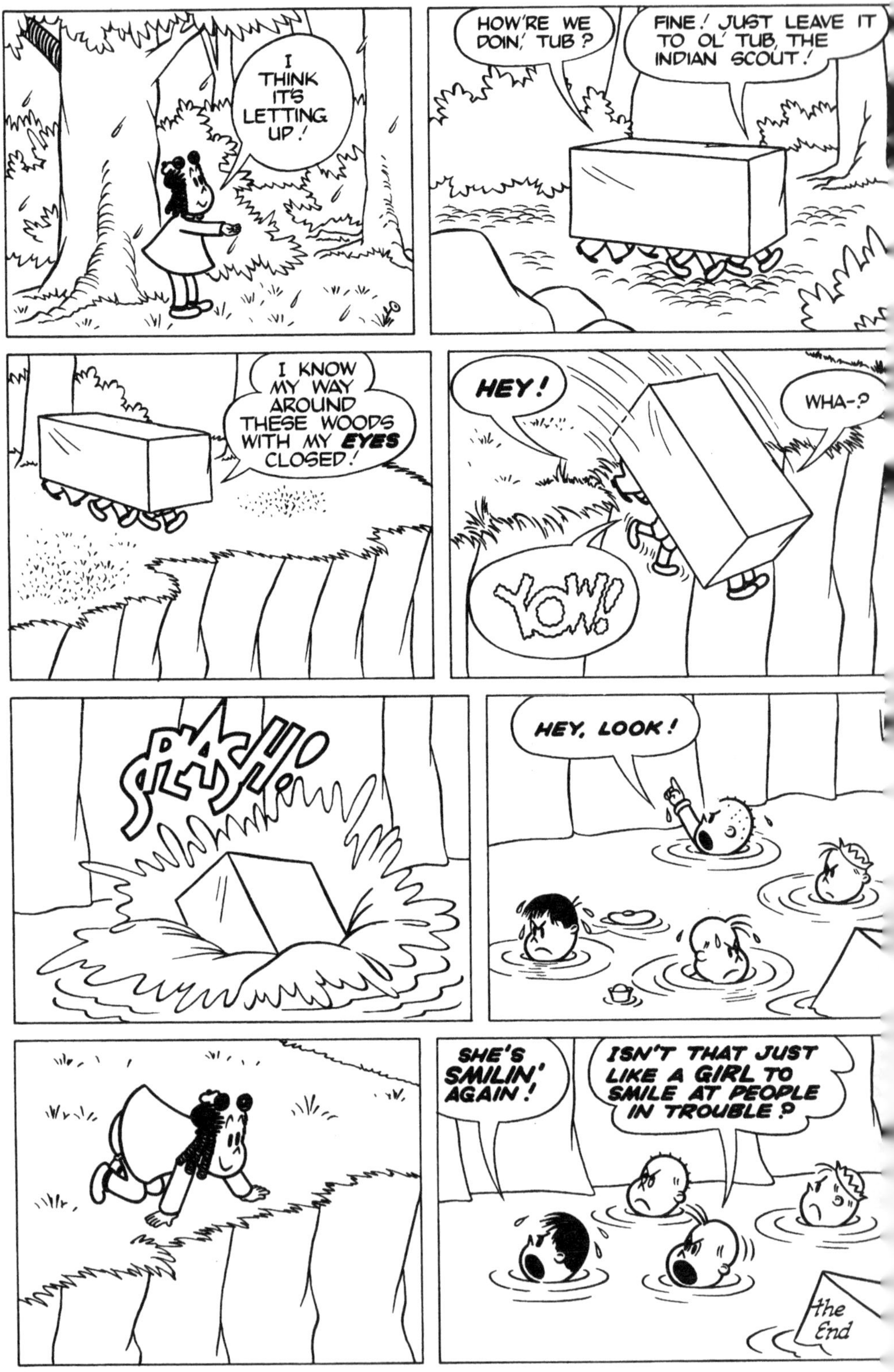
I THINK IT'S LETTING UP!
HOW'RE WE DOIN', TUB?
FINE! JUST LEAVE IT TO OL' TUB, THE INDIAN SCOUT!
I KNOW MY WAY AROUND THESE WOODS WITH MY **EYES** CLOSED!
HEY!
WHA-?
YOW!
SPLASH!
HEY, LOOK!
SHE'S SMILIN' AGAIN!
ISN'T THAT JUST LIKE A GIRL TO SMILE AT PEOPLE IN TROUBLE?
the End

marge's LITTLE LULU

GUESSING GAME

FELLERS! LOOK!!

HEY, KIDS! CAN YOU GUESS THE NUMBER OF MARBLES IN THIS BOWL?

A BIG PRIZE TO THE WINNER!

HERE'S A SLIP OF PAPER FOR EACH OF YOU...NOW ALL YOU HAVE TO DO IS WRITE YOUR NAME ON IT AND THE NUMBER OF MARBLES YOU THINK ARE IN THAT BOWL!

OBOY!

THE ONE WHO COMES **CLOSEST** TO THE RIGHT NUMBER WINS THE PRIZE — **FIVE** DOLLARS **WORTH OF MERCHANDISE!**

OBOY! WE C'N GET A COUPLA **BASEBALL MITTS!**

WAIT, FELLERS! DON'T WRITE ANYTHING DOWN YET!

OH, SURE, SURE!

ER...WE'D LIKE TO THINK IT OVER A LITTLE WHILE...

THE CONTEST ENDS AT TWELVE NOON TOMORROW! BE SURE TO HAVE YOUR SLIPS IN BEFORE THEN!

OKAY, FELLERS, LET'S GO!

BUT—

BUT—

LISTEN, FELLERS, WHAT'S THE USE OF TRYIN' TO GUESS HOW MANY MARBLES ARE IN THAT BOWL? LET'S BE SCIENTIFIC ABOUT IT!

SCIENTIFIC?

I AIN'T NO SCIENTIST!

ALL WE HAVE TO DO IS GET A **BOWL** EXACTLY THAT SIZE AN' FILL IT UP WITH **MARBLES!** THEN WE **COUNT** 'EM!

WOW! WE GOT A **FISH BOWL** AT HOME THAT'S JUST THAT **SIZE!**

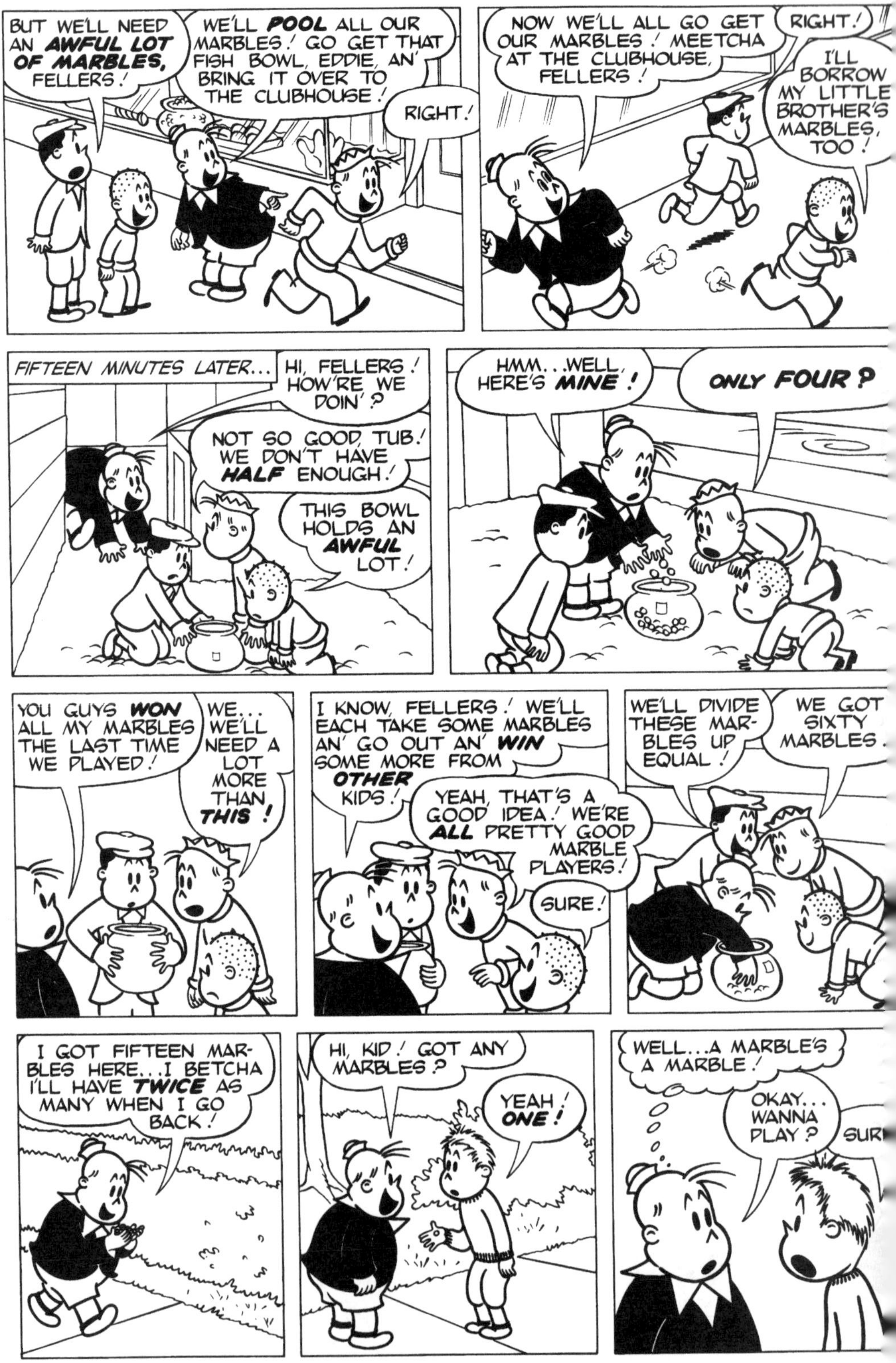

BUT WE'LL NEED AN AWFUL LOT OF MARBLES, FELLERS!
WE'LL POOL ALL OUR MARBLES! GO GET THAT FISH BOWL, EDDIE, AN' BRING IT OVER TO THE CLUBHOUSE!
RIGHT!
NOW WE'LL ALL GO GET OUR MARBLES! MEETCHA AT THE CLUBHOUSE, FELLERS!
RIGHT!
I'LL BORROW MY LITTLE BROTHER'S MARBLES, TOO!
FIFTEEN MINUTES LATER...
HI, FELLERS! HOW'RE WE DOIN'?
NOT SO GOOD, TUB! WE DON'T HAVE HALF ENOUGH!
THIS BOWL HOLDS AN AWFUL LOT!
HMM...WELL, HERE'S MINE!
ONLY FOUR?
YOU GUYS WON ALL MY MARBLES THE LAST TIME WE PLAYED!
WE... WE'LL NEED A LOT MORE THAN THIS!
I KNOW, FELLERS! WE'LL EACH TAKE SOME MARBLES AN' GO OUT AN' WIN SOME MORE FROM OTHER KIDS!
YEAH, THAT'S A GOOD IDEA! WE'RE ALL PRETTY GOOD MARBLE PLAYERS!
SURE!
WE'LL DIVIDE THESE MARBLES UP EQUAL!
WE GOT SIXTY MARBLES.
I GOT FIFTEEN MARBLES HERE...I BETCHA I'LL HAVE TWICE AS MANY WHEN I GO BACK!
HI, KID! GOT ANY MARBLES?
YEAH! ONE!
WELL...A MARBLE'S A MARBLE!
OKAY... WANNA PLAY?

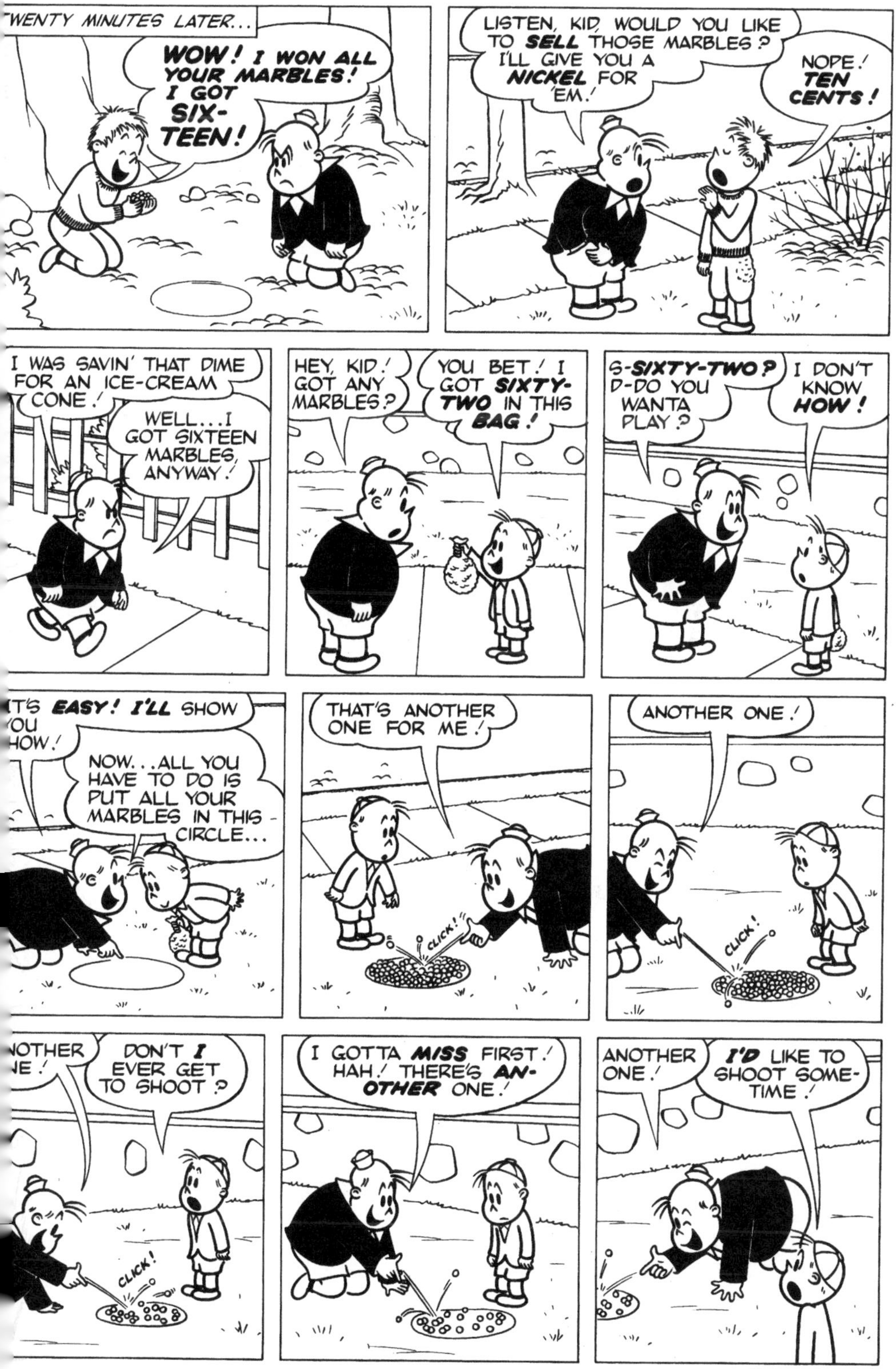
WENTY MINUTES LATER...
WOW! I WON ALL YOUR MARBLES! I GOT SIX-TEEN!
LISTEN, KID, WOULD YOU LIKE TO SELL THOSE MARBLES? I'LL GIVE YOU A NICKEL FOR 'EM!
NOPE! TEN CENTS!
I WAS SAVIN' THAT DIME FOR AN ICE-CREAM CONE!
WELL...I GOT SIXTEEN MARBLES ANYWAY!
HEY, KID! GOT ANY MARBLES?
YOU BET! I GOT SIXTY-TWO IN THIS BAG!
S-SIXTY-TWO? D-DO YOU WANTA PLAY?
I DON'T KNOW HOW!
T'S EASY! I'LL SHOW OU HOW!
NOW...ALL YOU HAVE TO DO IS PUT ALL YOUR MARBLES IN THIS CIRCLE...
THAT'S ANOTHER ONE FOR ME!
CLICK!
ANOTHER ONE!
CLICK!
NOTHER NE!
DON'T I EVER GET TO SHOOT?
CLICK!
I GOTTA MISS FIRST! HAH! THERE'S AN-OTHER ONE!
ANOTHER ONE!
I'D LIKE TO SHOOT SOME-TIME!

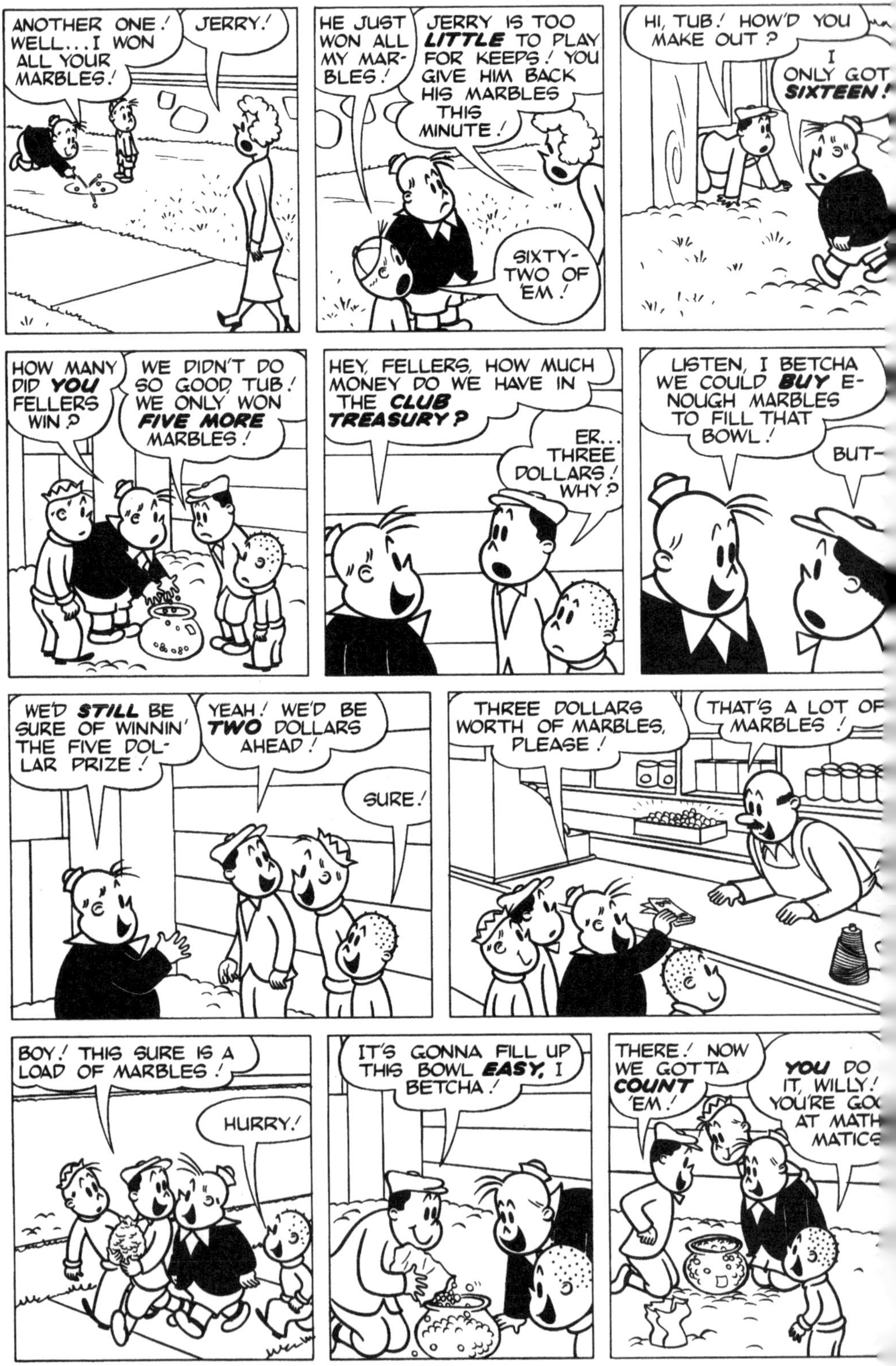
ANOTHER ONE! WELL... I WON ALL YOUR MARBLES!
JERRY!
HE JUST WON ALL MY MARBLES!
JERRY IS TOO LITTLE TO PLAY FOR KEEPS! YOU GIVE HIM BACK HIS MARBLES THIS MINUTE!
SIXTY-TWO OF 'EM!
HI, TUB! HOW'D YOU MAKE OUT?
I ONLY GOT SIXTEEN!
HOW MANY DID YOU FELLERS WIN?
WE DIDN'T DO SO GOOD TUB! WE ONLY WON FIVE MORE MARBLES!
HEY, FELLERS, HOW MUCH MONEY DO WE HAVE IN THE CLUB TREASURY?
ER... THREE DOLLARS! WHY?
LISTEN, I BETCHA WE COULD BUY ENOUGH MARBLES TO FILL THAT BOWL!
BUT—
WE'D STILL BE SURE OF WINNIN' THE FIVE DOLLAR PRIZE!
YEAH! WE'D BE TWO DOLLARS AHEAD!
SURE!
THREE DOLLARS WORTH OF MARBLES, PLEASE!
THAT'S A LOT OF MARBLES!
BOY! THIS SURE IS A LOAD OF MARBLES!
HURRY!
IT'S GONNA FILL UP THIS BOWL EASY, I BETCHA!
THERE! NOW WE GOTTA COUNT 'EM!
YOU DO IT, WILLY! YOU'RE GOO AT MATH MATICS

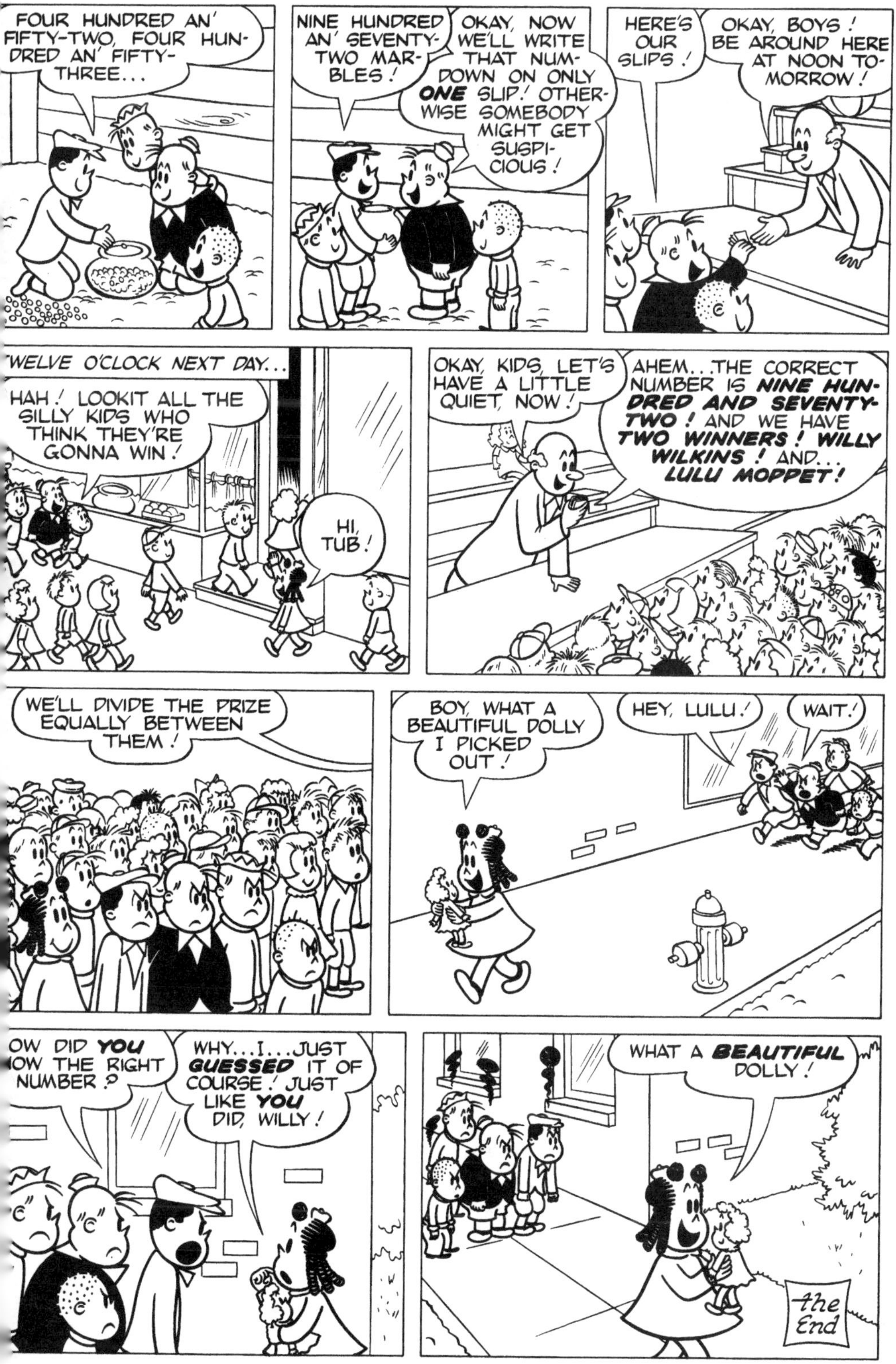
FOUR HUNDRED AN' FIFTY-TWO, FOUR HUNDRED AN' FIFTY-THREE...
NINE HUNDRED AN' SEVENTY-TWO MARBLES!
OKAY, NOW WE'LL WRITE THAT NUMBER DOWN ON ONLY **ONE** SLIP! OTHERWISE SOMEBODY MIGHT GET SUSPICIOUS!
HERE'S OUR SLIPS!
OKAY, BOYS! BE AROUND HERE AT NOON TOMORROW!
TWELVE O'CLOCK NEXT DAY...
HAH! LOOKIT ALL THE SILLY KIDS WHO THINK THEY'RE GONNA WIN!
HI, TUB!
OKAY, KIDS, LET'S HAVE A LITTLE QUIET, NOW!
AHEM...THE CORRECT NUMBER IS **NINE HUNDRED AND SEVENTY-TWO!** AND WE HAVE **TWO WINNERS! WILLY WILKINS!** AND... **LULU MOPPET!**
WE'LL DIVIDE THE PRIZE EQUALLY BETWEEN THEM!
BOY, WHAT A BEAUTIFUL DOLLY I PICKED OUT!
HEY, LULU!
WAIT!
OW DID **YOU** NOW THE RIGHT NUMBER?
WHY...I...JUST **GUESSED** IT OF COURSE! JUST LIKE **YOU** DID, WILLY!
WHAT A **BEAUTIFUL** DOLLY!
The End

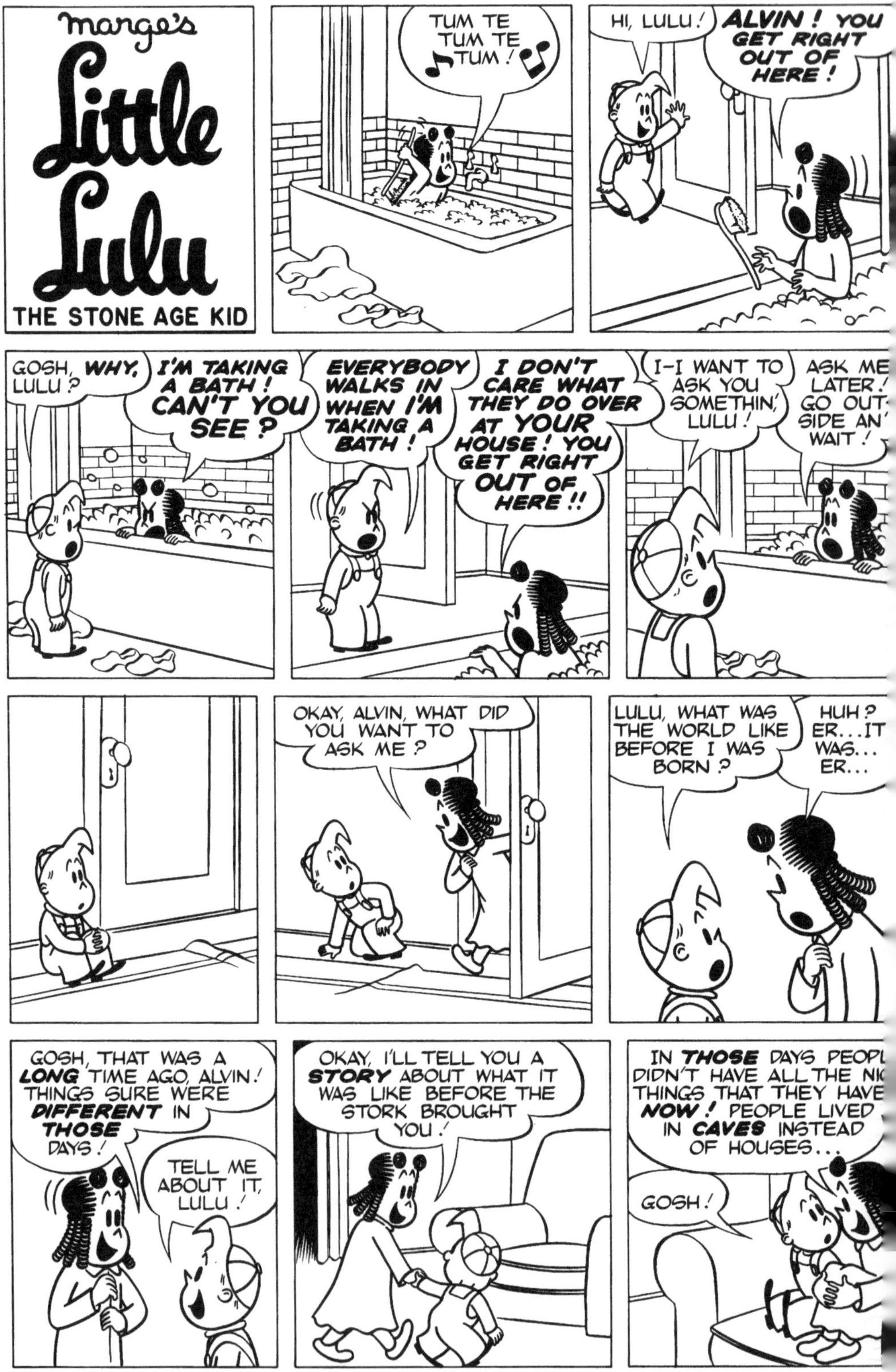
marge's
Little Lulu
THE STONE AGE KID
TUM TE TUM TE TUM!
HI, LULU!
ALVIN! YOU GET RIGHT OUT OF HERE!
GOSH, WHY, LULU?
I'M TAKING A BATH! CAN'T YOU SEE?
EVERYBODY WALKS IN WHEN I'M TAKING A BATH!
I DON'T CARE WHAT THEY DO OVER AT YOUR HOUSE! YOU GET RIGHT OUT OF HERE!!
I-I WANT TO ASK YOU SOMETHIN', LULU!
ASK ME LATER! GO OUT-SIDE AN' WAIT!
OKAY, ALVIN, WHAT DID YOU WANT TO ASK ME?
LULU, WHAT WAS THE WORLD LIKE BEFORE I WAS BORN?
HUH? ER...IT WAS... ER...
GOSH, THAT WAS A LONG TIME AGO, ALVIN! THINGS SURE WERE DIFFERENT IN THOSE DAYS!
TELL ME ABOUT IT, LULU!
OKAY, I'LL TELL YOU A STORY ABOUT WHAT IT WAS LIKE BEFORE THE STORK BROUGHT YOU!
IN THOSE DAYS PEOPL DIDN'T HAVE ALL THE NI THINGS THAT THEY HAVE NOW! PEOPLE LIVED IN CAVES INSTEAD OF HOUSES...
GOSH!

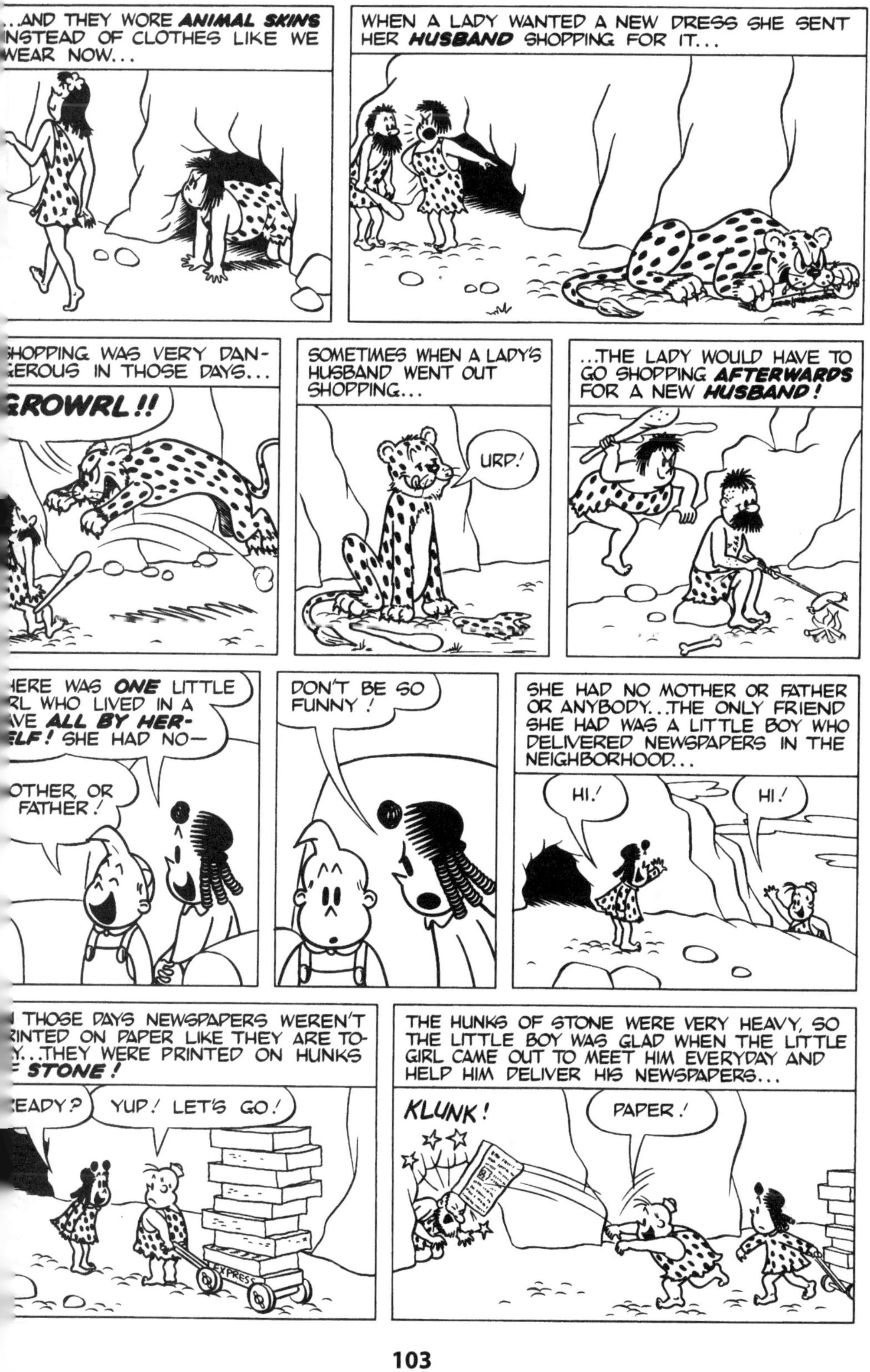
...AND THEY WORE ANIMAL SKINS NSTEAD OF CLOTHES LIKE WE WEAR NOW...
WHEN A LADY WANTED A NEW DRESS SHE SENT HER HUSBAND SHOPPING FOR IT...
HOPPING WAS VERY DANGEROUS IN THOSE DAYS...
GROWRL!!
SOMETIMES WHEN A LADY'S HUSBAND WENT OUT SHOPPING...
URP!
...THE LADY WOULD HAVE TO GO SHOPPING AFTERWARDS FOR A NEW HUSBAND!
HERE WAS ONE LITTLE RL WHO LIVED IN A VE ALL BY HERELF! SHE HAD NO—
OTHER OR FATHER!
DON'T BE SO FUNNY!
SHE HAD NO MOTHER OR FATHER OR ANYBODY...THE ONLY FRIEND SHE HAD WAS A LITTLE BOY WHO DELIVERED NEWSPAPERS IN THE NEIGHBORHOOD...
HI!
HI!
THOSE DAYS NEWSPAPERS WEREN'T RINTED ON PAPER LIKE THEY ARE TOY...THEY WERE PRINTED ON HUNKS STONE!
EADY?
YUP! LET'S GO!
EXPRESS
THE HUNKS OF STONE WERE VERY HEAVY, SO THE LITTLE BOY WAS GLAD WHEN THE LITTLE GIRL CAME OUT TO MEET HIM EVERYDAY AND HELP HIM DELIVER HIS NEWSPAPERS...
KLUNK!
PAPER!

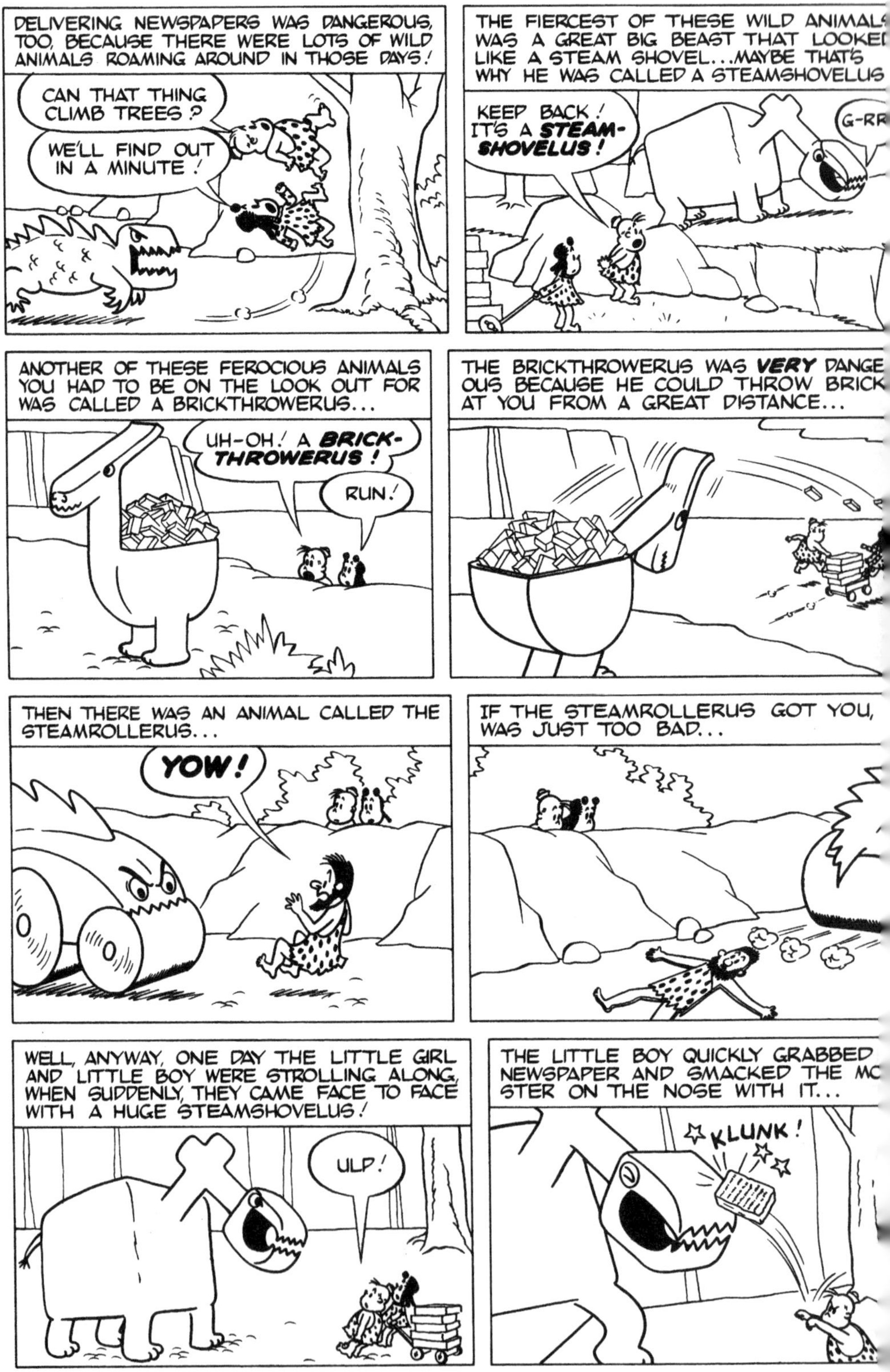
DELIVERING NEWSPAPERS WAS DANGEROUS, TOO, BECAUSE THERE WERE LOTS OF WILD ANIMALS ROAMING AROUND IN THOSE DAYS!
CAN THAT THING CLIMB TREES?
WE'LL FIND OUT IN A MINUTE!
THE FIERCEST OF THESE WILD ANIMALS WAS A GREAT BIG BEAST THAT LOOKE LIKE A STEAM SHOVEL...MAYBE THAT'S WHY HE WAS CALLED A STEAMSHOVELUS
KEEP BACK! IT'S A **STEAM-SHOVELUS!**
G-RR
ANOTHER OF THESE FEROCIOUS ANIMALS YOU HAD TO BE ON THE LOOK OUT FOR WAS CALLED A BRICKTHROWERUS...
UH-OH! A **BRICK-THROWERUS!**
RUN!
THE BRICKTHROWERUS WAS **VERY** DANGE OUS BECAUSE HE COULD THROW BRICK AT YOU FROM A GREAT DISTANCE...
THEN THERE WAS AN ANIMAL CALLED THE STEAMROLLERUS...
YOW!
IF THE STEAMROLLERUS GOT YOU, WAS JUST TOO BAD...
WELL, ANYWAY, ONE DAY THE LITTLE GIRL AND LITTLE BOY WERE STROLLING ALONG, WHEN SUDDENLY, THEY CAME FACE TO FACE WITH A HUGE STEAMSHOVELUS!
ULP!
THE LITTLE BOY QUICKLY GRABBED NEWSPAPER AND SMACKED THE MO STER ON THE NOSE WITH IT...
KLUNK!

GOSH, THE STEAMSHOVELUS WAS MAD! HE LET OUT A TERRIBLE ROAR AND CHARGED DOWN ON THE LITTLE KIDS...

ROAR!

RUN FER YOUR LIFE!

THEY TURNED AND RAN AS FAST AS THEY COULD TO THE NEAREST CAVE...

THE STEAMSHOVELUS WAS ONLY A FEW FEET BEHIND THEM WHEN THEY GOT SAFELY THROUGH THE DOOR...

BOY! THAT WAS *CLOSE*!

FOR A MOMENT THEY THOUGHT THEY WERE SAFE, BUT THEN THE STEAMSHOVELUS BEGAN TO TEAR AWAY AT THE FRONT OF THE CAVE...

HE'S COMIN' AFTER US! RUN!!

THE KIDS RAN FARTHER BACK INTO THE CAVE, AND THE STEAMSHOVELUS CHEWED HIS WAY AFTER THEM...

MEANWHILE, OTHER STEAMSHOVELUSES AND BRICKTHROWERUSES AND STEAMROLLERUSES HEARD ALL THE COMMOTION AND CAME RUNNING...

THE ANGRY STEAMSHOVELUSES IMMEDIATELY BEGAN CHEWING INTO ALL THE *OTHER* CAVES IN THE VILLAGE...

AND RIGHT BEHIND THEM THE EXCITED STEAMROLLERUSES ROLLED BACK AND FORTH IMPATIENTLY...

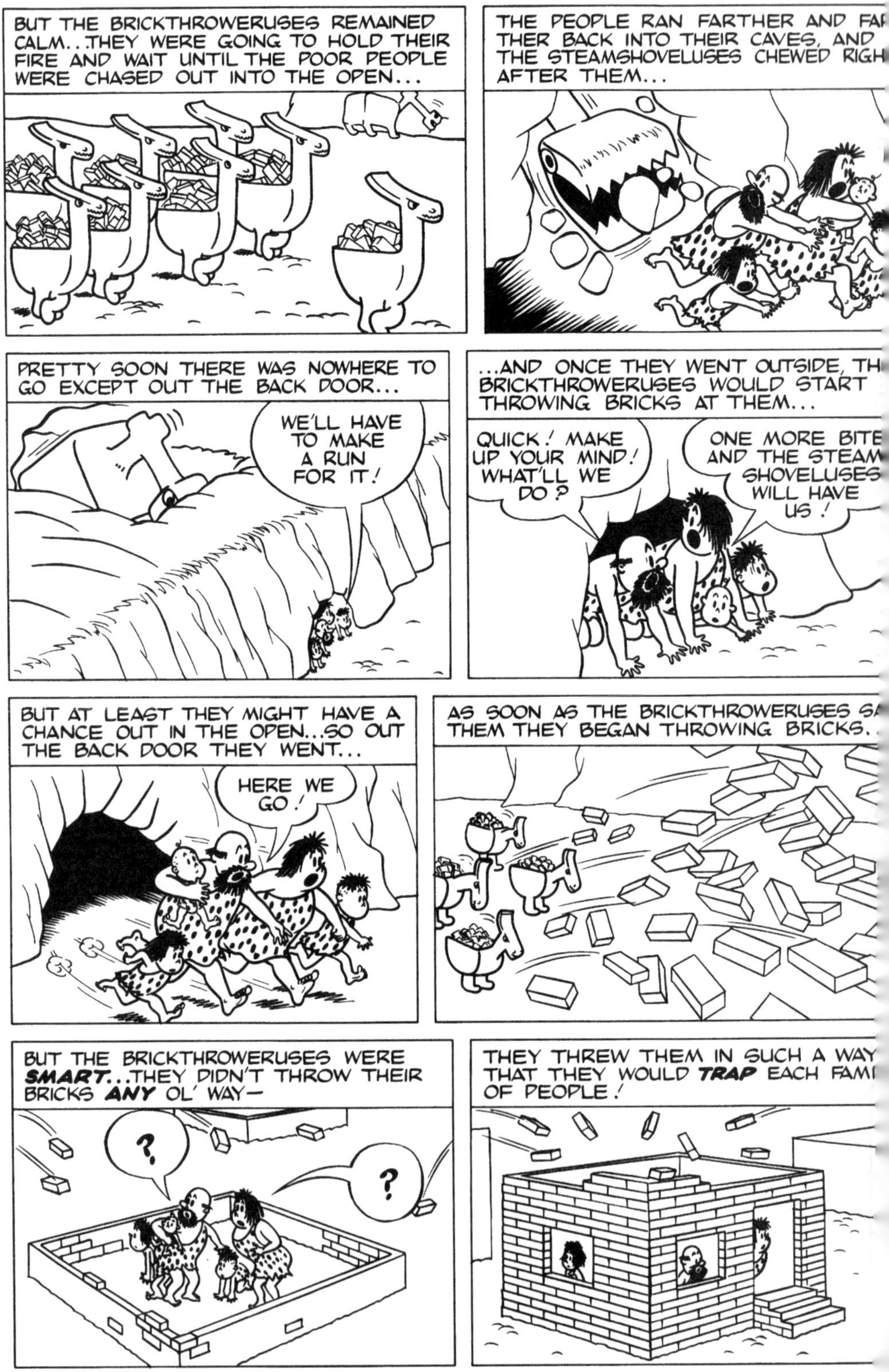
BUT THE BRICKTHROWERUSES REMAINED CALM...THEY WERE GOING TO HOLD THEIR FIRE AND WAIT UNTIL THE POOR PEOPLE WERE CHASED OUT INTO THE OPEN...
THE PEOPLE RAN FARTHER AND FAR THER BACK INTO THEIR CAVES, AND THE STEAMSHOVELUSES CHEWED RIGH AFTER THEM...
PRETTY SOON THERE WAS NOWHERE TO GO EXCEPT OUT THE BACK DOOR...
WE'LL HAVE TO MAKE A RUN FOR IT!
...AND ONCE THEY WENT OUTSIDE, TH BRICKTHROWERUSES WOULD START THROWING BRICKS AT THEM...
QUICK! MAKE UP YOUR MIND! WHAT'LL WE DO?
ONE MORE BITE AND THE STEAM SHOVELUSES WILL HAVE US!
BUT AT LEAST THEY MIGHT HAVE A CHANCE OUT IN THE OPEN...SO OUT THE BACK DOOR THEY WENT...
HERE WE GO!
AS SOON AS THE BRICKTHROWERUSES SA THEM THEY BEGAN THROWING BRICKS..
BUT THE BRICKTHROWERUSES WERE SMART...THEY DIDN'T THROW THEIR BRICKS ANY OL' WAY—
?
?
THEY THREW THEM IN SUCH A WAY THAT THEY WOULD TRAP EACH FAMI OF PEOPLE!

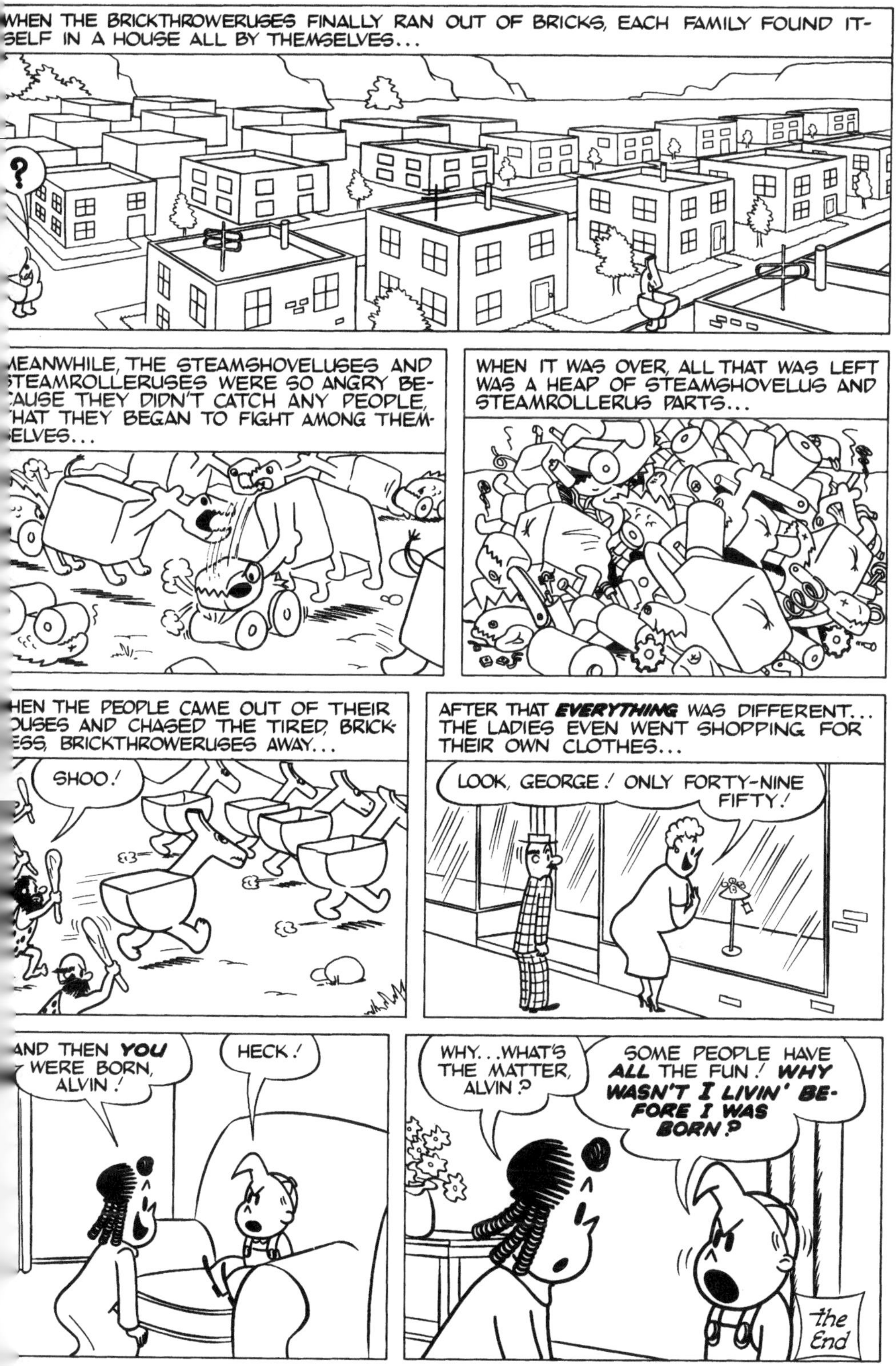
WHEN THE BRICKTHROWERUSES FINALLY RAN OUT OF BRICKS, EACH FAMILY FOUND IT-SELF IN A HOUSE ALL BY THEMSELVES...
?
MEANWHILE, THE STEAMSHOVELUSES AND STEAMROLLERUSES WERE SO ANGRY BE-CAUSE THEY DIDN'T CATCH ANY PEOPLE, THAT THEY BEGAN TO FIGHT AMONG THEM-SELVES...
WHEN IT WAS OVER, ALL THAT WAS LEFT WAS A HEAP OF STEAMSHOVELUS AND STEAMROLLERUS PARTS...
WHEN THE PEOPLE CAME OUT OF THEIR HOUSES AND CHASED THE TIRED, BRICK-LESS, BRICKTHROWERUSES AWAY...
SHOO!
AFTER THAT **EVERYTHING** WAS DIFFERENT... THE LADIES EVEN WENT SHOPPING FOR THEIR OWN CLOTHES...
LOOK, GEORGE! ONLY FORTY-NINE FIFTY!
AND THEN **YOU** WERE BORN, ALVIN!
HECK!
WHY...WHAT'S THE MATTER, ALVIN?
SOME PEOPLE HAVE **ALL** THE FUN! **WHY WASN'T I LIVIN' BE-FORE I WAS BORN?**
The End

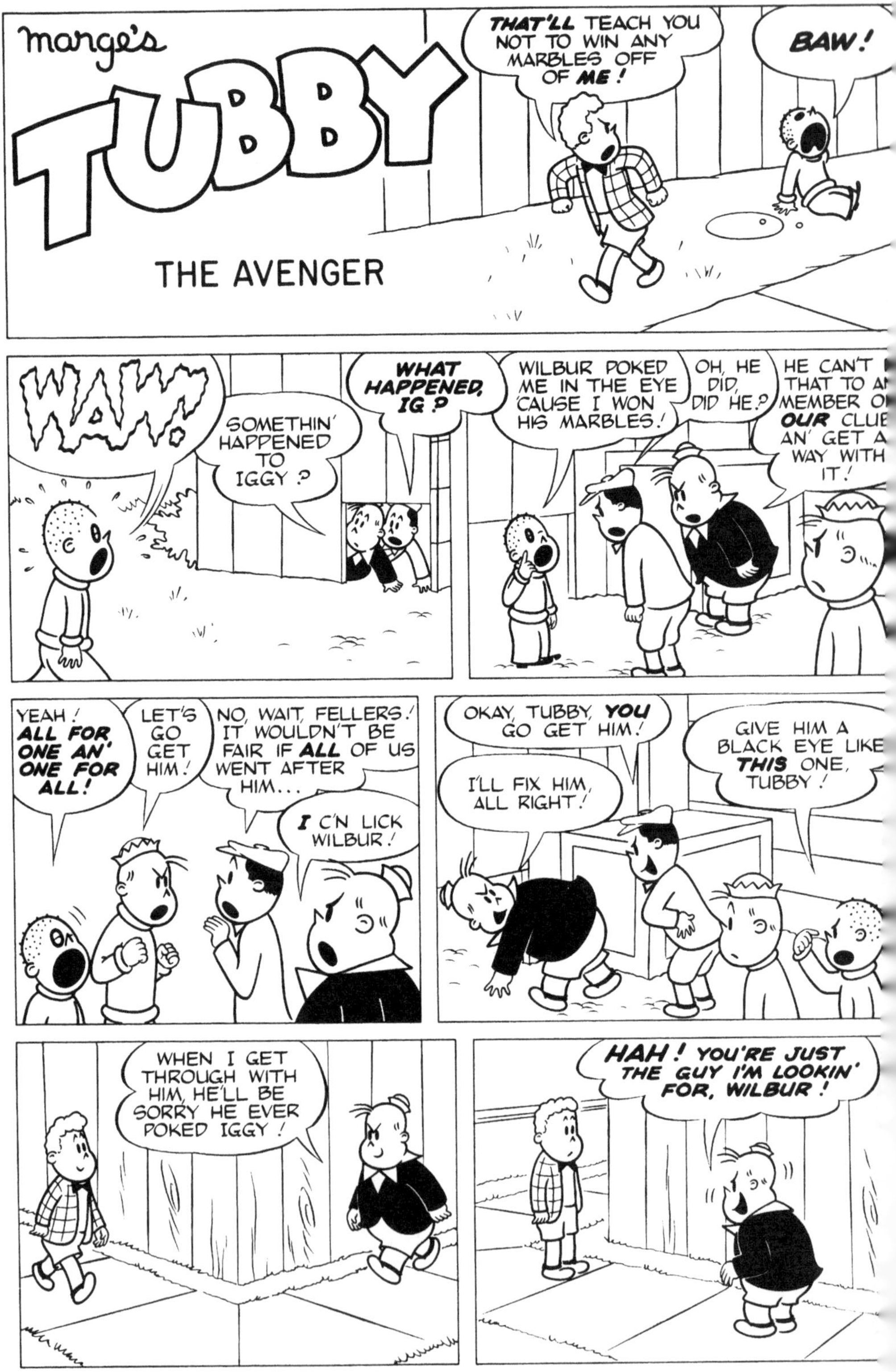
marge's
TUBBY
THE AVENGER
THAT'LL TEACH YOU NOT TO WIN ANY MARBLES OFF OF ME!
BAW!
WAW!
SOMETHIN' HAPPENED TO IGGY?
WHAT HAPPENED, IG?
WILBUR POKED ME IN THE EYE 'CAUSE I WON HIS MARBLES!
OH, HE DID, DID HE?
HE CAN'T THAT TO A MEMBER O OUR CLU AN' GET A WAY WITH IT!
YEAH! ALL FOR ONE AN' ONE FOR ALL!
LET'S GO GET HIM!
NO, WAIT, FELLERS! IT WOULDN'T BE FAIR IF ALL OF US WENT AFTER HIM...
I C'N LICK WILBUR!
OKAY, TUBBY, YOU GO GET HIM!
I'LL FIX HIM, ALL RIGHT!
GIVE HIM A BLACK EYE LIKE THIS ONE, TUBBY!
WHEN I GET THROUGH WITH HIM, HE'LL BE SORRY HE EVER POKED IGGY!
HAH! YOU'RE JUST THE GUY I'M LOOKIN' FOR, WILBUR!

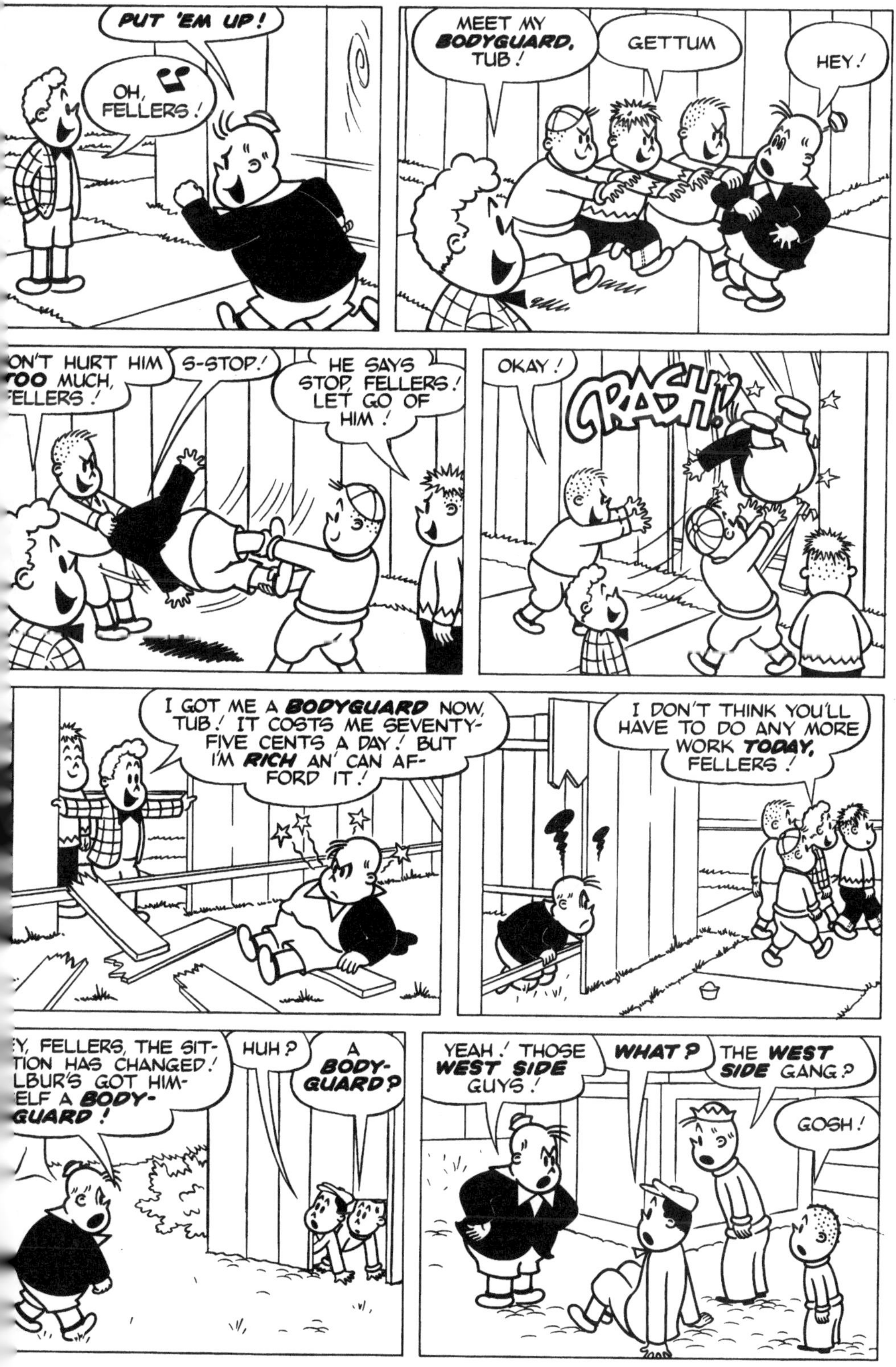
PUT 'EM UP!
OH, FELLERS!
MEET MY BODYGUARD, TUB!
GETTUM
HEY!
ON'T HURT HIM TOO MUCH, ELLERS!
S-STOP!
HE SAYS STOP, FELLERS! LET GO OF HIM!
OKAY!
CRASH!
I GOT ME A BODYGUARD NOW, TUB! IT COSTS ME SEVENTY-FIVE CENTS A DAY! BUT I'M RICH AN' CAN AF-FORD IT!
I DON'T THINK YOU'LL HAVE TO DO ANY MORE WORK TODAY, FELLERS!
Y, FELLERS, THE SIT-TION HAS CHANGED! LBUR'S GOT HIM-ELF A BODY-GUARD!
HUH?
A BODY-GUARD?
YEAH! THOSE WEST SIDE GUYS!
WHAT?
THE WEST SIDE GANG?
GOSH!

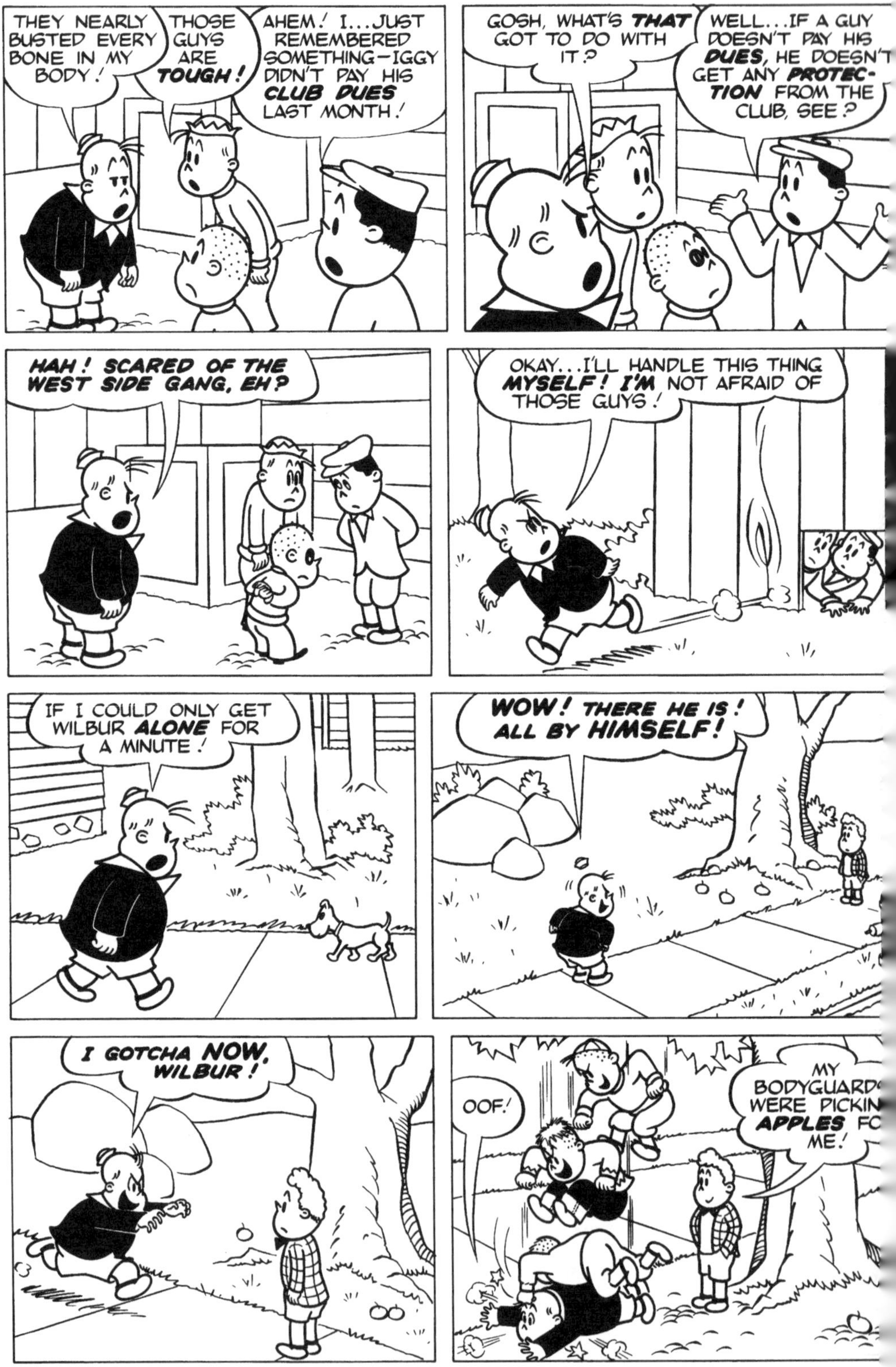
THEY NEARLY BUSTED EVERY BONE IN MY BODY!
THOSE GUYS ARE TOUGH!
AHEM! I...JUST REMEMBERED SOMETHING—IGGY DIDN'T PAY HIS CLUB DUES LAST MONTH!
GOSH, WHAT'S THAT GOT TO DO WITH IT?
WELL...IF A GUY DOESN'T PAY HIS DUES, HE DOESN'T GET ANY PROTECTION FROM THE CLUB, SEE?
HAH! SCARED OF THE WEST SIDE GANG, EH?
OKAY...I'LL HANDLE THIS THING MYSELF! I'M NOT AFRAID OF THOSE GUYS!
IF I COULD ONLY GET WILBUR ALONE FOR A MINUTE!
WOW! THERE HE IS! ALL BY HIMSELF!
I GOTCHA NOW, WILBUR!
OOF!
MY BODYGUARDS WERE PICKIN APPLES FO ME!

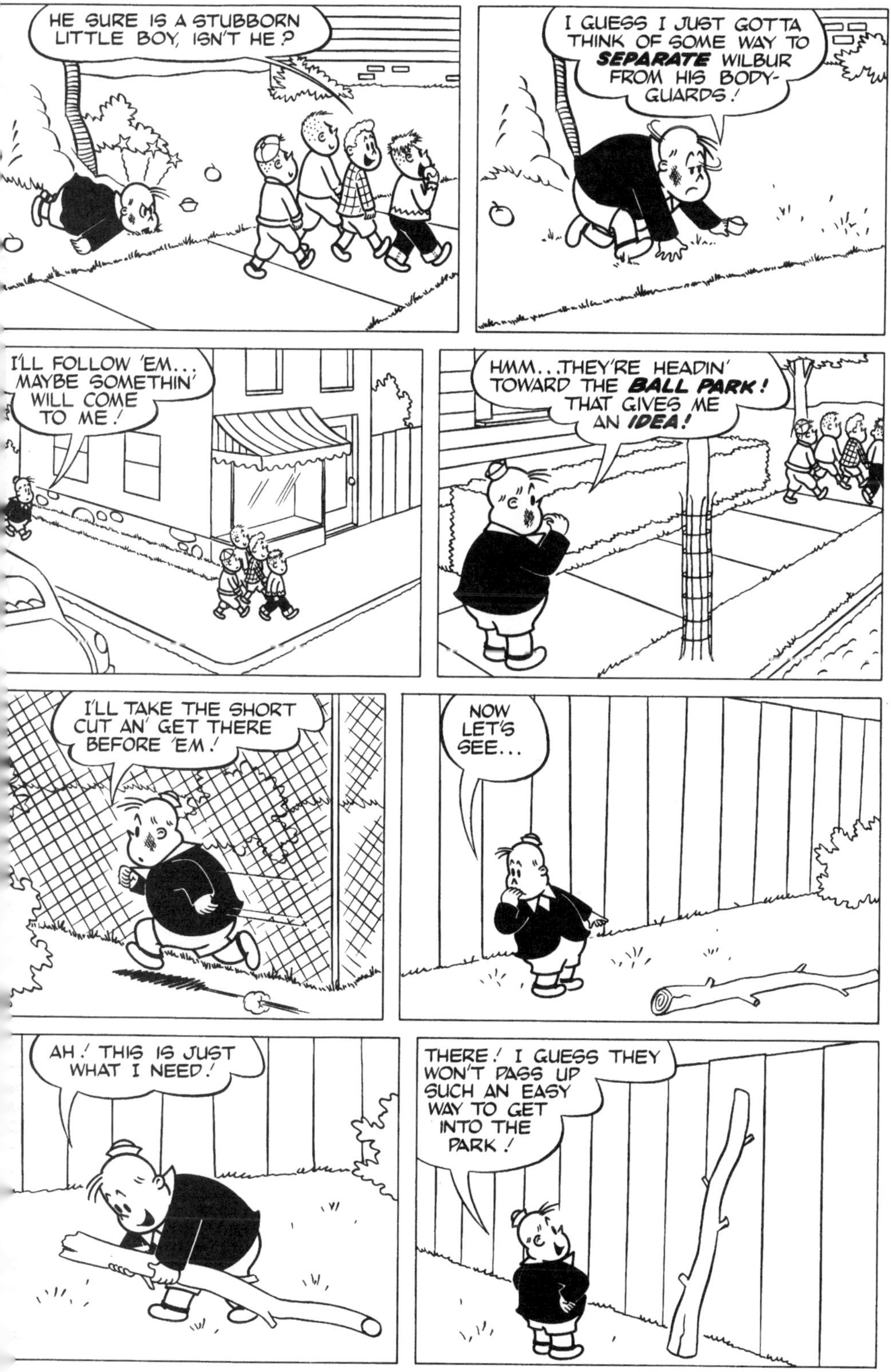
HE SURE IS A STUBBORN LITTLE BOY, ISN'T HE?
I GUESS I JUST GOTTA THINK OF SOME WAY TO **SEPARATE** WILBUR FROM HIS BODY-GUARDS!
I'LL FOLLOW 'EM... MAYBE SOMETHIN' WILL COME TO ME!
HMM...THEY'RE HEADIN' TOWARD THE **BALL PARK!** THAT GIVES ME AN **IDEA!**
I'LL TAKE THE SHORT CUT AN' GET THERE BEFORE 'EM!
NOW LET'S SEE...
AH! THIS IS JUST WHAT I NEED!
THERE! I GUESS THEY WON'T PASS UP SUCH AN EASY WAY TO GET INTO THE PARK!

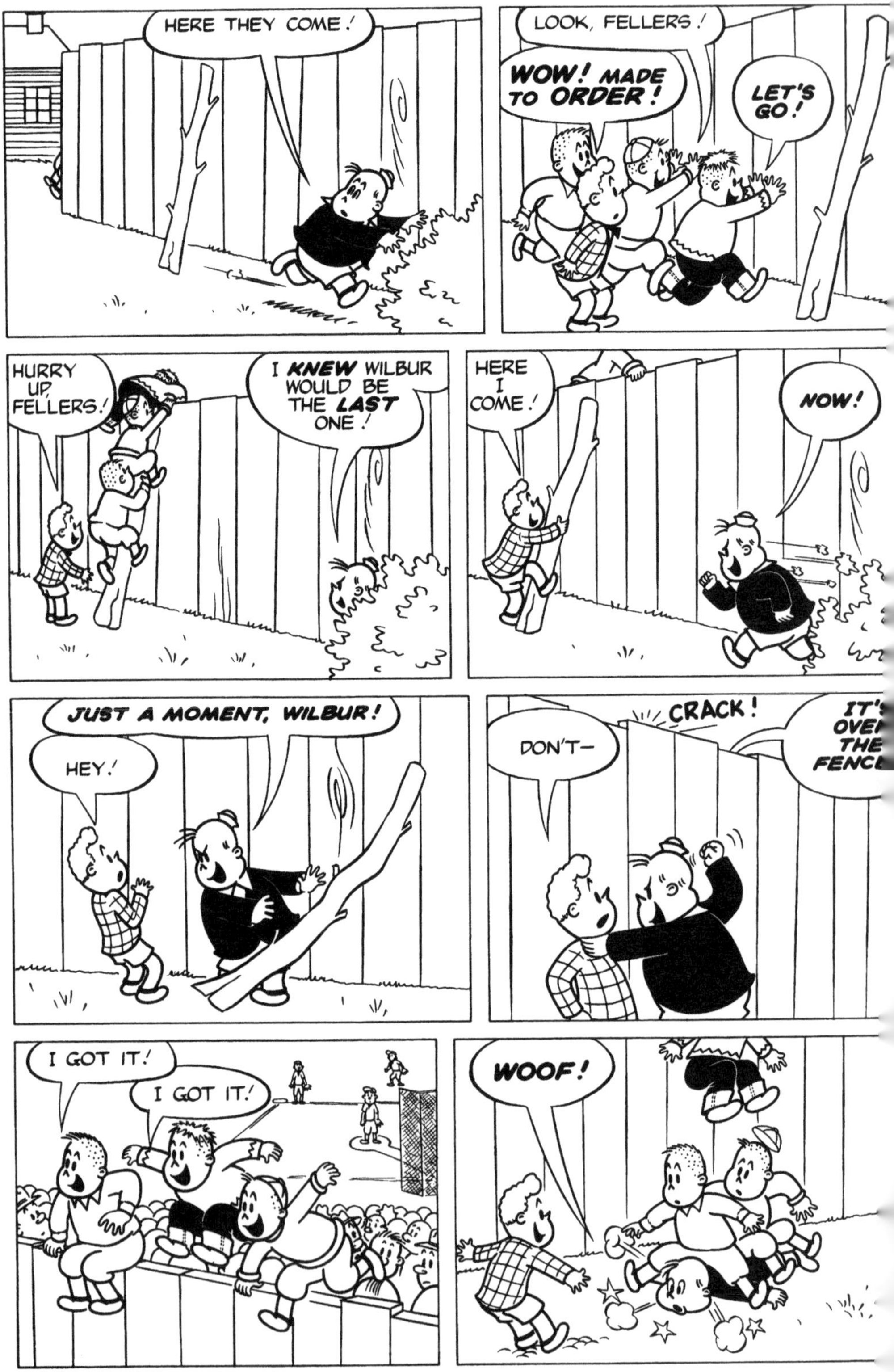
HERE THEY COME!
LOOK, FELLERS!
WOW! MADE TO ORDER!
LET'S GO!
HURRY UP, FELLERS!
I KNEW WILBUR WOULD BE THE LAST ONE!
HERE I COME!
NOW!
JUST A MOMENT, WILBUR!
HEY!
CRACK!
DON'T—
I GOT IT!
I GOT IT!
WOOF!

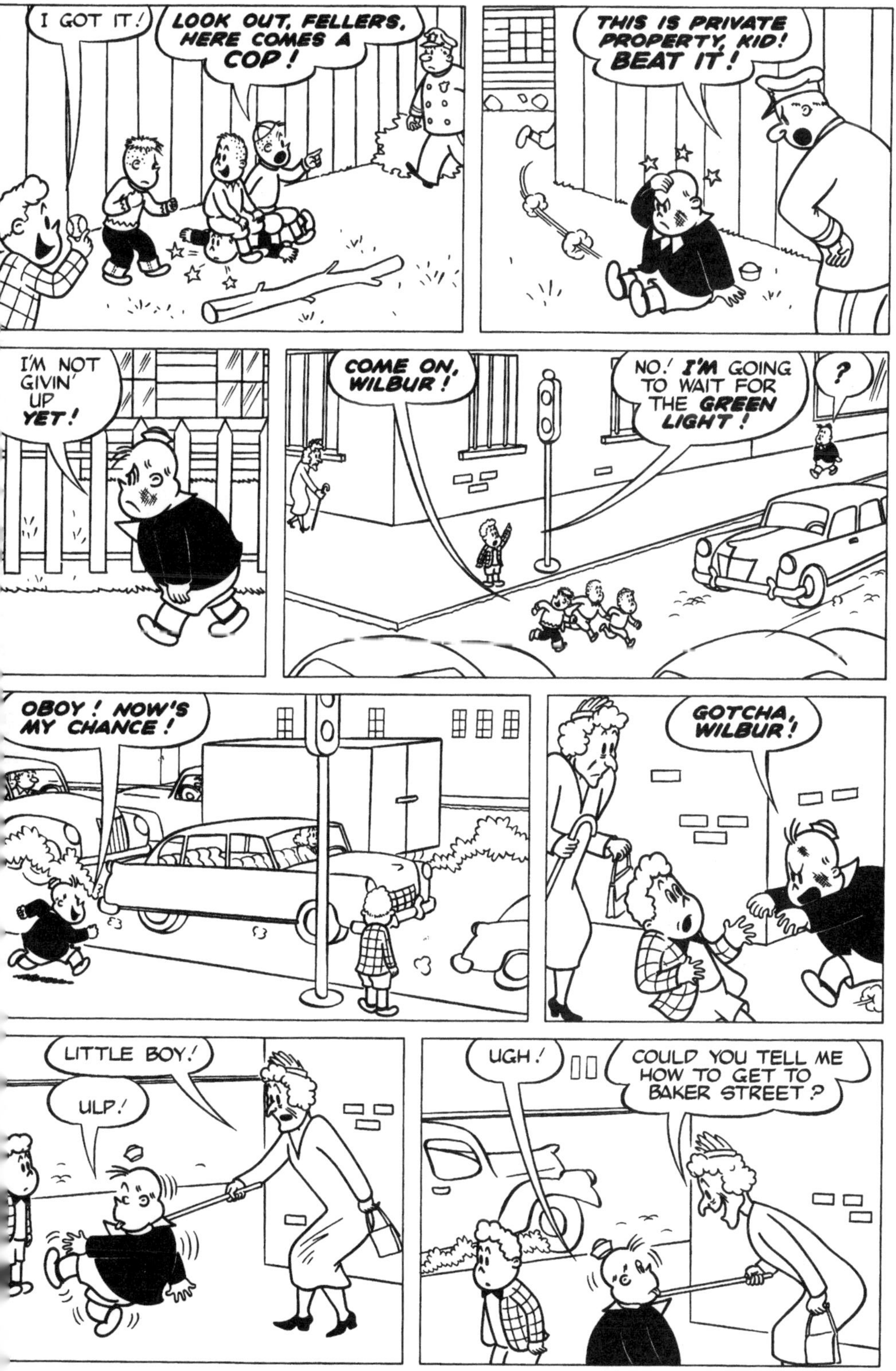
I GOT IT!
LOOK OUT, FELLERS, HERE COMES A COP!
THIS IS PRIVATE PROPERTY, KID! BEAT IT!
I'M NOT GIVIN' UP YET!
COME ON, WILBUR!
NO! I'M GOING TO WAIT FOR THE GREEN LIGHT!
?
OBOY! NOW'S MY CHANCE!
GOTCHA, WILBUR!
LITTLE BOY!
ULP!
UGH!
COULD YOU TELL ME HOW TO GET TO BAKER STREET?

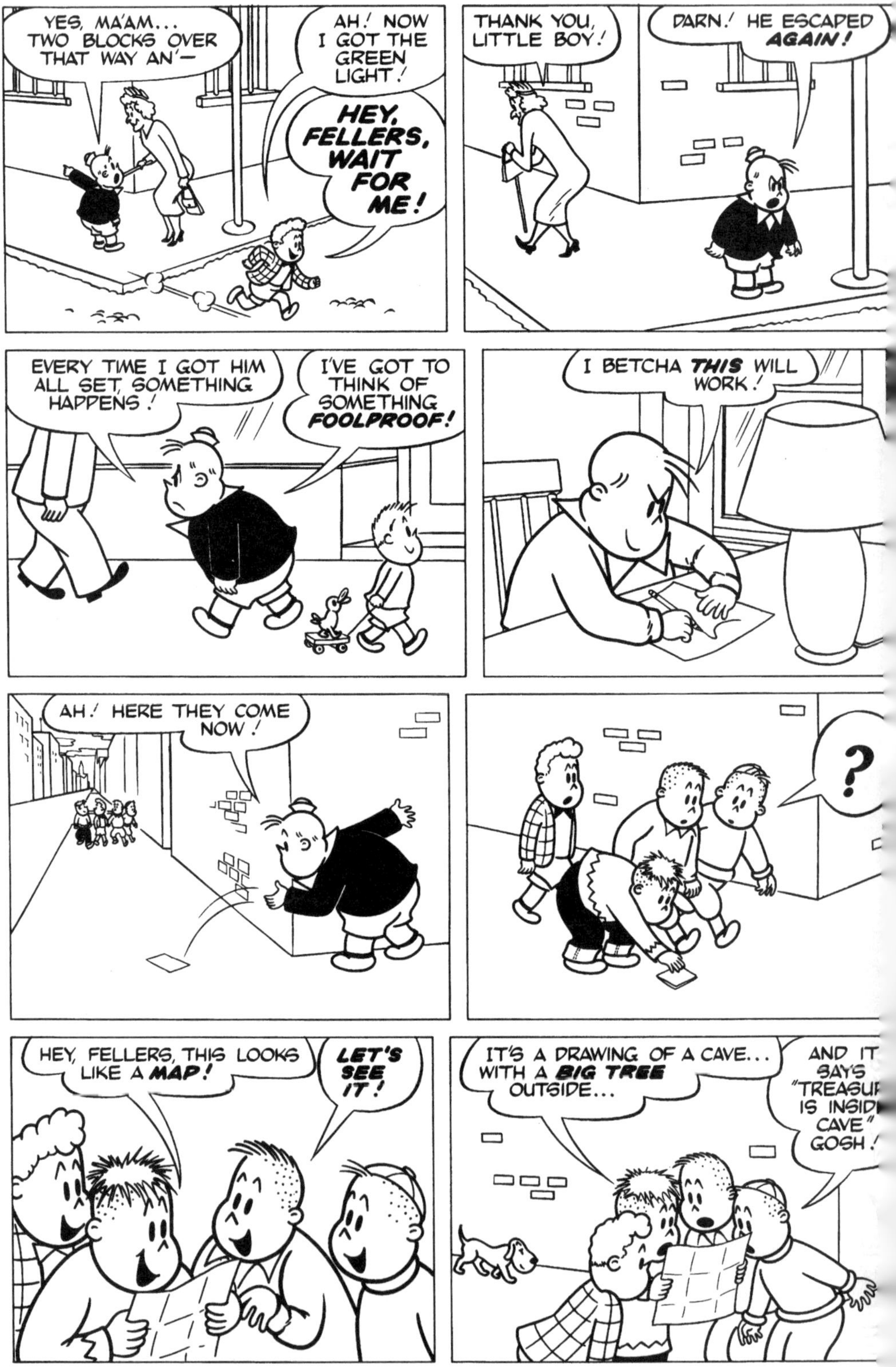
YES, MA'AM... TWO BLOCKS OVER THAT WAY AN'—
AH! NOW I GOT THE GREEN LIGHT!
HEY, FELLERS, WAIT FOR ME!
THANK YOU, LITTLE BOY!
DARN! HE ESCAPED AGAIN!
EVERY TIME I GOT HIM ALL SET, SOMETHING HAPPENS!
I'VE GOT TO THINK OF SOMETHING FOOLPROOF!
I BETCHA THIS WILL WORK!
AH! HERE THEY COME NOW!
?
HEY, FELLERS, THIS LOOKS LIKE A MAP!
LET'S SEE IT!
IT'S A DRAWING OF A CAVE... WITH A BIG TREE OUTSIDE...

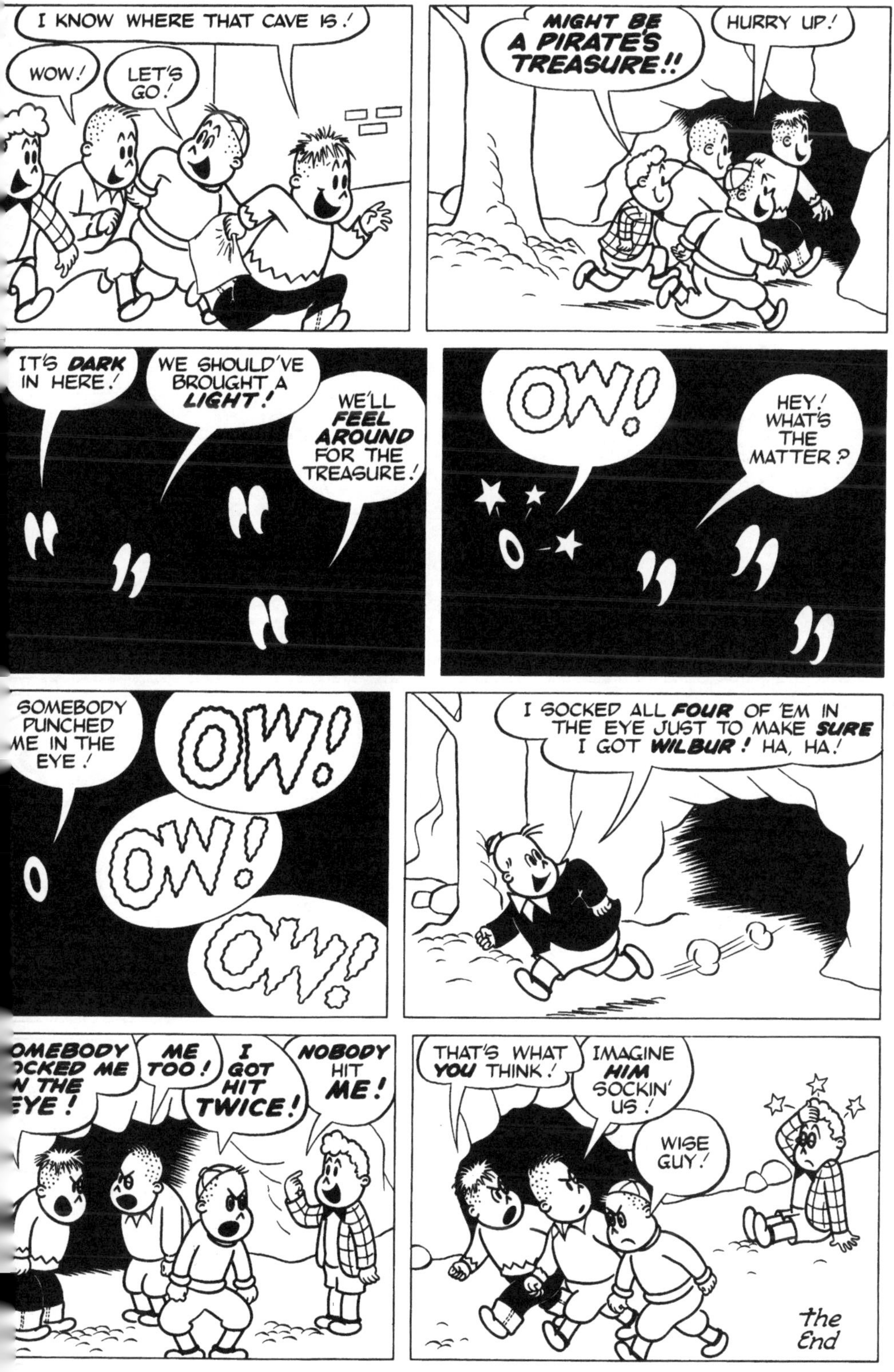
I KNOW WHERE THAT CAVE IS!
WOW!
LET'S GO!
MIGHT BE A PIRATE'S TREASURE!!
HURRY UP!
IT'S DARK IN HERE!
WE SHOULD'VE BROUGHT A LIGHT!
WE'LL FEEL AROUND FOR THE TREASURE!
OW!
HEY! WHAT'S THE MATTER?
SOMEBODY PUNCHED ME IN THE EYE!
OW!
OW!
OW!
I SOCKED ALL FOUR OF 'EM IN THE EYE JUST TO MAKE SURE I GOT WILBUR! HA, HA!
OMEBODY OCKED ME N THE EYE!
ME TOO!
I GOT HIT TWICE!
NOBODY HIT ME!
THAT'S WHAT YOU THINK!
IMAGINE HIM SOCKIN' US!
WISE GUY!
the End

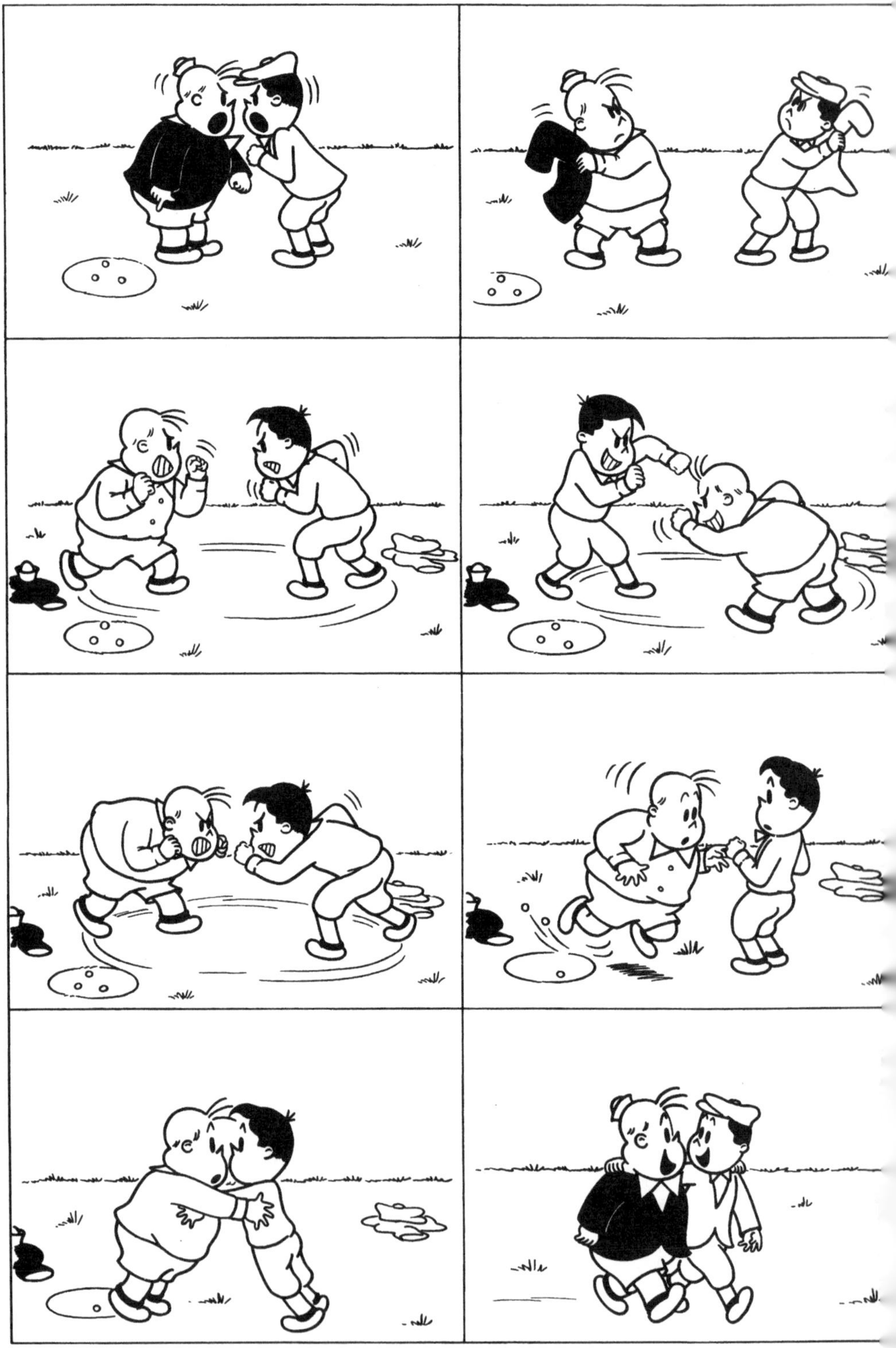

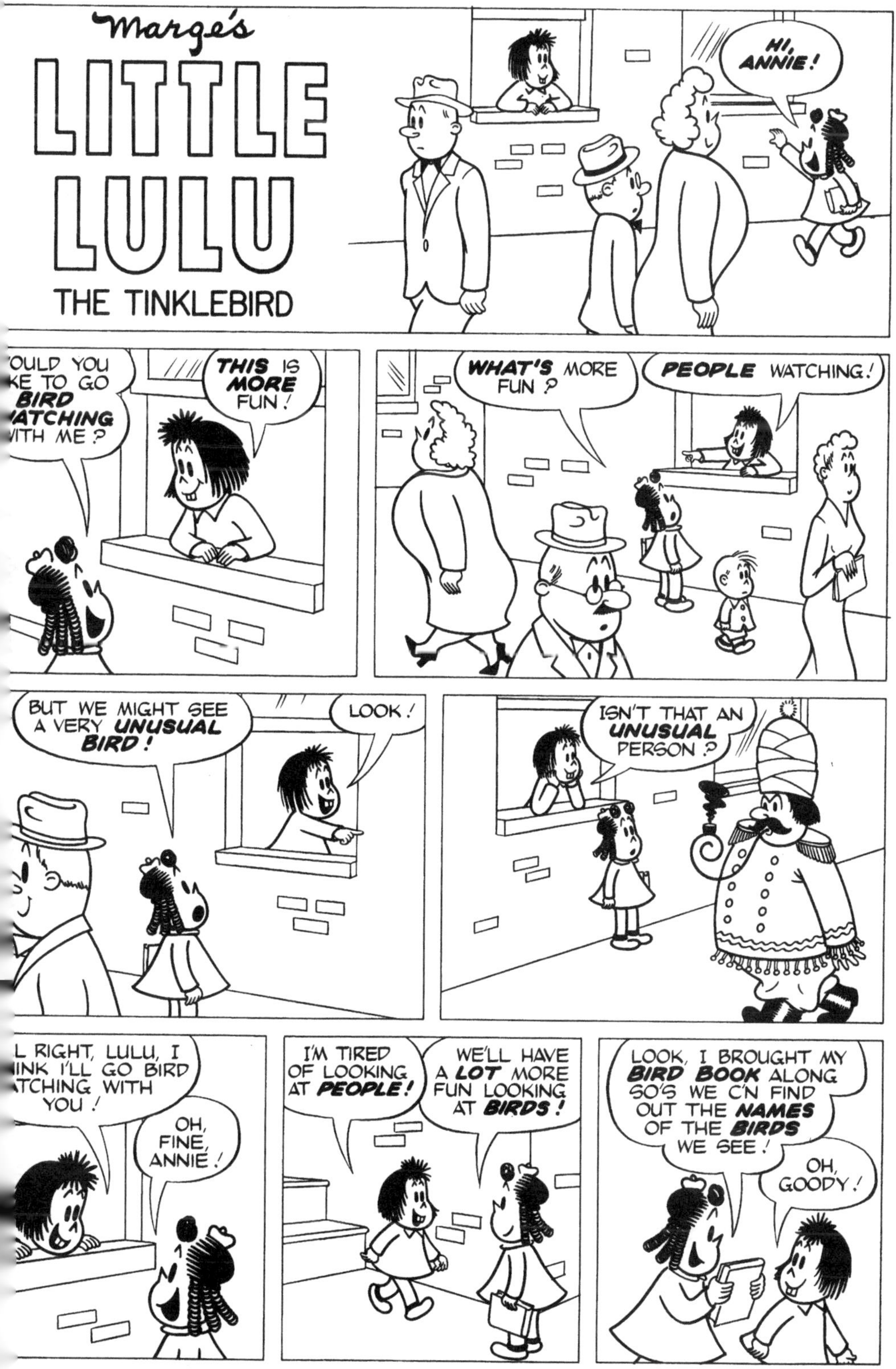
Marge's
LITTLE LULU
THE TINKLEBIRD
HI, ANNIE!
'OULD YOU KE TO GO BIRD ATCHING WITH ME?
THIS IS MORE FUN!
WHAT'S MORE FUN?
PEOPLE WATCHING!
BUT WE MIGHT SEE A VERY UNUSUAL BIRD!
LOOK!
ISN'T THAT AN UNUSUAL PERSON?
L RIGHT, LULU, I INK I'LL GO BIRD TCHING WITH YOU!
OH, FINE, ANNIE!
I'M TIRED OF LOOKING AT PEOPLE!
WE'LL HAVE A LOT MORE FUN LOOKING AT BIRDS!
LOOK, I BROUGHT MY BIRD BOOK ALONG SO'S WE C'N FIND OUT THE NAMES OF THE BIRDS WE SEE!
OH, GOODY!

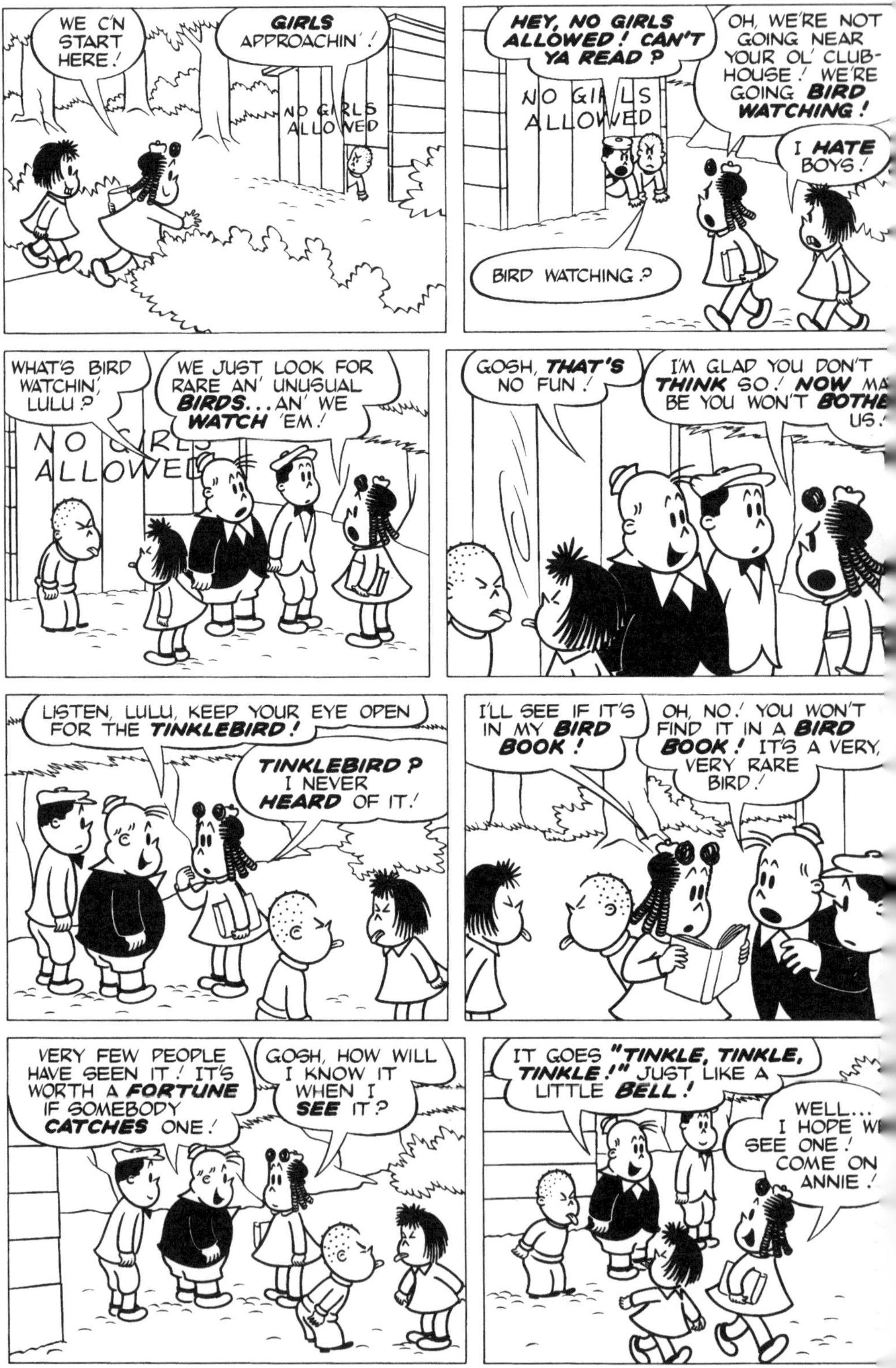
WE C'N START HERE!
GIRLS APPROACHIN'!
NO GIRLS ALLOWED
HEY, NO GIRLS ALLOWED! CAN'T YA READ?
NO GIRLS ALLOWED
OH, WE'RE NOT GOING NEAR YOUR OL' CLUB-HOUSE! WE'RE GOING BIRD WATCHING!
I HATE BOYS!
BIRD WATCHING?
WHAT'S BIRD WATCHIN', LULU?
WE JUST LOOK FOR RARE AN' UNUSUAL BIRDS... AN' WE WATCH 'EM!
GOSH, THAT'S NO FUN!
I'M GLAD YOU DON'T THINK SO! NOW MA BE YOU WON'T BOTHE US!
LISTEN, LULU, KEEP YOUR EYE OPEN FOR THE TINKLEBIRD!
TINKLEBIRD? I NEVER HEARD OF IT!
I'LL SEE IF IT'S IN MY BIRD BOOK!
OH, NO! YOU WON'T FIND IT IN A BIRD BOOK! IT'S A VERY, VERY RARE BIRD!
VERY FEW PEOPLE HAVE SEEN IT! IT'S WORTH A FORTUNE IF SOMEBODY CATCHES ONE!
GOSH, HOW WILL I KNOW IT WHEN I SEE IT?
IT GOES "TINKLE, TINKLE, TINKLE!" JUST LIKE A LITTLE BELL!
WELL... I HOPE WE SEE ONE! COME ON ANNIE!

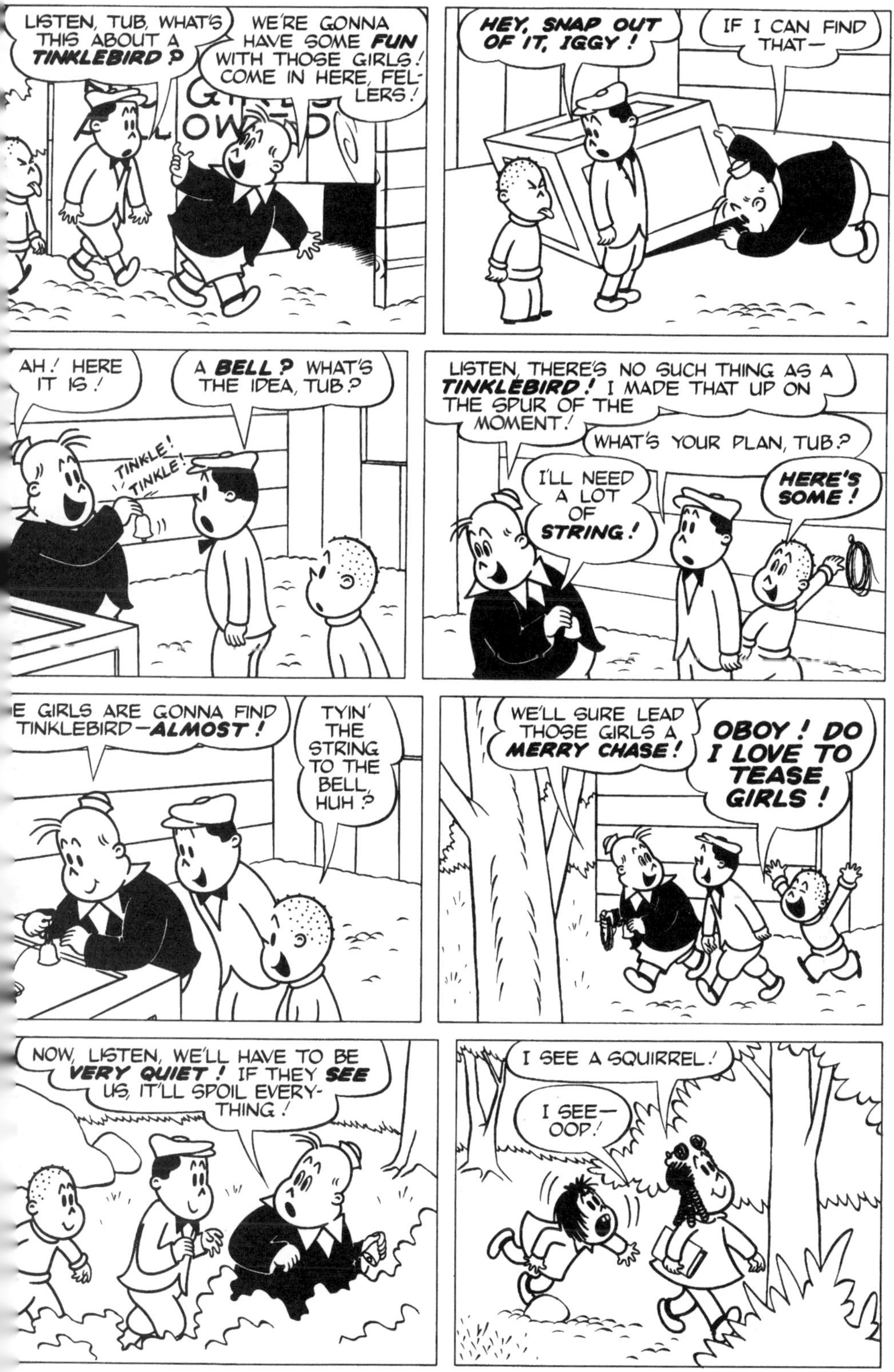
LISTEN, TUB, WHAT'S THIS ABOUT A TINKLEBIRD?
WE'RE GONNA HAVE SOME FUN WITH THOSE GIRLS! COME IN HERE, FELLERS!
HEY, SNAP OUT OF IT, IGGY!
IF I CAN FIND THAT—
AH! HERE IT IS!
A BELL? WHAT'S THE IDEA, TUB?
TINKLE! TINKLE!
LISTEN, THERE'S NO SUCH THING AS A TINKLEBIRD! I MADE THAT UP ON THE SPUR OF THE MOMENT!
WHAT'S YOUR PLAN, TUB?
I'LL NEED A LOT OF STRING!
HERE'S SOME!
E GIRLS ARE GONNA FIND TINKLEBIRD—ALMOST!
TYIN' THE STRING TO THE BELL, HUH?
WE'LL SURE LEAD THOSE GIRLS A MERRY CHASE!
OBOY! DO I LOVE TO TEASE GIRLS!
NOW, LISTEN, WE'LL HAVE TO BE VERY QUIET! IF THEY SEE US, IT'LL SPOIL EVERYTHING!
I SEE A SQUIRREL!
I SEE— OOP!

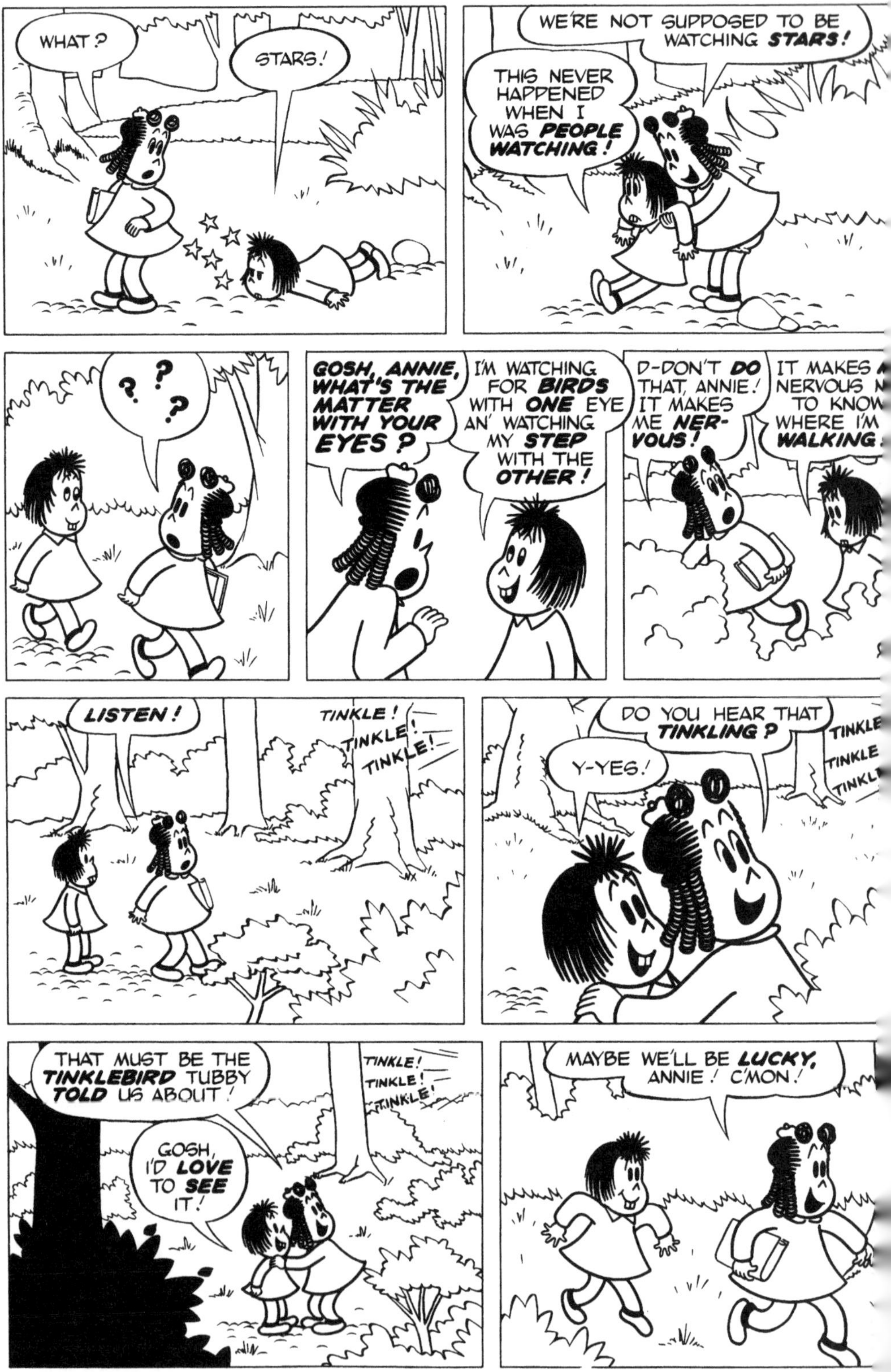

WHAT?
STARS!
WE'RE NOT SUPPOSED TO BE WATCHING **STARS!**
THIS NEVER HAPPENED WHEN I WAS **PEOPLE WATCHING!**
? ? ?
GOSH, ANNIE, WHAT'S THE MATTER WITH YOUR EYES?
I'M WATCHING FOR **BIRDS** WITH **ONE** EYE AN' WATCHING MY **STEP** WITH THE **OTHER!**
D-DON'T **DO** THAT, ANNIE! IT MAKES ME **NER-VOUS!**
IT MAKES NERVOUS TO KNOW WHERE I'M **WALKING**
LISTEN!
TINKLE! TINKLE! TINKLE!
DO YOU HEAR THAT **TINKLING?**
Y-YES!
TINKLE TINKLE
THAT MUST BE THE **TINKLEBIRD** TUBBY **TOLD** US ABOUT!
TINKLE! TINKLE! TINKLE!
GOSH, I'D **LOVE** TO **SEE** IT!
MAYBE WE'LL BE **LUCKY,** ANNIE! C'MON!

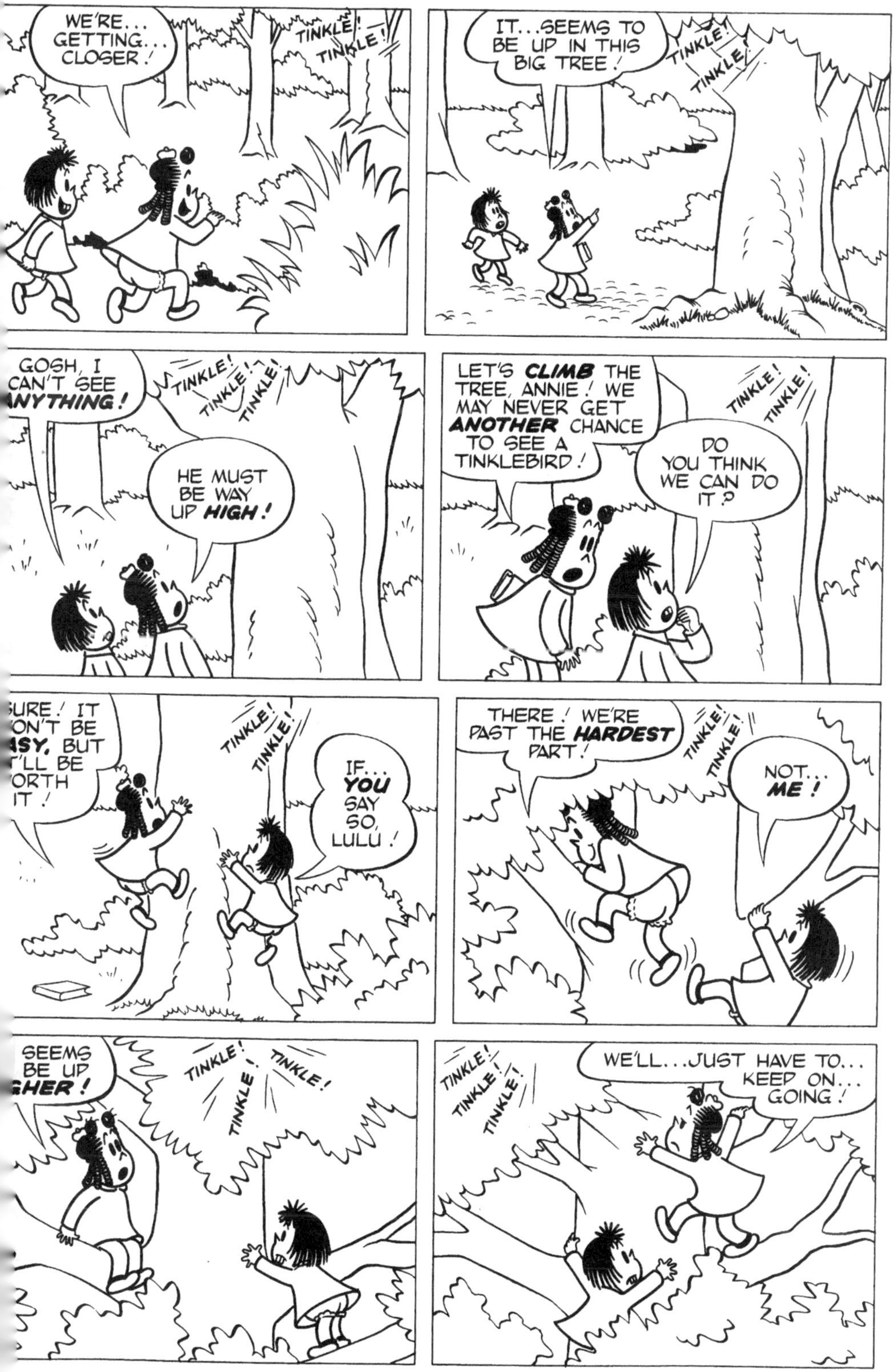
WE'RE... GETTING... CLOSER!
TINKLE! TINKLE!
IT...SEEMS TO BE UP IN THIS BIG TREE!
TINKLE! TINKLE!
GOSH, I CAN'T SEE ANYTHING!
TINKLE! TINKLE! TINKLE!
HE MUST BE WAY UP HIGH!
LET'S CLIMB THE TREE, ANNIE! WE MAY NEVER GET ANOTHER CHANCE TO SEE A TINKLEBIRD!
TINKLE! TINKLE!
DO YOU THINK WE CAN DO IT?
TINKLE! TINKLE!
IF... YOU SAY SO, LULU!
THERE! WE'RE PAST THE HARDEST PART!
TINKLE! TINKLE!
NOT... ME!
TINKLE! TINKLE! TINKLE!
TINKLE! TINKLE! TINKLE!
WE'LL...JUST HAVE TO... KEEP ON... GOING!

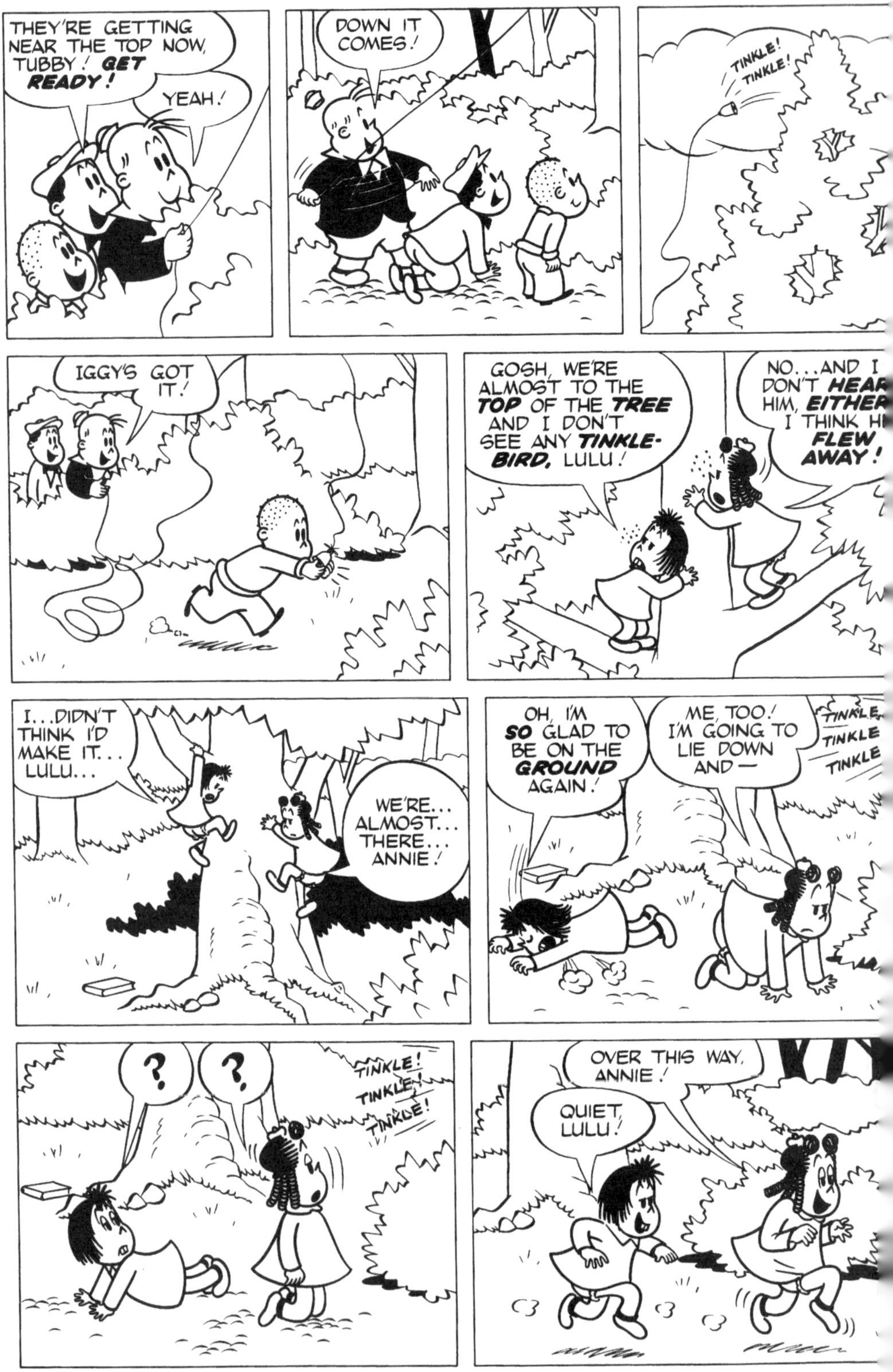
THEY'RE GETTING NEAR THE TOP NOW, TUBBY! GET READY!
YEAH!
DOWN IT COMES!
TINKLE! TINKLE!
IGGY'S GOT IT!
GOSH, WE'RE ALMOST TO THE TOP OF THE TREE AND I DON'T SEE ANY TINKLE-BIRD, LULU!
NO...AND I DON'T HEAR HIM, EITHER I THINK H FLEW AWAY!
I...DIDN'T THINK I'D MAKE IT... LULU...
WE'RE... ALMOST... THERE... ANNIE!
OH, I'M SO GLAD TO BE ON THE GROUND AGAIN!
ME, TOO! I'M GOING TO LIE DOWN AND—
TINKLE TINKLE TINKLE
?
?
TINKLE! TINKLE! TINKLE!
OVER THIS WAY, ANNIE!
QUIET, LULU!

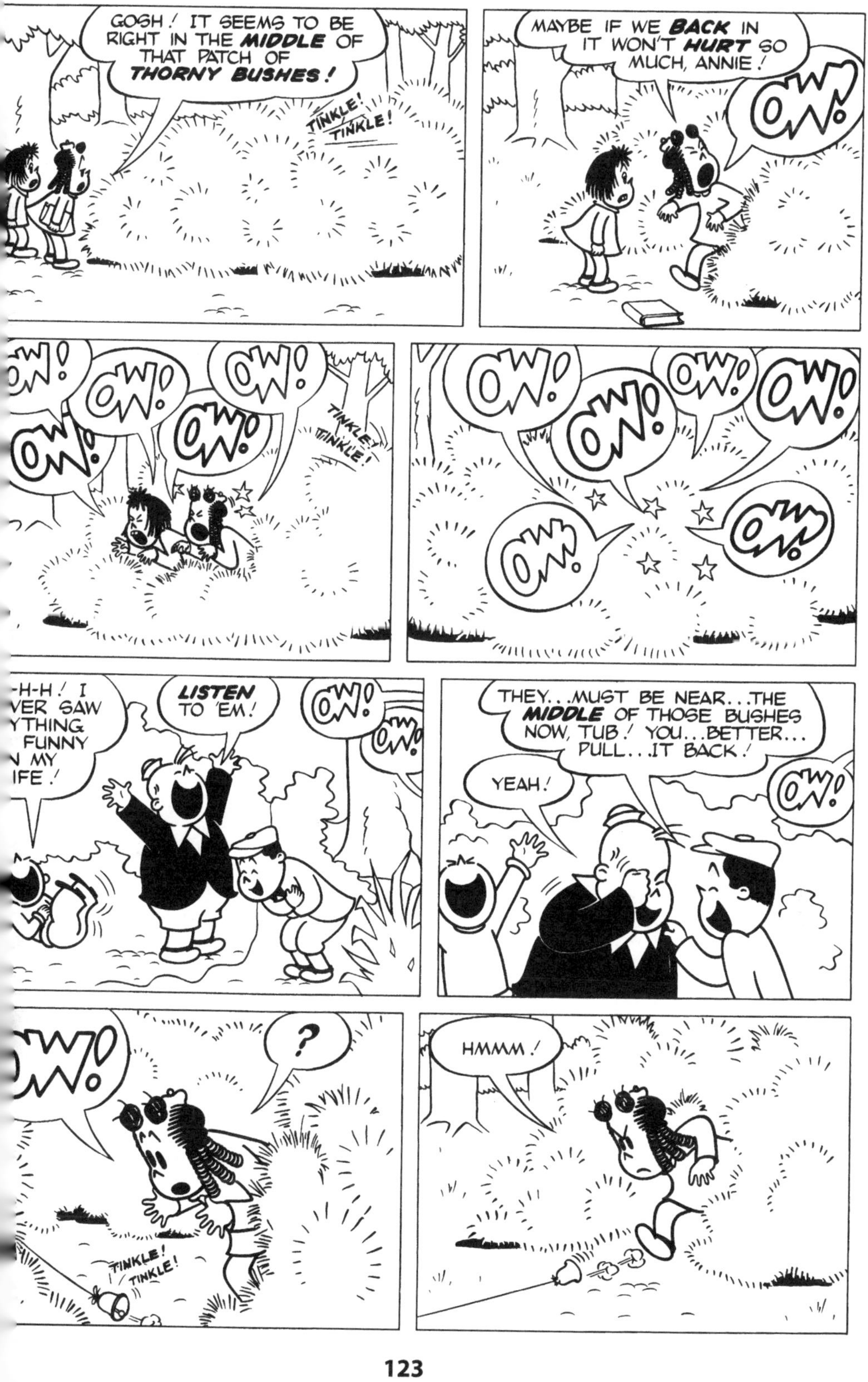
GOSH! IT SEEMS TO BE RIGHT IN THE **MIDDLE** OF THAT PATCH OF **THORNY BUSHES!**
TINKLE! TINKLE!
MAYBE IF WE **BACK** IN IT WON'T **HURT** SO MUCH, ANNIE!
OW!
OW!
OW!
OW!
OW!
OW!
TINKLE! TINKLE!
OW!
OW!
OW!
OW!
OW!
OW!
-H-H! I
VER SAW
YTHING
FUNNY
N MY
IFE!
LISTEN TO 'EM!
OW!
OW!
THEY...MUST BE NEAR...THE **MIDDLE** OF THOSE BUSHES NOW, TUB! YOU...BETTER... PULL...IT BACK!
YEAH!
OW!
OW!
?
TINKLE! TINKLE!
HMMM!

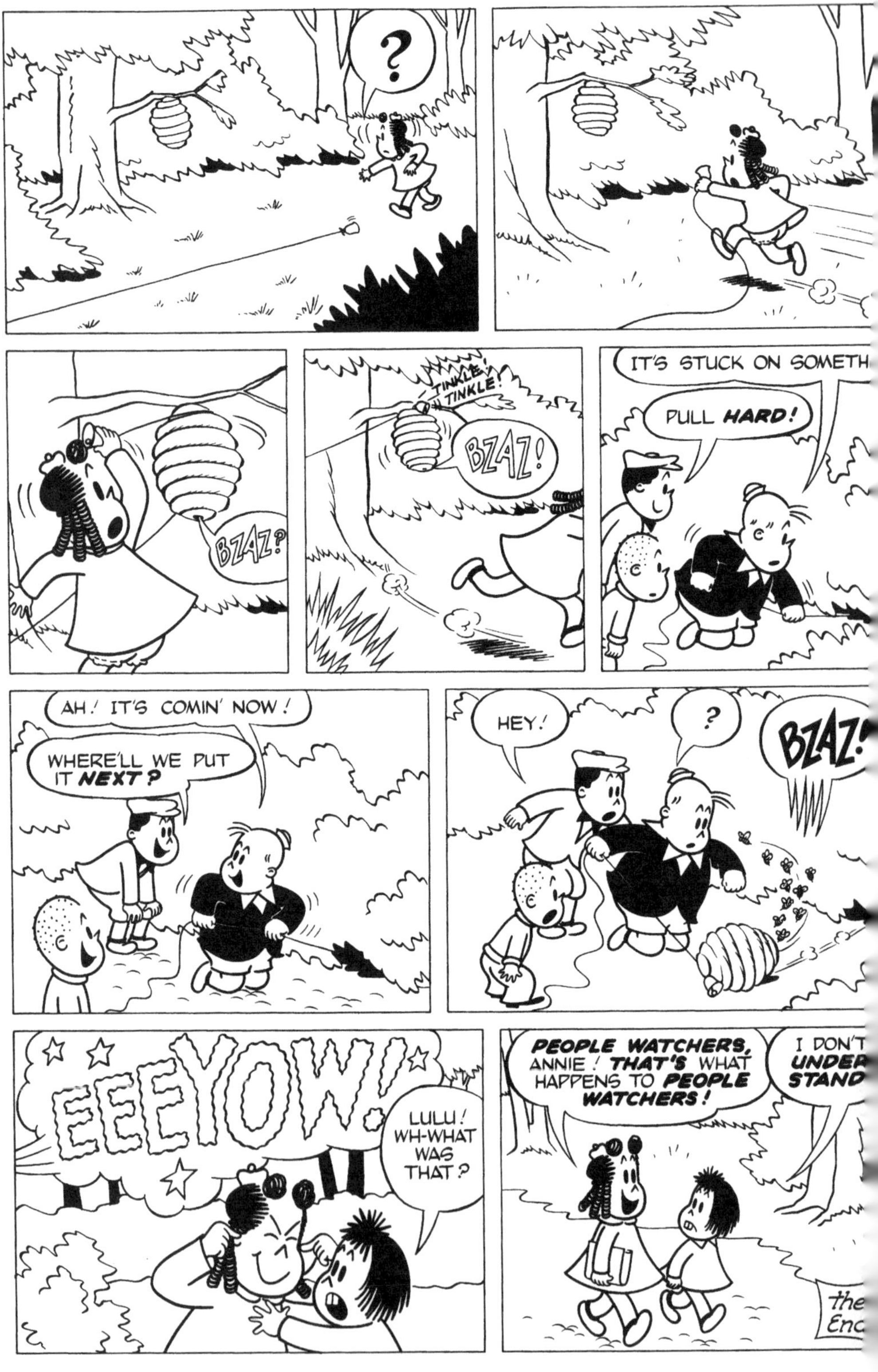
?
BZAZ?
TINKLE, TINKLE!
BZAZ!
IT'S STUCK ON SOMETH
PULL **HARD!**
AH! IT'S COMIN' NOW!
WHERE'LL WE PUT IT **NEXT?**
HEY!
?
BZAZ!
EEEYOW!
LULU! WH-WHAT WAS THAT?
PEOPLE WATCHERS, ANNIE! **THAT'S** WHAT HAPPENS TO **PEOPLE WATCHERS!**
I DON'T **UNDER STAND**
the Enc

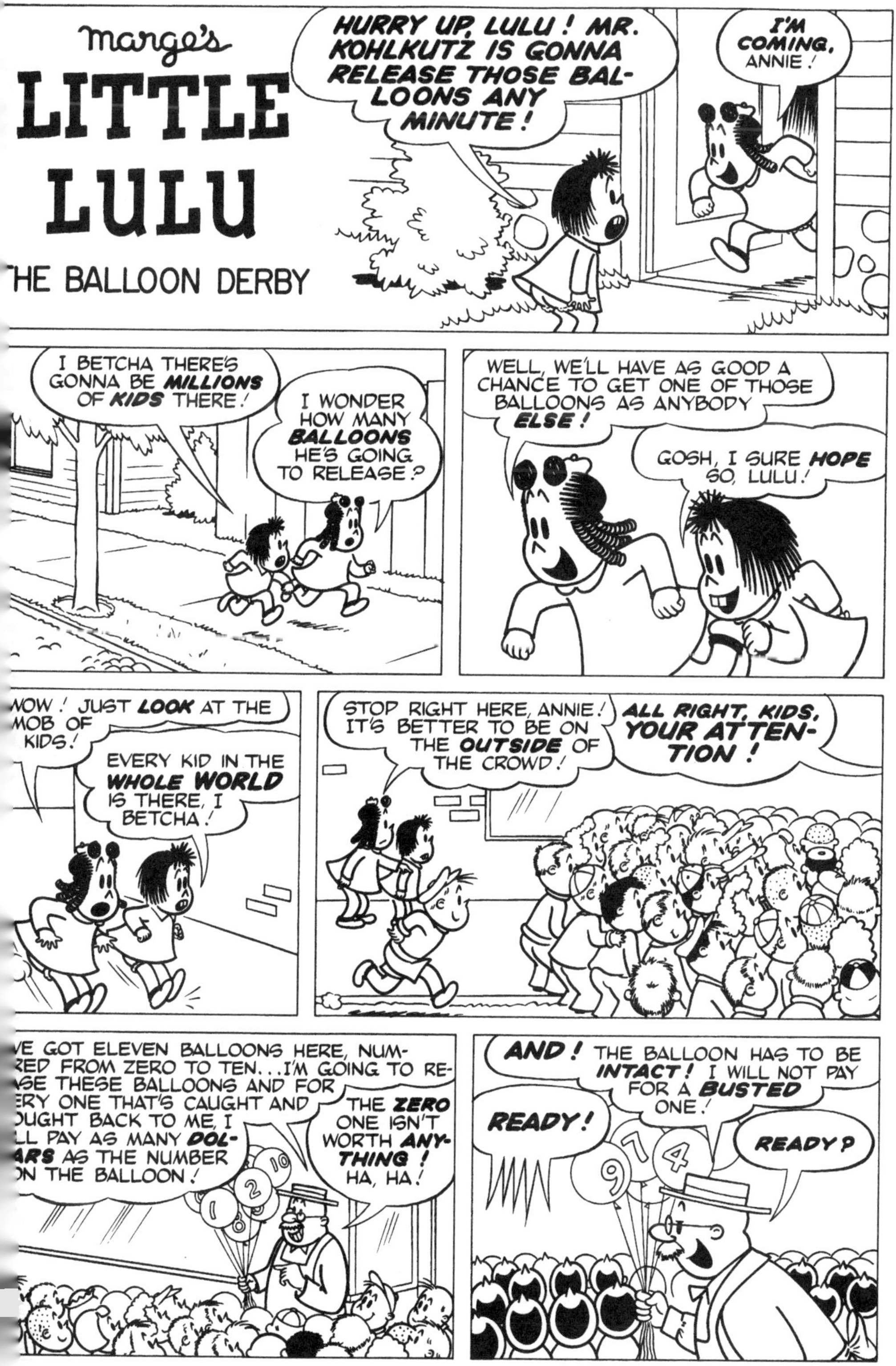
marge's
LITTLE LULU
THE BALLOON DERBY
HURRY UP, LULU! MR. KOHLKUTZ IS GONNA RELEASE THOSE BALLOONS ANY MINUTE!
I'M COMING, ANNIE!
I BETCHA THERE'S GONNA BE MILLIONS OF KIDS THERE!
I WONDER HOW MANY BALLOONS HE'S GOING TO RELEASE?
WELL, WE'LL HAVE AS GOOD A CHANCE TO GET ONE OF THOSE BALLOONS AS ANYBODY ELSE!
GOSH, I SURE HOPE SO, LULU!
WOW! JUST LOOK AT THE MOB OF KIDS!
EVERY KID IN THE WHOLE WORLD IS THERE, I BETCHA!
STOP RIGHT HERE, ANNIE! IT'S BETTER TO BE ON THE OUTSIDE OF THE CROWD!
ALL RIGHT, KIDS, YOUR ATTENTION!
WE GOT ELEVEN BALLOONS HERE, NUMBERED FROM ZERO TO TEN...I'M GOING TO RELEASE THESE BALLOONS AND FOR EVERY ONE THAT'S CAUGHT AND BROUGHT BACK TO ME, I WILL PAY AS MANY DOLLARS AS THE NUMBER ON THE BALLOON!
THE ZERO ONE ISN'T WORTH ANYTHING! HA, HA!
AND! THE BALLOON HAS TO BE INTACT! I WILL NOT PAY FOR A BUSTED ONE!
READY!
READY?

THERE'S A **STRONG WIND** BLOWING TO-DAY! YOU KIDS ARE GOING TO DO SOME **RUNNING!**

HEY! WHY AREN'T **YOU** CHASING THE BALLOONS, LIDDLE BOY?

OH... FIRE HYDRANT!

THIS BALLOON STUNT SURE WILL BE GOOD **ADVERTISING** FOR **KOHLKUTZ'S BUTCHER SHOP!**

YOW! MY GARDEN!

HEY, COME ON, KIDS! THERE'S A BALLOON STUCK WAY UP ON TOP OF THIS TREE!!

CRASH!

TAKE OFF YOUR HATS, GENTLEMEN, THAT WAS THE **OLDEST** AND MOST BEAUTIFUL TREE IN THE STATE!

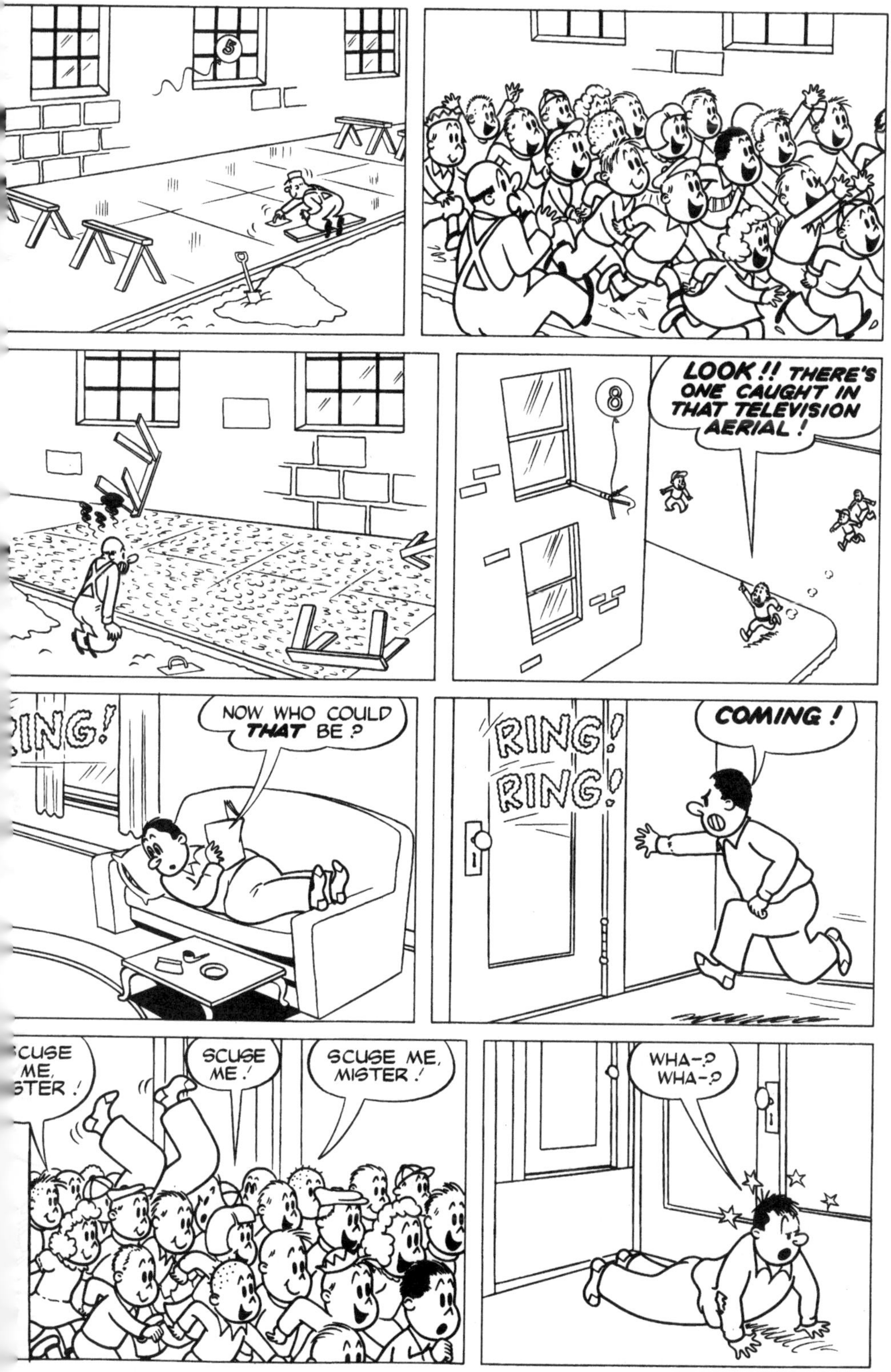

LOOK !! THERE'S ONE CAUGHT IN THAT TELEVISION AERIAL !
ING!
NOW WHO COULD *THAT* BE ?
RING! RING!
COMING !
CUSE ME, STER !
SCUSE ME !
SCUSE ME, MISTER !
WHA-? WHA-?

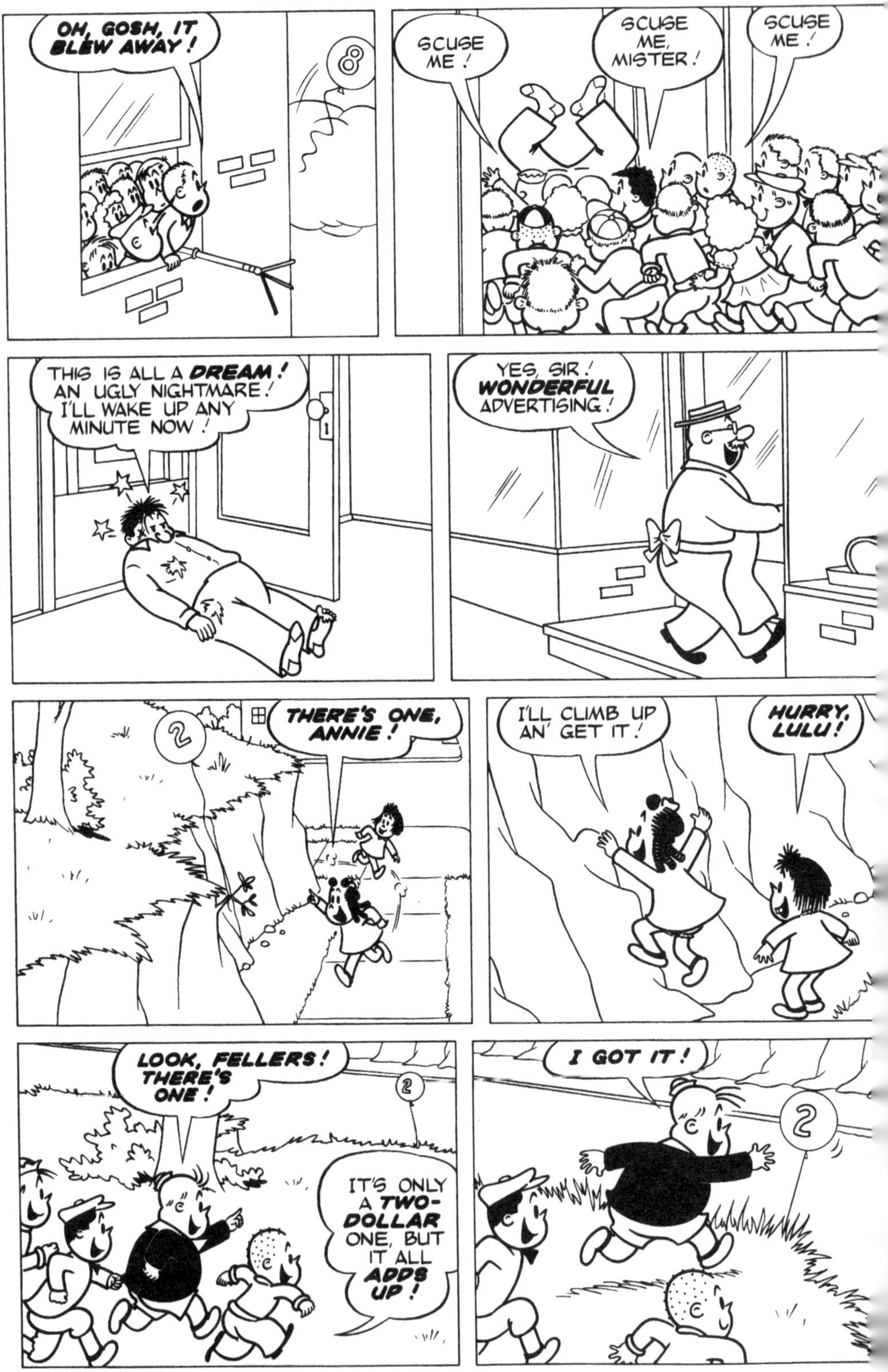
OH, GOSH, IT BLEW AWAY!
8
SCUSE ME!
SCUSE ME, MISTER!
SCUSE ME!
THIS IS ALL A DREAM! AN UGLY NIGHTMARE! I'LL WAKE UP ANY MINUTE NOW!
YES, SIR! WONDERFUL ADVERTISING!
2
THERE'S ONE, ANNIE!
I'LL CLIMB UP AN' GET IT!
HURRY, LULU!
LOOK, FELLERS! THERE'S ONE!
2
IT'S ONLY A TWO-DOLLAR ONE, BUT IT ALL ADDS UP!
I GOT IT!
2

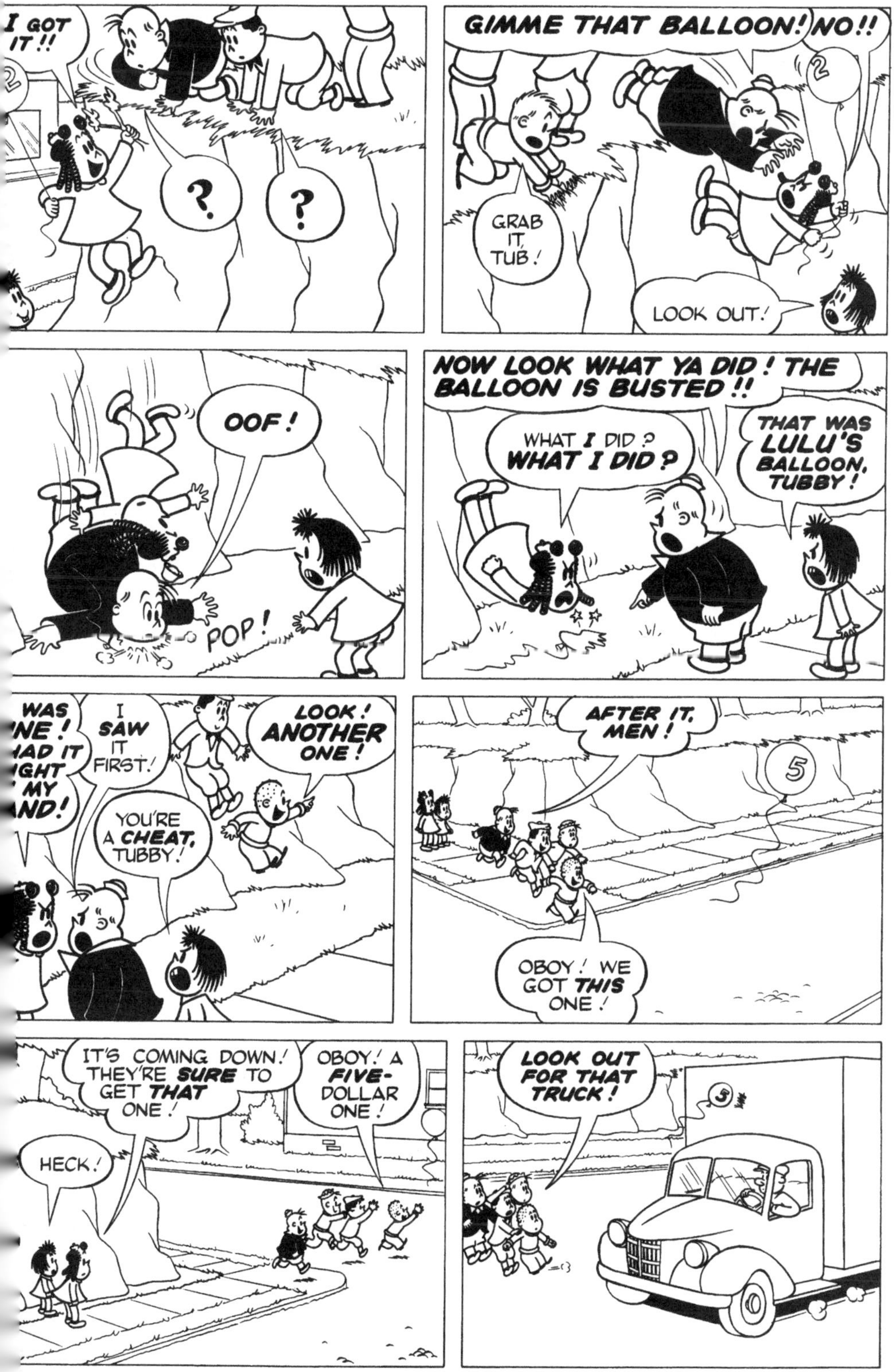
I GOT IT!!
?
?
GIMME THAT BALLOON!
NO!!
GRAB IT, TUB!
LOOK OUT!
OOF!
POP!
NOW LOOK WHAT YA DID! THE BALLOON IS BUSTED!!
WHAT I DID? WHAT I DID?
THAT WAS LULU'S BALLOON, TUBBY!
WAS
I SAW IT FIRST!
LOOK! ANOTHER ONE!
YOU'RE A CHEAT, TUBBY!
AFTER IT, MEN!
OBOY! WE GOT THIS ONE!
IT'S COMING DOWN! THEY'RE SURE TO GET THAT ONE!
OBOY! A FIVE-DOLLAR ONE!
HECK!
LOOK OUT FOR THAT TRUCK!

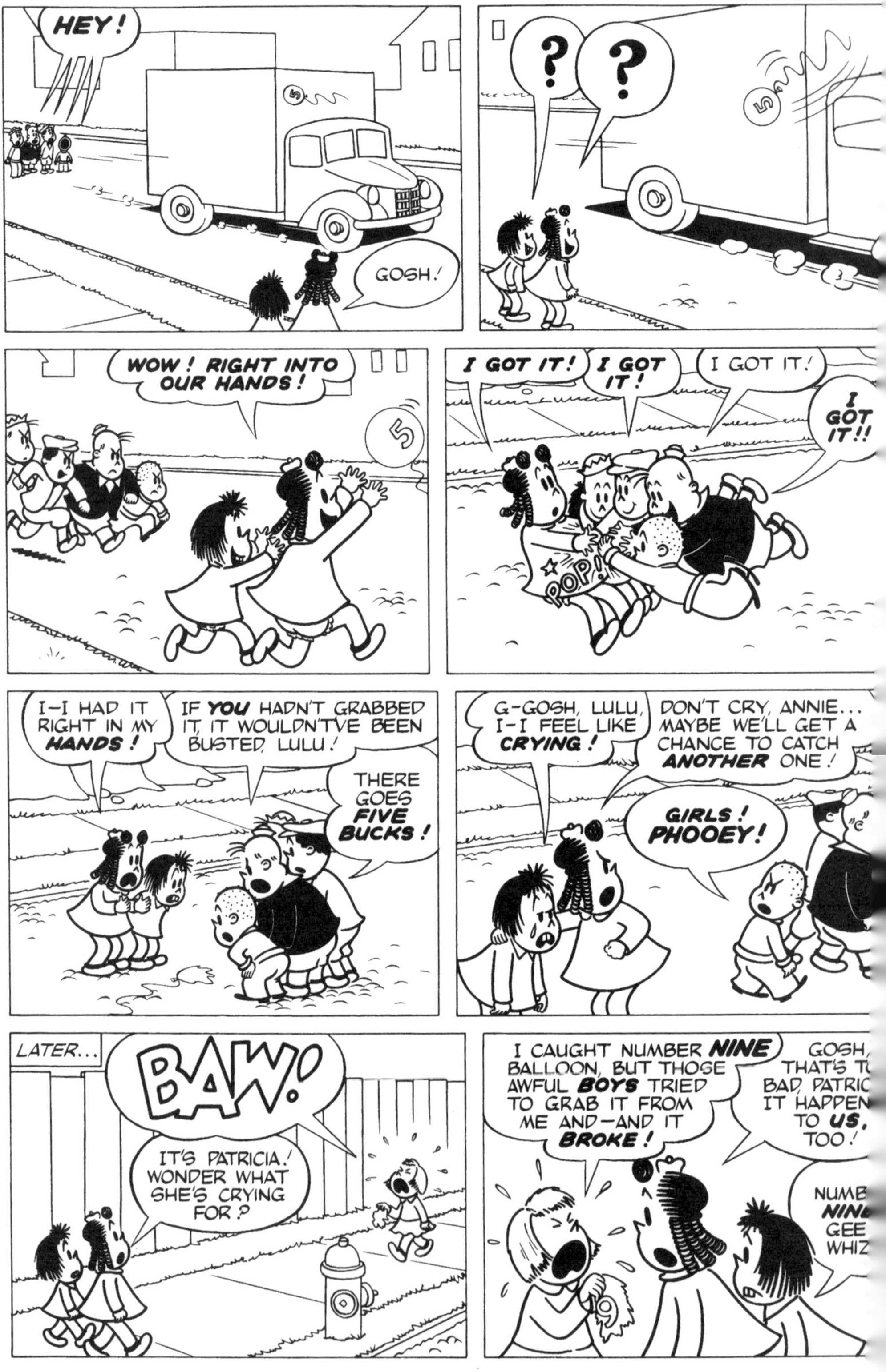
HEY!
GOSH!
?
?
WOW! RIGHT INTO OUR HANDS!
I GOT IT!
I GOT IT!
I GOT IT!
I GOT IT!!
POP!
I—I HAD IT RIGHT IN MY HANDS!
IF YOU HADN'T GRABBED IT, IT WOULDN'T'VE BEEN BUSTED, LULU!
THERE GOES FIVE BUCKS!
G-GOSH, LULU, I-I FEEL LIKE CRYING!
DON'T CRY, ANNIE... MAYBE WE'LL GET A CHANCE TO CATCH ANOTHER ONE!
GIRLS! PHOOEY!
LATER...
BAW!
IT'S PATRICIA! WONDER WHAT SHE'S CRYING FOR?
I CAUGHT NUMBER NINE BALLOON, BUT THOSE AWFUL BOYS TRIED TO GRAB IT FROM ME AND—AND IT BROKE!
GOSH, THAT'S T BAD, PATRIC IT HAPPEN TO US, TOO!
NUMB NIN GEE WHIZ

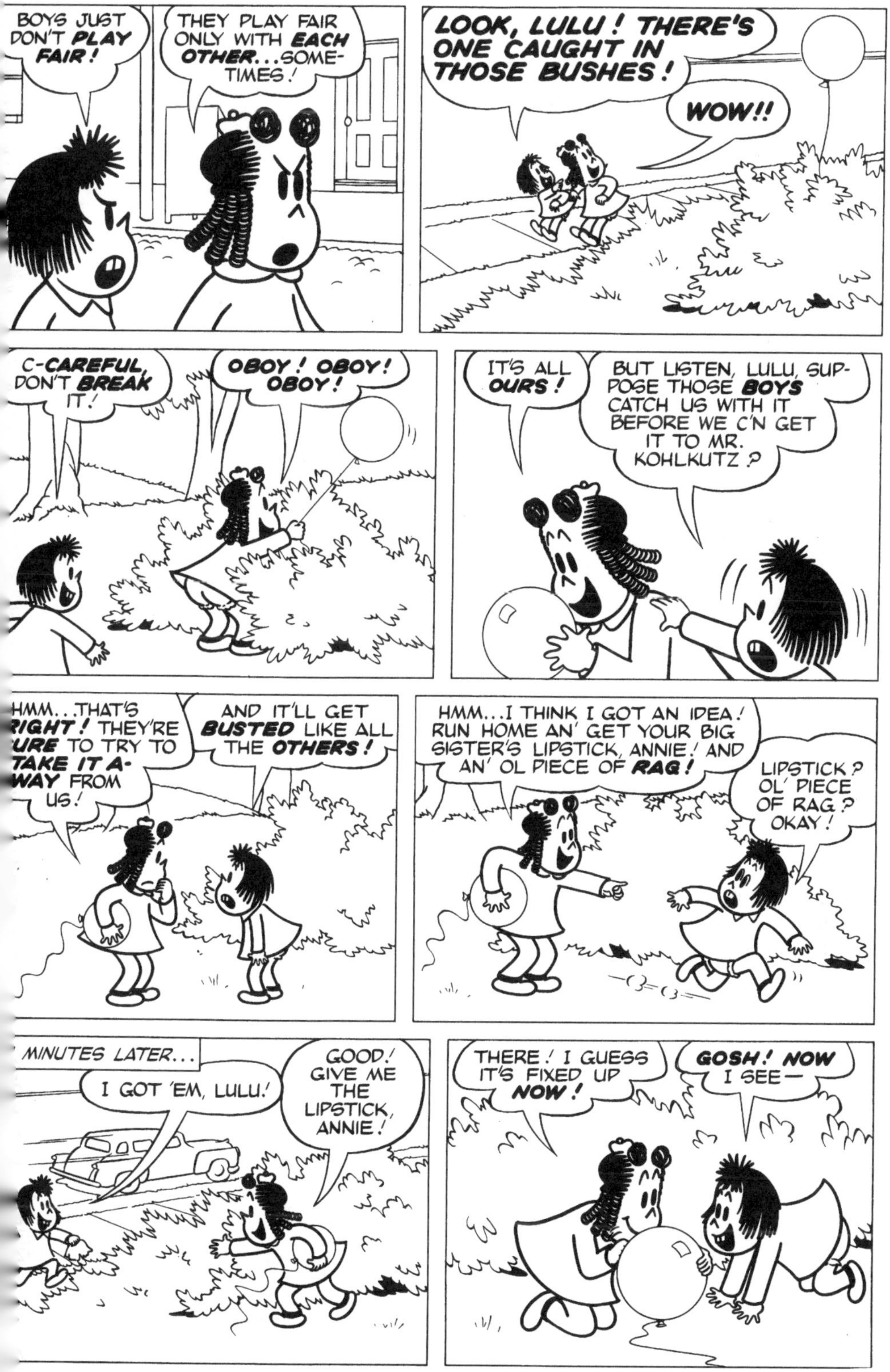

BOYS JUST DON'T **PLAY FAIR**!
THEY PLAY FAIR ONLY WITH **EACH OTHER**...SOME-TIMES!
LOOK, LULU! THERE'S ONE CAUGHT IN THOSE BUSHES!
WOW!!
C-**CAREFUL**, DON'T **BREAK** IT!
OBOY! OBOY! OBOY!
IT'S ALL **OURS**!
BUT LISTEN, LULU, SUP-POSE THOSE **BOYS** CATCH US WITH IT BEFORE WE C'N GET IT TO MR. KOHLKUTZ?
HMM...THAT'S **IGHT**! THEY'RE **URE** TO TRY TO **TAKE IT A-WAY** FROM US!
AND IT'LL GET **BUSTED** LIKE ALL THE **OTHERS**!
HMM...I THINK I GOT AN IDEA! RUN HOME AN' GET YOUR BIG SISTER'S LIPSTICK, ANNIE! AND AN' OL PIECE OF **RAG**!
LIPSTICK? OL' PIECE OF RAG? OKAY!
MINUTES LATER...
I GOT 'EM, LULU!
GOOD! GIVE ME THE LIPSTICK, ANNIE!
THERE! I GUESS IT'S FIXED UP **NOW**!
GOSH! NOW I SEE—

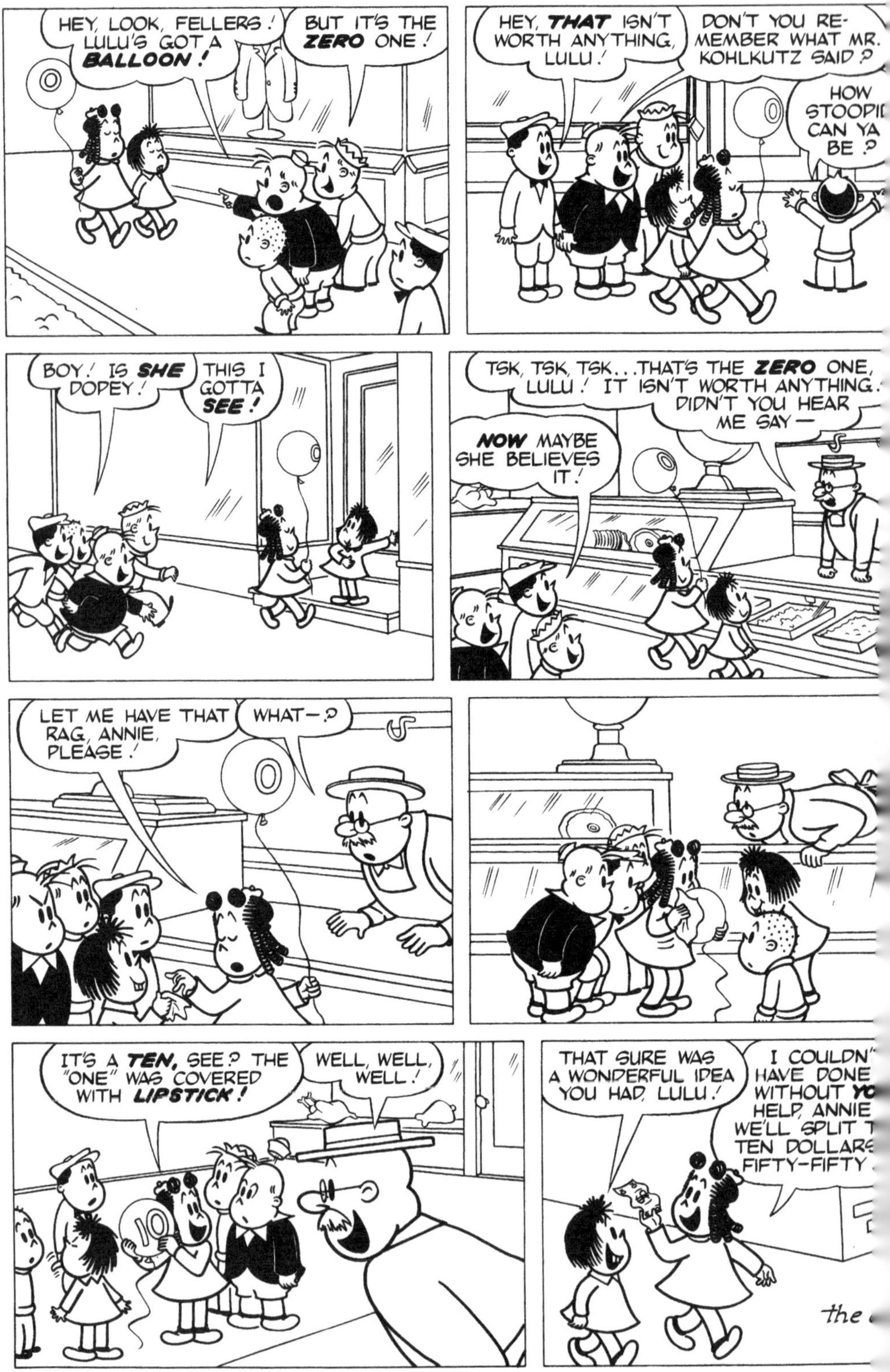

HEY, LOOK, FELLERS! LULU'S GOT A **BALLOON**!
BUT IT'S THE **ZERO** ONE!
HEY, **THAT** ISN'T WORTH ANYTHING, LULU!
DON'T YOU RE-MEMBER WHAT MR. KOHLKUTZ SAID?
HOW STOOPI CAN YA BE?
BOY! IS **SHE** DOPEY!
THIS I GOTTA **SEE**!
TSK, TSK, TSK...THAT'S THE **ZERO** ONE, LULU! IT ISN'T WORTH ANYTHING. DIDN'T YOU HEAR ME SAY—
NOW MAYBE SHE BELIEVES IT!
LET ME HAVE THAT RAG, ANNIE, PLEASE!
WHAT—?
IT'S A **TEN**, SEE? THE "ONE" WAS COVERED WITH **LIPSTICK**!
WELL, WELL, WELL!
THAT SURE WAS A WONDERFUL IDEA YOU HAD, LULU!
I COULDN' HAVE DONE WITHOUT YO HELP, ANNIE WE'LL SPLIT T TEN DOLLAR FIFTY-FIFTY

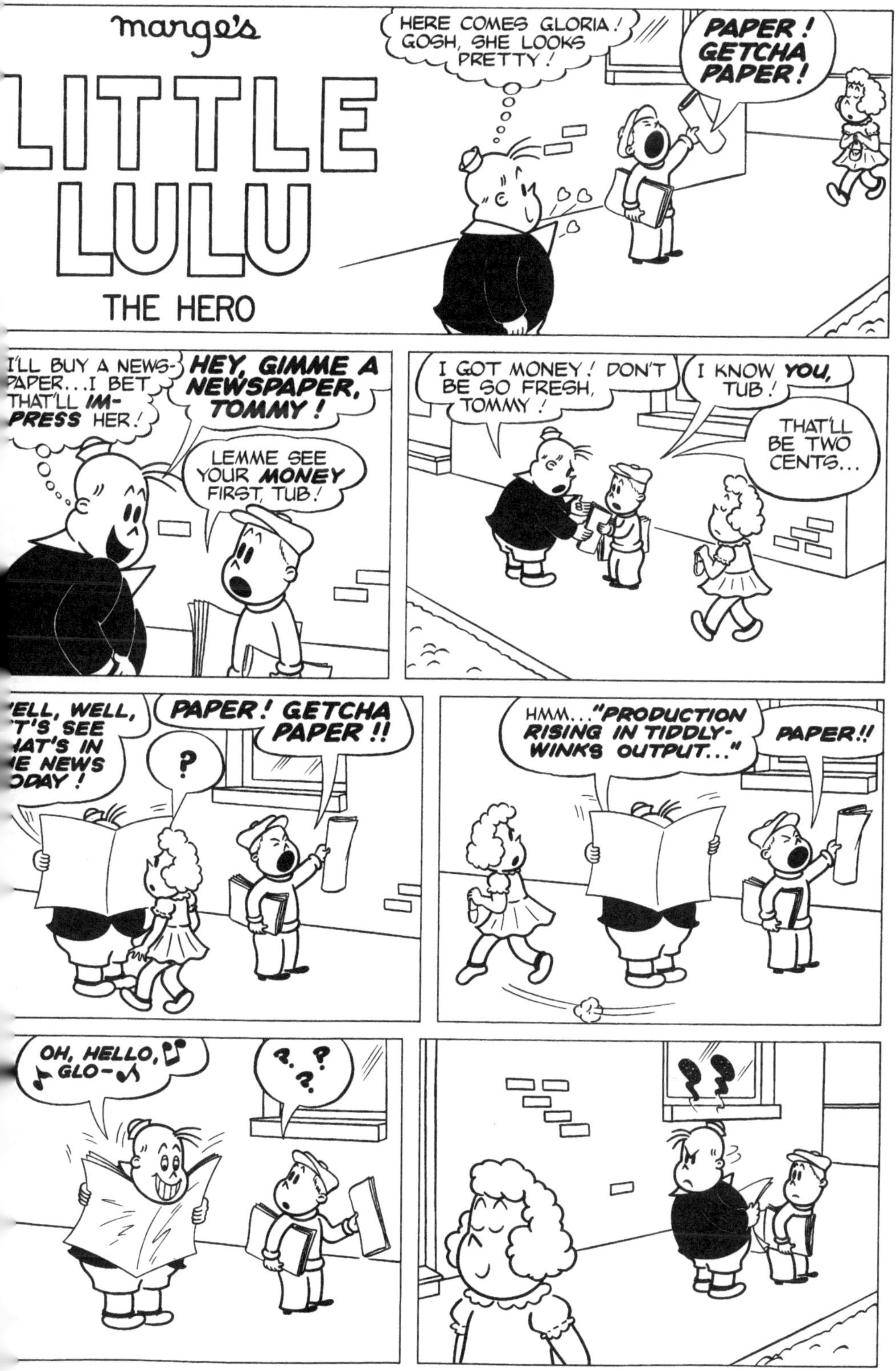
marge's
LITTLE LULU
THE HERO
HERE COMES GLORIA! GOSH, SHE LOOKS PRETTY!
PAPER! GETCHA PAPER!
I'LL BUY A NEWS-PAPER... I BET THAT'LL IM-PRESS HER!
HEY, GIMME A NEWSPAPER, TOMMY!
LEMME SEE YOUR MONEY FIRST, TUB!
I GOT MONEY! DON'T BE SO FRESH, TOMMY!
I KNOW YOU, TUB!
THAT'LL BE TWO CENTS...
ELL, WELL, T'S SEE HAT'S IN E NEWS ODAY!
PAPER! GETCHA PAPER!!
?
HMM... "PRODUCTION RISING IN TIDDLY-WINKS OUTPUT..."
PAPER!!
OH, HELLO, GLO-
? ? ?

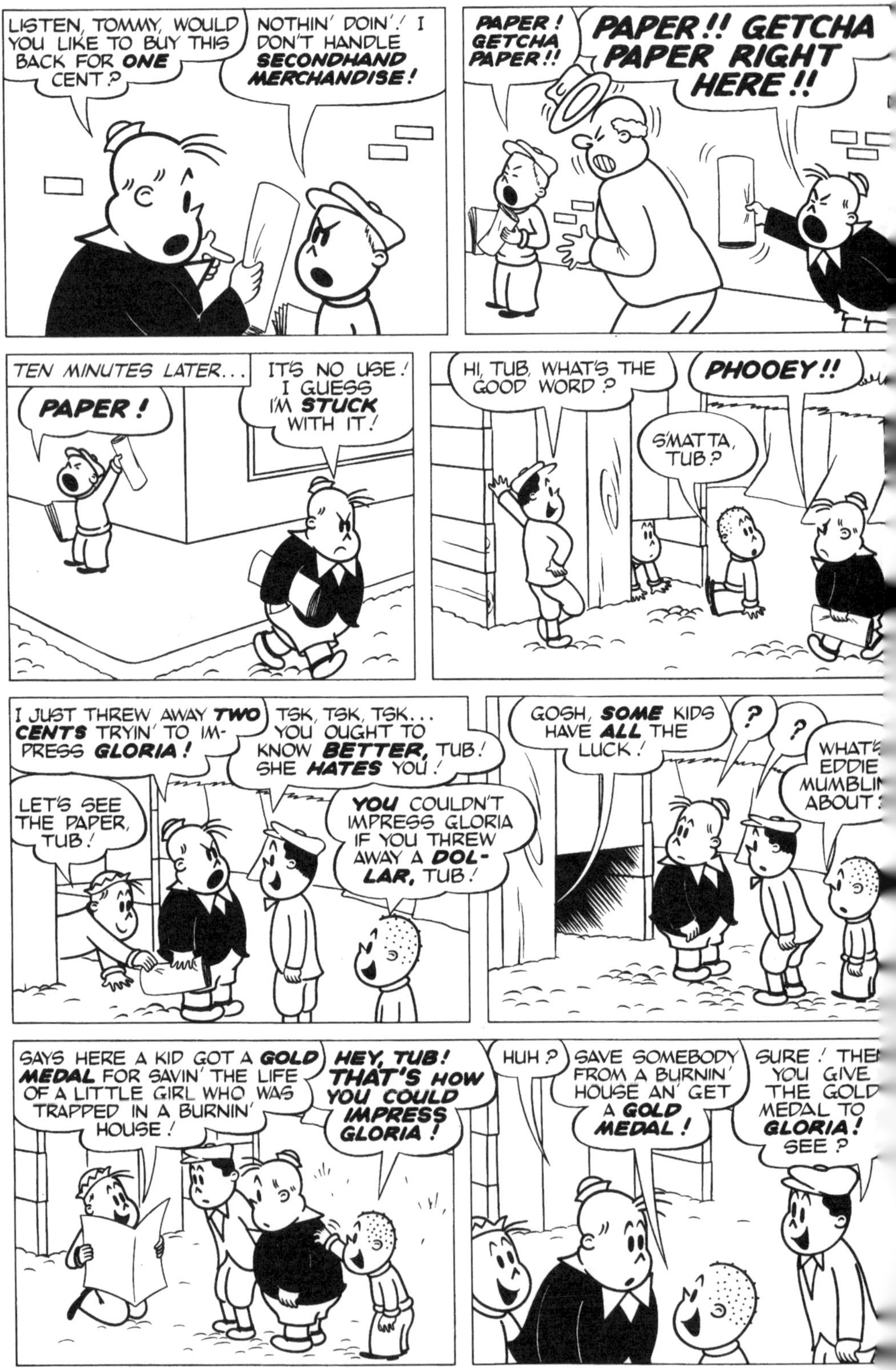
LISTEN, TOMMY, WOULD YOU LIKE TO BUY THIS BACK FOR ONE CENT?
NOTHIN' DOIN'! I DON'T HANDLE SECONDHAND MERCHANDISE!
PAPER! GETCHA PAPER!!
PAPER!! GETCHA PAPER RIGHT HERE!!
TEN MINUTES LATER...
PAPER!
IT'S NO USE! I GUESS I'M STUCK WITH IT!
HI, TUB, WHAT'S THE GOOD WORD?
PHOOEY!!
S'MATTA, TUB?
I JUST THREW AWAY TWO CENTS TRYIN' TO IMPRESS GLORIA!
TSK, TSK, TSK... YOU OUGHT TO KNOW BETTER, TUB! SHE HATES YOU!
LET'S SEE THE PAPER, TUB!
YOU COULDN'T IMPRESS GLORIA IF YOU THREW AWAY A DOLLAR, TUB!
GOSH, SOME KIDS HAVE ALL THE LUCK!
?
?
WHAT' EDDIE MUMBLI ABOUT
SAYS HERE A KID GOT A GOLD MEDAL FOR SAVIN' THE LIFE OF A LITTLE GIRL WHO WAS TRAPPED IN A BURNIN' HOUSE!
HEY, TUB! THAT'S HOW YOU COULD IMPRESS GLORIA!
HUH?
SAVE SOMEBODY FROM A BURNIN' HOUSE AN' GET A GOLD MEDAL!
SURE! THE YOU GIVE THE GOLD MEDAL TO GLORIA! SEE?

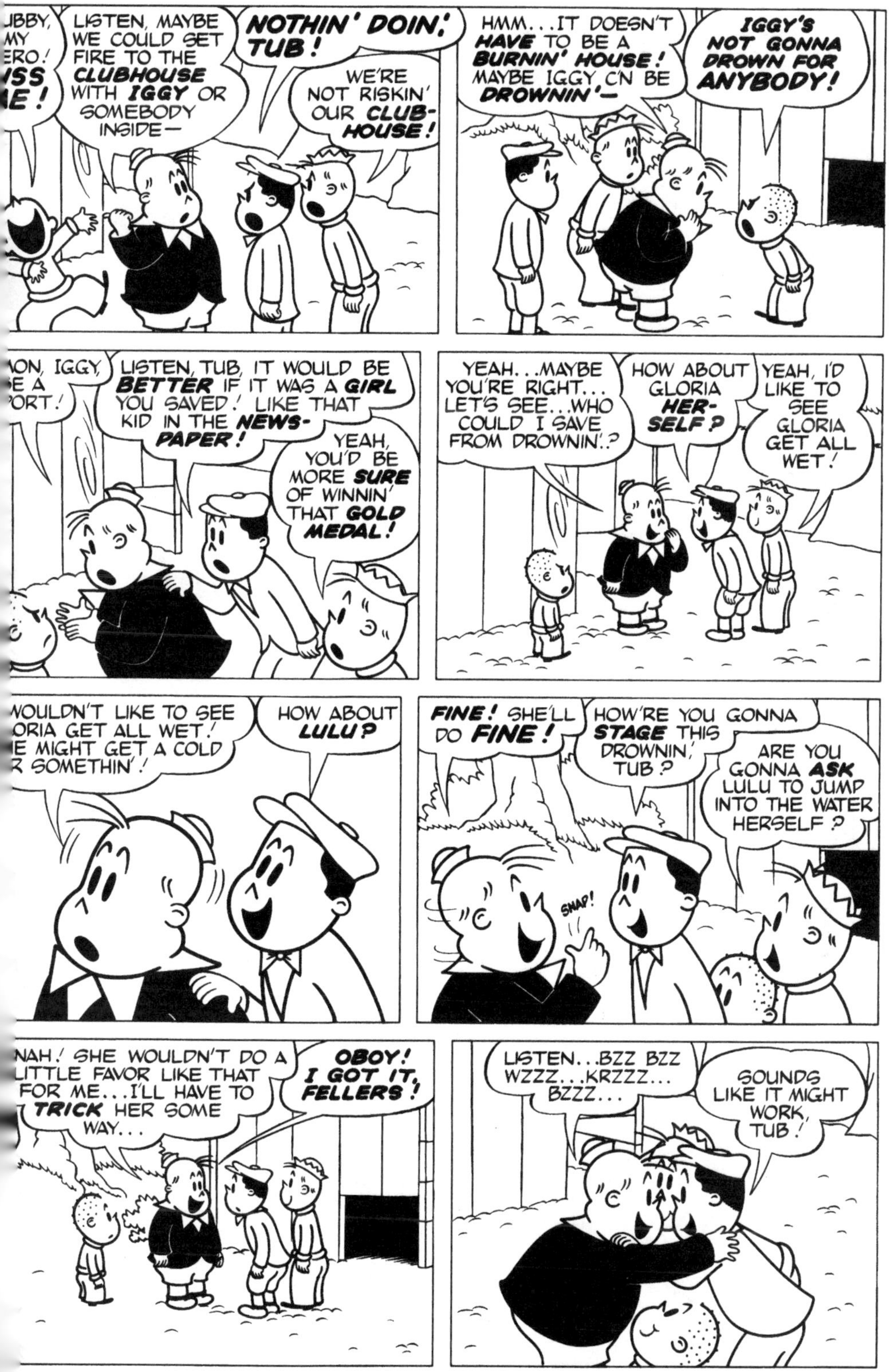

UBBY, MY ERO! ISS E!
LISTEN, MAYBE WE COULD SET FIRE TO THE CLUBHOUSE WITH IGGY OR SOMEBODY INSIDE—
NOTHIN' DOIN', TUB!
WE'RE NOT RISKIN' OUR CLUB-HOUSE!
HMM...IT DOESN'T HAVE TO BE A BURNIN' HOUSE! MAYBE IGGY C'N BE DROWNIN'—
IGGY'S NOT GONNA DROWN FOR ANYBODY!
ON, IGGY, E A ORT!
LISTEN, TUB, IT WOULD BE BETTER IF IT WAS A GIRL YOU SAVED! LIKE THAT KID IN THE NEWS-PAPER!
YEAH, YOU'D BE MORE SURE OF WINNIN' THAT GOLD MEDAL!
YEAH...MAYBE YOU'RE RIGHT... LET'S SEE...WHO COULD I SAVE FROM DROWNIN'..?
HOW ABOUT GLORIA HER-SELF?
YEAH, I'D LIKE TO SEE GLORIA GET ALL WET!
WOULDN'T LIKE TO SEE ORIA GET ALL WET! E MIGHT GET A COLD R SOMETHIN'!
HOW ABOUT LULU?
FINE! SHE'LL DO FINE!
SNAP!
HOW'RE YOU GONNA STAGE THIS DROWNIN', TUB?
ARE YOU GONNA ASK LULU TO JUMP INTO THE WATER HERSELF?
NAH! SHE WOULDN'T DO A LITTLE FAVOR LIKE THAT FOR ME...I'LL HAVE TO TRICK HER SOME WAY...
OBOY! I GOT IT, FELLERS!
LISTEN...BZZ BZZ WZZZ...KRZZZ... BZZZ...
SOUNDS LIKE IT MIGHT WORK, TUB!

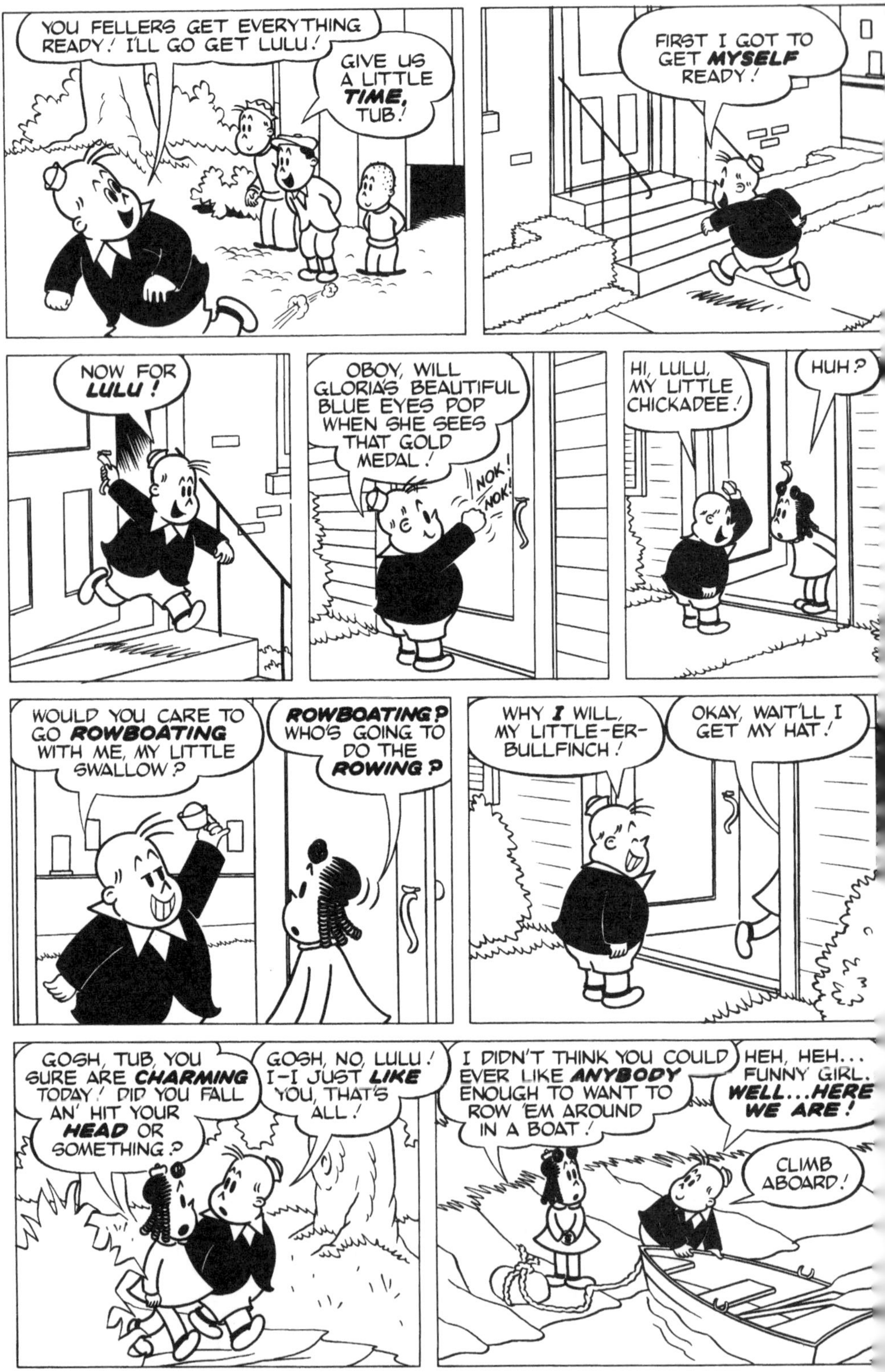
YOU FELLERS GET EVERYTHING READY! I'LL GO GET LULU!
GIVE US A LITTLE **TIME,** TUB!
FIRST I GOT TO GET **MYSELF** READY!
NOW FOR **LULU!**
OBOY, WILL GLORIA'S BEAUTIFUL BLUE EYES POP WHEN SHE SEES THAT GOLD MEDAL!
NOK! NOK!
HI, LULU, MY LITTLE CHICKADEE!
HUH?
WOULD YOU CARE TO GO **ROWBOATING** WITH ME, MY LITTLE SWALLOW?
ROWBOATING? WHO'S GOING TO DO THE **ROWING?**
WHY **I** WILL, MY LITTLE-ER-BULLFINCH!
OKAY, WAIT'LL I GET MY HAT!
GOSH, TUB, YOU SURE ARE **CHARMING** TODAY! DID YOU FALL AN' HIT YOUR **HEAD** OR SOMETHING?
GOSH, NO, LULU! I-I JUST **LIKE** YOU, THAT'S ALL!
I DIDN'T THINK YOU COULD EVER LIKE **ANYBODY** ENOUGH TO WANT TO ROW 'EM AROUND IN A BOAT!
HEH, HEH... FUNNY GIRL. **WELL...HERE WE ARE!**
CLIMB ABOARD!

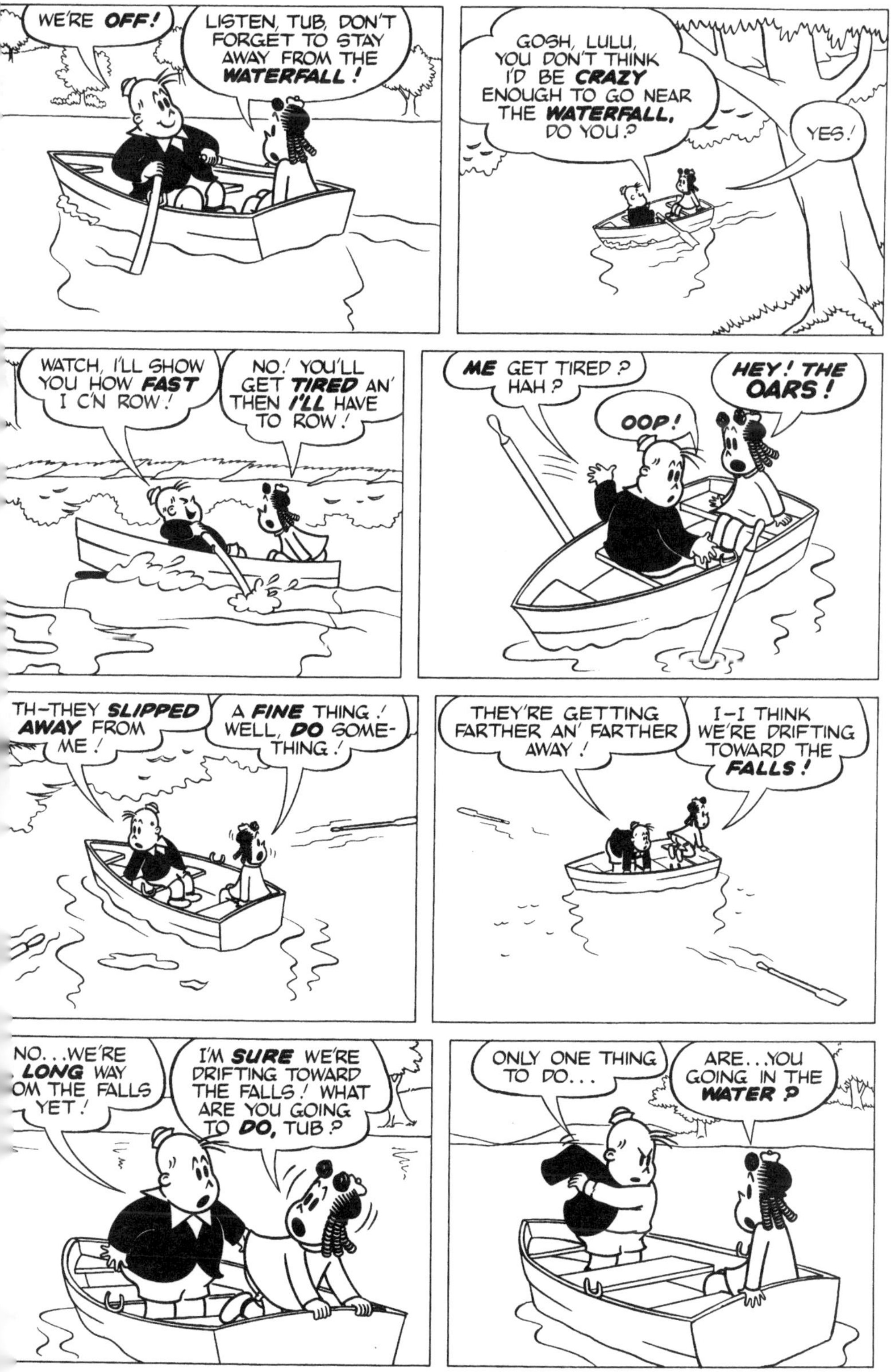
WE'RE OFF!
LISTEN, TUB, DON'T FORGET TO STAY AWAY FROM THE WATERFALL!
GOSH, LULU, YOU DON'T THINK I'D BE CRAZY ENOUGH TO GO NEAR THE WATERFALL, DO YOU?
YES!
WATCH, I'LL SHOW YOU HOW FAST I C'N ROW!
NO! YOU'LL GET TIRED AN' THEN I'LL HAVE TO ROW!
ME GET TIRED? HAH?
OOP!
HEY! THE OARS!
TH-THEY SLIPPED AWAY FROM ME!
A FINE THING! WELL, DO SOMETHING!
THEY'RE GETTING FARTHER AN' FARTHER AWAY!
I-I THINK WE'RE DRIFTING TOWARD THE FALLS!
NO...WE'RE LONG WAY OM THE FALLS YET!
I'M SURE WE'RE DRIFTING TOWARD THE FALLS! WHAT ARE YOU GOING TO DO, TUB?
ONLY ONE THING TO DO...
ARE...YOU GOING IN THE WATER?

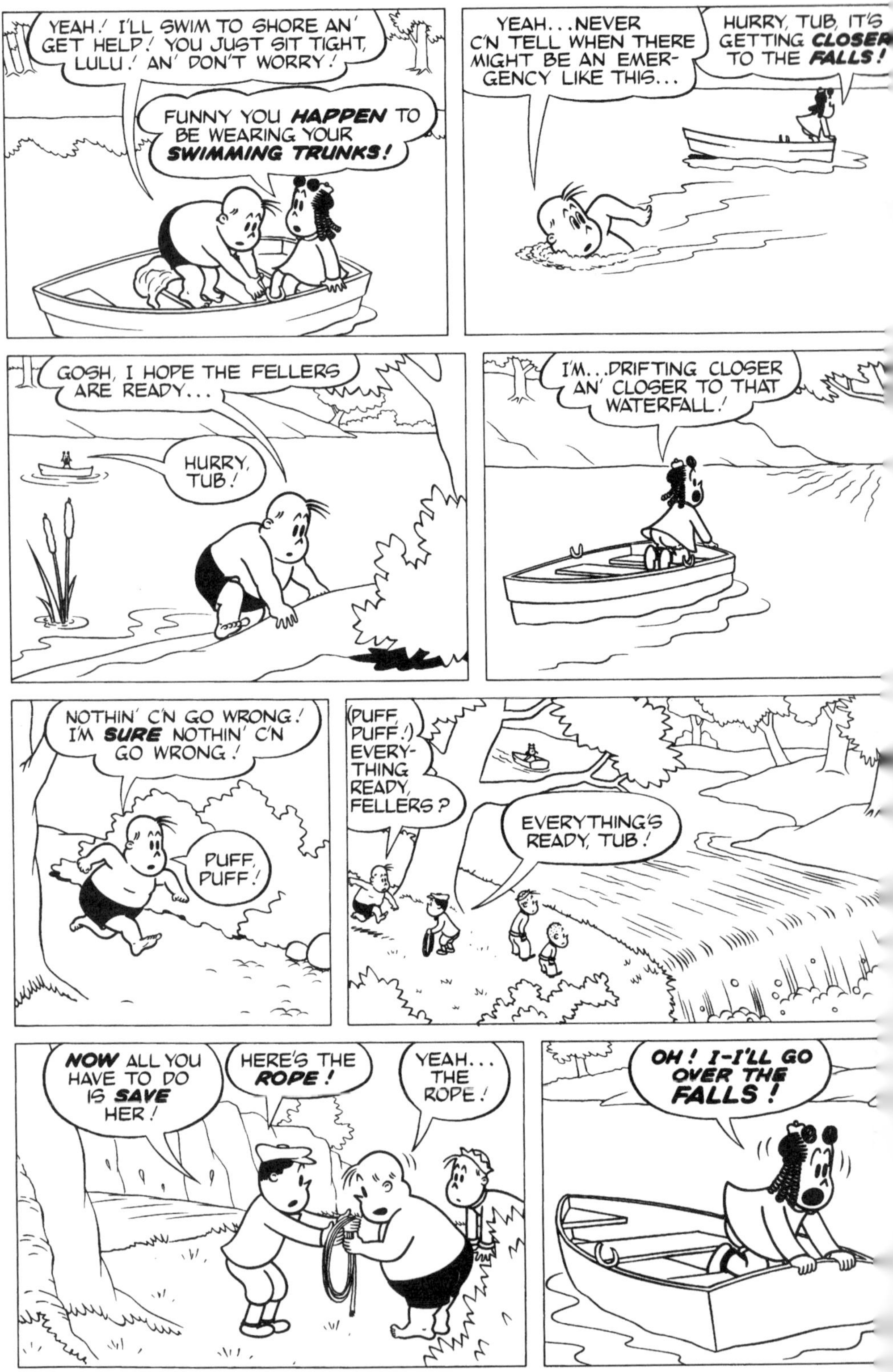
YEAH! I'LL SWIM TO SHORE AN' GET HELP! YOU JUST SIT TIGHT, LULU! AN' DON'T WORRY!
FUNNY YOU HAPPEN TO BE WEARING YOUR SWIMMING TRUNKS!
YEAH...NEVER C'N TELL WHEN THERE MIGHT BE AN EMERGENCY LIKE THIS...
HURRY, TUB, IT'S GETTING CLOSER TO THE FALLS!
GOSH, I HOPE THE FELLERS ARE READY...
HURRY, TUB!
I'M...DRIFTING CLOSER AN' CLOSER TO THAT WATERFALL!
NOTHIN' C'N GO WRONG! I'M SURE NOTHIN' C'N GO WRONG!
PUFF, PUFF!
(PUFF, PUFF!) EVERYTHING READY, FELLERS?
EVERYTHING'S READY, TUB!
NOW ALL YOU HAVE TO DO IS SAVE HER!
HERE'S THE ROPE!
YEAH... THE ROPE!
OH! I-I'LL GO OVER THE FALLS!

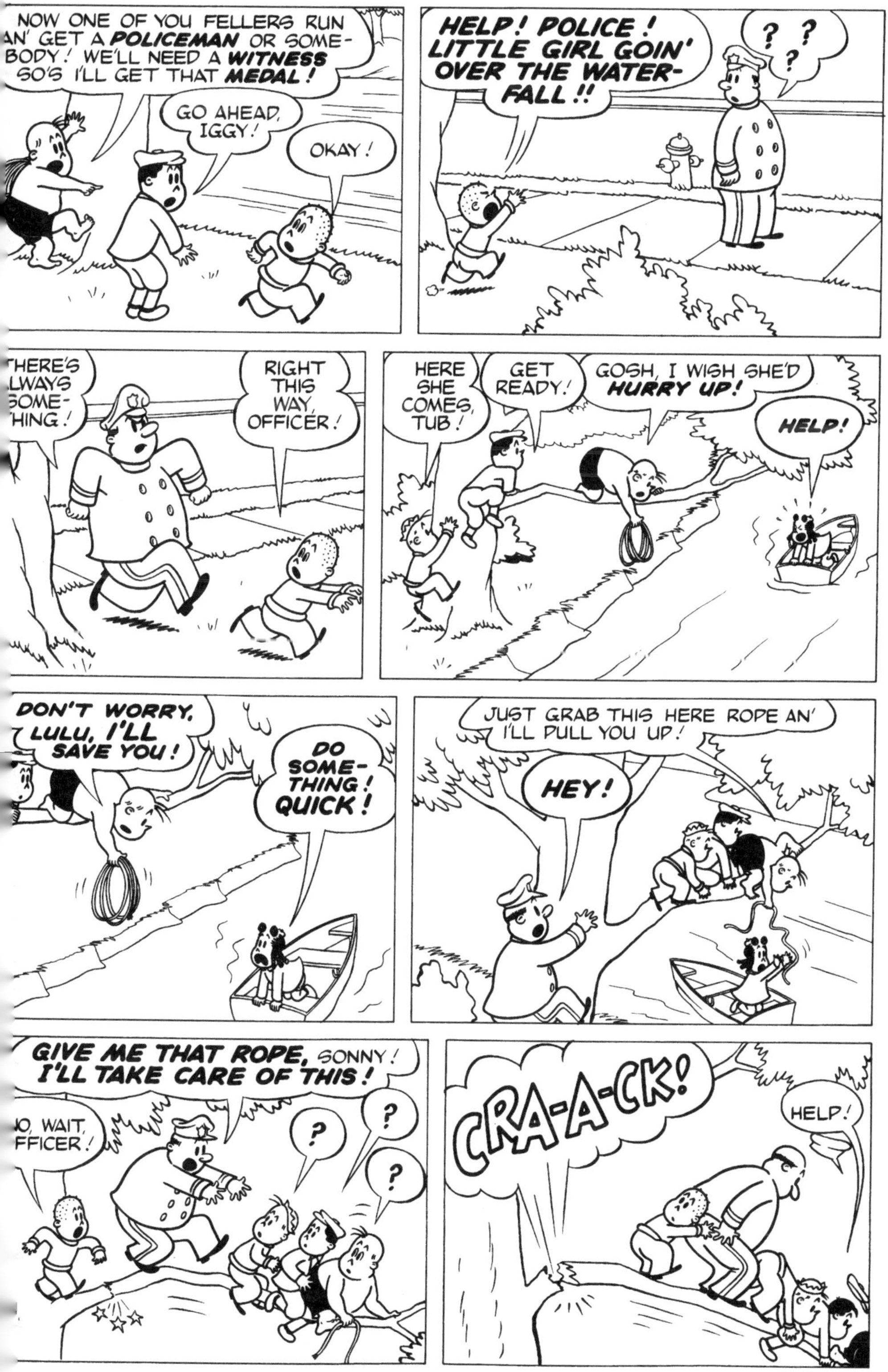

NOW ONE OF YOU FELLERS RUN AN' GET A POLICEMAN OR SOMEBODY! WE'LL NEED A WITNESS SO'S I'LL GET THAT MEDAL!
GO AHEAD, IGGY!
OKAY!
HELP! POLICE! LITTLE GIRL GOIN' OVER THE WATER-FALL!!
? ? ?
THERE'S ALWAYS SOMETHING!
RIGHT THIS WAY, OFFICER!
HERE SHE COMES, TUB!
GET READY!
GOSH, I WISH SHE'D HURRY UP!
HELP!
DON'T WORRY, LULU, I'LL SAVE YOU!
DO SOMETHING! QUICK!
JUST GRAB THIS HERE ROPE AN' I'LL PULL YOU UP!
HEY!
GIVE ME THAT ROPE, SONNY! I'LL TAKE CARE OF THIS!
NO, WAIT, OFFICER!
?
?
?
CRA-A-CK!
HELP!

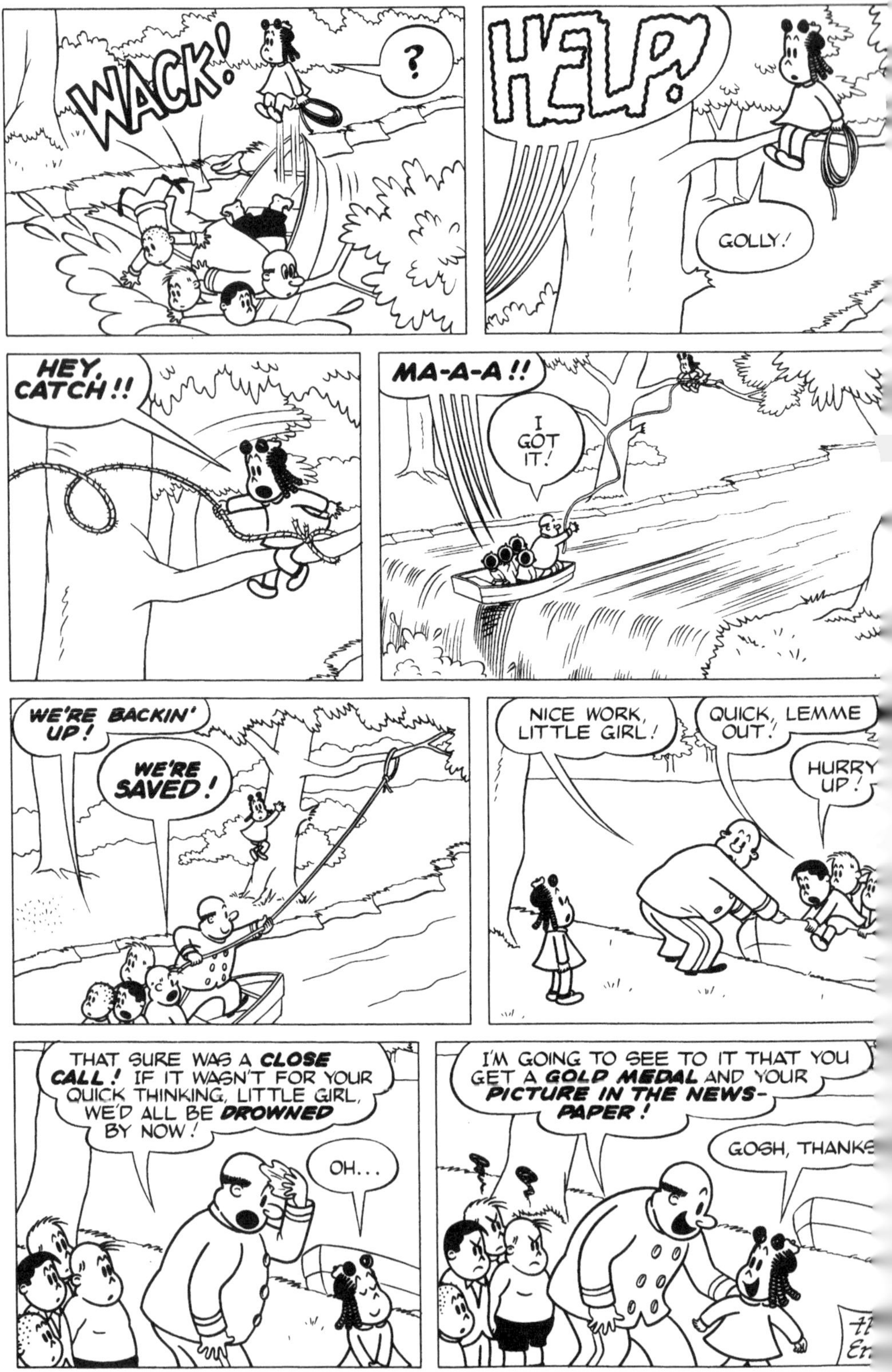

WACK!
?
HELP!
GOLLY!
HEY, CATCH!!
MA-A-A!!
I GOT IT!
WE'RE BACKIN' UP!
WE'RE SAVED!
NICE WORK, LITTLE GIRL!
QUICK, LEMME OUT!
HURRY UP!
THAT SURE WAS A CLOSE CALL! IF IT WASN'T FOR YOUR QUICK THINKING, LITTLE GIRL, WE'D ALL BE DROWNED BY NOW!
OH...
I'M GOING TO SEE TO IT THAT YOU GET A GOLD MEDAL AND YOUR PICTURE IN THE NEWS-PAPER!
GOSH, THANKS

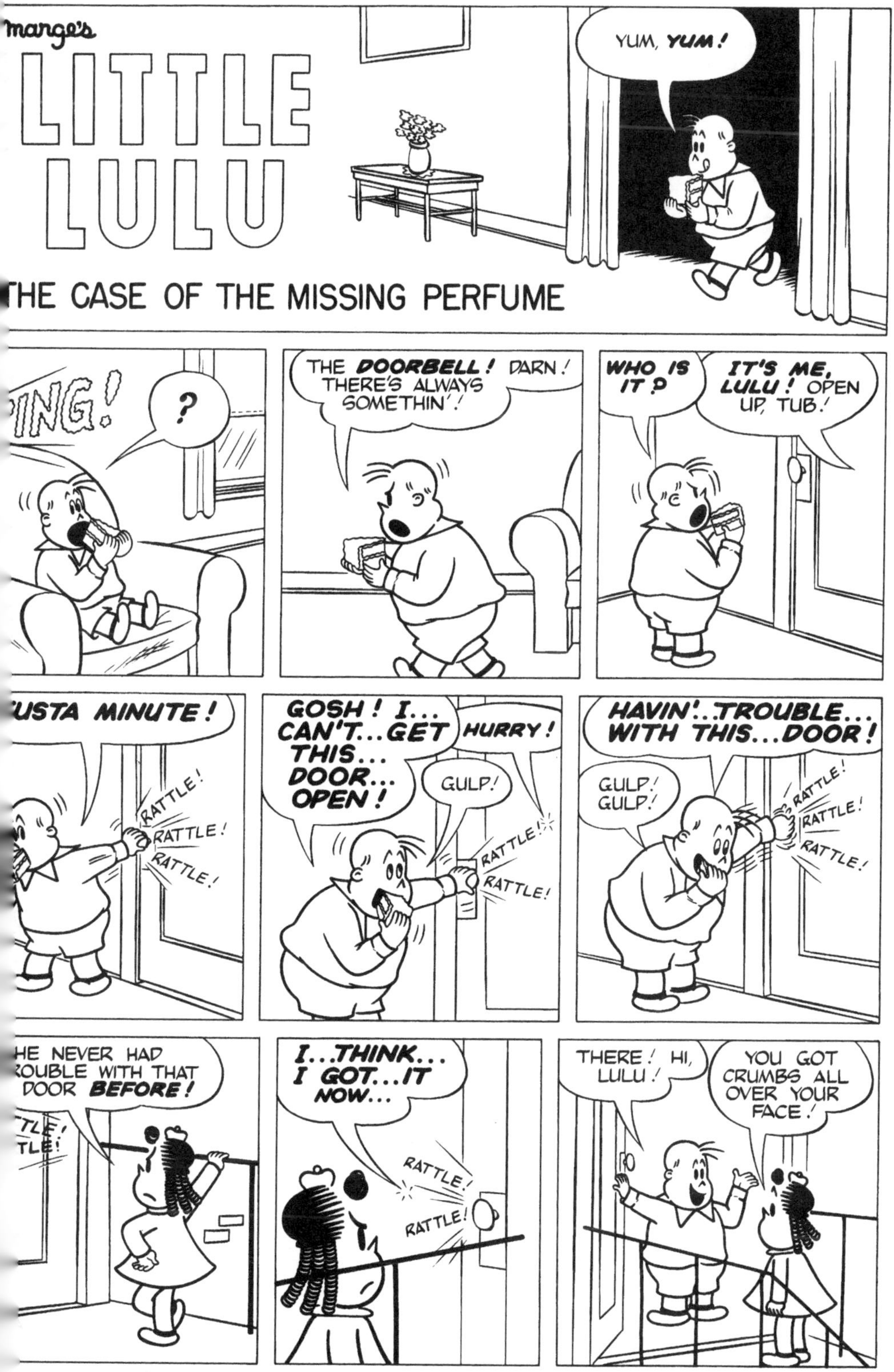
marge's
LITTLE LULU
THE CASE OF THE MISSING PERFUME
YUM, YUM!
ING!
?
THE DOORBELL! DARN! THERE'S ALWAYS SOMETHIN'!
WHO IS IT?
IT'S ME, LULU! OPEN UP, TUB!
USTA MINUTE!
RATTLE!
RATTLE!
RATTLE!
GOSH! I... CAN'T...GET THIS... DOOR... OPEN!
HURRY!
GULP!
RATTLE!
RATTLE!
HAVIN'...TROUBLE... WITH THIS...DOOR!
GULP! GULP!
RATTLE!
RATTLE!
RATTLE!
HE NEVER HAD
ROUBLE WITH THAT DOOR BEFORE!
I...THINK... I GOT...IT NOW...
RATTLE!
RATTLE!
THERE! HI, LULU!
YOU GOT CRUMBS ALL OVER YOUR FACE!

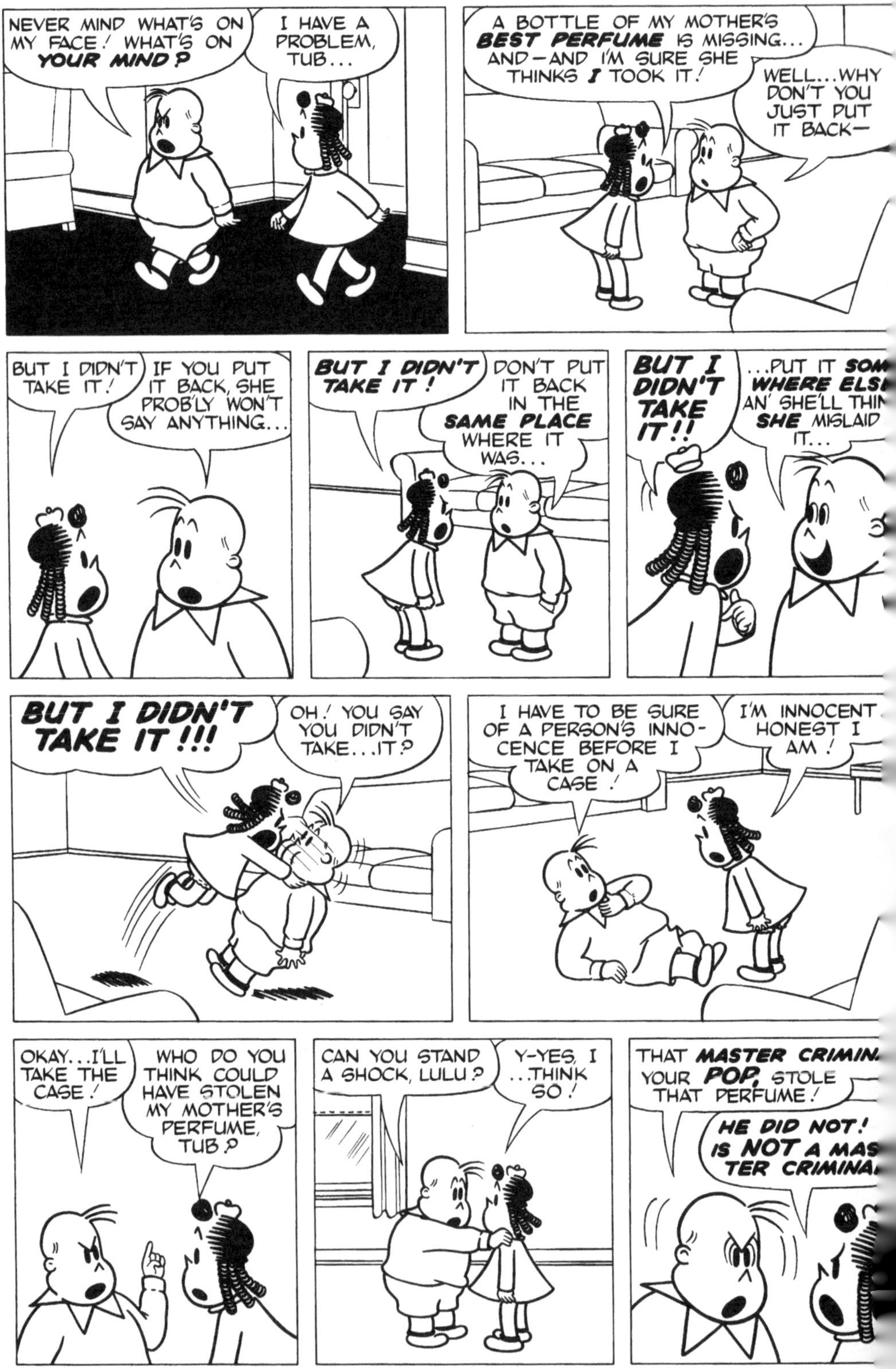

NEVER MIND WHAT'S ON MY FACE! WHAT'S ON **YOUR MIND?**
I HAVE A PROBLEM, TUB...
A BOTTLE OF MY MOTHER'S **BEST PERFUME** IS MISSING... AND—AND I'M SURE SHE THINKS **I** TOOK IT!
WELL...WHY DON'T YOU JUST PUT IT BACK—
BUT I DIDN'T TAKE IT!
IF YOU PUT IT BACK, SHE PROB'LY WON'T SAY ANYTHING...
BUT I DIDN'T TAKE IT!
DON'T PUT IT BACK IN THE **SAME PLACE** WHERE IT WAS...
BUT I DIDN'T TAKE IT!!
...PUT IT **SOM WHERE ELS** AN' SHE'LL THIN **SHE** MISLAID IT...
BUT I DIDN'T TAKE IT!!!
OH! YOU SAY YOU DIDN'T TAKE...IT?
I HAVE TO BE SURE OF A PERSON'S INNO-CENCE BEFORE I TAKE ON A CASE!
I'M INNOCENT HONEST I AM!
OKAY...I'LL TAKE THE CASE!
WHO DO YOU THINK COULD HAVE STOLEN MY MOTHER'S PERFUME, TUB?
CAN YOU STAND A SHOCK, LULU?
Y-YES, I ...THINK SO!
THAT **MASTER CRIMIN** YOUR **POP,** STOLE THAT PERFUME!
HE DID NOT! IS NOT A MAS TER CRIMINA

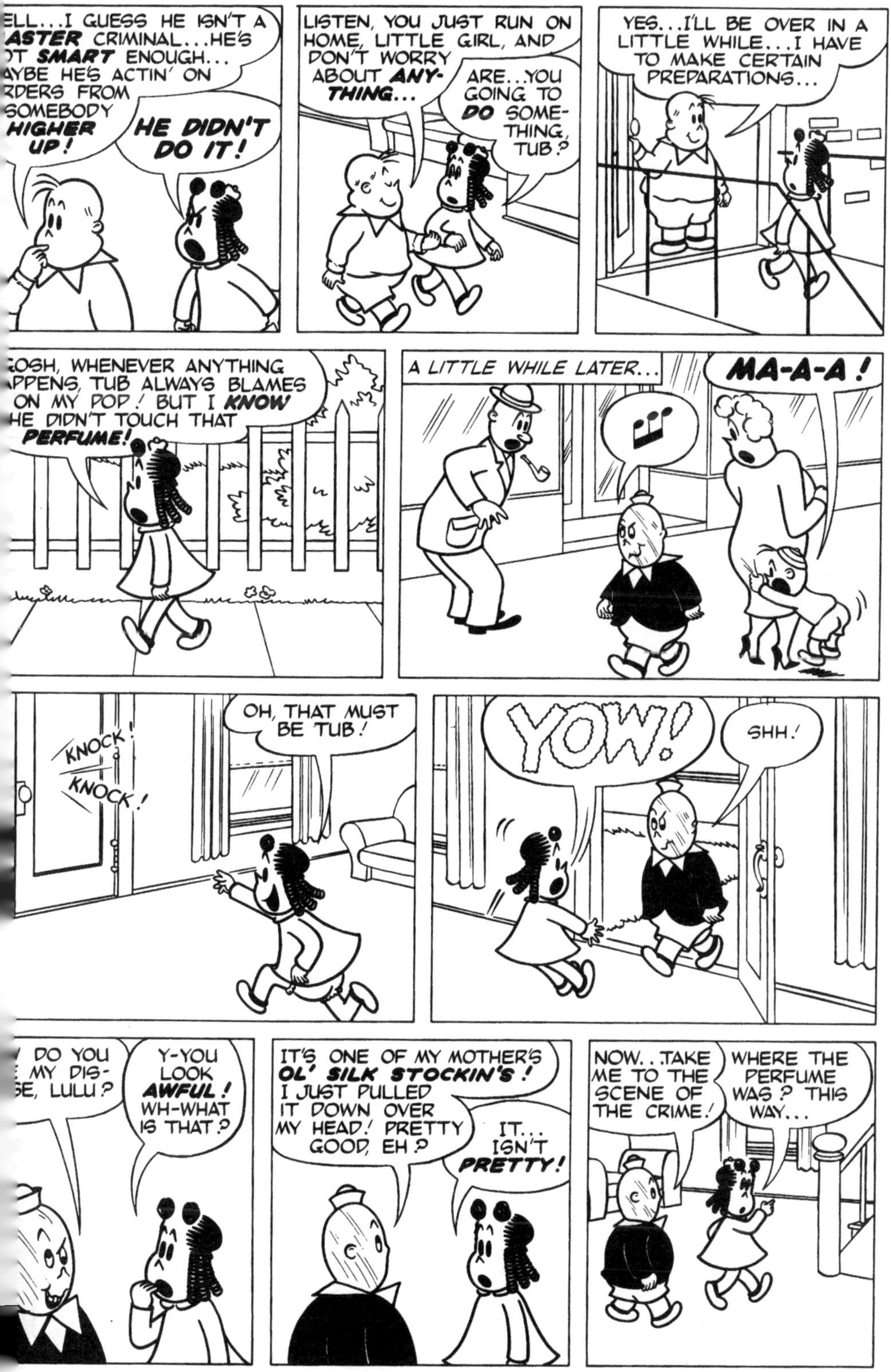
ELL...I GUESS HE ISN'T A ASTER CRIMINAL...HE'S OT SMART ENOUGH... AYBE HE'S ACTIN' ON RDERS FROM SOMEBODY HIGHER UP!
HE DIDN'T DO IT!
LISTEN, YOU JUST RUN ON HOME, LITTLE GIRL, AND DON'T WORRY ABOUT ANY-THING...
ARE...YOU GOING TO DO SOME-THING, TUB?
YES...I'LL BE OVER IN A LITTLE WHILE...I HAVE TO MAKE CERTAIN PREPARATIONS...
OSH, WHENEVER ANYTHING PPENS, TUB ALWAYS BLAMES ON MY POP! BUT I KNOW HE DIDN'T TOUCH THAT PERFUME!
A LITTLE WHILE LATER...
MA-A-A!
KNOCK!
KNOCK!
OH, THAT MUST BE TUB!
YOW!
SHH!
DO YOU E MY DIS- SE, LULU?
Y-YOU LOOK AWFUL! WH-WHAT IS THAT?
IT'S ONE OF MY MOTHER'S OL' SILK STOCKIN'S! I JUST PULLED IT DOWN OVER MY HEAD! PRETTY GOOD, EH?
IT... ISN'T PRETTY!
NOW...TAKE ME TO THE SCENE OF THE CRIME!
WHERE THE PERFUME WAS? THIS WAY...

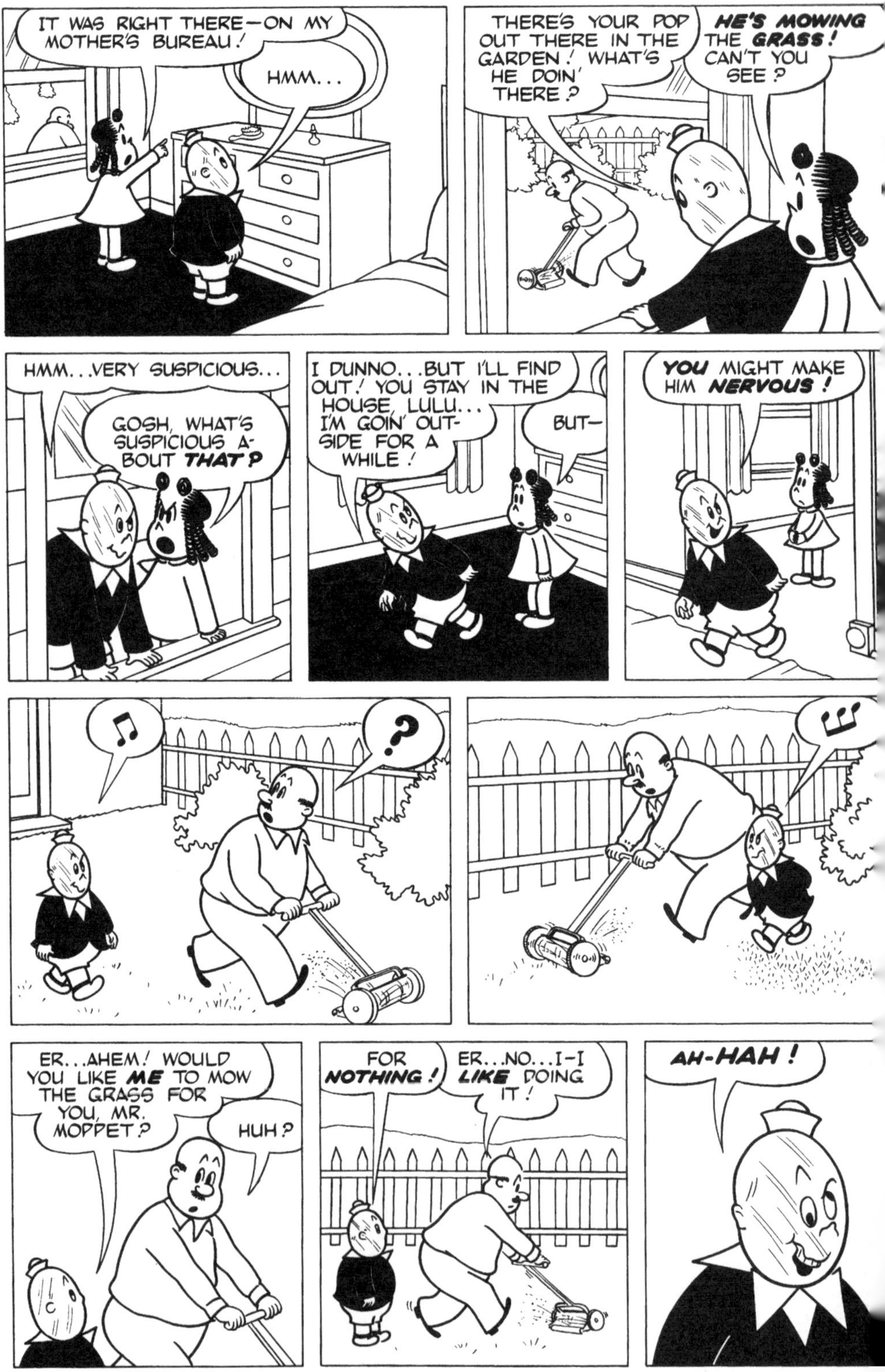
IT WAS RIGHT THERE—ON MY MOTHER'S BUREAU!
HMM...
THERE'S YOUR POP OUT THERE IN THE GARDEN! WHAT'S HE DOIN' THERE?
HE'S MOWING THE GRASS! CAN'T YOU SEE?
HMM...VERY SUSPICIOUS...
GOSH, WHAT'S SUSPICIOUS ABOUT THAT?
I DUNNO...BUT I'LL FIND OUT! YOU STAY IN THE HOUSE, LULU... I'M GOIN' OUTSIDE FOR A WHILE!
BUT—
YOU MIGHT MAKE HIM NERVOUS!
?
ER...AHEM! WOULD YOU LIKE ME TO MOW THE GRASS FOR YOU, MR. MOPPET?
HUH?
FOR NOTHING!
ER...NO...I-I LIKE DOING IT!
AH-HAH!

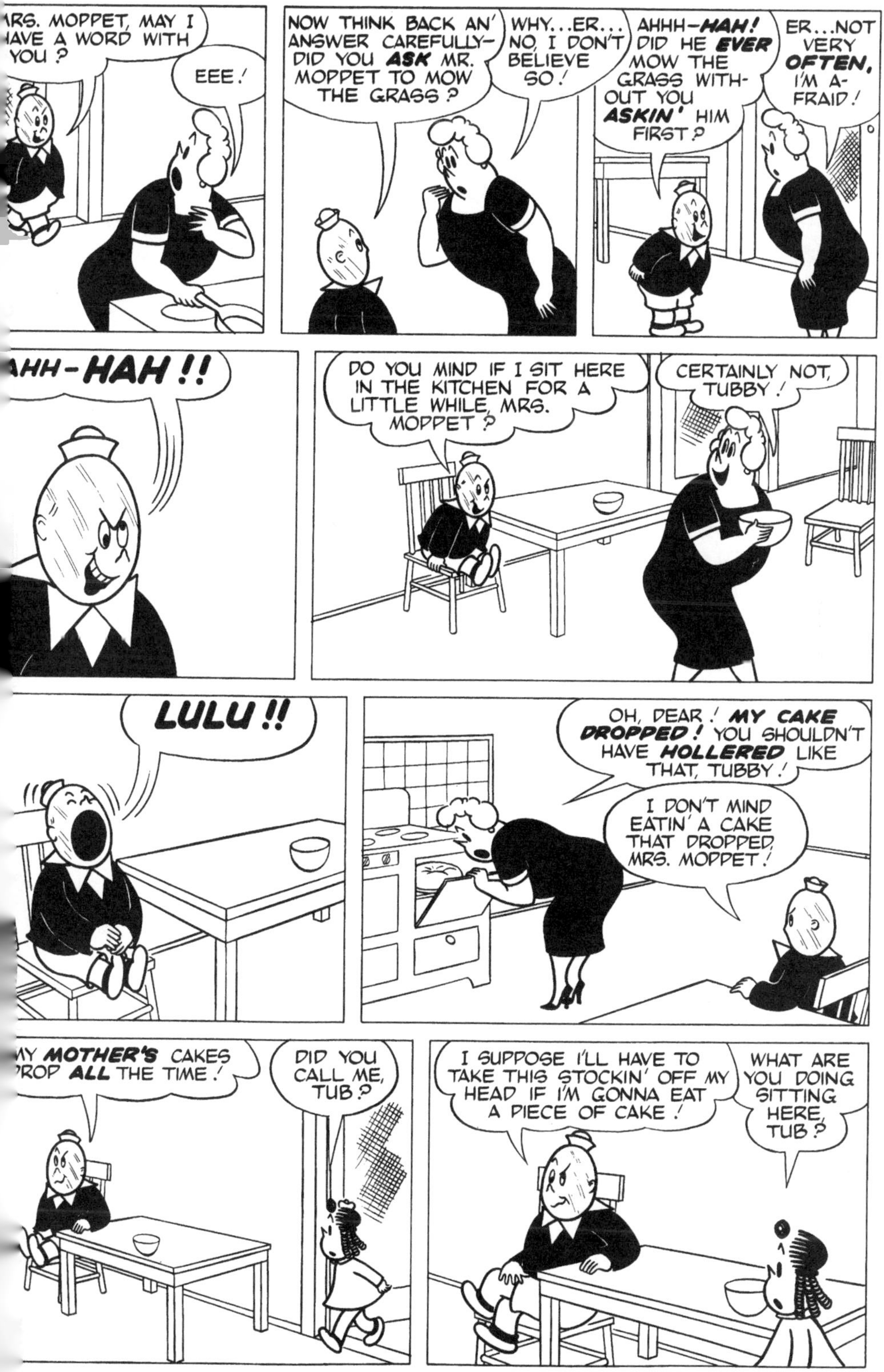

MRS. MOPPET, MAY I HAVE A WORD WITH YOU ?
EEE !
NOW THINK BACK AN' ANSWER CAREFULLY- DID YOU ASK MR. MOPPET TO MOW THE GRASS ?
WHY...ER... NO, I DON'T BELIEVE SO !
AHHH-HAH! DID HE EVER MOW THE GRASS WITH-OUT YOU ASKIN' HIM FIRST ?
ER...NOT VERY OFTEN, I'M A-FRAID !
AHH-HAH !!
DO YOU MIND IF I SIT HERE IN THE KITCHEN FOR A LITTLE WHILE, MRS. MOPPET ?
CERTAINLY NOT, TUBBY !
LULU !!
OH, DEAR ! MY CAKE DROPPED ! YOU SHOULDN'T HAVE HOLLERED LIKE THAT, TUBBY !
I DON'T MIND EATIN' A CAKE THAT DROPPED, MRS. MOPPET !
MY MOTHER'S CAKES DROP ALL THE TIME !
DID YOU CALL ME, TUB ?
I SUPPOSE I'LL HAVE TO TAKE THIS STOCKIN' OFF MY HEAD IF I'M GONNA EAT A PIECE OF CAKE !
WHAT ARE YOU DOING SITTING HERE, TUB ?

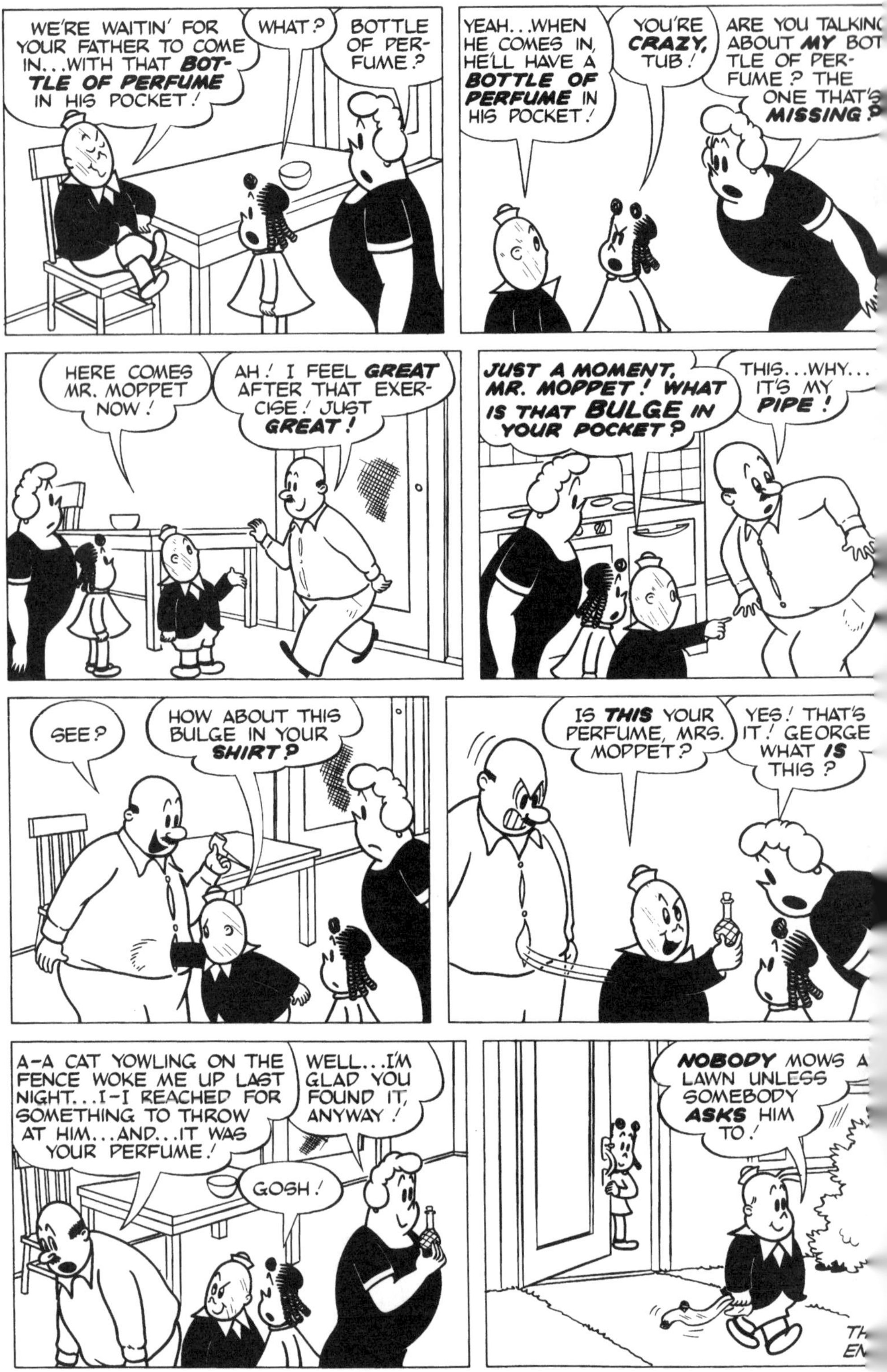
WE'RE WAITIN' FOR YOUR FATHER TO COME IN...WITH THAT **BOTTLE OF PERFUME** IN HIS POCKET!
WHAT?
BOTTLE OF PERFUME?
YEAH...WHEN HE COMES IN, HE'LL HAVE A **BOTTLE OF PERFUME** IN HIS POCKET!
YOU'RE **CRAZY,** TUB!
ARE YOU TALKING ABOUT **MY** BOTTLE OF PERFUME? THE ONE THAT'S **MISSING?**
HERE COMES MR. MOPPET NOW!
AH! I FEEL **GREAT** AFTER THAT EXERCISE! JUST **GREAT!**
JUST A MOMENT, MR. MOPPET! WHAT IS THAT BULGE IN YOUR POCKET?
THIS...WHY... IT'S MY **PIPE!**
SEE?
HOW ABOUT THIS BULGE IN YOUR **SHIRT?**
IS **THIS** YOUR PERFUME, MRS. MOPPET?
YES! THAT'S IT! GEORGE WHAT **IS** THIS?
A-A CAT YOWLING ON THE FENCE WOKE ME UP LAST NIGHT...I-I REACHED FOR SOMETHING TO THROW AT HIM...AND...IT WAS YOUR PERFUME!
WELL...I'M GLAD YOU FOUND IT, ANYWAY!
GOSH!
NOBODY MOWS A LAWN UNLESS SOMEBODY **ASKS** HIM TO!
TH
EN

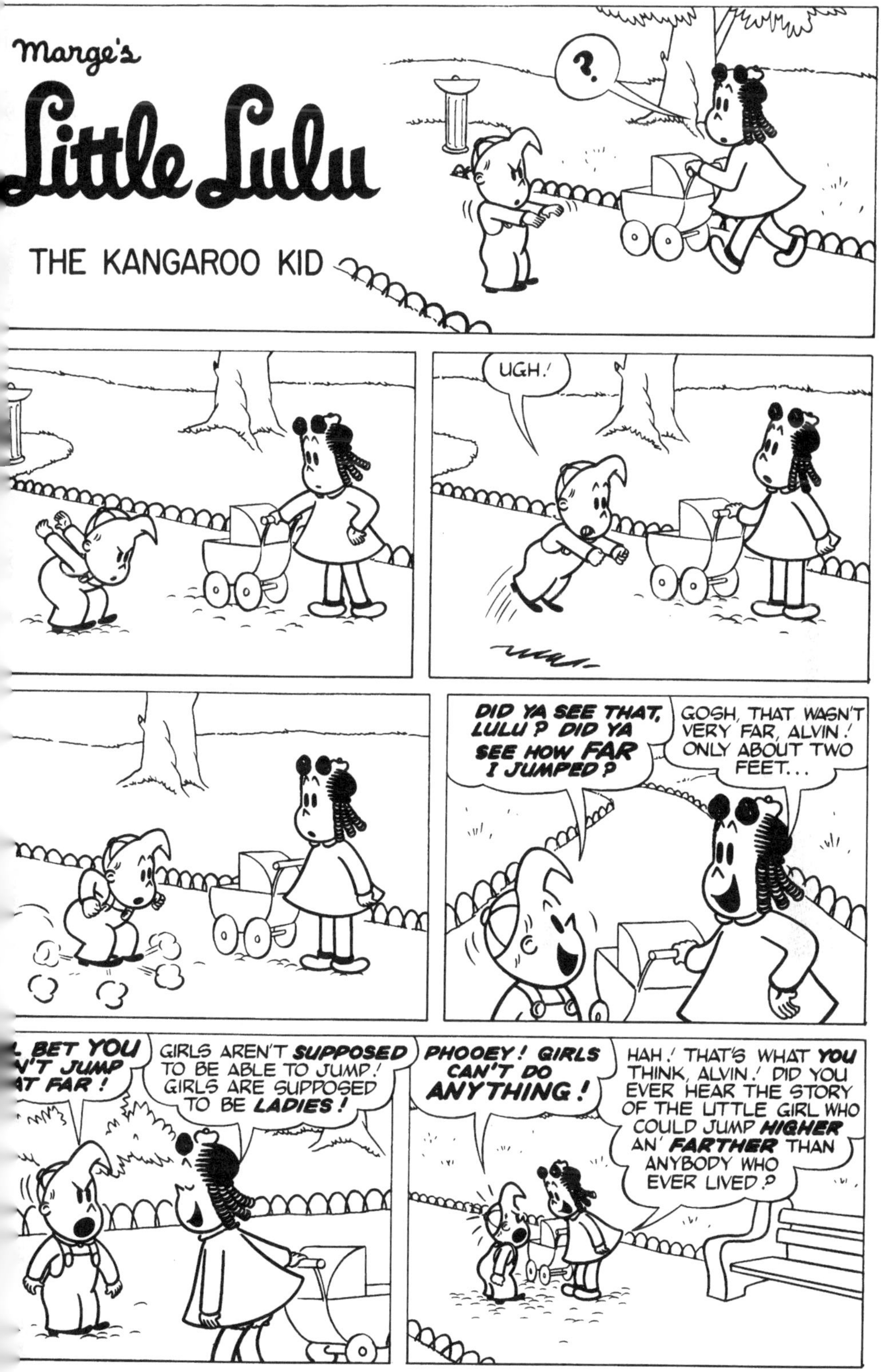
Marge's Little Lulu
THE KANGAROO KID
?
UGH!
DID YA SEE THAT, LULU? DID YA SEE HOW FAR I JUMPED?
GOSH, THAT WASN'T VERY FAR, ALVIN! ONLY ABOUT TWO FEET...
L BET YOU N'T JUMP AT FAR!
GIRLS AREN'T SUPPOSED TO BE ABLE TO JUMP! GIRLS ARE SUPPOSED TO BE LADIES!
PHOOEY! GIRLS CAN'T DO ANYTHING!
HAH! THAT'S WHAT YOU THINK, ALVIN! DID YOU EVER HEAR THE STORY OF THE LITTLE GIRL WHO COULD JUMP HIGHER AN' FARTHER THAN ANYBODY WHO EVER LIVED?

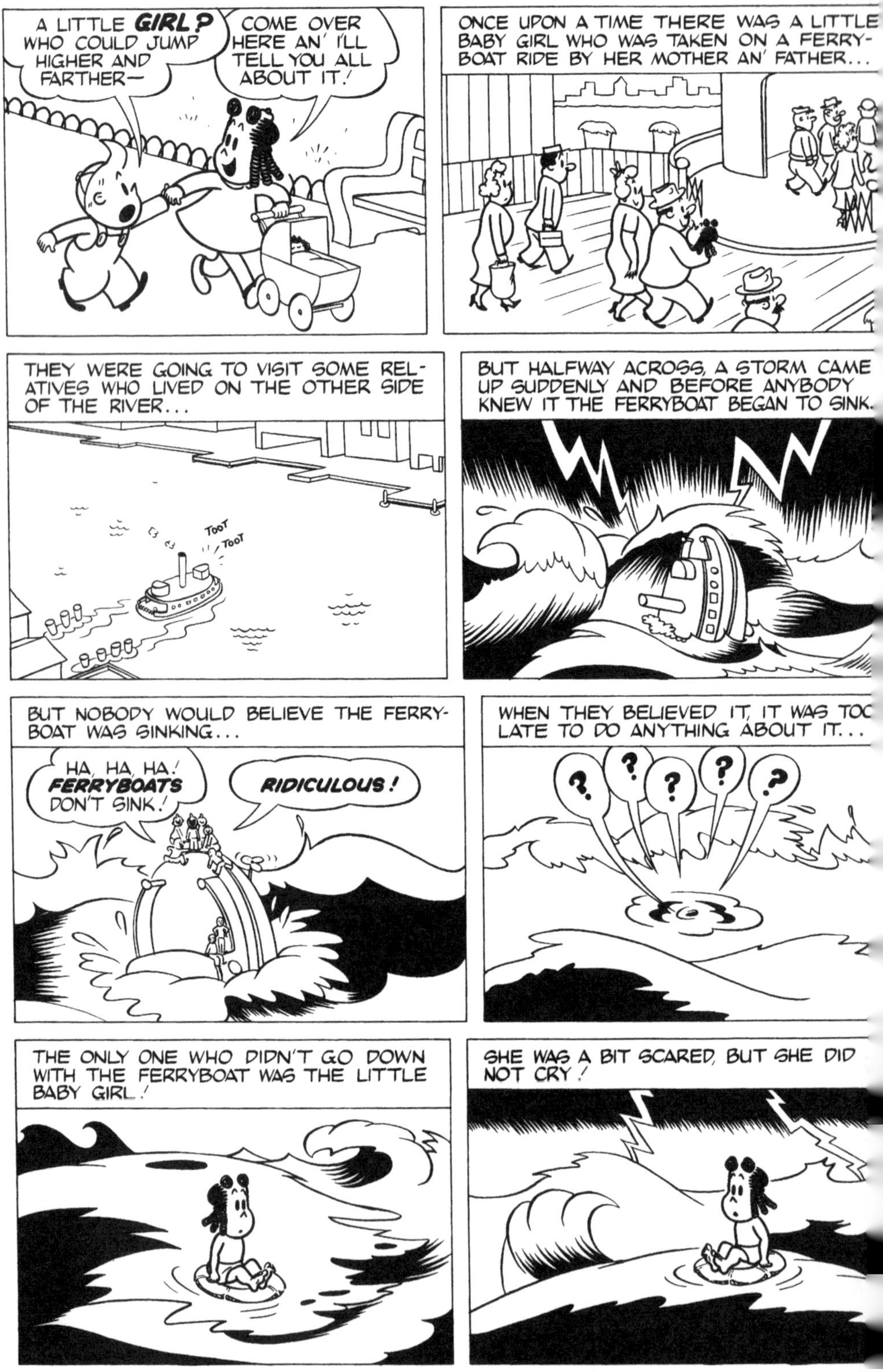

A LITTLE GIRL? WHO COULD JUMP HIGHER AND FARTHER—
COME OVER HERE AN' I'LL TELL YOU ALL ABOUT IT!
ONCE UPON A TIME THERE WAS A LITTLE BABY GIRL WHO WAS TAKEN ON A FERRY-BOAT RIDE BY HER MOTHER AN' FATHER...
THEY WERE GOING TO VISIT SOME REL-ATIVES WHO LIVED ON THE OTHER SIDE OF THE RIVER...
TOOT TOOT
BUT HALFWAY ACROSS, A STORM CAME UP SUDDENLY AND BEFORE ANYBODY KNEW IT THE FERRYBOAT BEGAN TO SINK.
BUT NOBODY WOULD BELIEVE THE FERRY-BOAT WAS SINKING...
HA, HA, HA! FERRYBOATS DON'T SINK!
RIDICULOUS!
WHEN THEY BELIEVED IT, IT WAS TOO LATE TO DO ANYTHING ABOUT IT...
? ? ? ? ?
THE ONLY ONE WHO DIDN'T GO DOWN WITH THE FERRYBOAT WAS THE LITTLE BABY GIRL!
SHE WAS A BIT SCARED, BUT SHE DID NOT CRY!

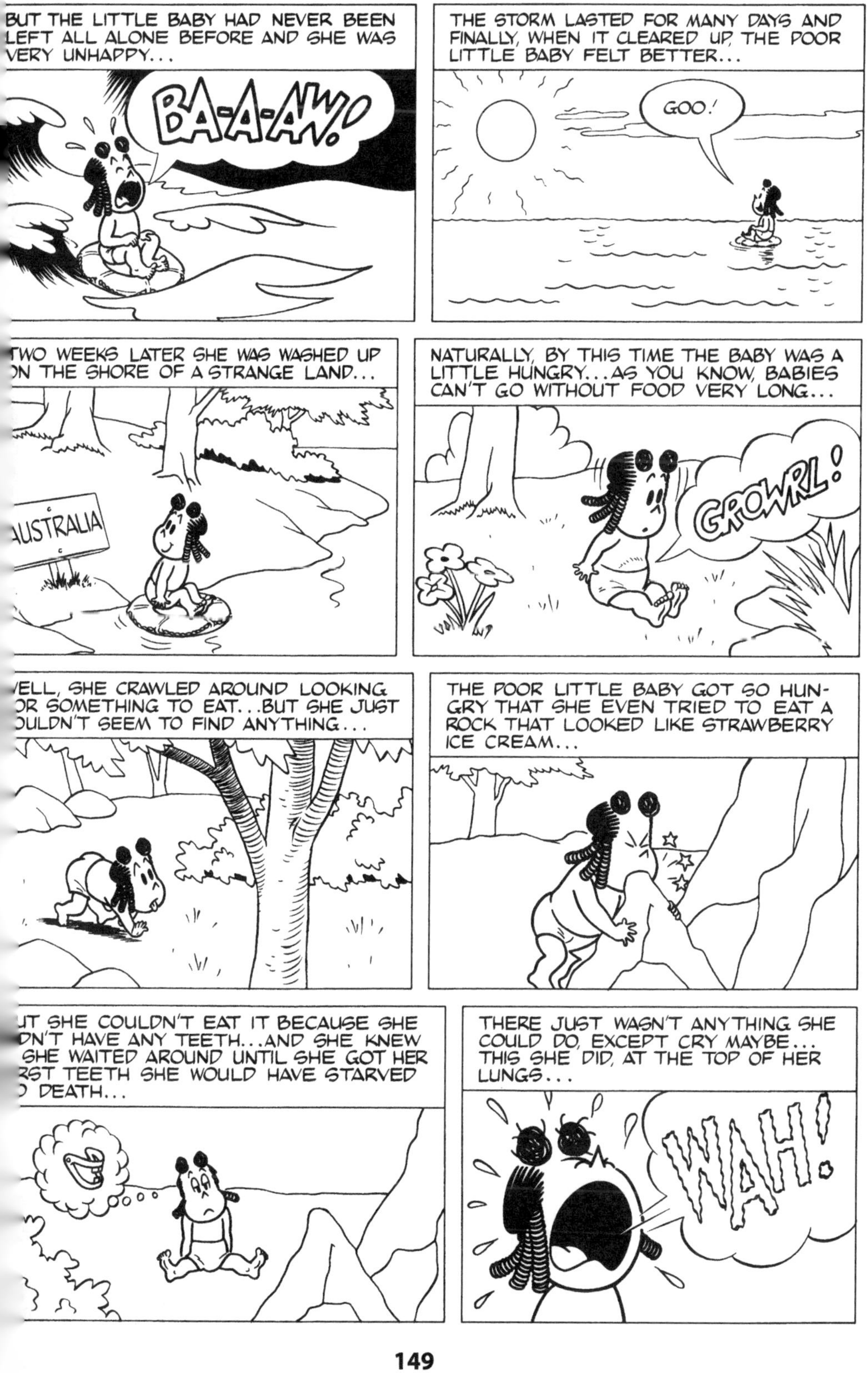

BUT THE LITTLE BABY HAD NEVER BEEN LEFT ALL ALONE BEFORE AND SHE WAS VERY UNHAPPY...
BA-A-AW!
THE STORM LASTED FOR MANY DAYS AND FINALLY, WHEN IT CLEARED UP, THE POOR LITTLE BABY FELT BETTER...
GOO!
TWO WEEKS LATER SHE WAS WASHED UP ON THE SHORE OF A STRANGE LAND...
AUSTRALIA
NATURALLY, BY THIS TIME THE BABY WAS A LITTLE HUNGRY...AS YOU KNOW, BABIES CAN'T GO WITHOUT FOOD VERY LONG...
GROWRL!
VELL, SHE CRAWLED AROUND LOOKING OR SOMETHING TO EAT...BUT SHE JUST OULDN'T SEEM TO FIND ANYTHING...
THE POOR LITTLE BABY GOT SO HUNGRY THAT SHE EVEN TRIED TO EAT A ROCK THAT LOOKED LIKE STRAWBERRY ICE CREAM...
UT SHE COULDN'T EAT IT BECAUSE SHE DN'T HAVE ANY TEETH...AND SHE KNEW SHE WAITED AROUND UNTIL SHE GOT HER RST TEETH SHE WOULD HAVE STARVED D DEATH...
THERE JUST WASN'T ANYTHING SHE COULD DO, EXCEPT CRY MAYBE... THIS SHE DID, AT THE TOP OF HER LUNGS...
WAH!

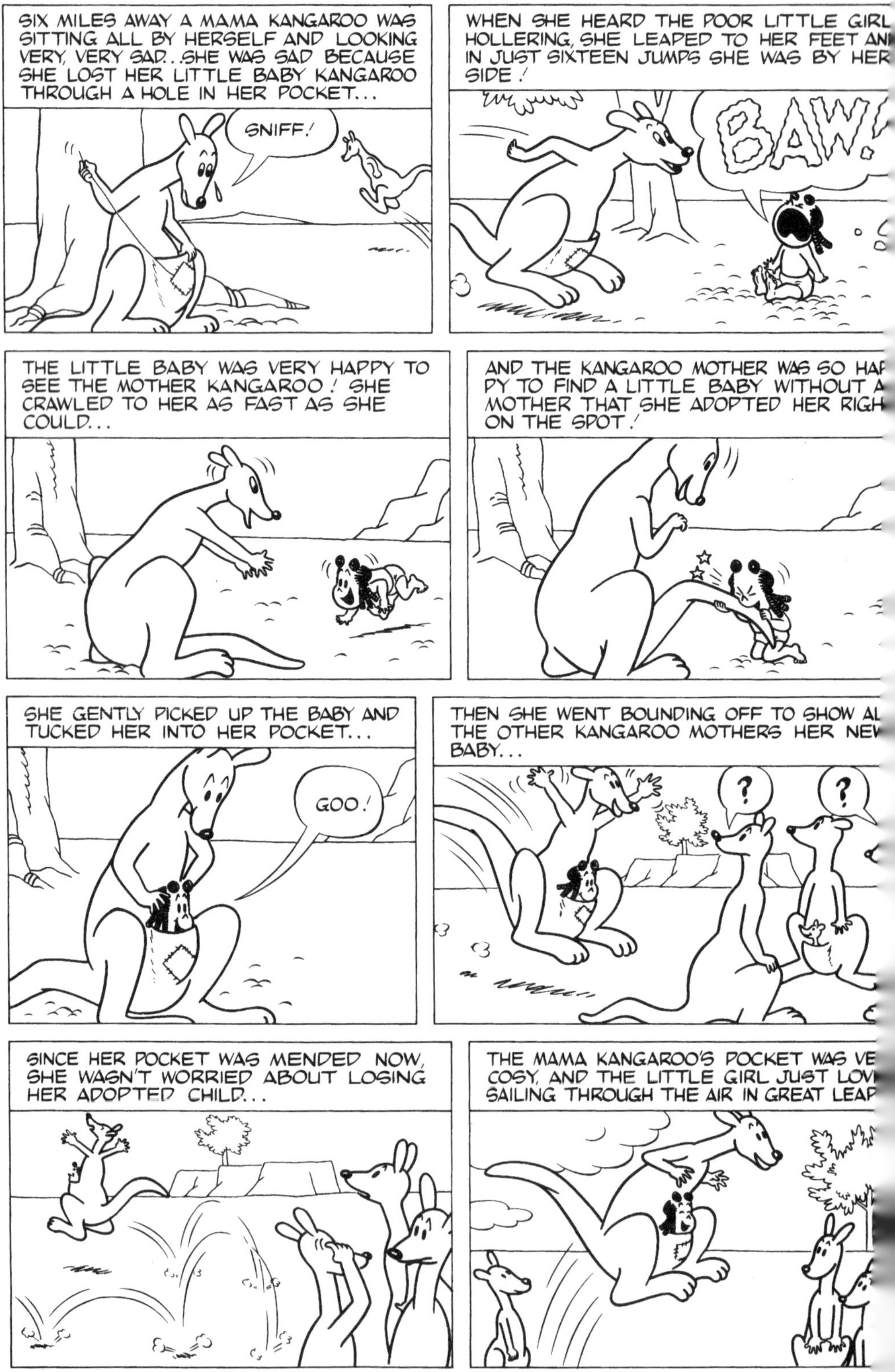
SIX MILES AWAY A MAMA KANGAROO WAS SITTING ALL BY HERSELF AND LOOKING VERY, VERY SAD..SHE WAS SAD BECAUSE SHE LOST HER LITTLE BABY KANGAROO THROUGH A HOLE IN HER POCKET...
SNIFF!
WHEN SHE HEARD THE POOR LITTLE GIRL HOLLERING, SHE LEAPED TO HER FEET AN IN JUST SIXTEEN JUMPS SHE WAS BY HER SIDE!
BAW!
THE LITTLE BABY WAS VERY HAPPY TO SEE THE MOTHER KANGAROO! SHE CRAWLED TO HER AS FAST AS SHE COULD...
AND THE KANGAROO MOTHER WAS SO HAP PY TO FIND A LITTLE BABY WITHOUT A MOTHER THAT SHE ADOPTED HER RIGH ON THE SPOT!
SHE GENTLY PICKED UP THE BABY AND TUCKED HER INTO HER POCKET...
GOO!
THEN SHE WENT BOUNDING OFF TO SHOW AL THE OTHER KANGAROO MOTHERS HER NEW BABY...
?
?
SINCE HER POCKET WAS MENDED NOW, SHE WASN'T WORRIED ABOUT LOSING HER ADOPTED CHILD...
THE MAMA KANGAROO'S POCKET WAS VE COSY, AND THE LITTLE GIRL JUST LOV SAILING THROUGH THE AIR IN GREAT LEAP

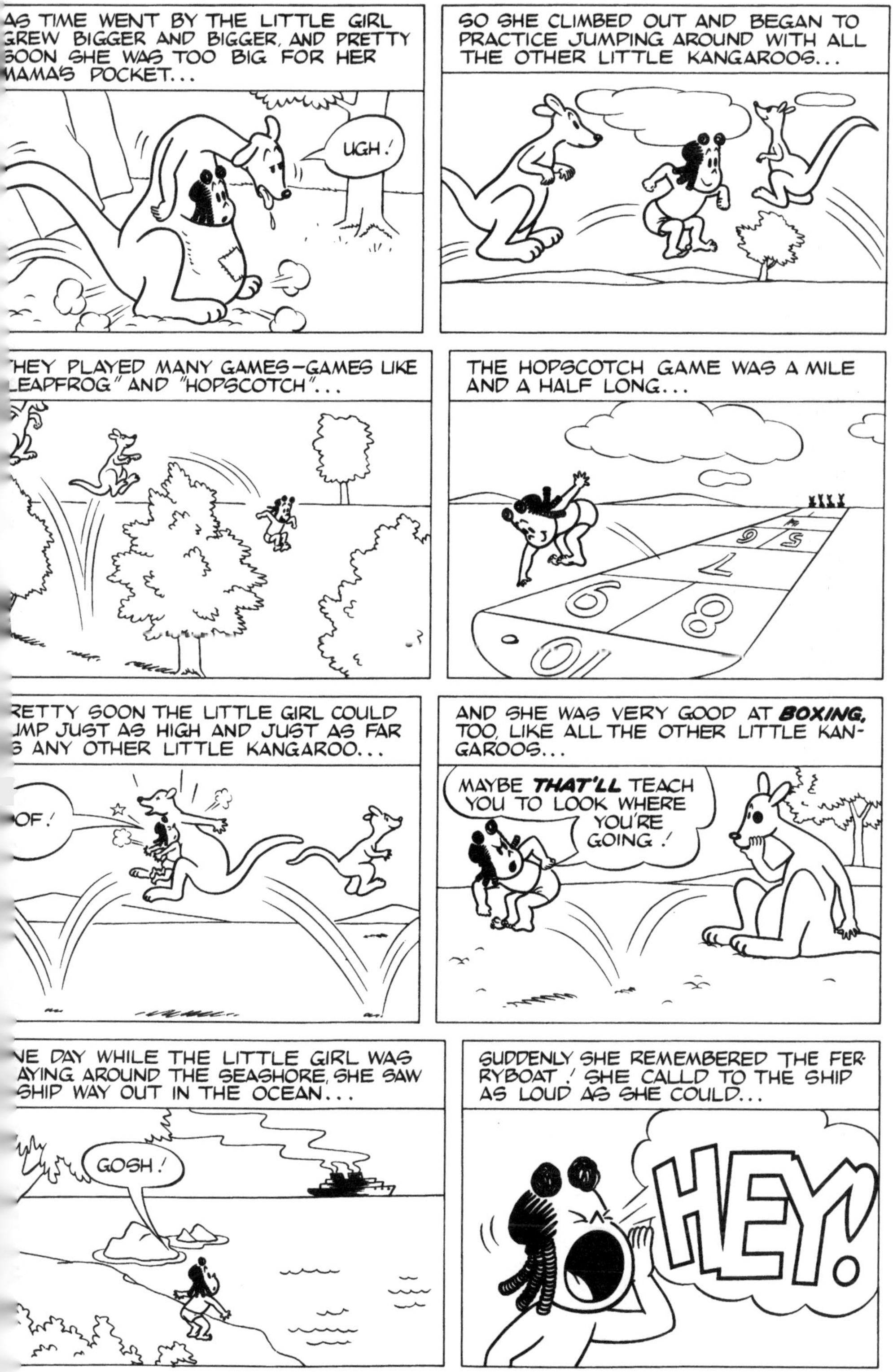

AS TIME WENT BY THE LITTLE GIRL GREW BIGGER AND BIGGER, AND PRETTY SOON SHE WAS TOO BIG FOR HER MAMA'S POCKET...
UGH!
SO SHE CLIMBED OUT AND BEGAN TO PRACTICE JUMPING AROUND WITH ALL THE OTHER LITTLE KANGAROOS...
HEY PLAYED MANY GAMES—GAMES LIKE EAPFROG" AND "HOPSCOTCH"...
THE HOPSCOTCH GAME WAS A MILE AND A HALF LONG...
RETTY SOON THE LITTLE GIRL COULD JMP JUST AS HIGH AND JUST AS FAR S ANY OTHER LITTLE KANGAROO...
OF!
AND SHE WAS VERY GOOD AT **BOXING,** TOO, LIKE ALL THE OTHER LITTLE KANGAROOS...
MAYBE ***THAT'LL*** TEACH YOU TO LOOK WHERE YOU'RE GOING!
NE DAY WHILE THE LITTLE GIRL WAS AYING AROUND THE SEASHORE, SHE SAW SHIP WAY OUT IN THE OCEAN...
GOSH!
SUDDENLY SHE REMEMBERED THE FERRYBOAT! SHE CALLD TO THE SHIP AS LOUD AS SHE COULD...
HEY!

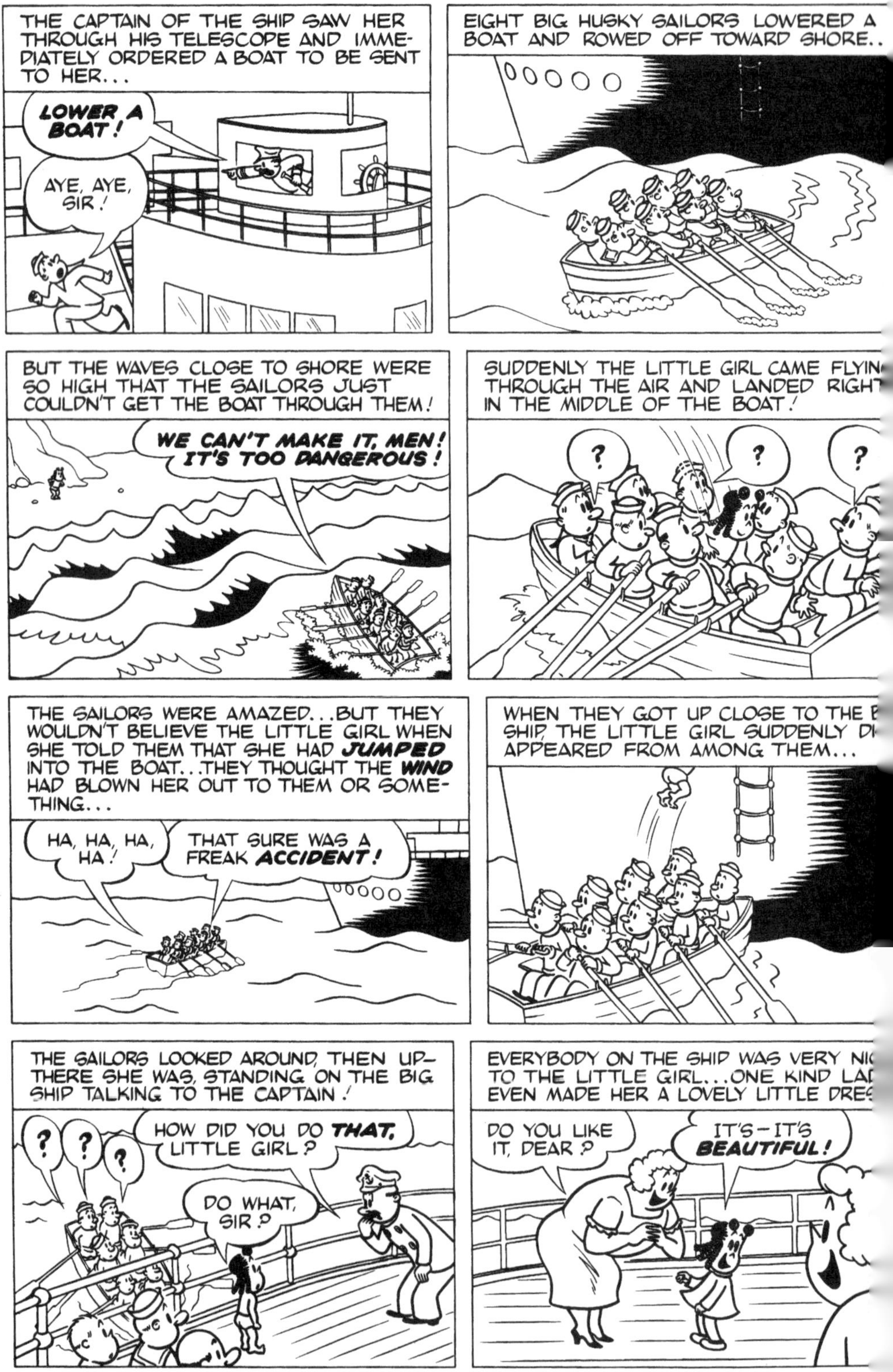
THE CAPTAIN OF THE SHIP SAW HER THROUGH HIS TELESCOPE AND IMMEDIATELY ORDERED A BOAT TO BE SENT TO HER...
LOWER A BOAT!
AYE, AYE, SIR!
EIGHT BIG HUSKY SAILORS LOWERED A BOAT AND ROWED OFF TOWARD SHORE..
BUT THE WAVES CLOSE TO SHORE WERE SO HIGH THAT THE SAILORS JUST COULDN'T GET THE BOAT THROUGH THEM!
WE CAN'T MAKE IT, MEN! IT'S TOO DANGEROUS!
SUDDENLY THE LITTLE GIRL CAME FLYIN
THROUGH THE AIR AND LANDED RIGHT
IN THE MIDDLE OF THE BOAT!
?
?
?
THE SAILORS WERE AMAZED...BUT THEY WOULDN'T BELIEVE THE LITTLE GIRL WHEN SHE TOLD THEM THAT SHE HAD JUMPED INTO THE BOAT...THEY THOUGHT THE WIND HAD BLOWN HER OUT TO THEM OR SOMETHING...
HA, HA, HA, HA!
THAT SURE WAS A FREAK ACCIDENT!
WHEN THEY GOT UP CLOSE TO THE B
SHIP, THE LITTLE GIRL SUDDENLY DI
APPEARED FROM AMONG THEM...
THE SAILORS LOOKED AROUND, THEN UP—THERE SHE WAS, STANDING ON THE BIG SHIP TALKING TO THE CAPTAIN!
?
?
?
HOW DID YOU DO THAT, LITTLE GIRL?
DO WHAT, SIR?
EVERYBODY ON THE SHIP WAS VERY NI
TO THE LITTLE GIRL...ONE KIND LA
EVEN MADE HER A LOVELY LITTLE DRE
DO YOU LIKE IT, DEAR?
IT'S—IT'S BEAUTIFUL!

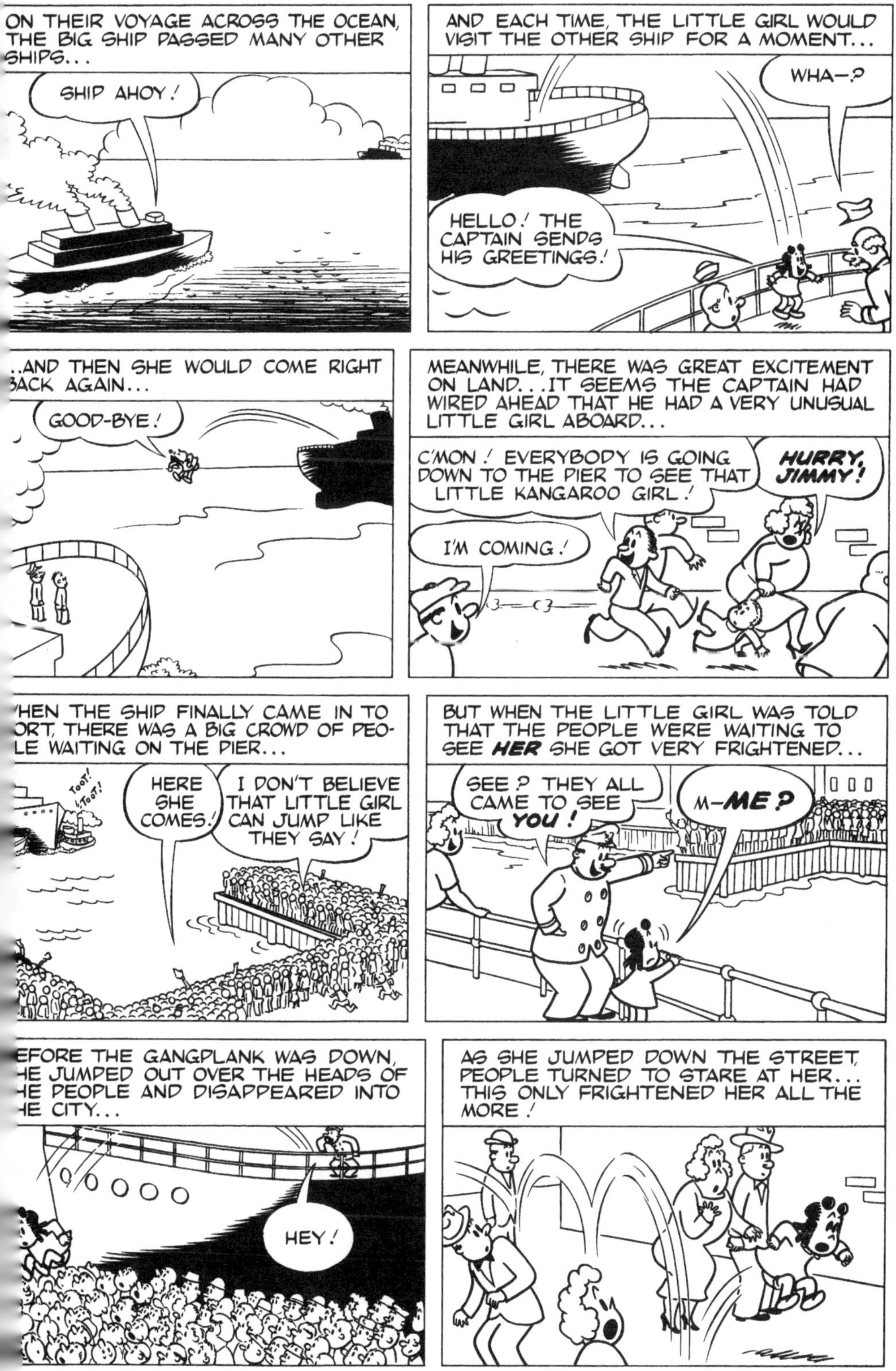
ON THEIR VOYAGE ACROSS THE OCEAN, THE BIG SHIP PASSED MANY OTHER SHIPS...
SHIP AHOY!
AND EACH TIME, THE LITTLE GIRL WOULD VISIT THE OTHER SHIP FOR A MOMENT...
WHA—?
HELLO! THE CAPTAIN SENDS HIS GREETINGS!
..AND THEN SHE WOULD COME RIGHT ACK AGAIN...
GOOD-BYE!
MEANWHILE, THERE WAS GREAT EXCITEMENT ON LAND...IT SEEMS THE CAPTAIN HAD WIRED AHEAD THAT HE HAD A VERY UNUSUAL LITTLE GIRL ABOARD...
C'MON! EVERYBODY IS GOING DOWN TO THE PIER TO SEE THAT LITTLE KANGAROO GIRL!
HURRY, JIMMY!
I'M COMING!
HEN THE SHIP FINALLY CAME IN TO ORT, THERE WAS A BIG CROWD OF PEO- LE WAITING ON THE PIER...
TOOT! TOOT!
HERE SHE COMES!
I DON'T BELIEVE THAT LITTLE GIRL CAN JUMP LIKE THEY SAY!
BUT WHEN THE LITTLE GIRL WAS TOLD THAT THE PEOPLE WERE WAITING TO SEE HER SHE GOT VERY FRIGHTENED...
SEE? THEY ALL CAME TO SEE YOU!
M-ME?
EFORE THE GANGPLANK WAS DOWN, HE JUMPED OUT OVER THE HEADS OF HE PEOPLE AND DISAPPEARED INTO HE CITY...
HEY!
AS SHE JUMPED DOWN THE STREET, PEOPLE TURNED TO STARE AT HER... THIS ONLY FRIGHTENED HER ALL THE MORE!

TO GET OUT OF SIGHT SHE JUMPED THROUGH THE WINDOW OF A BIG BUILDING...

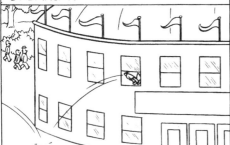

BUT WHEN SHE LANDED INSIDE SHE DISCOVERED SHE WAS RIGHT IN THE MIDDLE OF A **MILLION** PEOPLE!

?

SHE TOOK ANOTHER JUMP TO GET AWAY, BUT SHE WAS **TIRED** NOW AND IT WAS ONLY A **LITTLE** JUMP...

YOW!

OH, I'M SO TIRED!

YOW!

THEN SHE COLLAPSED ON HER FACE!

DID YOU SEE THAT JUMP?

SHE WON THE **CUP!**

PLOP!

WHEN SHE CAME TO, A MAN WAS HANDING HER A BIG, BEAUTIFUL, GOLD CUP, AND EVERYBODY WAS CHEERING!

TAKE IT, IT'S **YOURS!**

THE GREATEST JUMPER OF **ALL TIME!**

AND THEN SUDDENLY A LADY AND A MAN BURST THROUGH THE CROWD AND GRABBED HER UP IN THEIR ARMS! IT WAS HER DEAR **MOTHER** AND **FATHER!**

MY DARLING!

MY BABY!

MY MOM AN' POP!

THEY WEREN'T DROWNED IN THE FERRYBOAT AFTER ALL...IT SEEMS THEY WALKED ALONG THE SUBWAY TUNNEL THAT RUNS UNDER THE RIVER, AN'—

LISTEN, LULU, WHAT I WANNA KNOW IS—

CAN **YOU** JUMP TWO FEET?

ONLY **BOYS** AND **KANGAROOS** JUMP!

the End

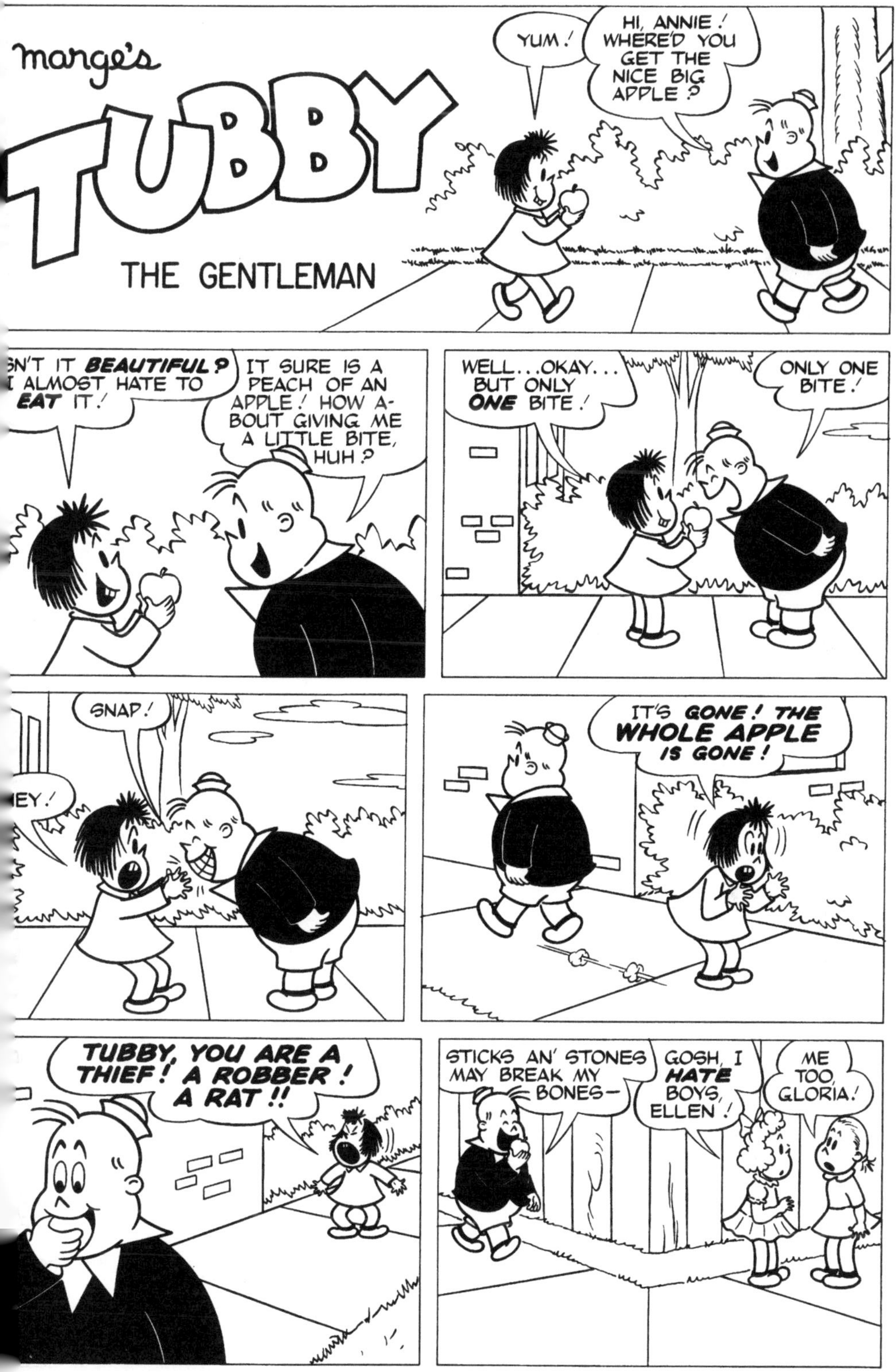
marge's
TUBBY
THE GENTLEMAN
YUM!
HI, ANNIE! WHERE'D YOU GET THE NICE BIG APPLE?
SN'T IT BEAUTIFUL? I ALMOST HATE TO EAT IT!
IT SURE IS A PEACH OF AN APPLE! HOW A-BOUT GIVING ME A LITTLE BITE, HUH?
WELL...OKAY... BUT ONLY ONE BITE!
ONLY ONE BITE!
SNAP!
EY!
IT'S GONE! THE WHOLE APPLE IS GONE!
TUBBY, YOU ARE A THIEF! A ROBBER! A RAT!!
STICKS AN' STONES MAY BREAK MY BONES—
GOSH, I HATE BOYS, ELLEN!
ME TOO, GLORIA!

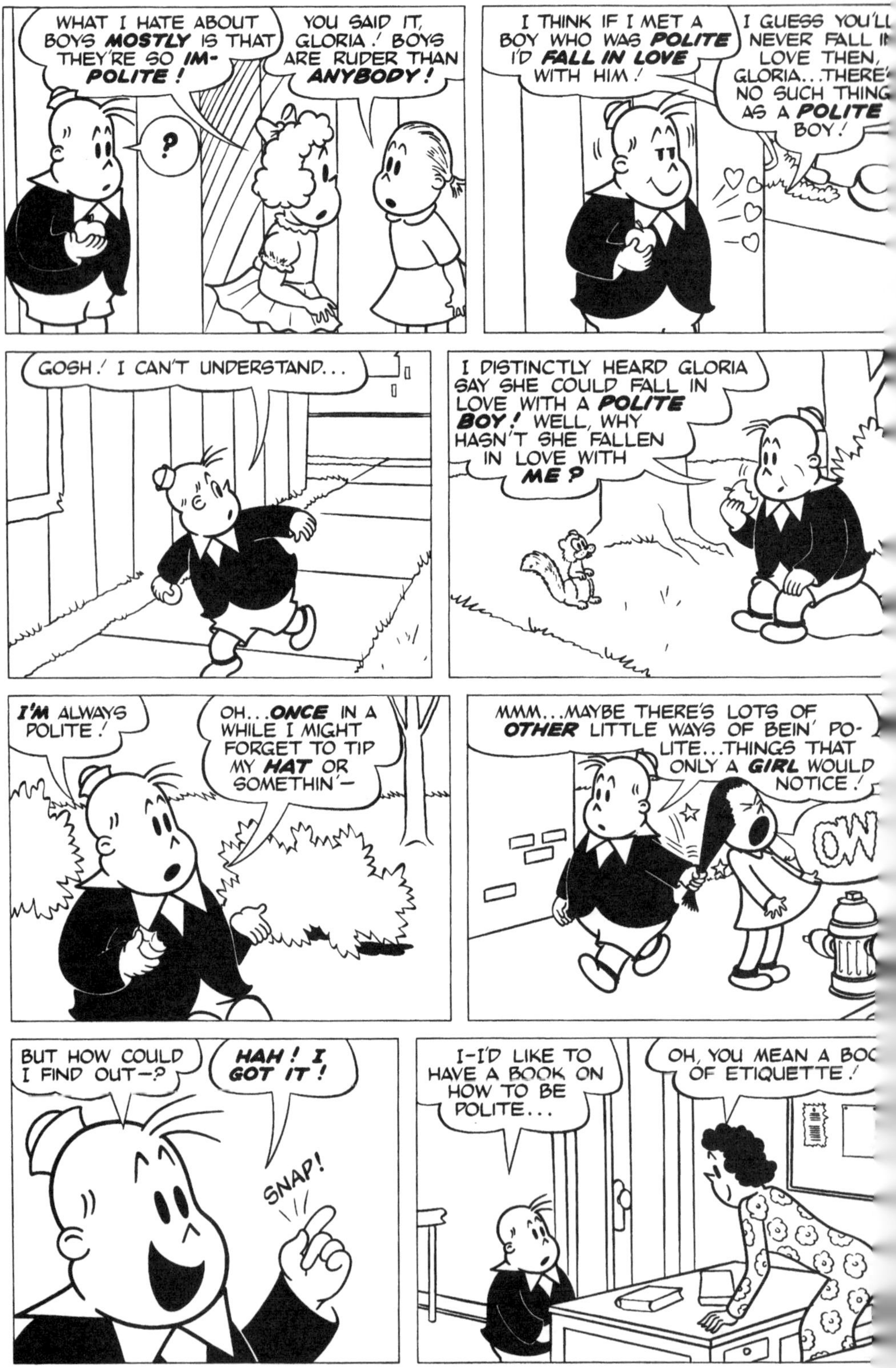
WHAT I HATE ABOUT BOYS **MOSTLY** IS THAT THEY'RE SO **IM-POLITE!**
YOU SAID IT, GLORIA! BOYS ARE RUDER THAN **ANYBODY!**
?
I THINK IF I MET A BOY WHO WAS **POLITE** I'D **FALL IN LOVE** WITH HIM!
I GUESS YOU'LL NEVER FALL IN LOVE THEN, GLORIA...THERE'S NO SUCH THING AS A **POLITE** BOY!
GOSH! I CAN'T UNDERSTAND...
I DISTINCTLY HEARD GLORIA SAY SHE COULD FALL IN LOVE WITH A **POLITE BOY!** WELL, WHY HASN'T SHE FALLEN IN LOVE WITH **ME?**
I'M ALWAYS POLITE!
OH...**ONCE** IN A WHILE I MIGHT FORGET TO TIP MY **HAT** OR SOMETHIN'—
MMM...MAYBE THERE'S LOTS OF **OTHER** LITTLE WAYS OF BEIN' PO-LITE...THINGS THAT ONLY A **GIRL** WOULD NOTICE!
OW
BUT HOW COULD I FIND OUT—?
HAH! I GOT IT!
SNAP!
I-I'D LIKE TO HAVE A BOOK ON HOW TO BE POLITE...
OH, YOU MEAN A BOOK OF ETIQUETTE!

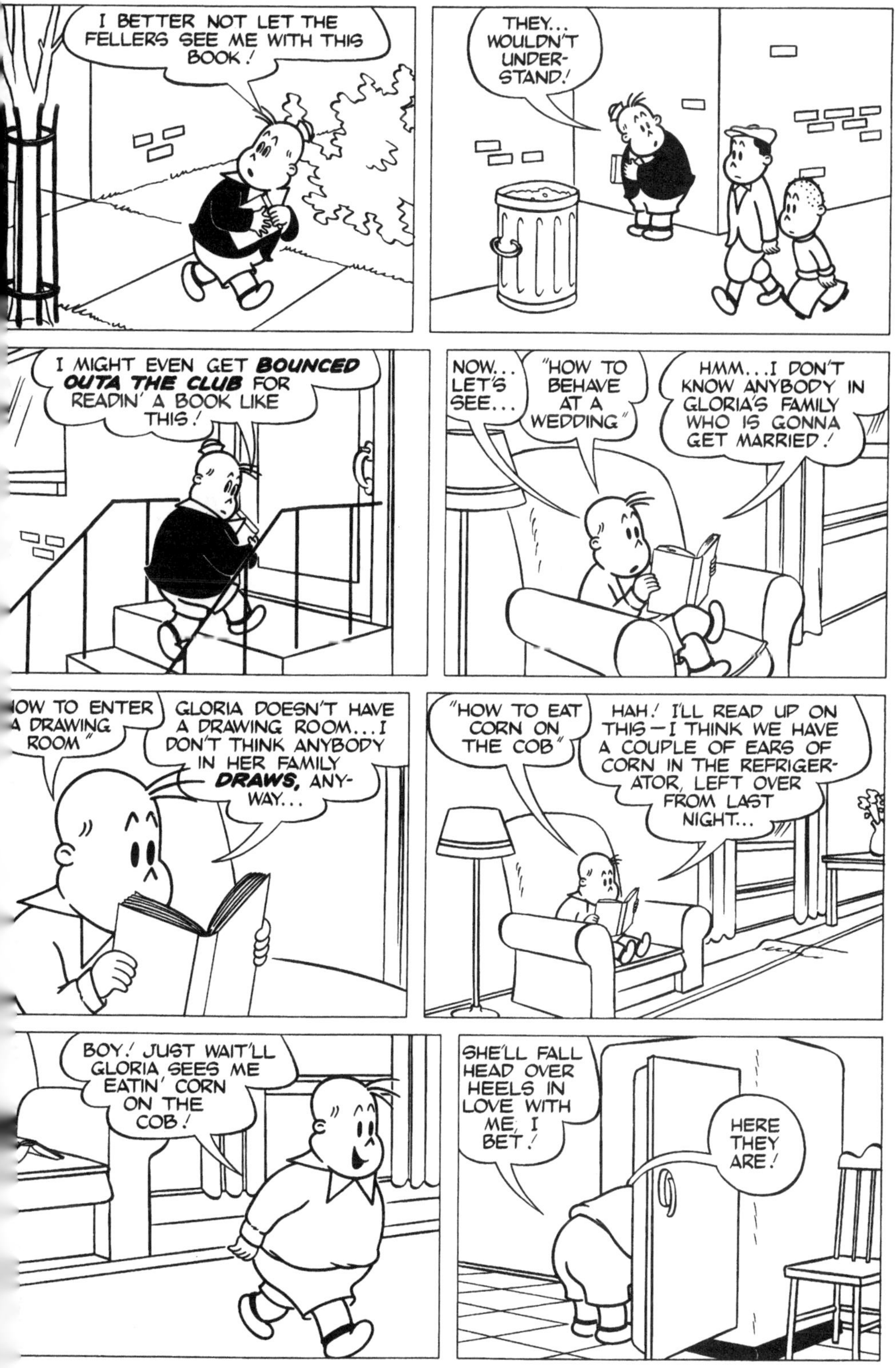
I BETTER NOT LET THE FELLERS SEE ME WITH THIS BOOK!
THEY... WOULDN'T UNDER-STAND!
I MIGHT EVEN GET **BOUNCED OUTA THE CLUB** FOR READIN' A BOOK LIKE THIS!
NOW... LET'S SEE...
"HOW TO BEHAVE AT A WEDDING"
HMM...I DON'T KNOW ANYBODY IN GLORIA'S FAMILY WHO IS GONNA GET MARRIED!
HOW TO ENTER A DRAWING ROOM"
GLORIA DOESN'T HAVE A DRAWING ROOM...I DON'T THINK ANYBODY IN HER FAMILY **DRAWS,** ANY-WAY...
"HOW TO EAT CORN ON THE COB"
HAH! I'LL READ UP ON THIS—I THINK WE HAVE A COUPLE OF EARS OF CORN IN THE REFRIGER-ATOR, LEFT OVER FROM LAST NIGHT...
BOY! JUST WAIT'LL GLORIA SEES ME EATIN' CORN ON THE COB!
SHE'LL FALL HEAD OVER HEELS IN LOVE WITH ME, I BET!
HERE THEY ARE!

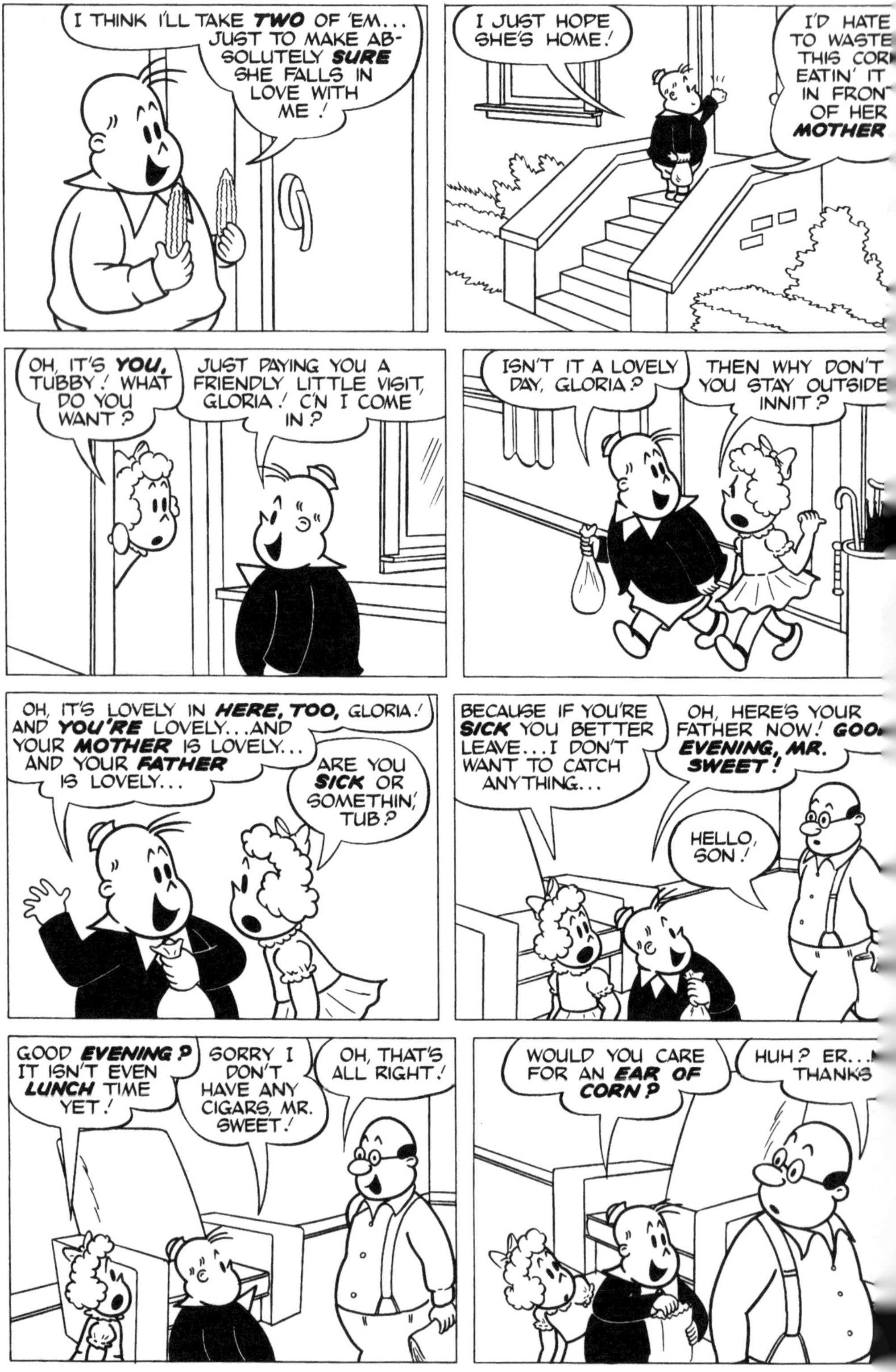
I THINK I'LL TAKE **TWO** OF 'EM... JUST TO MAKE ABSOLUTELY **SURE** SHE FALLS IN LOVE WITH ME!
I JUST HOPE SHE'S HOME!
I'D HATE TO WASTE THIS COR EATIN' IT IN FRONT OF HER **MOTHER**
OH, IT'S **YOU,** TUBBY! WHAT DO YOU WANT?
JUST PAYING YOU A FRIENDLY LITTLE VISIT, GLORIA! C'N I COME IN?
ISN'T IT A LOVELY DAY, GLORIA?
THEN WHY DON'T YOU STAY OUTSIDE INNIT?
OH, IT'S LOVELY IN **HERE, TOO,** GLORIA! AND **YOU'RE** LOVELY...AND YOUR **MOTHER** IS LOVELY... AND YOUR **FATHER** IS LOVELY...
ARE YOU **SICK** OR SOMETHIN', TUB?
BECAUSE IF YOU'RE **SICK** YOU BETTER LEAVE...I DON'T WANT TO CATCH ANYTHING...
OH, HERE'S YOUR FATHER NOW! **GOO EVENING, MR. SWEET!**
HELLO, SON!
GOOD **EVENING?** IT ISN'T EVEN **LUNCH** TIME YET!
SORRY I DON'T HAVE ANY CIGARS, MR. SWEET!
OH, THAT'S ALL RIGHT!
WOULD YOU CARE FOR AN **EAR OF CORN?**
HUH? ER... THANKS

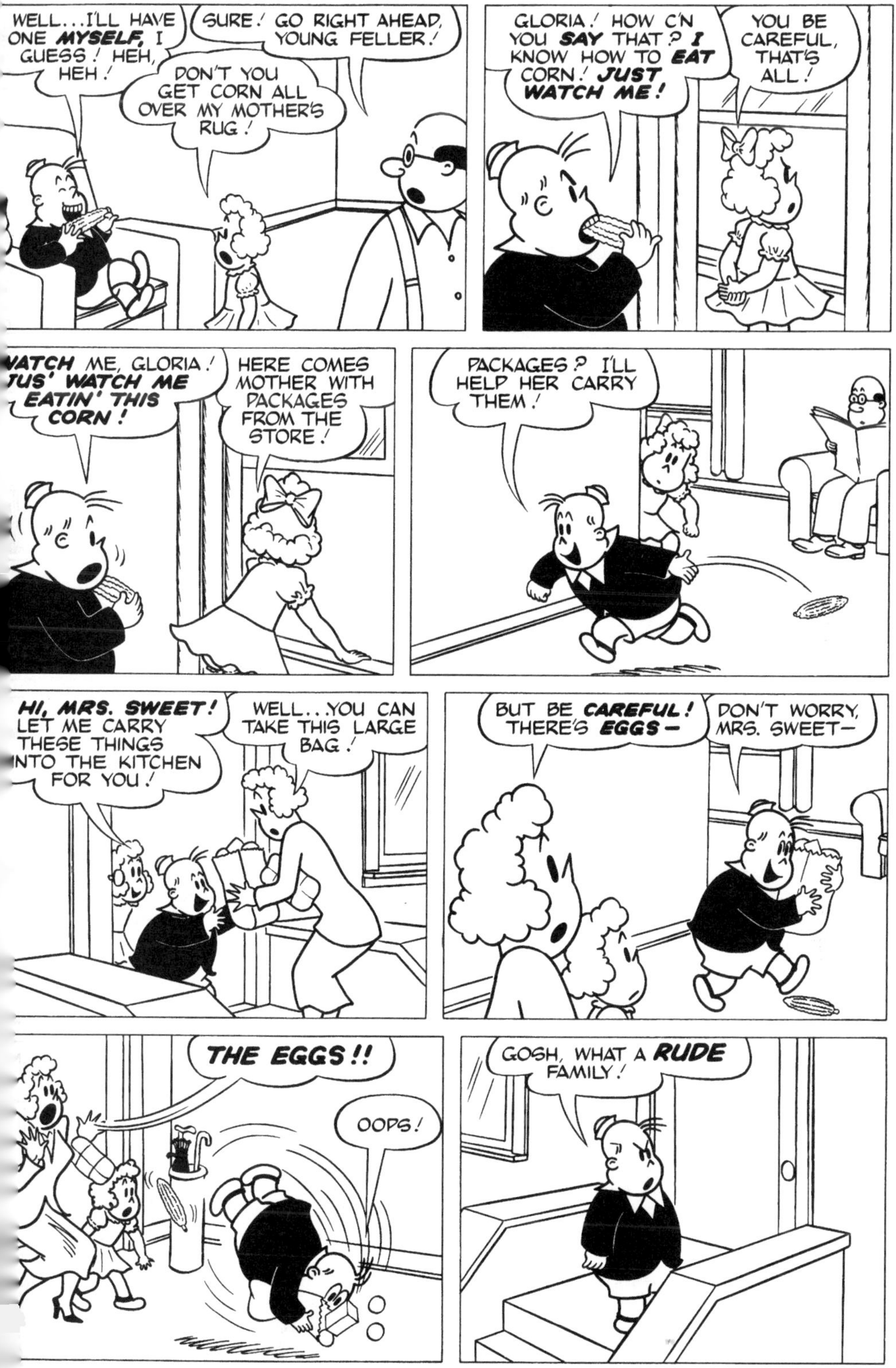
WELL...I'LL HAVE ONE MYSELF, I GUESS! HEH, HEH!
SURE! GO RIGHT AHEAD, YOUNG FELLER!
DON'T YOU GET CORN ALL OVER MY MOTHER'S RUG!
GLORIA! HOW C'N YOU SAY THAT? I KNOW HOW TO EAT CORN! JUST WATCH ME!
YOU BE CAREFUL, THAT'S ALL!
WATCH ME, GLORIA! JUS' WATCH ME EATIN' THIS CORN!
HERE COMES MOTHER WITH PACKAGES FROM THE STORE!
PACKAGES? I'LL HELP HER CARRY THEM!
HI, MRS. SWEET! LET ME CARRY THESE THINGS INTO THE KITCHEN FOR YOU!
WELL...YOU CAN TAKE THIS LARGE BAG!
BUT BE CAREFUL! THERE'S EGGS—
DON'T WORRY, MRS. SWEET—
THE EGGS!!
OOPS!
GOSH, WHAT A RUDE FAMILY!

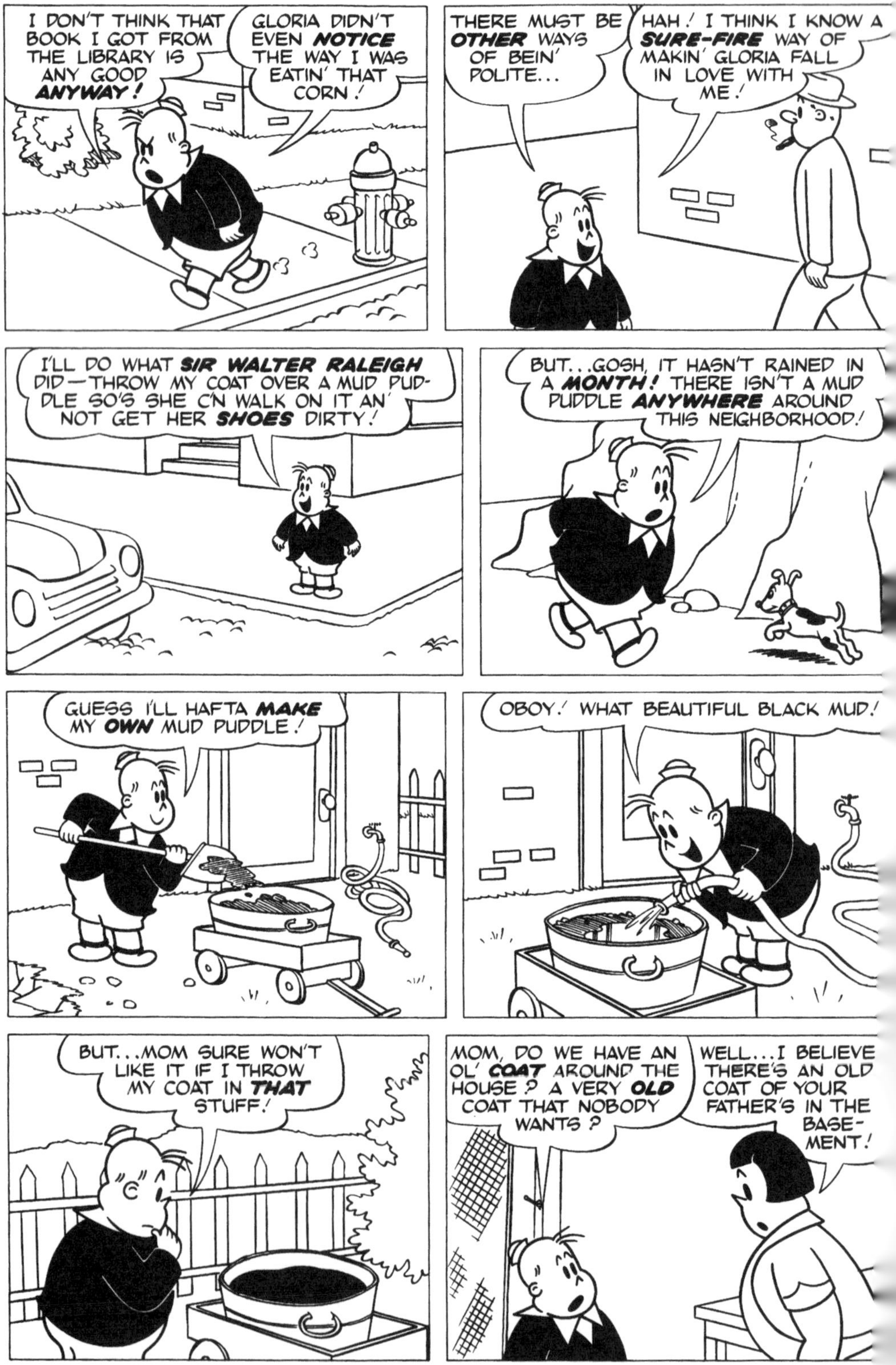
I DON'T THINK THAT BOOK I GOT FROM THE LIBRARY IS ANY GOOD ANYWAY!
GLORIA DIDN'T EVEN NOTICE THE WAY I WAS EATIN' THAT CORN!
THERE MUST BE OTHER WAYS OF BEIN' POLITE...
HAH! I THINK I KNOW A SURE-FIRE WAY OF MAKIN' GLORIA FALL IN LOVE WITH ME!
I'LL DO WHAT SIR WALTER RALEIGH DID—THROW MY COAT OVER A MUD PUDDLE SO'S SHE C'N WALK ON IT AN' NOT GET HER SHOES DIRTY!
BUT...GOSH, IT HASN'T RAINED IN A MONTH! THERE ISN'T A MUD PUDDLE ANYWHERE AROUND THIS NEIGHBORHOOD!
GUESS I'LL HAFTA MAKE MY OWN MUD PUDDLE!
OBOY! WHAT BEAUTIFUL BLACK MUD!
BUT...MOM SURE WON'T LIKE IT IF I THROW MY COAT IN THAT STUFF!
MOM, DO WE HAVE AN OL' COAT AROUND THE HOUSE? A VERY OLD COAT THAT NOBODY WANTS?
WELL...I BELIEVE THERE'S AN OLD COAT OF YOUR FATHER'S IN THE BASEMENT!

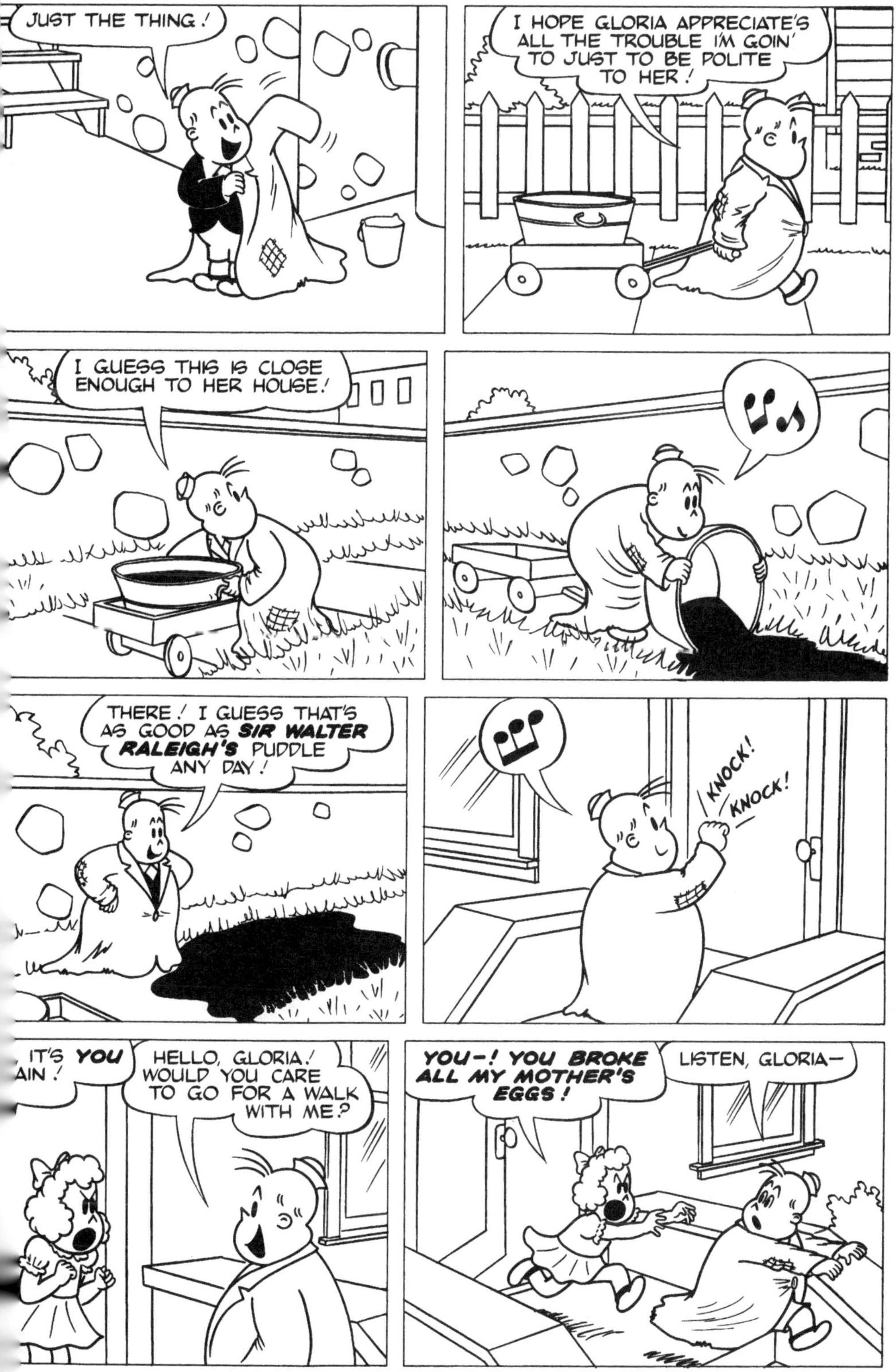
JUST THE THING!
I HOPE GLORIA APPRECIATE'S ALL THE TROUBLE I'M GOIN' TO JUST TO BE POLITE TO HER!
I GUESS THIS IS CLOSE ENOUGH TO HER HOUSE!
THERE! I GUESS THAT'S AS GOOD AS **SIR WALTER RALEIGH'S** PUDDLE ANY DAY!
KNOCK!
KNOCK!
IT'S **YOU** AIN!
HELLO, GLORIA! WOULD YOU CARE TO GO FOR A WALK WITH ME?
YOU—! YOU BROKE ALL MY MOTHER'S EGGS!
LISTEN, GLORIA—

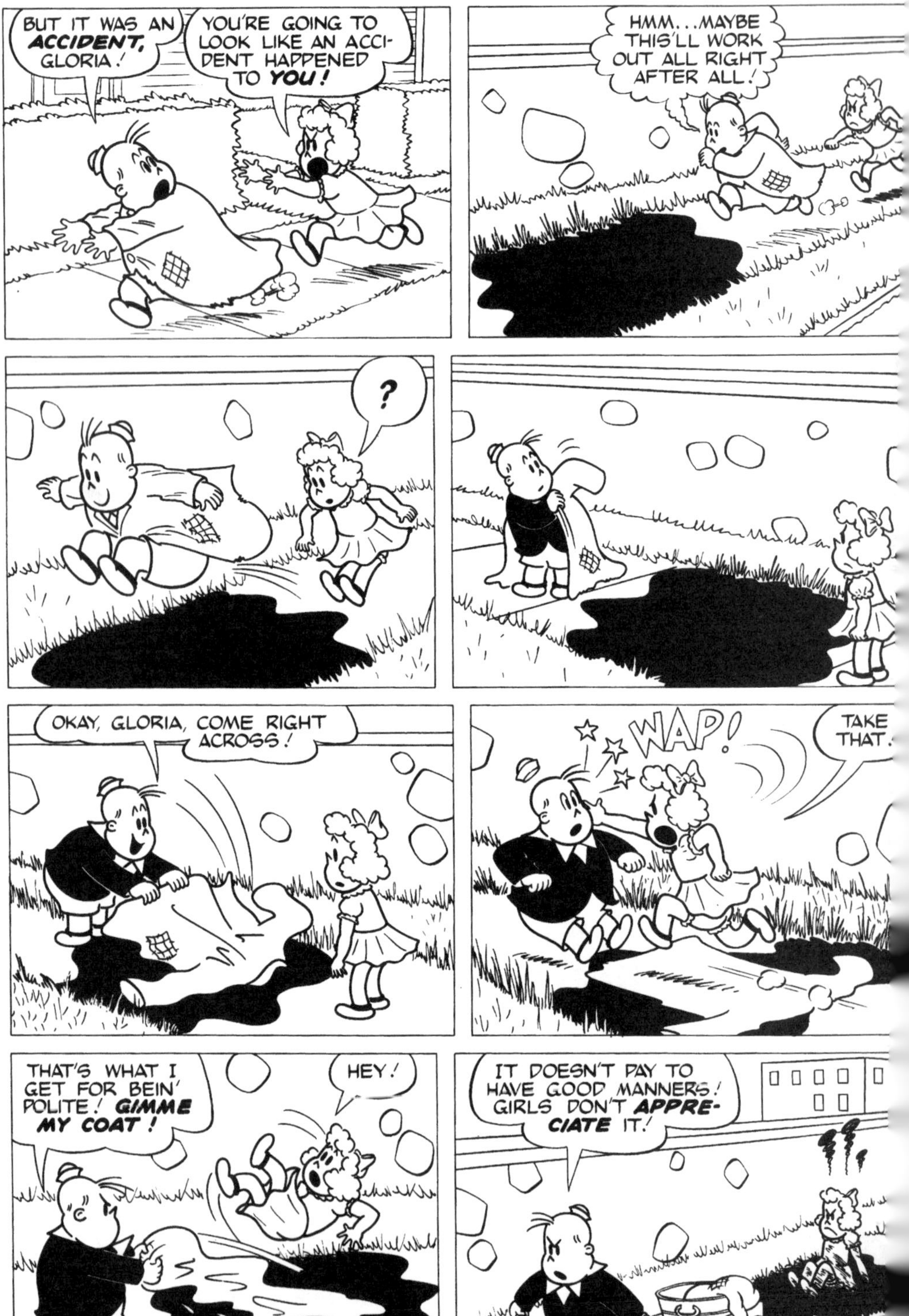
BUT IT WAS AN **ACCIDENT,** GLORIA!
YOU'RE GOING TO LOOK LIKE AN ACCIDENT HAPPENED TO **YOU!**
HMM...MAYBE THIS'LL WORK OUT ALL RIGHT AFTER ALL!
?
OKAY, GLORIA, COME RIGHT ACROSS!
WAP!
TAKE THAT.
THAT'S WHAT I GET FOR BEIN' POLITE! **GIMME MY COAT!**
HEY!
IT DOESN'T PAY TO HAVE GOOD MANNERS! GIRLS DON'T **APPRECIATE** IT!
THE END

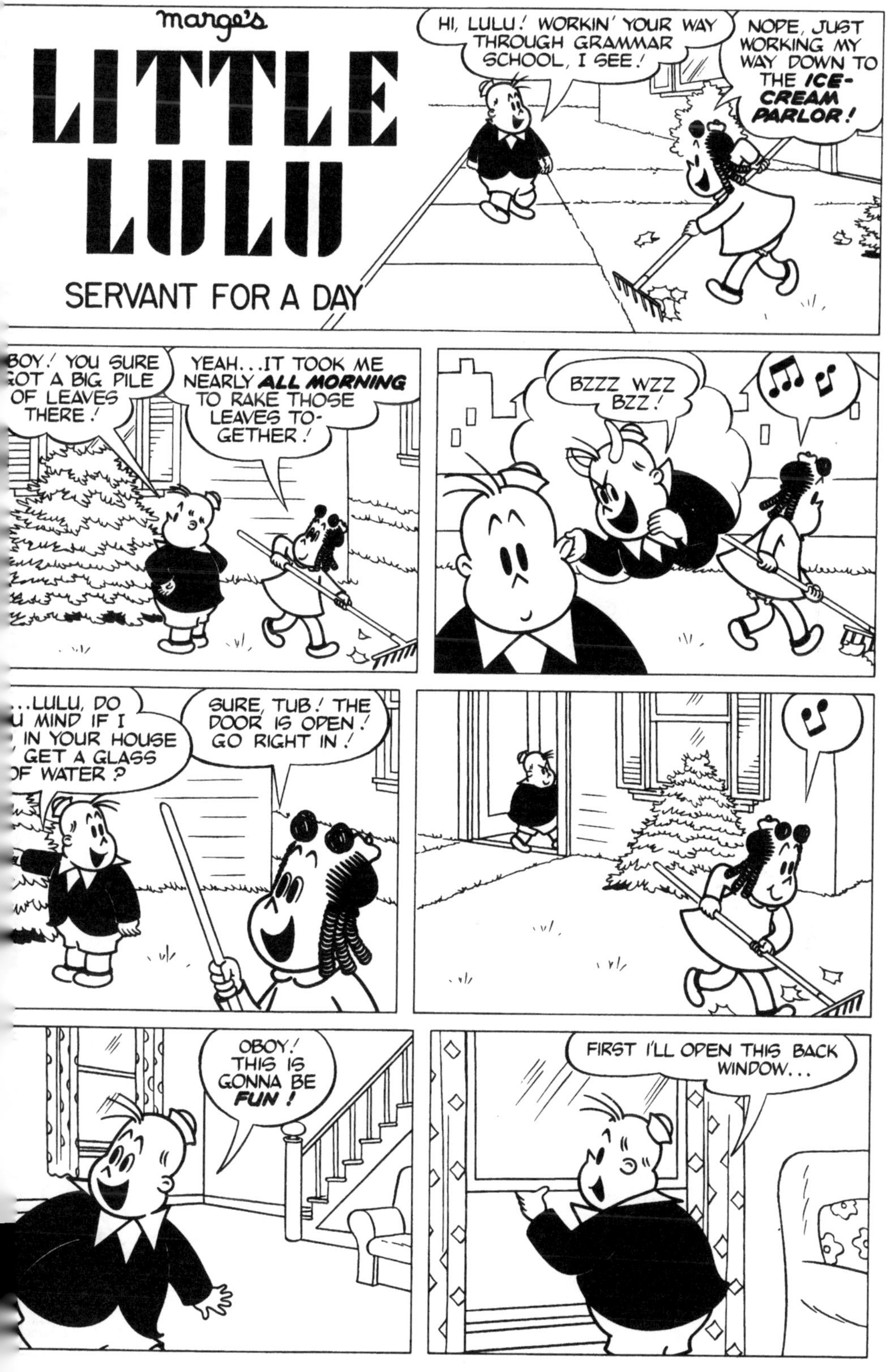
marge's
LITTLE LULU
SERVANT FOR A DAY
HI, LULU! WORKIN' YOUR WAY THROUGH GRAMMAR SCHOOL, I SEE!
NOPE, JUST WORKING MY WAY DOWN TO THE **ICE-CREAM PARLOR!**
BOY! YOU SURE GOT A BIG PILE OF LEAVES THERE!
YEAH...IT TOOK ME NEARLY **ALL MORNING** TO RAKE THOSE LEAVES TOGETHER!
BZZZ WZZ BZZ!
...LULU, DO U MIND IF I IN YOUR HOUSE GET A GLASS OF WATER?
SURE, TUB! THE DOOR IS OPEN! GO RIGHT IN!
OBOY! THIS IS GONNA BE **FUN!**
FIRST I'LL OPEN THIS BACK WINDOW...

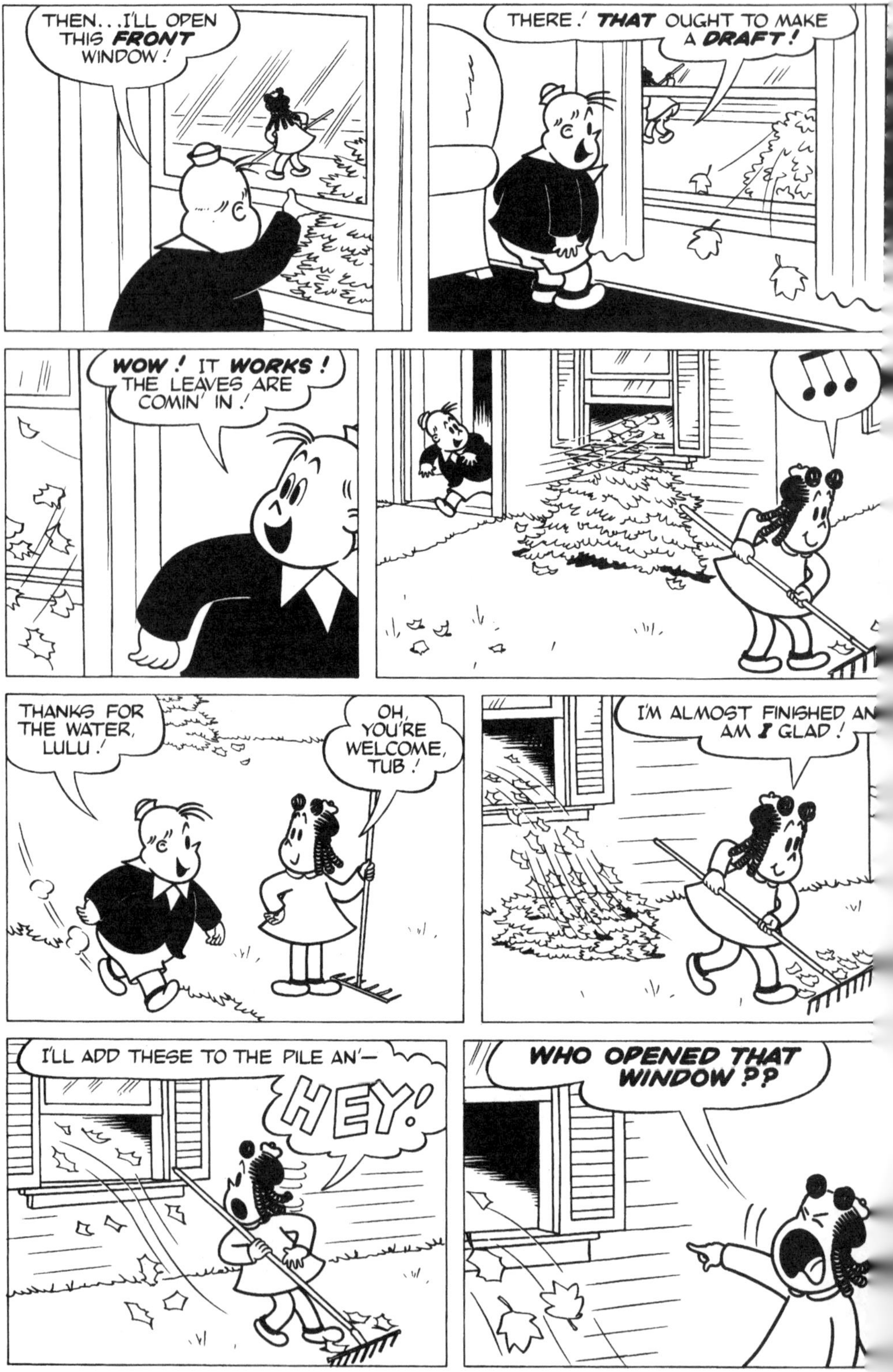
THEN...I'LL OPEN THIS **FRONT** WINDOW!
THERE! **THAT** OUGHT TO MAKE A **DRAFT**!
WOW! IT **WORKS**! THE LEAVES ARE COMIN' IN!
THANKS FOR THE WATER, LULU!
OH, YOU'RE WELCOME, TUB!
I'M ALMOST FINISHED AN AM **I** GLAD!
I'LL ADD THESE TO THE PILE AN'—
HEY!
WHO OPENED THAT WINDOW??

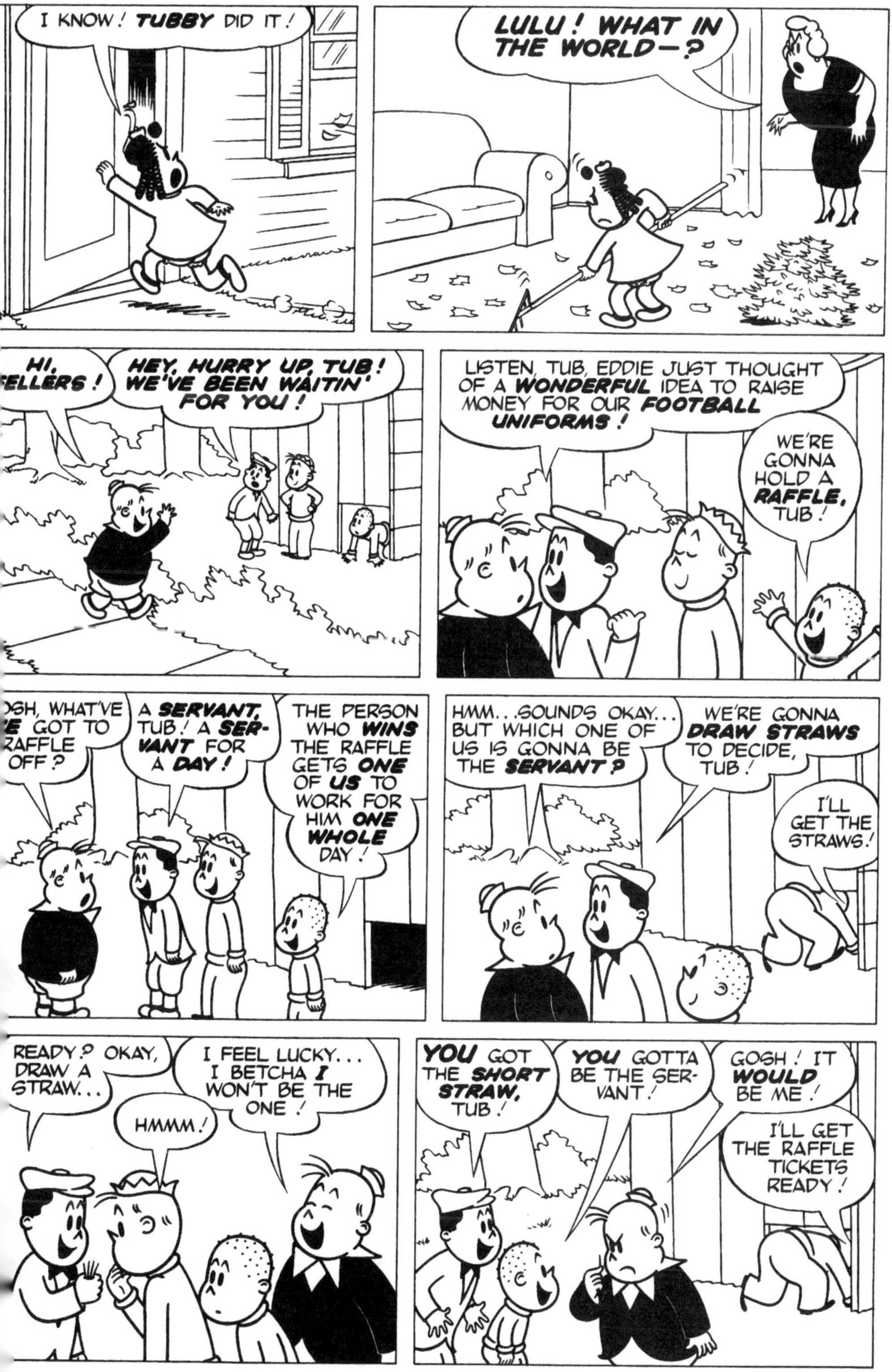
I KNOW! TUBBY DID IT!
LULU! WHAT IN THE WORLD—?
HI, FELLERS!
HEY, HURRY UP, TUB! WE'VE BEEN WAITIN' FOR YOU!
LISTEN, TUB, EDDIE JUST THOUGHT OF A WONDERFUL IDEA TO RAISE MONEY FOR OUR FOOTBALL UNIFORMS!
WE'RE GONNA HOLD A RAFFLE, TUB!
GOSH, WHAT'VE WE GOT TO RAFFLE OFF?
A SERVANT, TUB! A SERVANT FOR A DAY!
THE PERSON WHO WINS THE RAFFLE GETS ONE OF US TO WORK FOR HIM ONE WHOLE DAY!
HMM... SOUNDS OKAY... BUT WHICH ONE OF US IS GONNA BE THE SERVANT?
WE'RE GONNA DRAW STRAWS TO DECIDE, TUB!
I'LL GET THE STRAWS!
READY? OKAY, DRAW A STRAW...
HMMM!
I FEEL LUCKY... I BETCHA I WON'T BE THE ONE!
YOU GOT THE SHORT STRAW, TUB!
YOU GOTTA BE THE SERVANT!
GOSH! IT WOULD BE ME!
I'LL GET THE RAFFLE TICKETS READY!

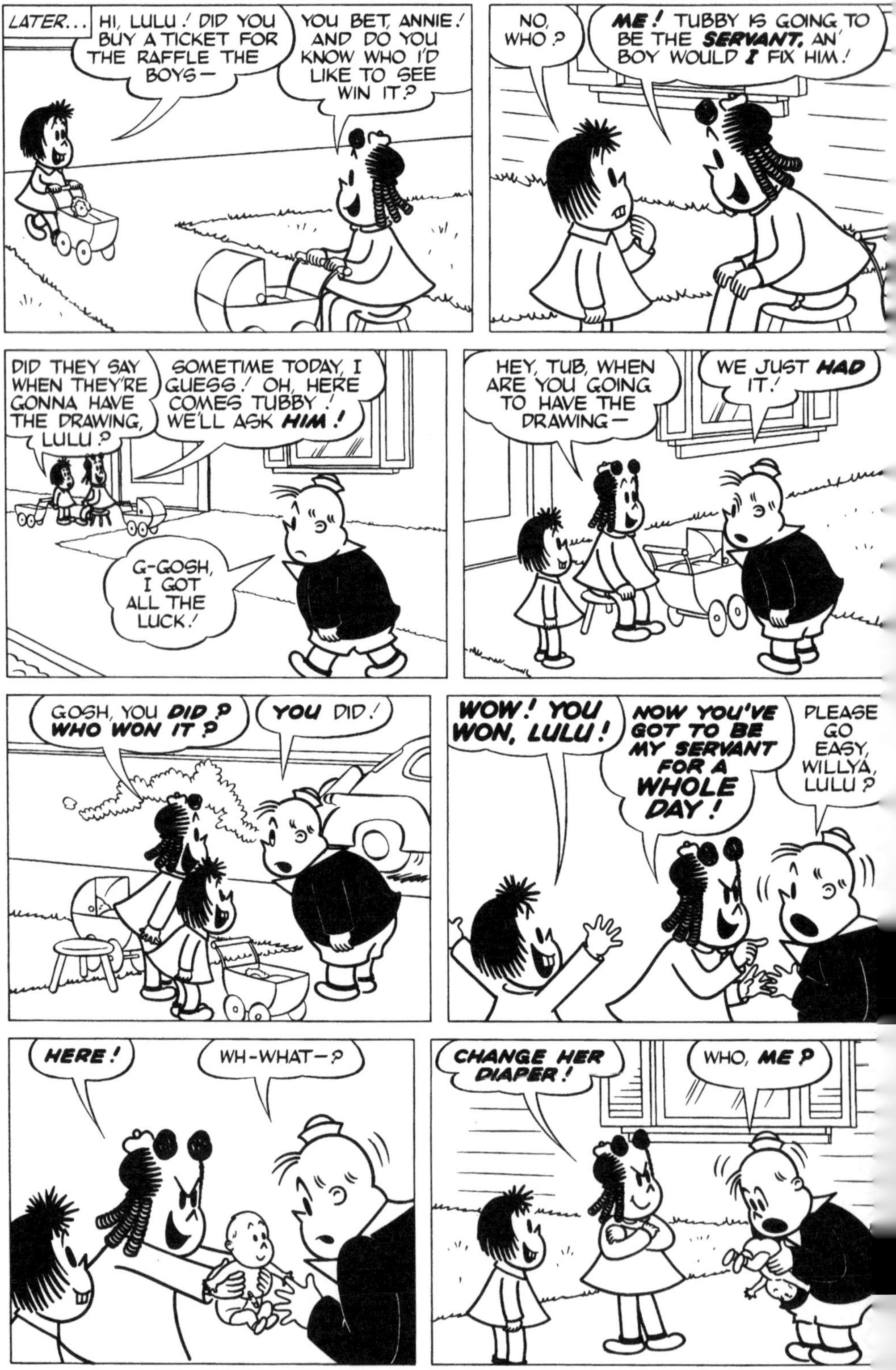

LATER...
HI, LULU! DID YOU BUY A TICKET FOR THE RAFFLE THE BOYS—
YOU BET, ANNIE! AND DO YOU KNOW WHO I'D LIKE TO SEE WIN IT?
NO, WHO?
ME! TUBBY IS GOING TO BE THE **SERVANT**, AN' BOY WOULD **I** FIX HIM!
DID THEY SAY WHEN THEY'RE GONNA HAVE THE DRAWING, LULU?
SOMETIME TODAY, I GUESS! OH, HERE COMES TUBBY! WE'LL ASK **HIM**!
G-GOSH, I GOT ALL THE LUCK!
HEY, TUB, WHEN ARE YOU GOING TO HAVE THE DRAWING—
WE JUST **HAD** IT!
GOSH, YOU **DID**? **WHO WON IT?**
YOU DID!
WOW! YOU WON, LULU!
NOW YOU'VE GOT TO BE MY SERVANT FOR A WHOLE DAY!
PLEASE GO EASY, WILLYA, LULU?
HERE!
WH-WHAT—?
CHANGE HER DIAPER!
WHO, **ME?**

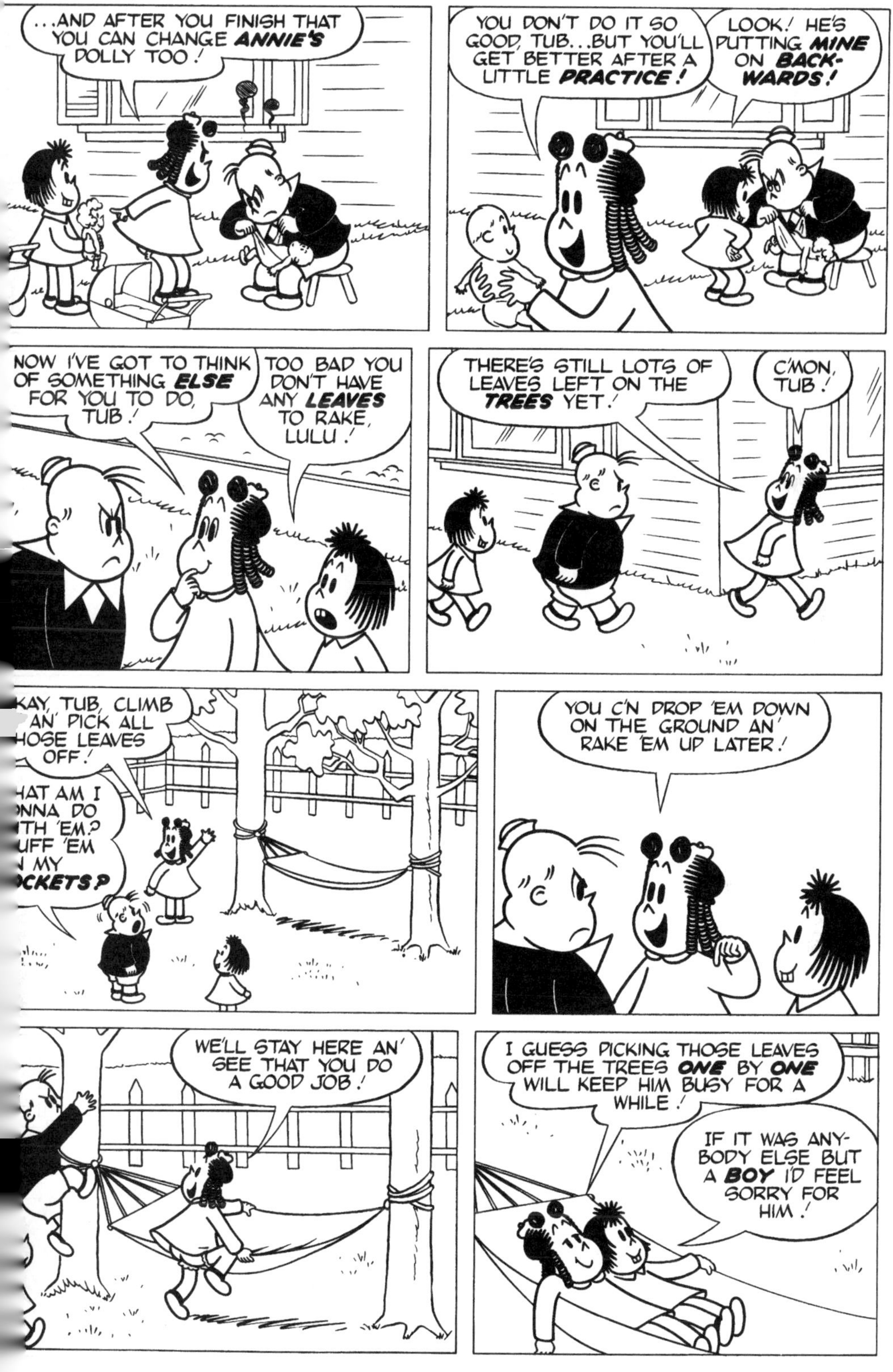
...AND AFTER YOU FINISH THAT YOU CAN CHANGE ANNIE'S DOLLY TOO!
YOU DON'T DO IT SO GOOD, TUB...BUT YOU'LL GET BETTER AFTER A LITTLE PRACTICE!
LOOK! HE'S PUTTING MINE ON BACK-WARDS!
NOW I'VE GOT TO THINK OF SOMETHING ELSE FOR YOU TO DO, TUB!
TOO BAD YOU DON'T HAVE ANY LEAVES TO RAKE, LULU!
THERE'S STILL LOTS OF LEAVES LEFT ON THE TREES YET!
C'MON, TUB!
KAY, TUB, CLIMB AN' PICK ALL HOSE LEAVES OFF!
HAT AM I ONNA DO ITH 'EM? UFF 'EM N MY OCKETS?
YOU C'N DROP 'EM DOWN ON THE GROUND AN' RAKE 'EM UP LATER!
WE'LL STAY HERE AN' SEE THAT YOU DO A GOOD JOB!
I GUESS PICKING THOSE LEAVES OFF THE TREES ONE BY ONE WILL KEEP HIM BUSY FOR A WHILE!
IF IT WAS ANY-BODY ELSE BUT A BOY I'D FEEL SORRY FOR HIM!

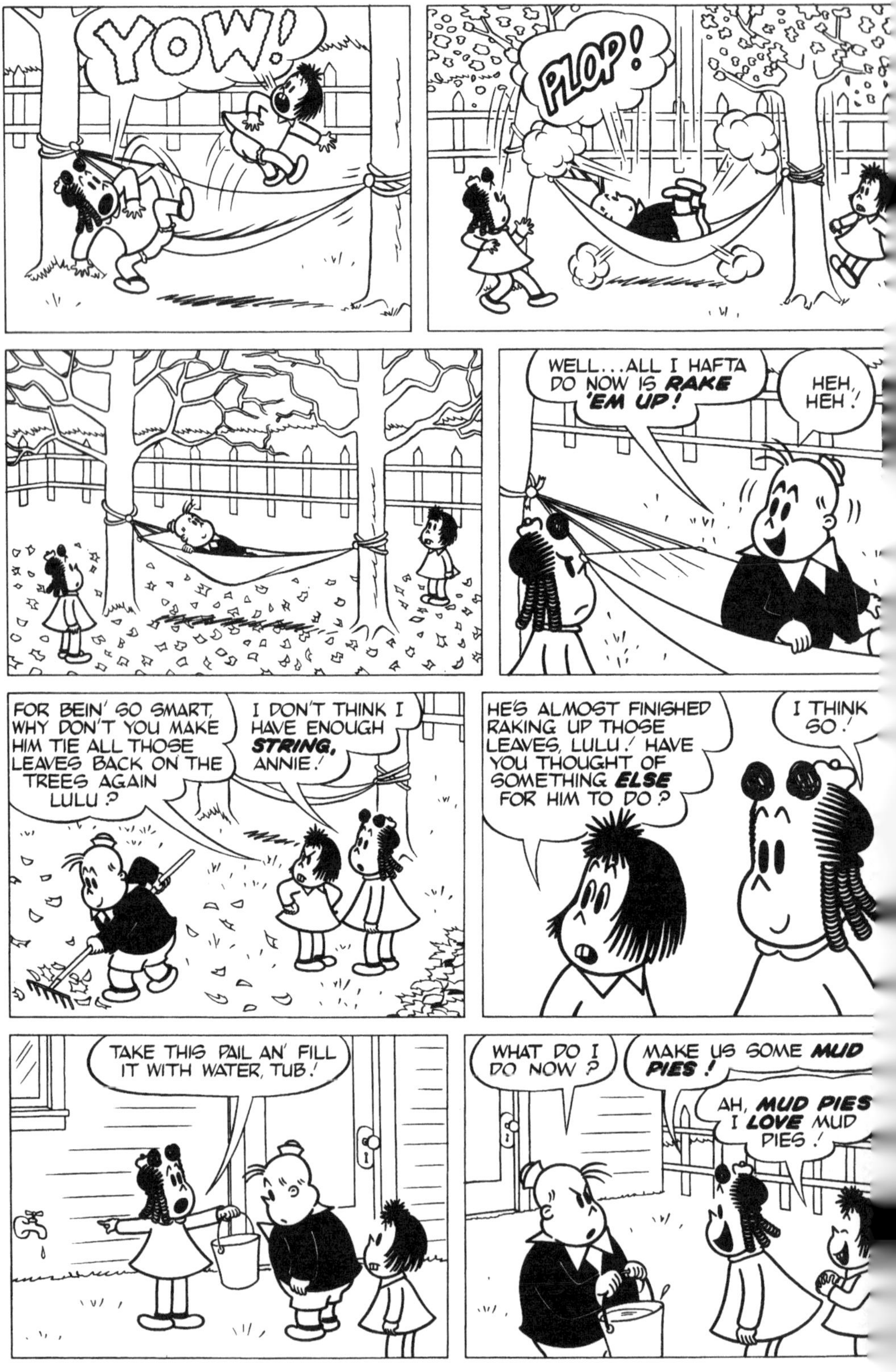
YOW!
PLOP!
WELL...ALL I HAFTA DO NOW IS RAKE 'EM UP!
HEH, HEH!
FOR BEIN' SO SMART, WHY DON'T YOU MAKE HIM TIE ALL THOSE LEAVES BACK ON THE TREES AGAIN LULU?
I DON'T THINK I HAVE ENOUGH STRING, ANNIE!
HE'S ALMOST FINISHED RAKING UP THOSE LEAVES, LULU! HAVE YOU THOUGHT OF SOMETHING ELSE FOR HIM TO DO?
I THINK SO!
TAKE THIS PAIL AN' FILL IT WITH WATER, TUB!
WHAT DO I DO NOW?
MAKE US SOME MUD PIES!
AH, MUD PIES I LOVE MUD PIES!

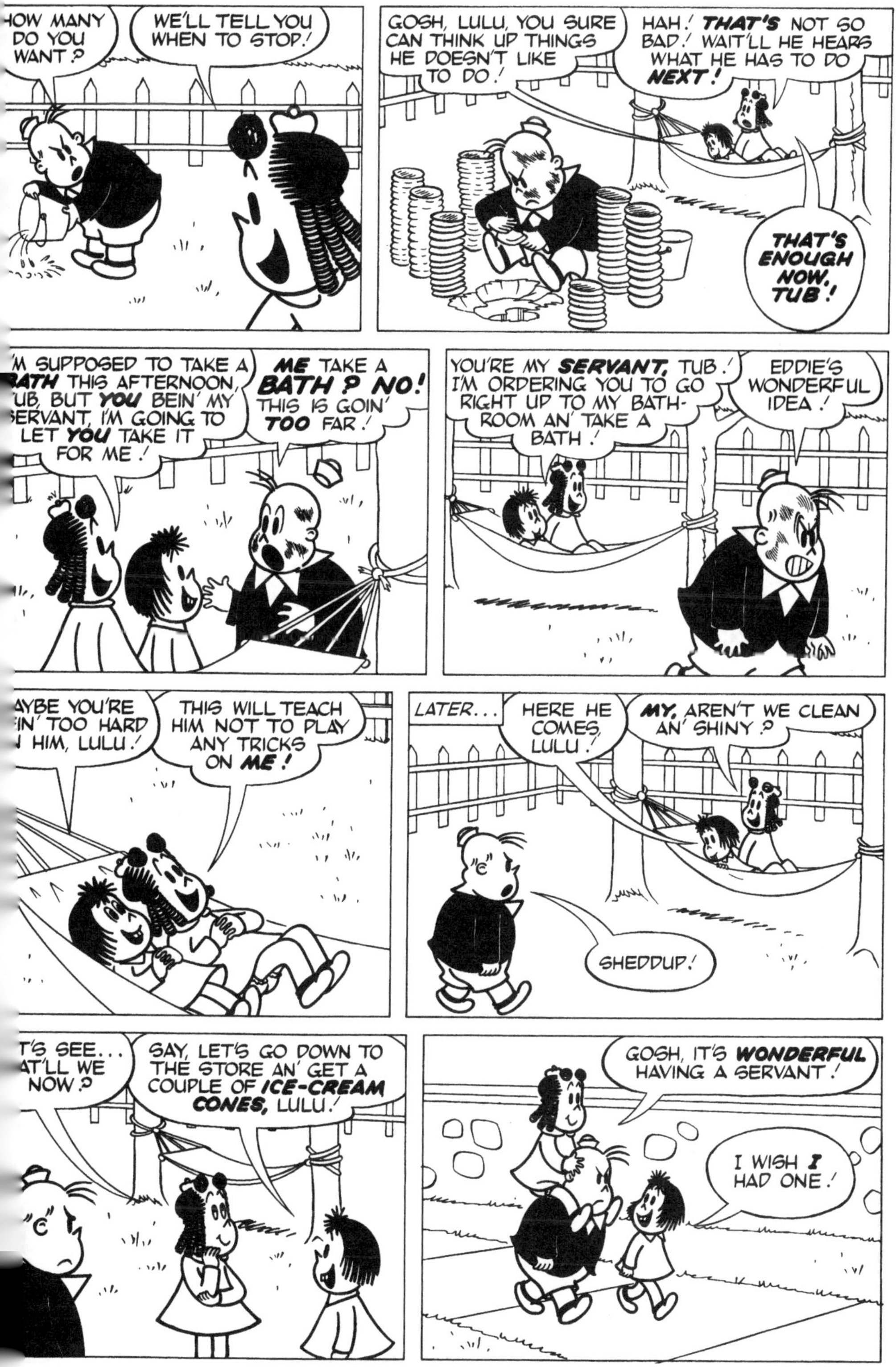

HOW MANY DO YOU WANT?
WE'LL TELL YOU WHEN TO STOP!
GOSH, LULU, YOU SURE CAN THINK UP THINGS HE DOESN'T LIKE TO DO!
HAH! THAT'S NOT SO BAD! WAIT'LL HE HEARS WHAT HE HAS TO DO NEXT!
THAT'S ENOUGH NOW, TUB!
I'M SUPPOSED TO TAKE A BATH THIS AFTERNOON, TUB, BUT YOU BEIN' MY SERVANT, I'M GOING TO LET YOU TAKE IT FOR ME!
ME TAKE A BATH? NO! THIS IS GOIN' TOO FAR!
YOU'RE MY SERVANT, TUB! I'M ORDERING YOU TO GO RIGHT UP TO MY BATH-ROOM AN' TAKE A BATH!
EDDIE'S WONDERFUL IDEA!
AYBE YOU'RE EIN' TOO HARD N HIM, LULU!
THIS WILL TEACH HIM NOT TO PLAY ANY TRICKS ON ME!
LATER...
HERE HE COMES, LULU!
MY, AREN'T WE CLEAN AN' SHINY?
SHEDDUP!
T'S SEE... AT'LL WE NOW?
SAY, LET'S GO DOWN TO THE STORE AN' GET A COUPLE OF ICE-CREAM CONES, LULU!
GOSH, IT'S WONDERFUL HAVING A SERVANT!
I WISH I HAD ONE!

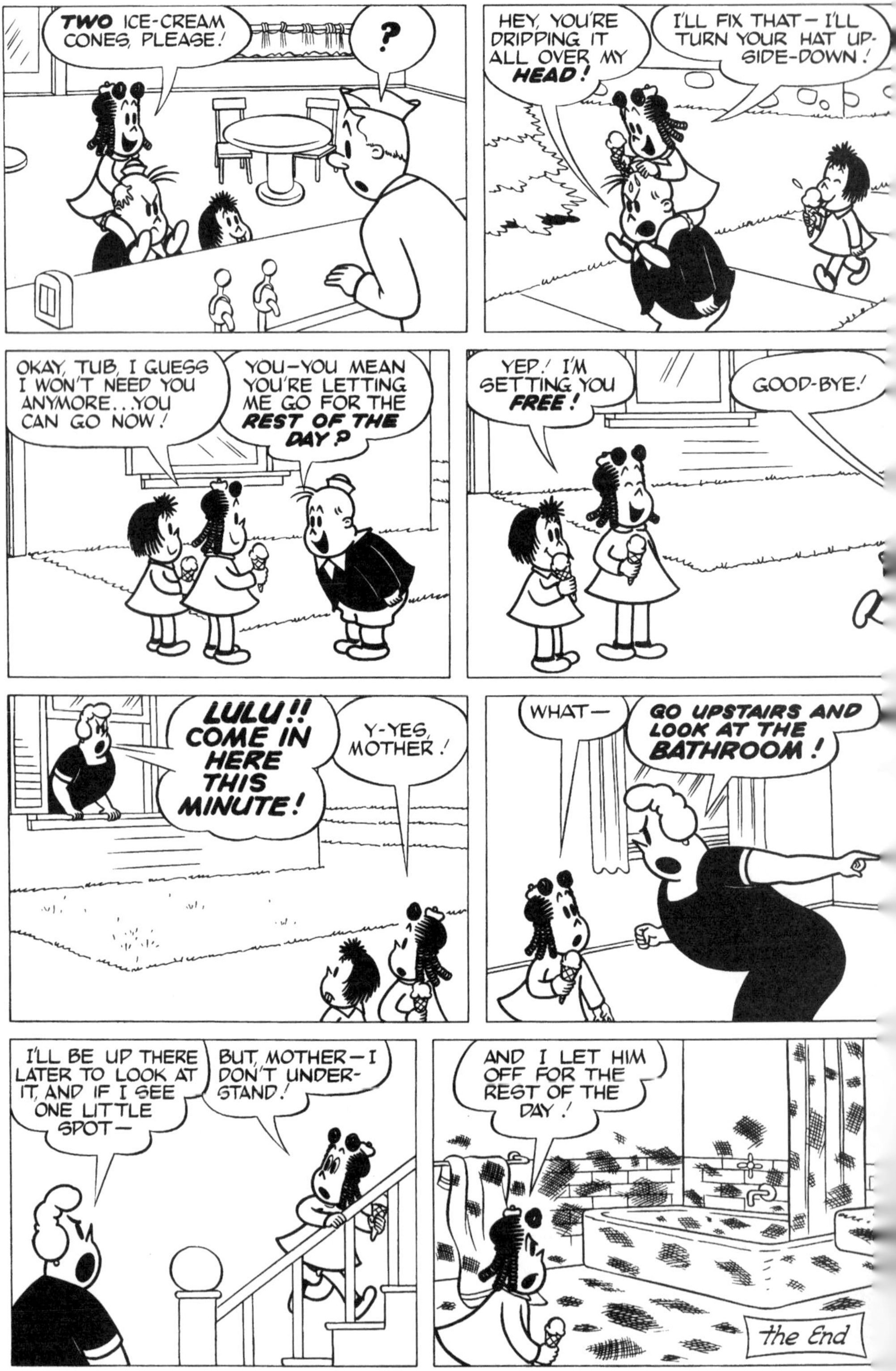
TWO ICE-CREAM CONES, PLEASE!
?
HEY, YOU'RE DRIPPING IT ALL OVER MY HEAD!
I'LL FIX THAT—I'LL TURN YOUR HAT UP-SIDE-DOWN!
OKAY, TUB, I GUESS I WON'T NEED YOU ANYMORE...YOU CAN GO NOW!
YOU—YOU MEAN YOU'RE LETTING ME GO FOR THE REST OF THE DAY?
YEP! I'M SETTING YOU FREE!
GOOD-BYE!
LULU!! COME IN HERE THIS MINUTE!
Y-YES, MOTHER!
WHAT—
GO UPSTAIRS AND LOOK AT THE BATHROOM!
I'LL BE UP THERE LATER TO LOOK AT IT, AND IF I SEE ONE LITTLE SPOT—
BUT, MOTHER—I DON'T UNDER-STAND!
AND I LET HIM OFF FOR THE REST OF THE DAY!
the End

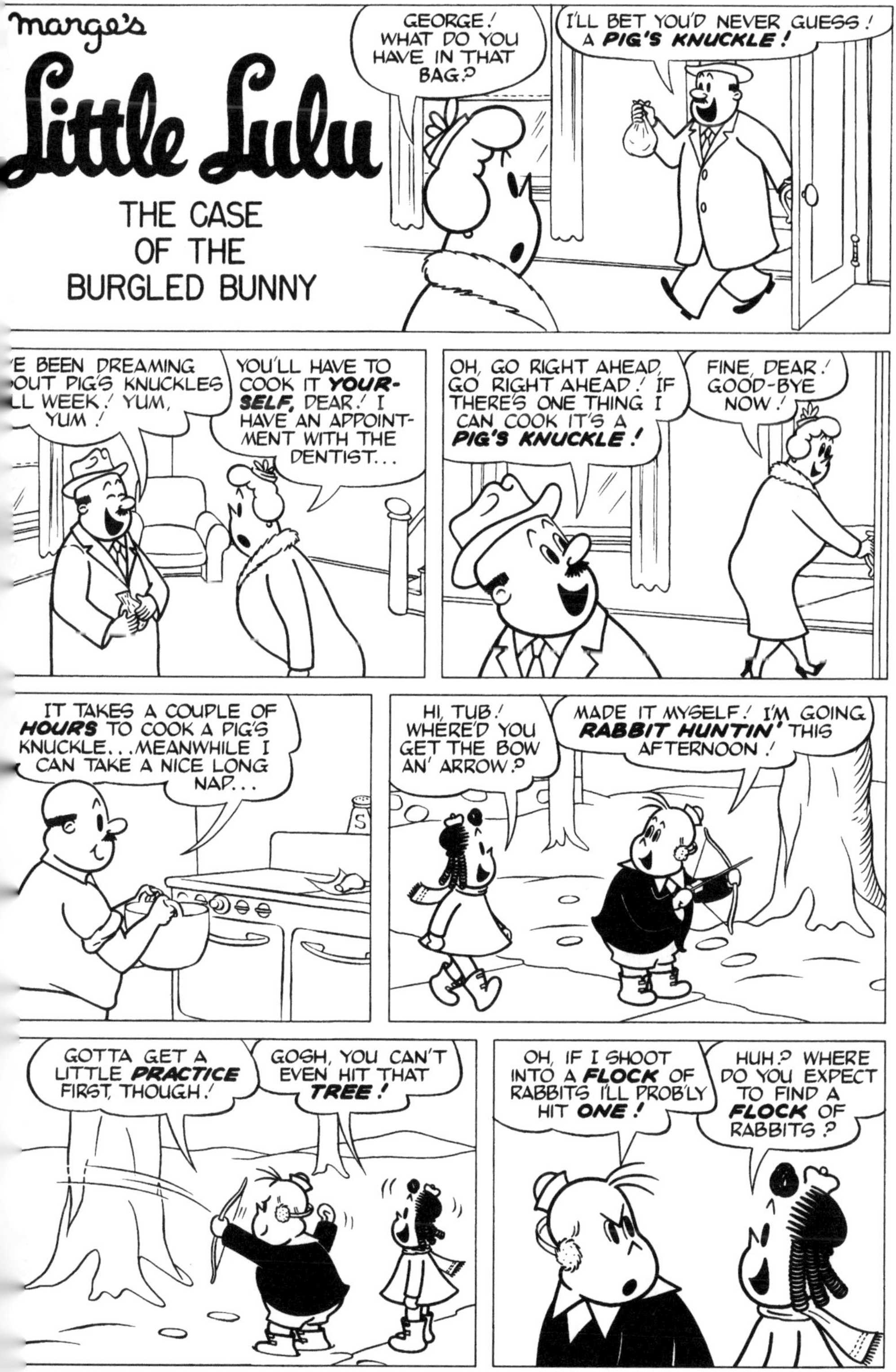
marge's
Little Lulu
THE CASE OF THE BURGLED BUNNY
GEORGE! WHAT DO YOU HAVE IN THAT BAG?
I'LL BET YOU'D NEVER GUESS! A PIG'S KNUCKLE!
'E BEEN DREAMING OUT PIG'S KNUCKLES LL WEEK! YUM, YUM!
YOU'LL HAVE TO COOK IT YOURSELF, DEAR! I HAVE AN APPOINTMENT WITH THE DENTIST...
OH, GO RIGHT AHEAD, GO RIGHT AHEAD! IF THERE'S ONE THING I CAN COOK IT'S A PIG'S KNUCKLE!
FINE, DEAR! GOOD-BYE NOW!
IT TAKES A COUPLE OF HOURS TO COOK A PIG'S KNUCKLE...MEANWHILE I CAN TAKE A NICE LONG NAP...
S
HI, TUB! WHERE'D YOU GET THE BOW AN' ARROW?
MADE IT MYSELF! I'M GOING RABBIT HUNTIN' THIS AFTERNOON!
GOTTA GET A LITTLE PRACTICE FIRST, THOUGH!
GOSH, YOU CAN'T EVEN HIT THAT TREE!
OH, IF I SHOOT INTO A FLOCK OF RABBITS I'LL PROB'LY HIT ONE!
HUH? WHERE DO YOU EXPECT TO FIND A FLOCK OF RABBITS?

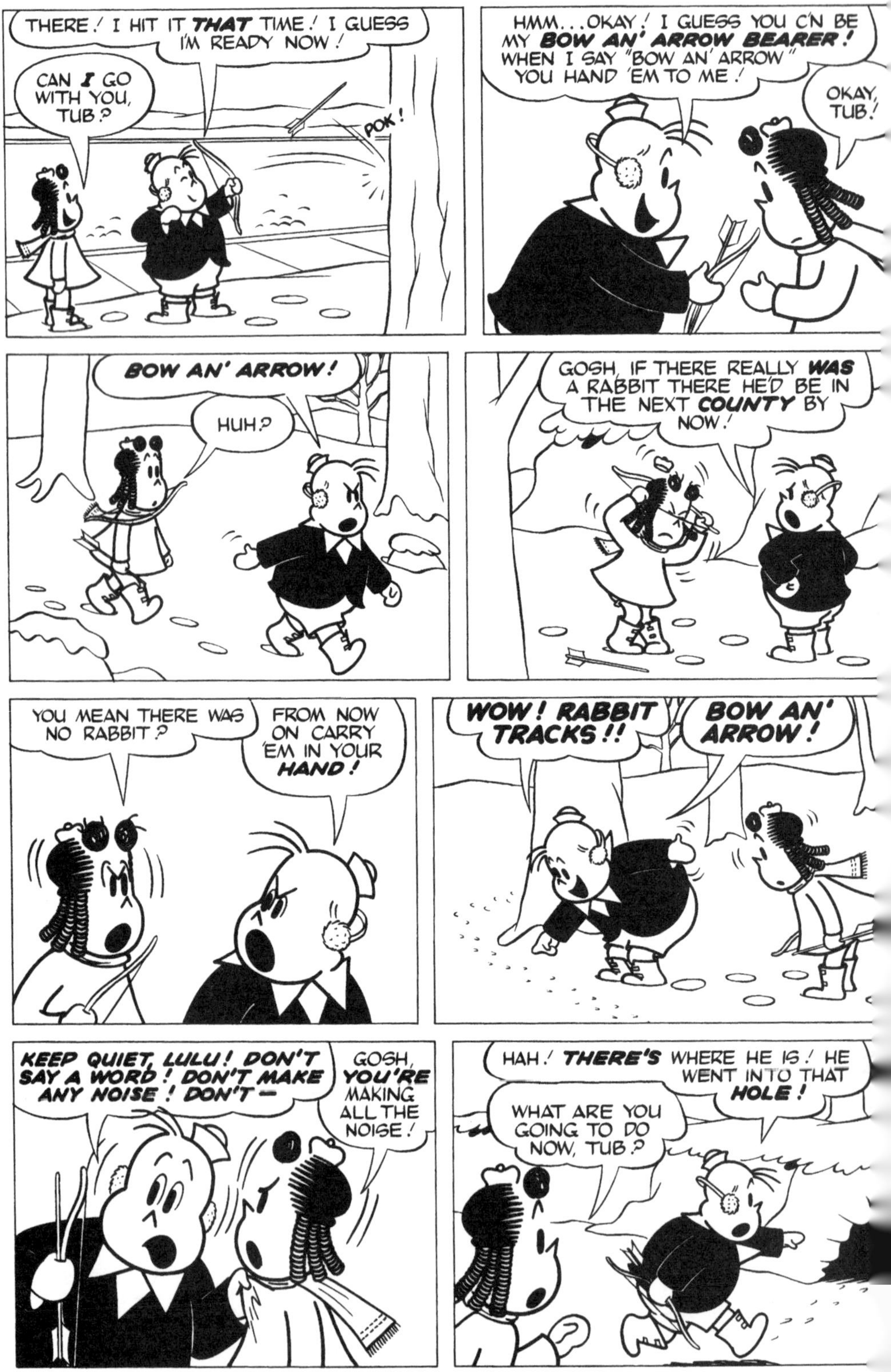
THERE! I HIT IT THAT TIME! I GUESS I'M READY NOW!
CAN I GO WITH YOU, TUB?
POK!
HMM...OKAY! I GUESS YOU C'N BE MY BOW AN' ARROW BEARER! WHEN I SAY "BOW AN' ARROW" YOU HAND 'EM TO ME!
OKAY, TUB!
BOW AN' ARROW!
HUH?
GOSH, IF THERE REALLY WAS A RABBIT THERE HE'D BE IN THE NEXT COUNTY BY NOW!
YOU MEAN THERE WAS NO RABBIT?
FROM NOW ON CARRY 'EM IN YOUR HAND!
WOW! RABBIT TRACKS!!
BOW AN' ARROW!
KEEP QUIET, LULU! DON'T SAY A WORD! DON'T MAKE ANY NOISE! DON'T—
GOSH, YOU'RE MAKING ALL THE NOISE!
HAH! THERE'S WHERE HE IS! HE WENT INTO THAT HOLE!
WHAT ARE YOU GOING TO DO NOW, TUB?

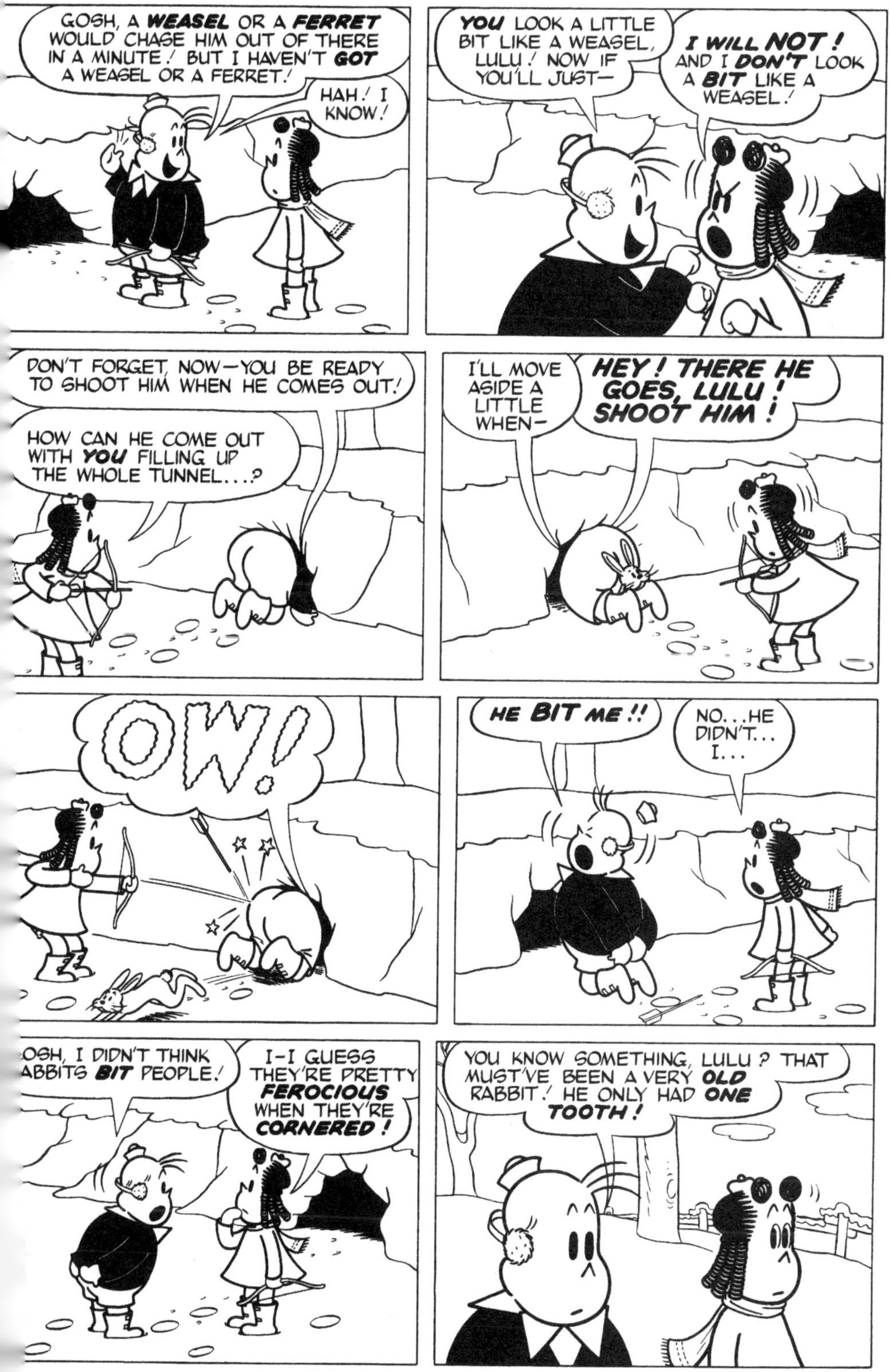
GOSH, A **WEASEL** OR A **FERRET** WOULD CHASE HIM OUT OF THERE IN A MINUTE! BUT I HAVEN'T **GOT** A WEASEL OR A FERRET!
HAH! I KNOW!
YOU LOOK A LITTLE BIT LIKE A WEASEL, LULU! NOW IF YOU'LL JUST—
I WILL NOT! AND I **DON'T** LOOK A **BIT** LIKE A WEASEL!
DON'T FORGET, NOW—YOU BE READY TO SHOOT HIM WHEN HE COMES OUT!
HOW CAN HE COME OUT WITH **YOU** FILLING UP THE WHOLE TUNNEL...?
I'LL MOVE ASIDE A LITTLE WHEN—
HEY! THERE HE GOES, LULU! SHOOT HIM!
OW!
HE BIT ME!!
NO...HE DIDN'T... I...
OSH, I DIDN'T THINK ABBITS **BIT** PEOPLE!
I-I GUESS THEY'RE PRETTY **FEROCIOUS** WHEN THEY'RE **CORNERED!**
YOU KNOW SOMETHING, LULU? THAT MUST'VE BEEN A VERY **OLD** RABBIT! HE ONLY HAD **ONE TOOTH!**

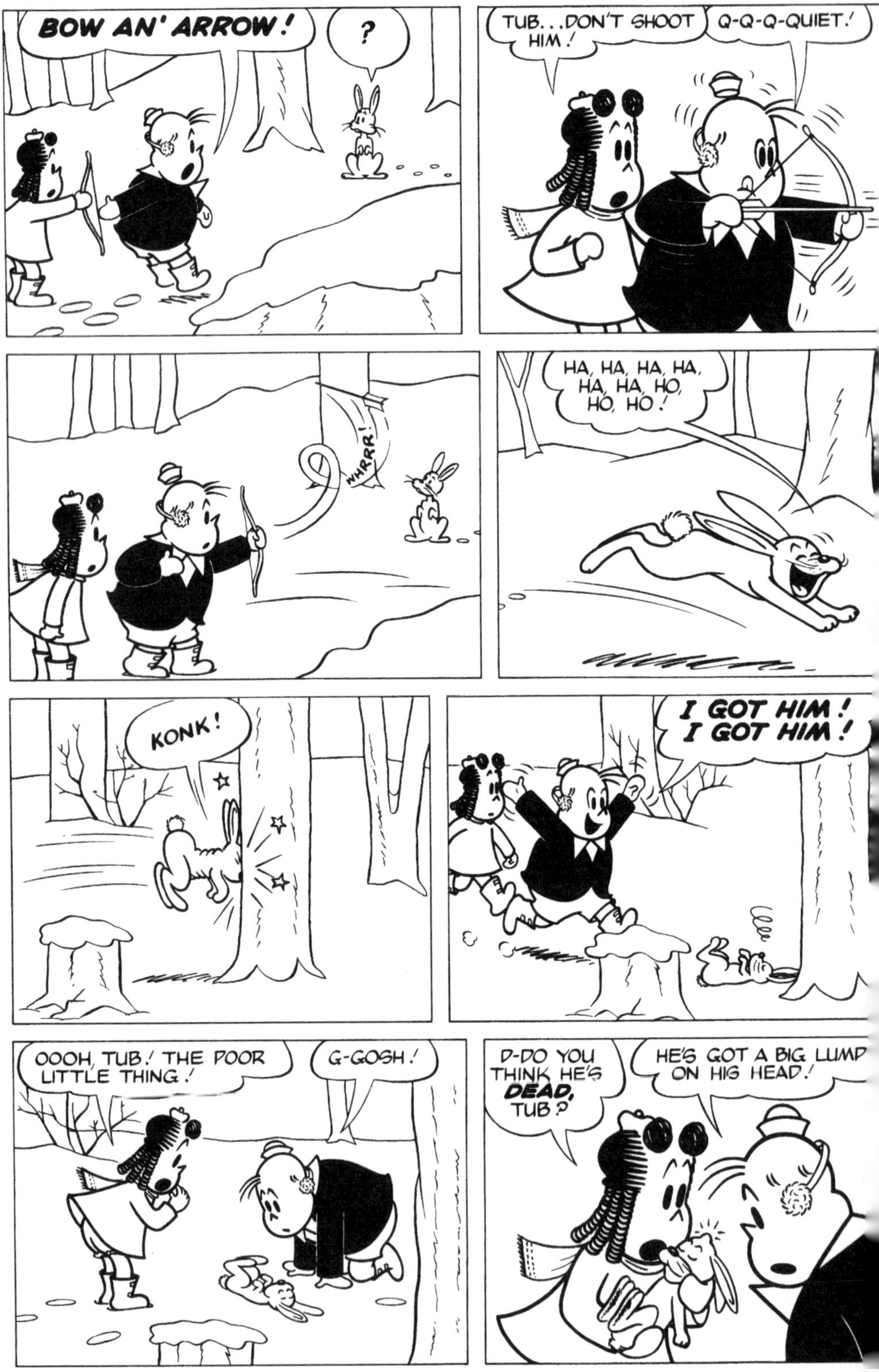
BOW AN' ARROW!
?
TUB...DON'T SHOOT HIM!
Q-Q-Q-QUIET!
WHRRR!
HA, HA, HA, HA, HA, HA, HO, HO, HO!
KONK!
I GOT HIM! I GOT HIM!
OOOH, TUB! THE POOR LITTLE THING!
G-GOSH!
D-DO YOU THINK HE'S DEAD, TUB?
HE'S GOT A BIG LUMP ON HIS HEAD!

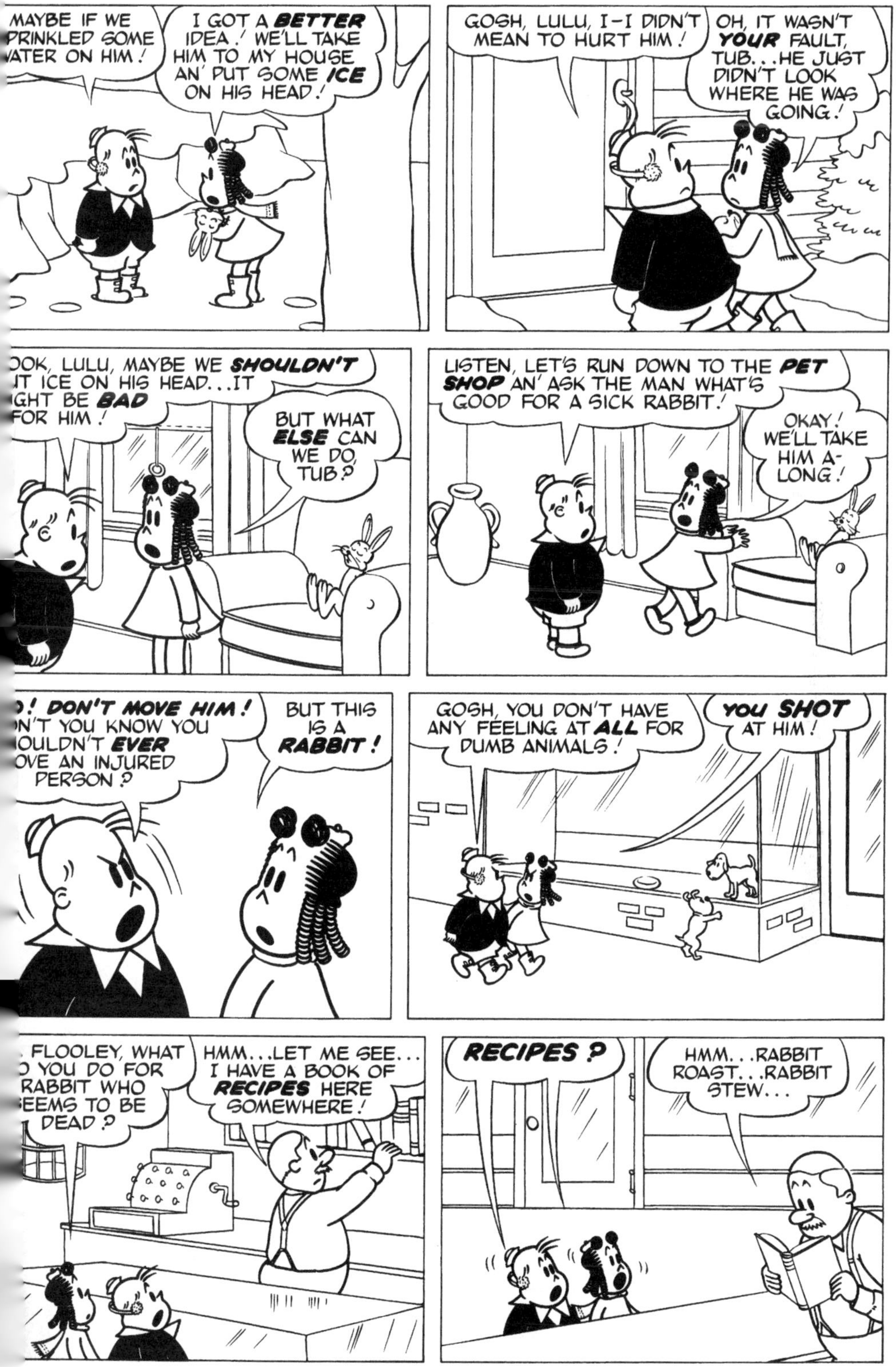

MAYBE IF WE PRINKLED SOME ATER ON HIM!
I GOT A BETTER IDEA! WE'LL TAKE HIM TO MY HOUSE AN' PUT SOME ICE ON HIS HEAD!
GOSH, LULU, I-I DIDN'T MEAN TO HURT HIM!
OH, IT WASN'T YOUR FAULT, TUB...HE JUST DIDN'T LOOK WHERE HE WAS GOING!
OOK, LULU, MAYBE WE SHOULDN'T IT ICE ON HIS HEAD...IT IGHT BE BAD FOR HIM!
BUT WHAT ELSE CAN WE DO, TUB?
LISTEN, LET'S RUN DOWN TO THE PET SHOP AN' ASK THE MAN WHAT'S GOOD FOR A SICK RABBIT!
OKAY! WE'LL TAKE HIM A-LONG!
O! DON'T MOVE HIM! N'T YOU KNOW YOU OULDN'T EVER OVE AN INJURED PERSON?
BUT THIS IS A RABBIT!
GOSH, YOU DON'T HAVE ANY FEELING AT ALL FOR DUMB ANIMALS!
YOU SHOT AT HIM!
FLOOLEY, WHAT O YOU DO FOR RABBIT WHO EEMS TO BE DEAD?
HMM...LET ME SEE... I HAVE A BOOK OF RECIPES HERE SOMEWHERE!
RECIPES?
HMM...RABBIT ROAST...RABBIT STEW...

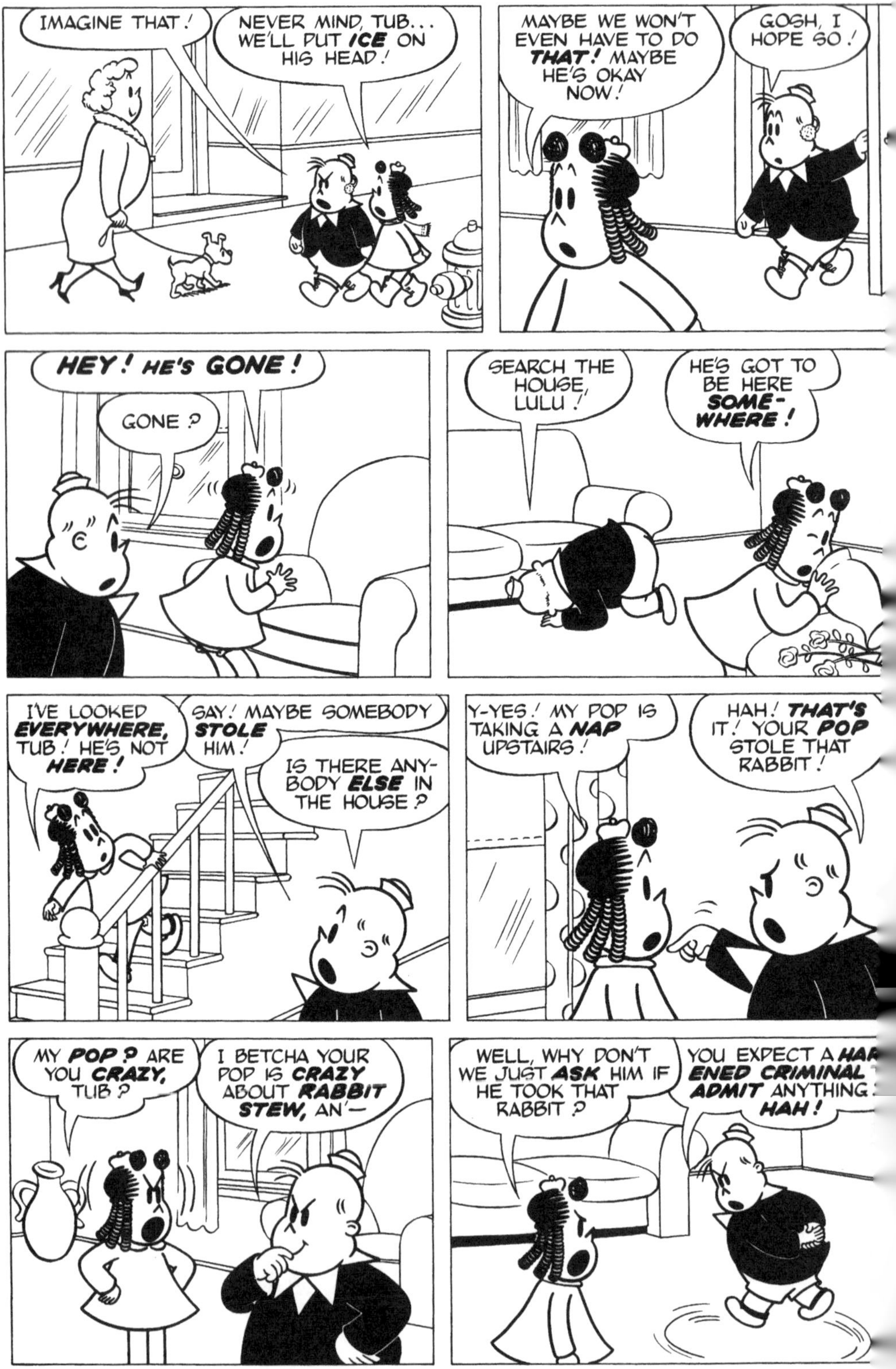
IMAGINE THAT!
NEVER MIND, TUB... WE'LL PUT ICE ON HIS HEAD!
MAYBE WE WON'T EVEN HAVE TO DO THAT! MAYBE HE'S OKAY NOW!
GOSH, I HOPE SO!
HEY! HE'S GONE!
GONE?
SEARCH THE HOUSE, LULU!
HE'S GOT TO BE HERE SOME-WHERE!
I'VE LOOKED EVERYWHERE, TUB! HE'S NOT HERE!
SAY! MAYBE SOMEBODY STOLE HIM!
IS THERE ANY-BODY ELSE IN THE HOUSE?
Y-YES! MY POP IS TAKING A NAP UPSTAIRS!
HAH! THAT'S IT! YOUR POP STOLE THAT RABBIT!
MY POP? ARE YOU CRAZY, TUB?
I BETCHA YOUR POP IS CRAZY ABOUT RABBIT STEW, AN'—
WELL, WHY DON'T WE JUST ASK HIM IF HE TOOK THAT RABBIT?
YOU EXPECT A HAR ENED CRIMINAL ADMIT ANYTHING HAH!

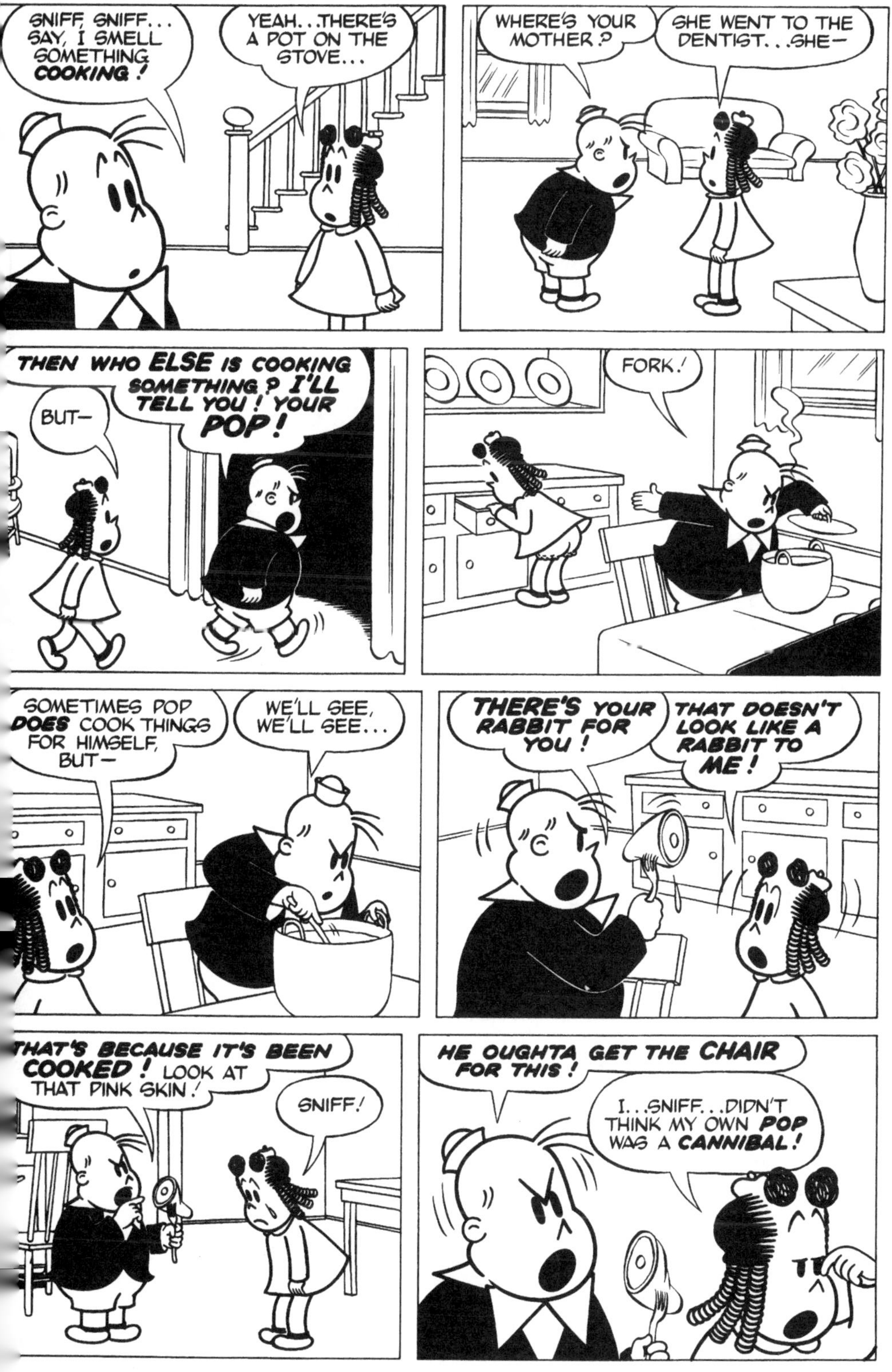
SNIFF, SNIFF... SAY, I SMELL SOMETHING COOKING!
YEAH...THERE'S A POT ON THE STOVE...
WHERE'S YOUR MOTHER?
SHE WENT TO THE DENTIST...SHE—
THEN WHO ELSE IS COOKING SOMETHING? I'LL TELL YOU! YOUR POP!
BUT—
FORK!
SOMETIMES POP DOES COOK THINGS FOR HIMSELF, BUT—
WE'LL SEE, WE'LL SEE...
THERE'S YOUR RABBIT FOR YOU!
THAT DOESN'T LOOK LIKE A RABBIT TO ME!
THAT'S BECAUSE IT'S BEEN COOKED! LOOK AT THAT PINK SKIN!
SNIFF!
HE OUGHTA GET THE CHAIR FOR THIS!
I...SNIFF...DIDN'T THINK MY OWN POP WAS A CANNIBAL!

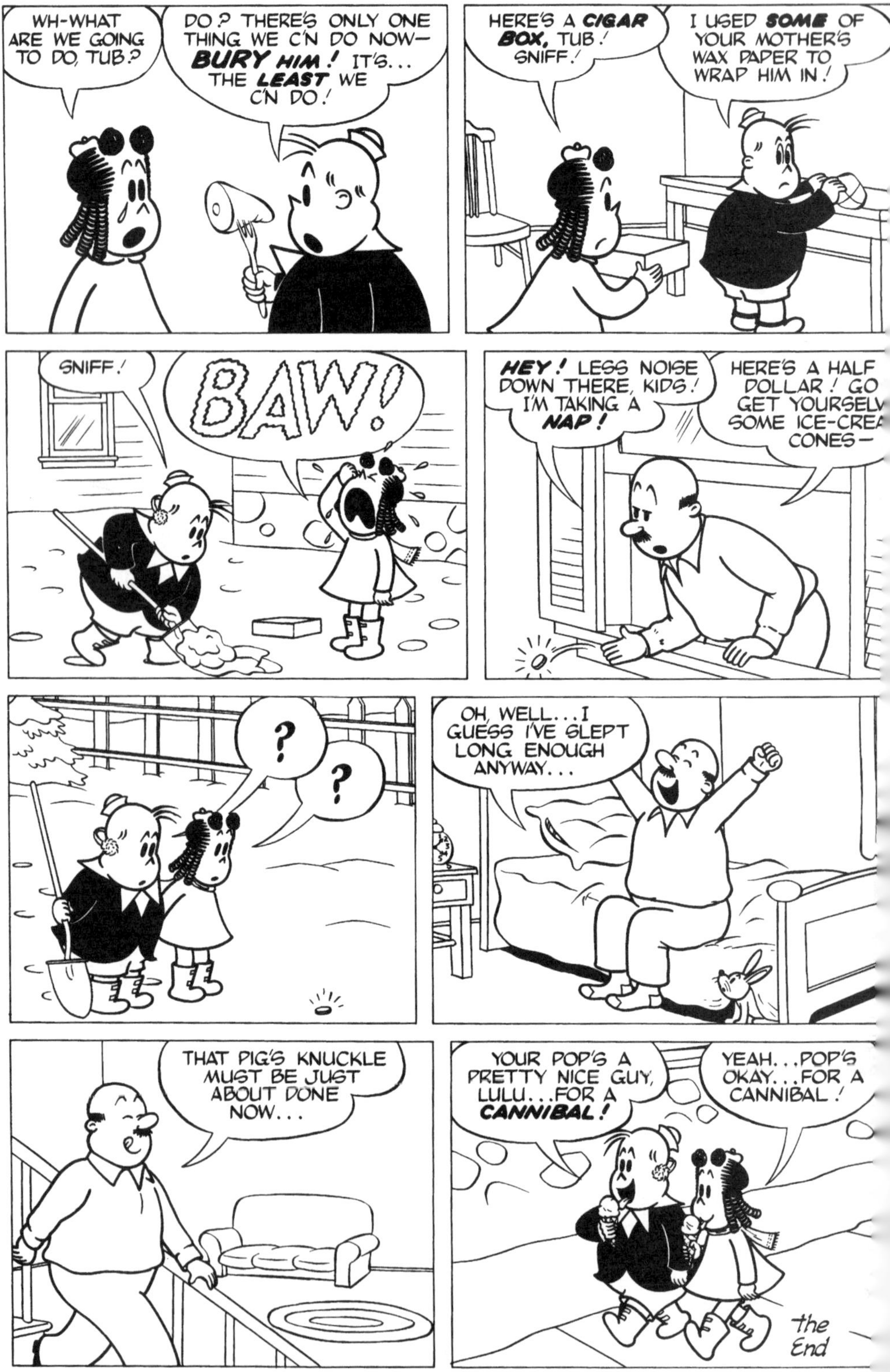
WH-WHAT ARE WE GOING TO DO, TUB?
DO? THERE'S ONLY ONE THING WE C'N DO NOW— BURY HIM! IT'S... THE LEAST WE C'N DO!
HERE'S A CIGAR BOX, TUB! SNIFF!
I USED SOME OF YOUR MOTHER'S WAX PAPER TO WRAP HIM IN!
SNIFF!
BAW!
HEY! LESS NOISE DOWN THERE, KIDS! I'M TAKING A NAP!
HERE'S A HALF DOLLAR! GO GET YOURSELV SOME ICE-CREA CONES—
?
?
OH, WELL... I GUESS I'VE SLEPT LONG ENOUGH ANYWAY...
THAT PIG'S KNUCKLE MUST BE JUST ABOUT DONE NOW...
YOUR POP'S A PRETTY NICE GUY, LULU... FOR A CANNIBAL!
YEAH... POP'S OKAY... FOR A CANNIBAL!
the End

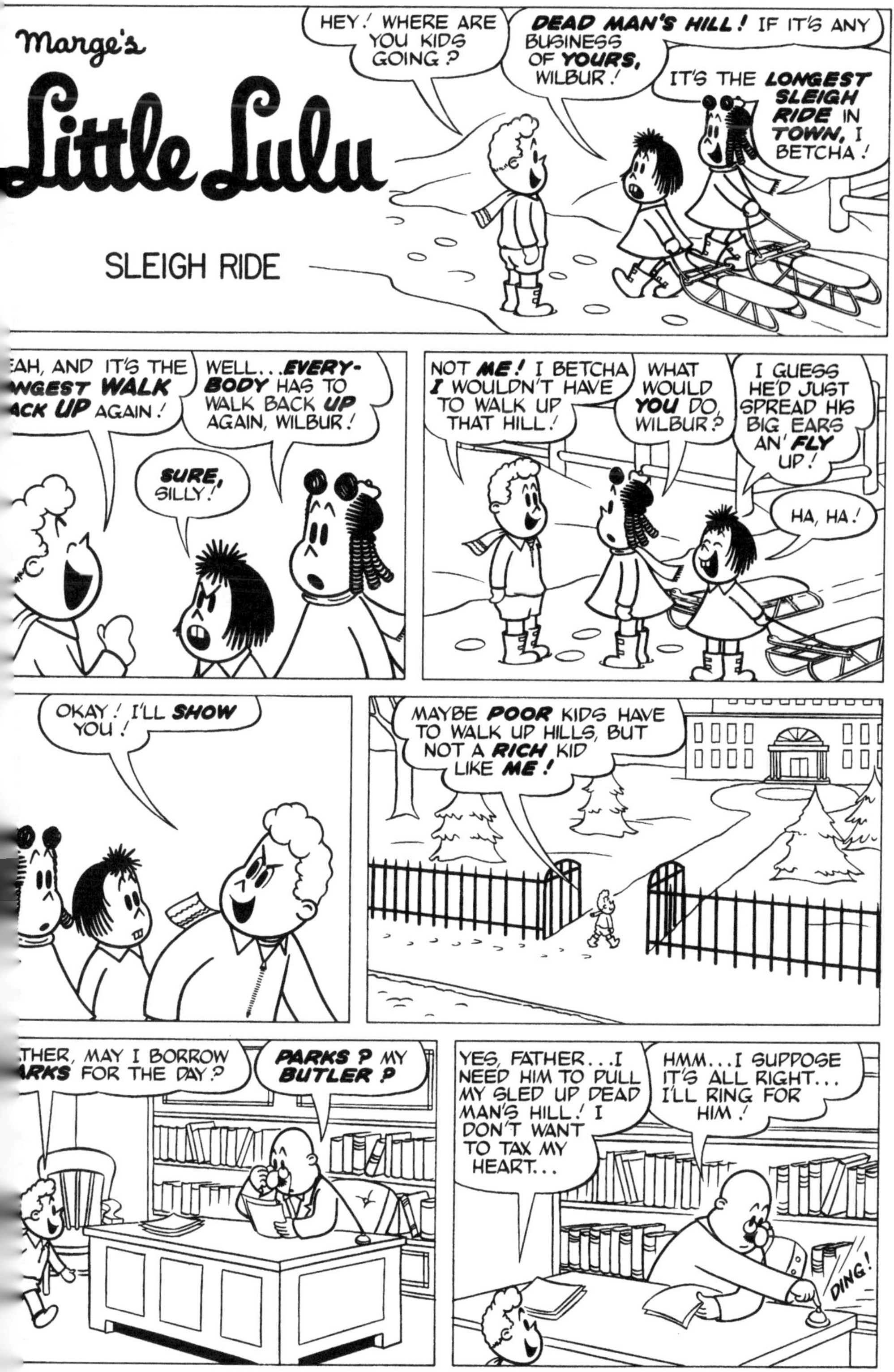
Marge's
Little Lulu
SLEIGH RIDE
HEY! WHERE ARE YOU KIDS GOING?
DEAD MAN'S HILL! IF IT'S ANY BUSINESS OF YOURS, WILBUR!
IT'S THE LONGEST SLEIGH RIDE IN TOWN, I BETCHA!
EAH, AND IT'S THE NGEST WALK ACK UP AGAIN!
SURE, SILLY!
WELL... EVERYBODY HAS TO WALK BACK UP AGAIN, WILBUR!
NOT ME! I BETCHA I WOULDN'T HAVE TO WALK UP THAT HILL!
WHAT WOULD YOU DO, WILBUR?
I GUESS HE'D JUST SPREAD HIS BIG EARS AN' FLY UP!
HA, HA!
OKAY! I'LL SHOW YOU!
MAYBE POOR KIDS HAVE TO WALK UP HILLS, BUT NOT A RICH KID LIKE ME!
THER, MAY I BORROW ARKS FOR THE DAY?
PARKS? MY BUTLER?
YES, FATHER... I NEED HIM TO PULL MY SLED UP DEAD MAN'S HILL! I DON'T WANT TO TAX MY HEART...
HMM... I SUPPOSE IT'S ALL RIGHT... I'LL RING FOR HIM!
DING!

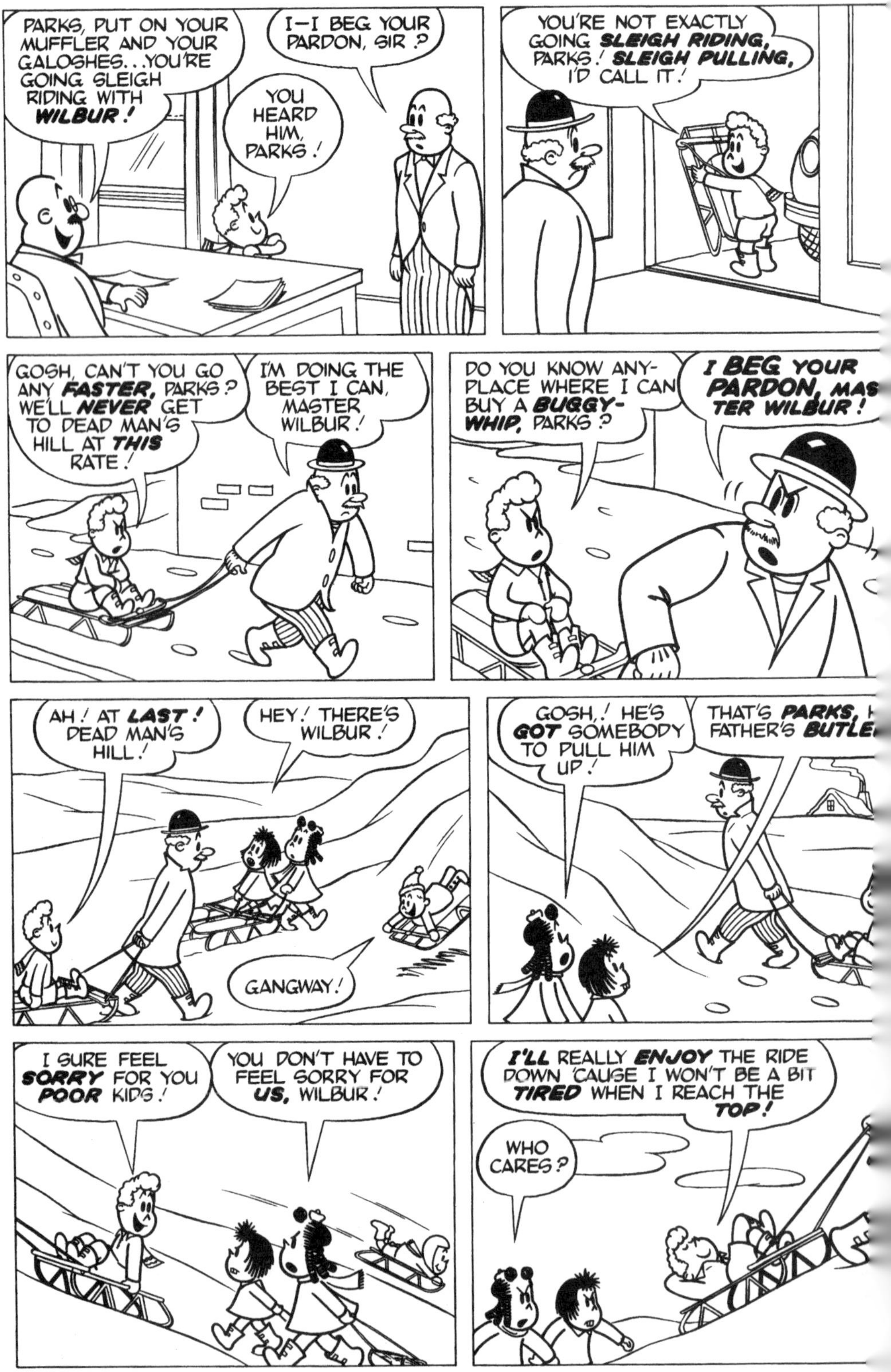
PARKS, PUT ON YOUR MUFFLER AND YOUR GALOSHES...YOU'RE GOING SLEIGH RIDING WITH WILBUR!
YOU HEARD HIM, PARKS!
I—I BEG YOUR PARDON, SIR?
YOU'RE NOT EXACTLY GOING SLEIGH RIDING, PARKS! SLEIGH PULLING, I'D CALL IT!
GOSH, CAN'T YOU GO ANY FASTER, PARKS? WE'LL NEVER GET TO DEAD MAN'S HILL AT THIS RATE!
I'M DOING THE BEST I CAN, MASTER WILBUR!
DO YOU KNOW ANY-PLACE WHERE I CAN BUY A BUGGY-WHIP, PARKS?
I BEG YOUR PARDON, MAS TER WILBUR!
AH! AT LAST! DEAD MAN'S HILL!
HEY! THERE'S WILBUR!
GANGWAY!
GOSH! HE'S GOT SOMEBODY TO PULL HIM UP!
THAT'S PARKS, FATHER'S BUTLE
I SURE FEEL SORRY FOR YOU POOR KIDS!
YOU DON'T HAVE TO FEEL SORRY FOR US, WILBUR!
I'LL REALLY ENJOY THE RIDE DOWN 'CAUSE I WON'T BE A BIT TIRED WHEN I REACH THE TOP!
WHO CARES?

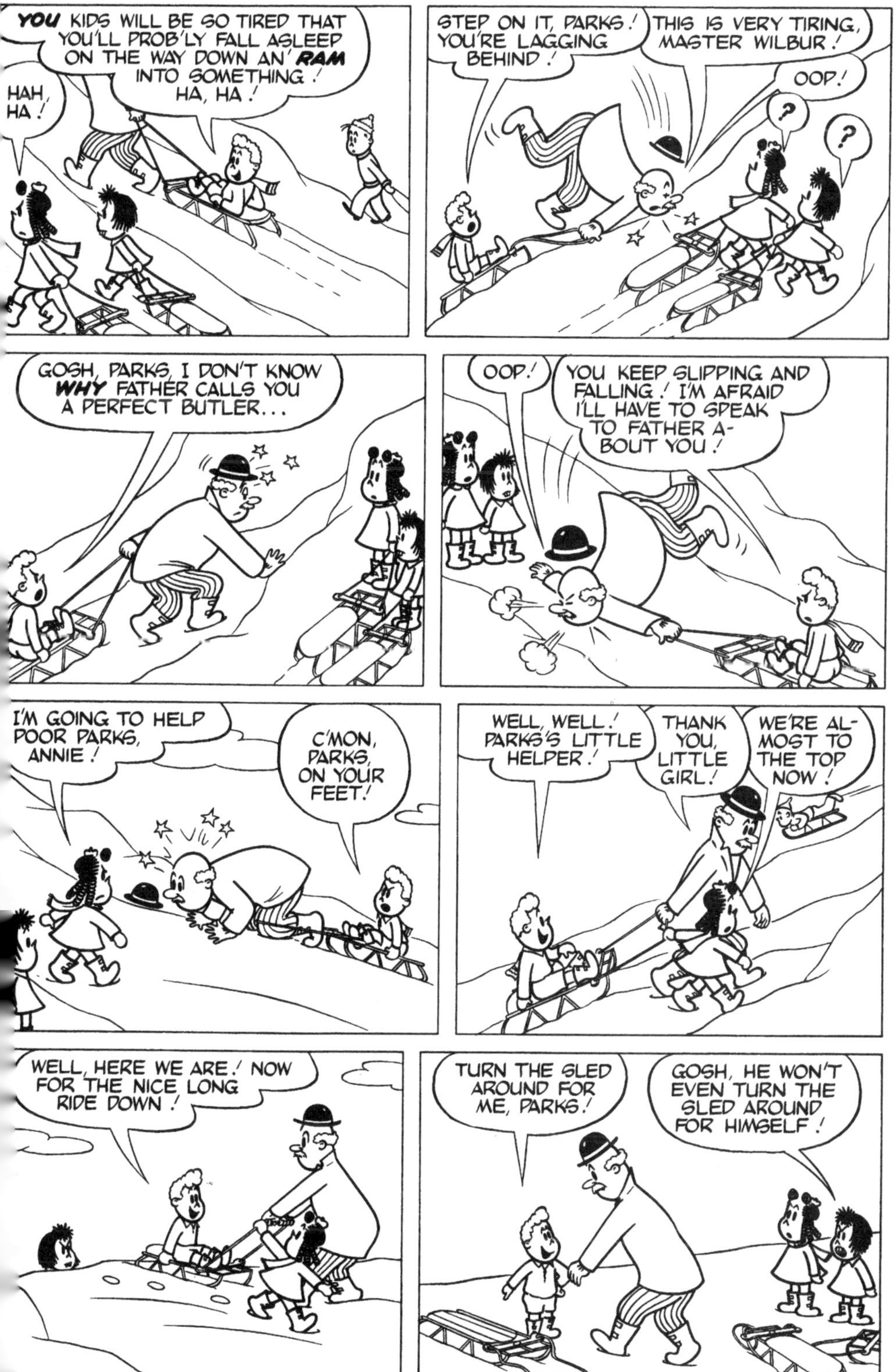
YOU KIDS WILL BE SO TIRED THAT YOU'LL PROB'LY FALL ASLEEP ON THE WAY DOWN AN' RAM INTO SOMETHING! HA, HA!
HAH, HA!
STEP ON IT, PARKS! YOU'RE LAGGING BEHIND!
THIS IS VERY TIRING, MASTER WILBUR!
OOP!
?
?
GOSH, PARKS, I DON'T KNOW WHY FATHER CALLS YOU A PERFECT BUTLER...
OOP!
YOU KEEP SLIPPING AND FALLING! I'M AFRAID I'LL HAVE TO SPEAK TO FATHER ABOUT YOU!
I'M GOING TO HELP POOR PARKS, ANNIE!
C'MON, PARKS, ON YOUR FEET!
WELL, WELL! PARKS'S LITTLE HELPER!
THANK YOU, LITTLE GIRL!
WE'RE ALMOST TO THE TOP NOW!
WELL, HERE WE ARE! NOW FOR THE NICE LONG RIDE DOWN!
TURN THE SLED AROUND FOR ME, PARKS!
GOSH, HE WON'T EVEN TURN THE SLED AROUND FOR HIMSELF!

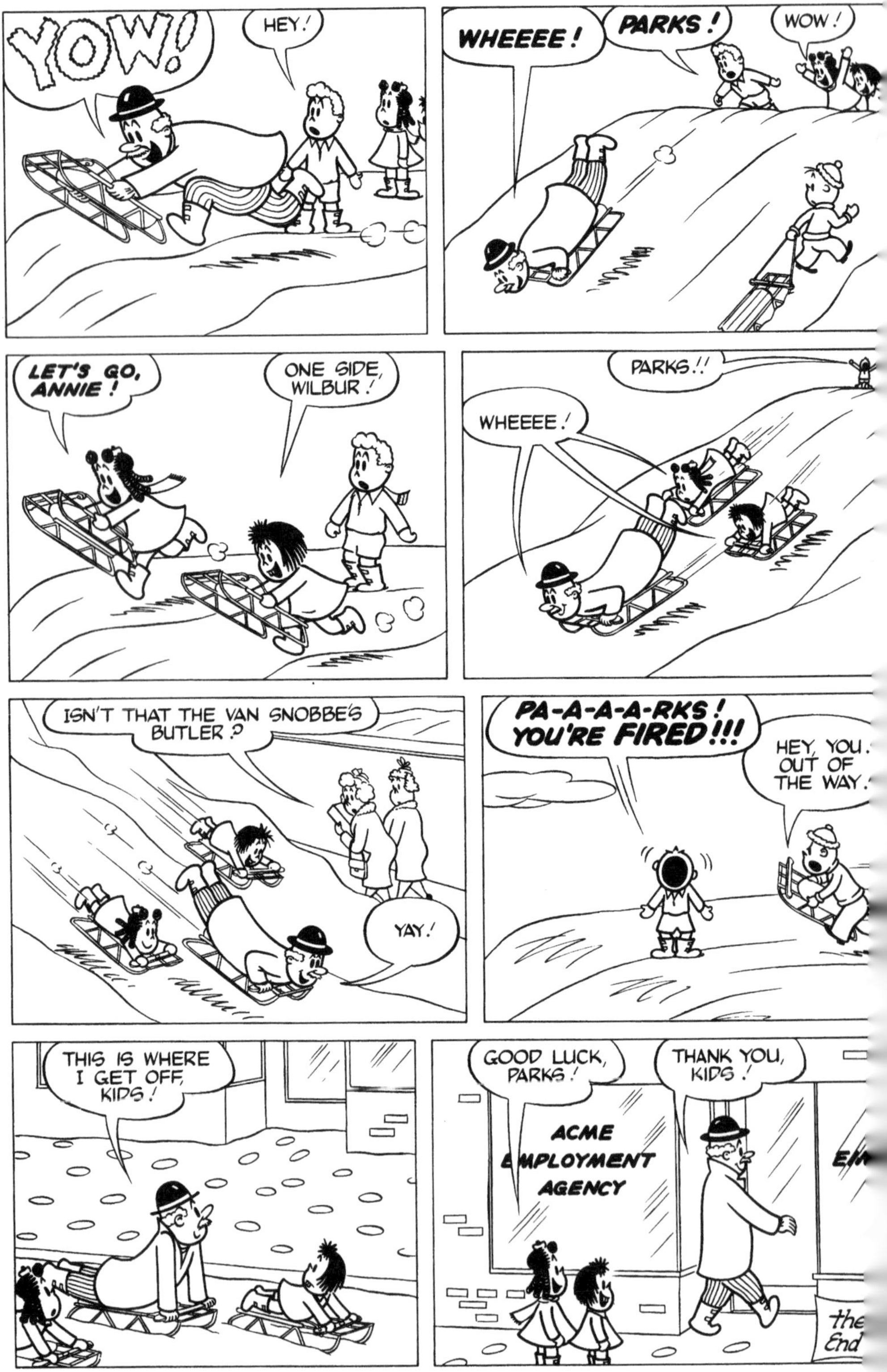
YOW!
HEY!
WHEEEE!
PARKS!
WOW!
LET'S GO, ANNIE!
ONE SIDE, WILBUR!
PARKS!!
WHEEEE!
ISN'T THAT THE VAN SNOBBE'S BUTLER?
YAY!
PA-A-A-A-RKS! YOU'RE FIRED!!!
HEY, YOU. OUT OF THE WAY.
THIS IS WHERE I GET OFF, KIDS!
GOOD LUCK, PARKS!
THANK YOU, KIDS!
ACME EMPLOYMENT AGENCY
the End

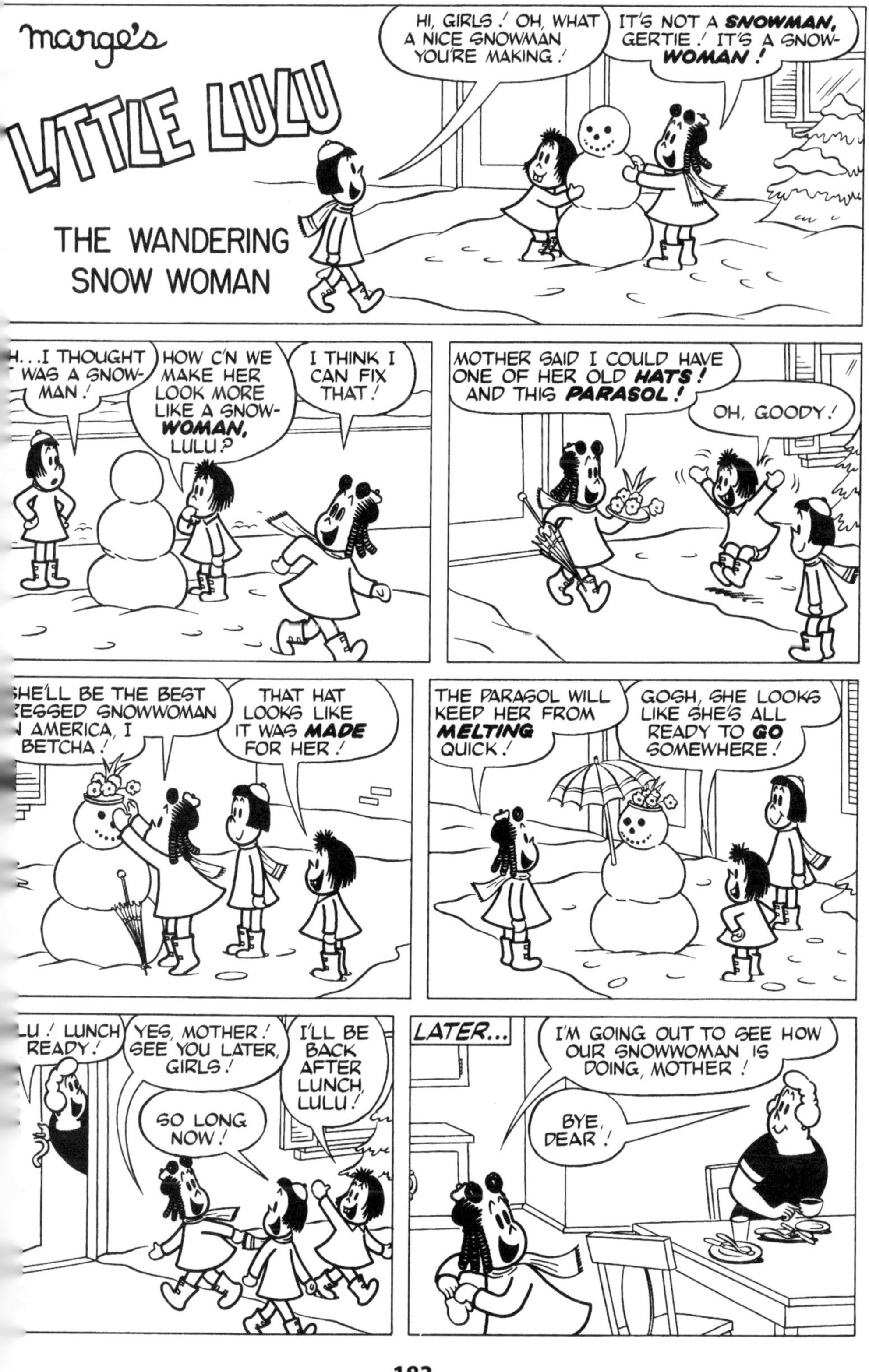
marge's
LITTLE LULU
THE WANDERING SNOW WOMAN
HI, GIRLS! OH, WHAT A NICE SNOWMAN YOU'RE MAKING!
IT'S NOT A **SNOWMAN,** GERTIE! IT'S A SNOW-**WOMAN!**
H...I THOUGHT T WAS A SNOW-MAN!
HOW C'N WE MAKE HER LOOK MORE LIKE A SNOW-**WOMAN,** LULU?
I THINK I CAN FIX THAT!
MOTHER SAID I COULD HAVE ONE OF HER OLD **HATS!** AND THIS **PARASOL!**
OH, GOODY!
HE'LL BE THE BEST RESSED SNOWWOMAN N AMERICA, I BETCHA!
THAT HAT LOOKS LIKE IT WAS **MADE** FOR HER!
THE PARASOL WILL KEEP HER FROM **MELTING** QUICK!
GOSH, SHE LOOKS LIKE SHE'S ALL READY TO **GO** SOMEWHERE!
LU! LUNCH READY!
YES, MOTHER! SEE YOU LATER, GIRLS!
I'LL BE BACK AFTER LUNCH, LULU!
SO LONG NOW!
LATER...
I'M GOING OUT TO SEE HOW OUR SNOWWOMAN IS DOING, MOTHER!
BYE, DEAR!

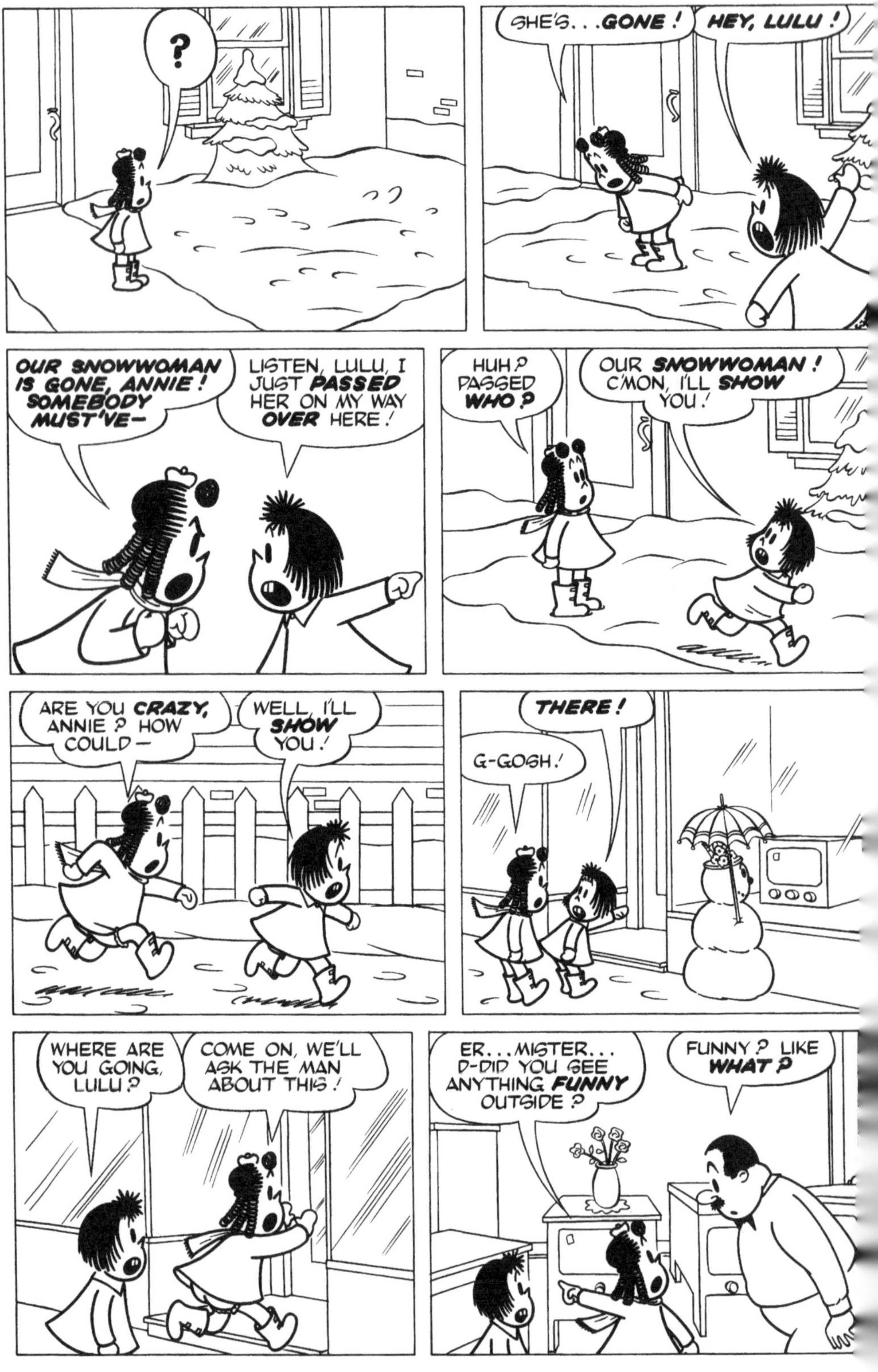
?
SHE'S...GONE!
HEY, LULU!
OUR SNOWWOMAN IS GONE, ANNIE! SOMEBODY MUST'VE—
LISTEN, LULU, I JUST PASSED HER ON MY WAY OVER HERE!
HUH? PASSED WHO?
OUR SNOWWOMAN! C'MON, I'LL SHOW YOU!
ARE YOU CRAZY, ANNIE? HOW COULD—
WELL, I'LL SHOW YOU!
THERE!
G-GOSH!
WHERE ARE YOU GOING, LULU?
COME ON, WE'LL ASK THE MAN ABOUT THIS!
ER...MISTER... D-DID YOU SEE ANYTHING FUNNY OUTSIDE?
FUNNY? LIKE WHAT?

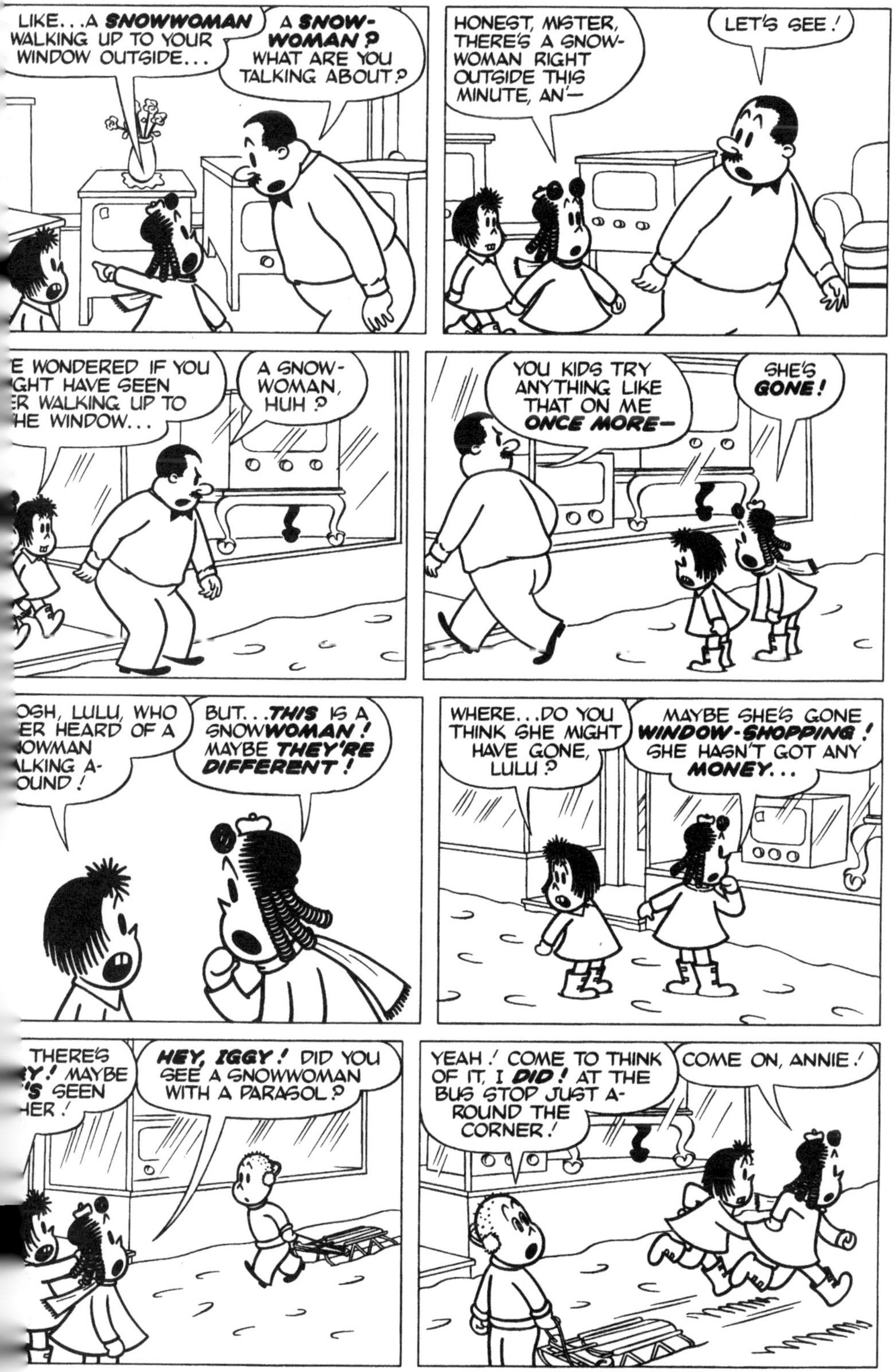
LIKE...A SNOWWOMAN WALKING UP TO YOUR WINDOW OUTSIDE...
A SNOW-WOMAN? WHAT ARE YOU TALKING ABOUT?
HONEST, MISTER, THERE'S A SNOW-WOMAN RIGHT OUTSIDE THIS MINUTE, AN'—
LET'S SEE!
E WONDERED IF YOU GHT HAVE SEEN ER WALKING UP TO HE WINDOW...
A SNOW-WOMAN, HUH?
YOU KIDS TRY ANYTHING LIKE THAT ON ME ONCE MORE—
SHE'S GONE!
OSH, LULU, WHO ER HEARD OF A OWMAN LKING A-OUND!
BUT...THIS IS A SNOWWOMAN! MAYBE THEY'RE DIFFERENT!
WHERE...DO YOU THINK SHE MIGHT HAVE GONE, LULU?
MAYBE SHE'S GONE WINDOW-SHOPPING! SHE HASN'T GOT ANY MONEY...
THERE'S Y! MAYBE 'S SEEN HER!
HEY, IGGY! DID YOU SEE A SNOWWOMAN WITH A PARASOL?
YEAH! COME TO THINK OF IT, I DID! AT THE BUS STOP JUST A-ROUND THE CORNER!
COME ON, ANNIE!

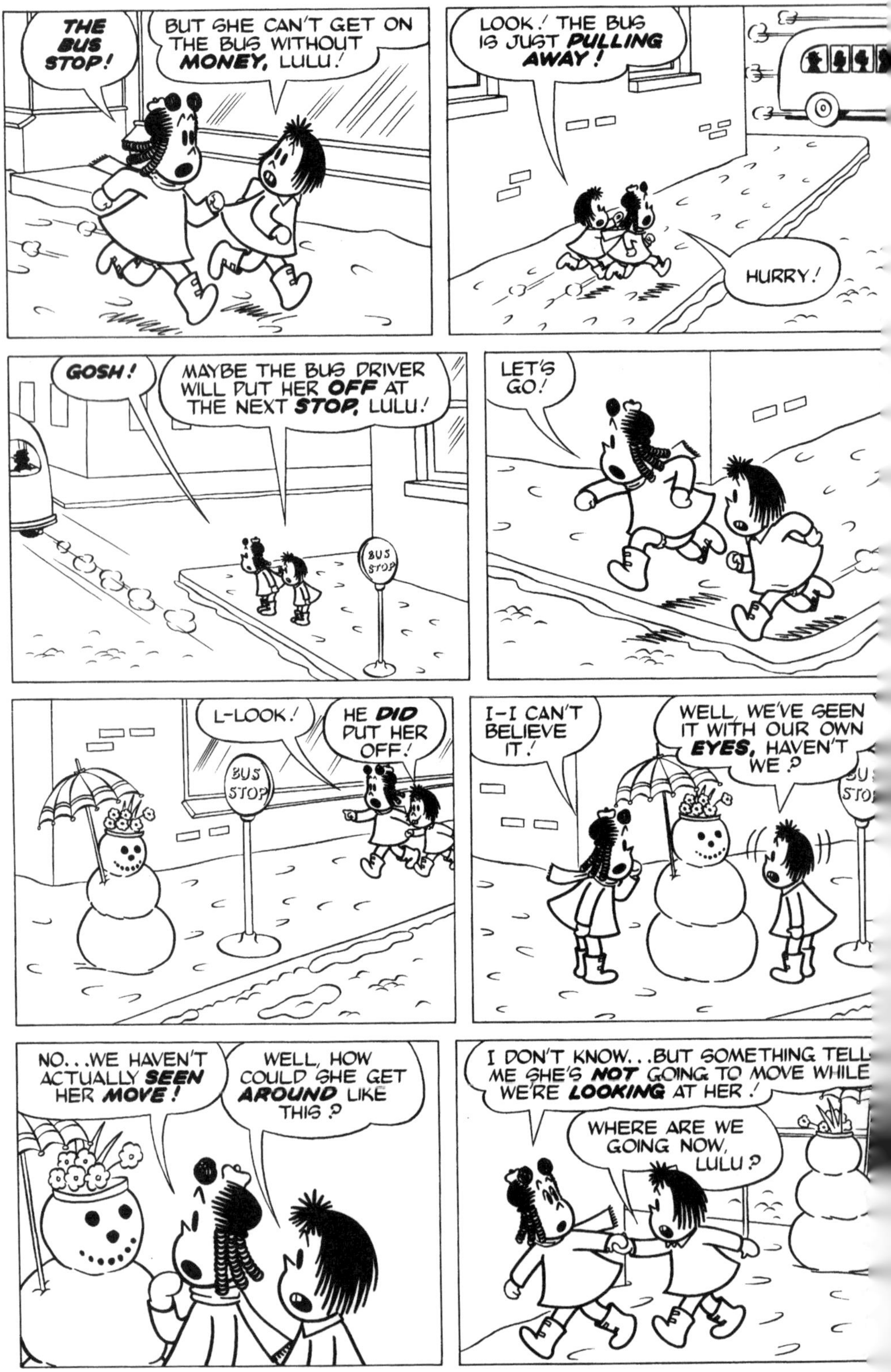
THE BUS STOP!
BUT SHE CAN'T GET ON THE BUS WITHOUT MONEY, LULU!
LOOK! THE BUS IS JUST PULLING AWAY!
HURRY!
GOSH!
MAYBE THE BUS DRIVER WILL PUT HER OFF AT THE NEXT STOP, LULU!
BUS STOP
LET'S GO!
L-LOOK!
HE DID PUT HER OFF!
BUS STOP
I-I CAN'T BELIEVE IT!
WELL, WE'VE SEEN IT WITH OUR OWN EYES, HAVEN'T WE?
NO...WE HAVEN'T ACTUALLY SEEN HER MOVE!
WELL, HOW COULD SHE GET AROUND LIKE THIS?
I DON'T KNOW...BUT SOMETHING TELL ME SHE'S NOT GOING TO MOVE WHILE WE'RE LOOKING AT HER!
WHERE ARE WE GOING NOW, LULU?

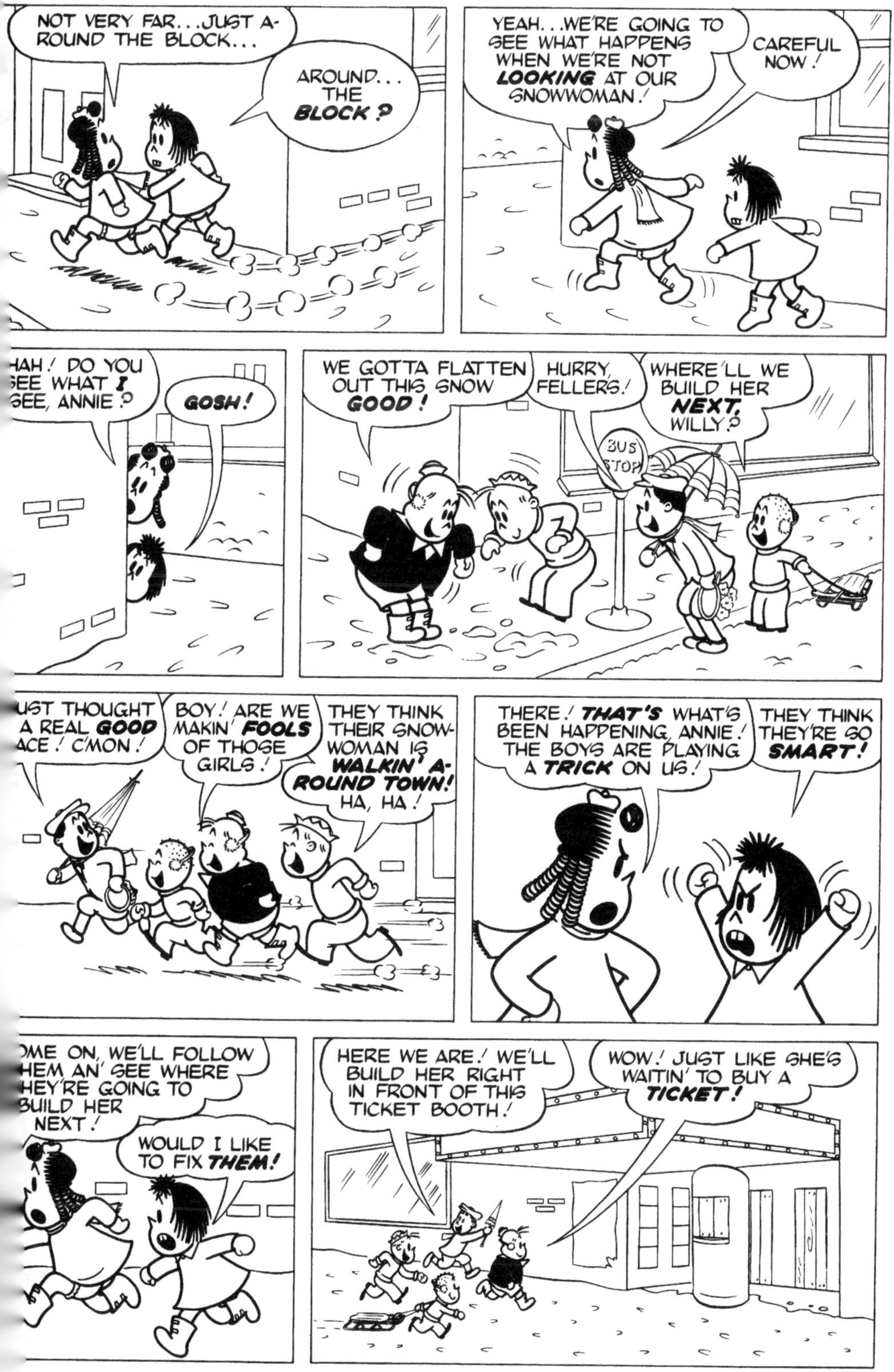
NOT VERY FAR...JUST A-ROUND THE BLOCK...
AROUND... THE **BLOCK?**
YEAH...WE'RE GOING TO SEE WHAT HAPPENS WHEN WE'RE NOT **LOOKING** AT OUR SNOWWOMAN!
CAREFUL NOW!
HAH! DO YOU SEE WHAT **I** SEE, ANNIE?
GOSH!
WE GOTTA FLATTEN OUT THIS SNOW **GOOD!**
HURRY, FELLERS!
WHERE'LL WE BUILD HER **NEXT,** WILLY?
BUS STOP
UST THOUGHT A REAL **GOOD** ACE! C'MON!
BOY! ARE WE MAKIN' **FOOLS** OF THOSE GIRLS!
THEY THINK THEIR SNOW-WOMAN IS **WALKIN' A-ROUND TOWN!** HA, HA!
THERE! **THAT'S** WHAT'S BEEN HAPPENING, ANNIE! THE BOYS ARE PLAYING A **TRICK** ON US!
THEY THINK THEY'RE SO **SMART!**
OME ON, WE'LL FOLLOW HEM AN' SEE WHERE HEY'RE GOING TO BUILD HER NEXT!
WOULD I LIKE TO FIX **THEM!**
HERE WE ARE! WE'LL BUILD HER RIGHT IN FRONT OF THIS TICKET BOOTH!
WOW! JUST LIKE SHE'S WAITIN' TO BUY A **TICKET!**

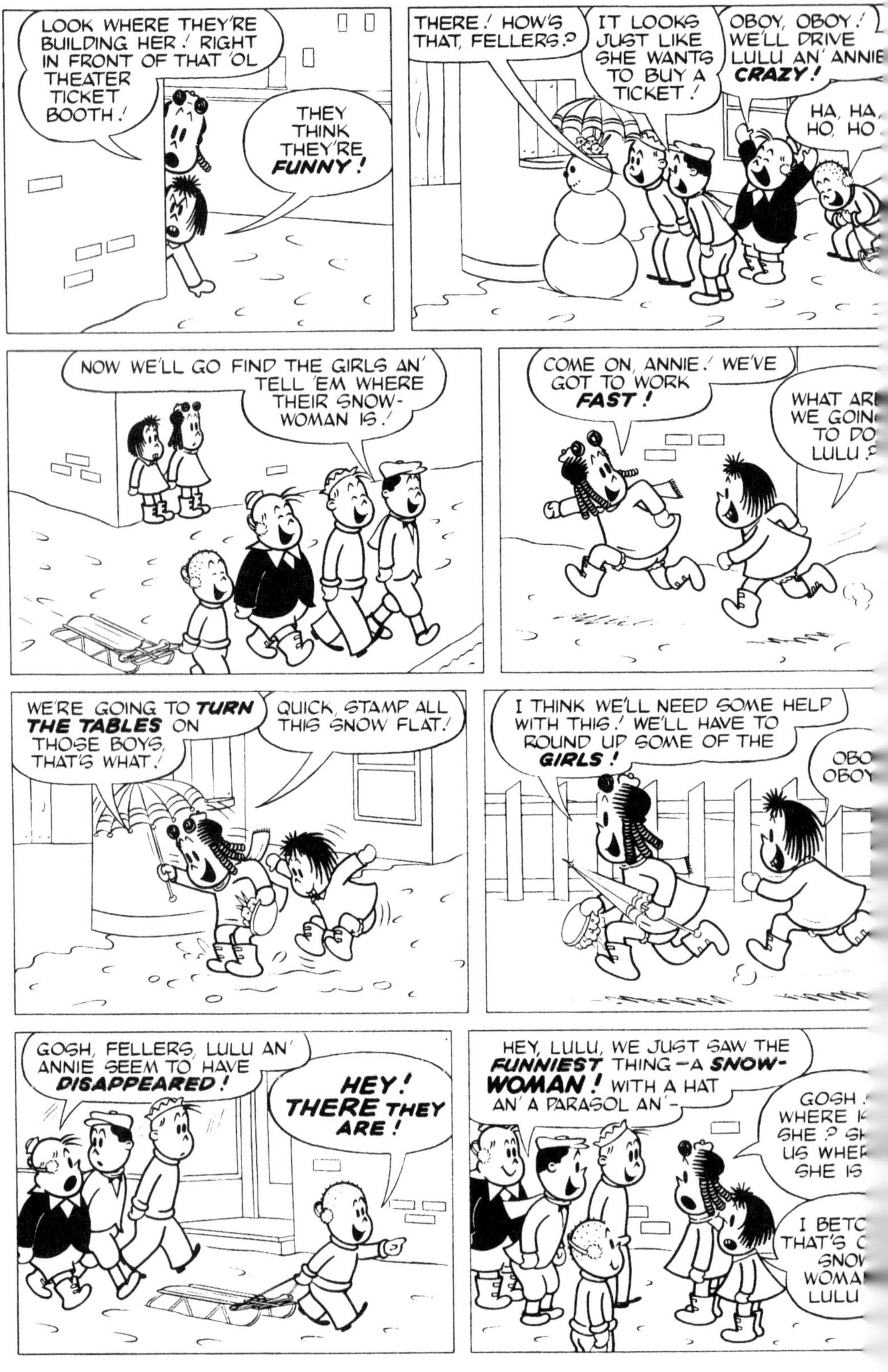

LOOK WHERE THEY'RE BUILDING HER! RIGHT IN FRONT OF THAT 'OL THEATER TICKET BOOTH!
THEY THINK THEY'RE **FUNNY**!
THERE! HOW'S THAT, FELLERS?
IT LOOKS JUST LIKE SHE WANTS TO BUY A TICKET!
OBOY, OBOY! WE'LL DRIVE LULU AN' ANNIE **CRAZY**!
HA, HA, HO, HO
NOW WE'LL GO FIND THE GIRLS AN' TELL 'EM WHERE THEIR SNOW-WOMAN IS!
COME ON, ANNIE! WE'VE GOT TO WORK **FAST**!
WHAT AR WE GOIN TO DO LULU?
WE'RE GOING TO **TURN THE TABLES** ON THOSE BOYS, THAT'S WHAT!
QUICK, STAMP ALL THIS SNOW FLAT!
I THINK WE'LL NEED SOME HELP WITH THIS! WE'LL HAVE TO ROUND UP SOME OF THE **GIRLS**!
OBO OBOY
GOSH, FELLERS, LULU AN' ANNIE SEEM TO HAVE **DISAPPEARED**!
HEY! THERE THEY ARE!
HEY, LULU, WE JUST SAW THE **FUNNIEST** THING—A **SNOW-WOMAN**! WITH A HAT AN' A PARASOL AN'—
GOSH! WHERE I SHE? SH US WHER SHE IS
I BETC THAT'S C SNOW WOMA LULU

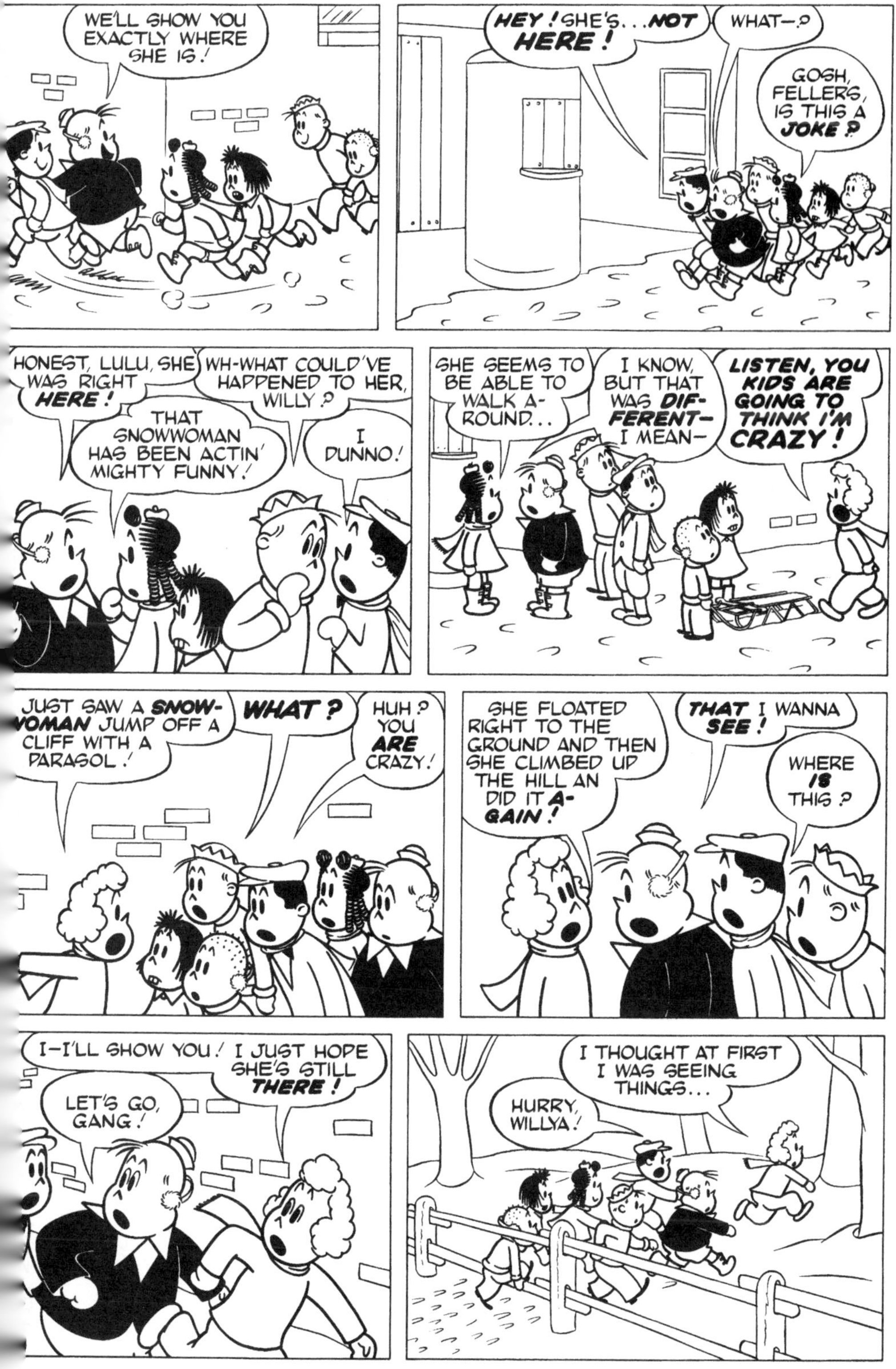
WE'LL SHOW YOU EXACTLY WHERE SHE IS!
HEY! SHE'S... NOT HERE!
WHAT—?
GOSH, FELLERS, IS THIS A JOKE?
HONEST, LULU, SHE WAS RIGHT HERE!
WH-WHAT COULD'VE HAPPENED TO HER, WILLY?
THAT SNOWWOMAN HAS BEEN ACTIN' MIGHTY FUNNY!
I DUNNO!
SHE SEEMS TO BE ABLE TO WALK A-ROUND...
I KNOW, BUT THAT WAS DIF-FERENT— I MEAN—
LISTEN, YOU KIDS ARE GOING TO THINK I'M CRAZY!
JUST SAW A SNOW-WOMAN JUMP OFF A CLIFF WITH A PARASOL!
WHAT?
HUH? YOU ARE CRAZY!
SHE FLOATED RIGHT TO THE GROUND AND THEN SHE CLIMBED UP THE HILL AN DID IT A-GAIN!
THAT I WANNA SEE!
WHERE IS THIS?
I—I'LL SHOW YOU! I JUST HOPE SHE'S STILL THERE!
LET'S GO, GANG!
I THOUGHT AT FIRST I WAS SEEING THINGS...
HURRY, WILLYA!

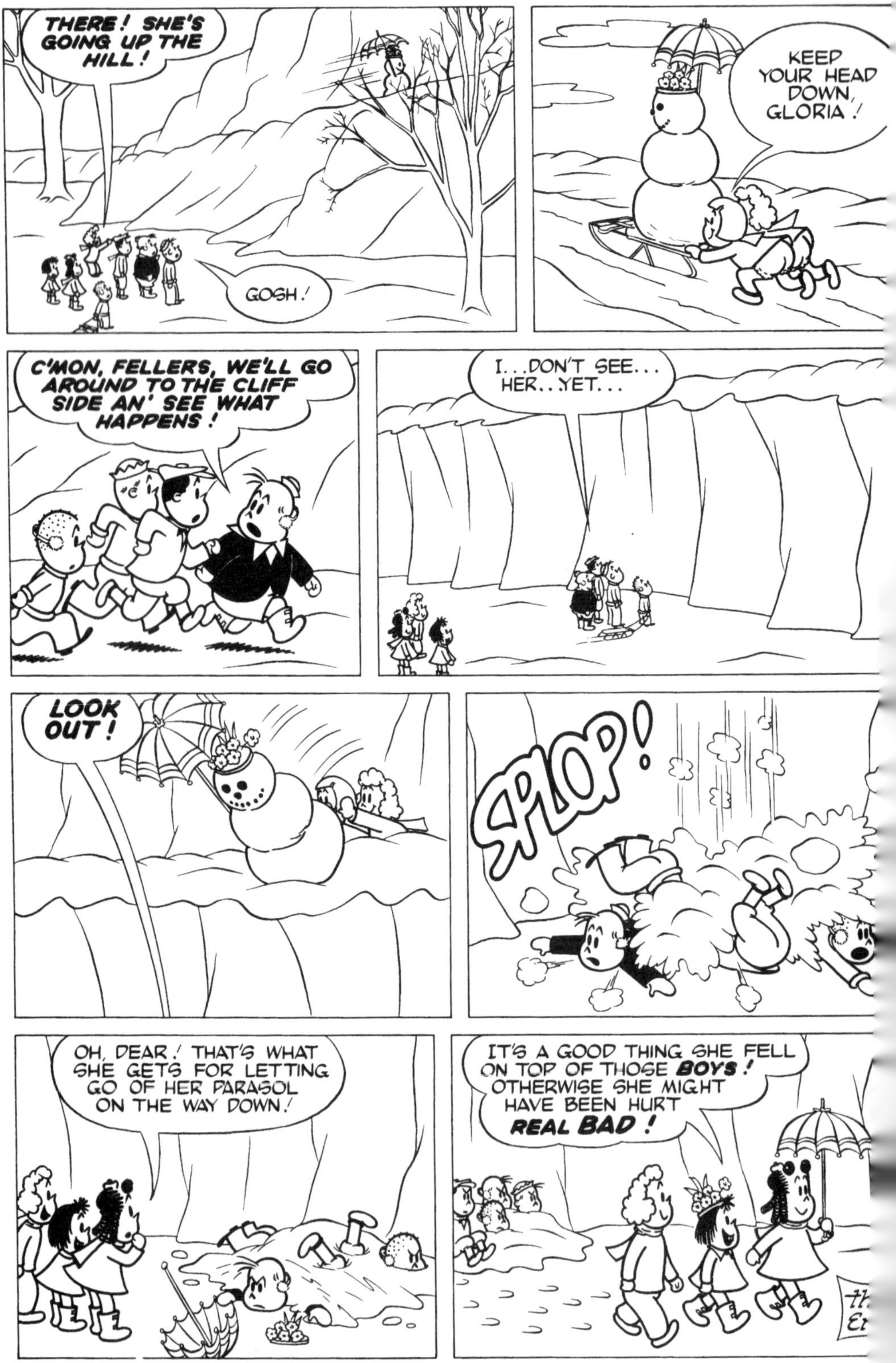
THERE! SHE'S GOING UP THE HILL!
GOSH!
KEEP YOUR HEAD DOWN, GLORIA!
C'MON, FELLERS, WE'LL GO AROUND TO THE CLIFF SIDE AN' SEE WHAT HAPPENS!
I...DON'T SEE... HER...YET...
LOOK OUT!
SPLOP!
OH, DEAR! THAT'S WHAT SHE GETS FOR LETTING GO OF HER PARASOL ON THE WAY DOWN!
IT'S A GOOD THING SHE FELL ON TOP OF THOSE BOYS! OTHERWISE SHE MIGHT HAVE BEEN HURT REAL BAD!

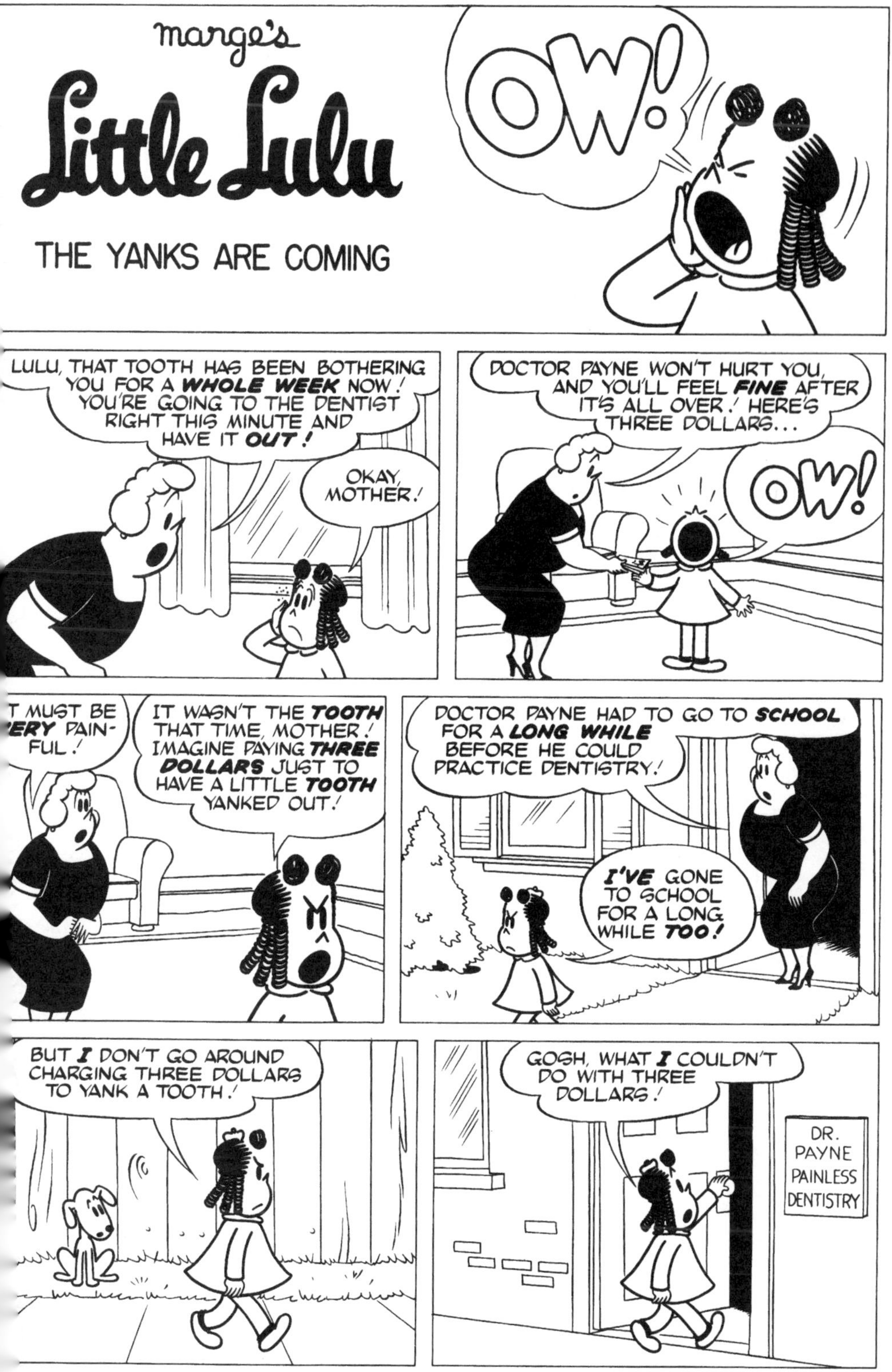
marge's
Little Lulu
THE YANKS ARE COMING
OW!
LULU, THAT TOOTH HAS BEEN BOTHERING YOU FOR A **WHOLE WEEK** NOW! YOU'RE GOING TO THE DENTIST RIGHT THIS MINUTE AND HAVE IT **OUT**!
OKAY, MOTHER!
DOCTOR PAYNE WON'T HURT YOU, AND YOU'LL FEEL **FINE** AFTER IT'S ALL OVER! HERE'S THREE DOLLARS...
OW!
T MUST BE ERY PAIN-FUL!
IT WASN'T THE **TOOTH** THAT TIME, MOTHER! IMAGINE PAYING **THREE DOLLARS** JUST TO HAVE A LITTLE **TOOTH** YANKED OUT!
DOCTOR PAYNE HAD TO GO TO **SCHOOL** FOR A **LONG WHILE** BEFORE HE COULD PRACTICE DENTISTRY!
I'VE GONE TO SCHOOL FOR A LONG WHILE **TOO**!
BUT **I** DON'T GO AROUND CHARGING THREE DOLLARS TO YANK A TOOTH!
GOSH, WHAT **I** COULDN'T DO WITH THREE DOLLARS!
DR. PAYNE PAINLESS DENTISTRY

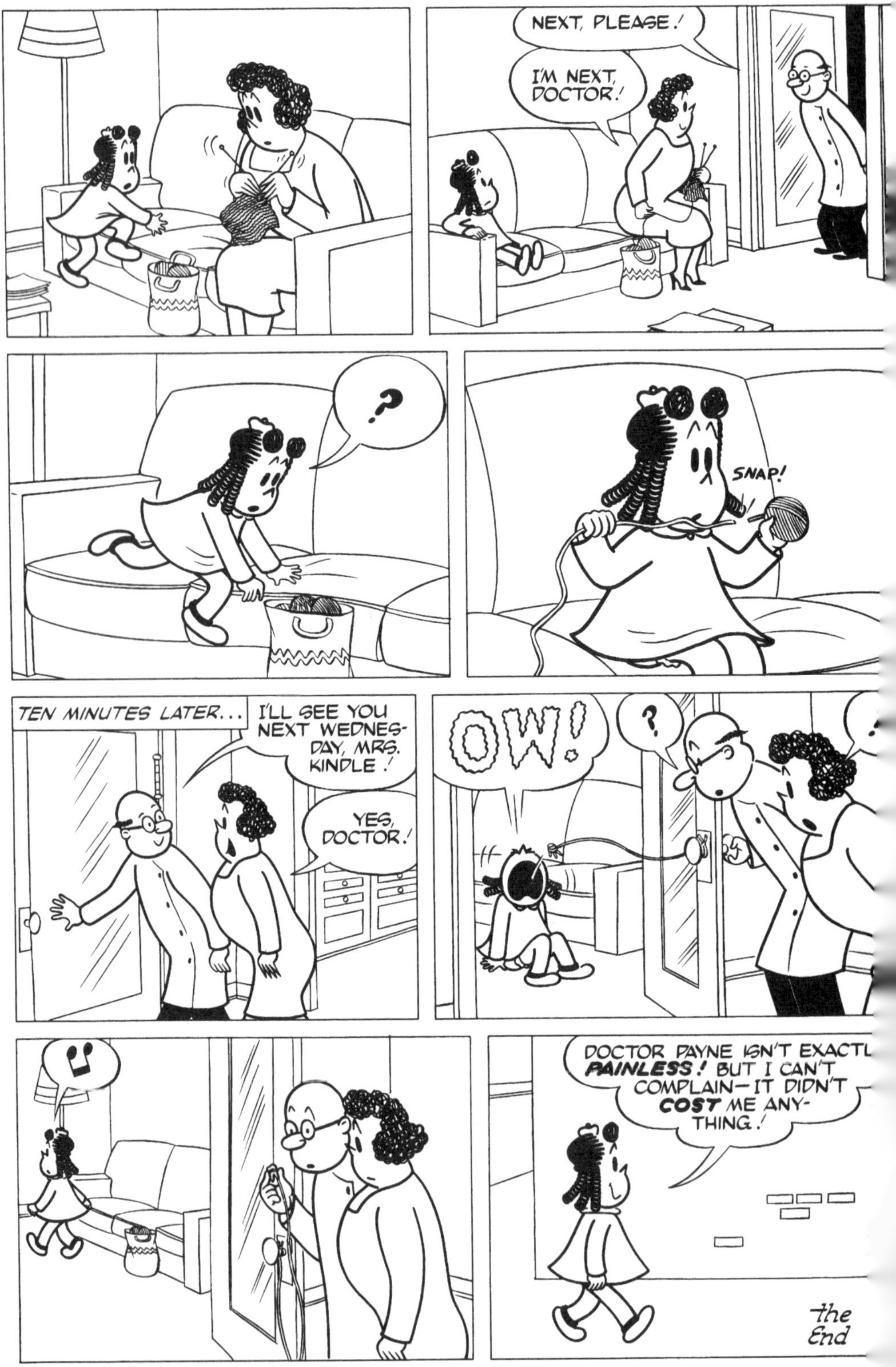
NEXT, PLEASE!
I'M NEXT, DOCTOR!
?
SNAP!
TEN MINUTES LATER...
I'LL SEE YOU NEXT WEDNES-DAY, MRS. KINDLE!
YES, DOCTOR!
OW!
?
DOCTOR PAYNE ISN'T EXACTL
PAINLESS! BUT I CAN'T COMPLAIN—IT DIDN'T COST ME ANY-THING!
The End

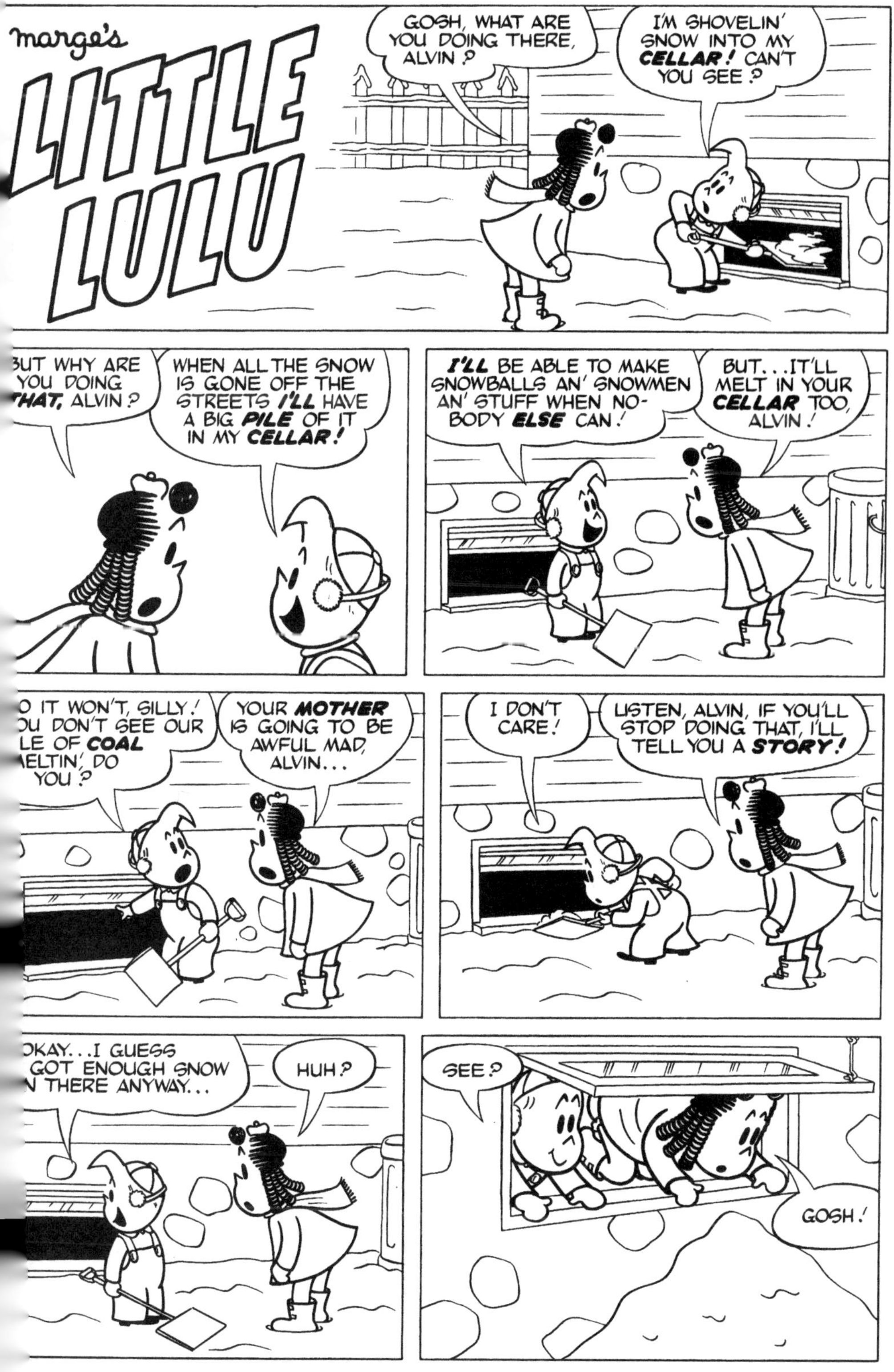
marge's
LITTLE LULU
GOSH, WHAT ARE YOU DOING THERE, ALVIN ?
I'M SHOVELIN' SNOW INTO MY CELLAR! CAN'T YOU SEE ?
BUT WHY ARE YOU DOING THAT, ALVIN ?
WHEN ALL THE SNOW IS GONE OFF THE STREETS I'LL HAVE A BIG PILE OF IT IN MY CELLAR!
I'LL BE ABLE TO MAKE SNOWBALLS AN' SNOWMEN AN' STUFF WHEN NOBODY ELSE CAN!
BUT...IT'LL MELT IN YOUR CELLAR TOO, ALVIN!
O IT WON'T, SILLY! OU DON'T SEE OUR LE OF COAL ELTIN', DO YOU ?
YOUR MOTHER IS GOING TO BE AWFUL MAD, ALVIN...
I DON'T CARE!
LISTEN, ALVIN, IF YOU'LL STOP DOING THAT, I'LL TELL YOU A STORY!
OKAY...I GUESS GOT ENOUGH SNOW N THERE ANYWAY...
HUH ?
SEE ?
GOSH!

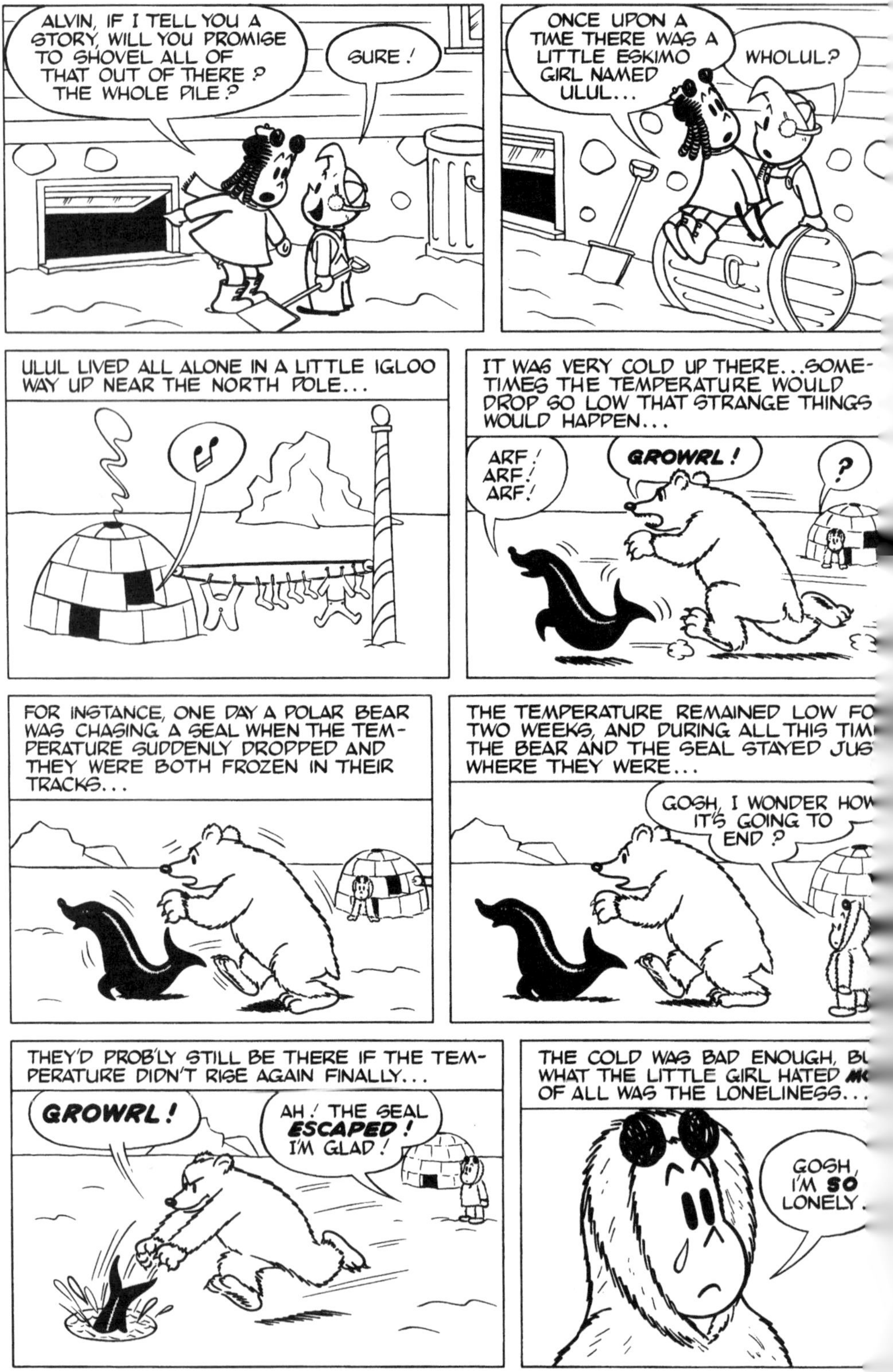
ALVIN, IF I TELL YOU A STORY, WILL YOU PROMISE TO SHOVEL ALL OF THAT OUT OF THERE? THE WHOLE PILE?
SURE!
ONCE UPON A TIME THERE WAS A LITTLE ESKIMO GIRL NAMED ULUL...
WHOLUL?
ULUL LIVED ALL ALONE IN A LITTLE IGLOO WAY UP NEAR THE NORTH POLE...
IT WAS VERY COLD UP THERE...SOMETIMES THE TEMPERATURE WOULD DROP SO LOW THAT STRANGE THINGS WOULD HAPPEN...
ARF! ARF! ARF!
GROWRL!
?
FOR INSTANCE, ONE DAY A POLAR BEAR WAS CHASING A SEAL WHEN THE TEMPERATURE SUDDENLY DROPPED AND THEY WERE BOTH FROZEN IN THEIR TRACKS...
THE TEMPERATURE REMAINED LOW FO TWO WEEKS, AND DURING ALL THIS TIM THE BEAR AND THE SEAL STAYED JUS WHERE THEY WERE...
GOSH, I WONDER HOW IT'S GOING TO END?
THEY'D PROB'LY STILL BE THERE IF THE TEMPERATURE DIDN'T RISE AGAIN FINALLY...
GROWRL!
AH! THE SEAL ESCAPED! I'M GLAD!
THE COLD WAS BAD ENOUGH, BU WHAT THE LITTLE GIRL HATED MO OF ALL WAS THE LONELINESS...
GOSH, I'M SO LONELY.

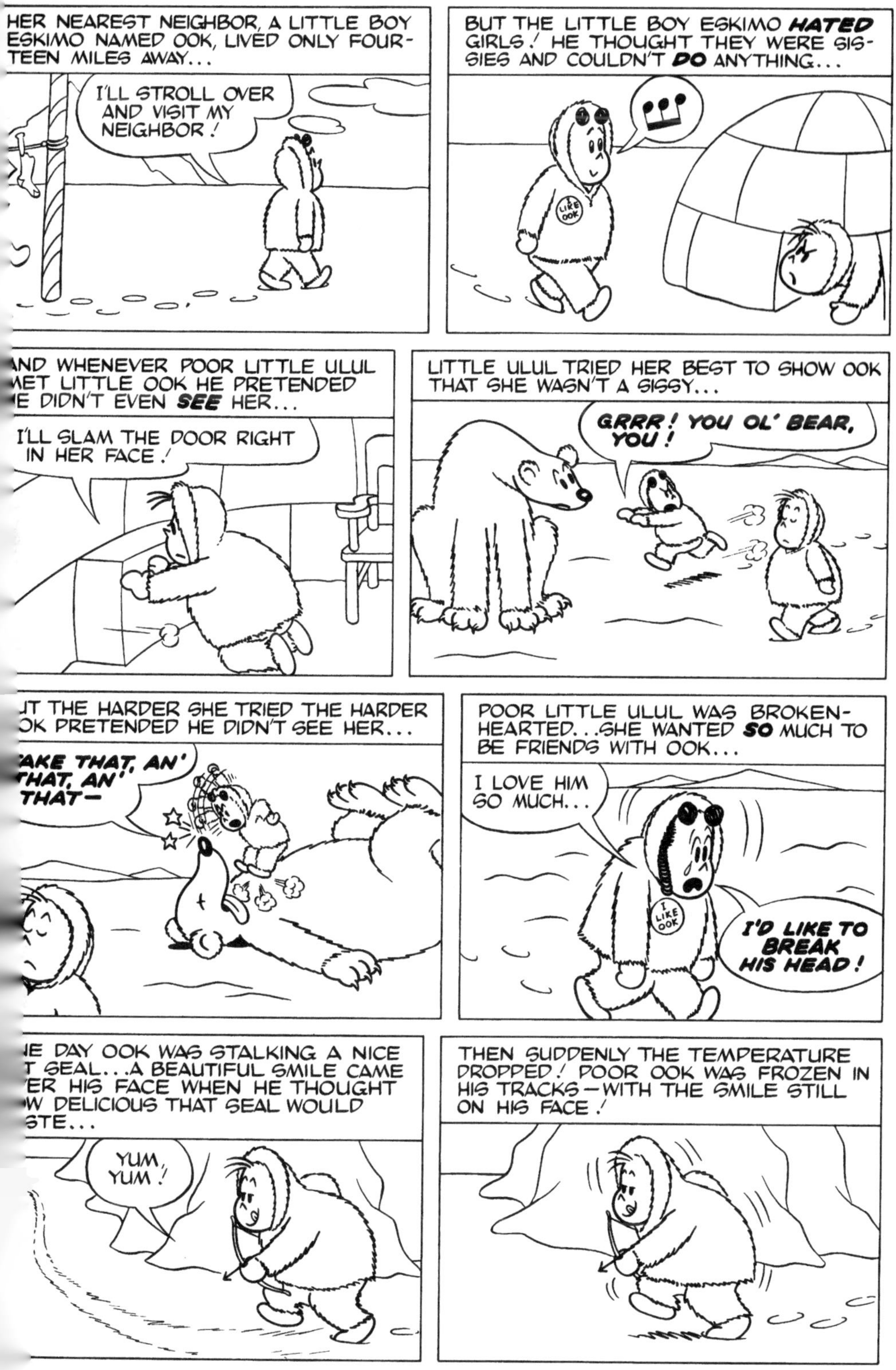
HER NEAREST NEIGHBOR, A LITTLE BOY ESKIMO NAMED OOK, LIVED ONLY FOURTEEN MILES AWAY...
I'LL STROLL OVER AND VISIT MY NEIGHBOR!
BUT THE LITTLE BOY ESKIMO **HATED** GIRLS! HE THOUGHT THEY WERE SISSIES AND COULDN'T **DO** ANYTHING...
I LIKE OOK
AND WHENEVER POOR LITTLE ULUL MET LITTLE OOK HE PRETENDED HE DIDN'T EVEN **SEE** HER...
I'LL SLAM THE DOOR RIGHT IN HER FACE!
LITTLE ULUL TRIED HER BEST TO SHOW OOK THAT SHE WASN'T A SISSY...
GRRR! YOU OL' BEAR, YOU!
UT THE HARDER SHE TRIED THE HARDER OK PRETENDED HE DIDN'T SEE HER...
AKE THAT, AN' THAT, AN' THAT—
POOR LITTLE ULUL WAS BROKEN-HEARTED...SHE WANTED **SO** MUCH TO BE FRIENDS WITH OOK...
I LOVE HIM SO MUCH...
I LIKE OOK
I'D LIKE TO BREAK HIS HEAD!
IE DAY OOK WAS STALKING A NICE T SEAL...A BEAUTIFUL SMILE CAME ER HIS FACE WHEN HE THOUGHT W DELICIOUS THAT SEAL WOULD STE...
YUM, YUM!
THEN SUDDENLY THE TEMPERATURE DROPPED! POOR OOK WAS FROZEN IN HIS TRACKS—WITH THE SMILE STILL ON HIS FACE!

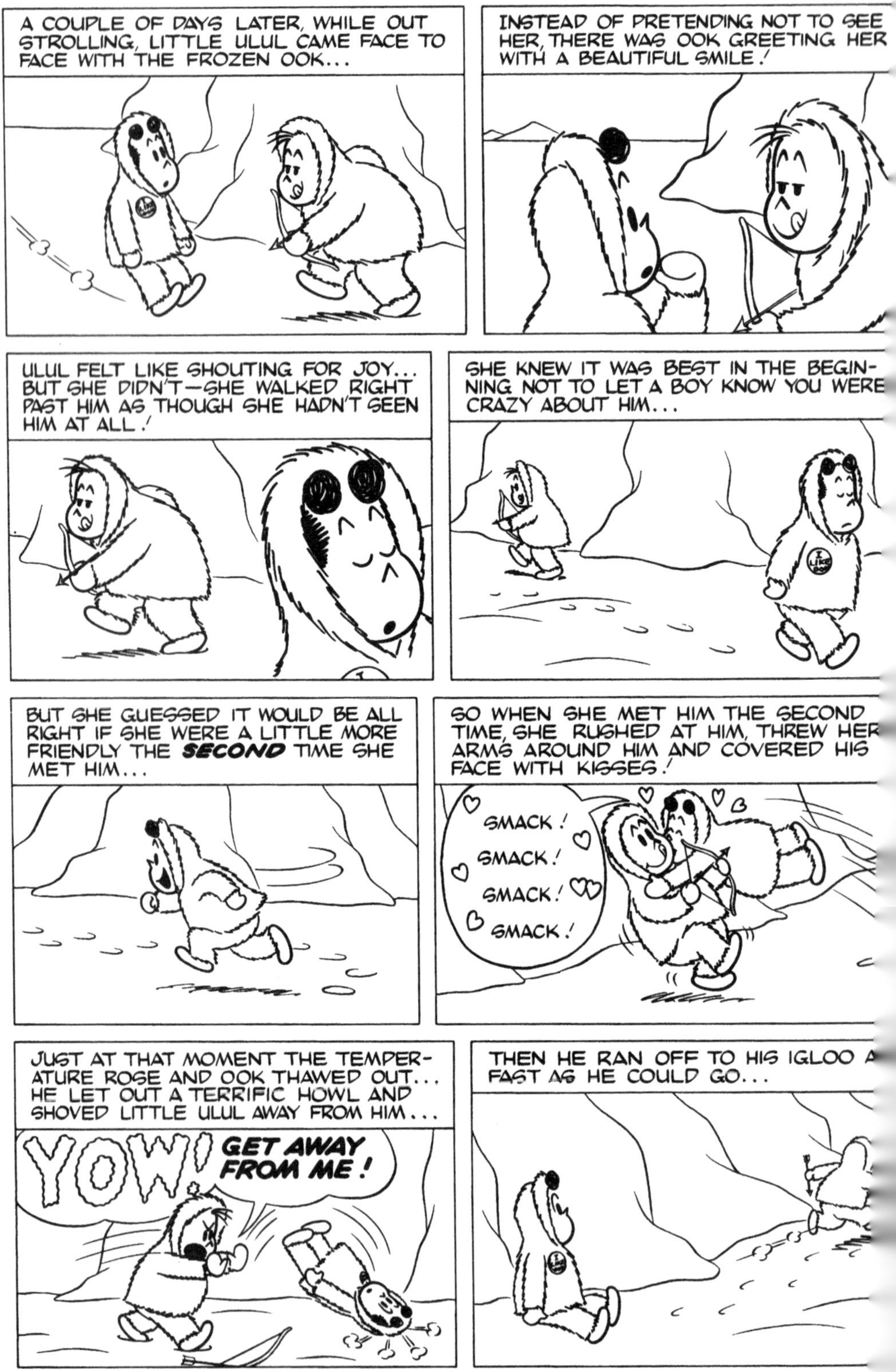
A COUPLE OF DAYS LATER, WHILE OUT STROLLING, LITTLE ULUL CAME FACE TO FACE WITH THE FROZEN OOK...
INSTEAD OF PRETENDING NOT TO SEE HER, THERE WAS OOK GREETING HER WITH A BEAUTIFUL SMILE!
ULUL FELT LIKE SHOUTING FOR JOY... BUT SHE DIDN'T—SHE WALKED RIGHT PAST HIM AS THOUGH SHE HADN'T SEEN HIM AT ALL!
SHE KNEW IT WAS BEST IN THE BEGINNING NOT TO LET A BOY KNOW YOU WERE CRAZY ABOUT HIM...
BUT SHE GUESSED IT WOULD BE ALL RIGHT IF SHE WERE A LITTLE MORE FRIENDLY THE ***SECOND*** TIME SHE MET HIM...
SO WHEN SHE MET HIM THE SECOND TIME, SHE RUSHED AT HIM, THREW HER ARMS AROUND HIM AND COVERED HIS FACE WITH KISSES!
SMACK! SMACK! SMACK! SMACK!
JUST AT THAT MOMENT THE TEMPERATURE ROSE AND OOK THAWED OUT... HE LET OUT A TERRIFIC HOWL AND SHOVED LITTLE ULUL AWAY FROM HIM...
YOW! **GET AWAY FROM ME!**
THEN HE RAN OFF TO HIS IGLOO AS FAST AS HE COULD GO...

POOR LITTLE ULUL WAS DUMBFOUNDED... SHE DIDN'T KNOW **WHAT** TO THINK...

G-GOSH, WHY DOES HE **HATE** ME LIKE THAT?

THEN A WONDERFUL IDEA CAME TO HER...SHE KNEW THAT THE BEST WAY TO MAKE A LITTLE BOY LIKE YOU WAS TO GIVE HIM SOMETHING **GOOD TO EAT!**

WOW! I'LL INVITE HIM TO **DINNER!!**

SO LITTLE ULUL GOT HER FISHING LINE AND WENT DOWN TO THE WATER'S EDGE...

I'LL HAVE A **CANDLE** ON THE TABLE AN' EVERYTHING!

SHE WAS HOPING SHE WOULD CATCH A NICE FAT FISH FOR OOK...

WHEN HE SEES WHAT A GOOD **COOK** I AM—

N A LITTLE WHILE SHE FELT A STRONG UG ON HER LINE AND SHE HAULED IN ITH ALL HER MIGHT...

UH-OH! A **BITE!**

THE FISH FOUGHT AS HARD AS HE COULD, BUT HE WAS NO MATCH FOR LITTLE ULUL...

MUST BE A **BIG** ONE!

A FEW MINUTES HE WAS LYING ON THE ICE AT THE FEET OF THE HAPPY LITTLE GIRL...

IT'S EVEN BIGGER THAN I THOUGHT!

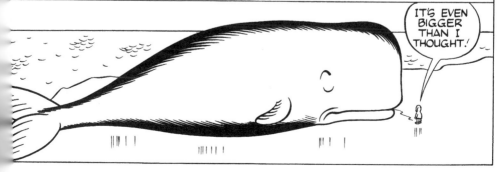

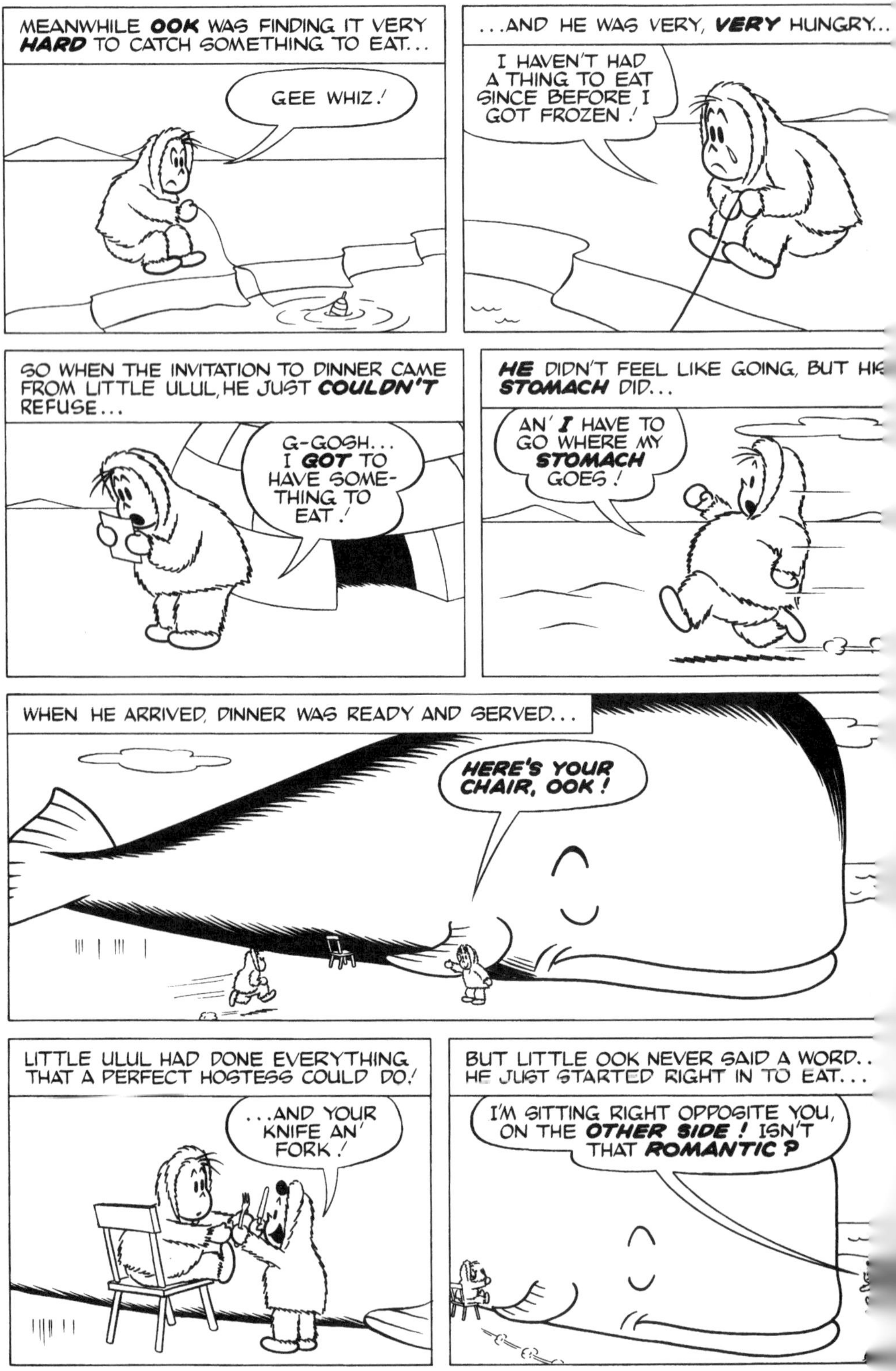

MEANWHILE **OOK** WAS FINDING IT VERY **HARD** TO CATCH SOMETHING TO EAT...
GEE WHIZ!
...AND HE WAS VERY, **VERY** HUNGRY...
I HAVEN'T HAD A THING TO EAT SINCE BEFORE I GOT FROZEN!
SO WHEN THE INVITATION TO DINNER CAME FROM LITTLE ULUL, HE JUST **COULDN'T** REFUSE...
G-GOSH... I **GOT** TO HAVE SOME-THING TO EAT!
HE DIDN'T FEEL LIKE GOING, BUT HIS **STOMACH** DID...
AN' **I** HAVE TO GO WHERE MY **STOMACH** GOES!
WHEN HE ARRIVED, DINNER WAS READY AND SERVED...
HERE'S YOUR CHAIR, OOK!
LITTLE ULUL HAD DONE EVERYTHING THAT A PERFECT HOSTESS COULD DO!
...AND YOUR KNIFE AN' FORK!
BUT LITTLE OOK NEVER SAID A WORD.. HE JUST STARTED RIGHT IN TO EAT...
I'M SITTING RIGHT OPPOSITE YOU, ON THE **OTHER SIDE!** ISN'T THAT **ROMANTIC?**

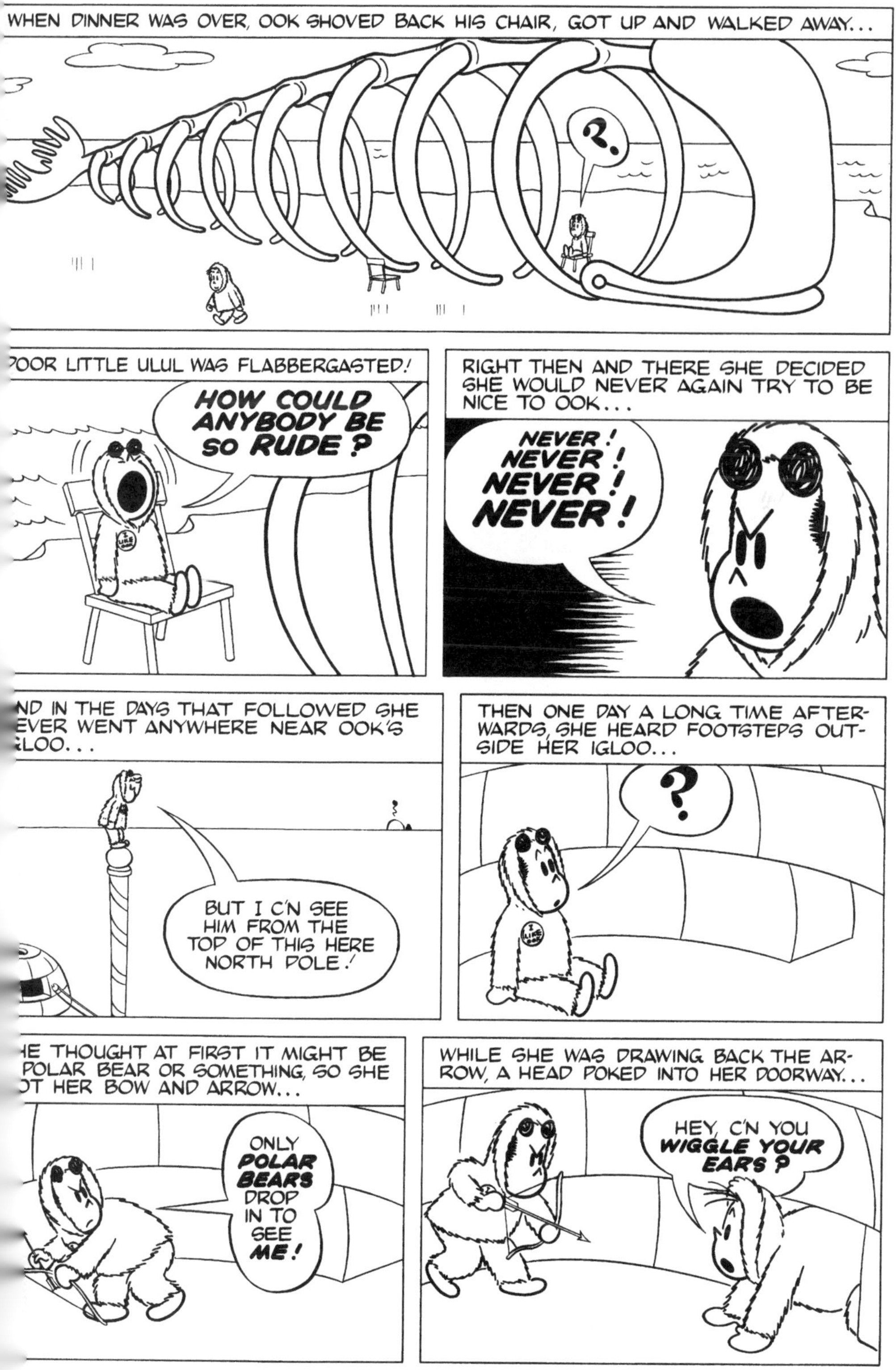

WHEN DINNER WAS OVER, OOK SHOVED BACK HIS CHAIR, GOT UP AND WALKED AWAY...
?.
POOR LITTLE ULUL WAS FLABBERGASTED!
HOW COULD ANYBODY BE SO RUDE?
RIGHT THEN AND THERE SHE DECIDED SHE WOULD NEVER AGAIN TRY TO BE NICE TO OOK...
NEVER! NEVER! NEVER! NEVER!
ND IN THE DAYS THAT FOLLOWED SHE EVER WENT ANYWHERE NEAR OOK'S LOO...
BUT I C'N SEE HIM FROM THE TOP OF THIS HERE NORTH POLE!
THEN ONE DAY A LONG TIME AFTERWARDS, SHE HEARD FOOTSTEPS OUTSIDE HER IGLOO...
?
HE THOUGHT AT FIRST IT MIGHT BE POLAR BEAR OR SOMETHING, SO SHE OT HER BOW AND ARROW...
ONLY POLAR BEARS DROP IN TO SEE ME!
WHILE SHE WAS DRAWING BACK THE ARROW, A HEAD POKED INTO HER DOORWAY...
HEY, C'N YOU WIGGLE YOUR EARS?

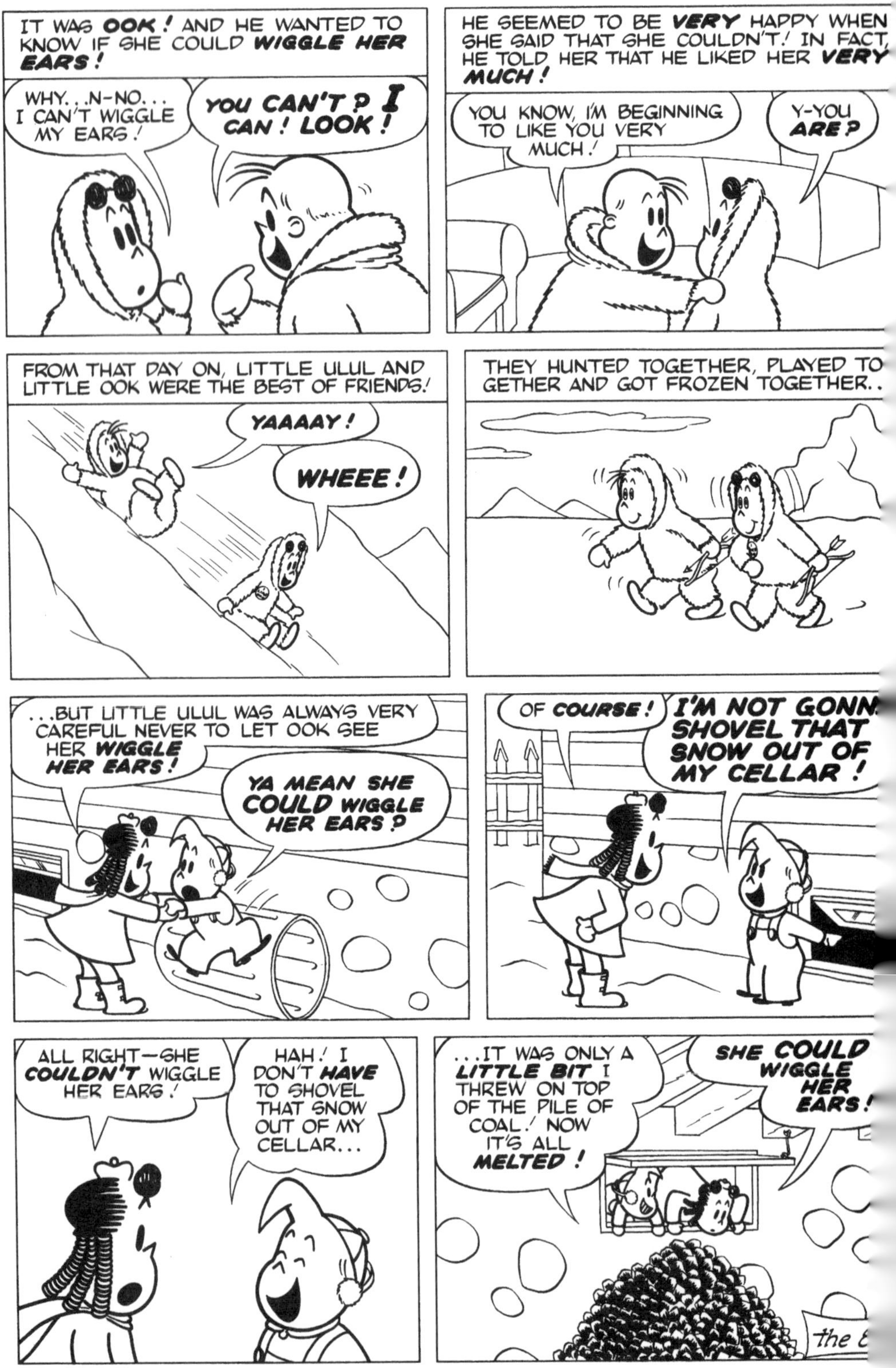
IT WAS OOK! AND HE WANTED TO KNOW IF SHE COULD WIGGLE HER EARS!
WHY...N-NO... I CAN'T WIGGLE MY EARS!
YOU CAN'T? I CAN! LOOK!
HE SEEMED TO BE VERY HAPPY WHEN SHE SAID THAT SHE COULDN'T! IN FACT, HE TOLD HER THAT HE LIKED HER VERY MUCH!
YOU KNOW, I'M BEGINNING TO LIKE YOU VERY MUCH!
Y-YOU ARE?
FROM THAT DAY ON, LITTLE ULUL AND LITTLE OOK WERE THE BEST OF FRIENDS!
YAAAAY!
WHEEE!
THEY HUNTED TOGETHER, PLAYED TOGETHER AND GOT FROZEN TOGETHER...
...BUT LITTLE ULUL WAS ALWAYS VERY CAREFUL NEVER TO LET OOK SEE HER WIGGLE HER EARS!
YA MEAN SHE COULD WIGGLE HER EARS?
OF COURSE!
I'M NOT GONN SHOVEL THAT SNOW OUT OF MY CELLAR!
ALL RIGHT—SHE COULDN'T WIGGLE HER EARS!
HAH! I DON'T HAVE TO SHOVEL THAT SNOW OUT OF MY CELLAR...
...IT WAS ONLY A LITTLE BIT I THREW ON TOP OF THE PILE OF COAL! NOW IT'S ALL MELTED!
SHE COULD WIGGLE HER EARS!
the e

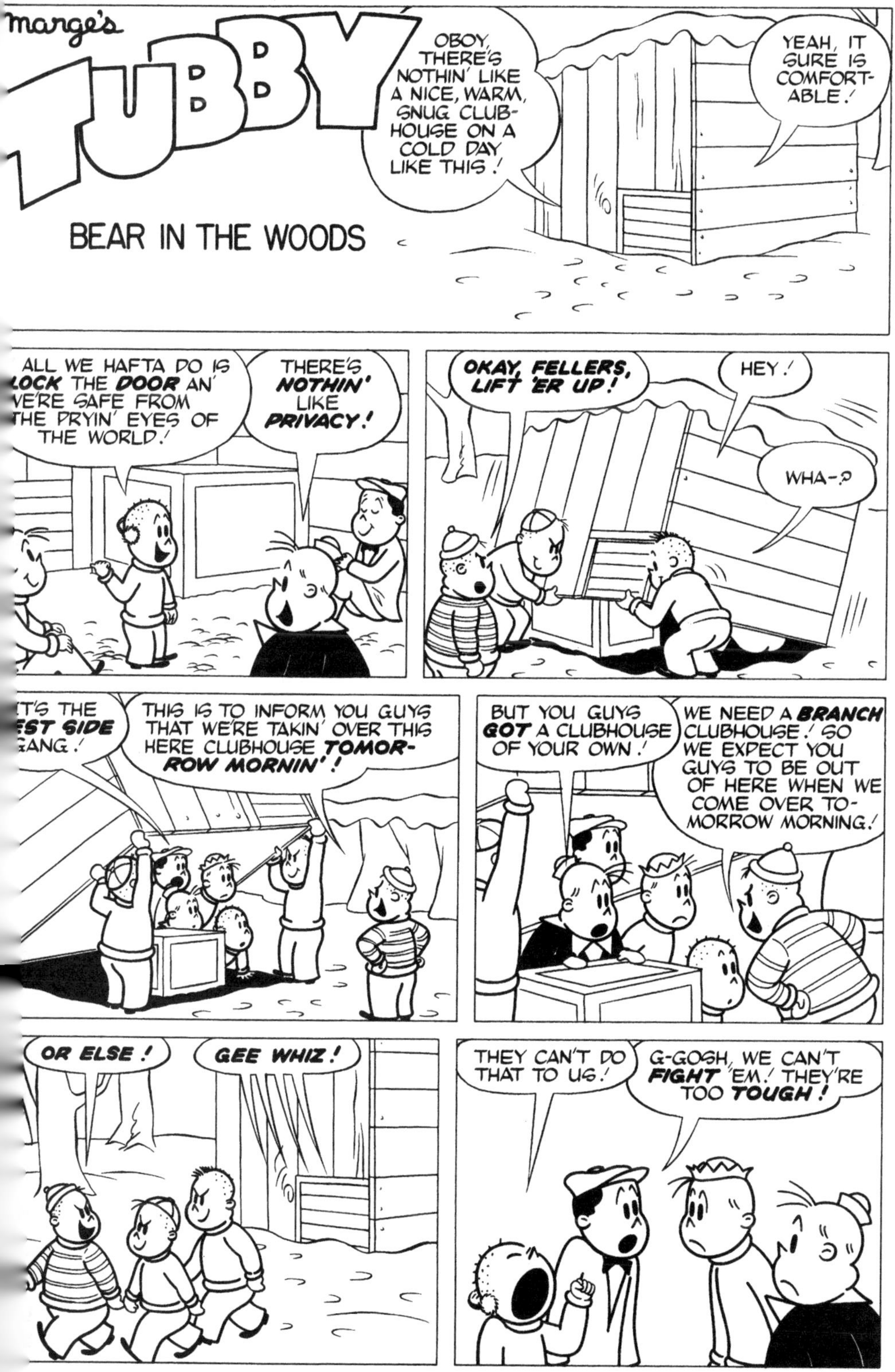

marge's TUBBY
BEAR IN THE WOODS
OBOY, THERE'S NOTHIN' LIKE A NICE, WARM, SNUG CLUB-HOUSE ON A COLD DAY LIKE THIS!
YEAH, IT SURE IS COMFORT-ABLE!
ALL WE HAFTA DO IS LOCK THE DOOR AN' WE'RE SAFE FROM THE PRYIN' EYES OF THE WORLD!
THERE'S NOTHIN' LIKE PRIVACY!
OKAY, FELLERS, LIFT 'ER UP!
HEY!
WHA-?
IT'S THE EST SIDE GANG!
THIS IS TO INFORM YOU GUYS THAT WE'RE TAKIN' OVER THIS HERE CLUBHOUSE TOMOR-ROW MORNIN'!
BUT YOU GUYS GOT A CLUBHOUSE OF YOUR OWN!
WE NEED A BRANCH CLUBHOUSE! SO WE EXPECT YOU GUYS TO BE OUT OF HERE WHEN WE COME OVER TO-MORROW MORNING!
OR ELSE!
GEE WHIZ!
THEY CAN'T DO THAT TO US!
G-GOSH, WE CAN'T FIGHT 'EM! THEY'RE TOO TOUGH!

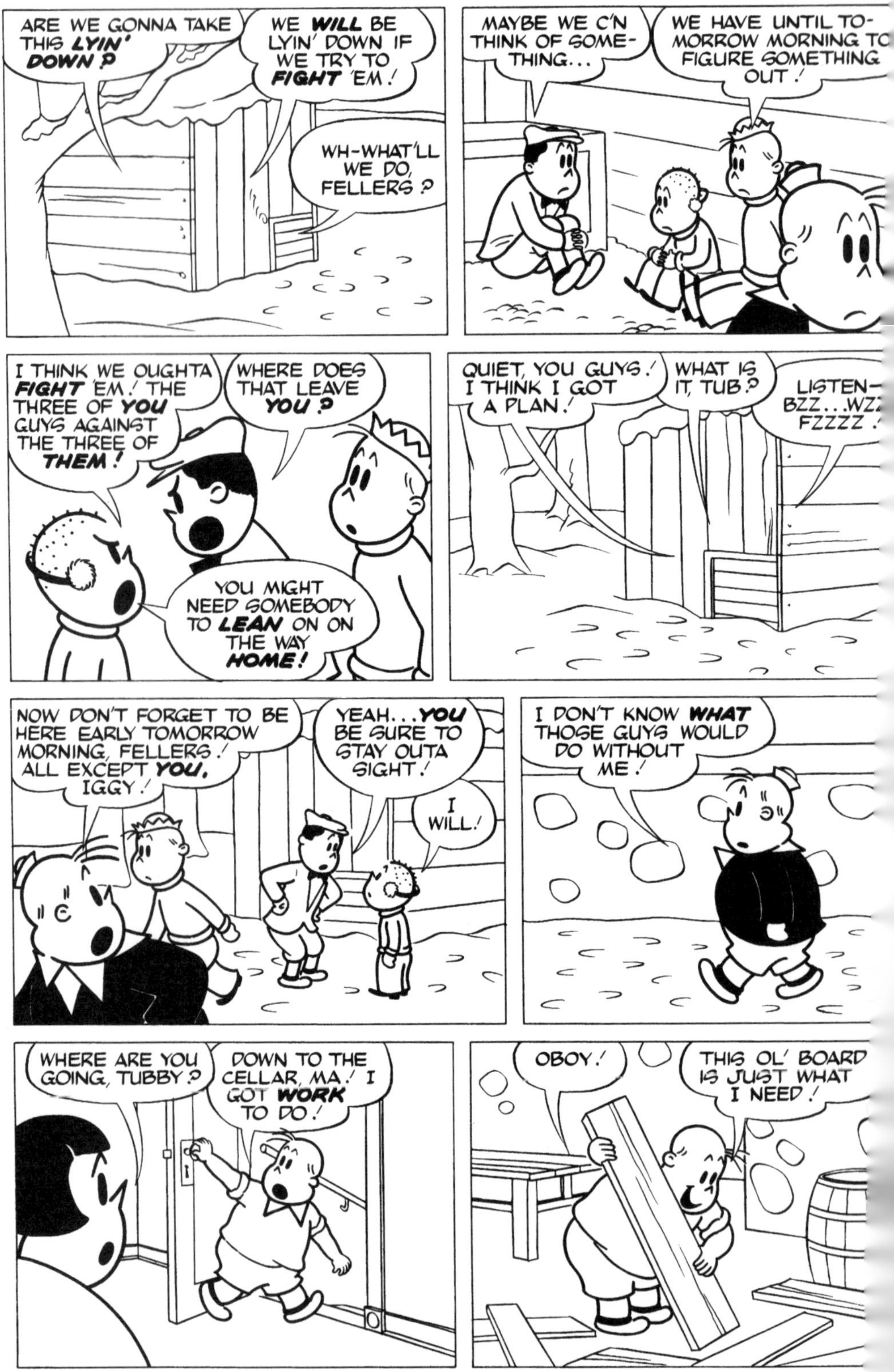

ARE WE GONNA TAKE THIS LYIN' DOWN ?
WE WILL BE LYIN' DOWN IF WE TRY TO FIGHT 'EM !
WH-WHAT'LL WE DO, FELLERS ?
MAYBE WE C'N THINK OF SOME-THING...
WE HAVE UNTIL TO-MORROW MORNING TO FIGURE SOMETHING OUT !
I THINK WE OUGHTA FIGHT 'EM ! THE THREE OF YOU GUYS AGAINST THE THREE OF THEM !
WHERE DOES THAT LEAVE YOU ?
YOU MIGHT NEED SOMEBODY TO LEAN ON ON THE WAY HOME !
QUIET, YOU GUYS ! I THINK I GOT A PLAN !
WHAT IS IT, TUB ?
LISTEN— BZZ...WZZ FZZZZ !
NOW DON'T FORGET TO BE HERE EARLY TOMORROW MORNING, FELLERS ! ALL EXCEPT YOU, IGGY !
YEAH...YOU BE SURE TO STAY OUTA SIGHT !
I WILL !
I DON'T KNOW WHAT THOSE GUYS WOULD DO WITHOUT ME !
WHERE ARE YOU GOING, TUBBY ?
DOWN TO THE CELLAR, MA ! I GOT WORK TO DO !
OBOY !
THIS OL' BOARD IS JUST WHAT I NEED !

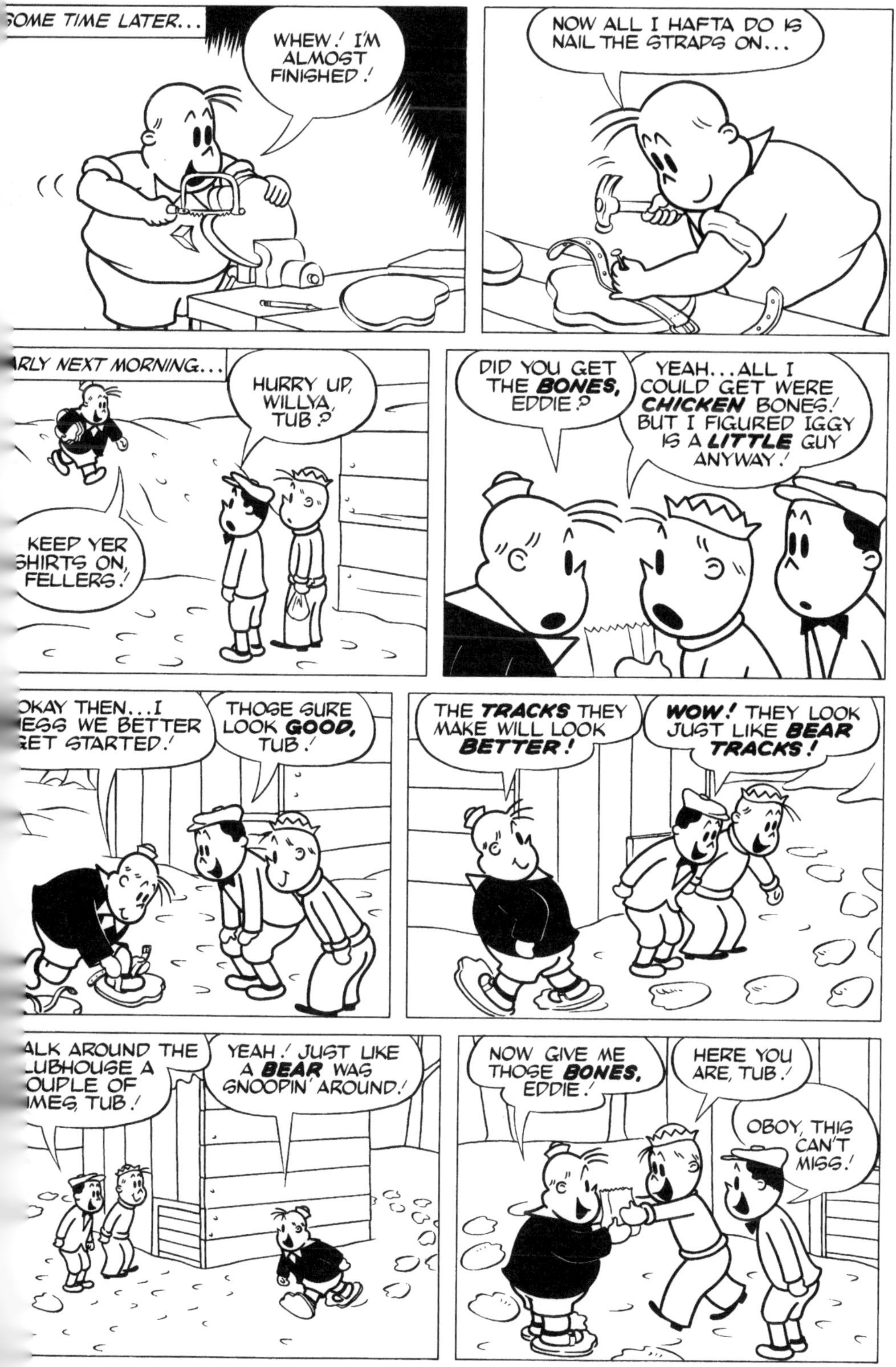
SOME TIME LATER...
WHEW! I'M ALMOST FINISHED!
NOW ALL I HAFTA DO IS NAIL THE STRAPS ON...
ARLY NEXT MORNING...
HURRY UP, WILLYA, TUB?
KEEP YER SHIRTS ON, FELLERS!
DID YOU GET THE BONES, EDDIE?
YEAH...ALL I COULD GET WERE CHICKEN BONES! BUT I FIGURED IGGY IS A LITTLE GUY ANYWAY!
OKAY THEN...I UESS WE BETTER GET STARTED!
THOSE SURE LOOK GOOD, TUB!
THE TRACKS THEY MAKE WILL LOOK BETTER!
WOW! THEY LOOK JUST LIKE BEAR TRACKS!
ALK AROUND THE LUBHOUSE A OUPLE OF IMES, TUB!
YEAH! JUST LIKE A BEAR WAS SNOOPIN' AROUND!
NOW GIVE ME THOSE BONES, EDDIE!
HERE YOU ARE, TUB!
OBOY, THIS CAN'T MISS!

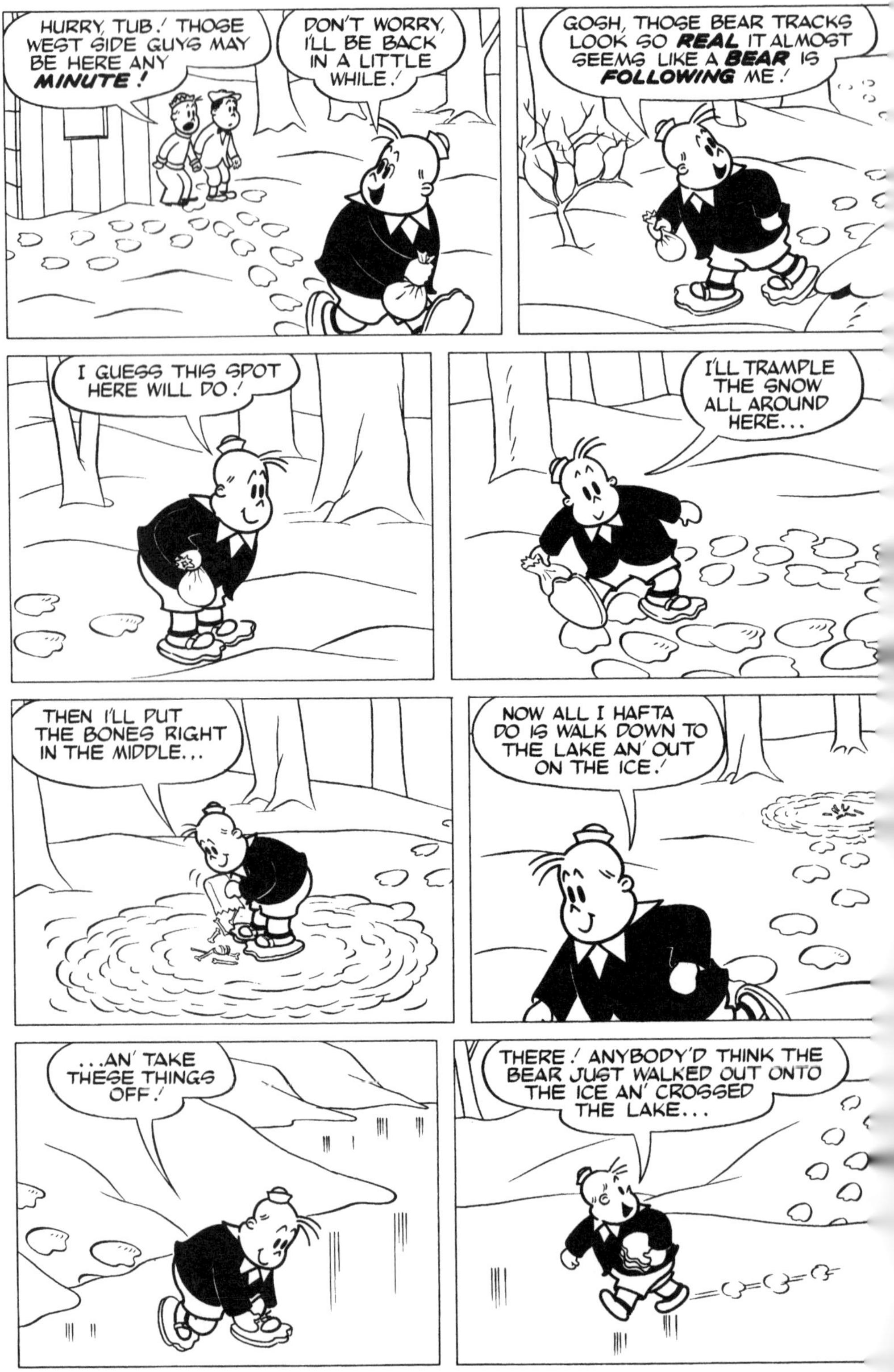
HURRY, TUB.! THOSE WEST SIDE GUYS MAY BE HERE ANY MINUTE!
DON'T WORRY, I'LL BE BACK IN A LITTLE WHILE.!
GOSH, THOSE BEAR TRACKS LOOK SO REAL IT ALMOST SEEMS LIKE A BEAR IS FOLLOWING ME.!
I GUESS THIS SPOT HERE WILL DO.!
I'LL TRAMPLE THE SNOW ALL AROUND HERE...
THEN I'LL PUT THE BONES RIGHT IN THE MIDDLE...
NOW ALL I HAFTA DO IS WALK DOWN TO THE LAKE AN' OUT ON THE ICE.!
...AN' TAKE THESE THINGS OFF.!
THERE.! ANYBODY'D THINK THE BEAR JUST WALKED OUT ONTO THE ICE AN' CROSSED THE LAKE...

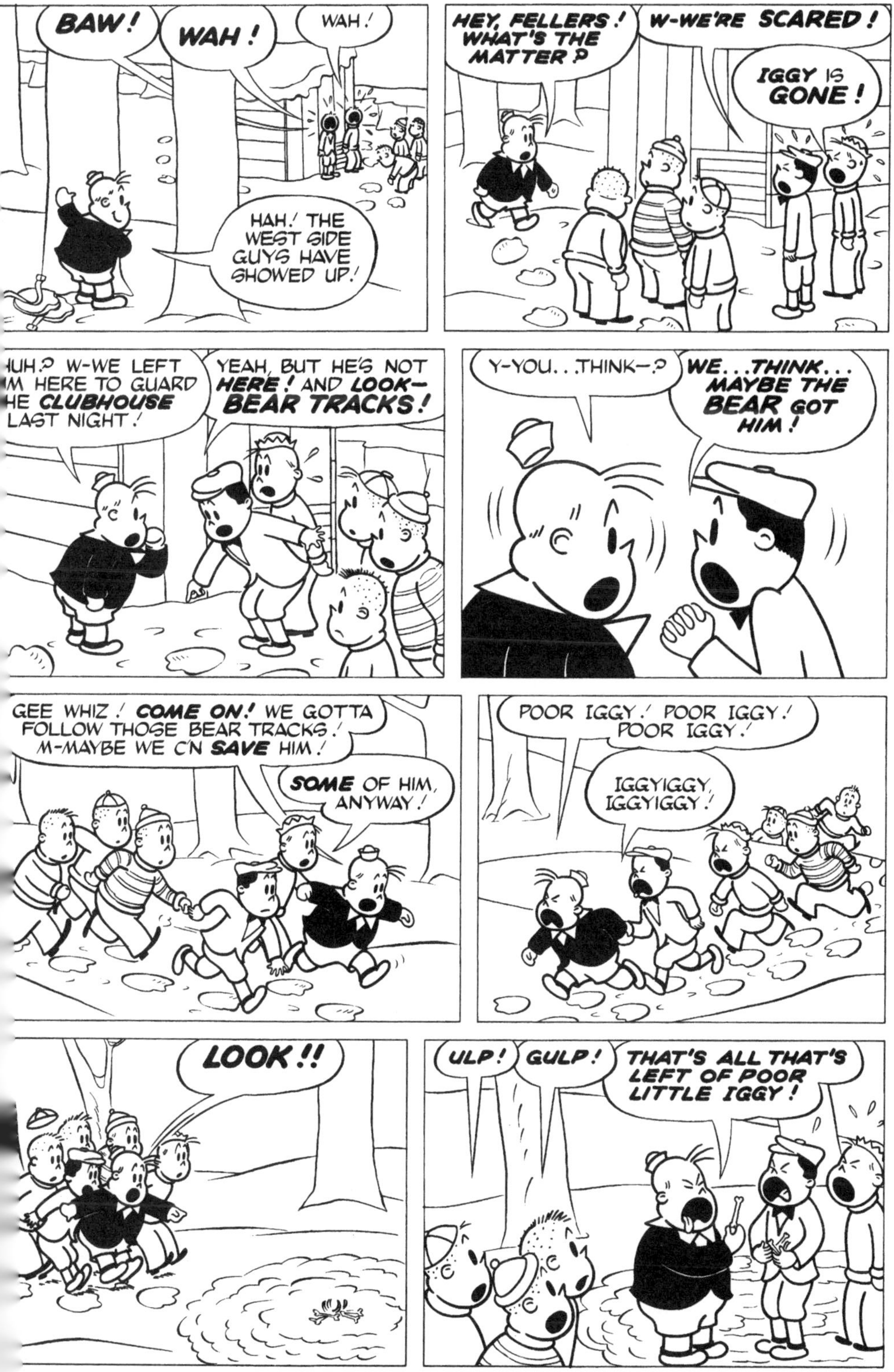
BAW!
WAH!
WAH!
HAH! THE WEST SIDE GUYS HAVE SHOWED UP!
HEY, FELLERS! WHAT'S THE MATTER?
W-WE'RE SCARED!
IGGY IS GONE!
HUH? W-WE LEFT M HERE TO GUARD HE CLUBHOUSE LAST NIGHT!
YEAH, BUT HE'S NOT HERE! AND LOOK—BEAR TRACKS!
Y-YOU...THINK—?
WE...THINK... MAYBE THE BEAR GOT HIM!
GEE WHIZ! COME ON! WE GOTTA FOLLOW THOSE BEAR TRACKS! M-MAYBE WE C'N SAVE HIM!
SOME OF HIM, ANYWAY!
POOR IGGY! POOR IGGY! POOR IGGY!
IGGYIGGY, IGGYIGGY!
LOOK!!
ULP!
GULP!
THAT'S ALL THAT'S LEFT OF POOR LITTLE IGGY!

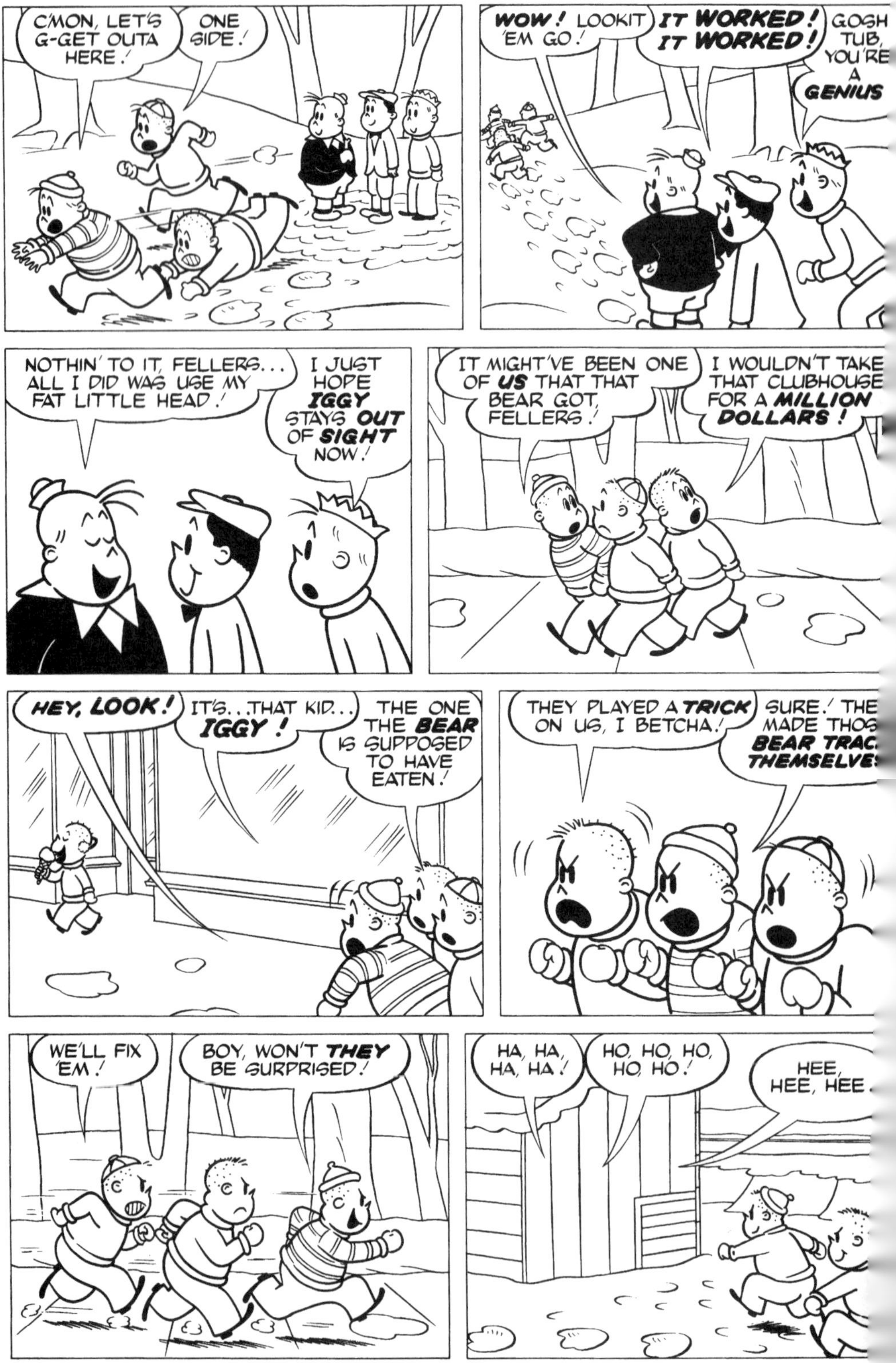
C'MON, LET'S G-GET OUTA HERE.!
ONE SIDE.!
WOW! LOOKIT 'EM GO.!
IT WORKED! IT WORKED!
GOSH TUB, YOU'RE A GENIUS
NOTHIN' TO IT, FELLERS... ALL I DID WAS USE MY FAT LITTLE HEAD.!
I JUST HOPE IGGY STAYS OUT OF SIGHT NOW.!
IT MIGHT'VE BEEN ONE OF US THAT THAT BEAR GOT, FELLERS.!
I WOULDN'T TAKE THAT CLUBHOUSE FOR A MILLION DOLLARS!
HEY, LOOK!
IT'S...THAT KID... IGGY!
THE ONE THE BEAR IS SUPPOSED TO HAVE EATEN.!
THEY PLAYED A TRICK ON US, I BETCHA.!
WE'LL FIX 'EM.!
BOY, WON'T THEY BE SURPRISED.!
HA, HA, HA, HA.!
HO, HO, HO, HO, HO.!
HEE, HEE, HEE

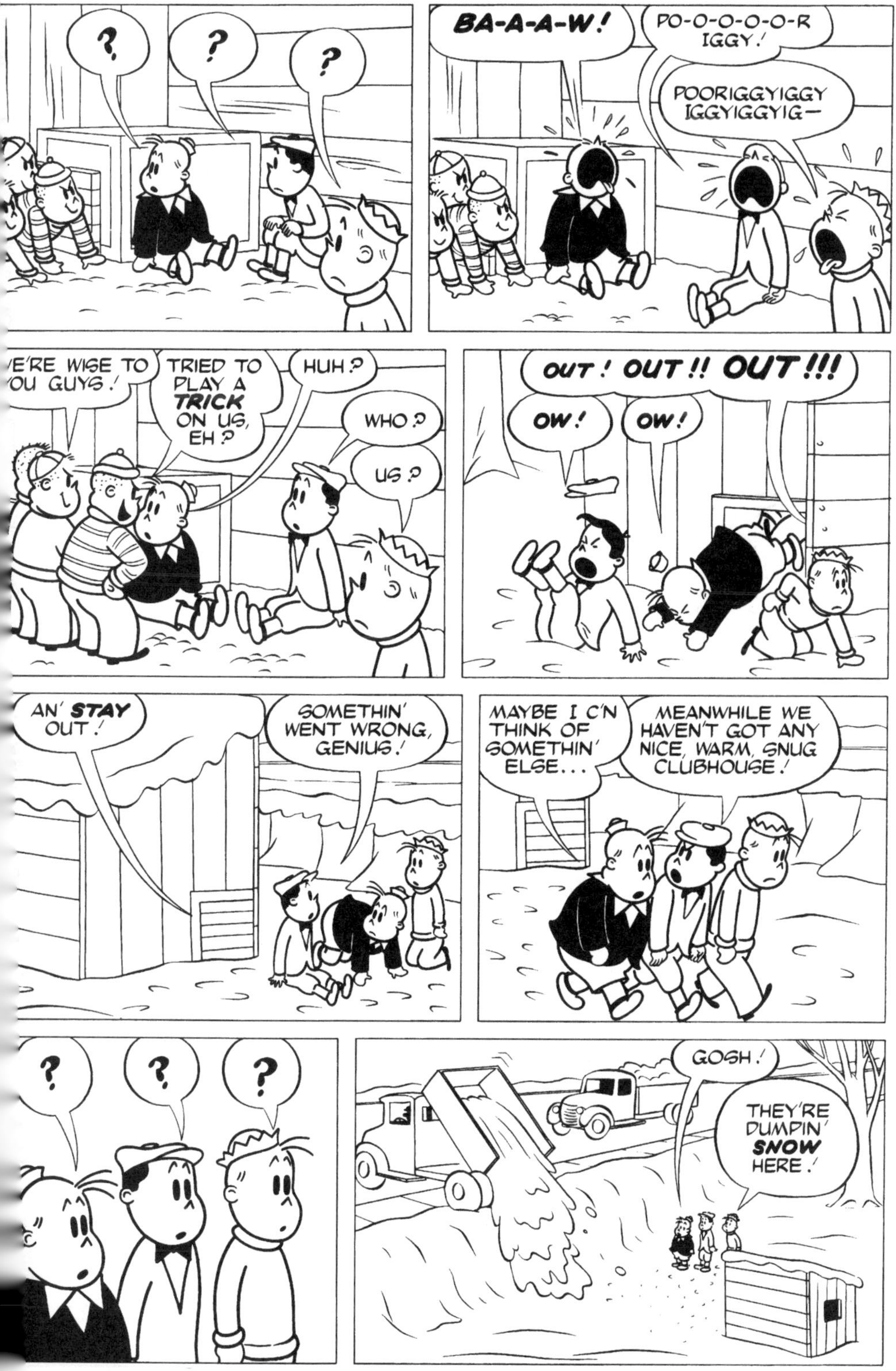
?
?
?
BA-A-A-W!
PO-O-O-O-O-R IGGY!
POORIGGYIGGY IGGYIGGYIG—
E'RE WISE TO OU GUYS!
TRIED TO PLAY A TRICK ON US, EH?
HUH?
WHO?
US?
OUT! OUT!! OUT!!!
OW!
OW!
AN' STAY OUT!
SOMETHIN' WENT WRONG, GENIUS!
MAYBE I C'N THINK OF SOMETHIN' ELSE...
MEANWHILE WE HAVEN'T GOT ANY NICE, WARM, SNUG CLUBHOUSE!
?
?
?
GOSH!
THEY'RE DUMPIN' SNOW HERE!

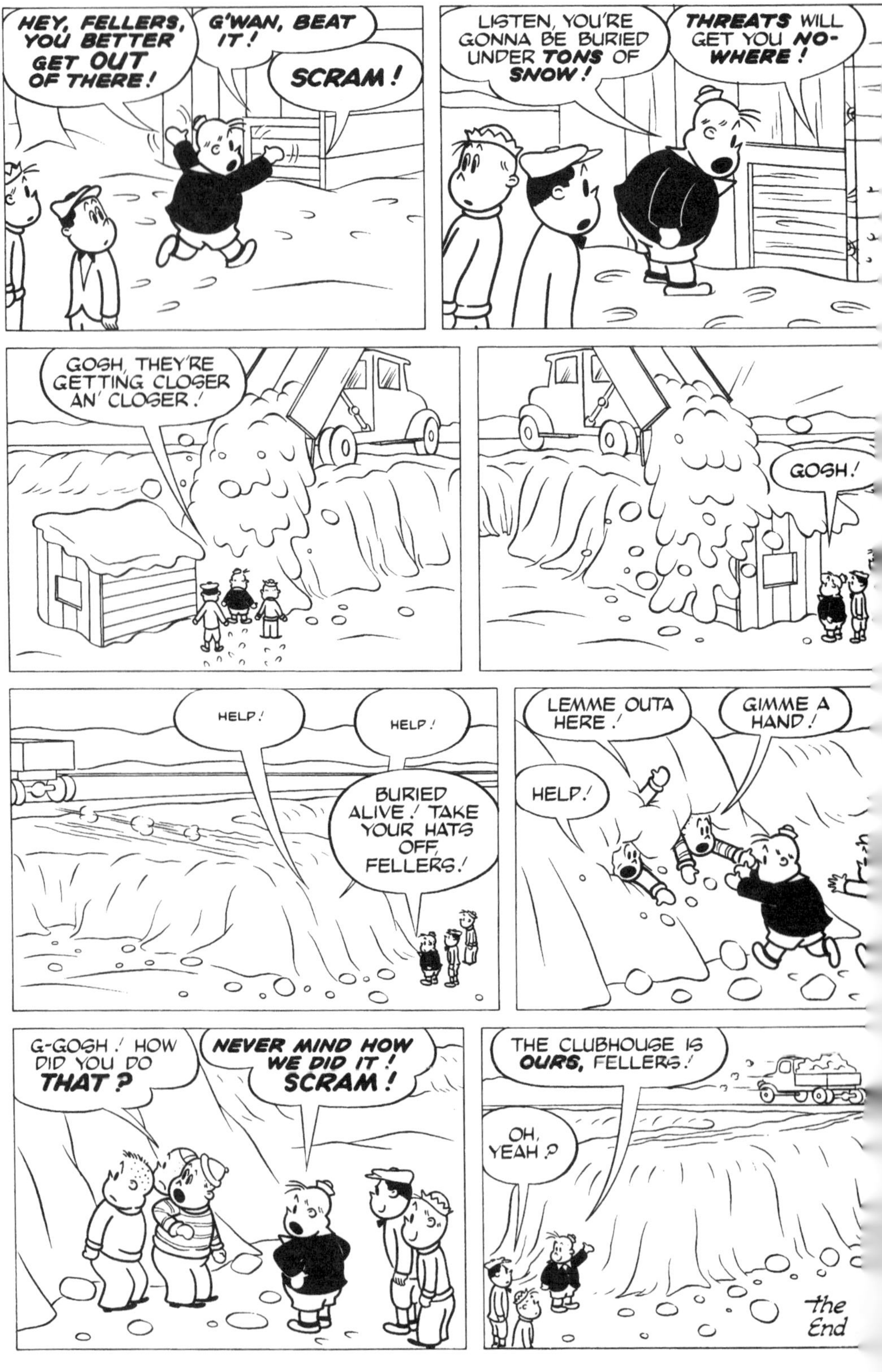
HEY, FELLERS, YOU BETTER GET OUT OF THERE!
G'WAN, BEAT IT!
SCRAM!
LISTEN, YOU'RE GONNA BE BURIED UNDER TONS OF SNOW!
THREATS WILL GET YOU NO-WHERE!
GOSH, THEY'RE GETTING CLOSER AN' CLOSER!
GOSH!
HELP!
HELP!
BURIED ALIVE! TAKE YOUR HATS OFF, FELLERS!
LEMME OUTA HERE!
GIMME A HAND!
HELP!
G-GOSH! HOW DID YOU DO THAT?
NEVER MIND HOW WE DID IT! SCRAM!
THE CLUBHOUSE IS OURS, FELLERS!
OH, YEAH?
the End

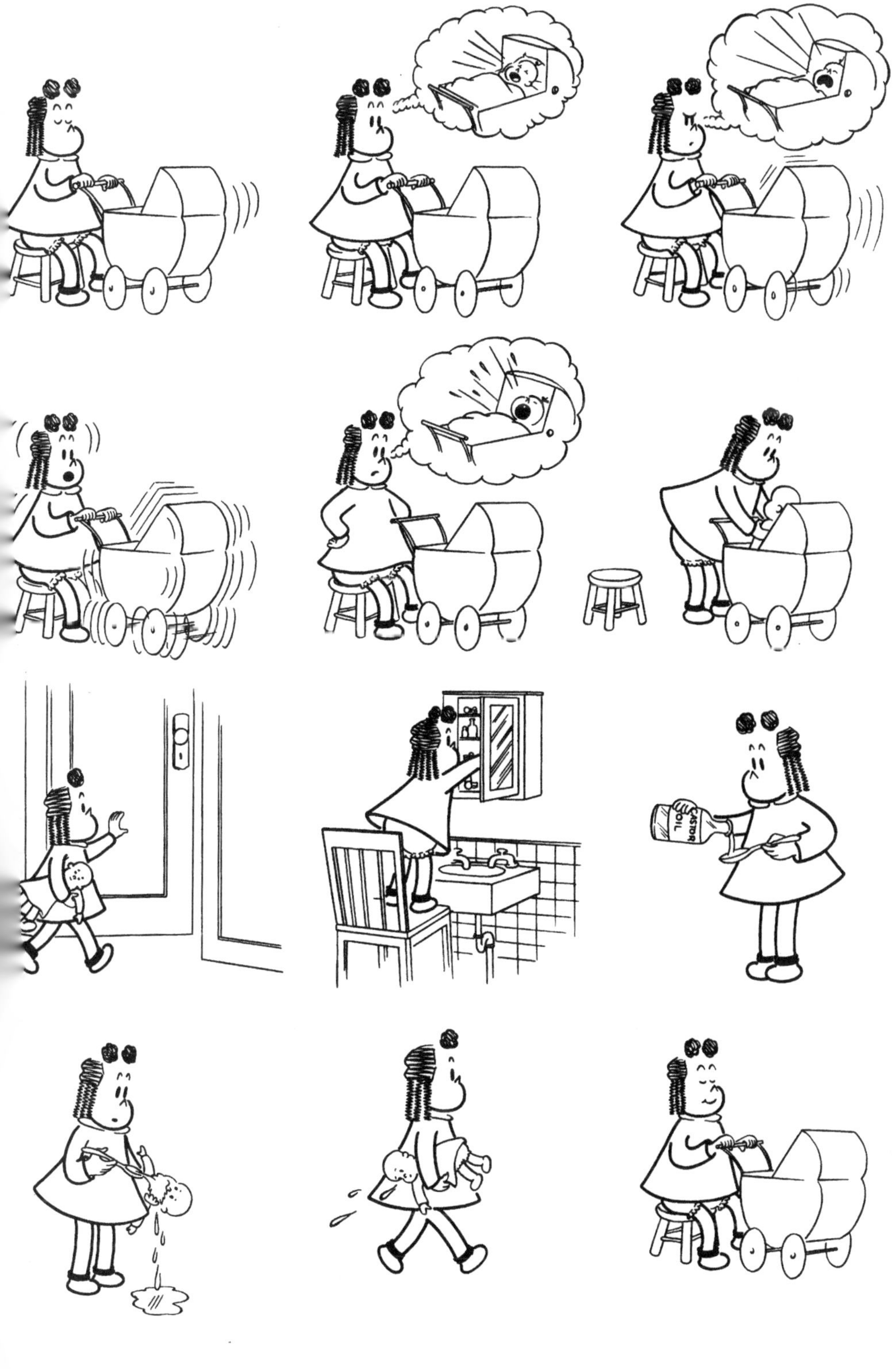
CASTOR OIL

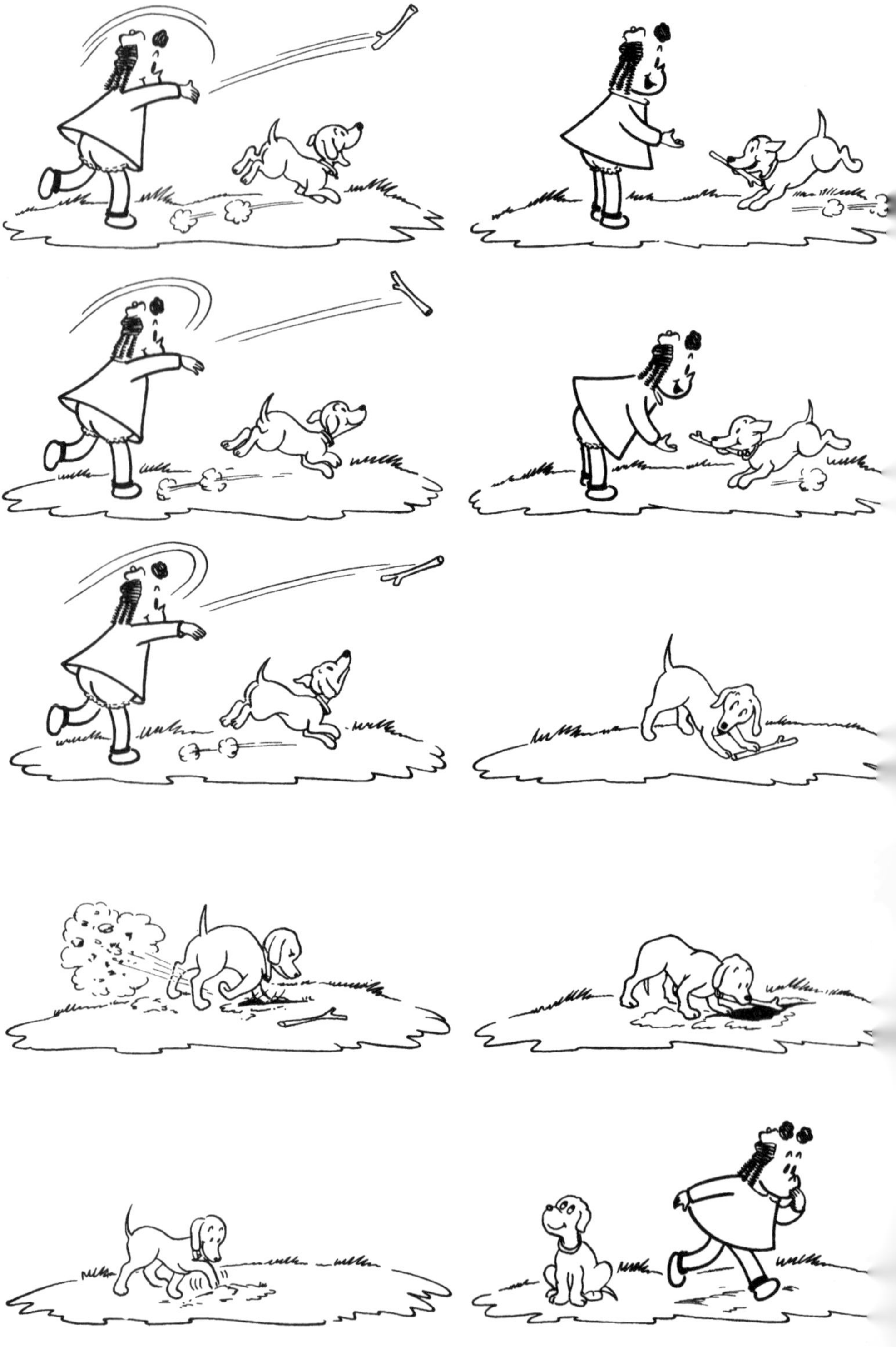

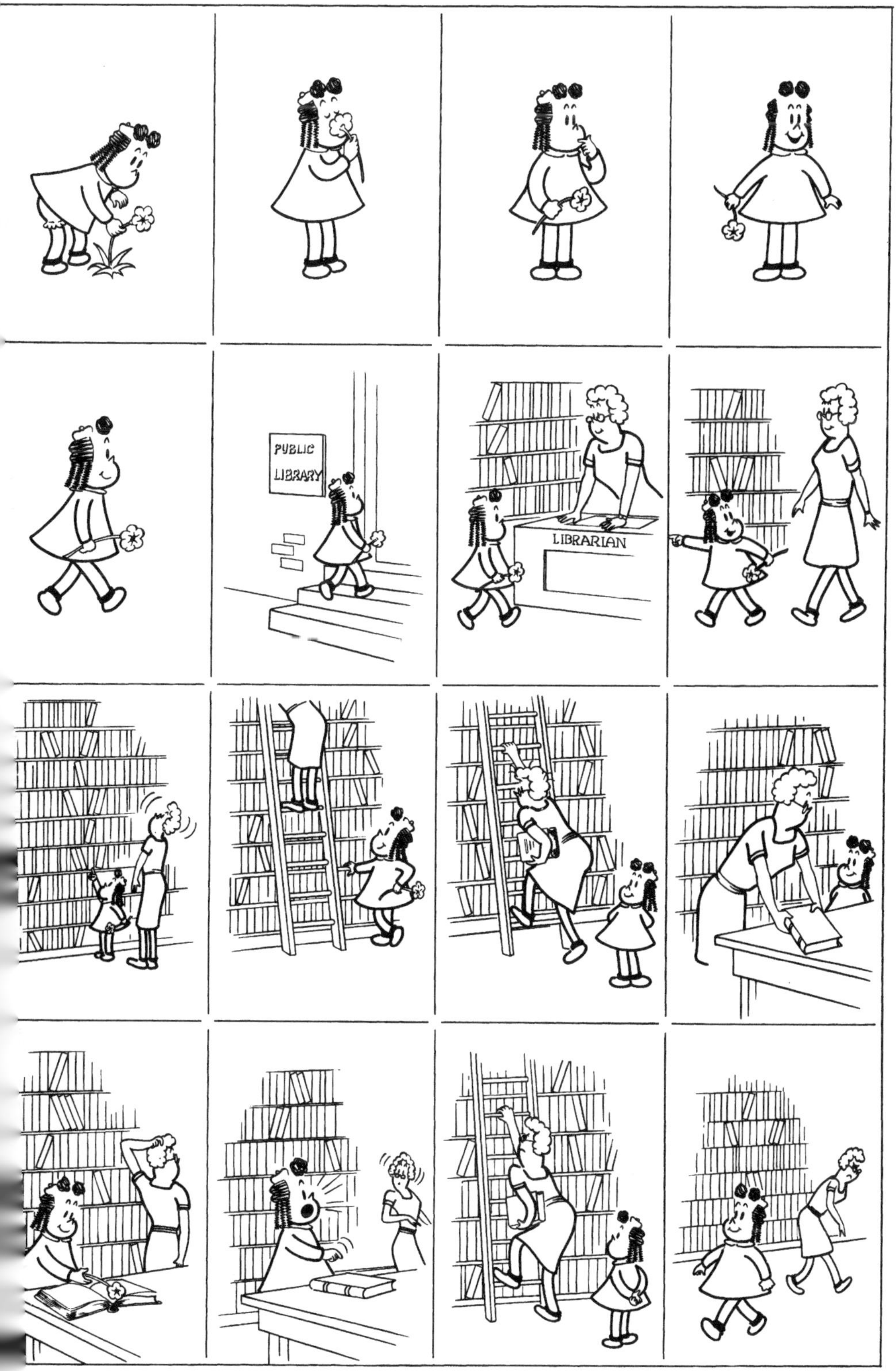
PUBLIC
LIBRARY
LIBRARIAN

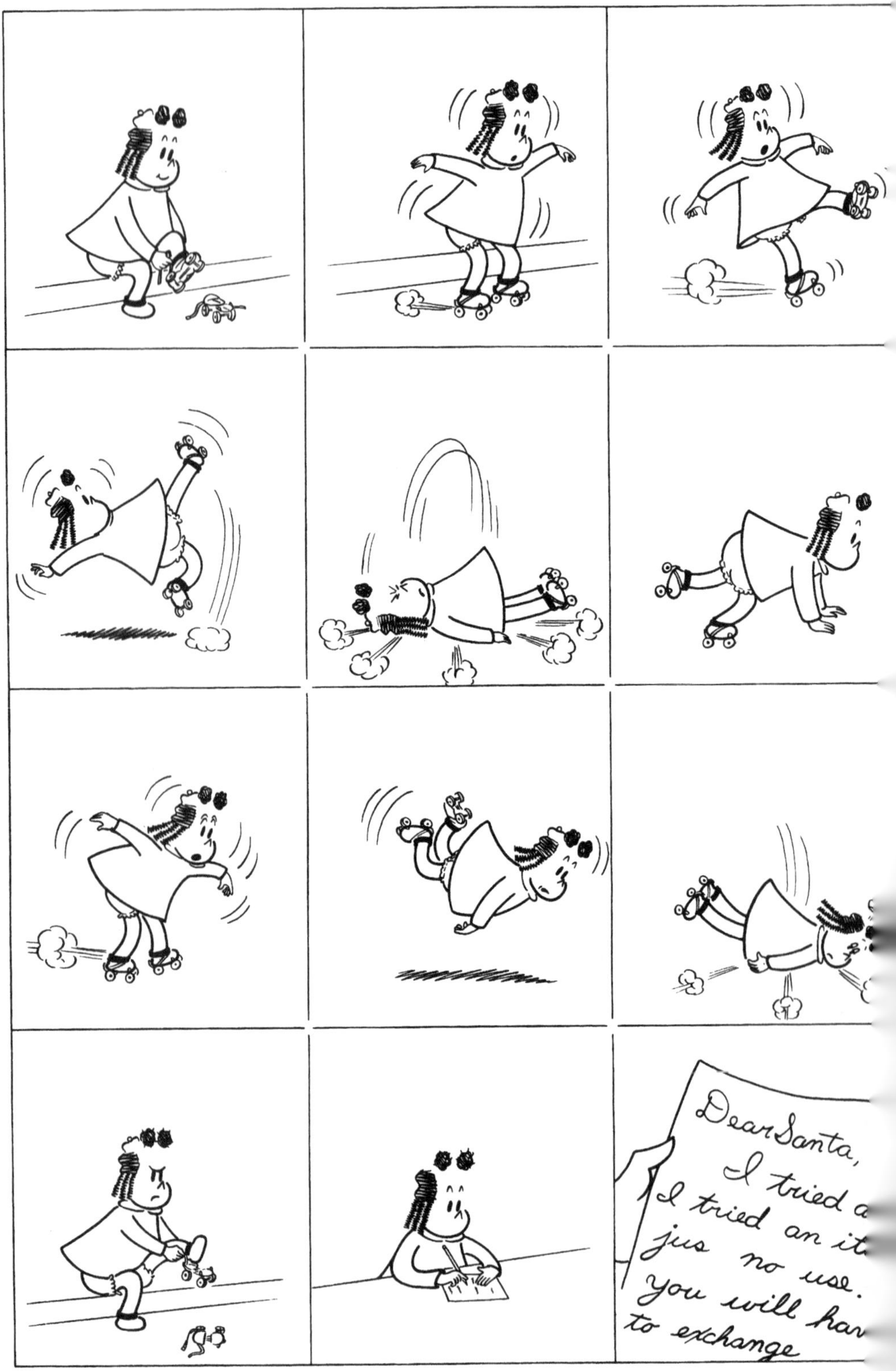
Dear Santa,
I tried a
I tried an it
jus no use.
you will hav
to exchange

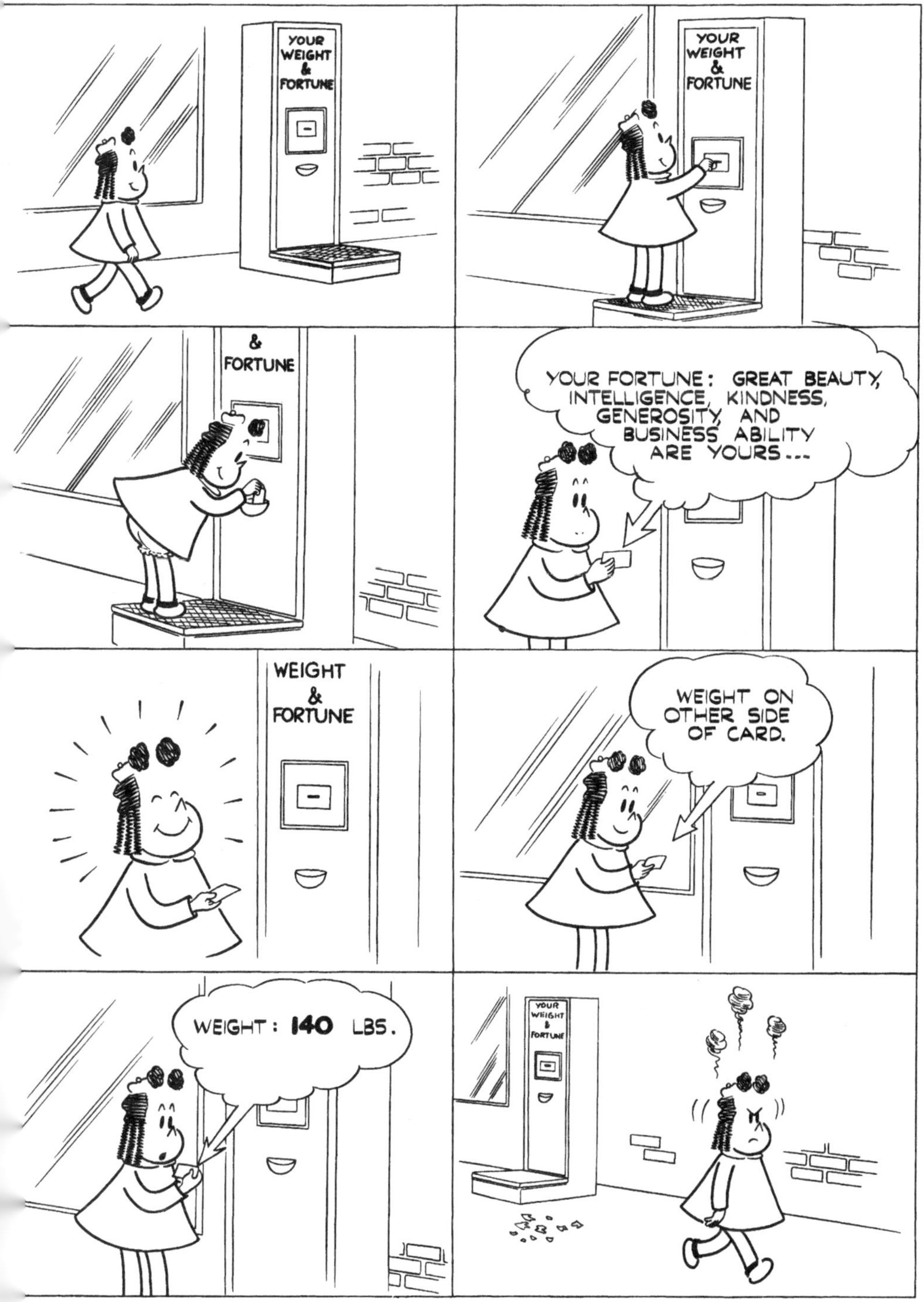
YOUR WEIGHT & FORTUNE
YOUR WEIGHT & FORTUNE
& FORTUNE
YOUR FORTUNE: GREAT BEAUTY, INTELLIGENCE, KINDNESS, GENEROSITY, AND BUSINESS ABILITY ARE YOURS...
WEIGHT & FORTUNE
WEIGHT ON OTHER SIDE OF CARD.
WEIGHT: 140 LBS.
YOUR WEIGHT & FORTUNE

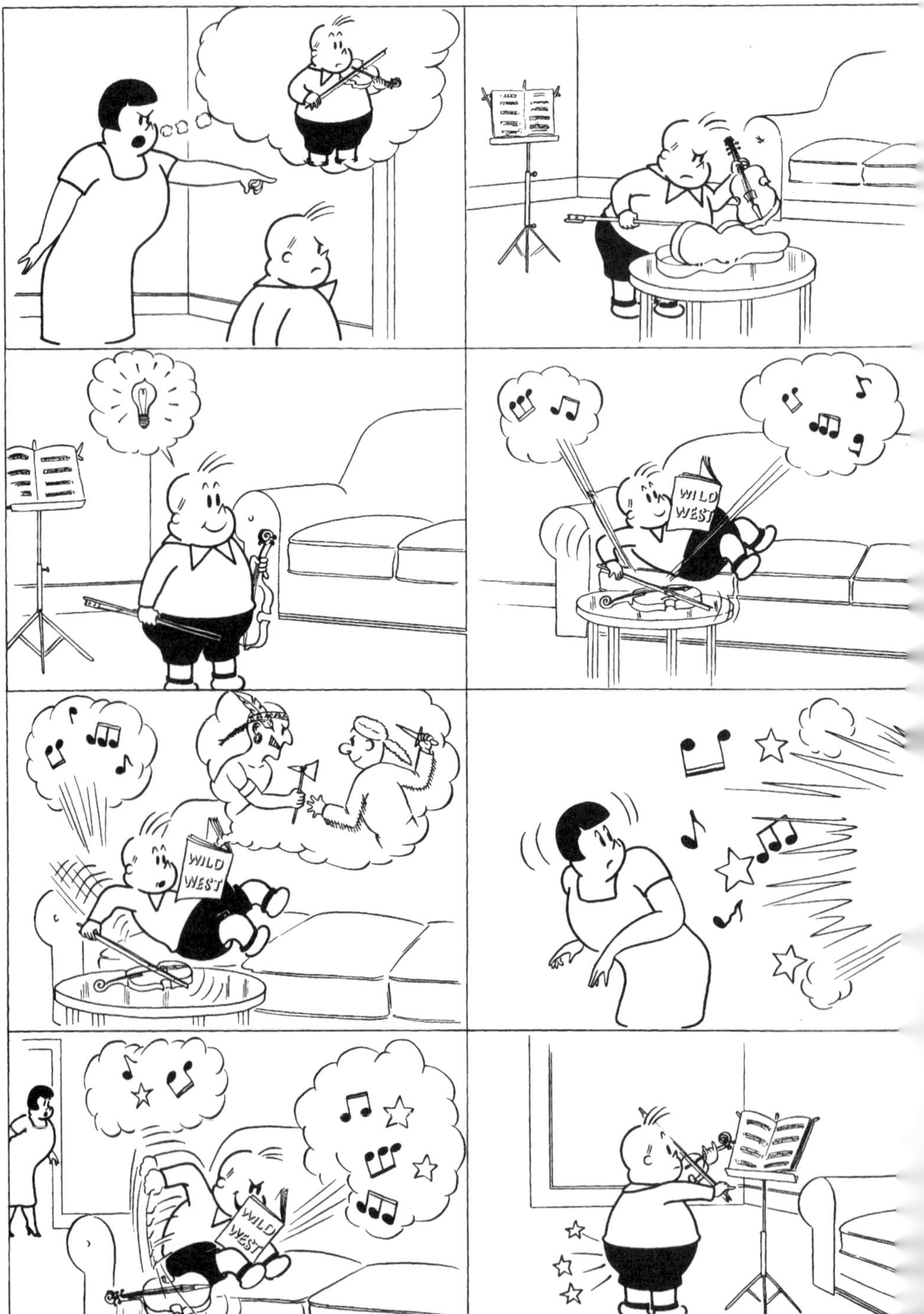
WILD WEST
WILD WEST
WILD WEST

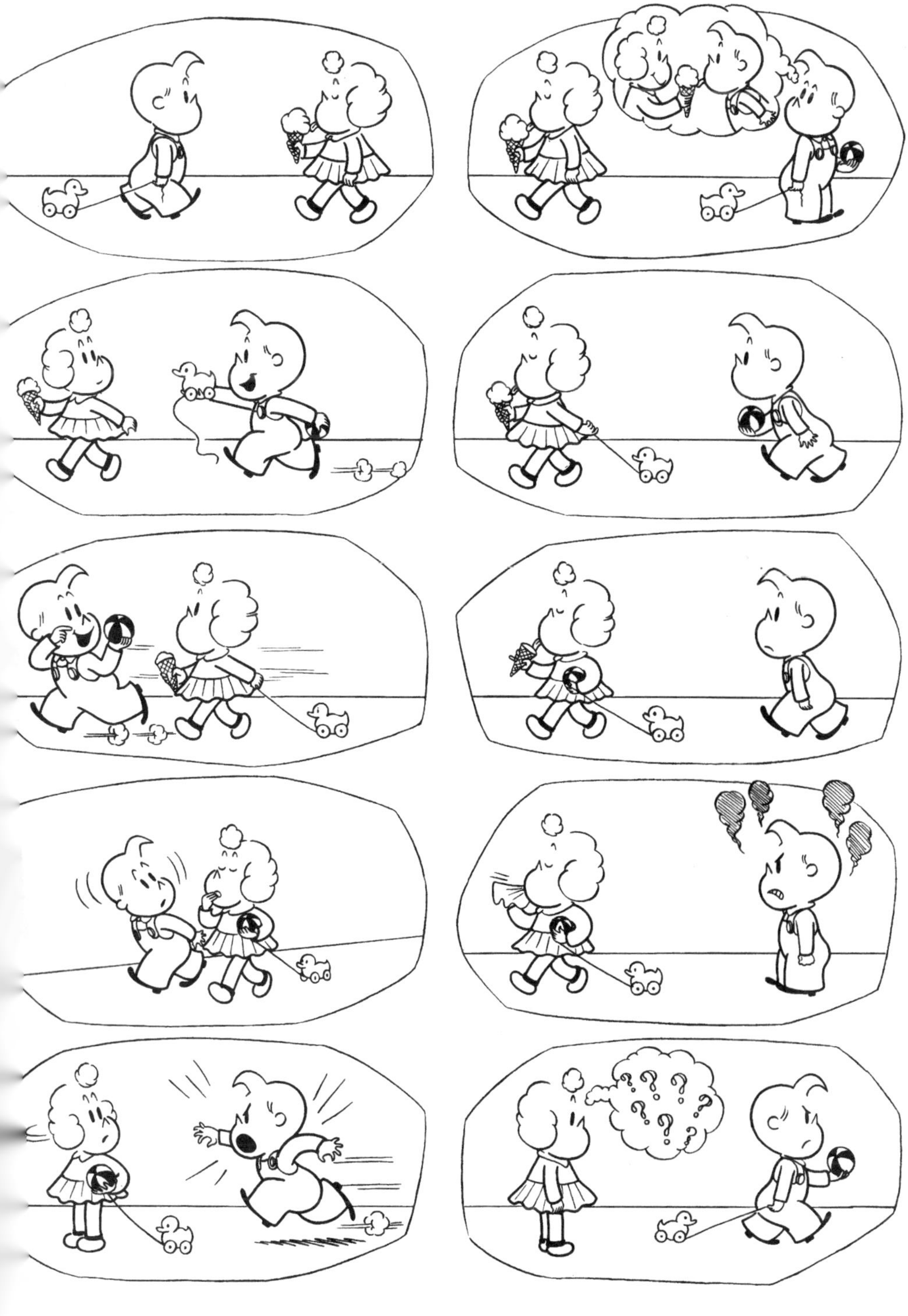
? ? ? ? ? ? ? ? ?

Little Lulu®

$9.95 Each!

Volume 1:
My Dinner with Lulu
ISBN-10: 1-59307-318-6
ISBN-13: 978-1-59307-318-3

Volume 2:
Sunday Afternoon
ISBN-10: 1-59307-345-3
ISBN-13: 978-1-59307-345-9

Volume 3:
Lulu in the Doghouse
ISBN-10: 1-59307-346-1
ISBN-13: 978-1-59307-346-6

Volume 4:
Lulu Goes Shopping
ISBN-10: 1-59307-270-8
ISBN-13: 978-1-59307-270-4

Volume 5:
Lulu Takes a Trip
ISBN-10: 1-59307-317-8
ISBN-13: 978-1-59307-317-6

Volume 6:
Letters to Santa
ISBN-10: 1-59307-386-0
ISBN-13: 978-1-59307-386-2

Volume 7:
Lulu's Umbrella Service
ISBN-10: 1-59307-399-2
ISBN-13: 978-1-59307-399-2

Volume 8:
Late for School
ISBN-10: 1-59307-453-0
ISBN-13: 978-1-59307-453-1

Volume 9:
Lucky Lulu
ISBN-10: 1-59307-471-9
ISBN-13: 978-1-59307-471-5

Volume 10:
All Dressed Up
ISBN-10: 1-59307-534-0
ISBN-13: 978-1-59307-534-7

Volume 11:
April Fools
ISBN-10: 1-59307-557-X
ISBN-13: 978-1-59307-557-6

Volume 12:
Leave It to Lulu
ISBN-10: 1-59307-620-7
ISBN-13: 978-1-59307-620-7

COMING IN DECEMBER!
Volume 13:
Too Much Fun
ISBN-10: 1-59307-621-5
ISBN-13: 978-1-59307-621-4

ALSO AVAILABLE!
Little Lulu Color Special
208 pages, full color
ISBN-10: 1-59307-613-4
ISBN-13: 978-1-59307-613-9
$13.95